The Editor

CLAUDIA L. JOHNSON is Professor of English at Princeton University. She is the author of *Jane Austen: Women, Politics and the Novel* and *Equivocal Beings: Politics, Gender, and Sentimentality in the 1790s* as well as many articles on eighteenth- and nineteenth-century literature.

MANSFIELD PARK

AUTHORITATIVE TEXT
CONTEXTS
CRITICISM

W. W. NORTON & COMPANY, INC.
Also Publishes

ENGLISH RENAISSANCE DRAMA: A NORTON ANTHOLOGY
edited by David Bevington et al.

THE NORTON ANTHOLOGY OF AFRICAN AMERICAN LITERATURE
edited by Henry Louis Gates Jr. and Nellie Y. McKay et al.

THE NORTON ANTHOLOGY OF AMERICAN LITERATURE
edited by Nina Baym et al.

THE NORTON ANTHOLOGY OF CHILDREN'S LITERATURE
edited by Jack Zipes et al.

THE NORTON ANTHOLOGY OF DRAMA
edited by J. Ellen Gainor, Stanton B. Garner Jr., and Martin Puchner

THE NORTON ANTHOLOGY OF ENGLISH LITERATURE
edited by M. H. Abrams and Stephen Greenblatt et al.

THE NORTON ANTHOLOGY OF LITERATURE BY WOMEN
edited by Sandra M. Gilbert and Susan Gubar

THE NORTON ANTHOLOGY OF MODERN AND CONTEMPORARY POETRY
edited by Jahan Ramazani, Richard Ellmann, and Robert O'Clair

THE NORTON ANTHOLOGY OF POETRY
edited by Margaret Ferguson, Mary Jo Salter, and Jon Stallworthy

THE NORTON ANTHOLOGY OF SHORT FICTION
edited by R. V. Cassill and Richard Bausch

THE NORTON ANTHOLOGY OF THEORY AND CRITICISM
edited by Vincent B. Leitch et al.

THE NORTON ANTHOLOGY OF WORLD LITERATURE
edited by Sarah Lawall et al.

THE NORTON FACSIMILE OF THE FIRST FOLIO OF SHAKESPEARE
prepared by Charlton Hinman

THE NORTON INTRODUCTION TO LITERATURE
edited by Alison Booth and Kelly J. Mays

THE NORTON READER
edited by Linda H. Peterson and John C. Brereton

THE NORTON SAMPLER
edited by Thomas Cooley

THE NORTON SHAKESPEARE, BASED ON THE OXFORD EDITION
edited by Stephen Greenblatt et al.

For a complete list of Norton Critical Editions, visit
www.wwnorton.com/college/English/nce_home.htm

A NORTON CRITICAL EDITION

Jane Austen

MANSFIELD PARK

AUTHORITATIVE TEXT

CONTEXTS

CRITICISM

Edited by

CLAUDIA L. JOHNSON

PRINCETON UNIVERSITY

W • W • NORTON & COMPANY • *New York* • *London*

Copyright © 1998 by W. W. Norton & Company, Inc.

The text of this book is composed in Electra with the display set
in Bernhard Modern.
Composition by PennSet, Inc.
Manufacturing by Courier Companies.

Library of Congress Cataloging-in-Publication Data
Austen, Jane, 1775–1817.
Mansfield Park : authoritative text, contexts, criticism / Jane
Austen ; edited by Claudia L. Johnson.
p.   cm. — (A Norton critical edition)
Includes bibliographical references.

ISBN 0-393-96791-3 (pbk.)

1. England — Social life and customs — 19th century — Fiction.
2. Young women — England — Fiction. 3. Austen, Jane, 1775–1817.
Mansfield Park. I. Johnson, Claudia L. II. Title.
PR4034.M3   1997
823'.7 — dc21   96-49462

W. W. Norton & Company, Inc.
500 Fifth Avenue, New York, N.Y. 10110
www.wwnorton.com

W. W. Norton & Company Ltd.
15 Carlisle Street, London W1D 3BS

9 0

Contents

Criticism   413

Acknowledgments

From the start, Jane Austen's work has had an uncanny power to create communities out of diverse persons, and it seems that an entire community of scholars, students, librarians, editors, and general readers has helped me in the preparation of this Norton Critical Edition. I would like first to thank the staffs of the Rare and Manuscript Collections of the Carl A. Kroch Library at Cornell University and of Rare Books and Special Collections at Princeton University for making their rich holdings in first editions and background material available to me. Margaret M. Sherry of Firestone Library was particularly helpful through every stage of this project. In addition, more colleagues and students than I can possibly mention here have advised me on matters ranging from the selection of background material to the choice of passages requiring explanatory footnotes; among these Nina Auerbach, Carol Kay, A. W. Litz, Anne K. Mellor, B. C. Southam, Patricia M. Spacks, Joseph Wiesenfarth, and Susan Wolfson offered advice for which I am especially grateful. I would also like to thank Patricia Latkin of Jane Austen Books in Chicago for helping me track down information about green goose, among other things; Henry Churchyard for the resources available on his Jane Austen website; and Mark Turner for running computerized word combination searches, which helped in several textual decisions.

I reserve my deepest thanks for Carol Bemis, Editor of the Norton Critical Editions, for her patience and encouragement; for Jan Fergus, whose knowledge of Austen's texts is matchless and whose assistance has been generous; and most of all for Sarah M. Anderson, whose formidable command of textual scholarship in all its rigors has saved me from many a blunder, and whose unstinting support has made everything possible.

Introduction

Jane Austen and *Mansfield Park*

Mansfield Park is an ambitious and difficult novel, the first composed and published exclusively in Jane Austen's adulthood. She was proud of it. Inclined to consider *Pride and Prejudice*, which she had just published, "rather too light & bright & sparkling," Austen wrote a novel with all the "shade" her earlier comic masterpiece lacked.[1] Of course, she knew full well that *Mansfield Park* was different from her previous work—"not half so entertaining," as she put it—but she was confident it would "sell well" and contribute to the modest but growing commercial success of her previous novels, a success which, as she confided to her brother Frank, "only made [her] long for more."[2] She had reason to suppose herself right. Within six months of its publication by Thomas Egerton in May 1813, Austen wrote her niece, "You will be glad to hear that the first Edit: of M.P. is all sold."[3] Naturally Austen supposed that Egerton would agree to a second edition. But Egerton declined. With the assistance of her brother Henry, Austen negotiated with John Murray, who published the second edition in February 1816 on commission.[4]

It is painful to consider the failure of this enterprise, which Austen entered into with such confidence. There are no contemporary reviews of *Mansfield Park*. The second edition of *Mansfield Park* hardly sold at all, and Austen had to pay Murray for its publication costs out of the profits she made from her next novel, *Emma*. And yet Austen still followed the fortunes of *Mansfield Park* closely. She carefully recorded even the silliest opinions about the novel voiced by her neighbors or relations. And when Murray sent her Sir Walter Scott's positive (anonymous) review of *Emma* in the prestigious *Quarterly Review*, she had nothing to say, except to protest "the total omission of Mansfield Park," adding with some asperity, "I cannot but be sorry that so clever a Man

---

1. *Jane Austen's Letters*, ed. Deirdre Le Faye (Oxford and New York: Oxford UP, 1995), 3rd ed., 203. The letter is dated February 4, 1813. Hereafter, I will indicate letters from this edition by date rather than page number.
2. *Letters*, July 3–6, 1813.
3. *Letters*, November 18–20, 1814.
4. David Gilson, *A Bibliography of Jane Austen* (Oxford: Clarendon Press, 1982) 59.

as the Reviewer of *Emma*, should consider it as unworthy of being noticed."[5]

In our own time, *Mansfield Park* has hardly been neglected. Instead, it is avidly read and has the distinction of being Austen's most controversial novel. This is largely because its apparent skepticism about wit, high spirits, and desire appears to announce an abrupt about-face from her previous work. Austen imagined that the overweening Emma Woodhouse would be the heroine no one would like much but herself, but posterity has found it far harder to like Fanny Price, with all her self-doubt and modesty. For some Fanny Price is a prig *extraordinaire*, and the novel the very acme of sanctimoniousness. "What became of Jane Austen?"[6] is the famous question Kingsley Amis asked when he turned in bewilderment from the sparkling *Pride and Prejudice* to the dour *Mansfield Park*, appalled to find that the author who "set out bravely to correct conventional notions of the desirable and virtuous" in other novels became in *this* novel "their slave." Many readers have agreed that something went wrong with Austen in *Mansfield Park*, and have sought the cause. Did Austen undergo a conversion to Evangelicalism, and thus on the grounds of religious principle dramatize the triumph of priggishness over playfulness, duty over desire? Or, elaborating this answer more psychologically, did she suffer some inner compulsion to revenge herself upon her own imagination, to scourge her wit, to punish the saucy Elizabeth Bennet by recasting her as that shallow, worldling-siren, Mary Crawford? Did she suffer some other sort of "crisis" which, with its attendant fatigue, made her yearn for stasis, submerging personality in principle, and foregoing energy for repose?[7]

Over and against these readers have been those who feel that *Mansfield Park* does not stand out as the oddball of Austen's canon, but is indeed her most central work insofar as it posits stability, authority, custom, sobriety, and staunch morality as values cultivated in the country houses of the Tory gentry. For such readers, Fanny and Edmund are attractive, sensible, and sympathetic despite their passing flaws; the rootless Crawfords are patently unfeeling, amoral, and materialistic; and the novel as a whole rigorously moral in meting out its rewards to the deserving and its punishments to the undeserving.

Of course, there are many intermediary positions as well, for *Mansfield Park* is a profoundly experimental novel, challenging to read in part because it refuses to let us repose our full confidence in *any* single character or mode: it is skeptical not only about witty heroines, after all, but also about ponderous paternal figures, who turn out to be mer-

---

5. *Letters*, April 1, 1816.
6. Kingsley Amis, "What Became of Jane Austen?" was originally published in *Spectator*, October 4, 1957, 339–40. I quote from the version printed in William Heath, ed., *Discussion of Jane Austen* (Boston: Heath and Company, 1961) 99–101.
7. For one of the most enduring discussion of this kind, see Lionel Trilling's essay on *Mansfield Park*, reprinted below, pp. 423–34.

cenary rather than judicious; about sober clergymen, who turn out to be benighted and self-deceiving rather than steady; about modest good girls, who are painfully inhibited and more than a little naive; and finally even about the values of the country estate itself, which, notably unlike its counterpart Pemberley in *Pride and Prejudice*, is here tainted by its association with the slave trade and Sir Thomas's "business" in Antigua.

Critical fortunes change. Squarely taking on such issues as class, gender, sexuality, religion, education, theatricality, and colonialism, *Mansfield Park* now appears to occupy a more critical place in Austen's canon and in literary and cultural history generally than that perennial favorite *Pride and Prejudice*. The present edition is designed to further this trend.

Mansfield Park is noticeably more allusive than Austen's other novels. In addition to the complete text of Elizabeth Inchbald's *Lovers' Vows*, I have provided other contextualizing material about education, female modesty, religion, theatricals, clerical responsibility, and landscape improvement, along with selections from William Cowper's poetry and contemporary remarks on that other, seldom-discussed play in the novel, *Henry VIII*. In addition, I have provided background material on the slave trade and its abolition, which is currently an urgent subject of critical interest—some debates in the House of Commons, of which Sir Thomas is a member, which represent the opinions of West Indian planters and Liverpool interests; and some selections from Thomas Clarkson, an author beloved of Austen, on the abolition of the slave trade.

Because these selections are comparatively generous, I have scaled back on nineteenth- and early-twentieth-century background material with a somewhat better conscience, declining to represent material from Austen's letters, on the grounds that relevant portions are cited in the Criticism section. It has been harder to pare down selections from modern criticism, as the interests of space required. The essays included here represent important, often competing, critical trends—such as feminism, historicism, poststructuralism, cultural studies, and the literary marketplace—and together they suggest how and why the controversy over this rich and complex novel is not likely to end soon. There has been much splendid scholarly work on this novel that I have not been able to include, and I have listed such work in the selected bibliography.

A Note on Money in Austen's Novels

Few subjects fascinate students reading Austen for the first time more than money, and for good reason: Austen's characters themselves are both extremely interested in their neighbors' annual incomes and extremely well-informed about them. Their houses, grounds, and gardens, their trips to London, their carriages, their servants, their governesses, their pianos, and the fruit on their tables are signs of wealth and status.

During Austen's time, one's wealth is typically described as a yearly disposable income, a figure in turn calculated by multiplying the principal of one's inheritance by 5 percent (the interest earned by investing in 5 percent government funds). But determining the actual value of money during Austen's time is a greater challenge. In recent years, those of us accustomed to currency based on dollars rather than pounds sterling have been advised to multiply each pound sterling by anywhere from 33, 60, or 200 times in order to determine dollar equivalences for the United States in the late twentieth century, formulas that would put Mr. Rushworth's yearly disposable income of £12,000 at around $396,000, $720,000 or $2,900,000 a year.[8] Of course, scholars and economists are also quick to add that such formulas are misleading. First, the economy during Austen's time was still principally landed and agrarian, which means among many other things that the basic cost of consumer items is not comparable to their cost today, in an urban and industrial economy. Cloth, for example, which was not mass manufactured, was very expensive, and food generally cheaper. Second, wealth itself was distributed among a much smaller number of people than is the case today. When G. E. Mingay says that only four hundred families among the landed gentry during Austen's time had annual incomes within the range of £5,000 and £50,000, with the average among these at £10,000 (Darcy's annual income in *Pride and Prejudice*), we get some idea of the fabulousness of Rushworth's £12,000 a year in *Mansfield Park*, and some insight into Sir Thomas's motives for wanting his daughter Maria to proceed with her marriage to Rushworth, even though he knows she does not love him.[9]

If the stupendous wealth of Rushworth is the upper limit in Austen's novels, at the lower end is what her characters call a "competence," which Edward Copeland has aptly defined as "the bottom line of gentility, increasing and decreasing with the pretensions of its possessor to

8. James Heldman recommends a ratio of $33.13/£1 for 1988 equivalences in "How Wealthy Is Mr. Darcy—Really," *Persuasions*, 12 (1990): 38–49; Margaret A. Doody recommends a $60/£1 ratio for 1990 in Appendix IV (on Finance) to her edition of Frances Burney's *The Wanderer; or, Female Difficulties* (Oxford: Oxford World Classics, 1991); a novel originally published in 1814, the same year as *Mansfield Park*; Julia Prewitt Brown recommends a $200/£1 ratio for 1985 in *A Reader's Guide to the Nineteenth-Century English Novel* (New York, Macmillan, 1985) 7–8.

9. *English Landed Society in the Eighteenth Century* (London: Routledge, & Kegan Paul, 1963) 26. Mingay's tables for the variability of annual incomes among genteel ranks can be summarized as follows: gentlemen between £300–£1,000; squires between £1,000–£3,000; wealthy gentry between £3,000–£5,000; and great landlords, between £5,000–£10,000. As Eric Hobsbawm points out, in 1800 "less than 14 percent of British families had an income of more than £50 per year, and of these only one-quarter earned more than £200 a year." See *The Age of Revolution, 1789–1848* (New York: New American Library, 1989) 36.

rank and status."[1] In *Mansfield Park*, Edmund's living at Thornton Lacey is £700 a year, and this figure, twice as much as what was minimally necessary for a bachelor, is the bottom range of a competence for a married couple. At the end of *Sense and Sensibility*, the sensible Elinor Dashwood attains her dream of a competence when she and Edward Ferrars marry on a combined annual income of £850. Mr. and Mrs. Norris had an income of about £1000, which makes Mrs. Norris's stinginess more irrational. Commanding an extremely ample fortune of £4,000 a year himself, Henry Crawford calls Edmund's income "a fine thing for a younger brother" partly because he assumes that Edmund will reside at Mansfield Park and that his living will be pocket money. The worldly Mary Crawford, with a taste for London life, is alarmed by Edmund's unambitious contentment with a competence. Five percent interest on her fortune of £20,000 would bring in £1,000 a year, and this money was more than a competence; indeed, it was sufficient even to cover some of the elegancies of genteel life, such as a carriage. Twice that much would be considered wealth for the minor gentry. More opulent luxuries such as a house in London required a yearly income of £5000 or more.[2]

Lower down on the social scale are the Prices in Portsmouth. Assuming that Mrs. Price took the same lump sum of £7000 to her unfortunate marriage that Lady Bertram brought to hers, she would bring £350 to her family annually, a figure that would be supplemented by the £45 a year Mr. Price brings in as a half-pay officer. Though hardly penurious, a yearly income of £395 is not enough to maintain the gentility Fanny has been used to at Mansfield Park, even if the Prices *can* afford two (bad) servants. Austen herself lived with her mother, sister, and one servant on around £460 a year, and when Mr. and Mrs. John Dashwood in *Sense and Sensibility* consign their stepmother and half-sisters to a similar income (£500 a year), Austen describes their rationalizations with bristling irony: "[W]hat on earth can four women want for more than that?—They will live so cheap! Their housekeeping will be nothing at all; they will keep no company, and can have no expences of any kind! Only conceive how comfortable they will be!"[3]

Things get lower still for Austen's characters, though not in *Mansfield Park*. Left a total of £1000 apiece at their great-uncle's death, the Dashwood sisters each contribute £50 a year to their maintenance at Barton Cottage, and even smaller income (calculated by the precise Mr. Collins on a 4 rather than 5 percent basis) awaits the Bennet sisters of *Pride and Prejudice* after their father's death. Mrs. Smith in *Persuasion* cannot afford a servant, which probably puts her income at £50. As a governess,

---

1. Edward Copeland's *Women Writing About Money* (Cambridge: Cambridge UP, 1995) 23. Throughout this discussion, I am extremely indebted to this splendidly informative work.
2. Copeland 15–32.
3. *The Novels of Jane Austen*, 3rd ed., ed. R. W. Chapman, vol. I, *Sense and Sensibility* (London: Oxford UP, 1933; rpt. 1982) 12; quoted in Copeland, p. 31.

Jane Fairfax in *Emma*, like Jane Eyre after her, could look forward to a salary of £30 a year. A common laborer would make around £25. In *Mansfield Park* Tom Bertram scoffs at Edmund's concern that the expenses from staging *Lovers' Vows* at home will amount to £20.

A Note on Austen and the Text of *Mansfield Park*

There is no extant autograph manuscript of *Mansfield Park*. The first edition (hereafter called A) was published in May 1814 by Thomas Egerton, who had also published Austen's earlier novels. The second edition (hereafter called B) was published by John Murray in February 1816. B is rightly considered authoritative not only because it contains fewer errors, but also because it incorporates Austen's corrections upon and additions to A. This edition, like all modern editions, is based on B. With only two, close printed versions to collate and no autograph to consult, the text of *Mansfield Park* is relatively unproblematic.

Comparing A and B gives us the chance to ponder Austen's relation to her own texts in distinctive ways. On December 11, 1815, she returned what was probably a corrected copy of A to Murray, saying "I return also, Mansfield Park, as ready for a 2d Edit: I beleive [sic], as I can make it.—"[4] The import of this remark is far from clear, and it is worth thinking about what she meant.[5] Is she saying, with mock self-deprecation, that her powers are not sufficient to make the novel completely ready for the second edition? Or, is she stating that she does not have the time or the leeway to do so? A collation of A and B shows that—with the exception of two paragraphs about William's ship in volume III—Austen's revisions are sparing, one is tempted even to say forbearing, and for an author celebrated for stylistic precision, this seems striking. Yet every bit as striking is the fact that the compositors of B, in resetting the text, go out of their way to follow A despite different house policies about punctuation and spelling, in the vast majority of cases printing the same words on each line, the same number of lines on each page, and, when the line endings do get out of sync, resuming as soon as possible. The reason for this is not hard to determine: using a relatively clean printed text as a guide ensures the greater speed and accuracy of the resetting. With this in mind, we may wonder—this is only speculation—if Austen (who was paying for publication costs) revised only sparingly because Murray advised her that

4. *Letters*, December 11, 1815. Chapman is also of the opinion that Austen was referring to a corrected copy of A. See *The Novels of Jane Austen*, 3rd ed., ed. R. W. Chapman (London: Oxford UP, 1934; rpt. 1966) xii.

5. There is no certain evidence that Austen read proof for B. It would be unusual not to do so. Austen gives a lively report about receiving and correcting page proof—or, "Sheets," as she called them—for Murray's edition of *Emma*. On November 24, 1815, she announces that the printer's boys bring the sheets and carry away the corrected ones. But the letters from early 1816—and there are not a lot of them—never mention "sheets" for *Mansfield Park*.

extensive corrections would increase the time and cost of publication, somewhat as editors today ask authors in the later stages of production to avoid all but essential changes.

This matter is important for readers of Austen because it invites us to ask how she, nothing if not a splendidly self-conscious author, regarded her work once it was a printed artifact. Did she expect a printed page to look like a manuscript page? Austen's extant fair copies, for example, frequently run conversations together in a single, long paragraph. Did she expect typesetters to indent for each new speaker? Similarly, Austen's extant manuscripts rarely indent for paragraphs. Was she conserving paper, assuming that a printed version of her handwritten page would indent in appropriate places? And what about the punctuation of stops? In the manuscripts Austen generally uses a period followed by a long dash (.—) for an endstop. Did she expect printers to delete the dashes, or did these kinds of dashes signify in some particular way? The printed texts are inconsistent, presumably omitting dashes most of the time, but retaining them in some contexts (e.g., in Lady Bertram's congratulations to Fanny on her marriage proposal, in some letters, and in some internal monologue). Did Austen care about spelling and punctuation?

Austen noted the appearance of typesetter's mistakes in Egerton's *Pride and Prejudice*—calling them "Typical errors"—and observed that she found one "blunder" in Volume III, "where two speeches are made into one."[6] We also know that she thought adding a " 'said he' or a 'said she' would sometimes make the dialogue more immediately clear." But such concern had its limits. Her quip " 'I do not write for such dull Elves / As have not a great deal of Ingenuity themselves' "— so often cited with respect to the weighty matters of interpretative practice, and in particular to irony—actually pertains to "Typical errors" alone.[7]

A contains many small errors. Due in part to the fact that its volumes were set by two different printers, its practice is inconsistent with regard to the spelling of many words (e.g., *chuse/choose*), to the capitalization of nouns and titles (e.g., *Father/father; Lady/lady*), to the separation of compounds (*Anybody/any body*), to the hyphenation of compounds (e.g., *head-ache/headache*); to the use of an apostrophe in some past tenses (e.g., *dress'd; blush'd*), among many other kinds of instances. But even after making allowances for such differences not merely among but also within the volumes of A, and after granting that punctuation and spelling were less regularized than today (despite the efforts of printers' manuals to recommend uniformity), A contains many distinctive errors. Among these are: (a) outright mistakes, as provable by context, and as corrected in B (e.g., *of* for *or*; *then* for *than*; *too* for *two*);

6. *Letters*, January 29, 1813, and February 4, 1813.
7. *Letters*, January 29, 1813.

(b) omitted or misplaced plural possessive apostrophes (e.g., *Lovers Vows* and/or *Lover's Vows* instead of *Lovers' Vows* throughout *A1*; *year's* for *years*'); (c) mis-set, inverted, dropped, or doubled letters (e.g., *themselvess, Crauford, prfiot, b en*; and (d) omitted spaces between words (e.g., *Ifeel, evenin*).

More troublesome, because impinging on matters Austen *did* care about, is the punctuation of dialogue. Sometimes A misplaces open- and close-quotation marks, which blurs dialogue and description, making it hard to register when speech stops and resumes. On one occasion, when Lady Bertram and Mrs. Norris discuss where Fanny will stay after Mr. Norris has died, A omits indenting for any of the speeches. This "error," if it is an error (it is "corrected" in B), probably results not from departing from Austen's faircopy, but from following it closely.

We have no record that Austen complained about these mistakes. But even more telling is the fact that even though most printers' errors are corrected in B—caught by Austen and/or by Murray's correctors—some carry over: e.g., the misnumbering of chapter fourteen in volume III, printed as *XVI* instead of *XIV*; the printing of *Miss* instead of *Mrs.*; the omission of spaces and apostrophes for plural possessives; and the misplacement of quotation marks in dialogue.

These mistakes are small, rarely hard even for dull elves to catch. It is precisely on this account that their carry-over from A to B obliges us to wonder what making *Mansfield Park* "as ready for a 2d Edit" as she could entailed for Austen. Possibly she wasn't a keen proofreader. But it is likelier that Austen did not consider punctuation her affair.[8] In any case, if it is true that Austen's corrected copy of A let stand such "Typical" errors as the mis-setting of quotation marks, then we must reconsider R. W. Chapman's notion that the "very slightness" of Austen's changes from A to B shows "some 'particularity' of revision" on her part.[9] "Particular" changes may be the advertent or inadvertent work of compositors. I would be wary of regarding any change in punctuation from A to B as "too good for the printer" and therefore probably Austen's, as Chapman sometimes does.[1] Even larger changes—such as A's "It is to be called Lovers Vows" as opposed to B's "It is to be Lovers' Vows"—should be eyed warily before we conclude that they show us Austen's hand at work.

8. Austen does report receiving a "modest" marginal query from the typesetter of *Emma* concerning her spelling of *arra-root* for *arrow-root*, and to my ear at least she sounds pleasantly surprised by the query. See *Letters*, November 26, 1815. Concerning punctuation, printers' manuals advised authors "to leave the pointing entirely to the printers, as from their constant practice they must have acquired a uniform mode of punctuation." See C. Stower *The Printer's Grammar; or, Introduction to the Art of Printing* (London, 1808) 80. On the corrector's role in ensuring uniform punctuation, see, Stower 213.
9. Chapman, xii.
1. See, for example, his note to page 421, line 22.

None of this questions the authority of B. It is meant rather to underscore the compositors' role not simply in the transmission but also in the very formation of our sense of Austen's artistry. We delight in reading Austen closely. And yet compositors' parts in paragraphing and punctuating, maybe even in some wording—matters from which we squeeze a lot of nuance—are greater than has been acknowledged. If Austen was a minute artist, a cameoist working on a "little bit (two Inches wide) of Ivory" with a fine "Brush,"[2] then she had a very definite sense of when her work was done. Once her work was printed, she does not appear to have worried over each brush stroke. Austen seems to have regarded matters "Typical" as to some extent distinguishable from and outside of her domain. What Woolf so eloquently described as "the rhythm and shapeliness and severity"[3] of Austen's sentences inheres more in the spoken word rather than in the printed page.

What Austen manifestly *did* care about was the authenticity of details. From her letters we know that as she was composing *Mansfield Park*, she inquired about local details—(e.g., was there a Government House at Gibraltar? what is the time frame for the ordination process? do hedgerows grow in Northamptonshire? could she use the name of ships in commission?)[4] Furthermore, between the publication of the first and second editions of *Mansfield Park*, she evidently consulted with her sailor brothers about Mr. Price's description of his son's ship as it left the inner harbor of Portsmouth to moor at Spithead. This section, unlike the "polite" converse she generally reports, is dense with jargon; and Austen's goal here is to represent not only Mr. Price's enthusiasm for the *Thrush* and his pride in his son, now a lieutenant, but also his obliviousness to Fanny. The last thing Austen wanted was to be faulted for failing to render nautical terms precisely when the wielding of this specialized speech was the whole point. Accordingly, for example, she changes *point* to *platform*, because Mr. Price could not have seen the *Thrush* from the Point; *alert*, a technical term about readiness inappropriate to the context, to *sharp*; *things* (evidently too nontechnical) to *mess*; *under weigh* (which implies being anchored) with *moorings*, since the water in Portsmouth harbor is too shallow for anchors. And the proud William rejoins with a new sentence—"*It's the best birth at Spithead*"—locating the Thrush more specifically, relative to the *sheer hulk*. The revised paragraphs, fully reproduced below (pp. 257–58), take up a total of two additional lines.

In this text, I follow the authority of B, noting where A differs significantly even when the error is fairly gross. I do not list variants in

2. *Letters*, December 16–17, 1816.
3. *The Common Reader*, first series (New York: Harcourt, Brace, & World, 1953) 139.
4. See *Letters*, January 24, 1813, January 29, 1813, and July 3–6, 1813.

punctuation and spelling unless they impinge upon the sense. A's practices in this regard are frequently inconsistent even within a volume printed by the same house. A's apparent carelessness, which results in errors such as quotation marks that are not closed, militates against its choice as the basis for an edition. B usually corrects errors at this level and demonstrates a higher level of self-consistency. Nevertheless, practices concerning punctuation, spelling, capitalization (Pug, pug), and the use of apostrophes to mark possessives (e.g., yours/your's) are in some flux during this period, and like Chapman but more consistently, I let such irregularity stand as long as it does not affect the comprehension of the text. In a relatively few instances, the reading of A is to be preferred to B, and such cases are always listed in the Textual Notes (below, pp. 322–25). Except in the case of egregious typographical errors and misplaced or missing quotation marks, which are corrected silently, when neither A nor B offers a correct reading, I have emended and noted the passage, mentioning Chapman's discussion of the matter if he and I differ in our interpretations.

Because Austen's contemporary readers apparently tolerated a wider range of inconsistency than readers would today, and because the precise extent to which Austen supervised the production of this text must remain a matter of conjecture, I have attempted to produce a conservative edition, different from Chapman's in small but pervasive ways. To be sure, Chapman's Works of Jane Austen was a monumental achievement: never before had anyone attempted to arrive at an "authoritative" text of Austen's novels by collating the editions published in her lifetime, checking them against available information in her letters, and reviewing and noting usages contemporary to her. Never before had any of the texts of any British novelist been treated with the care customarily reserved for classical authors and poets. I share the debt of generations of Austenian scholars to Chapman's texts and notes. His good judgment and good example have made many of my own editorial decisions immeasurably easier.

That said, it is also true that Chapman's practice, at its best so measured and careful, is sometimes capricious: sometimes he prefers the punctuation, spelling, or even substantives of A without justification or note; sometimes he emends A and B when they agree to good sense; sometimes he tidies punctuation and grammar, producing an amalgam of A and B. True, his emendations are not radical. But minute changes add up. Because one can easily assume that accidentals were the work of compositors in the first place, it is all too tempting to correct them in the belief that one knows what Austen was thinking. Convinced that—what with four different typesetters at work in A and B—there are already too many hands in Mansfield Park, I have tried not to smuggle in my own, to follow *B* more regularly than Chapman does, and to avoid introducing new variants in punctuation.[5] The resulting text is rawer and less lapidary than Chapman's—taking a different stand on several cruxes.

Claudia L. Johnson

---

5. There are two compositors for A: Sidney for vols. I and III and Roworth for vol. II. B employs three compositors: Moyes for vol. I, Roworth for vol. 2, and Davison for vol. III. It will be noted that Roworth also set the second volume for A.

The Text of
MANSFIELD PARK

MANSFIELD PARK:

A NOVEL.

IN THREE VOLUMES.

———◆———

BY THE

AUTHOR OF " PRIDE AND PREJUDICE."

———◆———

VOL. I.

SECOND EDITION.

London:

PRINTED FOR J. MURRAY, ALBEMARLE-STREET.

1816.

Volume I

Chapter I.

About thirty years ago, Miss Maria Ward of Huntingdon, with only seven thousand pounds, had the good luck to captivate Sir Thomas Bertram, of Mansfield Park, in the county of Northampton, and to be thereby raised to the rank of a baronet's[1] lady, with all the comforts and consequences of an handsome house and large income. All Huntingdon exclaimed on the greatness of the match, and her uncle, the lawyer, himself, allowed her to be at least three thousand pounds short of any equitable claim to it. She had two sisters to be benefited by her elevation; and such of their acquaintance as thought Miss Ward and Miss Frances quite as handsome as Miss Maria, did not scruple to predict their marrying with almost equal advantage. But there certainly are not so many men of large fortune in the world, as there are pretty women to deserve them. Miss Ward, at the end of half a dozen years, found herself obliged to be attached to the Rev. Mr. Norris, a friend of her brother-in-law, with scarcely any private fortune, and Miss Frances fared yet worse. Miss Ward's match, indeed, when it came to the point, was not contemptible, Sir Thomas being happily able to give his friend an income in the living[2] of Mansfield, and Mr. and Mrs. Norris began their career of conjugal felicity with very little less than a thousand a year. But Miss Frances married, in the common phrase, to disoblige her family, and by fixing on a Lieutenant of Marines, without education, fortune, or connections, did it very thoroughly. She could hardly have made a more untoward choice. Sir Thomas Bertram had interest,[3] which, from principle as well as pride, from a general wish of doing right, and a desire of seeing all that were connected with him in situations of respectability, he would have been glad to exert for the advantage of Lady Bertram's sister; but her husband's profession was such as no interest could reach; and before he had time to devise any other method of assisting them, an absolute breach between the sisters had

1. A baronet is the degree of hereditary honor below a baron and above a knight; a commoner, not a peer.
2. A benefice; a permanent appointment as rector or vicar, providing the holder with income from tithes. In most country churches, the principal landowner of a parish had the right to present livings, and often did so to younger sons and relations.
3. Influence.

taken place. It was the natural result of the conduct of each party, and such as a very imprudent marriage almost always produces. To save herself from useless remonstrance, Mrs. Price never wrote to her family on the subject till actually married. Lady Bertram, who was a woman of very tranquil feelings, and a temper remarkably easy and indolent, would have contented herself with merely giving up her sister, and thinking no more of the matter: but Mrs. Norris had a spirit of activity, which could not be satisfied till she had written a long and angry letter to Fanny, to point out the folly of her conduct, and threaten her with all its possible ill consequences. Mrs. Price in her turn was injured and angry; and an answer which comprehended each sister in its bitterness, and bestowed such very disrespectful reflections on the pride of Sir Thomas, as Mrs. Norris could not possibly keep to herself, put an end to all intercourse between them for a considerable period.

Their homes were so distant, and the circles in which they moved so distinct, as almost to preclude the means of ever hearing of each other's existence during the eleven following years, or at least to make it very wonderful to Sir Thomas, that Mrs. Norris should ever have it in her power to tell them, as she now and then did in an angry voice, that Fanny had got another child. By the end of eleven years, however,* Mrs. Price could no longer afford to cherish pride or resentment, or to lose one connection that might possibly assist her. A large and still increasing family, an husband disabled for active service, but not the less equal to company and good liquor, and a very small income to supply their wants, made her eager to regain the friends she had so carelessly sacrificed; and she addressed Lady Bertram in a letter which spoke so much contrition and despondence, such a superfluity of children, and such a want of almost every thing else, as could not but dispose them all to a reconciliation. She was preparing for her ninth lying-in, and after bewailing the circumstance, and imploring their countenance as sponsors to the expected child, she could not conceal how important she felt they might be to the future maintenance of the eight already in being. Her eldest was a boy of ten years old, a fine spirited fellow who longed to be out in the world; but what could she do? Was there any chance of his being hereafter useful to Sir Thomas in the concerns of his West Indian property?[4] No situation would be beneath him—or what did Sir Thomas think of Woolwich?[5] or how could a boy be sent out to the East?[6]

The letter was not unproductive. It re-established peace and kindness. Sir Thomas sent friendly advice and professions, Lady Bertram dispatched money and baby-linen, and Mrs. Norris wrote the letters.

4. Sir Thomas has a sugar plantation in Antigua, one of England's oldest colonies in the West Indies.
5. A garrison town on the Thames, east of London, site of the Royal Arsenal and Royal Military Academy, where William could be trained or employed.
6. The East Indies.

Such were its immediate effects, and within a twelvemonth a more important advantage to Mrs. Price resulted from it. Mrs. Norris was often observing to the others, that she could not get her poor sister and her family out of her head, and that much as they had all done for her, she seemed to be wanting to do more: and at length she could not but own it to be her wish, that poor Mrs. Price should be relieved from the charge and expense of one child entirely out of her great number. "What if they were among them to undertake the care of her eldest daughter, a girl now nine years old, of an age to require more attention than her poor mother could possibly give? The trouble and expense of it to them, would be nothing compared with the benevolence of the action." Lady Bertram agreed with her instantly. "I think we cannot do better," said she, "let us send for the child."

Sir Thomas could not give so instantaneous and unqualified a consent. He debated and hesitated;—it was a serious charge;—a girl so brought up must be adequately provided for, or there would be cruelty instead of kindness in taking her from her family. He thought of his own four children—of his two sons—of cousins in love, &c.;—but no sooner had he deliberately begun to state his objections, than Mrs. Norris interrupted him with a reply to them all whether stated or not.

"My dear Sir Thomas, I perfectly comprehend you, and do justice to the generosity and delicacy of your notions, which indeed are quite of a piece with your general conduct; and I entirely agree with you in the main as to the propriety of doing every thing one could by way of providing for a child one had in a manner taken into one's own hands; and I am sure I should be the last person in the world to withhold my mite upon such an occasion. Having no children of my own, who should I look to in any little matter I may ever have to bestow, but the children of my sisters?—and I am sure Mr. Norris is too just—but you know I am a woman of few words and professions. Do not let us be frightened from a good deed by a trifle. Give a girl an education, and introduce her properly into the world, and ten to one but she has the means of settling well, without farther expense to any body. A niece of our's, Sir Thomas, I may say, or, at least of *your's*, would not grow up in this neighbourhood without many advantages. I don't say she would be so handsome as her cousins. I dare say she would not; but she would be introduced into the society of this country under such very favourable circumstances as, in all human probability, would get her a creditable establishment. You are thinking of your sons—but do not you know that of all things upon earth *that* is the least likely to happen; brought up, as they would be, always together like brothers and sisters? It is morally impossible. I never knew an instance of it. It is, in fact, the only sure way of providing against the connection. Suppose her a pretty girl, and seen by Tom or Edmund for the first time seven years hence, and I dare say there would be mischief. The very idea of her having been suffered to grow up at a distance from us all in poverty and neglect, would be enough to make either of the dear sweet-tempered boys in love with her. But breed her up with them from this time, and suppose her even to have the beauty of an angel, and she will never be more to either than a sister."

"There is a great deal of truth in what you say," replied Sir Thomas, "and far be it from me to throw any fanciful impediment in the way of a plan which would be so consistent with the relative situations of each. I only meant to observe, that it ought not to be lightly engaged in, and that to make it really serviceable to Mrs. Price, and creditable to ourselves, we must secure to the child, or consider ourselves engaged to secure to her hereafter, as circumstances may arise, the provision of a gentlewoman, if no such establishment should offer as you are so sanguine in expecting."

"I thoroughly understand you," cried Mrs. Norris; "you are every thing that is generous and considerate, and I am sure we shall never disagree on this point. Whatever I can do, as you well know, I am always ready enough to do for the good of those I love; and, though I could never feel for this little girl the hundredth part of the regard I bear your own dear children, nor consider her, in any respect, so much my own, I should hate myself if I were capable of neglecting her. Is not she a sister's child? and could I bear to see her want, while I had a bit of bread to give her? My dear Sir Thomas, with all my faults I have a warm heart: and, poor as I am, would rather deny myself the necessaries of life, than do an ungenerous thing. So, if you are not against it, I will write to my poor sister to-morrow, and make the proposal; and, as soon as matters are settled, I will engage to get the child to Mansfield; you shall have no trouble about it. My own trouble, you know, I never regard. I will send Nanny to London on purpose, and she may have a bed at her cousin, the sadler's, and the child be appointed to meet her there. They may easily get her from Portsmouth to town by the coach, under the care of any creditable person that may chance to be going. I dare say there is always some reputable trades-man's wife or other going up."

Except to the attack on Nanny's cousin, Sir Thomas no longer made any objection, and a more respectable, though less economical rendez-vous being accordingly substituted, every thing was considered as set-tled, and the pleasures of so benevolent a scheme were already enjoyed. The division of gratifying sensations ought not, in strict justice, to have been equal; for Sir Thomas was fully resolved to be the real and con-sistent patron of the selected child, and Mrs. Norris had not the least intention of being at any expense whatever in her maintenance. As far as walking, talking, and contriving reached, she was thoroughly benev-olent, and nobody knew better how to dictate liberality to others: but her love of money was equal to her love of directing, and she knew quite as well how to save her own as to spend that of her friends. Having married on a narrower income than she had been used to look forward to, she had, from the first, fancied a very strict line of economy necessary; and what was begun as a matter of prudence, soon grew into a matter of choice, as an object of that needful solicitude, which there were no children to supply. Had there been a family to provide for, Mrs. Norris might never have saved her money; but having no care of that kind, there was nothing to impede her frugality, or lessen the comfort of making a yearly addition to an income which they had never lived up to. Under this infatuating principle, counteracted by no real affection for her sister, it was impossible for her to aim at more than the credit of projecting and arranging so expensive a charity; though perhaps she might so little know herself, as to walk home to the Parsonage after this conversation, in the happy belief of being the most liberal-minded sister and aunt in the world.

When the subject was brought forward again, her views were more fully explained; and, in reply to Lady Bertram's calm inquiry of "Where shall the child come to first, sister, to you or to us?" Sir Thomas heard, with some surprise, that it would be totally out of Mrs. Norris's power to take any share in the personal charge of her. He had been considering her as a particularly welcome addition at the Parsonage, as a desirable companion to an aunt who had no children of her own; but he found himself wholly mistaken. Mrs. Norris was sorry to say, that the little girl's staying with them, at least as things then were, was quite out of the question. Poor Mr. Norris's indifferent state of health made it an impossibility: he could no more bear* the noise of a child than he could fly; if indeed he should ever get well of his gouty complaints, it would be a different matter: she should then be glad to take her turn, and think nothing of the inconvenience; but just now, poor Mr. Norris took up every moment of her time, and the very mention of such a thing she was sure would distract him.

"Then she had better come to us,*" said Lady Bertram with the utmost composure. After a short pause, Sir Thomas added with dignity, "Yes, let her home be in this house. We will endeavour to do our duty by her, and she will at least have the advantage of companions of her own age, and of a regular instructress."

"Very true," cried Mrs. Norris, "which are both very important considerations: and it will be just the same to Miss Lee, whether she has three girls to teach, or only two—there can be no difference. I only wish I could be more useful; but you see I do all in my power. I am not one of those that spare their own trouble; and Nanny shall fetch her, however it may put me to inconvenience to have my chief counsellor away for three days. I suppose, sister, you will put the child in the little white attic, near the old nurseries. It will be much the best place for her, so near Miss Lee, and not far from the girls, and close by the housemaids, who could either of them help to dress* her you know, and take care of her clothes, for I suppose you would not think it fair to expect Ellis to wait on her as well as the others. Indeed, I do not see that you could possibly place her any where else.

Lady Bertram made no opposition.

"I hope she will prove a well-disposed girl," continued Mrs. Norris, "and be sensible of her uncommon good fortune in having such friends."

"Should her disposition be really bad," said Sir Thomas, "we must not, for our own children's sake, continue her in the family; but there is no reason to expect so great an evil. We shall probably see much to wish altered in her, and must prepare ourselves for gross ignorance, some meanness of opinions, and very distressing vulgarity of manner; but these are not incurable faults—nor, I trust, can they be dangerous for her associates. Had my daughters* been *younger* than herself, I should have considered the introduction of such a companion, as a matter of very serious moment; but as it is, I hope there can be nothing to fear for *them*, and every thing to hope for *her*, from the association."

"That is exactly what I think," cried Mrs. Norris, "and what I was saying to my husband this morning. It will be an education for the child said I, only being with her cousins; if Miss Lee taught her nothing, she would learn to be good and clever from *them*."

"I hope she will not tease my poor pug," said Lady Bertram; "I have but just got Julia to leave it alone."

"There will be some difficulty in our way, Mrs. Norris," observed Sir Thomas, "as to the distinction proper to be made between the girls as they grow up; how to preserve in the minds of my *daughters* the consciousness of what they are, without making them think too lowly of their cousin; and how, without depressing her spirits too far, to make her remember that she is not a *Miss Bertram*. I should wish to see them very good friends, and would, on no account, authorize in my girls the smallest degree of arrogance towards their relation; but still they cannot be equals. Their rank, fortune, rights, and expectations, will always be different. It is a point of great delicacy, and you must assist us in our endeavours to choose exactly the right line of conduct."

Mrs. Norris was quite at his service; and though she perfectly agreed with him as to its being a most difficult thing, encouraged him to hope that between them it would be easily managed.

It will be readily believed that Mrs. Norris did not write to her sister in vain. Mrs. Price seemed rather surprised that a girl should be fixed on, when she had so many fine boys, but accepted the offer most thankfully, assuring them of her daughter's being a very well-disposed, good-humoured girl, and trusting they would never have cause to throw her off. She spoke of her farther as somewhat delicate and puny, but was sanguine in the hope of her being materially better for change of air.

Poor woman! she probably thought change of air might agree with many of her children.

Chapter II.

The little girl performed her long journey in safety, and at Northampton was met by Mrs. Norris, who thus regaled in the credit of being foremost to welcome her, and in the importance of leading her in to the others, and recommending her to their kindness.

Fanny Price[1] was at this time just ten years old, and though there might not be much in her first appearance to captivate, there was, at least, nothing to disgust her relations. She was small of her age, with no glow of complexion, nor any other striking beauty; exceedingly timid and shy, and shrinking from notice; but her air, though awkward, was not vulgar, her voice was sweet, and when she spoke, her countenance was pretty. Sir Thomas and Lady Bertram received her very kindly, and Sir Thomas seeing how much she needed encouragement, tried to be all that was conciliating; but he had to work against a most untoward gravity of deportment—and Lady Bertram, without taking half so much trouble, or speaking one word where he spoke ten, by the mere aid of a good-humoured smile, became immediately the less awful[2] character of the two.

The young people were all at home, and sustained their share in the introduction very well, with much good humour, and no embarrassment, at least on the part of the sons, who at seventeen and sixteen, and tall of their age, had all the grandeur of men in the eyes of their little cousin. The two girls were more at a loss from being younger and in greater awe of their father, who addressed them on the occasion with rather an injudicious particularity. But they were too much used to company and praise, to have any thing like natural shyness, and their confidence increasing from their cousin's total want of it, they were soon able to take a full survey of her face and her frock in easy indifference.

They were a remarkably fine family, the sons very well-looking, the daughters decidedly handsome, and all of them well-grown and forward of their age, which produced as striking a difference between the cousins in person, as education had given to their address; and no one would have supposed the girls so nearly of an age as they really were. There was in fact but two years between the youngest and Fanny. Julia Bertram was only twelve, and Maria but a year older. The little visitor meanwhile was as unhappy* as possible. Afraid of every body, ashamed

---

1. This name may derive from George Crabbe's *Parish Register* (1807), part II, where "Fanny Price" is a virtuous and long-suffering young woman pursued by a rakish gentleman.
2. Awesome; filling one with terror and dread.

of herself, and longing for the home she had left, she knew not how to look up, and could scarcely speak to be heard, or without crying. Mrs. Norris had been talking to her the whole way from Northampton of her wonderful good fortune, and the extraordinary degree of gratitude and good behaviour which it ought to produce, and her consciousness of misery was therefore increased by the idea of its being a wicked thing for her not to be happy. The fatigue too, of so long a journey, became soon no trifling evil. In vain were the well-meant condescensions of Sir Thomas, and all the officious prognostications of Mrs. Norris that she would be a good girl; in vain did Lady Bertram smile and make her sit on the sofa with herself and pug, and vain was even the sight of a gooseberry tart towards giving her comfort; she could scarcely swallow two mouthfuls before tears interrupted her, and sleep seeming to be her likeliest friend, she was taken to finish her sorrows in bed.

"This is not a very promising beginning," said Mrs. Norris when Fanny had left the room.—"After all that I said to her as we came along, I thought she would have behaved better; I told her how much might depend upon her acquitting herself well at first. I wish there may not be a little sulkiness of temper—her poor mother had a good deal; but we must make allowances for such a child—and I do not know that her being sorry to leave her home is really against her, for, with all its faults, it *was* her home, and she cannot as yet understand how much she has changed for the better; but then there is moderation in all things."

It required a longer time, however, than Mrs. Norris was inclined to allow, to reconcile Fanny to the novelty of Mansfield Park, and the separation from every body she had been used to. Her feelings were very acute, and too little understood to be properly attended to. Nobody meant to be unkind, but nobody put themselves out of their way to secure her comfort.

The holiday allowed to the Miss Bertrams the next day on purpose to afford leisure for getting acquainted with, and entertaining their young cousin, produced little union. They could not but hold her cheap on finding that she had but two sashes, and had never learnt French; and when they perceived her to be little struck with the duet they were so good as to play, they could do no more than make her a generous present of some of their least valued toys, and leave her to herself, while they adjourned to whatever might be the favourite holiday sport of the moment, making artificial flowers or wasting gold paper.

Fanny, whether near or from her cousins, whether in the school-room, the drawing-room, or the shrubbery, was equally forlorn, finding something to fear in every person and place. She was disheartened by Lady Bertram's silence, awed by Sir Thomas's grave looks, and quite overcome by Mrs. Norris's admonitions. Her elder cousins mortified her by reflections on her size, and abashed her by noticing her shyness;

Miss Lee wondered at her ignorance, and the maid-servants sneered at her clothes; and when to these sorrows was added the idea of the brothers and sisters among whom she had always been important as playfellow, instructress, and nurse, the despondence that sunk her little heart was severe.

The grandeur of the house astonished, but could not console her. The rooms were too large for her to move in with ease; whatever she touched she expected to injure, and she crept about in constant terror of something or other; often retreating towards her own chamber to cry; and the little girl who was spoken of in the drawing-room when she left it at night, as seeming so desirably sensible of her peculiar good fortune, ended every day's sorrows by sobbing herself to sleep. A week had passed in this way, and no suspicion of it conveyed by her quiet passive manner, when she was found one morning by her cousin Edmund, the youngest of the sons, sitting crying on the attic stairs.

"My dear little cousin," said he with all the gentleness of an excellent nature, "what can be the matter?" And sitting down by her, was at great pains to overcome her shame in being so surprised, and persuade her to speak openly. "Was she ill? or was any body angry with her? or had she quarrelled with Maria and Julia? or was she puzzled about any thing in her lesson that he could explain? Did she, in short, want any thing he could possibly get her, or do for her?" For a long while no answer could be obtained beyond a "no, no—not at all—no, thank you;" but he still persevered, and no sooner had he begun to revert to her own home, than her increased sobs explained to him where the grievance lay. He tried to console her.

"You are sorry to leave Mamma, my dear little Fanny," said he, "which shows you to be a very good girl; but you must remember that you are with relations and friends, who all love you, and wish to make you happy. Let us walk out in the park,[3] and you shall tell me all about your brothers and sisters."

On pursuing the subject, he found that dear as all these brothers and sisters generally were, there was one among them who ran more in her thoughts than the rest. It was William whom she talked of most and wanted most to see. William, the eldest, a year older than herself, her constant companion and friend; her advocate with her mother (of whom he was the darling) in every distress. "William did not like she should come away—he had told her he should miss her very much indeed." "But William will write to you, I dare say." "Yes, he had promised he would, but he had told *her* to write first." "And when shall you do it?" She hung her head and answered, hesitatingly, "she did not know; she had not any paper."

"If that be all your difficulty, I will furnish you with paper and every

3. The area of land, containing woods, lakes, pasturage, etc., surrounding a large country house.

other material, and you may write your letter whenever you choose. Would it make you happy to write to William?"

"Yes, very."

"Then let it be done now. Come with me into the breakfast-room, we shall find every thing there, and be sure of having the room to ourselves."

"But, cousin—will it go to the post?"

"Yes, depend upon me it shall; it shall go with the other letters; and as your uncle will frank[4] it, it will cost William nothing."

"My uncle!" repeated Fanny with a frightened look.

"Yes, when you have written the letter, I will take it to my father to frank."

Fanny thought it a bold measure, but offered no farther resistance; and they went together into the breakfast-room, where Edmund prepared her paper, and ruled her lines with all the good will that her brother could himself have felt, and probably with somewhat more exactness. He continued with her the whole time of her writing, to assist her with his penknife or his orthography, as either were wanted; and added to these attentions, which she felt very much, a kindness to her brother, which delighted her beyond all the rest. He wrote with his own hand his love to his cousin William, and sent him half a guinea under the seal.[5] Fanny's feelings on the occasion were such as she believed herself incapable of expressing; but her countenance and a few artless words fully conveyed all their gratitude and delight, and her cousin began to find her an interesting object. He talked to her more, and from all that she said, was convinced of her having an affectionate heart, and a strong desire of doing right; and he could perceive her to be farther entitled to attention, by great sensibility of her situation, and great timidity. He had never knowingly given her pain, but he now felt that she required more positive kindness, and with that view endeavoured, in the first place, to lessen her fears of them all, and gave her especially a great deal of good advice as to playing with Maria and Julia, and being as merry as possible.

From this day Fanny grew more comfortable.[6] She felt that she had a friend, and the kindness of her cousin Edmund gave her better spirits with every body else. The place became less strange, and the people less formidable; and if there were some amongst them whom she could not cease to fear, she began at least to know their ways, and to catch

---

4. As a member of parliament, Sir Thomas could post letters free, by signing the envelope; otherwise, recipients paid the cost of postage, based on weight and distance.
5. Envelopes were made by folding the sheets of a letter from the top and bottom and sealing them with wax. Here, Edmund also uses the seal to affix a coin. Guineas and half-guineas were first issued in 1663 for English trade in Africa. In Austen's time, guineas and half-guineas were handsome gold coins, worth twenty-one shillings and ten shillings six pence respectively, whose use carried great prestige. They were not minted after 1813.
6. Consolable, capable of being cheered.

the best manner of conforming to them. The little rusticities and awk-wardnesses which had at first made grievous inroads on the tranquillity of all, and not least of herself, necessarily wore away, and she was no longer materially afraid to appear before her uncle, nor did her aunt Norris's voice make her start very much. To her cousins she became occasionally an acceptable companion. Though unworthy, from infe-riority of age and strength, to be their constant associate, their pleasures and schemes were sometimes of a nature to make a third very useful, especially when that third was of an obliging, yielding temper; and they could not but own, when their aunt inquired into her faults, or their brother Edmund urged her claims to their kindness, that "Fanny was good-natured enough."

Edmund was uniformly kind himself, and she had nothing worse to endure on the part of Tom, than that sort of merriment which a young man of seventeen will always think fair with a child of ten. He was just entering into life, full of spirits, and with all the liberal dispositions of an eldest son, who feels born only for expense and enjoyment. His kindness to his little cousin was consistent with his situation and rights: he made her some very pretty presents, and laughed at her.

As her appearance and spirits improved, Sir Thomas and Mrs. Norris thought with greater satisfaction of their benevolent plan; and it was pretty soon decided between them, that though far from clever, she showed a tractable disposition, and seemed likely to give them little trouble. A mean opinion of her abilities was not confined to *them*. Fanny could read, work,[7] and write, but she had been taught nothing more; and as her cousins found her ignorant of many things with which they had been long familiar, they thought her prodigiously stupid, and for the first two or three weeks were continually bringing some fresh report of it into the drawing-room. "Dear Mamma, only think, my cousin cannot put the map of Europe together[8]—or my cousin cannot tell the principal rivers in Russia—or she never heard of Asia Minor—or she does not know the difference between water-colours and crayons!—How strange!—Did you ever hear any thing so stupid?"

"My dear," their considerate aunt would reply; "it is very bad, but you must not expect every body to be as forward and quick at learning as yourself."

"But, aunt, she is really so very ignorant!—Do you know, we asked her last night, which way she would go to get to Ireland; and she said, she should cross to the Isle of Wight. She thinks of nothing but the Isle of Wight, and she calls it *the Island*,[9] as if there were no other island in the world. I am sure I should have been ashamed of myself,

---

7. Do needlework.
8. Geography puzzles were commonly used as an aid in instruction. Austen may be ironic as well, for the "map of Europe" was jumbled in the wake of the Napoleonic Wars.
9. Fanny's geography shows her attachment to her Portsmouth home, where the Isle of Wight looms just off the coast.

if I had not known better long before I was so old as she is. I cannot
remember the time when I did not know a great deal that she has not
the least notion of yet. How long ago it is, aunt, since we used to repeat
the chronological order of the kings of England, with the dates of their
accession, and most of the principal events of their reigns!"

"Yes," added the other; "and of the Roman emperors as low as Se-
verus; besides a great deal of the Heathen Mythology, and all the Met-
als, Semi-Metals, Planets, and distinguished philosophers."

"Very true, indeed, my dears, but you are blessed with wonderful
memories, and your poor cousin has probably none at all. There is a
vast deal of difference in memories, as well as in every thing else, and
therefore you must make allowance for your cousin, and pity her deficiency. And remember that, if you are ever so forward and clever
yourselves, you should always be modest; for, much as you know already, there is a great deal more for you to learn."

"Yes, I know there is, till I am seventeen. But I must tell you another
thing of Fanny, so odd and so stupid. Do you know, she says she does
not want to learn either music or drawing."

"To be sure, my dear, that is very stupid indeed, and shows a great
want of genius[1] and emulation. But, all things considered, I do not
know whether it is not as well that it should be so, for, though you
know (owing to me) your papa and mamma are so good as to bring
her up with you, it is not at all necessary that she should be as accomplished as you are;—on the contrary, it is much more desirable that
there should be a difference."

Such were the counsels by which Mrs. Norris assisted to form her
nieces' minds; and it is not very wonderful that with all their promising
talents and early information, they should be entirely deficient in the
less common acquirements of self-knowledge, generosity, and humility.
In every thing but disposition, they were admirably taught. Sir Thomas
did not know what was wanting, because, though a truly anxious father,
he was not outwardly affectionate, and the reserve of his manner repressed all the flow of their spirits before him.

To the education of her daughters, Lady Bertram paid not the smallest attention. She had not time for such cares. She was a woman who
spent her days in sitting nicely dressed on a sofa, doing some long piece
of needle-work, of little use and no beauty, thinking more of her pug
than her children, but very indulgent to the latter, when it did not put
herself to inconvenience, guided in every thing important by Sir Thomas, and in smaller concerns by her sister. Had she possessed greater
leisure for the service of her girls, she would probably have supposed
it unnecessary, for they were under the care of a governess, with proper
masters, and could want nothing more. As for Fanny's being stupid at

---

1. Aptitude.

learning, "she could only say it was very unlucky, but some people *were* stupid, and Fanny must take more pains; she did not know what else was to be done; and except her being so dull, she must add, she saw no harm in the poor little thing—and always found her very handy and quick in carrying messages, and fetching what she wanted."

Fanny, with all her faults of ignorance and timidity, was fixed at Mansfield Park, and learning to transfer in its favour much of her attachment to her former home, grew up there not unhappily among her cousins. There was no positive ill-nature in Maria or Julia; and though Fanny was often mortified by their treatment of her, she thought too lowly of her own claims to feel injured by it.

From about the time of her entering the family, Lady Bertram, in consequence of a little ill-health, and a great deal of indolence, gave up the house in town, which she had been used to occupy every spring, and remained wholly in the country, leaving Sir Thomas to attend his duty in Parliament, with whatever increase or diminution of comfort might arise from her absence. In the country, therefore, the Miss Bertrams continued to exercise their memories, practise their duets, and grow tall and womanly; and their father saw them becoming in person, manner, and accomplishments, every thing that could satisfy his anxiety. His eldest son was careless and extravagant, and had already given him much uneasiness; but his other children promised him nothing but good. His daughters he felt, while they retained the name of Bertram, must be giving it new grace, and in quitting it he trusted would extend its respectable alliances; and the character of Edmund, his strong good sense and uprightness of mind, bid most fairly for utility, honour, and happiness to himself and all his connections. He was to be a clergyman.

Amid the cares and the complacency which his own children suggested, Sir Thomas did not forget to do what he could for the children of Mrs. Price; he assisted her liberally in the education and disposal of her sons as they became old enough for a determinate pursuit: and Fanny, though almost totally separated from her family, was sensible of the truest satisfaction in hearing of any kindness towards them, or of any thing at all promising in their situation or conduct. Once, and once only in the course of many years, had she the happiness of being with William. Of the rest she saw nothing; nobody seemed to think of her ever going amongst them again, even for a visit, nobody at home seemed to want her; but William determining, soon after her removal, to be a sailor, was invited to spend a week with his sister in Northamptonshire, before he went to sea. Their eager affection in meeting, their exquisite delight in being together, their hours of happy mirth, and moments of serious conference, may be imagined; as well as the sanguine views and spirits of the boy even to the last, and the misery of the girl when he left her. Luckily the visit happened in the Christmas holidays, when she could directly look for comfort to her cousin Edmund; and he told her such charming things of what William was to do, and be hereafter, in consequence of his profession, as made her gradually admit that the separation might have some use. Edmund's friendship never failed her: his leaving Eton for Oxford made no change in his kind dispositions, and only afforded more frequent opportunities of proving them. Without any display of doing more than the rest, or any fear of doing too much, he was always true to her interests, and considerate of her feelings, trying to make her good qualities understood, and to conquer the diffidence which prevented their being more apparent; giving her advice, consolation, and encouragement.

Kept back as she was by every body else, his single support could not bring her forward, but his attentions were otherwise of the highest importance in assisting the improvement of her mind, and extending its pleasures. He knew her to be clever, to have a quick apprehension as well as good sense, and a fondness for reading, which, properly directed, must be an education in itself. Miss Lee taught her French, and heard her read the daily portion of History; but he recommended the books which charmed her leisure hours, he encouraged her taste, and corrected her judgment; he made reading useful by talking to her of what she read, and heightened its attraction by judicious praise. In return for such services she loved him better than any body in the world except William; her heart was divided between the two.

Chapter III.

The first event of any importance in the family was the death of Mr. Norris, which happened when Fanny was about fifteen, and necessarily introduced alterations and novelties. Mrs. Norris, on quitting the parsonage, removed first to the park, and afterwards to a small house of Sir Thomas's in the village, and consoled herself for the loss of her husband by considering that she could do very well without him, and for her reduction of income by the evident necessity of stricter economy.

The living was hereafter for Edmund, and had his uncle died a few years sooner, it would have been duly given to some friend to hold til he were old enough for orders. But Tom's extravagance had, previous to that event, been so great, as to render a different disposal of the next presentation necessary, and the younger brother must help to pay for the pleasures of the elder.[1] There was another family-living actually held for Edmund; but though this circumstance had made the arrange-

---

1. Instead of giving the living to Edmund, Sir Thomas sells it to Dr. Grant to raise money to cover Tom's debts. Since livings were tenured appointments, Edmund has no chance for the Mansfield living until Dr. Grant dies.

ment somewhat easier to Sir Thomas's conscience, he could not but feel it to be an act of injustice, and he earnestly tried to impress his eldest son with the same conviction, in the hope of its producing a better effect than any thing he had yet been able to say or do.

"I blush for you, Tom," said he, in his most dignified manner; "I blush for the expedient which I am driven on, and I trust I may pity your feelings as a brother on the occasion. You have robbed Edmund for ten, twenty, thirty years, perhaps for life, of more than half the income which ought to be his. It may hereafter be in my power, or in your's (I hope it will), to procure him better preferment; but it must not be forgotten, that no benefit of that sort would have been beyond his natural claims on us, and that nothing can, in fact, be an equivalent for the certain advantage which he is now obliged to forego through the urgency of your debts."

Tom listened with some shame and some sorrow; but escaping as quickly as possible, could soon with cheerful selfishness reflect, 1st, that he had not been half so much in debt as some of his friends; 2dly, that his father had made a most tiresome piece of work of it; and 3dly, that the future incumbent, whoever he might be, would, in all probability, die very soon.

On Mr. Norris's death, the presentation became the right of a Dr. Grant, who came consequently to reside at Mansfield, and on proving to be a hearty man of forty-five, seemed likely to disappoint Mr. Bertram's calculations. But "no, he was a short-neck'd, apoplectic sort of fellow, and, plied well with good things, would soon pop off."

He had a wife about fifteen years his junior, but no children, and they entered the neighbourhood with the usual fair report of being very respectable, agreeable people.

The time was now come when Sir Thomas expected his sister-in-law to claim her share in their niece, the change in Mrs. Norris's situation, and the improvement in Fanny's age, seeming not merely to do away any former objection to their living together, but even to give it the most decided eligibility; and as his own circumstances were rendered less fair than heretofore, by some recent losses on his West India Estate,[2] in addition to his eldest son's extravagance, it became not undesirable to himself to be relieved from the expense of her support, and the obligation of her future provision. In the fulness of his belief that such a thing must be, he mentioned its probability to his wife; and the first time of the subject's occurring to her again, happening to be when Fanny was present, she calmly observed to her, "So, Fanny, you are going to leave us, and live with my sister. How shall you like it?"

2. At the time, Sir Thomas's sugar plantation on his West Indies estate could be losing money for several reasons: decreased crop production stemming from exhausted soil; increased competition from other sugar-producing islands; and/or increased production costs resulting from the abolition of the slave trade in 1807.

Fanny was too much surprised to do more than repeat her aunt's words, "Going to leave you?"

"Yes, my dear, why should you be astonished? You have been five years with us, and my sister always meant to take you when Mr. Norris died. But you must come up and tack on my patterns all the same."

The news was as disagreeable to Fanny as it had been unexpected. She had never received kindness from her aunt Norris, and could not love her.

"I shall be very sorry to go away," said she, with a faltering voice.

"Yes, I dare say you will; *that's* natural enough. I suppose you have had as little to vex you, since you came into this house, as any creature in the world."

"I hope I am not ungrateful, aunt," said Fanny, modestly. "No, my dear; I hope not. I have always found you a very good girl."

"And am I never to live here again?"

"Never, my dear; but you are sure of a comfortable home. It can make very little difference to you, whether you are in one house or the other."

Fanny left the room with a very sorrowful heart; she could not feel the difference to be so small, she could not think of living with her aunt with any thing like satisfaction. As soon as she met with Edmund, she told him her distress.

"Cousin," said she, "something is going to happen which I do not like at all; and though you have often persuaded me into being reconciled to things that I disliked at first, you will not be able to do it now. I am going to live entirely with my aunt Norris."

"Indeed!"

"Yes, my aunt Bertram has just told me so. It is quite settled. I am to leave Mansfield Park, and go to the White house, I suppose, as soon as she is removed there."

"Well, Fanny, and if the plan were not unpleasant to you, I should call it an excellent one."

"Oh! Cousin!"

"It has every thing else in its favour. My aunt is acting like a sensible woman in wishing for you. She is choosing a friend and companion exactly where she ought, and I am glad her love of money does not interfere. You will be what you ought to be to her. I hope it does not distress you very much, Fanny."

"Indeed it does. I cannot like it. I love this house and every thing in it. I shall love nothing there. You know how uncomfortable I feel with her."

"I can say nothing for her manner to you as a child; but it was the same with us all, or nearly so. She never knew how to be pleasant to children. But you are now of an age to be treated better; I think she *is* behaving better already; and when you are her only companion, you *must* be important to her."

"I can never be important to any one."

"What is to prevent you?"

"Every thing—my situation—my foolishness and awkwardness."

"As to your foolishness and awkwardness, my dear Fanny, believe me, you never have a shadow of either, but in using the words so improperly. There is no reason in the world why you should not be important where you are known. You have good sense, and a sweet temper, and I am sure you have a grateful heart, that could never receive kindness without wishing to return it. I do not know any better qualifications for a friend and companion."

"You are too kind," said Fanny, colouring at such praise; "how shall I ever thank you as I ought, for thinking so well of me. Oh! cousin, if I am to go away, I shall remember your goodness, to the last moment of my life."

"Why, indeed, Fanny, I should hope to be remembered at such a distance as the White house. You speak as if you were going two hundred miles off, instead of only across the park. But you will belong to us almost as much as ever. The two families will be meeting every day in the year. The only difference will be, that living with your aunt, you will necessarily be brought forward, as you ought to be. *Here*, there are too many, whom you can hide behind; but with *her* you will be forced to speak for yourself."

"Oh! do not say so."

"I must say it, and say it with pleasure. Mrs. Norris is much better fitted than my mother for having the charge of you now. She is of a temper to do a great deal for any body she really interests herself about, and she will force you to do justice to your natural powers."

Fanny sighed, and said, "I cannot see things as you do; but I ought to believe you to be right rather than myself, and I am very much obliged to you for trying to reconcile me to what must be. If I could suppose my aunt really to care for me, it would be delightful to feel myself of consequence to any body!—*Here*, I know I am of none, and yet I love the place so well."

"The place, Fanny, is what you will not quit, though you quit the house. You will have as free a command of the park and gardens as ever. Even *your* constant little heart need not take fright at such a nominal change. You will have the same walks to frequent, the same library to choose from, the same people to look at, the same horse to ride."

"Very true. Yes, dear old grey poney. Ah! cousin, when I remember how much I used to dread riding, what terrors it gave me to hear it talked of as likely to do me good;—(Oh! how I have trembled at my uncle's opening his lips if horses were talked of) and then think of the kind pains you took to reason and persuade me out of my fears, and convince me that I should like it after a little while, and feel how right you proved to be, I am inclined to hope you may always prophesy as well."

"And I am quite convinced that your being with Mrs. Norris, will be as good for your mind, as riding has been for your health—and as much for your ultimate happiness, too."

So ended their discourse, which, for any very appropriate service it could render Fanny, might as well have been spared, for Mrs. Norris had not the smallest intention of taking her. It had never occurred to her, on the present occasion, but as a thing to be carefully avoided. To prevent its being expected, she had fixed on the smallest habitation which could rank as genteel among the buildings of Mansfield parish; the White house being only just large enough to receive herself and her servants, and allow a spare room for a friend, of which she made a very particular point;—the spare-rooms at the parsonage had never been wanted, but the absolute necessity of a spare-room for a friend was now never forgotten. Not all her precautions, however, could save her from being suspected of something better; or, perhaps, her very display of the importance of a spare-room, might have misled Sir Thomas to suppose it really intended for Fanny. Lady Bertram soon brought the matter to a certainty, by carelessly observing to Mrs. Norris,—

"I think, sister, we need not keep Miss Lee any longer, when Fanny goes to live with you?"

Mrs. Norris almost started. "Live with me, dear Lady Bertram, what do you mean?"

"Is not she to live with you?—I thought you had settled it with Sir Thomas?"

"Me! never. I never spoke a syllable about it to Sir Thomas, nor he to me. Fanny live with me! the last thing in the world for me to think of, or for any body to wish that really knows us both. Good heaven! what could I do with Fanny?—Me! a poor helpless, forlorn widow, unfit for any thing, my spirits quite broke down, what could I do with a girl at her time of life, a girl of fifteen! the very age of all others to need most attention and care, and put the cheerfullest spirits to the test. Sure Sir Thomas could not seriously expect such a thing! Sir Thomas is too much my friend. Nobody that wishes me well, I am sure, would propose it. How came Sir Thomas to speak to you about it?"

"Indeed, I do not know. I suppose he thought it best."

"But what did he say?—He could not say he *wished* me to take Fanny. I am sure in his heart he could not wish me to do it."

"No, he only said he thought it very likely—and I thought so too.

We both thought it would be a comfort to you. But if you do not like it, there is no more to be said. She is no incumbrance here."

"Dear sister! If you consider my unhappy state, how can she be any comfort to me? Here am I a poor desolate widow, deprived of the best of husbands, my health gone in attending and nursing him, my spirits still worse, all my peace in this world destroyed, with barely enough to support me in the rank of a gentlewoman, and enable me to live so as not to disgrace the memory of the dear departed—what possible comfort could I have in taking such a charge upon me as Fanny! If I could wish it for my own sake, I would not do so unjust a thing by the poor girl. She is in good hands, and sure of doing well. I must struggle through my sorrows and difficulties as I can."

"Then you will not mind living by yourself quite alone?"

"Dear Lady Bertram! what am I fit for but solitude? Now and then I shall hope to have a friend in my little cottage (I shall always have a bed for a friend); but the most part of my future days will be spent in utter seclusion. If I can but make both ends meet, that's all I ask for."

"I hope, sister, things are not so very bad with you neither—considering Sir Thomas* says you will have six hundred a year."

"Lady Bertram, I do not complain. I know I cannot live as I have done, but I must retrench where I can, and learn to be a better manager. I *have been* a liberal housekeeper enough, but I shall not be ashamed to practise economy now. My situation is as much altered as my income. A great many things were due from poor Mr. Norris as clergyman of the parish, that cannot be expected from me. It is unknown how much was consumed in our kitchen by odd comers and goers. At the White house, matters must be better looked after. I *must* live within my income, or I shall be miserable; and I own it would give me great satisfaction to be able to do rather more—to lay by a little at the end of the year."

"I dare say you will. You always do, don't you?"

"My object, Lady Bertram, is to be of use to those that come after me. It is for your children's good that I wish to be richer. I have nobody else to care for, but I should be very glad to think I could leave a little trifle among them, worth their having."

"You are very good, but do not trouble yourself about them. They are sure of being well provided for. Sir Thomas will take care of that."

"Why, you know Sir Thomas's means will be rather straitened, if the Antigua estate is to make such poor returns."

"Oh! *that* will soon be settled. Sir Thomas has been writing about it, I know."

"Well, Lady Bertram," said Mrs. Norris, moving to go, "I can only say that my sole desire is to be of use to your family—and so if Sir Thomas should ever speak again about my taking Fanny, you will be able to say, that my health and spirits put it quite out of the question —besides that, I really should not have a bed to give her, for I must keep a spare room for a friend.

Lady Bertram repeated enough of this conversation to her husband, to convince him how much he had mistaken his sister-in-law's views; and she was from that moment perfectly safe from all expectation, or the slightest allusion to it from him. He could not but wonder at her refusing to do any thing for a niece, whom she had been so forward to adopt; but as she took early care to make him, as well as Lady Bertram, understand that whatever she possessed was designed for their family, he soon grew reconciled to a distinction, which at the same time that it was advantageous and complimentary to them, would enable him better to provide for Fanny himself.

Fanny soon learnt how unnecessary had been her fears of a removal; and her spontaneous, untaught felicity on the discovery, conveyed some consolation to Edmund for his disappointment in what he had expected to be so essentially serviceable to her. Mrs. Norris took possession of the White house, the Grants arrived at the parsonage, and these events over, every thing at Mansfield went on for some time as usual.

The Grants showing a disposition to be friendly and sociable, gave great satisfaction in the main among their new acquaintance. They had their faults, and Mrs. Norris soon found them out. The Dr. was very fond of eating, and would have a good dinner every day; and Mrs. Grant, instead of contriving to gratify him at little expense, gave her cook as high wages as they did at Mansfield Park, and was scarcely ever seen in her offices.[3] Mrs. Norris could not speak with any temper of such grievances, nor of the quantity of butter and eggs that were regularly consumed in the house. "Nobody loved plenty and hospitality more than herself—nobody more hated pitiful[4] doings—the parsonage she believed had never been wanting in comforts of any sort, had never borne a bad character in *her time*, but this was a way of going on that she could not understand. A fine lady in a country parsonage was quite out of place. *Her* store-room she thought might have been good enough for Mrs. Grant to go into. Enquire where she would, she could not find out that Mrs. Grant had ever had more than five thousand pounds."

Lady Bertram listened without much interest to this sort of invective. She could not enter into the wrongs of an economist, but she felt all the injuries of beauty in Mrs. Grant's being so well settled in life without being handsome, and expressed her astonishment on that point almost as often, though not so diffusely, as Mrs. Norris discussed the other.

These opinions had been hardly canvassed a year, before another

3. The kitchen and pantries.
4. Scrimping, mean.

event arose of such importance in the family, as might fairly claim some place in the thoughts and conversation of the ladies. Sir Thomas found it expedient to go to Antigua himself, for the better arrangement of his affairs, and he took his eldest son with him in the hope of detaching him from some bad connections at home. They left England with the probability of being nearly a twelve-month absent.

The necessity of the measure in a pecuniary light, and the hope of its utility to his son, reconciled Sir Thomas to the effort of quitting the rest of his family, and of leaving his daughters to the direction of others at their present most interesting time of life. He could not think Lady Bertram quite equal to supply his place with them, or rather to perform what should have been her own; but in Mrs. Norris's watchful attention, and in Edmund's judgment, he had sufficient confidence to make him go without fears for their conduct.

Lady Bertram did not at all like to have her husband leave her; but she was not disturbed by any alarm for his safety, or solicitude for his comfort, being one of those persons who think nothing can be danger-ous or difficult, or fatiguing to any body but themselves.

The Miss Bertrams were much to be pitied on the occasion; not for their sorrow, but for their want of it. Their father was no object of love to them, he had never seemed the friend of their pleasures, and his absence was unhappily most welcome. They were relieved by it from all restraint; and without aiming at one gratification that would probably have been forbidden by Sir Thomas, they felt themselves immediately at their own disposal, and to have every indulgence within their reach. Fanny's relief, and her consciousness of it, were quite equal to her cousins', but a more tender nature suggested that her feelings were ungrateful, and she really grieved because she could not grieve. "Sir Thomas, who had done so much for her and her brothers, and who was gone perhaps never to return! that she should see him go without a tear!—it was a shameful insensibility." He had said to her moreover, on the very last morning, that he hoped she might see William again in the course of the ensuing winter, and had charged her to write and invite him to Mansfield as soon as the squadron to which he belonged should be known to be in England. "This was so thoughtful and kind!"—and would he only have smiled upon her and called her "my dear Fanny," while he said it, every former frown or cold address might have been forgotten. But he had ended his speech in a way to sink her in sad mortification, by adding, "If William does come to Mansfield, I hope you may be able to convince him that the many years which have passed since you parted, have not been spent on your side entirely without improvement—though I fear he must find his sister at sixteen in some respects too much like his sister at ten." She cried bitterly over this reflection when her uncle was gone; and her cousins, on seeing her with red eyes, set her down as a hypocrite.

Chapter IV.

Tom Bertram had of late spent so little of his time at home, that he could be only nominally missed; and Lady Bertram was soon astonished to find how very well they did even without his father, how well Edmund could supply his place in carving, talking to the steward, writing to the attorney, settling with the servants, and equally saving her from all possible fatigue or exertion in every particular, but that of directing her letters.

The earliest intelligence of the travellers' safe arrival in Antigua after a favourable voyage, was received; though not before Mrs. Norris had been indulging in very dreadful fears, and trying to make Edmund participate them whenever she could get him alone; and as she depended on being the first person made acquainted with any fatal catastrophe, she had already arranged the manner of breaking it to all the others, when Sir Thomas's assurances of their both being alive and well, made it necessary to lay by her agitation and affectionate preparatory speeches for a while.

The winter came and passed without their being called for; the accounts continued perfectly good;—and Mrs. Norris in promoting gaieties for her nieces, assisting their toilettes, displaying their accomplishments, and looking about for their future husbands, had so much to do as, in addition to all her own household cares, some interference in those of her sister, and Mrs. Grant's wasteful doings to overlook, left her very little occasion to be occupied even in fears for the absent.

The Miss Bertrams were now fully established among the belles of the neighbourhood; and as they joined to beauty and brilliant acquirements, a manner naturally easy, and carefully formed to general civility and obligingness, they possessed its favour as well as its admiration. Their vanity was in such good order, that they seemed to be quite free from it, and gave themselves no airs; while the praises attending such behaviour, secured, and brought round by their aunt, served to strengthen them in believing they had no faults.

Lady Bertram did not go into public with her daughters. She was too indolent even to accept a mother's gratification in witnessing their success and enjoyment at the expense of any personal trouble, and the charge was made over to her sister, who desired nothing better than a post of such honourable representation, and very thoroughly relished the means it afforded her of mixing in society without having horses to hire.

Fanny had no share in the festivities of the season; but she enjoyed being avowedly useful as her aunt's companion, when they called away the rest of the family; and as Miss Lee had left Mansfield, she naturally became every thing to Lady Bertram during the night of a ball or a party. She talked to her, listened to her, read to her; and the tranquillity of such evenings, her perfect security in such a *tête-à-tête* from any sound of unkindness, was unspeakably welcome to a mind which had seldom known a pause in its alarms or embarrassments. As to her cousins' gaieties, she loved to hear an account of them, especially of the balls, and whom Edmund had danced with; but thought too lowly of her own situation to imagine she should ever be admitted to the same, and listened therefore without an idea of any nearer concern in them. Upon the whole, it was a comfortable winter to her; for though it brought no William to England, the never failing hope of his arrival was worth much.

The ensuing spring deprived her of her valued friend the old grey poney, and for some time she was in danger of feeling the loss in her health as well as in her affections, for in spite of the acknowledged importance of her riding on horseback, no measures were taken for mounting her again, "because," as it was observed by her aunts, "she might ride one of her cousins'* horses at any time when they did not want them;" and as the Miss Bertrams regularly wanted their horses every fine day, and had no idea of carrying their obliging manners to the sacrifice of any real pleasure, that time of course never came. They took their cheerful rides in the fine mornings of April and May; and Fanny either sat at home the whole day with one aunt, or walked beyond her strength at the instigation of the other; Lady Bertram holding exercise to be as unnecessary for every body as it was unpleasant to herself; and Mrs. Norris, who was walking all day, thinking every body ought to walk as much. Edmund was absent at this time, or the evil would have been earlier remedied. When he returned to understand how Fanny was situated, and perceived* its ill effects, there seemed with him but one thing to be done, and that "Fanny must have a horse," was the resolute declaration with which he opposed whatever could be urged by the supineness of his mother, or the economy of his aunt, to make it appear unimportant. Mrs. Norris could not help thinking that some steady old thing might be found among the numbers belonging to the Park, that would do vastly well, or that one might be borrowed of the steward, or that perhaps Dr. Grant might now and then lend them the poney he sent to the post. She could not but consider it as absolutely unnecessary, and even improper, that Fanny should have a regular lady's horse of her own in the style of her cousins. She was sure Sir Thomas had never intended it; and she must say, that to be making such a purchase in his absence, and adding to the great expenses of his stable at a time when a large part of his income was unsettled, seemed to her very unjustifiable. "Fanny must have a horse," was Edmund's only reply. Mrs. Norris could not see it in the same light. Lady Bertram did; she entirely agreed with her son as to the necessity of it, and as to its being considered necessary by his father;—

she only pleaded against there being any hurry, she only wanted him to wait till Sir Thomas's return, and then Sir Thomas might settle it all himself. He would be at home in September, and where would be the harm of only waiting till September?

Though Edmund was much more displeased with his aunt than with his mother, as evincing least regard for her niece, he could not help paying more attention to what she said, and at length determined on a method of proceeding which would obviate the risk of his father's thinking he had done too much, and at the same time procure for Fanny the immediate means of exercise, which he could not bear she should be without. He had three horses of his own, but not one that would carry a woman. Two of them were hunters; the third, a useful road-horse:[1] this third he resolved to exchange for one that his cousin might ride; he knew where such a one was to be met with, and having once made up his mind, the whole business was soon completed. The new mare proved a treasure; with a very little trouble, she became exactly calculated for the purpose, and Fanny was then put in almost full possession of her. She had not supposed before, that any thing could ever suit her like the old grey poney; but her delight in Edmund's mare was far beyond any former pleasure of the sort; and the addition it was ever receiving in the consideration of that kindness from which her pleasure sprung, was beyond all her words to express. She regarded her cousin as an example of every thing good and great, as possessing worth, which no one but herself could ever appreciate, and as entitled to such gratitude from her, as no feelings could be strong enough to pay. Her sentiments towards him were compounded of all that was respectful, grateful, confiding, and tender.

As the horse continued in name as well as fact, the property of Edmund, Mrs. Norris could tolerate its being for Fanny's use; and had Lady Bertram ever thought about her own objection again, he might have been excused in her eyes, for not waiting till Sir Thomas's return in September, for when September came, Sir Thomas was still abroad, and without any near prospect of finishing his business. Unfavourable circumstances had suddenly arisen at a moment when he was beginning to turn all his thoughts towards England, and the very great uncertainty in which every thing was then involved, determined him on sending home his son, and waiting the final arrangement by himself. Tom arrived safely, bringing an excellent account of his father's health; but to very little purpose, as far as Mrs. Norris was concerned. Sir Thomas's sending away his son, seemed to her so like a parent's care, under the influence of a foreboding of evil to himself, that she could not help feeling dreadful presentiments; and as the long evenings of

---

1. Road-horses were saddled only for use on roads; hunters were more spirited, were adapted for use especially in fox hunting, and were trained for speed, endurance, and jumping through fields.

autumn came on, was so terribly haunted by these ideas, in the sad solitariness of her cottage, as to be obliged to take daily refuge in the dining room of the park. The return of winter engagements, however, was not without its effect; and in the course of their progress, her mind became so pleasantly occupied in superintending the fortunes of her eldest niece, as tolerably to quiet her nerves. "If poor Sir Thomas were fated never to return, it would be peculiarly consoling to see their dear Maria well married," she very often thought; always when they were in the company of men of fortune, and particularly on the introduction of a young man who had recently succeeded to one of the largest estates and finest places in the country.

Mr. Rushworth was from the first struck with the beauty of Miss Bertram, and being inclined to marry, soon fancied himself in love. He was a heavy young man, with not more than common sense; but as there was nothing disagreeable in his figure or address, the young lady was well pleased with her conquest. Being now in her twenty-first year, Maria Bertram was beginning to think matrimony a duty; and as a marriage with Mr. Rushworth would give her the enjoyment of a larger income than her father's, as well as ensure her the house in town, which was now a prime object, it became, by the same rule of moral obligation, her evident duty to marry Mr. Rushworth if she could. Mrs. Norris was most zealous in promoting the match, by every suggestion and contrivance, likely to enhance its desirableness to either party; and, among other means, by seeking an intimacy with the gentleman's mother, who at present lived with him, and to whom she even forced Lady Bertram to go through ten miles of indifferent road, to pay a morning visit. It was not long before a good understanding took place between this lady and herself. Mrs. Rushworth acknowledged herself very desirous that her son should marry, and declared that of all the young ladies she had ever seen, Miss Bertram seemed, by her amiable qualities and accomplishments, the best adapted to make him happy. Mrs. Norris accepted the compliment, and admired the nice discernment of character which could so well distinguish merit. Maria was indeed the pride and delight of them all—perfectly faultless—an angel; and of course, so surrounded by admirers, must be difficult in her choice; but yet as far as Mrs. Norris could allow herself to decide on so short an acquaintance, Mr. Rushworth appeared precisely the young man to deserve and attach her.

After dancing with each other at a proper number of balls, the young people justified these opinions, and an engagement, with a due reference to the absent Sir Thomas, was entered into, much to the satisfaction of their respective families, and of the general lookers-on of the neighbourhood, who had, for many weeks past, felt the expediency of Mr. Rushworth's marrying Miss Bertram.

It was some months before Sir Thomas's consent could be received;

but in the mean while, as no one felt a doubt of his most cordial pleasure in the connection, the intercourse of the two families was carried on without restraint, and no other attempt made at secrecy, than Mrs. Norris's talking of it every where as a matter not to be talked of at present.

Edmund was the only one of the family who could see a fault in the business; but no representation of his aunt's could induce him to find Mr. Rushworth a desirable companion. He could allow his sister to be the best judge of her own happiness, but he was not pleased that her happiness should centre in a large income; nor could he refrain from often saying to himself, in Mr. Rushworth's company, "If this man had not twelve thousand a year, he would be a very stupid fellow."

Sir Thomas, however, was truly happy in the prospect of an alliance so unquestionably advantageous, and of which he heard nothing but the perfectly good and agreeable. It was a connection exactly of the right sort; in the same county, and the same interest;[2] and his most hearty concurrence was conveyed as soon as possible. He only conditioned that the marriage should not take place before his return, which he was again looking eagerly forward to. He wrote in April, and had strong hopes of settling every thing to his entire satisfaction, and leaving Antigua before the end of the summer.

Such was the state of affairs in the month of July, and Fanny had just reached her eighteenth year, when the society of the village received an addition in the brother and sister of Mrs. Grant, a Mr. and Miss Crawford, the children of her mother by a second marriage. They were young people of fortune. The son had a good estate in Norfolk, the daughter twenty thousand pounds. As children, their sister had been always very fond of them; but, as her own marriage had been soon followed by the death of their common parent, which left them to the care of a brother of their father, of whom Mrs. Grant knew nothing, she had scarcely seen them since. In their uncle's house they had found a kind home. Admiral and Mrs. Crawford, though agreeing in nothing else, were united in affection for these children, or at least were no farther adverse in their feelings than that each had their favourite, to whom they showed the greatest fondness of the two. The Admiral delighted in the boy, Mrs. Crawford doated on the girl; and it was the lady's death which now obliged her *protegée*, after some months further trial at her uncle's house, to find another home. Admiral Crawford was a man of vicious conduct, who chose, instead of retaining his niece, to bring his mistress under his own roof; and to this Mrs. Grant was indebted for her sister's proposal of coming to her, a measure quite as welcome on one side, as it could be expedient on the other; for Mrs. Grant having by this time run through the usual resources of ladies

2. Having shared political or economic concerns.

residing in the country without a family of children; having more than filled her favourite sitting room with pretty furniture, and made a choice collection of plants and poultry, was very much in want of some variety at home. The arrival, therefore, of a sister whom she had always loved, and now hoped to retain with her as long as she remained single, was highly agreeable; and her chief anxiety was lest Mansfield should not satisfy the habits of a young woman who had been mostly used to London.

Miss Crawford was not entirely free from similar apprehensions, though they arose principally from doubts of her sister's style of living and tone of society; and it was not till after she had tried in vain to persuade her brother to settle with her at his own country-house, that she could resolve to hazard herself among her other relations. To any thing like a permanence of abode, or limitation of society, Henry Crawford had, unluckily, a great dislike; he could not accommodate his sister in an article of such importance, but he escorted her, with the utmost kindness, into Northamptonshire, and as readily engaged to fetch her away again at half an hour's notice, whenever she were weary of the place.

The meeting was very satisfactory on each side. Miss Crawford found a sister without preciseness or rusticity—a sister's husband who looked the gentleman, and a house commodious and well fitted up; and Mrs. Grant received in those whom she hoped to love better than ever, a young man and woman of very prepossessing appearance. Mary Crawford was remarkably pretty; Henry, though not handsome, had air and countenance; the manners of both were lively and pleasant, and Mrs. Grant immediately gave them credit for every thing else. She was delighted with each, but Mary was her dearest object; and having never been able to glory in beauty of her own, she thoroughly enjoyed the power of being proud of her sister's. She had not waited her arrival to look out for a suitable match for her; she had fixed on Tom Bertram; the eldest son of a Baronet was not too good for a girl of twenty thousand pounds, with all the elegance and accomplishments which Mrs. Grant foresaw in her; and being a warm-hearted, unreserved woman, Mary had not been three hours in the house before she told her what she had planned.

Miss Crawford was glad to find a family of such consequence so very near them, and not at all displeased either at her sister's early care, or the choice it had fallen on. Matrimony was her object, provided she could marry well, and having seen Mr. Bertram in town, she knew that objection could no more be made to his person than to his situation in life. While she treated it as a joke, therefore, she did not forget to think of it seriously. The scheme was soon repeated to Henry.

"And now," added Mrs. Grant, "I have thought of something to make it quite complete. I should dearly love to settle you both in this country, and therefore, Henry, you shall marry the youngest Miss Bertram, a nice, handsome, good-humoured, accomplished girl, who will make you very happy."

Henry bowed and thanked her.

"My dear sister," said Mary, "if you can persuade him into any thing of the sort, it will be a fresh matter of delight to me, to find myself allied to any body so clever, and I shall only regret that you have not half-a-dozen daughters to dispose of. If you can persuade Henry to marry, you must have the address of a Frenchwoman. All that English abilities can do, has been tried already. I have three very particular friends who have been all dying for him in their turn; and the pains which they, their mothers, (very clever women,) as well as my dear aunt and myself, have taken to reason, coax, or trick him into marrying, is inconceivable! He is the most horrible flirt that can be imagined. If your Miss Bertrams do not like to have their hearts broke, let them avoid Henry."

"My dear brother, I will not believe this of you."

"No, I am sure you are too good. You will be kinder than Mary. You will allow for the doubts of youth and inexperience. I am of a cautious temper, and unwilling to risk my happiness in a hurry. Nobody can think more highly of the matrimonial state than myself. I consider the blessing of a wife as most justly described in those discreet lines of the poet, "Heaven's *last* best gift."[3]

"There, Mrs. Grant, you see how he dwells on one word, and only look at his smile. I assure you he is very detestable—the admiral's lessons have quite spoiled him."

"I pay very little regard," said Mrs. Grant, "to what any young person says on the subject of marriage. If they profess a disinclination for it, I only set it down that they have not yet seen the right person."

Dr. Grant laughingly congratulated Miss Crawford on feeling no disinclination to the state herself.

"Oh! yes, I am not at all ashamed of it. I would have every body marry if they can do it properly; I do not like to have people throw themselves away; but every body should marry as soon as they can do it to advantage."

Chapter V.

The young people were pleased with each other from the first. On each side there was much to attract, and their acquaintance soon promised as early an intimacy as good manners would warrant. Miss Crawford's beauty did her no disservice with the Miss Bertrams. They were too

3. From Adam's description of Eve in John Milton's *Paradise Lost* 5.19.

handsome themselves to dislike any woman for being so too, and were almost as much charmed as their brothers, with her lively dark eye, clear brown complexion, and general prettiness. Had she been tall, full formed, and fair, it might have been more of a trial; but as it was, there could be no comparison, and she was most allowably a sweet pretty girl, while they were the finest young women in the country.

Her brother was not handsome; no, when they first saw him, he was absolutely plain, black and plain; but still he was the gentleman, with a pleasing address. The second meeting proved him not so very plain; he was plain, to be sure, but then he had so much countenance, and his teeth were so good, and he was so well made, that one soon forgot he was plain; and after a third interview, after dining in company with him at the parsonage, he was no longer allowed to be called so by any body. He was, in fact, the most agreeable young man the sisters had ever known, and they were equally delighted with him. Miss Bertram's engagement made him in equity the property of Julia, of which Julia was fully aware, and before he had been at Mansfield a week, she was quite ready to be fallen in love with.

Maria's notions on the subject were more confused and indistinct. She did not want to see or understand. "There could be no harm in her liking an agreeable man—every body knew her situation—Mr. Crawford must take care of himself." Mr. Crawford did not mean to be in any danger; the Miss Bertrams were worth pleasing, and were ready to be pleased; and he began with no object but of making them like him. He did not want them to die of love; but with sense and temper which ought to have made him judge and feel better, he allowed himself great latitude on such points.

"I like your Miss Bertrams exceedingly, sister," said he, as he returned from attending them to their carriage after the said dinner visit; "they are very elegant, agreeable girls."

"So they are, indeed, and I am delighted to hear you say it. But you like Julia best."

"Oh! yes, I like Julia best."

"But do you really? for Miss Bertram is in general thought the handsomest."

"So I should suppose. She has the advantage in every feature, and I prefer her countenance—but I like Julia best. Miss Bertram is certainly the handsomest, and I have found her the most agreeable, but I shall always like Julia best, because you order me."

"I shall not talk to you, Henry, but I know you *will* like her best at last."

"Do not I tell you, that I like her best *at first*?"

"And besides, Miss Bertram is engaged. Remember that, my dear brother. Her choice is made."

"Yes, and I like her the better for it. An engaged woman is always more agreeable than a disengaged. She is satisfied with herself. Her cares are over, and she feels that she may exert all her powers of pleasing without suspicion. All is safe with a lady engaged; no harm can be done."

"Why as to that—Mr. Rushworth is a very good sort of young man, and it is a great match for her."

"But Miss Bertram does not care three straws for him; *that* is your opinion of your intimate friend. *I* do not subscribe to it. I am sure Miss Bertram is very much attached to Mr. Rushworth. I could see it in her eyes, when he was mentioned. I think too well of Miss Bertram to suppose she would ever give her hand without her heart."

"Mary, how shall we manage him?"

"We must leave him to himself I believe. Talking does no good. He will be taken in at last."

"But I would not have him *taken in*, I would not have him duped; I would have it all fair and honourable."

"Oh! dear—Let him stand his chance and be taken in. It will do just as well. Every body is taken in at some period or other."

"Not always in marriage, dear Mary."

"In marriage especially. With all due respect to such of the present company as chance to be married, my dear Mrs. Grant, there is not one in a hundred of either sex, who is not taken in when they marry. Look where I will, I see that it *is* so; and I feel that it *must* be so, when I consider that it is, of all transactions, the one in which people expect most from others, and are least honest themselves."

"Ah! You have been in a bad school for matrimony, in Hill Street."

"My poor aunt had certainly little cause to love the state; but, however, speaking from my own observation, it is a manœuvring business. I know so many who have married in the full expectation and confidence of some one particular advantage in the connection, or accomplishment or good quality in the person, who have found themselves entirely deceived, and been obliged to put up with exactly the reverse! What is this, but a take in?"

"My dear child, there must be a little imagination here. I beg your pardon, but I cannot quite believe you. Depend upon it, you see but half. You see the evil, but you do not see the consolation. There will be little rubs and disappointments every where, and we are all apt to expect too much; but then, if one scheme of happiness fails, human nature turns to another; if the first calculation is wrong, we make a second better; we find comfort somewhere—and those evil-minded observers, dearest Mary, who make much of a little, are more taken in and deceived than the parties themselves."

"Well done, sister! I honour your *esprit du corps*.[1] When I am a wife,

1. Group spirit. In this novel, the use of French phrases connotes a wit and worldliness that contrast with the sedate and retired style of life at Mansfield Park.

I mean to be just as staunch myself; and I wish my friends in general would be so too. It would save me many a heart-ache."

"You are as bad as your brother, Mary; but we will cure you both. Mansfield shall cure you both—and without any taking in. Stay with us and we will cure you."

The Crawfords, without wanting to be cured, were very willing to stay. Mary was satisfied with the parsonage as a present home, and Henry equally ready to lengthen his visit. He had come, intending to spend only a few days with them, but Mansfield promised well, and there was nothing to call him elsewhere. It delighted Mrs. Grant to keep them both with her, and Dr. Grant was exceedingly well contented to have it so; a talking pretty young woman like Miss Crawford, is always pleasant society to an indolent, stay-at-home man; and Mr. Crawford's being his guest was an excuse for drinking claret every day.

The Miss Bertrams' admiration of Mr. Crawford was more rapturous than any thing which Miss Crawford's habits made her likely to feel. She acknowledged, however, that the Mr. Bertrams were very fine young men, that two such young men were not often seen together even in London, and that their manners, particularly those of the eldest, were very good. *He* had been much in London, and had more liveliness and gallantry than Edmund, and must, therefore, be preferred; and, indeed, his being the eldest was another strong claim. She had felt an early presentiment that she *should* like the eldest best. She knew it was her way.

Tom Bertram must have been thought pleasant, indeed, at any rate; he was the sort of young man to be generally liked, his agreeableness was of the kind to be oftener found agreeable than some endowments of a higher stamp, for he had easy manners, excellent spirits, a large acquaintance, and a great deal to say; and the reversion of Mansfield Park, and a baronetcy, did no harm to all this. Miss Crawford soon felt, that he and his situation might do. She looked about her with due consideration, and found almost every thing in his favour, a park, a real park five miles round, a spacious modern-built house, so well placed and well screened as to deserve to be in any collection of engravings of gentlemen's seats in the kingdom, and wanting only to be completely new furnished—pleasant sisters, a quiet mother, and an agreeable man himself—with the advantage of being tied up from much gaming at present, by a promise to his father, and of being Sir Thomas hereafter. It might do very well; she believed she should accept him; and she began accordingly to interest herself a little about the horse which he had to run at the B—— races.

These races were to call him away not long after their acquaintance began; and as it appeared that the family did not, from his usual goings on, expect him back again for many weeks, it would bring his passion to an early proof. Much was said on his side to induce her to attend the races, and schemes were made for a large party to them, with all the eagerness of inclination, but it would only do to be talked of.

And Fanny, what was *she* doing and thinking all this while? and what was *her* opinion of the new-comers? Few young ladies of eighteen could be less called on to speak their opinion than Fanny. In a quiet way, very little attended to, she paid her tribute of admiration to Miss Crawford's beauty; but as she still continued to think Mr. Crawford very plain, in spite of her two cousins having repeatedly proved the contrary, she never mentioned *him*. The notice which she excited herself, was to this effect. "I begin now to understand you all, except Miss Price," said Miss Crawford, as she was walking with the Mr. Bertrams. "Pray, is she out,[2] or is she not?—I am puzzled.—She dined at the parsonage, with the rest of you, which seemed like being *out*; and yet she says so little, that I can hardly suppose she *is*."

Edmund, to whom this was chiefly addressed, replied, "I believe I know what you mean—but I will not undertake to answer the question. My cousin is grown up. She has the age and sense of a woman, but the outs and not outs are beyond me."

"And yet in general, nothing can be more easily ascertained. The distinction is so broad. Manners as well as appearance are, generally speaking, so totally different. Till now, I could not have supposed it possible to be mistaken as to a girl's being out or not. A girl not out, has always the same sort of dress; a close bonnet for instance, looks very demure, and never says a word. You may smile—but it is so I assure you—and except that it is sometimes carried a little too far, it is all very proper. Girls should be quiet and modest. The most objectionable part is, that the alteration of manners on being introduced into company is frequently too sudden. They sometimes pass in such very little time from reserve to quite the opposite—to confidence! *That* is the faulty part of the present system. One does not like to see a girl of eighteen or nineteen so immediately up to every thing—and perhaps when one has seen her hardly able to speak the year before. Mr. Bertram, I dare say *you* have sometimes met with such changes."

"I believe I have; but this is hardly fair; I see what you are at. You are quizzing[3] me and Miss Anderson."

"No indeed. Miss Anderson! I do not know who or what you mean. I am quite in the dark. But I *will* quiz you with a great deal of pleasure, if you will tell me what about."

"Ah! you carry it off very well, but I cannot be quite so far imposed on. You must have had Miss Anderson in your eye, in describing an altered young lady. You paint too accurately for mistake. It was exactly so. The Andersons of Baker Street. We were speaking of them the other

---

2. Being or coming *out* refers to a woman's being formally presented to society as mature and marriageable.
3. Poking fun at; ridiculing.

day, you know. Edmund, you have heard me mention Charles Anderson. The circumstance was precisely as this lady has represented it. When Anderson first introduced me to his family, about two years ago, his sister was not *out*, and I could not get her to speak to me. I sat there an hour one morning waiting for Anderson, with only her and a little girl or two in the room—the governess being sick or run away, and the mother in and out every moment with letters of business; and I could hardly get a word or a look from the young lady—nothing like a civil answer—she screwed up her mouth, and turned from me with such an air! I did not see her again for a twelvemonth. She was then *out*. I met her at Mrs. Holford's—and did not recollect her. She came up to me, claimed me as an acquaintance, stared me out of countenance, and talked and laughed till I did not know which way to look. I felt that I must be the jest of the room at the time—and Miss Crawford, it is plain, has heard the story."

"And a very pretty story it is, and with more truth in it, I dare say, than does credit to Miss Anderson. It is too common a fault. Mothers certainly have not yet got quite the right way of managing their daughters. I do not know where the error lies. I do not pretend to set people right, but I do see that they are often wrong."

"Those who are showing the world what female manners *should be*," said Mr. Bertram, gallantly, "are doing a great deal to set them right."

"The error is plain enough," said the less courteous Edmund; "such girls are ill brought up. They are given wrong notions from the beginning. They are always acting upon motives of vanity—and there is no more real modesty in their behaviour *before* they appear in public than afterwards."

"I do not know," replied Miss Crawford hesitatingly. "Yes, I cannot agree with you there. It is certainly the modestest part of the business. It is much worse to have girls *not out*, give themselves the same airs and take the same liberties as if they were, which I *have* seen done. *That* is worse than any thing—quite disgusting!"

"Yes, *that* is very inconvenient indeed," said Mr. Bertram. "It leads one astray; one does not know what to do. The close bonnet and demure air you describe so well, (and nothing was ever juster,) tell one what is expected; but I got into a dreadful scrape last year from the want of them. I went down to Ramsgate[4] for a week with a friend last September—just after my return from the West Indies—my friend Sneyd—you have heard me speak of Sneyd, Edmund; his father and mother and sisters were there, all new to me. When we reached Albion place they were out; we went after them, and found them on the pier. Mrs. and the two Miss Sneyds, with others of their acquaintance. I made my bow in form, and as Mrs. Sneyd was surrounded by men,

4. A coastal resort in Kent.

attached myself to one of her daughters, walked by her side all the way home, and made myself as agreeable as I could; the young lady perfectly easy in her manners, and as ready to talk as to listen. I had not a suspicion that I could be doing any thing wrong. They looked just the same; both well dressed, with veils and parasols like other girls; but I afterwards found that I had been giving all my attention to the youngest, who was not *out*, and had most excessively offended the eldest. Miss Augusta ought not to have been noticed for the next six months, and Miss Sneyd, I believe, has never forgiven me."

"That was bad indeed. Poor Miss Sneyd! Though I have no younger sister, I feel for her. To be neglected before one's time, must be very vexatious. But it was entirely the mother's fault. Miss Augusta should have been with her governess. Such half and half doings never prosper. But now I must be satisfied about Miss Price. Does she go to balls? Does she dine out every where, as well as at my sister's?"

"No," replied Edmund, "I do not think she has ever been to a ball. My mother seldom goes into company herself, and dines no where but with Mrs. Grant, and Fanny stays at home with *her*."

"Oh! then the point is clear. Miss Price is *not* out."

Chapter VI.

Mr. Bertram set off for ———, and Miss Crawford was prepared to find a great chasm in their society, and to miss him decidedly in the meetings which were now becoming almost daily between the families; and on their all dining together at the park soon after his going, she retook her chosen place near the bottom of the table, fully expecting to feel a most melancholy difference in the change of masters. It would be a very flat business, she was sure. In comparison with his brother, Edmund would have nothing to say. The soup would be sent round in a most spiritless manner, wine drank without any smiles, or agreeable trifling, and the venison cut up without supplying one pleasant anecdote of any former haunch, or a single entertaining story about "my friend such a one." She must try to find amusement in what was passing at the upper end of the table, and in observing Mr. Rushworth, who was now making his appearance at Mansfield, for the first time since the Crawfords' arrival. He had been visiting a friend in a neighbouring county, and that friend having recently had his grounds laid out by an improver,[1] Mr. Rushworth was returned with his head full of the subject, and very eager to be improving his own place in the same way; and though not saying much to the purpose, could talk of nothing else.

1. "Improvement" is a resonant word in this novel, here referring to the eighteenth-century fashion for landscape design. The novel considers other efforts of improvement as well, e.g., Edmund's efforts to improve Fanny's mind.

The subject had been already handled in the drawing-room; it was revived in the dining-parlour. Miss Bertram's attention and opinion was evidently his chief aim; and though her deportment showed rather conscious superiority than any solicitude to oblige him, the mention of Sotherton Court, and the ideas attached to it, gave her a feeling of complacency, which prevented her from being very ungracious.

"I wish you could see Compton," said he, "it is the most complete thing! I never saw a place so altered in my life. I told Smith I did not know where I was. The approach *now* is one of the finest things in the country. You see the house in the most surprising manner. I declare when I got back to Sotherton yesterday, it looked like a prison—quite a dismal old prison."

"Oh! for shame!" cried Mrs. Norris. "A prison, indeed! Sotherton Court is the noblest old place in the world."

"It wants improvement, ma'am, beyond any thing. I never saw a place that wanted so much improvement in my life; and it is so forlorn, that I do not know what can be done with it."

"No wonder that Mr. Rushworth should think so at present," said Mrs. Grant to Mrs. Norris, with a smile; "but depend upon it, Sotherton will have *every* improvement in time which his heart can desire."

"I must try to do something with it," said Mr. Rushworth, "but I do not know what. I hope I shall have some good friend to help me."

"Your best friend upon such an occasion," said Miss Bertram, calmly, "would be Mr. Repton,[2] I imagine."

"That is what I was thinking of. As he has done so well by Smith, I think I had better have him at once. His terms are five guineas a day."

"Well, and if they were *ten*," cried Mrs. Norris, "I am sure *you* need not regard it. The expense need not be any impediment. If I were you, I should not think of the expense. I would have every thing done in the best style, and made as nice as possible. Such a place as Sotherton Court deserves every thing that taste and money can do. You have space to work upon there, and grounds that will well reward you. For my own part, if I had any thing within the fiftieth part of the size of Sotherton, I should be always planting and improving, for naturally I am excessively fond of it. It would be too ridiculous for me to attempt any thing where I am now, with my little half acre. It would be quite a burlesque. But if I had more room, I should take a prodigious delight in improving and planting. We did a vast deal in that way at the parsonage; we made it quite a different place from what it was when we first had it. You young ones do not remember much about it, perhaps. But if dear Sir Thomas were here, he could tell you what improvements we made; and a great deal more would have been done, but for poor

---

2. Humphry Repton (1752–1818) was the most famous landscape designer of the time, successor to Lancelot "Capability" Brown (1716–1783); his services were expensive. See "Contexts," below, pp. 382–87.

Mr. Norris's sad state of health. He could hardly ever get out, poor man, to enjoy any thing, and *that* disheartened me from doing several things that Sir Thomas and I used to talk of. If it had not been for *that*, we should have carried on the garden wall, and made the plantation to shut out the churchyard, just as Dr. Grant has done. We were always doing something, as it was. It was only the spring twelvemonth before Mr. Norris's death, that we put in the apricot against the stable wall, which is now grown such a noble tree, and getting to such perfection, sir," addressing herself then to Dr. Grant.

"The tree thrives well beyond a doubt, madam," replied Dr. Grant. "The soil is good; and I never pass it without regretting, that the fruit should be so little worth the trouble of gathering."

"Sir, it is a moor park,[3] we bought it as a moor park, and it cost us —that is, it was a present from Sir Thomas, but I saw the bill, and I know it cost seven shillings, and was charged as a moor park."

"You were imposed on, ma'am," replied Dr. Grant; "these potatoes have as much the flavour of a moor park apricot, as the fruit from that tree. It is an insipid fruit at the best; but a good apricot is eatable, which none from my garden are."

"The truth is, ma'am," said Mrs. Grant, pretending to whisper across the table to Mrs. Norris, "that Dr. Grant hardly knows what the natural taste of our apricot is; he is scarcely ever indulged with one, for it is so valuable a fruit, with a little assistance, and ours is such a remarkably large, fair sort, that what with early tarts and preserves, my cook contrives to get them all."

Mrs. Norris, who had begun to redden, was appeased, and, for a little while, other subjects took place of the improvements of Sotherton. Dr. Grant and Mrs. Norris were seldom good friends; their acquaintance had begun in dilapidations,[4] and their habits were totally dissimilar.

After a short interruption, Mr. Rushworth began again. "Smith's place is the admiration of all the country; and it was a mere nothing before Repton took it in hand. I think I shall have Repton."

"Mr. Rushworth," said Lady Bertram, "if I were you, I would have a very pretty shrubbery. One likes to get out into a shrubbery in fine weather."

Mr. Rushworth was eager to assure her ladyship of his acquiescence, and tried to make out something complimentary; but between his submission to *her* taste, and his having always intended the same himself, with the super-added objects of professing attention to the comfort of ladies in general, and of insinuating, that there was one only whom he was anxious to please, he grew puzzled; and Edmund was glad to put

3. A variety of apricot.
4. From canon law; expenses charged to a clergyman or his heirs for wear and tear to the house and property held during his encumbancy. The stingy Mrs. Norris resents having to pay for repairing what is now Dr. Grant's.

an end to his speech by a proposal of wine. Mr. Rushworth, however, though not usually a great talker, had still more to say on the subject next his heart. "Smith has not much above a hundred acres altogether in his grounds, which is little enough, and makes it more surprising that the place can have been so improved. Now, at Sotherton, we have a good seven hundred, without reckoning the water meadows;[5] so that I think, if so much could be done at Compton, we need not despair. There have been two or three fine old trees cut down that grew too near the house, and it opens the prospect amazingly, which makes me think that Repton, or any body of that sort, would certainly have the avenue at Sotherton down; the avenue that leads from the west front to the top of the hill you know," turning to Miss Bertram particularly as he spoke. But Miss Bertram thought it most becoming to reply:

"The avenue! Oh! I do not recollect it. I really know very little of Sotherton."

Fanny, who was sitting on the other side of Edmund, exactly opposite Miss Crawford, and who had been attentively listening, now looked at him, and said in a low voice,

"Cut down an avenue! What a pity! Does not it make you think of Cowper?" 'Ye fallen avenues, once more I mourn your fate unmerited.'[6]

He smiled as he answered, "I am afraid the avenue stands a bad chance, Fanny."

"I should like to see Sotherton before it is cut down, to see the place as it is now, in its old state; but I do not suppose I shall."

"Have you never been there? No, you never can; and unluckily it is out of distance for a ride. I wish we could contrive it."

"Oh! it does not signify. Whenever I do see it, you will tell me how it has been altered."

"I collect," said Miss Crawford, "that Sotherton is an old place, and a place of some grandeur. In any particular style of building?"

"The house was built in Elizabeth's time, and is a large, regular, brick building—heavy, but respectable* looking, and has many good rooms. It is ill placed. It stands in one of the lowest spots of the park; in that respect, unfavourable for improvement. But the woods are fine, and there is a stream, which, I dare say, might be made a good deal of. Mr. Rushworth is quite right, I think, in meaning to give it a modern dress, and I have no doubt that it will be all done extremely well."

Miss Crawford listened with submission, and said to herself, "He is a well bred man; he makes the best of it."

"I do not wish to influence Mr. Rushworth," he continued, "but had I a place to new fashion, I should not put myself into the hands of an

---

5. Meadows periodically overflowed by a stream.
6. Famous lines from William Cowper's *The Task* 1.338–39. See also Ann Radcliffe's *The Mysteries of Udolpho* (1794), vol. I, ch. 1, where St. Aubert laments that trees on his ancestral estate will be cut down.

improver. I would rather have an inferior degree of beauty, of my own choice, and acquired progressively. I would rather abide by my own blunders than by his."

"*You* would know what you were about of course—but that would not suit *me*. I have no eye or ingenuity for such matters, but as they are before me; and had I a place of my own in the country, I should be most thankful to any Mr. Repton who would undertake it, and give me as much beauty as he could for my money; and I should never look at it, till it was complete."

"It would be delightful to *me* to see the progress of it all," said Fanny.

"Ay—you have been brought up to it. It was no part of my education; and the only dose I ever had, being administered by not the first favourite in the world, has made me consider improvements *in hand* as the greatest of nuisances. Three years ago, the admiral, my honoured uncle, bought a cottage at Twickenham for us all to spend our summers in; and my aunt and I went down to it quite in raptures; but it being excessively pretty, it was soon found necessary to be improved; and for three months we were all dirt and confusion, without a gravel walk to step on, or a bench fit for use. I would have every thing as complete as possible in the country, shrubberies and flower gardens, and rustic seats innumerable; but it must be all done without my care. Henry is different, he loves to be doing."

Edmund was sorry to hear Miss Crawford, whom he was much disposed to admire, speak so freely of her uncle. It did not suit his sense of propriety, and he was silenced, till induced by further smiles and liveliness, to put the matter by for the present.

"Mr. Bertram," said she, "I have tidings of my harp at last. I am assured that it is safe at Northampton; and there it has probably been these ten days, in spite of the solemn assurances we have so often received to the contrary." Edmund expressed his pleasure and surprise. "The truth is, that our inquiries were too direct; we sent a servant, we went ourselves: this will not do seventy miles from London—but this morning we heard of it in the right way. It was seen by some farmer, and he told the miller, and the miller told the butcher, and the butcher's son-in-law left word at the shop."

"I am very glad that you have heard of it, by whatever means; and hope there will be no farther delay."

"I am to have it to-morrow; but how do you think it is to be conveyed? Not by a waggon or cart;—Oh! no, nothing of that kind could be hired in the village. I might as well have asked for porters and a hand-barrow."

"You would find it difficult, I dare say, just now, in the middle of a very late hay harvest, to hire a horse and cart?"

"I was astonished to find what a piece of work was made of it! To want a horse and cart in the country seemed impossible, so I told my maid to speak for one directly; and as I cannot look out of my dressing-closet without seeing one farm yard, nor walk in the shrubbery without passing another, I thought it would be only ask and have, and was rather grieved that I could not give the advantage to all. Guess my surprise, when I found that I had been asking the most unreasonable, most impossible thing in the world, had offended all the farmers, all the labourers, all the hay in the parish. As for Dr. Grant's bailiff, I believe I had better keep out of *his* way; and my brother-in-law himself, who is all kindness in general, looked rather black upon me, when he found what I had been at."

"You could not be expected to have thought on the subject before, but when you *do* think of it, you must see the importance of getting in the grass. The hire of a cart at any time, might not be so easy as you suppose; our farmers are not in the habit of letting them out; but in harvest, it must be quite out of their power to spare a horse."

"I shall understand all your ways in time; but coming down with the true London maxim, that every thing is to be got with money, I was a little embarrassed at first by the sturdy independence of your country customs. However, I am to have my harp fetched tomorrow. Henry, who is good-nature itself, has offered to fetch it in his barouche.[7] Will it not be honourably conveyed?"

Edmund spoke of the harp as his favourite instrument, and hoped to be soon allowed to hear her. Fanny had never heard the harp at all, and wished for it very much.

"I shall be most happy to play to you both," said Miss Crawford; "at least, as long as you can like to listen; probably much longer, for I dearly love music myself, and where the natural taste is equal, the player must always be best off, for she is gratified in more ways than one. Now, Mr. Bertram, if you write to your brother, I entreat you to tell him that my harp *is* come, he heard so much of my misery about it. And you may say, if you please, that I shall prepare my most plaintive airs against his return, in compassion to his feelings, as I know his horse will lose."

"If I write, I will say whatever you wish me; but I do not at present foresee any occasion for writing."

"No, I dare say, nor if he were to be gone a twelvemonth, would you ever write to him, nor he to you, if it could be helped. The occasion would never be foreseen. What strange creatures brothers are! You would not write to each other but upon the most urgent necessity in the world; and when obliged to take up the pen to say that such a horse is ill, or such a relation dead, it is done in the fewest possible words. You have but one style among you. I know it perfectly. Henry, who is in every other respect exactly what a brother should be, who loves me,

---

7. A four-wheeled carriage, having an outside front seat for the driver and seats inside for two couples facing each other.

consults me, confides in me, and will talk to me by the hour together, has never yet turned the page in a letter; and very often it is nothing more than, 'Dear Mary, I am just arrived. Bath seems full, and every thing as usual. Your's sincerely.' That is the true manly style; that is a complete brother's letter."

"When they are at a distance from all their family," said Fanny, colouring for William's sake, "they can write long letters."

"Miss Price has a brother at sea," said Edmund, "whose excellence as a correspondent, makes her think you too severe upon us."

"At sea, has she?—In the King's service of course."

Fanny would rather have had Edmund tell the story, but his determined silence obliged her to relate her brother's situation; her voice was animated in speaking of his profession, and the foreign stations he had been on, but she could not mention the number of years that he had been absent without tears in her eyes. Miss Crawford civilly wished him an early promotion.

"Do you know any thing of my cousin's captain?" said Edmund; "Captain Marshall? You have a large acquaintance in the navy, I conclude?"

"Among Admirals, large enough; but," with an air of grandeur, "we know very little of the inferior ranks. Post captains may be very good sort of men, but they do not belong to *us*. Of various admirals I could tell you a great deal; of them and their flags, and the gradation of their pay, and their bickerings and jealousies. But in general, I can assure you that they are all passed over, and all very ill used. Certainly, my home at my uncle's brought me acquainted with a circle of admirals. Of *Rears*, and *Vices*,[8] I saw enough. Now, do not be suspecting me of a pun, I entreat."

Edmund again felt grave, and only replied, "It is a noble profession."

"Yes, the profession is well enough under two circumstances; if it make the fortune, and there be discretion in spending it. But, in short, it is not a favourite profession of mine. It has never worn an amiable form to *me*."

Edmund reverted to the harp, and was again very happy in the prospect of hearing her play.

The subject of improving grounds meanwhile was still under consideration among the others; and Mrs. Grant could not help addressing her brother, though it was calling his attention from Miss Julia Bertram. "My dear Henry, have *you* nothing to say? You have been an improver yourself, and from what I hear of Everingham, it may vie with any place in England. Its natural beauties, I am sure, are great. Everingham as it *used* to be was perfect in my estimation; such a happy fall of ground, and such timber! What would not I give to see it again!"

8. Grades within the rank of admiral.

"Nothing could be so gratifying to me as to hear your opinion of it," was his answer. "But I fear there would be some disappointment. You would not find it equal to your present ideas. In extent it is a mere nothing—you would be surprised at its insignificance; and as for improvement, there was very little for me to do; too little—I should like to have been busy much longer."

"You are fond of the sort of thing?" said Julia.

"Excessively: but what with the natural advantages of the ground, which pointed out even to a very young eye what little remained to be done, and my own consequent resolutions, I had not been of age three months before Everingham was all that it is now. My plan was laid at Westminster—a little altered perhaps at Cambridge, and at one and twenty executed. I am inclined to envy Mr. Rushworth for having so much happiness yet before him. I have been a devourer of my own."

"Those who see quickly, will resolve quickly and act quickly," said Julia. "*You* can never want employment. Instead of envying Mr. Rushworth, you should assist him with your opinion."

Mrs. Grant hearing the latter part of this speech, enforced it warmly, persuaded that no judgment could be equal to her brother's; and as Miss Bertram caught at the idea likewise, and gave it her full support, declaring that in her opinion it was infinitely better to consult with friends and disinterested advisers, than immediately to throw the business into the hands of a professional man, Mr. Rushworth was very ready to request the favour of Mr. Crawford's assistance; and Mr. Crawford after properly depreciating his own abilities, was quite at his service in any way that could be useful. Mr. Rushworth then began to propose Mr. Crawford's doing him the honour of coming over to Sotherton, and taking a bed there; when Mrs. Norris, as if reading in her two nieces' minds their little approbation of a plan which was to take Mr. Crawford away, interposed with an amendment. "There can be no doubt of Mr. Crawford's willingness; but why should not more of us go?—Why should not we make a little party? Here are many that would be interested in your improvements, my dear Mr. Rushworth, and that would like to hear Mr. Crawford's opinion on the spot, and that might be of some small use to you with *their* opinions; and for my own part I have been long wishing to wait upon your good mother again; nothing but having no horses of my own, could have made me so remiss; but now I could go and sit a few hours with Mrs. Rushworth while the rest of you walked about and settled things, and then we could all return to a late dinner here, or dine at Sotherton just as might be most agreeable to your mother, and have a pleasant drive home by moonlight. I dare say Mr. Crawford would take my two nieces and me in his barouche, and Edmund can go on horseback, you know, sister, and Fanny will stay at home with you."

Lady Bertram made no objection, and every one concerned in the going, was forward in expressing their ready concurrence, excepting Edmund, who heard it all and said nothing.

Chapter VII.

"Well Fanny, and how do you like Miss Crawford *now*?" said Edmund the next day, after thinking some time on the subject himself. "How did you like her yesterday?"

"Very well—very much. I like to hear her talk. She entertains me; and she is so extremely pretty, that I have great pleasure in looking at her."

"It is her countenance that is so attractive. She has a wonderful play of feature! But was there nothing in her conversation that struck you Fanny, as not quite right?"

"Oh! yes, she ought not to have spoken of her uncle as she did. I was quite astonished. An uncle with whom she has been living so many years, and who, whatever his faults may be, is so very fond of her brother, treating him, they say, quite like a son. I could not have believed it!"

"I thought you would be struck. It was very wrong—very indecorous."

"And very ungrateful I think."

"Ungrateful is a strong word. I do not know that her uncle has any claim to her *gratitude*; his wife certainly had; and it is the warmth of her respect for her aunt's memory which misleads her here. She is awkwardly circumstanced. With such warm feelings and lively spirits it must be difficult to do justice to her affection for Mrs. Crawford, without throwing a shade on the admiral. I do not pretend to know which was most to blame in their disagreements, though the admiral's present conduct might incline one to the side of his wife: but it is natural and amiable that Miss Crawford should acquit her aunt entirely. I do not censure her *opinions*; but there certainly *is* impropriety in making them public."

"Do not you think," said Fanny, after a little consideration, "that this impropriety is a reflection itself upon Mrs. Crawford, as her niece has been entirely brought up by her? She cannot have given her right notions of what was due to the admiral."

"That is a fair remark. Yes, we must suppose the faults of the niece to have been those of the aunt; and it makes one more sensible of the disadvantages she has been under. But I think her present home must do her good. Mrs. Grant's manners are just what they ought to be. She speaks of her brother with a very pleasing affection."

"Yes, except as to his writing her such short letters. She made me almost laugh; but I cannot rate so very highly the love or good nature of a brother, who will not give himself the trouble of writing any thing worth reading, to his sisters, when they are separated. I am sure William would never have used *me* so, under any circumstances. And what right had she to suppose, that *you* would not write long letters when you were absent?"

"The right of a lively mind, Fanny, seizing whatever may contribute to its own amusement or that of others; perfectly allowable, when untinctured by ill humour or roughness; and there is not a shadow of either in the countenance or manner of Miss Crawford, nothing sharp, or loud, or coarse. She is perfectly feminine, except in the instances we have been speaking of. *There* she cannot be justified. I am glad you saw it all as I did."

Having formed her mind and gained her affections, he had a good chance of her thinking like him; though at this period, and on this subject, there began now to be some danger of dissimilarity, for he was in a line of admiration of Miss Crawford, which might lead him where Fanny could not follow. Miss Crawford's attractions did not lessen. The harp arrived, and rather added to her beauty, wit, and good humour, for she played with the greatest obligingness, with an expression and taste which were peculiarly becoming, and there was something clever to be said at the close of every air. Edmund was at the parsonage every day to be indulged with his favourite instrument; one morning secured an invitation for the next, for the lady could not be unwilling to have a listener, and every thing was soon in a fair train.

A young woman, pretty, lively, with a harp as elegant as herself; and both placed near a window, cut down to the ground, and opening on a little lawn, surrounded by shrubs in the rich foliage of summer, was enough to catch any man's heart. The season, the scene, the air, were all favourable to tenderness and sentiment. Mrs. Grant and her tambour frame[1] were not without their use; it was all in harmony; and as every thing will turn to account when love is once set going, even the sandwich tray, and Dr. Grant doing the honours of it, were worth looking at. Without studying the business, however, or knowing what he was about, Edmund was beginning, at the end of a week of such intercourse, to be a good deal in love; and to the credit of the lady it may be added, that without his being a man of the world or an elder brother, without any of the arts of flattery or the gaieties of small talk, he began to be agreeable to her. She felt it to be so, though she had not foreseen and could hardly understand it; for he was not pleasant by any common rule, he talked no nonsense, he paid no compliments, his opinions were unbending, his attentions tranquil and simple. There was a charm, perhaps, in his sincerity, his steadiness, his integrity, which Miss Craw-

---

1. A circular frame, consisting of two closely fitting hoops by means of which fabric is stretched for embroidery work.

ford might be equal to feel, though not equal to discuss with herself. She did not think very much about it, however; he pleased her for the present; she liked to have him near her; it was enough.

Fanny could not wonder that Edmund was at the parsonage every morning; she would gladly have been there too, might she have gone in uninvited and unnoticed to hear the harp; neither could she wonder, that when the evening stroll was over, and the two families parted again, he should think it right to attend Mrs. Grant and her sister to their home, while Mr. Crawford was devoted to the ladies of the park; but she thought it a very bad exchange, and if Edmund were not there to mix the wine and water for her, would rather go without it than not. She was a little surprised that he could spend so many hours with Miss Crawford, and not see more of the sort of fault which he had already observed, and of which *she* was almost always reminded by a something of the same nature whenever she was in her company; but so it was. Edmund was fond of speaking to her of Miss Crawford, but he seemed to think it enough that the admiral had since been spared; and she scrupled to point out her own remarks to him, lest it should appear like ill-nature. The first actual pain which Miss Crawford occasioned her, was the consequence of an inclination to learn to ride, which the former caught soon after her being settled at Mansfield from the example of the young ladies at the park, and which, when Edmund's acquaintance with her increased, led to his encouraging the wish, and the offer of his own quiet mare for the purpose of her first attempts, as the best fitted for a beginner that either stable could furnish. No pain, no injury, however, was designed by him to his cousin in this offer: *she* was not to lose a day's exercise by it. The mare was only to be taken down to the parsonage half an hour before her ride were to begin; and Fanny, on its being first proposed, so far from feeling slighted, was almost overpowered with gratitude that he should be asking her leave for it.

Miss Crawford made her first essay with great credit to herself, and no inconvenience to Fanny. Edmund, who had taken down the mare and presided at the whole, returned with it in excellent time, before either Fanny or the steady old coachman, who always attended her when she rode without her cousins, were ready to set forward. The second day's trial was not so guiltless. Miss Crawford's enjoyment of riding was such, that she did not know how to leave off. Active and fearless, and, though rather small, strongly made, she seemed formed for a horsewoman; and to the pure genuine pleasure of the exercise, something was probably added in Edmund's attendance and instructions, and something more in the conviction of very much surpassing her sex in general by her early progress, to make her unwilling to dismount. Fanny was ready and waiting, and Mrs. Norris was beginning to scold her for not being gone, and still no horse was announced, no

Edmund appeared. To avoid her aunt, and look for him, she went out.

The houses, though scarcely half a mile apart, were not within sight of each other; but by walking fifty yards from the hall door, she could look down the park, and command a view of the parsonage and all its demesnes, gently rising beyond the village road; and in Dr. Grant's meadow she immediately saw the group—Edmund and Miss Crawford both on horseback, riding side by side, Dr. and Mrs. Grant, and Mr. Crawford, with two or three grooms, standing about and looking on. A happy party it appeared to her—all interested in one object—cheerful beyond a doubt, for the sound of merriment ascended even to her. It was a sound which did not make *her* cheerful; she wondered that Edmund should forget her, and felt a pang. She could not turn her eyes from the meadow, she could not help watching all that passed. At first Miss Crawford and her companion made the circuit of the field, which was not small, at a foot's pace; then, at *her* apparent suggestion, they rose into a canter; and to Fanny's timid nature it was most astonishing to see how well she sat. After a few minutes, they stopt entirely, Edmund was close to her, he was speaking to her, he was evidently directing her management of the bridle, he had hold of her hand; she saw it, or the imagination supplied what the eye could not reach. She must not wonder at all this; what could be more natural than that Edmund should be making himself useful, and proving his good-nature by any one? She could not but think indeed that Mr. Crawford might as well have saved him the trouble; that it would have been particularly proper and becoming in a brother to have done it himself; but Mr. Crawford, with all his boasted good-nature, and all his coachmanship, probably knew nothing of the matter, and had no active kindness in comparison of Edmund. She began to think it rather hard upon the mare to have such double duty; if she were forgotten the poor mare should be remembered.

Her feelings for one and the other were soon a little tranquillized, by seeing the party in the meadow disperse, and Miss Crawford still on horseback, but attended by Edmund on foot, pass through a gate into the lane, and so into the park, and make towards the spot where she stood. She began then to be afraid of appearing rude and impatient; and walked to meet them with a great anxiety to avoid the suspicion.

"My dear Miss Price," said Miss Crawford, as soon as she was at all within hearing, "I am come to make my own apologies for keeping you waiting—but I have nothing in the world to say for myself—I knew it was very late, and that I was behaving extremely ill; and, therefore, if you please, you must forgive me. Selfishness must always be forgiven you know, because there is no hope of a cure."

Fanny's answer was extremely civil, and Edmund added his conviction that she could be in no hurry. "For there is more than time enough for my cousin to ride twice as far as she ever goes," said he, "and you have been promoting her comfort by preventing her from setting off half an hour sooner; clouds are now coming up, and she will not suffer from the heat as she would have done then. I wish *you* may not be fatigued by so much exercise. I wish you had saved yourself this walk home."

"No part of it fatigues me but getting off this horse, I assure you," said she, as she sprang down with his help; "I am very strong. Nothing ever fatigues me, but doing what I do not like. Miss Price, I give way to you with a very bad grace; but I sincerely hope you will have a pleasant ride, and that I may have nothing but good to hear of this dear, delightful, beautiful animal."

The old coachman, who had been waiting about with his own horse, now joining them, Fanny was lifted on her's, and they set off across another part of the park; her feelings of discomfort not lightened by seeing, as she looked back, that the others were walking down the hill together to the village; nor did her attendant do her much good by his comments on Miss Crawford's great cleverness as a horsewoman, which he had been watching with an interest almost equal to her own.

"It is a pleasure to see a lady with such a good heart for riding!" said he. "I never see one sit a horse better. She did not seem to have a thought of fear. Very different from you, miss, when you first began, six years ago come next Easter. Lord bless me! how you did tremble when Sir Thomas first had you put on!"

In the drawing-room Miss Crawford was also celebrated. Her merit in being gifted by nature with strength and courage was fully appreciated by the Miss Bertrams; her delight in riding was like their own; her early excellence in it was like their own, and they had great pleasure in praising it.

"I was sure she would ride well," said Julia; "she has the make for it. Her figure is as neat as her brother's."

"Yes," added Maria, "and her spirits are as good, and she has the same energy of character. I cannot but think that good horsemanship has a great deal to do with the mind."

When they parted at night, Edmund asked Fanny whether she meant to ride the next day.

"No, I do not know, not if you want the mare," was her answer. "I do not want her at all for myself," said he; "but whenever you are next inclined to stay at home, I think Miss Crawford would be glad to have her for a longer time—for a whole morning in short. She has a great desire to get as far as Mansfield common,[2] Mrs. Grant has been telling her of its fine views, and I have no doubt of her being perfectly equal to it. But any morning will do for this. She would be extremely sorry

2. Unenclosed land used by the community. The trend of enclosing commons had not yet reached Northamptonshire.

to interfere with you. It would be very wrong if she did.—*She* rides only for pleasure, *you* for health."

"I shall not ride to-morrow, certainly," said Fanny; "I have been out very often lately, and would rather stay at home. You know I am strong enough now to walk very well."

Edmund looked pleased, which must be Fanny's comfort, and the ride to Mansfield common took place the next morning;—the party included all the young people but herself, and was much enjoyed at the time, and doubly enjoyed again in the evening discussion. A successful scheme of this sort generally brings on another; and the having been to Mansfield-common, disposed them all for going somewhere else the day after. There were many other views to be shewn, and though the weather was hot, there were shady lanes wherever they wanted to go. A young party is always provided with a shady lane. Four fine mornings successively were spent in this manner, in shewing the Crawfords the country, and doing the honours of its finest spots. Every thing answered; it was all gaiety and good-humour, the heat only supplying inconvenience enough to be talked of with pleasure—till the fourth day, when the happiness of one of the party was exceedingly clouded. Miss Bertram was the one. Edmund and Julia were invited to dine at the parsonage, and *she* was excluded. It was meant and done by Mrs. Grant, with perfect good humour, on Mr. Rushworth's account, who was partly expected at the park that day; but it was felt as a very grievous injury, and her good manners were severely taxed to conceal her vexation and anger, till she reached home. As Mr. Rushworth did *not* come, the injury was increased, and she had not even the relief of shewing her power over him; she could only be sullen to her mother, aunt, and cousin, and throw as great a gloom as possible over their dinner and dessert.

Between ten and eleven, Edmund and Julia walked into the drawing-room, fresh with the evening air, glowing and cheerful, the very reverse of what they found in the three ladies sitting there, for Maria would scarcely raise her eyes from her book, and Lady Bertram was half asleep; and even Mrs. Norris, discomposed by her niece's ill-humour, and having asked one or two questions about the dinner, which were not immediately attended to, seemed almost determined to say no more. For a few minutes, the brother and sister were too eager in their praise of the night and their remarks on the stars, to think beyond themselves; but when the first pause came, Edmund, looking around, said, "But where is Fanny?—Is she gone to bed?"

"No, not that I know of," replied Mrs. Norris; "she was here a moment ago."

Her own gentle voice speaking from the other end of the room, which was a very long one, told them that she was on the sofa. Mrs. Norris began scolding.

"That is a very foolish trick, Fanny, to be idling away all the evening upon a sofa. Why cannot you come and sit here, and employ yourself as *we* do?—If you have no work of your own, I can supply you from the poor-basket.[3] There is all the new calico that was bought last week, not touched yet. I am sure I almost broke my back by cutting it out. You should learn to think of other people; and take my word for it, it is a shocking trick for a young person to be always lolling upon a sofa."

Before half this was said, Fanny was returned to her seat at the table, and had taken up her work again; and Julia, who was in high good-humour, from the pleasures of the day, did her the justice of exclaiming, "I must say, ma'am, that Fanny is as little upon the sofa as any body in the house."

"Fanny," said Edmund, after looking at her attentively; "I am sure you have the headach?"

She could not deny it, but said it was not very bad.

"I can hardly believe you," he replied; "I know your looks too well. How long have you had it?"

"Since a little before dinner. It is nothing but the heat."

"Did you go out in the heat?"

"Go out! to be sure she did," said Mrs. Norris; "would you have her stay within such a fine day as this? Were not we *all* out? Even your mother was out to-day for above an hour."

"Yes, indeed, Edmund," added her ladyship, who had been thoroughly awakened by Mrs. Norris's sharp reprimand to Fanny; "I was out above an hour. I sat three quarters of an hour in the flower garden, while Fanny cut the roses, and very pleasant it was I assure you, but very hot. It was shady enough in the alcove, but I declare I quite dreaded the coming home again."

"Fanny has been cutting roses, has she?"

"Yes, and I am afraid they will be the last this year. Poor thing! *She* found it hot enough, but they were so full blown, that one could not wait."

"There was no help for it certainly," rejoined Mrs. Norris, in a rather softened voice; "but I question whether her headach might not be caught *then*, sister. There is nothing so likely to give it as standing and stooping in a hot sun. But I dare say it will be well tomorrow. Suppose you let her have your aromatic vinegar;[4] I always forget to have mine filled."

"She has got it," said Lady Bertram; "she has had it ever since she came back from your house the second time."

"What!" cried Edmund; "has she been walking as well as cutting roses; walking across the hot park to your house, and doing it twice, ma'am?—No wonder her head aches."

3. A sewing basket containing material for making clothes for the poor.
4. Used like smelling salts to revive the weak or fainting.

Mrs. Norris was talking to Julia, and did not hear.

"I was afraid it would be too much for her," said Lady Bertram; "but when the roses were gathered, your aunt wished to have them, and then you know they must be taken home."

"But were there roses enough to oblige her to go twice?"

"No; but they were to be put into the spare room to dry; and, unluckily, Fanny forgot to lock the door of the room and bring away the key, so she was obliged to go again."

Edmund got up and walked about the room, saying, "And could nobody be employed on such an errand but Fanny?—Upon my word, ma'am, it has been a very ill-managed business."

"I am sure I do not know how it was to have been done better," cried Mrs. Norris, unable to be longer deaf; "unless I had gone myself indeed; but I cannot be in two places at once; and I was talking to Mr. Green at that very time about your mother's dairymaid, by *her* desire, and had promised John Groom to write to Mrs. Jefferies about his son, and the poor fellow was waiting for me half an hour. I think nobody can justly accuse me of sparing myself upon any occasion, but really I cannot do every thing at once. And as for Fanny's just stepping down to my house for me, it is not much above a quarter of a mile, I cannot think I was unreasonable to ask it. How often do I pace it three times a-day, early and late, ay and in all weathers too, and say nothing about it."

"I wish Fanny had half your strength, ma'am."

"If Fanny would be more regular in her exercise, she would not be knocked up[5] so soon. She has not been out on horseback now this long while, and I am persuaded, that when she does not ride, she ought to walk. If she had been riding before, I should not have asked it of her. But I thought it would rather do her good after being stooping among the roses; for there is nothing so refreshing as a walk after a fatigue of that kind; and though the sun was strong, it was not so very hot. Between ourselves, Edmund," nodding significantly at his mother, "it* was cutting the roses, and dawdling about in the flower-garden, that did the mischief."

"I am afraid it was, indeed," said the more candid Lady Bertram, who had overheard her, "I am very much afraid she caught the headach there, for the heat was enough to kill any body. It was as much as I could bear myself. Sitting and calling to Pug, and trying to keep him from the flower-beds, was almost too much for me."

Edmund said no more to either lady; but going quietly to another table, on which the supper tray yet remained, brought a glass of Madeira[6] to Fanny, and obliged her to drink the greater part. She wished

5. Tired.
6. A sweet, amber-colored wine which could be used medicinally either to revive or to settle one's spirits.

to be able to decline it; but the tears which a variety of feelings created, made it easier to swallow than to speak.

Vexed as Edmund was with his mother and aunt, he was still more angry with himself. His own forgetfulness of her was worse than any thing which they had done. Nothing of this would have happened had she been properly considered; but she had been left four days together without any choice of companions or exercise, and without any excuse for avoiding whatever her unreasonable aunts might require. He was ashamed to think that for four days together she had not had the power of riding, and very seriously resolved, however unwilling he must be to check a pleasure of Miss Crawford's, that it should never happen again.

Fanny went to bed with her heart as full as on the first evening of her arrival at the Park. The state of her spirits had probably had its share in her indisposition; for she had been feeling neglected, and been struggling against discontent and envy for some days past. As she leant on the sofa, to which she had retreated that she might not be seen, the pain of her mind had been much beyond that in her head; and the sudden change which Edmund's kindness had then occasioned, made her hardly know how to support herself.

Chapter VIII.

Fanny's rides recommenced the very next day, and as it was a pleasant fresh-feeling morning, less hot than the weather had lately been, Edmund trusted that her losses both of health and pleasure would be soon made good. While she* was gone, Mr. Rushworth arrived, escorting his mother, who came to be civil, and to shew her civility especially,* in urging the execution of the plan for visiting Sotherton, which had been started a fortnight before, and which, in consequence of her subsequent absence from home, had since lain dormant. Mrs. Norris and her nieces were all well pleased with its revival, and an early day was named, and agreed to, provided Mr. Crawford should be disengaged; the young ladies did not forget that stipulation, and though Mrs. Norris would willingly have answered for his being so, they would neither authorize the liberty, nor run the risk; and at last on a hint from Miss Bertram, Mr. Rushworth discovered that the properest thing to be done, was for him to walk down to the parsonage directly, and call on Mr. Crawford, and inquire whether Wednesday would suit him or not.

Before his return Mrs. Grant and Miss Crawford came in. Having been out some time, and taken a different route to the house, they had not met him. Comfortable hopes, however, were given that he would find Mr. Crawford at home. The Sotherton scheme was mentioned of course. It was hardly possible indeed that any thing else should be talked of, for Mrs. Norris was in high spirits about it, and Mrs. Rush--

worth, a well-meaning, civil, prosing, pompous woman, who thought nothing of consequence, but as it related to her own and her son's concerns, had not yet given over pressing Lady Bertram to be of the party. Lady Bertram constantly declined it; but her placid manner of refusal made Mrs. Rushworth still think she wished to come, till Mrs. Norris's more numerous words and louder tone convinced her of the truth.

"The fatigue would be too much for my sister, a great deal too much I assure you, my dear Mrs. Rushworth. Ten miles there, and ten back, you know. You must excuse my sister on this occasion, and accept of our two dear girls and myself without her. Sotherton is the only place that could give her a *wish* to go so far, but it cannot be indeed. She will have a companion in Fanny Price you know, so it will all do very well; and as for Edmund, as he is not here to speak for himself, I will answer for his being most happy to join the party. He can go on horse-back, you know."

Mrs. Rushworth being obliged to yield to Lady Bertram's staying at home, could only be sorry. "The loss of her Ladyship's company would be a great drawback, and she should have been extremely happy to have seen the young lady too, Miss Price, who had never been at Sotherton yet, and it was a pity she should not see the place."

"You are very kind, you are all kindness, my dear madam," cried Mrs. Norris; "but as to Fanny, she will have opportunities in plenty of seeing Sotherton. She has time enough before her; and her going now is quite out of the question. Lady Bertram could not possibly spare her."

"Oh! no—I cannot do without Fanny."

Mrs. Rushworth proceeded next, under the conviction that every body must be wanting to see Sotherton, to include Miss Crawford in the invitation; and though Mrs.* Grant, who had not been at the trouble of visiting Mrs. Rushworth on her coming into the neighbourhood, civilly declined it on her own account, she was glad to secure any pleasure for her sister; and Mary, properly pressed and persuaded, was not long in accepting her share of the civility. Mr. Rushworth came back from the parsonage successful; and Edmund made his appearance just in time to learn what had been settled for Wednesday, to attend Mrs. Rushworth to her carriage, and walk half way down the park with the two other ladies.

On his return to the breakfast-room, he found Mrs. Norris trying to make up her mind as to whether Miss Crawford's being of the party were desirable or not, or whether her brother's barouche would not be full without her. The Miss Bertrams laughed at the idea, assuring her that the barouche would hold four perfectly well, independent of the box, on which *one* might go with him.

"But why is it necessary," said Edmund, "that Crawford's carriage, or his *only* should be employed? Why is no use to be made of my mother's chaise? I could not, when the scheme was first mentioned the other day, understand why a visit from the family were not to be made in the carriage of the family."

"What!" cried Julia: "go box'd up three in a post-chaise[1] in this weather, when we may have seats in a barouche! No, my dear Edmund, that will not quite do."

"Besides," said Maria, "I know that Mr. Crawford depends upon taking us. After what passed at first, he would claim it as a promise."

"And my dear Edmund," added Mrs. Norris, "taking out *two* carriages when *one* will do, would* be trouble for nothing; and between ourselves, coachman is not very fond of the roads between this and Sotherton; he always complains bitterly of the narrow lanes scratching his carriage, and you know one should not like to have dear Sir Thomas when he comes home find all the varnish scratched off."

"That would not be a very handsome reason for using Mr. Crawford's," said Maria; "but the truth is, that Wilcox is a stupid old fellow, and does not know how to drive. I will answer for it that we shall find no inconvenience from narrow roads on Wednesday."

"There is no hardship, I suppose, nothing unpleasant," said Edmund, "in going on the barouche box."[2]

"Unpleasant!" cried Maria: "Oh! dear, I believe it would be generally thought the favourite seat. There can be no comparison as to one's view of the country. Probably, Miss Crawford will choose the barouche box herself."

"There can be no objection then to Fanny's going with you; there can be no doubt of your having room for her."

"Fanny!" repeated Mrs. Norris; "my dear Edmund, there is no idea of her going with us. She stays with her aunt. I told Mrs. Rushworth so. She is not expected."

"You can have no reason I imagine madam," said he, addressing his mother, "for wishing Fanny *not* to be of the party, but as it relates to yourself, to your own comfort. If you could do without her, you would not wish to keep her at home?"

"To be sure not, but I *cannot* do without her."

"You can, if I stay at home with you, as I mean to do."

There was a general cry out at this.

"Yes," he continued, "there is no necessity for my going, and I mean to stay at home. Fanny has a great desire to see Sotherton. I know she wishes it very much. She has not often a gratification of the kind, and I am sure ma'am you would be glad to give her the pleasure now?"

"Oh! yes, very glad, if your aunt sees no objection."

1. A closed carriage, carrying two or four people facing forward, drawn by horses that would be changed at each post.
2. A driver's seat.

Mrs. Norris was very ready with the only objection which could re-main, their having positively assured Mrs. Rushworth, that Fanny could not go, and the very strange appearance there would consequently be in taking her, which seemed to her a difficulty quite impossible to be got over. It must have the strangest appearance! It would be something so very unceremonious, so bordering on disrespect for Mrs. Rushworth, whose own manners were such a pattern of good-breeding and atten-tion, that she really did not feel equal to it. Mrs. Norris had no affection for Fanny, and no wish of procuring her pleasure at any time, but her opposition to Edmund *now* arose more from partiality for her own scheme because it *was* her own, than from any thing else. She felt that she had arranged every thing extremely well, and that any alteration must be for the worse. When Edmund, therefore, told her in reply, as he did when she would give him the hearing, that she need not distress herself on Mrs. Rushworth's account, because he had taken the oppor-tunity as he walked with her through the hall, of mentioning Miss Price as one who would probably be of the party, and had directly received a very sufficient invitation for his* cousin, Mrs. Norris was too much vexed to submit with a very good grace, and would only say, "Very well, very well, just as you choose, settle it your own way, I am sure I do not care about it."

"It seems very odd," said Maria, "that you should be staying at home instead of Fanny."

"I am sure she ought to be very much obliged to you," added Julia, hastily leaving the room as she spoke, from a consciousness that she ought to offer to stay at home herself.

"Fanny will feel quite as grateful as the occasion requires," was Ed-mund's only reply, and the subject dropt.

Fanny's gratitude when she heard the plan, was in fact much greater than her pleasure. She felt Edmund's kindness with all, and more than all, the sensibility which he, unsuspicious of her fond attachment, could be aware of; but that he should forego any enjoyment on her account gave her pain, and her own satisfaction in seeing Sotherton would be nothing without him.

The next meeting of the two Mansfield families produced another alteration in the plan, and one that was admitted with general appro-bation. Mrs. Grant offered herself as companion for the day to Lady Bertram in lieu of her son, and Dr. Grant was to join them at dinner. Lady Bertram was very well pleased to have it so, and the young ladies were in spirits again. Even Edmund was very thankful for an arrange-ment which restored him to his share of the party; and Mrs. Norris thought it an excellent plan, and had it at her tongue's end, and was on the point of proposing it when Mrs. Grant spoke.

Wednesday was fine, and soon after breakfast the barouche arrived, Mr. Crawford driving his sisters; and as every body was ready, there was

nothing to be done but for Mrs. Grant to alight and the others to take
their places. The place of all places, the envied seat, the post of honour,
was unappropriated. To whose happy lot was it to fall? While each of
the Miss Bertrams were meditating how best, and with most appearance
of obliging the others, to secure it, the matter was settled by Mrs.
Grant's saying, as she stepped from the carriage, "As there are five of
you, it will be better that one should sit with Henry, and as you were
saying lately, that you wished you could drive, Julia, I think this will
be a good opportunity for you to take a lesson."

Happy Julia! Unhappy Maria! The former was on the barouche-box
in a moment, the latter took her seat within, in gloom and mortification; and the carriage drove off amid the good wishes of the two
remaining ladies, and the barking of pug in his mistress's arms.

Their road was through a pleasant country; and Fanny, whose rides
had never been extensive, was soon beyond her knowledge, and was
very happy in observing all that was new, and admiring all that was
pretty. She was not often invited to join in the conversation of the
others, nor did she desire it. Her own thoughts and reflections were
habitually her best companions; and in observing the appearance of the
country, the bearings of the roads, the difference of soil, the state of
the harvest, the cottages, the cattle, the children, she found entertainment that could only have been heightened by having Edmund to
speak to of what she felt. That was the only point of resemblance between her and the lady who sat by her; in every thing but a value for
Edmund, Miss Crawford was very unlike her. She had none of Fanny's
delicacy of taste, of mind, of feeling; she saw nature, inanimate nature,
with little observation; her attention was all for men* and women, her
talents for the light and lively. In looking back after Edmund, however,
when there was any stretch of road behind them, or when he gained
on them in ascending a considerable hill, they were united, and a
"there he is" broke at the same moment from them both, more than
once.

For the first seven miles Miss Bertram had very little real comfort;
her prospect always ended in Mr. Crawford and her sister sitting side
by side full of conversation and merriment; and to see only his expressive profile as he turned with a smile to Julia, or to catch the laugh of
the other was a perpetual source of irritation, which her own sense of
propriety could but just smooth over. When Julia looked back, it was
with a countenance of delight, and whenever she spoke to them, it was
in the highest spirits; "her view of the country was charming, she wished
they could all see it, &c." but her only offer of exchange was addressed
to Miss Crawford, as they gained the summit of a long hill, and was
not more inviting than this, "Here is a fine burst of country. I wish you
had my seat, but I dare say you will not take it, let me press you ever

so much," and Miss Crawford could hardly answer, before they were moving again at a good pace.

When they came within the influence of Sotherton associations, it was better for Miss Bertram, who might be said to have two strings to her bow.[3] She had Rushworth-feelings, and Crawford-feelings, and in the vicinity of Sotherton, the former had considerable effect. Mr. Rushworth's consequence was hers. She could not tell Miss Crawford that "those woods belonged to Sotherton," she could not carelessly observe that "she believed it was now all Mr. Rushworth's property on each side of the road," without elation of heart; and it was a pleasure to increase with their approach to the capital freehold[4] mansion, and ancient manorial residence of the family, with all its rights of Court-Leet and Court-Baron.[5]

"Now we shall have no more rough road, Miss Crawford, our difficulties are over. The rest of the way is such as it ought to be. Mr. Rushworth has made it since he succeeded to the estate. Here begins the village. Those cottages are really a disgrace. The church spire is reckoned remarkably handsome. I am glad the church is not so close to the Great House as often happens in old places. The annoyance of the bells must be terrible. There is the parsonage; a tidy looking house, and I understand the clergyman and his wife are very decent people. Those are alms-houses, built by some of the family. To the right is the steward's house; he is a very respectable man. Now we are coming to the lodge gates; but we have nearly a mile through the park still. It is not ugly, you see, at this end; there is some fine timber, but the situation of the house is dreadful. We go down hill to it for half-a-mile, and it is a pity, for it would not be an ill-looking place if it had a better approach."

Miss Crawford was not slow to admire; she pretty well guessed Miss Bertram's feelings, and made it a point of honour to promote her enjoyment to the utmost. Mrs. Norris was all delight and volubility; and even Fanny had something to say in admiration, and might be heard with complacency. Her eye was eagerly taking in every thing within her reach; and after being at some pains to get a view of the house, and observing that "it was a sort of building which she could not look at but with respect," she added, "Now, where is the avenue? The house fronts the east, I perceive. The avenue, therefore, must be at the back of it. Mr. Rushworth talked of the west front."

"Yes, it is exactly behind the house; begins at a little distance, and ascends for half-a-mile to the extremity of the grounds. You may see

3. A proverbial English expression, alluding to Cupid's bow and arrow; i.e., Maria has inspired two admirers at once.
4. Unencumbered property that can be passed on freely to one's heirs.
5. Manorial courts, where civil and criminal cases are tried before a lord or his agent.

something of it here—something of the more distant trees. It is oak entirely."

Miss Bertram could now speak with decided information of what she had known nothing about, when Mr. Rushworth had asked her opinion, and her spirits were in as happy a flutter as vanity and pride could furnish, when they drove up to the spacious stone steps before the principal entrance.

Chapter IX.

Mr. Rushworth was at the door to receive his fair lady, and the whole party were welcomed by him with due attention. In the drawing-room they were met with equal cordiality by the mother, and Miss Bertram had all the distinction with each that she could wish. After the business of arriving was over, it was first necessary to eat, and the doors were thrown open to admit them through one or two intermediate rooms into the appointed dining-parlour, where a collation was prepared with abundance and elegance. Much was said, and much was ate, and all went well. The particular object of the day was then considered. How would Mr. Crawford like, in what manner would he choose, to take a survey of the grounds?—Mr. Rushworth mentioned his curricle.[1] Mr. Crawford suggested the greater desirableness of some carriage which might convey more than two. "To be depriving themselves of the advantage of other eyes and other judgments, might be an evil even beyond the loss of present pleasure."

Mrs. Rushworth proposed that the chaise should be taken also; but this was scarcely received as an amendment; the young ladies neither smiled nor spoke. Her next proposition of shewing the house to such of them as had not been there before, was more acceptable, for Miss Bertram was pleased to have its size displayed, and all were glad to be doing something.

The whole party rose accordingly, and under Mrs. Rushworth's guidance were shewn through a number of rooms, all lofty, and many large, and amply furnished in the taste of fifty years back, with shining floors, solid mahogany, rich damask, marble, gilding and carving, each handsome in its way. Of pictures there were abundance, and some few good, but the larger part were family portraits, no longer any thing to any body but Mrs. Rushworth, who had been at great pains to learn all that the housekeeper could teach, and was now almost equally well qualified to shew the house. On the present occasion, she addressed herself chiefly to Miss Crawford and Fanny, but there was no comparison in the willingness of their attention, for Miss Crawford, who had seen .

1. Lightweight, two-wheeled carriage.

scores of great houses, and cared for none of them, had only the appearance of civilly listening, while Fanny, to whom every thing was almost as interesting as it was new, attended with unaffected earnestness to all that Mrs. Rushworth could relate of the family in former times, its rise and grandeur, regal visits and loyal efforts,[2] delighted to connect any thing with history already known, or warm her imagination with scenes of the past.

The situation of the house excluded the possibility of much prospect from any of the rooms, and while Fanny and some of the others were attending Mrs. Rushworth, Henry Crawford was looking grave and shaking his head at the windows. Every room on the west front looked across a lawn to the beginning of the avenue immediately beyond tall iron palisades and gates.

Having visited many more rooms than could be supposed to be of any other use than to contribute to the window tax,[3] and find employment for housemaids, "Now," said Mrs. Rushworth, "we are coming to the chapel, which properly we ought to enter from above, and look down upon; but as we are quite among friends, I will take you in this way, if you will excuse me."

They entered. Fanny's imagination had prepared her for something grander than a mere, spacious, oblong room, fitted up for the purpose of devotion—with nothing more striking or more solemn than the profusion of mahogany,[4] and the crimson velvet cushions appearing over the ledge of the family gallery above. "I am disappointed,"* said she, in a low voice, to Edmund. "This is not my idea of a chapel. There is nothing awful here, nothing melancholy, nothing grand. Here are no aisles, no arches, no inscriptions, no banners. No banners, cousin, to be 'blown by the night wind of Heaven.' No signs that a 'Scottish monarch sleeps below.' "[5]

"You forget, Fanny, how lately all this has been built, and for how confined a purpose, compared with the old chapels of castles and monasteries. It was only for the private use of the family. They have been buried, I suppose, in the parish church. *There* you must look for the banners and the achievements."

"It was foolish of me not to think of all that, but I am disappointed."

Mrs. Rushworth began her relation. "This chapel was fitted up as

---

2. The suggestion may be that Rushworth's ancestors were loyal to the House of Stuart, sympathizing with the Jacobites in the uprisings of 1715 and 1745.

3. A tax on glass windows, first levied in 1695 and repealed in 1851.

4. R. W. Chapman finds Austen's usage anachronistic: the chapel was fitted up during the reign of James II (1685–89), but mahogany was not used in furnishings until the eighteenth century. Yet since the narrator states that the rooms were furnished with "solid mahogany" in "the taste of fifty years back" (i.e., around 1760), the mistake may be Mrs. Rushworth's, as she brags about the venerableness of her house.

5. Fanny is recalling verses X and XII from canto II of Sir Walter Scott's *Lay of the Last Minstrel* (1805): "Full many a scutcheon and banner riven, / Shook to the cold night-wind of heaven / . . . They sate them down on a marble stone / (A Scottish monarch slept below)."

you see it, in James the Second's time. Before that period, as I understand, the pews were only wainscot; and there is some reason to think
that the linings and cushions of the pulpit and family-seat were only
purple cloth; but this is not quite certain. It is a handsome chapel, and
was formerly in constant use both morning and evening. Prayers were
always read in it by the domestic chaplain, within the memory of many.
But the late Mr. Rushworth left it off."

"Every generation has its improvements," said Miss Crawford, with
a smile, to Edmund.

Mrs. Rushworth was gone to repeat her lesson to Mr. Crawford; and
Edmund, Fanny, and Miss Crawford, remained in a cluster together.

"It is a pity," cried Fanny, "that the custom should have been discontinued. It was a valuable part of former times. There is something
in a chapel and chaplain so much in character with a great house, with
one's ideas of what such a household should be! A whole family assembling regularly for the purpose of prayer, is fine!"

"Very fine indeed!" said Miss Crawford, laughing. "It must do the
heads of the family a great deal of good to force all the poor housemaids
and footmen to leave business and pleasure, and say their prayers here
twice a day, while they are inventing excuses themselves for staying
away."

"*That* is hardly Fanny's idea of a family assembling," said Edmund.
"If the master and mistress do *not* attend themselves, there must be
more harm than good in the custom."

"At any rate, it is safer to leave people to their own devices on such
subjects. Every body likes to go their own way—to choose their own
time and manner of devotion. The obligation of attendance, the formality, the restraint, the length of time—altogether it is a formidable
thing, and what nobody likes: and if the good people who used to kneel
and gape in that gallery could have foreseen that the time would ever
come when men and women might lie another ten minutes in bed,
when they woke with a headach, without danger of reprobation, because chapel was missed, they would have jumped with joy and envy.
Cannot you imagine with what unwilling feelings the former belles of
the house of Rushworth did many a time repair to this chapel? The
young Mrs. Eleanors and Mrs. Bridgets—starched up into seeming piety, but with heads full of something very different—especially if the
poor chaplain were not worth looking at—and, in those days, I fancy
parsons were very inferior even to what they are now."

For a few moments she was unanswered. Fanny coloured and looked
at Edmund, but felt too angry for speech; and *he* needed a little recollection before he could say, "Your lively mind can hardly be serious
even on serious subjects. You have given us an amusing sketch, and
human nature cannot say it was not so. We must all feel *at times* the
difficulty of fixing our thoughts as we could wish; but if you are sup-

posing it a frequent thing, that is to say, a weakness grown into a habit from neglect, what could be expected from the *private* devotions of such persons? Do you think the minds which are suffered, which are indulged in wanderings in a chapel, would be more collected in a closet?"[6]

"Yes, very likely. They would have two chances at least in their favour. There would be less to distract the attention from without, and it would not be tried so long."

"The mind which does not struggle against itself under *one* circumstance, would find objects to distract it in the *other*, I believe; and the influence of the place and of example may often rouse better feelings than are begun with. The greater length of the service, however, I admit to be sometimes too hard a stretch upon the mind. One wishes it were not so—but I have not yet left Oxford long enough to forget what chapel prayers are."

While this was passing, the rest of the party being scattered about the chapel, Julia called Mr. Crawford's attention to her sister, by saying, "Do look at Mr. Rushworth and Maria, standing side by side, exactly as if the ceremony were going to be performed. Have not they completely the air of it?"

Mr. Crawford smiled his acquiescence, and stepping forward to Maria, said, in a voice which she only could hear, "I do not like to see Miss Bertram so near the altar."

Starting, the lady instinctively moved a step or two, but recovering herself in a moment, affected to laugh, and asked him, in a tone not much louder, "if he would give her away?"

"I am afraid I should do it very awkwardly," was his reply, with a look of meaning.

Julia joining them at the moment, carried on the joke.

"Upon my word, it is really a pity that it should not take place directly, if we had but a proper license, for here we are altogether, and nothing in the world could be more snug and pleasant." And she talked and laughed about it with so little caution, as to catch the comprehension of Mr. Rushworth and his mother, and expose her sister to the whispered gallantries of her lover, while Mrs. Rushworth spoke with proper smiles and dignity of its being a most happy event to her whenever it took place.

"If Edmund were but in orders!" cried Julia, and running to where he stood with Miss Crawford and Fanny; "My dear Edmund, if you were but in orders now, you might perform the ceremony directly. How unlucky that you are not ordained, Mr. Rushworth and Maria are quite ready."

Miss Crawford's countenance, as Julia spoke, might have amused a

6. A small room.

disinterested observer. She looked almost aghast under the new idea she was receiving. Fanny pitied her. "How distressed she will be at what she said just now," passed across her mind.

"Ordained!" said Miss Crawford; "what, are you to be a clergyman?"

"Yes, I shall take orders soon after my father's return—probably at Christmas."

Miss Crawford rallying her spirits, and recovering her complexion, replied only, "If I had known this before, I would have spoken of the cloth with more respect," and turned the subject.

The chapel was soon afterwards left to the silence and stillness which reigned in it with few interruptions throughout the year. Miss Bertram, displeased with her sister, led the way, and all seemed to feel that they had been there long enough.

The lower part of the house had been now entirely shown, and Mrs. Rushworth, never weary in the cause, would have proceeded towards the principal stair-case, and taken them through all the rooms above, if her son had not interposed with a doubt of there being time enough. "For if," said he, with the sort of self-evident proposition which many a clearer head does not always avoid—"we are *too* long going over the house, we shall not have time for what is to be done out of doors. It is past two, and we are to dine at five."

Mrs. Rushworth submitted, and the question of surveying the grounds, with the who and the how, was likely to be more fully agitated, and Mrs. Norris was beginning to arrange by what junction of carriages and horses most could be done, when the young people, meeting with an outward door, temptingly open on a flight of steps which led immediately to turf and shrubs, and all the sweets of pleasure-grounds, as by one impulse, one wish for air and liberty, all walked out.

"Suppose we turn down here for the present," said Mrs. Rushworth, civilly taking the hint and following them. "Here are the greatest number of our plants, and here are the curious pheasants."

"Query," said Mr. Crawford, looking round him, "whether we may not find something to employ us here, before we go farther? I see walls of great promise. Mr. Rushworth, shall we summon a council on this lawn?"

"James," said Mrs. Rushworth to her son, "I believe the wilderness will be new to all the party. The Miss Bertrams have never seen the wilderness yet."

No objection was made, but for some time there seemed no inclination to move in any plan, or to any distance. All were attracted at first by the plants or the pheasants, and all dispersed about in happy independence. Mr. Crawford was the first to move forward, to examine the capabilities of that end of the house. The lawn, bounded on each side by a high wall, contained beyond the first planted ærea, a bowling-green, and beyond the bowling-green a long terrace walk, backed by iron palissades, and commanding a view over them into the tops of the trees of the wilderness immediately adjoining. It was a good spot for fault-finding. Mr. Crawford was soon followed by Miss Bertram and Mr. Rushworth, and when after a little time the others began to form into parties, these three were found in busy consultation on the terrace by Edmund, Miss Crawford and Fanny, who seemed as naturally to unite, and who after a short participation of their regrets and difficulties, left them and walked on. The remaining three, Mrs. Rushworth, Mrs. Norris, and Julia, were still far behind; for Julia, whose happy star no longer prevailed, was obliged to keep by the side of Mrs. Rushworth, and restrain her impatient feet to that lady's slow pace, while her aunt, having fallen in with the housekeeper, who was come out to feed the pheasants, was lingering behind in gossip with her. Poor Julia, the only one out of the nine not tolerably satisfied with their lot, was now in a state of complete penance, and as different from the Julia of the barouche-box as could well be imagined. The politeness which she had been brought up to practise as a duty, made it impossible for her to escape; while the want of that higher species of self-command, that just consideration of others, that knowledge of her own heart, that principle of right which had not formed any essential part of her education, made her miserable under it.

"This is insufferably hot," said Miss Crawford when they had taken one turn on the terrace, and were drawing a second time to the door in the middle which opened to the wilderness. "Shall any of us object to being comfortable? Here is a nice little wood, if one can but get into it. What happiness if the door should not be locked!—but of course it is, for in these great places, the gardeners are the only people who can go where they like."

The door, however, proved not to be locked, and they were all agreed in turning joyfully through it, and leaving the unmitigated glare of day behind. A considerable flight of steps landed them in the wilderness, which was a planted wood of about two acres, and though chiefly of larch and laurel, and beech cut down, and though laid out with too much regularity, was darkness and shade, and natural beauty, compared with the bowling-green and the terrace. They all felt the refreshment of it, and for some time could only walk and admire. At length, after a short pause, Miss Crawford began with, "So you are to be a clergyman, Mr. Bertram. This is rather a surprise to me."

"Why should it surprise you? You must suppose me designed for some profession, and might perceive that I am neither a lawyer, nor a soldier, nor a sailor."

"Very true; but, in short, it had not occurred to me. And you know there is generally an uncle or a grandfather to leave a fortune to the second son."

"A very praiseworthy practice," said Edmund, "but not quite universal. I am one of the exceptions, and *being* one, must do something for myself."

"But why are you to be a clergyman? I thought *that* was always the lot of the youngest, where there were many to choose before him."

"Do you think the church itself never chosen then?"

"*Never* is a black word. But yes, in the *never* of conversation which means *not very often*, I do think it. For what is to be done in the church? Men love to distinguish themselves, and in either of the other lines, distinction may be gained, but not in the church. A clergyman is nothing."

"The *nothing* of conversation has its gradations, I hope, as well as the *never*. A clergyman cannot be high in state or fashion. He must not head mobs, or set the ton[7] in dress. But I cannot call that situation nothing, which has the charge of all that is of the first importance to mankind, individually or collectively considered, temporally and eternally—which has the guardianship of religion and morals, and consequently of the manners which result from their influence. No one here can call the *office* nothing. If the man who holds it is so, it is by the neglect of his duty, by foregoing its just importance, and stepping out of his place to appear what he ought not to appear."

"*You* assign greater consequence to the clergyman than one has been used to hear given, or than I can quite comprehend. One does not see much of this influence and importance in society, and how can it be acquired where they are so seldom seen themselves? How can two sermons a week, even supposing them worth hearing, supposing the preacher to have the sense to prefer Blair's[8] to his own, do all that you speak of? govern the conduct and fashion the manners of a large congregation for the rest of the week? One scarcely sees a clergyman out of his pulpit."

"*You* are speaking of London, *I* am speaking of the nation at large."

"The metropolis, I imagine, is a pretty fair sample of the rest."

"Not, I should hope, of the proportion of virtue to vice throughout the kingdom. We do not look in great cities for our best morality. It is not there, that respectable people of any denomination can do most good; and it certainly is not there, that the influence of the clergy can be most felt. A fine preacher is followed and admired; but it is not in fine preaching only that a good clergyman will be useful in his parish and his neighbourhood, where the parish and neighbourhood are of a size capable of knowing his private character, and observing his general conduct, which in London can rarely be the case. The clergy are lost there in the crowds of their parishioners. They are known to the largest

---

7. Fashion; tone.
8. Hugh Blair (1718–1800) was a well-known Scottish divine and professor of rhetoric whose best-selling sermons (5 vols., 1777–1801) were often mined by clergymen who did not write their own every week.

part only as preachers. And with regard to their influencing public manners, Miss Crawford must not misunderstand me, or suppose I mean to call them the arbiters of good breeding, the regulators of refinement and courtesy, the masters of the ceremonies of life. The *manners* I speak of, might rather be called *conduct*, perhaps, the result of good principles; the effect, in short, of those doctrines which it is their duty to teach and recommend; and it will, I believe, be every where found, that as the clergy are, or are not what they ought to be, so are the rest of the nation."

"Certainly," said Fanny with gentle earnestness.

"There," cried Miss Crawford, "you have quite convinced Miss Price already."

"I wish I could convince Miss Crawford too."

"I do not think you ever will," said she with an arch smile; "I am just as much surprised now as I was at first that you should intend to take orders. You really are fit for something better. Come, do change your mind. It is not too late. Go into the law."

"Go into the law! with as much ease as I was told to go into this wilderness."

"Now you are going to say something about law being the worst wilderness of the two, but I forestall you; remember I have forestalled you."

"You need not hurry when the object is only to prevent my saying a bon-mot,[9] for there is not the least wit in my nature. I am a very matter of fact, plain spoken being, and may blunder on the borders of a repartee for half an hour together without striking it out."

A general silence succeeded. Each was thoughtful. Fanny made the first interruption by saying, "I wonder that I should be tired with only walking in this sweet wood; but the next time we come to a seat, if it is not disagreeable to you, I should be glad to sit down for a little while."

"My dear Fanny," cried Edmund, immediately drawing her arm within his, "how thoughtless I have been! I hope you are not very tired. Perhaps," turning to Miss Crawford, "my other companion may do me the honour of taking an arm."

"Thank you, but I am not at all tired." She took it, however, as she spoke, and the gratification of having her do so, of feeling such a connection for the first time, made him a little forgetful of Fanny. "You scarcely touch me," said he. "You do not make me of any use. What a difference in the weight of a woman's arm from that of a man! At Oxford I have been a good deal used to have a man lean on me for the length of a street, and you are only a fly in the comparison."

"I am really not tired, which I almost wonder at; for we must have walked at least a mile in this wood. Do not you think we have?"

9. A witticism; a clever or apt saying.

"Not half a mile," was his sturdy answer; for he was not yet so much in love as to measure distance, or reckon time, with feminine lawlessness.

"Oh! you do not consider how much we have wound about. We have taken such a very serpentine course; and the wood itself must be half a mile long in a straight line, for we have never seen the end of it yet, since we left the first great path."

"But if you remember, before we left that first great path, we saw directly to the end of it. We looked down the whole vista, and saw it closed by iron gates, and it could not have been more than a furlong[1] in length."

"Oh! I know nothing of your furlongs, but I am sure it is a very long wood; and that we have been winding in and out ever since we came into it; and therefore when I say that we have walked a mile in it, I must speak within compass."

"We have been exactly a quarter of an hour here," said Edmund, taking out his watch. "Do you think we are walking four miles an hour?"

"Oh! do not attack me with your watch. A watch is always too fast or too slow. I cannot be dictated to by a watch."

A few steps farther brought them out at the bottom of the very walk they had been talking of; and standing back, well shaded and sheltered, and looking over a ha-ha[2] into the park, was a comfortable-sized bench, on which they all sat down.

"I am afraid you are very tired, Fanny," said Edmund, observing her; "why would not you speak sooner? This will be a bad day's amusement for you, if you are to be knocked up. Every sort of exercise fatigues her so soon, Miss Crawford, except riding."

"How abominable in you, then, to let me engross her horse as I did all last week! I am ashamed of you and of myself, but it shall never happen again."

"*Your* attentiveness and consideration make me more sensible of my own neglect. Fanny's interest seems in safer hands with you than with me."

"That she should be tired now, however, gives me no surprise; for there is nothing in the course of one's duties so fatiguing as what we have been doing this morning—seeing a great house, dawdling from one room to another—straining one's eyes and one's attention—hearing what one does not understand—admiring what one does not care for. —It is generally allowed to be the greatest bore in the world, and Miss Price has found it so, though she did not know it."

"I shall soon be rested," said Fanny; "to sit in the shade on a fine day, and look upon verdure, is the most perfect refreshment."

1. A measure of distance equivalent to one-eighth of a mile, or 220 yards.
2. A sunken fence, constructed so as not to interfere with the view of the landscape.

After sitting a little while, Miss Crawford was up again. "I must move," said she, "resting fatigues me.—I have looked across the ha-ha till I am weary. I must go and look through that iron gate at the same view, without being able to see it so well."

Edmund left the seat likewise. "Now, Miss Crawford, if you will look up the walk, you will convince yourself that it cannot be half a mile long, or half half a mile."

"It is an immense distance," said she; "I see *that* with a glance."

He still reasoned with her, but in vain. She would not calculate, she would not compare. She would only smile and assert. The greatest degree of rational consistency could not have been more engaging, and they talked with mutual satisfaction. At last it was agreed, that they should endeavour to determine the dimensions of the wood by walking a little more about it. They would go to one end of it, in the line they were then in (for there was a straight green walk along the bottom by the side of the ha-ha,) and perhaps turn a little way in some other direction, if it seemed likely to assist them, and be back in a few minutes. Fanny said she was rested, and would have moved too, but this was not suffered. Edmund urged her remaining where she was with an earnestness which she could not resist, and she was left on the bench to think with pleasure of her cousin's care, but with great regret that she was not stronger. She watched them till they had turned the corner, and listened till all sound of them had ceased.

Chapter X.

A quarter of an hour, twenty minutes, passed away, and Fanny was still thinking of Edmund, Miss Crawford, and herself, without interruption from any one. She began to be surprised at being left so long, and to listen with an anxious desire of hearing their steps and their voices again. She listened, and at length she heard; she heard voices and feet approaching; but she had just satisfied herself that it was not those she wanted, when Miss Bertram, Mr. Rushworth, and Mr. Crawford, issued from the same path which she had trod herself, and were before her.

"Miss Price all alone!" and "My dear Fanny, how comes this?" were the first salutations. She told her story. "Poor dear Fanny," cried her cousin, "how ill you have been used by them! You had better have staid with us."

Then seating herself with a gentleman on each side, she resumed the conversation which had engaged them before, and discussed the possibility of improvements with much animation. Nothing was fixed on—but Henry Crawford was full of ideas and projects, and, generally speaking, whatever he proposed was immediately approved, first by her, and then by Mr. Rushworth, whose principal business seemed to be to hear the others, and who scarcely risked an original thought of his own beyond a wish that they had seen his friend Smith's place.

After some minutes spent in this way, Miss Bertram observing the iron gate, expressed a wish of passing through it into the park, that their views and their plans might be more comprehensive. It was the very thing of all others to be wished, it was the best, it was the only way of proceeding with any advantage, in Henry Crawford's opinion; and he directly saw a knoll not half a mile off, which would give them exactly the requisite command of the house. Go therefore they must to that knoll; and through that gate; but the gate was locked. Mr. Rushworth wished he had brought the key; he had been very near thinking whether he should not bring the key; he was determined he would never come without the key again; but still this did not remove the present evil. They could not get through; and as Miss Bertram's inclination for so doing did by no means lessen, it ended in Mr. Rushworth's declaring outright that he would go and fetch the key. He set off accordingly.

"It is undoubtedly the best thing we can do now, as we are so far from the house already," said Mr. Crawford, when he was gone.

"Yes, there is nothing else to be done. But now, sincerely, do not you find the place altogether worse than you expected?"

"No, indeed, far otherwise. I find it better, grander, more complete in its style, though that style may not be the best. And to tell you the truth," speaking rather lower, "I do not think that *I* shall ever see Sotherton again with so much pleasure as I do now. Another summer will hardly improve it to me."

After a moment's embarrassment the lady replied, "You are too much a man of the world not to see with the eyes of the world. If other people think Sotherton improved, I have no doubt that you will."

"I am afraid I am not quite so much the man of the world as might be good for me in some points. My feelings are not quite so evanescent, nor my memory of the past under such easy dominion as one finds to be the case with men of the world."

This was followed by a short silence. Miss Bertram began again. "You seemed to enjoy your drive here very much this morning. I was glad to see you so well entertained. You and Julia were laughing the whole way."

"Were we? Yes, I believe we were; but I have not the least recollection at what. Oh! I believe I was relating to her some ridiculous stories of an old Irish groom of my uncle's. Your sister loves to laugh."

"You think her more light-hearted than I am."

"More easily amused," he replied, "consequently you know," smiling, "better company. I could not have hoped to entertain *you* with Irish anecdotes during a ten miles' drive."

"Naturally, I believe, I am as lively as Julia, but I have more to think of now."

"You have undoubtedly—and there are situations in which very high spirits would denote insensibility. Your prospects, however, are too fair to justify want of spirits. You have a very smiling scene before you."

"Do you mean literally or figuratively? Literally, I conclude. Yes, certainly, the sun shines and the park looks very cheerful. But unluckily that iron gate, that ha-ha, give me a feeling of restraint and hardship. I cannot get out, as the starling said."[1] As she spoke, and it was with expression, she walked to the gate; he followed her. "Mr. Rushworth is so long fetching this key!"

"And for the world you would not get out without the key and without Mr. Rushworth's authority and protection, or I think you might with little difficulty pass round the edge of the gate, here, with my assistance; I think it might be done, if you really wished to be more at large, and could allow yourself to think it not prohibited."

"Prohibited! nonsense! I certainly can get out that way, and I will. Mr. Rushworth will be here in a moment you know—we shall not be out of sight."

"Or if we are, Miss Price will be so good as to tell him, that he will find us near that knoll, the grove of oak on the knoll."

Fanny, feeling all this to be wrong, could not help making an effort to prevent it. "You will hurt yourself, Miss Bertram," she cried, "you will certainly hurt yourself against those spikes—you will tear your gown—you will be in danger of slipping into the ha-ha. You had better not go."

Her cousin was safe on the other side, while these words were spoken, and smiling with all the good-humour of success, she said, "Thank you, my dear Fanny, but I and my gown are alive and well, and so good bye."

Fanny was again left to her solitude, and with no increase of pleasant feelings, for she was sorry for almost all that she had seen and heard, astonished at Miss Bertram, and angry with Mr. Crawford. By taking a circuitous, and as it appeared to her, very unreasonable direction to the knoll, they were soon beyond her eye; and for some minutes longer she remained without sight or sound of any companion. She seemed to have the little wood all to herself. She could almost have thought, that Edmund and Miss Crawford had left it, but that it was impossible for Edmund to forget her so entirely.

She was again roused from disagreeable musings by sudden footsteps, somebody was coming at a quick pace down the principal walk. She expected Mr. Rushworth, but it was Julia, who hot and out of breath, and with a look of disappointment, cried out on seeing her, "Heyday! Where are the others? I thought Maria and Mr. Crawford were with you."

---

1. Maria is quoting from Laurence Sterne's famous *A Sentimental Journey* (1768), "The Passport: The Hotel at Paris," featuring the misadventures of a caged bird.

Fanny explained.

"A pretty trick, upon my word! I cannot see them any where," looking eagerly into the park. "But they cannot be very far off, and I think I am equal to as much as Maria, even without help."

"But, Julia, Mr. Rushworth will be here in a moment with the key. Do wait for Mr. Rushworth."

"Not I, indeed. I have had enough of the family for one morning. Why, child, I have but this moment escaped from his horrible mother. Such a penance as I have been enduring, while you were sitting here so composed and so happy! It might have been as well, perhaps, if you had been in my place, but you always contrive to keep out of these scrapes."

This was a most unjust reflection, but Fanny could allow for it, and let it pass; Julia was vexed, and her temper was hasty, but she felt that it would not last, and therefore taking no notice, only asked her if she had not seen Mr. Rushworth.

"Yes, yes, we saw him. He was posting away as if upon life and death, and could but just spare time to tell us his errand, and where you all were."

"It is a pity that he should have so much trouble for nothing."

"*That* is Miss Maria's concern. I am not obliged to punish myself for *her* sins. The mother I could not avoid, as long as my tiresome aunt was dancing about with the housekeeper, but the son I *can* get away from."

And she immediately scrambled across the fence, and walked away, not attending to Fanny's last question of whether she had seen any thing of Miss Crawford and Edmund. The sort of dread in which Fanny now sat of seeing Mr. Rushworth prevented her thinking so much of their continued absence, however, as she might have done. She felt that he had been very ill-used, and was quite unhappy in having to communicate what had passed. He joined her within five minutes after Julia's exit; and though she made the best of the story, he was evidently mortified and displeased in no common degree. At first he scarcely said any thing; his looks only expressed his extreme surprise and vexation, and he walked to the gate and stood there, without seeming to know what to do.

"They desired me to stay—my cousin Maria charged me to say that you would find them at that knoll, or thereabouts."

"I do not believe I shall go any further," said he sullenly; "I see nothing of them. By the time I get to the knoll, they may be gone some where else. I have had walking enough."

And he sat down with a most gloomy countenance by Fanny.

"I am very sorry," said she; "it is very unlucky." And she longed to be able to say something more to the purpose.

After an interval of silence, "I think they might as well have staid for me," said he.

"Miss Bertram thought you would follow her."

"I should not have had to follow her if she had staid."

This could not be denied, and Fanny was silenced. After another pause, he went on: "Pray, Miss Price, are you such a great admirer of this Mr. Crawford as some people are? For my part, I can see nothing in him."

"I do not think him at all handsome."

"Handsome! Nobody can call such an under-sized man handsome. He is not five foot nine. I should not wonder if he was not more than five foot eight. I think he is an ill-looking fellow. In my opinion, these Crawfords are no addition at all. We did very well without them."

A small sigh escaped Fanny here, and she did not know how to contradict him.

"If I had made any difficulty about fetching the key, there might have been some excuse, but I went the very moment she said she wanted it."

"Nothing could be more obliging than your manner, I am sure, and I dare say you walked as fast as you could; but still it is some distance, you know, from this spot to the house, quite into the house; and when people are waiting, they are bad judges of time, and every half minute seems like five."

He got up and walked to the gate again, and "wished he had had the key about him at the time." Fanny thought she discerned in his standing there, an indication of relenting, which encouraged her to another attempt, and she said, therefore, "It is a pity you should not join them. They expected to have a better view of the house from that part of the park, and will be thinking how it may be improved; and nothing of that sort, you know, can be settled without you."

She found herself more successful in sending away, than in retaining a companion. Mr. Rushworth was worked on. "Well," said he, "if you really think I had better go; it would be foolish to bring the key for nothing." And letting himself out, he walked off without further ceremony.

Fanny's thoughts were now all engrossed by the two who had left her so long ago, and getting quite impatient, she resolved to go in search of them. She followed their steps along the bottom walk, and had just turned up into another, when the voice and the laugh of Miss Crawford once more caught her ear; the sound approached, and a few more windings brought them before her. They were just returned into the wilderness from the park, to which a side gate, not fastened, had tempted them very soon after their leaving her, and they had been across a portion of the park into the very avenue which Fanny had been hoping the whole morning to reach at last; and had been sitting down under one of the trees. This was their history. It was evident that they had been spending their time pleasantly, and were not aware of the length of their absence. Fanny's best consolation was in being assured that Edmund had wished for her very much, and that he should certainly have come back for her, had she not been tired already; but this was not quite sufficient to do away the pain of having been left a whole hour, when he had talked of only a few minutes, nor to banish the sort of curiosity she felt, to know what they had been conversing about all that time; and the result of the whole was to her disappointment and depression, as they prepared, by general agreement, to return to the house.

On reaching the bottom of the steps to the terrace, Mrs. Rushworth and Mrs. Norris presented themselves at the top, just ready for the wilderness, at the end of an hour and half from their leaving the house. Mrs. Norris had been too well employed to move faster. Whatever cross accidents had occurred to intercept the pleasures of her nieces, she had found a morning[2] of complete enjoyment—for the housekeeper, after a great many courtesies on the subject of pheasants, had taken her to the dairy, told her all about their cows, and given her the receipt[3] for a famous cream cheese; and since Julia's leaving them, they had been met by the gardener, with whom she had made a most satisfactory acquaintance, for she had set him right as to his grandson's illness, convinced him it was an ague, and promised him a charm[4] for it; and he, in return, had shewn her all his choicest nursery of plants, and actually presented her with a very curious specimen of heath.

On this rencontre they all returned to the house together, there to lounge away the time as they could with sofas, and chit-chat, and Quarterly Reviews,[5] till the return of the others, and the arrival of dinner. It was late before the Miss Bertrams and the two gentlemen came in, and their ramble did not appear to have been more than partially agreeable, or at all productive of any thing useful with regard to the object of the day. By their own accounts they had been all walking after each other, and the junction which had taken place at last seemed, to Fanny's observation, to have been as much too late for re-establishing harmony, as it confessedly had been for determining on any alteration. She felt, as she looked at Julia and Mr. Rushworth, that her's was not the only dissatisfied bosom amongst them; there was gloom on the face of each.

2. In Austen's novels, any time before dinner, served between 5 and 7 P.M., later hours being more fashionable.
3. Recipe.
4. Practicing what we now consider "folk" medicine, Mrs. Norris promises the gardener some amulet to relieve his son's affliction.
5. Periodicals featuring reviews of and by prominent writers. The Tory *Quarterly Review* (begun in 1809 by John Murray, publisher of *Emma, Persuasion, Northanger Abbey*, and the 2nd ed. of *Mansfield Park*) and the Whig *Edinburgh Review* (begun in 1802) enjoyed a wide circulation.

Mr. Crawford and Miss Bertram were much more gay, and she thought that he was taking particular pains, during dinner, to do away any little resentment of the other two, and restore general good humour.

Dinner was soon followed by tea and coffee, a ten miles' drive home allowed no waste of hours, and from the time of their sitting down to table, it was a quick succession of busy nothings till the carriage came to the door, and Mrs. Norris, having fidgetted about, and obtained a few pheasant's eggs and a cream cheese from the housekeeper, and made abundance of civil speeches to Mrs. Rushworth, was ready to lead the way. At the same moment Mr. Crawford approaching Julia, said, "I hope I am not to lose my companion, unless she is afraid of the evening air in so exposed a seat." The request had not been foreseen, but was very graciously received, and Julia's day was likely to end almost as well as it began. Miss Bertram had made up her mind to something different, and was a little disappointed—but her conviction of being really the one preferred, comforted her under it, and enabled her to receive Mr. Rushworth's parting attentions as she ought. He was certainly better pleased to hand her into the barouche than to assist her in ascending the box—and his complacency seemed confirmed by the arrangement.

"Well, Fanny, this has been a fine day for you, upon my word!" said Mrs. Norris, as they drove through the park. "Nothing but pleasure from beginning to end! I am sure you ought to be very much obliged to your aunt Bertram and me, for contriving to let you go. A pretty good day's amusement you have had!"

Maria was just discontented enough to say directly, "I think you have done pretty well yourself, ma'am. Your lap seems full of good things, and here is a basket of something between us, which has been knocking my elbow unmercifully."

"My dear, it is only a beautiful little heath, which that nice old gardener would make me take; but if it is in your way, I will have it in my lap directly. There Fanny, you shall carry that parcel for me—take great care of it—do not let it fall; it is a cream cheese, just like the excellent one we had at dinner. Nothing would satisfy that good old Mrs. Whitaker, but my taking one of the cheeses. I stood out as long as I could, till the tears almost came into her eyes, and I knew it was just the sort that my sister would be delighted with. That Mrs. Whitaker is a treasure! She was quite shocked when I asked her whether wine was allowed at the second table, and she has turned away two house-maids for wearing white gowns. Take care of the cheese, Fanny. Now I can manage the other parcel and the basket very well."

"What else have you been spunging?" said Maria, half pleased that Sotherton should be so complimented.

"Spunging, my dear! It is nothing but four of those beautiful pheasant's eggs, which Mrs. Whitaker would quite force upon me; she would not take a denial. She said it must be such an amusement to me, as she understood I lived quite alone, to have a few living creatures of that sort; and so to be sure it will. I shall get the dairy maid to set them under the first spare hen, and if they come to good I can have them moved to my own house and borrow a coop; and it will be a great delight to me in my lonely hours to attend to them. And if I have good luck, your mother shall have some."

It was a beautiful evening, mild and still,[6] and the drive was as pleasant as the serenity of nature could make it; but when Mrs. Norris ceased speaking it was altogether a silent drive to those within. Their spirits were in general exhausted—and to determine whether the day had afforded most pleasure or pain, might occupy the meditations of almost all.

Chapter XI.

The day at Sotherton, with all its imperfections, afforded the Miss Bertrams much more agreeable feelings than were derived from the letters from Antigua, which soon afterwards reached Mansfield. It was much pleasanter to think of Henry Crawford than of their father; and to think of their father in England again within a certain period, which these letters obliged them to do, was a most unwelcome exercise.

November was the black month fixed for his return. Sir Thomas wrote of it with as much decision as experience and anxiety could authorize. His business was so nearly concluded as to justify him in proposing to take his passage in the September packet,[1] and he consequently looked forward with the hope of being with his beloved family again early in November.

Maria was more to be pitied than Julia, for to her the father brought a husband, and the return of the friend most solicitous for her happiness, would unite her to the lover, on whom she had chosen that happiness should depend. It was a gloomy prospect, and all that she could do was to throw a mist over it, and hope when the mist cleared away, she should see something else. It would hardly be *early* in November, there were generally delays, a bad passage or *something*; that favouring *something* which every body who shuts their eyes while they look, or their understandings while they reason, feels the comfort of. It would probably be the middle of November at least; the middle of November

---

6. Compare William Wordsworth's sonnet "It is a beauteous evening, calm and free" (1802/07). Austen might also be recollecting Ann Radcliffe's "It was a still and beautiful night" from *The Mysteries of Udolpho* (1794), vol. I, ch. 4. Radcliffe was widely esteemed for her poetic evocations of consciousness interacting with landscape.
1. A boat carrying mail as well as goods and passengers.

was three months off. Three months comprised thirteen weeks. Much might happen in thirteen weeks.

Sir Thomas would have been deeply mortified by a suspicion of half that his daughters felt on the subject of his return, and would hardly have found consolation in a knowledge of the interest it excited in the breast of another young lady. Miss Crawford, on walking up with her brother to spend the evening at Mansfield Park, heard the good news; and though seeming to have no concern in the affair beyond politeness, and to have vented all her feelings in a quiet congratulation, heard it with an attention not so easily satisfied. Mrs. Norris gave the particulars of the letters, and the subject was dropt; but after tea, as Miss Crawford was standing at an open window with Edmund and Fanny looking out on a twilight scene, while the Miss Bertrams, Mr. Rushworth, and Henry Crawford, were all busy with candles at the piano-forte she suddenly revived it by turning round towards the group, and saying, "How happy Mr. Rushworth looks! He is thinking of November."

Edmund looked round at Mr. Rushworth too, but had nothing to say. "Your father's return will be a very interesting event."

"It will, indeed, after such an absence; an absence not only long, but including so many dangers."

"It will be the fore-runner also of other interesting events; your sister's marriage, and your taking orders."

"Yes."

"Don't be affronted," said she laughing; "but it does put me in mind of some of the old heathen heroes, who after performing great exploits in a foreign land, offered sacrifices to the gods on their safe return."

"There is no sacrifice in the case," replied Edmund with a serious smile, and glancing at the piano-forte again, "it is entirely her own doing."

"Oh! yes, I know it is. I was merely joking. She has done no more than what every young woman would do; and I have no doubt of her being extremely happy. My other sacrifice of course you do not understand."

"My taking orders I assure you is quite as voluntary as Maria's marrying."

"It is fortunate that your inclination and your father's convenience should accord so well. There is a very good living kept for you, I understand, hereabouts."

"Which you suppose has biassed me."

"But *that* I am sure it has not," cried Fanny.

"Thank you for your good word, Fanny, but it is more than I would affirm myself. On the contrary, the knowing that there was such a provision for me, probably did bias me. Nor can I think it wrong that it should. There was no natural disinclination to be overcome, and I see no reason why a man should make a worse clergyman for knowing that he will have a competence[2] early in life. I was in safe hands. I hope I should not have been influenced myself in a wrong way, and I am sure my father was too conscientious to have allowed it. I have no doubt that I was biassed, but I think it was blamelessly."

"It is the same sort of thing," said Fanny, after a short pause, "as for the son of an admiral to go into the navy, or the son of a general to be in the army, and nobody sees any thing wrong in that. Nobody wonders that they should prefer the line where their friends can serve them best, or suspects them to be less in earnest in it than they appear."

"No, my dear Miss Price, and for reasons good. The profession, either navy or army, is its own justification. It has every thing in its favour; heroism, danger, bustle, fashion. Soldiers and sailors are always acceptable in society. Nobody can wonder that men are soldiers and sailors."

"But the motives of a man who takes orders with the certainty of preferment,[3] may be fairly suspected, you think?" said Edmund. "To be justified in your eyes, he must do it in the most complete uncertainty of any provision."

"What! take orders without a living! No, that is madness indeed, absolute madness!"

"Shall I ask you how the church is to be filled, if a man is neither to take orders with a living, nor without? No, for you certainly would not know what to say. But I must beg some advantage to the clergyman from your own argument. As he cannot be influenced by those feelings which you rank highly as temptation and reward to the soldier and sailor in their choice of a profession, as heroism, and noise, and fashion are all against him, he ought to be less liable to the suspicion of wanting sincerity or good intentions in the choice of his."

"Oh! no doubt he is very sincere in preferring an income ready made, to the trouble of working for one; and has the best intentions of doing nothing all the rest of his days but eat, drink, and grow fat. It is indolence Mr. Bertram, indeed. Indolence and love of ease—a want of all laudable ambition, of taste for good company, or of inclination to take the trouble of being agreeable, which make men clergymen. A clergyman has nothing to do but to be slovenly and selfish—read the newspaper, watch the weather, and quarrel with his wife. His curate does all the work, and the business of his own life is to dine."

"There are such clergymen, no doubt, but I think they are not so common as to justify Miss Crawford in esteeming it their general character. I suspect that in this comprehensive and (may I say) commonplace censure, you are not judging from yourself, but from prejudiced

---

2. "A sufficiency of means for living comfortably" (OED). See "Introduction," above, pp. xiii–xvi.

3. A church appointment or promotion bringing financial or social advantage.

persons, whose opinions you have been in the habit of hearing. It is impossible that your own observation can have given you much knowledge of the clergy. You can have been personally acquainted with very few of a set of men you condemn so conclusively. You are speaking what you have been told at your uncle's table."

"I speak what appears to me the general opinion; and where an opinion is general, it is usually correct. Though *I* have not seen much of the domestic lives of clergymen, it is seen by too many to leave any deficiency of information."

"Where any one body of educated men, of whatever denomination, are condemned indiscriminately, there must be a deficiency of information, or (smiling) of something else. Your uncle, and his brother admirals, perhaps, knew little of clergymen beyond the chaplains whom, good or bad, they were always wishing away."

"Poor William! He has met with great kindness from the chaplain of the Antwerp," was a tender apostrophe of Fanny's, very much to the purpose of her own feelings, if not of the conversation.

"I have been so little addicted to take my opinions from my uncle," said Miss Crawford, "that I can hardly suppose;—and since you push me so hard, I must observe, that I am not entirely without the means of seeing what clergymen are, being at this present time the guest of my own brother, Dr. Grant. And though Dr. Grant is most kind and obliging to me, and though he is really a gentleman, and I dare say a good scholar and clever, and often preaches good sermons, and is very respectable, I see him to be an indolent selfish bon vivant, who must have his palate consulted in every thing, who will not stir a finger for the convenience of any one, and who, moreover, if the cook makes a blunder, is out of humour with his excellent wife. To own the truth, Henry and I were partly driven out this very evening, by a disappointment about a green goose,[4] which he could not get the better of. My poor sister was forced to stay and bear it."

"I do not wonder at your disapprobation, upon my word. It is a great defect of temper, made worse by a very faulty habit of self-indulgence; and to see your sister suffering from it, must be exceedingly painful to such feelings as your's. Fanny, it goes against us. We cannot attempt to defend Dr. Grant."

"No," replied Fanny, "but we need not give up his profession for all that; because, whatever profession Dr. Grant had chosen, he would have taken a —— not a good temper into it; and as he must either in the navy or army have had a great many more people under his command than he has now, I think more would have been made unhappy by him as a sailor or soldier than as a clergyman. Besides, I cannot but suppose that whatever there may be to wish otherwise in Dr. Grant,

4. A young goose, three or four months old.

would have been in a greater danger of becoming worse in a more active and worldly profession, where he would have had less time and obligation—where he might have escaped that knowledge of himself, the *frequency*, at least, of that knowledge which it is impossible he should escape as he is now. A man—a sensible man like Dr. Grant, cannot be in the habit of teaching others their duty every week, cannot go to church twice every Sunday and preach such very good sermons in so good a manner as he does, without being the better for it himself. It must make him think, and I have no doubt that he oftener endeavours to restrain himself than he would if he had been any thing but a clergyman."

"We cannot prove the contrary, to be sure—but I wish you a better fate Miss Price, than to be the wife of a man whose amiableness depends upon his own sermons; for though he may preach himself into a good humour every Sunday, it will be bad enough to have him quarrelling about green geese from Monday morning till Saturday night."

"I think the man who could often quarrel with Fanny," said Edmund, affectionately, "must be beyond the reach of any sermons."

Fanny turned farther into the window; and Miss Crawford had only time to say in a pleasant manner, "I fancy Miss Price has been more used to deserve praise than to hear it;" when being earnestly invited by the Miss Bertrams to join in a glee,[5] she tripped off to the instrument, leaving Edmund looking after her in an ecstasy of admiration of all her many virtues, from her obliging manners down to her light and graceful tread.

"There goes good humour I am sure," said he presently. "There goes a temper which would never give pain! How well she walks! and how readily she falls in with the inclination of others! joining them the moment she is asked. What a pity," he added, after an instant's reflection, "that she should have been in such hands!"

Fanny agreed to it, and had the pleasure of seeing him continue at the window with her, in spite of the expected glee; and of having his eyes soon turned like her's towards the scene without, where all that was solemn and soothing, and lovely, appeared in the brilliancy of an unclouded night, and the contrast of the deep shade of the woods. Fanny spoke her feelings. "Here's harmony!" said she, "Here's repose! Here's what may leave all painting and all music behind, and what poetry only can attempt to describe. Here's what may tranquillize every care, and lift the heart to rapture! When I look out on such a night as this, I feel as if there could be neither wickedness nor sorrow in the world; and there certainly would be less of both if the sublimity of Nature were more attended to, and people were carried more out of themselves by contemplating such a scene."

5. A vocal composition for three or more parts.

"I like to hear your enthusiasm, Fanny. It is a lovely night, and they are much to be pitied who have not been taught to feel in some degree as you do—who have not at least been given a taste for nature in early life. They lose a great deal."

"*You* taught me to think and feel on the subject, cousin." "I had a very apt scholar. There's Arcturus looking very bright."

"Yes, and the bear. I wish I could see Cassiopeia."

"We must go out on the lawn for that. Should you be afraid?"

"Not in the least. It is a great while since we have had any star-gazing."

"Yes, I do not know how it has happened." The glee began. "We will stay till this is finished, Fanny," said he, turning his back on the window; and as it advanced, she had the mortification of seeing him advance too, moving forward by gentle degrees towards the instrument, and when it ceased, he was close by the singers, among the most urgent in requesting to hear the glee again.

Fanny sighed alone at the window till scolded away by Mrs. Norris's threats of catching cold.

Chapter XII.

Sir Thomas was to return in November, and his eldest son had duties to call him earlier home. The approach of September brought tidings of Mr. Bertram first in a letter to the gamekeeper, and then in a letter to Edmund; and by the end of August, he arrived himself, to be gay, agreeable, and gallant again as occasion served, or Miss Crawford demanded, to tell of races and Weymouth,[1] and parties and friends, to which she might have listened six weeks before with some interest, and altogether to give her the fullest conviction, by the power of actual comparison, of her preferring his younger brother.

It was very vexatious, and she was heartily sorry for it; but so it was; and so far from now meaning to marry the elder, she did not even want to attract him beyond what the simplest claims of conscious beauty required; his lengthened absence from Mansfield, without any thing but pleasure in view, and his own will to consult, made it perfectly clear that he did not care about her; and his indifference was so much more than equalled by her own, that were he now to step forth the owner of Mansfield Park, the Sir Thomas complete, which he was to be in time, she did not believe she could accept him.

The season and duties which brought Mr. Bertram back to Mansfield, took Mr. Crawford into Norfolk. Everingham could not do with-

---

1. A fashionable seaside resort on the southern coast, frequented by the royal family. Calling it "a shocking place . . . without recommendation of any kind," Austen preferred less built-up coastal towns, such as nearby Lyme Regis.

out him in the beginning of September. He went for a fortnight; a fortnight of such dulness to the Miss Bertrams, as ought to have put them both on their guard, and made even Julia admit in her jealousy of her sister, the absolute necessity of distrusting his attentions, and wishing him not to return; and a fortnight of sufficient leisure in the intervals of shooting and sleeping, to have convinced the gentleman that he ought to keep longer away, had he been more in the habit of examining his own motives, and of reflecting to what the indulgence of his idle vanity was tending; but, thoughtless and selfish from prosperity and bad example, he would not look beyond the present moment. The sisters, handsome, clever, and encouraging, were an amusement to his sated mind; and finding nothing in Norfolk to equal the social pleasures of Mansfield, he gladly returned to it at the time appointed, and was welcomed thither quite as gladly by those whom he came to trifle with farther.

Maria, with only Mr. Rushworth to attend to her, and doomed to the repeated details of his day's sport, good or bad, his boast of his dogs, his jealousy of his neighbours, his doubts of their qualification,[2] and his zeal after poachers,—subjects which will not find their way to female feelings without some talent on one side, or some attachment on the other, had missed Mr. Crawford grievously; and Julia, unengaged and unemployed, felt all the right of missing him much more. Each sister believed herself the favourite. Julia might be justified in so doing by the hints of Mrs. Grant, inclined to credit what she wished, and Maria by the hints of Mr. Crawford himself. Every thing returned into the same channel as before his absence; his manners being to each so animated and agreeable, as to lose no ground with either, and just stopping short of the consistence, the steadiness, the solicitude, and the warmth which might excite general notice.

Fanny was the only one of the party who found any thing to dislike; but since the day at Sotherton, she could never see Mr. Crawford with either sister without observation, and seldom without wonder or censure; and had her confidence in her own judgment been equal to her exercise of it in every other respect, had she been sure that she was seeing clearly, and judging candidly, she would probably have made some important communications to her usual confidant. As it was, however, she only hazarded a hint, and the hint was lost. "I am rather surprised," said she, "that Mr. Crawford should come back again so soon, after being here so long before, full seven weeks; for I had understood he was so very fond of change and moving about, that I thought something would certainly occur when he was once gone, to take him elsewhere. He is used to much gayer places than Mansfield."

2. In the legal sense, having the right to hunt and kill game.

"It is to his credit," was Edmund's answer, "and I dare say it gives his sister pleasure. She does not like his unsettled habits."

"What a favourite he is with my cousins!"

"Yes, his manners to women are such as must please. Mrs. Grant, I believe, suspects him of a preference for Julia; I have never seen much symptom of it, but I wish it may be so. He has no faults but what a serious attachment would remove."

"If Miss Bertram were not engaged," said Fanny, cautiously, "I could sometimes almost think that he admired her more than Julia."

"Which is, perhaps, more in favour of his liking Julia best, than you, Fanny, may be aware; for I believe it often happens, that a man, before he has quite made up his own mind, will distinguish the sister or intimate friend of the woman he is really thinking of, more than the woman herself. Crawford has too much sense to stay here if he found himself in any danger from Maria; and I am not at all afraid for her, after such a proof as she has given, that her feelings are not strong."

Fanny supposed she must have been mistaken, and meant to think differently in future; but with all that submission to Edmund could do, and all the help of the coinciding looks and hints which she occasionally noticed in some of the others, and which seemed to say that Julia was Mr. Crawford's choice, she knew not always what to think. She was privy, one evening, to the hopes of her aunt Norris on this subject, as well as to her feelings, and the feelings of Mrs. Rushworth, on a point of some similarity, and could not help wondering as she listened; and glad would she have been not to be obliged to listen, for it was while all the other young people were dancing, and she sitting, most unwillingly, among the chaperons at the fire, longing for the reentrance of her elder cousin, on whom all her own hopes of a partner then depended. It was Fanny's first ball, though without the preparation or splendour of many a young lady's first ball, being the thought only of the afternoon, built on the late acquisition of a violin player in the servants' hall, and the possibility of raising five couple with the help of Mrs. Grant and a new intimate friend of Mr. Bertram's just arrived on a visit. It had, however, been a very happy one to Fanny through four dances, and she was quite grieved to be losing even a quarter of an hour.—While waiting and wishing, looking now at the dancers and now at the door, this dialogue between the two above-mentioned ladies was forced on her.

"I think, ma'am," said Mrs. Norris—her eyes directed towards Mr. Rushworth and Maria, who were partners for the second time—"we shall see some happy faces again now."

"Yes, ma'am, indeed"—replied the other, with a stately simper—"there will be some satisfaction in looking on *now*, and I think it was rather a pity they should have been obliged to part. Young folks in their situation should be excused complying with the common forms.—I wonder my son did not propose it."

"I dare say he did, ma'am.—Mr. Rushworth is never remiss. But dear Maria has such a strict sense of propriety, so much of that true delicacy which one seldom meets with now-a-days, Mrs. Rushworth, that wish of avoiding particularity!—Dear ma'am, only look at her face at this moment;—how different from what it was the two last dances!"

Miss Bertram did indeed look happy, her eyes were sparkling with pleasure, and she was speaking with great animation, for Julia and her partner, Mr. Crawford, were close to her; they were all in a cluster together. How she had looked before, Fanny could not recollect, for she had been dancing with Edmund herself, and had not thought about her.

Mrs. Norris continued, "It is quite delightful, ma'am, to see young people so properly happy, so well suited, and so much the thing! I cannot but think of dear Sir Thomas's delight. And what do you say, ma'am, to the chance of another match? Mr. Rushworth has set a good example, and such things are very catching."

Mrs. Rushworth, who saw nothing but her son, was quite at a loss. "The couple above, ma'am. Do you see no symptoms there?"

"Oh! dear—Miss Julia and Mr. Crawford. Yes, indeed, a very pretty match. What is his property?"

"Four thousand a year."

"Very well.—Those who have not more, must be satisfied with what they have.—Four thousand a year is a pretty estate, and he seems a very genteel, steady young man, so I hope Miss Julia will be very happy."

"It is not a settled thing, ma'am, yet.—We only speak of it among friends. But I have very little doubt it *will be*.—He is growing extremely particular in his attentions."

Fanny could listen no farther. Listening and wondering were all suspended for a time, for Mr. Bertram was in the room again, and though feeling it would be a great honour to be asked by him, she thought it must happen. He came towards their little circle; but instead of asking her to dance, drew a chair near her, and gave her an account of the present state of a sick horse, and the opinion of the groom, from whom he had just parted. Fanny found that it was not to be, and in the modesty of her nature immediately felt that she had been unreasonable in expecting it. When he had told of his horse, he took a newspaper from the table, and looking over it said in a languid way, "If you want to dance, Fanny, I will stand up with you."—With more than equal civility the offer was declined;—she did not wish to dance.—"I am glad of it," said he in a much brisker tone, and throwing down the newspaper again—"for I am tired to death. I only wonder how the good people can keep it up so long—They had need be *all* in love, to find any amusement in such folly—and so they are, I fancy.—If you look at them, you may see they are so many couple of lovers—all but Yates and Mrs. Grant—and, between ourselves, she, poor woman! must want a lover as much as any one of them. A desperate dull life her's must be with the doctor," making a sly face as he spoke towards the chair of the latter, who proving, however, to be close at his elbow, made so instantaneous a change of expression and subject necessary, as Fanny, in spite of every thing, could hardly help laughing at.—"A strange business this in America,[3] Dr. Grant!—What is your opinion?—I always come to you to know what I am to think of public matters."

"My dear Tom," cried his aunt soon afterwards, "as you are not dancing, I dare say you will have no objection to join us in a rubber;[4] shall you?"—then, leaving her seat, and coming to him to enforce the proposal, added in a whisper—"We want to make a table for Mrs. Rushworth, you know.—Your mother is quite anxious about it, but cannot very well spare time to sit down herself, because of her fringe.[5] Now, you and I and Dr. Grant will just do; and though we play but half-crowns, you know you may bet half-guineas with him."

"I should be most happy," replied he aloud, and jumping up with alacrity, "it would give me the greatest pleasure—but that I am this moment going to dance. Come, Fanny,"—taking her hand—"do not be dawdling any longer, or the dance will be over."

Fanny was led off very willingly, though it was impossible for her to feel much gratitude towards her cousin, or distinguish, as he certainly did, between the selfishness of another person and his own.

"A pretty modest request upon my word!" he indignantly exclaimed as they walked away. "To want to nail me to a card table for the next two hours with herself and Dr. Grant, who are always quarrelling, and that poking old woman, who knows no more of whist than of algebra. I wish my good aunt would be a little less busy! And to ask me in such a way too! without ceremony, before them all, so as to leave me no possibility of refusing! That is what I dislike most particularly. It raises my spleen more than any thing, to have the pretence of being asked, of being given a choice, and at the same time addressed in such a way as to oblige one to do the very thing—whatever it be! If I had not luckily thought of standing up with you, I could not have got out of it. It is a great deal too bad. But when my aunt has got a fancy in her head, nothing can stop her."

3. Some critics, following R. W. Chapman's dating according to the almanacs of 1808–09, maintain that Tom is referring to any now-forgotten news item to change the subject. Others, placing the action during 1812, according to the publication date of George Crabbe's *Tales in Verse* (1812), suggest that he alludes to war with the United States.
4. A set of three or five games, of which one party must win the majority in order to win the set.
5. Lady Bertram cannot play because she is busy sewing a fringed border.

Chapter XIII.

The Honourable[1] John Yates, this new friend, had not much to recommend him beyond habits of fashion and expense, and being the younger son of a lord with a tolerable independence; and Sir Thomas would probably have thought his introduction at Mansfield by no means desirable. Mr. Bertram's acquaintance with him had begun at Weymouth, where they had spent ten days together in the same society, and the friendship, if friendship it might be called, had been proved and perfected by Mr. Yates's being invited to take Mansfield in his way, whenever he could, and by his promising to come; and he did come rather earlier than had been expected, in consequence of the sudden breaking-up of a large party assembled for gaiety at the house of another friend, which he had left Weymouth to join. He came on the wings of disappointment, and with his head full of acting, for it had been a theatrical party; and the play, in which he had borne a part, was within two days of representation, when the sudden death of one of the nearest connections of the family had destroyed the scheme and dispersed the performers. To be so near happiness, so near fame, so near the long paragraph in praise of the private theatricals at Ecclesford, the seat of the Right Hon. Lord Ravenshaw, in Cornwall, which would of course have immortalized the whole party for at least a twelvemonth! and being so near, to lose it all, was an injury to be keenly felt, and Mr. Yates could talk of nothing else. Ecclesford and its theatre, with its arrangements and dresses, rehearsals and jokes, was his never-failing subject, and to boast of the past his only consolation.

Happily for him, a love of the theatre is so general, an itch for acting so strong among young people, that he could hardly out-talk the interest of his hearers. From the first casting of the parts, to the epilogue, it was all bewitching, and there were few who did not wish to have been a party concerned, or would have hesitated to try their skill. The play had been Lovers' Vows,[2] and Mr. Yates was to have been Count Cassel. "A trifling part," said he, "and not at all to my taste, and such a one as I certainly would not accept again; but I was determined to make no difficulties. Lord Ravenshaw and the duke had appropriated the only two characters worth playing before I reached Ecclesford; and though Lord Ravenshaw offered to resign his to me, it was impossible to take it, you know. I was sorry for *him* that he should have so mistaken his powers, for he was no more equal to the Baron! A little man, with a

---

1. A title bestowed on all the children of peers, and on the younger sons of earls. The narrator stresses that Tom's friend is a member of the aristocracy.
2. An adaptation of August Friedrich Ferdinand von Kotzebue's *Das Kind der Liebe* (1791) by Elizabeth Inchbald; often staged in London and in Bath when Austen lived there (1801–05). See "Contexts," below, pp. 329–75.

weak voice, always hoarse after the first ten minutes! It must have injured the piece materially; but *I* was resolved to make no difficulties.
Sir Henry thought the duke not equal to Frederick, but that was because Sir Henry wanted the part himself; whereas it was certainly in
the best hands of the two. I was surprised to see Sir Henry such a stick.
Luckily the strength of the piece did not depend upon him. Our Agatha
was inimitable, and the duke was thought very great by many. And
upon the whole it would certainly have gone off wonderfully."

"It was a hard case, upon my word;" and, "I do think you were very
much to be pitied;" were the kind responses of listening sympathy.

"It is not worth complaining about, but to be sure the poor old
dowager could not have died at a worse time; and it is impossible to
help wishing, that the news could have been suppressed for just the
three days we wanted. It was but three days; and being only a grandmother, and all happening two hundred miles off, I think there would
have been no great harm, and it *was* suggested, I know; but Lord Ravenshaw, who I suppose is one of the most correct men in England,
would not hear of it."

"An after-piece[3] instead of a comedy," said Mr. Bertram. "Lovers'
Vows were at an end, and Lord and Lady Ravenshaw left to act My*
Grandmother[4] by themselves. Well, the jointure[5] may comfort *him*; and
perhaps, between friends, he began to tremble for his credit and his
lungs in the Baron, and was not sorry to withdraw; and to make *you*
amends, Yates, I think we must raise a little theatre at Mansfield, and
ask you to be our manager."

This, though the thought of the moment, did not end with the moment; for the inclination to act was awakened, and in no one more
strongly than in him who was now master of the house; and who having
so much leisure as to make almost any novelty a certain good, had
likewise such a degree of lively talents and comic taste, as were exactly
adapted to the novelty of acting. The thought returned again and again.
"Oh! for the Ecclesford theatre and scenery to try something with."
Each sister could echo the wish; and Henry Crawford, to whom, in all
the riot of his gratifications it was yet an untasted pleasure, was quite
alive at the idea. "I really believe," said he, "I could be fool enough at
this moment to undertake any character that ever was written, from
Shylock or Richard III. down to the singing hero of a farce in his scarlet
coat and cocked hat. I feel as if I could be any thing or every thing, as
if I could rant and storm, or sigh, or cut capers in any tragedy or comedy
in the English language. Let us be doing something. Be it only half a
play—an act—a scene; what should prevent us? Not these countenances

3. A short drama staged after the main play.
4. *My Grandmother* (1793/94), a musical farce by Prince Hoare, often revived.
5. Property settled by a husband on his wife for her use after his death.

I am sure," looking towards the Miss Bertrams, "and for a theatre, what signifies a theatre? We shall be only amusing ourselves. Any room in this house might suffice."

"We must have a curtain," said Tom Bertram, "a few yards of green baize for a curtain, and perhaps that may be enough."

"Oh! quite enough," cried Mr. Yates, "with only just a side wing or two run up, doors in flat, and three or four scenes to be let down; nothing more would be necessary on such a plan as this. For mere amusement among ourselves, we should want nothing more."

"I believe we must be satisfied with *less*," said Maria. "There would not be time, and other difficulties would arise. We must rather adopt Mr. Crawford's views, and make the *performance*, not the *theatre*, our object. Many parts of our best plays are independent of scenery."

"Nay," said Edmund, who began to listen with alarm. "Let us do nothing by halves. If we are to act, let it be in a theatre completely fitted up with pit, box, and gallery, and let us have a play entire from beginning to end; so as it be a German play, no matter what, with a good tricking, shifting after-piece, and a figure-dance, and a horn-pipe, and a song between the acts. If we do not out do Ecclesford, we do nothing."

"Now, Edmund, do not be disagreeable," said Julia. "Nobody loves a play better than you do, or can have gone much farther to see one."

"True, to see real acting, good hardened real acting; but I would hardly walk from this room to the next to look at the raw efforts of those who have not been bred to the trade,—a set of gentlemen and ladies, who have all the disadvantages of education and decorum to struggle through."

After a short pause, however, the subject still continued, and was discussed with unabated eagerness, every one's inclination increasing by the discussion, and a knowledge of the inclination of the rest; and though nothing was settled but that Tom Bertram would prefer a comedy, and his sisters and Henry Crawford a tragedy, and that nothing in the world could be easier than to find a piece which would please them all, the resolution to act something or other, seemed so decided, as to make Edmund quite uncomfortable. He was determined to prevent it, if possible, though his mother, who equally heard the conversation which passed at table, did not evince the least disapprobation.

The same evening afforded him an opportunity of trying his strength. Maria, Julia, Henry Crawford, and Mr. Yates, were in the billiard-room. Tom returning from them into the drawing-room, where Edmund was standing thoughtfully by the fire, while Lady Bertram was on the sofa at a little distance, and Fanny close beside her arranging her work, thus began as he entered. "Such a horribly vile billiard-table as ours, is not to be met with, I believe, above ground! I can stand it no longer, and I think, I may say, that nothing shall ever tempt me to it again. But one good thing I have just ascertained. It is the very room for a theatre, precisely the shape and length for it, and the doors at the farther end, communicating with each other as they may be made to do in five minutes, by merely moving the book-case in my father's room, is the very thing we could have desired, if we had set down to wish for it. And my father's room will be an excellent green-room.[6] It seems to join the billiard-room on purpose."

"You are not serious, Tom, in meaning to act?" said Edmund in a low voice, as his brother approached the fire.

"Not serious! never more so, I assure you. What is there to surprise you in it?"

"I think it would be very wrong. In a *general* light, private theatricals are open to some objections, but as *we* are circumstanced, I must think it would be highly injudicious, and more than injudicious, to attempt any thing of the kind. It would show great want of feeling on my father's account, absent as he is, and in some degree of constant danger; and it would be imprudent, I think, with regard to Maria, whose situation is a very delicate one, considering every thing, extremely delicate."

"You take up a thing so seriously! as if we were going to act three times a week till my father's return, and invite all the country. But it is not to be a display of that sort. We mean nothing but a little amusement among ourselves, just to vary the scene, and exercise our powers in something new. We want no audience, no publicity. We may be trusted, I think, in choosing some play most perfectly unexceptionable, and I can conceive no greater harm or danger to any of us in conversing in the elegant written language of some respectable author than in chattering in words of our own. I have no fears, and no scruples. And as to my father's being absent, it is so far from an objection, that I consider it rather as a motive; for the expectation of his return must be a very anxious period to my mother, and if we can be the means of amusing that anxiety, and keeping up her spirits for the next few weeks, I shall think our time very well spent, and so I am sure will he.—It is a *very* anxious period for her."

As he said this, each looked towards their mother. Lady Bertram, sunk back in one corner of the sofa, the picture of health, wealth, ease, and tranquillity, was just falling into a gentle doze, while Fanny was getting through the few difficulties of her work for her.

Edmund smiled and shook his head.

"By Jove! this won't do"—cried Tom, throwing himself into a chair with a hearty laugh. "To* be sure, my dear mother, your anxiety—I was unlucky there."

"What is the matter?" asked her ladyship in the heavy tone of one half roused,—"I was not asleep."

---

6. A room where actors and actresses wait between scenes.

"Oh! dear, no ma'am—nobody suspected you—Well, Edmund," he continued, returning to the former subject, posture, and voice, as soon as Lady Bertram began to nod again—"But *this* I *will* maintain—that we shall be doing no harm."

"I cannot agree with you—I am convinced that my father would totally disapprove it."

"And I am convinced to the contrary.—Nobody is fonder of the exercise of talent in young people, or promotes it more, than my father; and for any thing of the acting, spouting, reciting kind, I think he has always a decided taste. I am sure he encouraged it in us as boys. How many a time have we mourned over the dead body of Julius Cæsar, and *to be'd* and *not** to be'd*, in this very room, for his amusement! And I am sure, *my name was Norval,*[7] every evening of my life through one Christmas holidays."

"It was a very different thing.—You must see the difference yourself. My father wished us, as school-boys, to speak well, but he would never wish his grown up daughters to be acting plays. His sense of decorum is strict."

"I know all that," said Tom, displeased. "I know my father as well as you do, and I'll take care that his daughters do nothing to distress him. Manage your own concerns, Edmund, and I'll take care of the rest of the family."

"If you are resolved on acting," replied the persevering Edmund, "I must hope it will be in a very small and quiet way; and I think a theatre ought not to be attempted.—It would be taking liberties with my father's house in his absence which could not be justified."

"For every thing of that nature, I will be answerable,"—said Tom, in a decided tone.—"His house shall not be hurt. I have quite as great an interest in being careful of his house as you can have; and as to such alterations as I was suggesting just now, such as moving a bookcase, or unlocking a door, or even as using the billiard-room for the space of a week without playing at billiards in it, you might just as well suppose he would object to our sitting more in this room, and less in the breakfast-room, than we did before he went away, or to my sister's* piano forte being moved from one side of the room to the other.—Absolute nonsense!"

"The innovation, if not wrong as an innovation, will be wrong as an expense."

"Yes, the expense of such an undertaking would be prodigious! Perhaps it might cost a whole twenty pounds.—Something of a Theatre we must have undoubtedly, but it will be on the simplest plan;—a green curtain and a little carpenter's work—and that's all; and as the carpenter's work may be all done at home by Christopher Jackson himself, it

---

7. This speech, from the second act of the immensely popular *Douglas, a Tragedy* (1756/57) by Rev. John Home (1722–1808), was a set piece for elocutionists.

will be too absurd to talk of expense;—and as long as Jackson is employed, every thing will be right with Sir Thomas.—Don't imagine that nobody in this house can see or judge but yourself.—Don't act yourself, if you do not like it, but don't expect to govern every body else."

"No, as to acting myself," said Edmund, "*that* I absolutely protest against."

Tom walked out of the room as he said it, and Edmund was left to sit down and stir the fire in thoughtful vexation.

Fanny, who had heard it all, and borne Edmund company in every feeling throughout the whole, now ventured to say, in her anxiety to suggest some comfort, "Perhaps they may not be able to find any play to suit them. Your brother's taste, and your sisters', seem very different."

"I have no hope there, Fanny. If they persist in the scheme they will find something—I shall speak to my sisters, and try to dissuade *them*, and that is all I can do."

"I should think my aunt Norris would be on your side."

"I dare say she would; but she has no influence with either Tom or my sisters that could be of any use; and if I cannot convince them myself, I shall let things take their course, without attempting it through her. Family squabbling is the greatest evil of all, and we had better do any thing than be altogether by the ears."[8]

His sisters, to whom he had an opportunity of speaking the next morning, were quite as impatient of his advice, quite as unyielding to his representation, quite as determined in the cause of pleasure, as Tom.—Their mother had no objection to the plan, and they were not in the least afraid of their father's disapprobation.—There could be no harm in what had been done in so many respectable families, and by so many women of the first consideration; and it must be scrupulousness run mad, that could see any thing to censure in a plan like their's, comprehending only brothers and sisters, and intimate friends, and which would never be heard of beyond themselves. Julia *did* seem inclined to admit that Maria's situation might require particular caution and delicacy—but that could not extend to *her*—*she* was at liberty; and Maria evidently considered her engagement as only raising her so much more above restraint, and leaving her less occasion than Julia, to consult either father or mother. Edmund had little to hope, but he was still urging the subject, when Henry Crawford entered the room, fresh from the Parsonage, calling out, "No want of hands in our Theatre, Miss Bertram. No want of under strappers[9]—My sister desires her love, and hopes to be admitted into the company, and will be happy to take the part of any old Duenna or tame Confidante, that you may not like to do yourselves."

Maria gave Edmund a glance, which meant, "What say you now?

8. At variance.
9. Petty fellows, underlings.

Can we be wrong if Mary Crawford feels the same?" And Edmund silenced, was obliged to acknowledge that the charm of acting might well carry fascination to the mind of genius; and with the ingenuity of love, to dwell more on the obliging, accommodating purport of the message than on any thing else.

The scheme advanced. Opposition was vain; and as to Mrs. Norris, he was mistaken in supposing she would wish to make any. She started no difficulties that were not talked down in five minutes by her eldest nephew and niece, who were all-powerful with her; and, as the whole arrangement was to bring very little expense to any body, and none at all to herself, as she foresaw in it all the comforts of hurry, bustle and importance, and derived the immediate advantage of fancying herself obliged to leave her own house, where she had been living a month at her own cost, and take up her abode in their's, that every hour might be spent in their service; she was, in fact, exceedingly delighted with the project.

Chapter XIV.

Fanny seemed nearer being right than Edmund had supposed. The business of finding a play that would suit every body, proved to be no trifle; and the carpenter had received his orders and taken his measurements, had suggested and removed at least two sets of difficulties, and having made the necessity of an enlargement of plan and expense fully evident, was already at work, while a play was still to seek. Other preparations were also in hand. An enormous roll of green baize had arrived from Northampton, and been cut out by Mrs. Norris (with a saving, by her good management, of full three quarters of a yard), and was actually forming into a curtain by the house-maids, and still the play was wanting; and as two or three days passed away in this manner, Edmund began almost to hope that none might ever be found.

There were, in fact, so many things to be attended to, so many people to be pleased, so many best characters required, and above all, such a need that the play should be at once both tragedy and comedy, that there did seem as little chance of a decision, as any thing pursued by youth and zeal could hold out.

On the tragic side were the Miss Bertrams, Henry Crawford, and Mr. Yates; on the comic, Tom Bertram, not *quite* alone, because it was evident that Mary Crawford's wishes, though politely kept back, inclined the same way; but his determinateness and his power, seemed to make allies unnecessary; and independent of this great irreconcileable difference, they wanted a piece containing very few characters in the whole, but every character first-rate, and three principal women. All the best plays were run over in vain. Neither Hamlet, nor Macbeth, nor Othello, nor Douglas, nor the Gamester, presented any thing that could satisfy even the tragedians; and the Rivals, the School for Scandal, Wheel of Fortune, Heir at Law,[1] and a long etcetera, were successively dismissed with yet warmer objections. No piece could be proposed that did not supply somebody with a difficulty, and on one side or the other it was a continual repetition of, "Oh! no, *that* will never do. Let us have no ranting tragedies. Too many characters—Not a tolerable woman's part in the play—Any thing but *that*, my dear Tom. It would be impossible to fill it up—One could not expect any body to take such a part—Nothing but buffoonery from beginning to end. *That* might do, perhaps, but for the low parts—If I *must* give my opinion, I have always thought it the most insipid play in the English language—I do not wish to make objections, I shall be happy to be of any use, but I think we could not choose worse."

Fanny looked on and listened, not unamused to observe the selfishness which, more or less disguised, seemed to govern them all, and wondering how it would end. For her own gratification she could have wished that something might be acted, for she had never seen even half a play, but every thing of higher consequence was against it.

"This will never do," said Tom Bertram at last. "We are wasting time most abominably. Something must be fixed on. No matter what, so that something is chosen. We must not be so nice. A few characters,* too many must not frighten us. We must *double* them. We must descend a little. If a part is insignificant, the greater our credit in making any thing of it. From this moment *I* make no difficulties. I take any part you choose to give me, so as it be comic. Let it but be comic, I condition for nothing more."

For about the fifth time he then proposed the Heir at Law, doubting only whether to prefer Lord Duberley or Dr. Pangloss for himself, and very earnestly, but very unsuccessfully, trying to persuade the others that there were some fine tragic parts in the rest of the Dramatis Personæ.

The pause which followed this fruitless effort was ended by the same speaker, who taking up one of the many volumes of plays that lay on the table, and turning it over, suddenly exclaimed, "Lovers' Vows! And why should not Lovers' Vows do for *us* as well as for the Ravenshaws? How came it never to be thought of before? It strikes me as if it would do exactly. What say you all?—Here are two capital tragic parts for Yates and Crawford, and here is the rhyming butler for me—if nobody else wants it—a trifling part, but the sort of thing I should not dislike, and as I said before, I am determined to take any-thing and do my best.

1. *The Gamester* (1753) by Edward Moore (1712–1757); *Heir at Law* (1797/1800) by George Colman the Younger (1762–1836); *The Rivals* (1775) and *School for Scandal* (1777) by Richard Brinsley Sheridan (1751–1816); *Wheel of Fortune* (1795) by Richard Cumberland (1732–1811): these plays were often performed and printed during the late eighteenth and early nineteenth centuries.

And as for the rest, they may be filled up by any-body. It is only Count Cassel and Anhalt."

The suggestion was generally welcome. Every body was growing weary of indecision, and the first idea with every body was, that nothing had been proposed before so likely to suit them all. Mr. Yates was particularly pleased; he had been sighing and longing to do the Baron at Ecclesford, had grudged every rant of Lord Ravenshaw's, and been forced to re-rant it all in his own room. To* storm through Baron Wildenhaim was the height of his theatrical ambition, and with the advantage of knowing half the scenes by heart already, he did now with the greatest alacrity offer his services for the part. To do him justice, however, he did not resolve to appropriate it—for remembering that there was some very good ranting ground in Frederick, he professed an equal willingness for that. Henry Crawford was ready to take either. Whichever Mr. Yates did not choose, would perfectly satisfy him, and a short parley of compliment ensued. Miss Bertram feeling all the interest of an Agatha in the question, took on her to decide it, by observing to Mr. Yates, that this was a point in which height and figure ought to be considered, and that *his* being the tallest, seemed to fit him peculiarly for the Baron. She was acknowledged to be quite right, and the two parts being accepted accordingly, she was certain of the proper Frederick. Three of the characters were now cast, besides Mr. Rushworth, who was always answered for by Maria as willing to do any thing; when Julia, meaning like her sister to be Agatha, began to be scrupulous on Miss Crawford's account.

"This is not behaving well by the absent," said she. "Here are not women enough. Amelia and Agatha may do for Maria and me, but here is nothing for your sister, Mr. Crawford."

Mr. Crawford desired *that* might not be thought of; he was very sure his sister had no wish of acting, but as she might be useful, and that she would not allow herself to be considered in the present case. But this was immediately opposed by Tom Bertram, who asserted the part of Amelia to be in every respect the property of Miss Crawford if she would accept it. "It falls as naturally, as necessarily to her," said he, "as Agatha does to one or other of my sisters. It can be no sacrifice on their side, for it is highly comic."

A short silence followed. Each sister looked anxious; for each felt the best claim to Agatha, and was hoping to have it pressed on her by the rest. Henry Crawford, who meanwhile had taken up the play, and with seeming carelessness was turning over the first act, soon settled the business. "I must entreat Miss *Julia* Bertram," said he, "not to engage in the part of Agatha, or it will be the ruin of all my solemnity. You must not, indeed you must not—(turning to her.) I could not stand your countenance dressed up in woe and paleness. The many laughs we have had together would infallibly come across me, and Frederick and his knapsack would be obliged to run away."

Pleasantly, courteously it was spoken; but the manner was lost in the matter to Julia's feelings. She saw a glance at Maria, which confirmed the injury to herself; it was a scheme—a trick; she was slighted, Maria was preferred; the smile of triumph which Maria was trying to suppress shewed how well it was understood, and before Julia could command herself enough to speak, her brother gave his weight against her too, by saying, "Oh! yes, Maria must be Agatha. Maria will be the best Agatha. Though Julia fancies she prefers tragedy, I would not trust her in it. There is nothing of tragedy about her. She has not the look of it. Her features are not tragic features, and she walks too quick, and speaks too quick, and would not keep her countenance. She had better do the old countrywoman; the Cottager's wife; you had, indeed, Julia. Cottager's wife is a very pretty part I assure you. The old lady relieves the high-flown benevolence of her husband with a good deal of spirit. You shall be Cottager's wife."

"Cottager's wife!" cried Mr. Yates. "What are you talking of? The most trivial, paltry, insignificant part; the merest common-place—not a tolerable speech in the whole. Your sister do that! It is an insult to propose it. At Ecclesford the governess was to have done it. We all agreed that it could not be offered to any body else. A little more justice, Mr. Manager, if you please. You do not deserve the office, if you cannot appreciate the talents of your company a little better."

"Why as to *that*, my good friend, till I and my company have really acted there must be some guess-work; but I mean no disparagement to Julia. We cannot have two Agathas, and we must have one Cottager's wife; and I am sure I set her the example of moderation myself in being satisfied with the old Butler. If the part is trifling she will have more credit in making something of it; and if she is so desperately bent against every thing humorous, let her take Cottager's speeches instead of Cottager's wife's, and so change the parts all through; *he* is solemn and pathetic enough I am sure. It could make no difference in the play; and as for Cottager himself, when he has got his wife's speeches, I would undertake him with all my heart."

"With all your partiality for Cottager's wife," said Henry Crawford, "it will be impossible to make any thing of it fit for your sister, and we must not suffer her good nature to be imposed on. We must not *allow* her to accept the part. She must not be left to her own complaisance. Her talents will be wanted in Amelia. Amelia is a character more difficult to be well represented than even Agatha. I consider Amelia as the most difficult character in the whole piece. It requires great powers, great nicety, to give her playfulness and simplicity without extravagance. I have seen good actresses fail in the part. Simplicity, indeed, is beyond the reach of almost every actress by profession. It requires a delicacy of feeling which they have not. It requires a gentlewoman—a Julia Bertram. You *will* undertake it I hope?" turning to her with a look of anxious entreaty, which softened her a little; but while she hesitated what to say, her brother again interposed with Miss Crawford's better claim.

"No, no, Julia must not be Amelia. It is not at all the part for her. She would not like it. She would not do well. She is too tall and robust. Amelia should be a small, light, girlish, skipping figure. It is fit for Miss Crawford and Miss Crawford only. She looks the part, and I am persuaded will do it admirably."

Without attending to this, Henry Crawford continued his supplication. "You must oblige us," said he, "indeed you must. When you have studied the character, I am sure you will feel it suit you. Tragedy may be your choice, but it will certainly appear that comedy chooses *you*. You will be to visit me in prison with a basket of provisions; you will not refuse to visit me in prison? I think I see you coming in with your basket."

The influence of his voice was felt. Julia wavered: but was he only trying to soothe and pacify her, and make her overlook the previous affront? She distrusted him. The slight had been most determined. He was, perhaps, but at treacherous play with her. She looked suspiciously at her sister; Maria's countenance was to decide it; if she were vexed and alarmed—but Maria looked all serenity and satisfaction, and Julia well knew that on this ground Maria could not be happy but at her expense. With hasty indignation therefore, and a tremulous voice, she said to him, "You do not seem afraid of not keeping your countenance when I come in with a basket of provisions—though one might have supposed—but it is only as Agatha that I was to be so overpowering!" —She stopped—Henry Crawford looked rather foolish, and as if he did not know what to say. Tom Bertram began again,

"Miss Crawford must be Amelia.—She will be an excellent Amelia."

"Do not be afraid of *my* wanting the character," cried Julia with angry quickness;—"I am *not* to be Agatha, and I am sure I will do nothing else; and as to Amelia, it is of all parts in the world the most disgusting to me. I quite detest her. An odious, little, pert, unnatural, impudent girl. I have always protested against comedy, and this is comedy in its worst form." And so saying, she walked hastily out of the room, leaving awkward feelings to more than one, but exciting small compassion in any except Fanny, who had been a quiet auditor of the whole, and who could not think of her as under the agitations of *jealousy*, without great pity.

A short silence succeeded her leaving them; but her brother soon returned to business and Lovers' Vows, and was eagerly looking over the play, with Mr. Yates's help, to ascertain what scenery would be necessary—while Maria and Henry Crawford conversed together in an under voice, and the declaration with which she began of, "I am sure I would give up the part to Julia most willingly, but that though I shall probably do it very ill, I feel persuaded *she* would do it worse," was doubtless receiving all the compliments it called for.

When this had lasted some time, the division of the party was completed by Tom Bertram and Mr. Yates walking off together to consult farther in the room now beginning to be called *the Theatre*, and Miss Bertram's resolving to go down to the Parsonage herself with the offer of Amelia to Miss Crawford; and Fanny remained alone.

The first use she made of her solitude was to take up the volume which had been left on the table, and begin to acquaint herself with the play of which she had heard so much. Her curiosity was all awake, and she ran through it with an eagerness which was suspended only by intervals of astonishment, that it could be chosen in the present instance—that it could be proposed and accepted in a private Theatre! Agatha and Amelia appeared to her in their different ways so totally improper for home representation—the situation of one, and the language of the other, so unfit to be expressed by any woman of modesty, that she could hardly suppose her cousins could be aware of what they were engaging in; and longed to have them roused as soon as possible by the remonstrance which Edmund would certainly make.

Chapter XV.

Miss Crawford accepted the part very readily, and soon after Miss Bertram's return from the Parsonage, Mr. Rushworth arrived, and another character was consequently cast. He had the offer of Count Cassel and Anhalt, and at first did not know which to choose, and wanted Miss Bertram to direct him, but upon being made to understand the different style of the characters, and which was which, and recollecting that he had once seen the play in London, and had thought Anhalt a very stupid fellow, he soon decided for the Count. Miss Bertram approved the decision, for the less he had to learn the better; and though she could not sympathize in his wish that the Count and Agatha might be to act together, nor wait very patiently while he was slowly turning over the leaves with the hope of still discovering such a scene, she very kindly took his part in hand, and curtailed every speech that admitted being shortened;—besides pointing out the necessity of his being very much dressed, and choosing his colours. Mr. Rushworth liked the idea of his finery very well, though affecting to despise it, and was too much engaged with what his own appearance would be, to think of the others, or draw any of those conclusions, or feel any of that displeasure, which Maria had been half prepared for.

Thus much was settled before Edmund, who had been out all the morning, knew any thing of the matter; but when he entered the drawing-room before dinner, the buz of discussion was high between Tom, Maria, and Mr. Yates; and Mr. Rushworth stepped forward with great alacrity to tell him the agreeable news.

"We have got a play," said he.—"It is to be* Lovers' Vows; and I am to be Count Cassel, and am to come in first with a blue dress, and a pink satin cloak, and afterwards am to have another fine fancy suit by way of a shooting dress.—I do not know how I shall like it."

Fanny's eyes followed Edmund, and her heart beat for him as she heard this speech, and saw his look, and felt what his sensations must be.

"Lovers' Vows!"—in a tone of the greatest amazement, was his only reply to Mr. Rushworth; and he turned towards his brother and sisters as if hardly doubting a contradiction.

"Yes," cried Mr. Yates.—"After all our debatings and difficulties, we find there is nothing that will suit us altogether so well, nothing so unexceptionable, as Lovers' Vows. The wonder is that it should not have been thought of before. My stupidity was abominable, for here we have all the advantage of what I saw at Ecclesford; and it is so useful to have any thing of a model!—We have cast almost every part."

"But what do you do for women?" said Edmund gravely, and looking at Maria.

Maria blushed in spite of herself as she answered, "I take the part which Lady Ravenshaw was to have done, and (with a bolder eye) Miss Crawford is to be Amelia."

"I should not have thought it the sort of play to be so easily filled up, with us," replied Edmund, turning away to the fire where sat his mother, aunt, and Fanny, and seating himself with a look of great vexation.

Mr. Rushworth followed him to say, "I come in three times, and have two and forty speeches. That's something, is not it?—But I do not much like the idea of being so fine.—I shall hardly know myself in a blue dress, and a pink satin cloak."

Edmund could not answer him.—In a few minutes Mr. Bertram was called out of the room to satisfy some doubts of the carpenter, and being accompanied by Mr. Yates, and followed soon afterwards by Mr. Rushworth, Edmund almost immediately took the opportunity of saying, "I cannot before Mr. Yates speak what I feel as to this play, without reflecting on his friends at Ecclesford—but I must now, my dear Maria, tell you, that I think it exceedingly unfit for private representation, and that I hope you will give it up.—I cannot but suppose you will when you have read it carefully over.—Read only the first Act aloud, to either your mother or aunt, and see how you can approve it.—It will not be necessary to send you to your father's judgment, I am convinced."

"We see things very differently," cried Maria—"I am perfectly acquainted with the play, I assure you—and with a very few omissions, and so forth, which will be made, of course, I can see nothing objectionable in it; and I am not the *only* young woman you find, who thinks it very fit for private representation."

"I am sorry for it," was his answer—"But in this matter it is *you* who are to lead. *You* must set the example.—If others have blundered, it is your place to put them right, and shew them what true delicacy is.— In all points of decorum, *your* conduct must be law to the rest of the party."

This picture of her consequence had some effect, for no one loved better to lead than Maria;—and with far more good humour she answered, "I am much obliged to you, Edmund;—you mean very well, I am sure—but I still think you see things too strongly; and I really cannot undertake to harangue all the rest upon a subject of this kind.—*There* would be the greatest indecorum I think."

"Do you imagine that I could have such an idea in my head? No— let your conduct be the only harangue.—Say that, on examining the part, you feel yourself unequal to it, that you find it requiring more exertion and confidence than you can be supposed to have.—Say this with firmness, and it will be quite enough.—All who can distinguish, will understand your motive.—The play will be given up, and your delicacy honoured as it ought."

"Do not act any thing improper, my dear," said Lady Bertram. "Sir Thomas would not like it.—Fanny, ring the bell; I must have my dinner.—To be sure Julia is dressed by this time."

"I am convinced, madam," said Edmund, preventing Fanny, "that Sir Thomas would not like it."

"There, my dear, do you hear what Edmund says?"

"If I were to decline the part," said Maria with renewed zeal, "Julia would certainly take it."

"What!"—cried Edmund, "if she knew your reasons!"

"Oh! she might think the difference between us—the difference in our situations—that *she* need not be so scrupulous as *I* might feel necessary. I am sure she would argue so. No, you must excuse me, I cannot retract my consent. It is too far settled; every body would be so disappointed. Tom would be quite angry: and if we are so very nice, we shall never act any thing."

"I was just going to say the very same thing," said Mrs. Norris. "If every play is to be objected to, you will act nothing—and the preparations will be all so much money thrown away—and I am sure *that* would be a discredit to us all. I do not know the play; but, as Maria says, if there is any thing a little too warm (and it is so with most of them) it can be easily left out.—We must not be over precise Edmund. As Mr. Rushworth is to act too, there can be no harm.—I only wish

Tom had known his own mind when the carpenters began, for there was the loss of half a day's work about those side-doors.—The curtain will be a good job, however. The maids do their work very well, and I think we shall be able to send back some dozens of the rings.—There is no occasion to put them so very close together. I *am* of some use I hope in preventing waste and making the most of things. There should always be one steady head to superintend so many young ones. I forgot to tell Tom of something that happened to me this very day.—I had been looking about me in the poultry yard, and was just coming out, when who should I see but Dick Jackson making up to the servants' hall door with two bits of deal board in his hand, bringing them to father, you may be sure; mother had chanced to send him a message to father, and then father had bid him bring up them two bits of board, for he could not no how do without them. I knew what all this meant, for the servants' dinner bell was ringing at the very moment over our heads, and as I hate such encroaching people, (the Jacksons are very encroaching, I have always said so,—just the sort of people to get all they can),* I said to the boy directly—(a great lubberly fellow of ten years old you know, who ought to be ashamed of himself,) *I'll* take the boards to your father, Dick; so get you home again as fast as you can. —The boy looked very silly and turned away without offering a word, for I believe I might speak pretty sharp; and I dare say it will cure him of coming marauding about the house for one while,—I hate such greediness—so good as your father is to the family, employing the man all the year round!"

Nobody was at the trouble of an answer; the others soon returned, and Edmund found that to have endeavoured to set them right must be his only satisfaction.

Dinner passed heavily. Mrs. Norris related again her triumph over Dick Jackson, but neither play nor preparation were otherwise much talked of, for Edmund's disapprobation was felt even by his brother, though he would not have owned it. Maria, wanting Henry Crawford's animating support, thought the subject better avoided. Mr. Yates, who was trying to make himself agreeable to Julia, found her gloom less impenetrable on any topic than that of his regret at her secession from their company, and Mr. Rushworth having only his own part, and his own dress in his head, had soon talked away all that could be said of either.

But the concerns of the theatre were suspended only for an hour or two; there was still a great deal to be settled; and the spirits of evening giving fresh courage, Tom, Maria, and Mr. Yates, soon after their being re-assembled in the drawing-room, seated themselves in committee at a separate table, with the play open before them, and were just getting deep in the subject when a most welcome interruption was given by the entrance of Mr. and Miss Crawford, who, late and dark and dirty as it was, could not help coming, and were received with the most grateful joy.

"Well, how do you go on?" and "What have you settled?" and "Oh! we can do nothing without you," followed the first salutations; and Henry Crawford was soon seated with the other three at the table, while his sister made her way to Lady Bertram, and with pleasant attention was complimenting *her*. "I must really congratulate your ladyship," said she, "on the play being chosen; for though you have borne it with exemplary patience, I am sure you must be sick of all our noise and difficulties. The actors may be glad, but the by-standers must be infinitely more thankful for a decision; and I do sincerely give you joy, madam, as well as Mrs. Norris, and every body else who is in the same predicament," glancing half fearfully, half slily, beyond Fanny to Edmund.

She was very civilly answered by Lady Bertram, but Edmund said nothing. His being only a by-stander was not disclaimed. After continuing in chat with the party round the fire a few minutes, Miss Crawford returned to the party round the table; and standing by them, seemed to interest herself in their arrangements till, as if struck by a sudden recollection, she exclaimed, "My good friends, you are most composedly at work upon these cottages and ale-houses, inside and out—but pray let me know my fate in the meanwhile. Who is to be Anhalt? What gentleman among you am I to have the pleasure of making love to?"

For a moment no one spoke; and then many spoke together to tell the same melancholy truth—that they had not yet got any Anhalt. "Mr. Rushworth was to be Count Cassel, but no one had yet undertaken Anhalt."

"I had my choice of the parts," said Mr. Rushworth; "but I thought I should like the Count best—though I do not much relish the finery I am to have."

"You chose very wisely, I am sure," replied Miss Crawford, with a brightened look. "Anhalt is a heavy part."

"*The Count* has two and forty speeches," returned Mr. Rushworth, "which is no trifle."

"I am not at all surprised," said Miss Crawford, after a short pause, "at this want of an Anhalt. Amelia deserves no better. Such a forward young lady may well frighten the men."

"I should be but too happy in taking the part if it were possible," cried Tom, "but unluckily the Butler and Anhalt are in together. I will not entirely give it up, however—I will try what can be done—I will look it over again."

"Your *brother* should take the part," said Mr. Yates, in a low voice. "Do not you think he would?"

"*I* shall not ask him," replied Tom, in a cold, determined manner.

Miss Crawford talked of something else, and soon afterwards rejoined the party at the fire. "They do not want me at all," said she, seating herself. "I only puzzle them, and oblige them to make civil speeches. Mr. Edmund Bertram, as you do not act yourself, you will be a disinterested adviser; and, therefore, I apply to *you*. What shall we do for an Anhalt? Is it practicable for any of the others to double it? What is your advice?"

"My advice," said he, calmly, "is that you change the play."

"*I* should have no objection," she replied; "for though I should not particularly dislike the part of Amelia if well supported—that is, if every thing went well—I shall be sorry to be an inconvenience—but as they do not choose to hear your advice at *that table*—(looking round)—it certainly will not be taken."

Edmund said no more.

"If *any* part could tempt *you* to act, I suppose it would be Anhalt," observed the lady, archly, after a short pause—"for he is a clergyman you know."

"*That* circumstance would by no means tempt me," he replied, "for I should be sorry to make the character ridiculous by bad acting. It must be very difficult to keep Anhalt from appearing a formal, solemn lecturer; and the man who chooses the profession itself, is, perhaps, one of the last who would wish to represent it on the stage."

Miss Crawford was silenced; and with some feelings of resentment and mortification, moved her chair considerably nearer the tea-table, and gave all her attention to Mrs. Norris, who was presiding there.

"Fanny," cried Tom Bertram, from the other table, where the conference was eagerly carrying on, and the conversation incessant, "we want your services."

Fanny was up in a moment, expecting some errand, for the habit of employing her in that way was not yet overcome, in spite of all that Edmund could do.

"Oh! we do not want to disturb you from your seat. We do not want your *present* services. We shall only want you in our play. You must be Cottager's wife."

"Me!" cried Fanny, sitting down again with a most frightened look. "Indeed you must excuse me. I could not act any thing if you were to give me the world. No, indeed, I cannot act."

"Indeed but you must, for we cannot excuse you. It need not frighten you; it is a nothing of a part, a mere nothing, not above half a dozen speeches altogether, and it will not much signify if nobody hears a word you say, so you may be as creepmouse as you like, but we must have you to look at."

"If you are afraid of half a dozen speeches," cried Mr. Rushworth, "what would you do with such a part as mine? I have forty-two to learn."

"It is not that I am afraid of learning by heart," said Fanny, shocked to find herself at that moment the only speaker in the room, and to feel that almost every eye was upon her; "but I really cannot act."

"Yes, yes, you can act well enough for *us*. Learn your part, and we will teach you all the rest. You have only two scenes, and as I shall be Cottager, I'll put you in and push you about; and you will do it very well I'll answer for it."

"No, indeed, Mr. Bertram, you must excuse me. You cannot have an idea. It would be absolutely impossible for me. If I were to undertake it, I should only disappoint you."

"Phoo! Phoo! Do not be so shame-faced. You'll do it very well. Every allowance will be made for you. We do not expect perfection. You must get a brown gown, and a white apron, and a mob cap,[1] and we must make you a few wrinkles, and a little of the crows-foot at the corner of your eyes, and you will be a very proper, little old woman."

"You must excuse me, indeed you must excuse me," cried Fanny, growing more and more red from excessive agitation, and looking distressfully at Edmund, who was kindly observing her, but unwilling to exasperate his brother by interference, gave her only an encouraging smile. Her entreaty had no effect on Tom; he only said again what he had said before; and it was not merely Tom, for the requisition was now backed by Maria and Mr. Crawford, and Mr. Yates, with an urgency which differed from his, but in being more gentle or more ceremonious, and which altogether was quite overpowering to Fanny; and before she could breathe after it, Mrs. Norris completed the whole, by thus addressing her in a whisper at once angry and audible: "What a piece of work here is about nothing,—I am quite ashamed of you, Fanny, to make such a difficulty of obliging your cousins in a trifle of this sort,—So kind as they are to you!—Take the part with a good grace, and let us hear no more of the matter, I entreat."

"Do not urge her, madam," said Edmund. "It is not fair to urge her in this manner.—You see she does not like to act.—Let her choose for herself as well as the rest of us.—Her judgment may be quite as safely trusted.—Do not urge her any more."

"I am not going to urge her,"—replied Mrs. Norris sharply, "but I shall think her a very obstinate, ungrateful girl, if she does not do what her aunt and cousins wish her—very ungrateful indeed, considering who and what she is."

Edmund was too angry to speak; but Miss Crawford looking for a moment with astonished eyes at Mrs. Norris, and then at Fanny, whose tears were beginning to show themselves, immediately said with some keenness, "I do not like my situation; this *place* is too hot for me"—and moved away her chair to the opposite side of the table close to Fanny, saying to her in a kind low whisper as she placed herself, "Never

---

1. A woman's cap, having a full crown and fastening around the chin.

mind, my dear Miss Price—this is a cross evening,—every body is cross and teasing—but do not let us mind them;" and with pointed attention continued to talk to her and endeavour to raise her spirits, in spite of being out of spirits herself.—By a look at her brother, she prevented any farther entreaty from the theatrical board, and the really good feelings by which she was almost purely governed, were rapidly restoring her to all the little she had lost in Edmund's favour.

Fanny did not love Miss Crawford; but she felt very much obliged to her for her present kindness; and when from taking notice of her work and wishing *she* could work as well, and begging for the pattern, and supposing Fanny was now preparing for her *appearance* as of course she would come out[2] when her cousin was married, Miss Crawford proceeded to inquire if she had heard lately from her brother at sea, and said that she had quite a curiosity to see him, and imagined him a very fine young man, and advised Fanny to get his picture drawn before he went to sea again—She* could not help admitting it to be very agreeable flattery, or help listening, and answering with more animation than she had intended.

The consultation upon the play still went on, and Miss Crawford's attention was first called from Fanny by Tom Bertram's telling her, with infinite regret, that he found it absolutely impossible for him to undertake the part of Anhalt in addition to the Butler;—he had been most anxiously trying to make it out to be feasible,—but it would not do,—he must give it up.—"But there will not be the smallest difficulty in filling it," he added.—"We have but to speak the word; we may pick and choose.—I could name at this moment at least six young men within six miles of us, who are wild to be admitted into our company, and there are one or two that would not disgrace us.—I should not be afraid to trust either of the Olivers or Charles Maddox.—Tom Oliver is a very clever fellow, and Charles Maddox is as gentlemanlike a man as you will see any where, so I will take my horse early to-morrow morning, and ride over to Stoke, and settle with one of them."

While he spoke, Maria was looking apprehensively round at Edmund in full expectation that he must oppose such an enlargement of the plan as this—so contrary to all their first protestations; but Edmund said nothing.—After a moment's thought, Miss Crawford calmly replied, "As far as I am concerned, I can have no objection to any thing that you all think eligible. Have I ever seen either of the gentlemen?—Yes, Mr. Charles Maddox dined at my sister's one day, did not he Henry?—A quiet-looking young man. I remember him. Let *him* be applied to, if you please, for it will be less unpleasant to me than to have a perfect stranger."

Charles Maddox was to be the man.—Tom repeated his resolution

---

2. Mary Crawford is referring to Fanny's debut in society, see above, p. 36, n. 2.

of going to him early on the morrow; and though Julia, who had
scarcely opened her lips before, observed in a sarcastic manner, and
with a glance, first at Maria, and then at Edmund, that "the Mansfield
Theatricals would enliven the whole neighbourhood exceedingly"—
Edmund still held his peace, and shewed his feelings only by a determined gravity.

"I am not very sanguine as to our play"—said Miss Crawford in an
under voice, to Fanny, after some consideration; "and I can tell Mr.
Maddox, that I shall shorten some of *his* speeches, and a great many
of *my own*, before we rehearse together.—It will be very disagreeable,
and by no means what I expected."

Chapter XVI.

It was not in Miss Crawford's power to talk Fanny into any real forgetfulness of what had passed.—When the evening was over, she went to
bed full of it, her nerves still agitated by the shock of such an attack
from her cousin Tom, so public and so persevered in, and her spirits
sinking under her aunt's unkind reflection and reproach. To be called
into notice in such a manner, to hear that it was but the prelude to
something so infinitely worse, to be told that she must do what was so
impossible as to act; and then to have the charge of obstinacy and
ingratitude follow it, enforced with such a hint at the dependence of
her situation, had been too distressing at the time, to make the remembrance when she was alone much less so,—especially with the super-
added dread of what the morrow might produce in continuation of the
subject. Miss Crawford had protected her only for the time; and if she
were applied to again among themselves with all the authoritative urgency that Tom and Maria were capable of; and Edmund perhaps
away—what should she do? She fell asleep before she could answer the
question, and found it quite as puzzling when she awoke the next
morning. The little white attic, which had continued her sleeping room
ever since her first entering the family, proving incompetent to suggest
any reply, she had recourse, as soon as she was dressed, to another
apartment, more spacious and more meet for walking about in, and
thinking, and of which she had now for some time been almost equally
mistress. It had been their school-room; so called till the Miss Bertrams
would not allow it to be called so any longer, and inhabited as such to
a later period. There Miss Lee had lived, and there they had read and
written, and talked and laughed, till within the last three years, when
she had quitted them.—The room had then become useless, and for
some time was quite deserted, except by Fanny, when she visited her
plants, or wanted one of the books, which she was still glad to keep
there, from the deficiency of space and accommodation in her little

chamber above;—but gradually, as her value for the comforts of it increased, she had added to her possessions, and spent more of her time
there; and having nothing to oppose her, had so naturally and so art-
lessly worked herself into it, that it was now generally admitted to be
her's. The East room as it had been called, ever since Maria Bertram
was sixteen, was now considered Fanny's, almost as decidedly as the
white attic;—the smallness of the one making the use of the other so
evidently reasonable, that the Miss Bertrams, with every superiority in
their own apartments, which their own sense of superiority could demand, were entirely approving it;—and Mrs. Norris having stipulated
for there never being a fire in it on Fanny's account, was tolerably
resigned to her having the use of what nobody else wanted, though the
terms in which she sometimes spoke of the indulgence, seemed to
imply that it was the best room in the house.

The aspect was so favourable, that even without a fire it was habitable
in many an early spring, and late autumn morning, to such a willing
mind as Fanny's, and while there was a gleam of sunshine, she hoped
not to be driven from it entirely, even when winter came. The comfort
of it in her hours of leisure was extreme. She could go there after any
thing unpleasant below, and find immediate consolation in some pursuit, or some train of thought at hand.—Her plants, her books—of
which she had been a collector, from the first hour of her commanding
a shilling—her writing desk, and her works of charity and ingenuity,
were all within her reach;—or if indisposed for employment, if nothing
but musing would do, she could scarcely see an object in that room
which had not an interesting remembrance connected with it.—Every
thing was a friend, or bore her thoughts to a friend; and though there
had been sometimes much of suffering to her—though her motives had
been often misunderstood, her feelings disregarded, and her comprehension under-valued; though she had known the pains of tyranny, of
ridicule, and neglect, yet almost every recurrence of either had led to
something consolatory; her aunt Bertram had spoken for her, or Miss
Lee had been encouraging, or what was yet more frequent or more
dear—Edmund had been her champion and her friend;—he had supported her cause, or explained her meaning, he had told her not to
cry, or had given her some proof of affection which made her tears
delightful—and the whole was now so blended together, so harmonized
by distance, that every former affliction had its charm. The room was
most dear to her, and she would not have changed its furniture for the
handsomest in the house, though what had been originally plain, had
suffered all the ill-usage of children—and its greatest elegancies and
ornaments were a faded footstool of Julia's work, too ill done for the
drawing-room, three transparencies,[1] made in a rage for transparencies,

1. Such pictures, drawn on transparent material and stuck on windowpanes in order to be il-
luminated from behind, were popular at this time.

for the three lower panes of one window, where Tintern Abbey held its station between a cave in Italy, and a moonlight lake in Cumberland;[2] a collection of family profiles thought unworthy of being anywhere else, over the mantle-piece, and by their side and pinned against the wall, a small sketch of a ship sent four years ago from the Mediterranean by William, with H. M. S. Antwerp at the bottom, in letters as tall as the mainmast.

To this nest of comforts Fanny now walked down to try its influence on an agitated, doubting spirit—to see if by looking at Edmund's profile she could catch any of his counsel, or by giving air to her geraniums she might inhale a breeze of mental strength herself. But she had more than fears of her own perseverance to remove; she had begun to feel undecided as to what she *ought to do*; and as she walked round the room her doubts were increasing. Was she *right* in refusing what was so warmly asked, so strongly wished for? What* might be so essential to a scheme on which some of those to whom she owed the greatest complaisance, had set their hearts? Was it not ill-nature—selfishness—and a fear of exposing herself? And would Edmund's judgment, would his persuasion of Sir Thomas's disapprobation of the whole, be enough to justify her in a determined denial in spite of all the rest? It would be so horrible to her to act, that she was inclined to suspect the truth and purity of her own scruples, and as she looked around her, the claims of her cousins to being obliged, were strengthened by the sight of present upon present that she had received from them. The table between the windows was covered with work-boxes and netting-boxes,[3] which had been given her at different times, principally by Tom; and she grew bewildered as to the amount of the debt which all these kind remembrances produced. A tap at the door roused her in the midst of this attempt to find her way to her duty, and her gentle "come in," was answered by the appearance of one, before whom all her doubts were wont to be laid. Her eyes brightened at the sight of Edmund.

"Can I speak with you, Fanny, for a few minutes?" said he.

"Yes, certainly."

"I want to consult. I want your opinion."

"My opinion!" she cried, shrinking from such a compliment, highly as it gratified her.

"Yes, your advice and opinion. I do not know what to do. This acting scheme gets worse and worse you see. They have chosen almost as bad a play as they could; and now, to complete the business, are going to ask the help of a young man very slightly known to any of us. This is

---

2. Tintern Abbey is a ruined abbey on the River Wye in Monmouthshire; Cumberland is a county in northwest England, including much of the celebrated Lake District. These places were described by William Gilpin (1724–1804), whose illustrated picturesque tours throughout the British Isles were publications Austen admired, and later by William Wordsworth, in such poems as "Lines Composed a Few Miles Above Tintern Abbey" (1798).

3. Boxes to store mesh fabric (i.e., netting) on which decorative patterns are worked with needles.

the end of all the privacy and propriety which was talked about at first. I know no harm of Charles Maddox; but the excessive intimacy which must spring from his being admitted among us in this manner, is highly objectionable, the *more* than intimacy—the familiarity. I cannot think of it with any patience—and it does appear to me an evil of such magnitude as must, *if possible*, be prevented. Do not you see it in the same light?"

"Yes, but what can be done? Your brother is so determined?"

"There is but *one* thing to be done, Fanny. I must take Anhalt myself. I am well aware that nothing else will quiet Tom."

Fanny could not answer him.

"It is not at all what I like," he continued. "No man can like being driven into the *appearance* of such inconsistency. After being known to oppose the scheme from the beginning, there is absurdity in the face of my joining them *now*, when they are exceeding their first plan in every respect; but I can think of no other alternative. Can you, Fanny?"

"No," said Fanny, slowly, "not immediately—but——"

"But what? I see your judgment is not with me. Think it a little over. Perhaps you are not so much aware as I am, of the mischief that *may*, of the unpleasantness* that *must*, arise from a young man's being received in this manner—domesticated among us—authorized to come at all hours—and placed suddenly on a footing which must do away all restraints. To think only of the license which every rehearsal must tend to create. It is all very bad! Put yourself in Miss Crawford's place, Fanny. Consider what it would be to act Amelia with a stranger. She has a right to be felt for, because she evidently feels for herself. I heard enough of what she said to you last night, to understand her unwillingness to be acting with a stranger; and as she probably engaged in the part with different expectations—perhaps, without considering the subject enough to know what was likely to be, it would be ungenerous, it would be really wrong to expose her to it. Her feelings ought to be respected. Does not it strike you so, Fanny? You hesitate."

"I am sorry for Miss Crawford; but I am more sorry to see you drawn in to do what you had resolved against, and what you are known to think will be disagreeable to my uncle. It will be such a triumph to the others!"

"They will not have much cause of triumph, when they see how infamously I act. But, however, triumph there certainly will be, and I must brave it. But if I can be the means of restraining the publicity of the business, of limiting the exhibition, of concentrating our folly, I shall be well repaid. As I am now, I have no influence, I can do nothing; I have offended them, and they will not hear me; but when I have put them in good humour by this concession, I am not without hopes of persuading them to confine the representation within a much smaller circle than they are now in the high road for. This will be a material gain. My object is to confine it to Mrs. Rushworth and the Grants. Will not this be worth gaining?"

"Yes, it will be a great point."

"But still it has not your approbation. Can you mention any other measure by which I have a chance of doing equal good?"

"No, I cannot think of any thing else."

"Give me your approbation, then, Fanny. I am not comfortable without it."

"Oh! cousin."

"If you are against me, I ought to distrust myself—and yet—— But it is absolutely impossible to let Tom go on in this way, riding about the country in quest of any body who can be persuaded to act—no matter whom; the look of a gentleman is to be enough. I thought *you* would have entered more into Miss Crawford's feelings."

"No doubt she will be very glad. It must be a great relief to her," said Fanny, trying for greater warmth of manner.

"She never appeared more amiable than in her behaviour to you last night. It gave her a very strong claim on my good will."

"She *was* very kind indeed, and I am glad to have her spared.". . . .*

She could not finish the generous effusion. Her conscience stopt her in the middle, but Edmund was satisfied.

"I shall walk down immediately after breakfast," said he, "and am sure of giving pleasure there. And now, dear Fanny, I will not interrupt you any longer. You want to be reading. But I could not be easy till I had spoken to you, and come to a decision. Sleeping or waking, my head has been full of this matter all night. It is an evil—but I am certainly making it less than it might be. If Tom is up, I shall go to him directly and get it over; and when we meet at breakfast we shall be all in high good humour at the prospect of acting the fool together with such unanimity. *You* in the meanwhile will be taking a trip into China, I suppose. How does Lord Macartney[4] go on?—(opening a volume on the table and then taking up some others.) And here are Crabbe's Tales, and the Idler,[5] at hand to relieve you, if you tire of your great book. I admire your little establishment exceedingly; and as soon as I am gone, you will empty your head of all this nonsense of acting, and sit comfortably down to your table. But do not stay here to be cold."

---

4. George, Lord Macartney (1737–1806), diplomat and author of *Plates to His Embassy to China* (1796). Fanny is probably reading John Barrow, *Some Account of the Public Life, and a Selection from the Unpublished Writings of the Earl of Macartney* (1807).

5. George Crabbe published his *Tales in Verse* in 1812. The *Idler* was a popular series of essays written by Samuel Johnson (1709–1784) between 1758 and 1760, and often collected and reprinted. Johnson and Crabbe were among Austen's favorite writers. Notably absent among Fanny's books are novels.

He went; but there was no reading, no China, no composure for Fanny. He had told her the most extraordinary, the most inconceivable, the most unwelcome news; and she could think of nothing else. To be acting! After all his objections—objections so just and so public! After all that she had heard him say, and seen him look, and known him to be feeling. Could it be possible? Edmund so inconsistent. Was he not deceiving himself? Was he not wrong? Alas! it was all Miss Crawford's doing. She had seen her influence in every speech, and was miserable. The doubts and alarms as to her own conduct, which had previously distressed her, and which had all slept while she listened to him, were become of little consequence now. This deeper anxiety swallowed them up. Things should take their course; she cared not how it ended. Her cousins might attack, but could hardly tease her. She was beyond their reach; and if at last obliged to yield—no matter—it was all misery *now*.

Chapter XVII.

It was, indeed, a triumphant day to Mr. Bertram and Maria. Such a victory over Edmund's discretion had been beyond their hopes, and was most delightful. There was no longer any thing to disturb them in their darling project, and they congratulated each other in private on the jealous weakness to which they attributed the change, with all the glee of feelings gratified in every way. Edmund might still look grave, and say he did not like the scheme in general, and must disapprove the play in particular; their point was gained; he was to act, and he was driven to it by the force of selfish inclinations only. Edmund had descended from that moral elevation which he had maintained before, and they were both as much the better as the happier for the descent.

They behaved very well, however, *to him* on the occasion, betraying no exultation beyond the lines about the corners of the mouth, and seemed to think it as great an escape to be quit of the intrusion of Charles Maddox, as if they had been forced into admitting him against their inclination. "To have it quite in their own family circle was what they had particularly wished. A stranger among them would have been the destruction of all their comfort," and when Edmund, pursuing that idea, gave a hint of his hope as to the limitation of the audience, they were ready, in the complaisance of the moment, to promise any thing. It was all good humour and encouragement. Mrs. Norris offered to contrive his dress, Mr. Yates assured him, that Anhalt's last scene with the Baron admitted a good deal of action and emphasis, and Mr. Rushworth undertook to count his speeches.

"Perhaps," said Tom, "*Fanny* may be more disposed to oblige us now. Perhaps you may persuade *her*."

"No, she is quite determined. She certainly will not act."

"Oh! very well." And not another word was said: but Fanny felt herself again in danger, and her indifference to the danger was beginning to fail her already.

There were not fewer smiles at the parsonage than at the park on this change in Edmund; Miss Crawford looked very lovely in her's, and entered with such an instantaneous renewal of cheerfulness into the whole affair, as could have but one effect on him. "He was certainly right in respecting such feelings; he was glad he had determined on it." And the morning wore away in satisfactions very sweet, if not very sound. One advantage resulted from it to Fanny; at the earnest request of Miss Crawford, Mrs. Grant had with her usual good humour agreed to undertake the part for which Fanny had been wanted—and this was all that occurred to gladden *her* heart during the day; and even this, when imparted by Edmund, brought a pang with it, for it was Miss Crawford to whom she was obliged, it was Miss Crawford whose kind exertions were to excite her gratitude, and whose merit in making them was spoken of with a glow of admiration. She was safe; but peace and safety were unconnected* here. Her mind had been never farther from peace. She could not feel that she had done wrong herself, but she was disquieted in every other way. Her heart and her judgment were equally against Edmund's decision; she could not acquit his unsteadiness; and his happiness under it made her wretched. She was full of jealousy and agitation. Miss Crawford came with looks of gaiety which seemed an insult, with friendly expressions towards herself which she could hardly answer calmly. Every body around her was gay and busy, prosperous and important, each had their object of interest, their part, their dress, their favourite scene, their friends and confederates, all were finding employment in consultations and comparisons, or diversion in the playful conceits they suggested. She alone was sad and insignificant; she had no share in any thing; she might go or stay, she might be in the midst of their noise, or retreat from it to the solitude of the East room, without being seen or missed. She could almost think any thing would have been preferable to this. Mrs. Grant was of consequence; *her* good nature had honourable mention—her taste and her time were considered—her presence was wanted—she was sought for and attended, and praised; and Fanny was at first in some danger of envying her the character she had accepted. But reflection brought better feelings, and shewed her that Mrs. Grant was entitled to respect, which could never have belonged to *her*, and that had she received even the greatest, she could never have been easy in joining a scheme which, considering only her uncle, she must condemn altogether.

Fanny's heart was not absolutely the only saddened one amongst them, as she soon began to acknowledge herself.—Julia was a sufferer too, though not quite so blamelessly.

Henry Crawford had trifled with her feelings; but she had very long allowed and even sought his attentions, with a jealously of her sister so reasonable as ought to have been their cure; and now that the conviction of his preference for Maria had been forced on her, she submitted to it without any alarm for Maria's situation, or any endeavour at rational tranquillity for herself.—She either sat in gloomy silence, wrapt in such gravity as nothing could subdue, no curiosity touch, no wit amuse; or allowing the attentions of Mr. Yates, was talking with forced gaiety to him alone, and ridiculing the acting of the others.

For a day or two after the affront was given, Henry Crawford had endeavoured to do it away by the usual attack of gallantry and compliment, but he had not cared enough about it to persevere against a few repulses; and becoming soon too busy with his play to have time for more than one flirtation, he grew indifferent to the quarrel, or rather thought it a lucky occurrence, as quietly putting an end to what might ere long have raised expectations in more than Mrs. Grant.—She was not pleased to see Julia excluded from the play, and sitting by disregarded; but as it was not a matter which really involved her happiness, as Henry must be the best judge of his own, and as he did assure her, with a most persuasive smile, that neither he nor Julia had ever had a serious thought of each other, she could only renew her former caution as to the elder sister, entreat him not to risk his tranquillity by too much admiration there, and then gladly take her share in any thing that brought cheerfulness to the young people in general, and that did so particularly promote the pleasure of the two so dear to her.

"I rather wonder Julia is not in love with Henry," was her observation to Mary.

"I dare say she is," replied Mary, coldly. "I imagine both sisters are."

"Both! no, no, that must not be. Do not give him a hint of it. Think of Mr. Rushworth."

"You had better tell Miss Bertram to think of Mr. Rushworth. It may do *her* some good. I often think of Mr. Rushworth's property and independence, and wish them in other hands—but I never think of *him*. A man might represent the county with such an estate; a man might escape a profession and represent the county."

"I dare say he *will* be in parliament soon. When Sir Thomas comes, I dare say he will be in for some borough, but there has been nobody to put him in the way of doing any thing yet."

"Sir Thomas is to achieve mighty things when he comes home," said Mary, after a pause. "Do you remember Hawkins Browne's 'Address to Tobacco,' in imitation of Pope?—

"Blest leaf! whose aromatic gales dispense
"To Templars modesty, to Parsons sense."[1]

I will parody them:

Blest Knight! whose dictatorial looks dispense
To Children affluence, to Rushworth sense.

Will not that do, Mrs. Grant? Every thing seems to depend upon Sir Thomas's return."

"You will find his consequence very just and reasonable when you see him in his family, I assure you. I do not think we do so well without him. He has a fine dignified manner, which suits the head of such a house, and keeps every body in their place. Lady Bertram seems more of a cipher now than when he is at home; and nobody else can keep Mrs. Norris in order. But, Mary, do not fancy that Maria Bertram cares for Henry. I am sure *Julia* does not, or she would not have flirted as she did last night with Mr. Yates; and though he and Maria are very good friends, I think she likes Sotherton too well to be inconstant."

"I would not give much for Mr. Rushworth's chance, if Henry stept in before the articles[2] were signed."

"If you have such a suspicion, something must be done, and as soon as the play is all over, we will talk to him seriously, and make him know his own mind; and if he means nothing, we will send him off, though he is Henry, for a time."

Julia *did* suffer, however, though Mrs. Grant discerned it not, and though it escaped the notice of many of her own family likewise. She had loved, she did love still, and she had all the suffering which a warm temper and a high spirit were likely to endure under the disappointment of a dear, though irrational hope, with a strong sense of ill-usage. Her heart was sore and angry, and she was capable only of angry consolations. The sister with whom she was used to be on easy terms, was now become her greatest enemy; they were alienated from each other, and Julia was not superior to the hope of some distressing end to the attentions which were still carrying on there, some punishment to Maria for conduct so shameful towards herself, as well as towards Mr. Rushworth. With no material fault of temper, or difference of opinion, to prevent their being very good friends while their interests were the same, the sisters, under such a trial as this, had not affection or principle enough to make them merciful or just, to give them honour or compassion. Maria felt her triumph, and pursued her purpose careless of Julia; and Julia could never see Maria distinguished by Henry

---

1. From Isaac Hawkins Browne's "A Pipe of Tobacco: in Imitation of Six Several Authors" (originally published in 1736), parodying Colley Cibber, Ambrose Philips, James Thomson, Edward Young, Alexander Pope, and Jonathan Swift. Reprinted in Robert Dodsley's *A Collection of Poems, by Different Hands* (1748), vol. 2, which Austen knew.
2. Items stipulated in a contract; here, a marriage contract.

Crawford, without trusting that it would create jealousy, and bring a public disturbance at last.

Fanny saw and pitied much of this in Julia; but there was no outward fellowship between them. Julia made no communication, and Fanny took no liberties. They were two solitary sufferers, or connected only by Fanny's consciousness.

The inattention of the two brothers and the aunt to Julia's discomposure, and their blindness to its true cause, must be imputed to the fulness of their own minds. They were totally preoccupied. Tom was engrossed by the concerns of his theatre, and saw nothing that did not immediately relate to it. Edmund, between his theatrical and his real part, between Miss Crawford's claims and his own conduct, between love and consistency, was equally unobservant; and Mrs. Norris was too busy in contriving and directing the general little matters of the company, superintending their various dresses with economical expedient, for which nobody thanked her, and saving, with delighted integrity, half-a-crown here and there to the absent Sir Thomas, to have leisure for watching the behaviour, or guarding the happiness of his daughters.

Chapter XVIII.

Every thing was now in a regular train; theatre, actors, actresses, and dresses, were all getting forward: but though no other great impediments arose, Fanny found, before many days were past, that it was not all uninterrupted enjoyment to the party themselves, and that she had not to witness the continuance of such unanimity and delight, as had been almost too much for her at first. Every body began to have their vexation. Edmund had many. Entirely against *his* judgment, a scene painter arrived from town, and was at work, much to the increase of the expenses, and what was worse, of the eclat[1] of their proceedings; and his brother, instead of being really guided by him as to the privacy of the representation, was giving an invitation to every family who came in his way. Tom himself began to fret over the scene painter's slow progress, and to feel the miseries of waiting. He had learned his part—all his parts—for he took every trifling one that could be united with the Butler, and began to be impatient to be acting; and every day thus unemployed, was tending to increase his sense of the insignificance of all his parts together, and make him more ready to regret that some other play had not been chosen.

Fanny, being always a very courteous listener, and often the only listener at hand, came in for the complaints and distresses of most of them. *She* knew that Mr. Yates was in general thought to rant dread-

1. Acclaim; here with pejorative connotations about publicity, i.e., creating a sensation or a "scene."

fully, that Mr. Yates was disappointed in Henry Crawford, that Tom Bertram spoke so quick he would be unintelligible, that Mrs. Grant spoilt every thing by laughing, that Edmund was behind-hand with his part, and that it was misery to have any thing to do with Mr. Rushworth, who was wanting a prompter through every speech. She knew, also, that poor Mr. Rushworth could seldom get any body to rehearse with him; *his* complaint came before her as well as the rest; and so decided to her eye was her cousin Maria's avoidance of him, and so needlessly often the rehearsal of the first scene between her and Mr. Crawford, that she had soon all the terror of other complaints from *him.*—So far from being all satisfied and all enjoying, she found every body requiring something they had not, and giving occasion of discontent to the others.—Every body had a part either too long or too short;—nobody would attend as they ought, nobody would remember on which side they were to come in—nobody but the complainer would observe any directions.

Fanny believed herself to derive as much innocent enjoyment from the play as any of them;—Henry Crawford acted well, and it was a pleasure to *her* to creep into the theatre, and attend the rehearsal of the first act—in spite of the feelings it excited in some speeches for Maria.—Maria she also thought acted well—too well;—and after the first rehearsal or two, Fanny began to be their only audience—and sometimes as prompter, sometimes as spectator—was often very useful.—As far as she could judge, Mr. Crawford was considerably the best actor of all; he had more confidence than Edmund, more judgment than Tom, more talent and taste than Mr. Yates.—She did not like him as a man, but she must admit him to be the best actor, and on this point there were not many who differed from her. Mr. Yates, indeed, exclaimed against his tameness and insipidity—and the day came at last, when Mr. Rushworth turned to her with a black look, and said—"Do you think there is any thing so very fine in all this? For the life and soul of me, I cannot admire him;—and between ourselves, to see such an undersized, little, mean-looking man, set up for a fine actor, is very ridiculous in my opinion."

From this moment there was a return of his former jealousy, which Maria, from increasing hopes of Crawford, was at little pains to remove; and the chances of Mr. Rushworth's ever attaining to the knowledge of his two and forty speeches became much less. As to his ever making any thing *tolerable* of them, nobody had the smallest idea of that except his mother—*She*, indeed, regretted that his part was not more considerable, and deferred coming over to Mansfield till they were forward enough in their rehearsal to comprehend all his scenes, but the others aspired at nothing beyond his remembering the catchword,[2] and the

2. A cue; the last word in an actor's speech, which serves as a prompt to the next actor.

first line of his speech, and being able to follow the prompter through the rest. Fanny, in her pity and kind-heartedness, was at great pains to teach him how to learn, giving him all the helps and directions in her power, trying to make an artificial memory for him, and learning every word of his part herself, but without his being much the forwarder.

Many uncomfortable, anxious, apprehensive feelings she certainly had; but with all these, and other claims on her time and attention, she was as far from finding herself without employment or utility amongst them, as without a companion in uneasiness; quite as far from having no demand on her leisure as on her compassion. The gloom of her first anticipations was proved to have been unfounded. She was occasionally useful to all; she was perhaps as much at peace as any.

There was a great deal of needle-work to be done moreover, in which her help was wanted; and that Mrs. Norris thought her quite as well off as the rest, was evident by the manner in which she claimed it: "Come Fanny," she cried, "these are fine times for you, but you must not be always walking from one room to the other and doing the look-ings on, at your ease, in this way,—I want you here.—I have been slaving myself till I can hardly stand, to contrive Mr. Rushworth's cloak without sending for any more satin; and now I think you may give me your help in putting it together.—There are but three seams, you may do them in a trice.—It would be lucky for me if I had nothing but the executive part to do.—*You* are best off, I can tell you; but if nobody did more than *you*, we should not get on very fast."

Fanny took the work very quietly, without attempting any defence; but her kinder aunt Bertram observed on her behalf,

"One cannot wonder, sister, that Fanny *should* be delighted; it is all new to her, you know,—you and I used to be very fond of a play ourselves—and so am I still;—and as soon as I am a little more at leisure, *I* mean to look in at their rehearsals too. What is the play about, Fanny, you have never told me?"

"Oh! sister, pray do not ask her now; for Fanny is not one of those who can talk and work at the same time.—It is about Lovers' Vows."

"I believe," said Fanny to her aunt Bertram, "there will be three acts rehearsed to-morrow evening, and that will give you an opportunity of seeing all the actors at once."

"You had better stay till the curtain is hung," interposed Mrs. Norris—"the curtain will be hung in a day or two,—there is very little sense in a play without a curtain—and I am much mistaken if you do not find it draw up into very handsome festoons."

Lady Bertram seemed quite resigned to waiting.—Fanny did not share her aunt's composure; she thought of the morrow a great deal,— for if the three acts were rehearsed, Edmund and Miss Crawford would then be acting together for the first time;—the third act would bring a scene between them which interested her most particularly, and which she was longing and dreading to see how they would perform. The whole subject of it was love—a marriage of love was to be described by the gentleman, and very little short of a declaration of love be made by the lady.

She had read, and read the scene again with many painful, many wondering emotions, and looked forward to their representation of it as a circumstance almost too interesting. She did not *believe* they had yet rehearsed it, even in private.

The morrow came, the plan for the evening continued, and Fanny's consideration of it did not become less agitated. She worked very diligently under her aunt's directions, but her diligence and her silence concealed a very absent, anxious mind; and about noon she made her escape with her work to the East room, that she might have no concern in another, and, as she deemed it, most unnecessary rehearsal of the first act, which Henry Crawford was just proposing, desirous at once of having her time to herself, and of avoiding the sight of Mr. Rushworth. A glimpse, as she passed through the hall, of the two ladies walking up from the parsonage, made no change in her wish of retreat, and she worked and meditated in the East room, undisturbed, for a quarter of an hour, when a gentle tap at the door was followed by the entrance of Miss Crawford.

"Am I right?—Yes; this is the East room. My dear Miss Price, I beg your pardon, but I have made my way to you on purpose to entreat your help."

Fanny, quite surprised, endeavoured to show herself mistress of the room by her civilities, and looked at the bright bars of her empty grate with concern.

"Thank you—I am quite warm, very warm. Allow me to stay here a little while, and do have the goodness to hear me my third act. I have brought my book, and if you would but rehearse it with me, I should be *so* obliged! I came here to-day intending to rehearse it with Edmund—by ourselves—against the evening, but he is not in the way; and if he *were*, I do not think I could go through it with *him*, till I have hardened myself a little, for really there *is* a speech or two—You will be so good, won't you?"

Fanny was most civil in her assurances, though she could not give them in a very steady voice.

"Have you ever happened to look at the part I mean?" continued Miss Crawford, opening her book. "Here it is. I did not think much of it at first—but, upon my word—. There, look at *that* speech, and *that*, and *that*. How am I ever to look him in the face and say such things? Could you do it? But then he is your cousin, which makes all the difference. You must rehearse it with me, that I may fancy *you* him, and get on by degrees. You *have* a look of *his* sometimes."

"Have I?—I will do my best with the greatest readiness—but I must *read* the part, for I can *say* very little of it."

"*None* of it, I suppose. You are to have the book of course. Now for it. We must have two chairs at hand for you to bring forward to the front of the stage. There—very good schoolroom chairs, not made for a theatre, I dare say; much more fitted for little girls to sit and kick their feet against when they are learning a lesson. What would your governess and your uncle say to see them used for such a purpose? Could Sir Thomas look in upon us just now, he would bless himself, for we are rehearsing all over the house. Yates is storming away in the dining room. I heard him as I came up stairs, and the theatre is engaged of course by those indefatigable rehearsers, Agatha and Frederick. If *they* are not perfect, I *shall* be surprised. By the bye, I looked in upon them five minutes ago, and it happened to be exactly at one of the times when they were trying *not* to embrace, and Mr. Rushworth was with me. I thought he began to look a little queer, so I turned it off as well as I could, by whispering to him, 'We shall have an excellent Agatha, there is something so *maternal* in her manner, so completely *maternal* in her voice and countenance.' Was not that well done of me? He brightened up directly. Now for my soliloquy."

She began, and Fanny joined in with all the modest feeling which the idea of representing Edmund was so strongly calculated to inspire; but with looks and voice so truly feminine, as to be no very good picture of a man. With such an Anhalt, however, Miss Crawford had courage enough and they had got through half the scene, when a tap at the door brought a pause, and the entrance of Edmund the next moment, suspended it all.

Surprise, consciousness, and pleasure, appeared in each of the three on this unexpected meeting; and as Edmund was come on the very same business that had brought Miss Crawford, consciousness and pleasure were likely to be more than momentary in *them*. He too had his book, and was seeking Fanny, to ask her to rehearse with him, and help him to prepare* for the evening, without knowing Miss Crawford to be in the house; and great was the joy and animation of being thus thrown together—of comparing schemes—and sympathizing in praise of Fanny's kind offices.

She could not equal them in their warmth. *Her* spirits sank under the glow of theirs, and she felt herself becoming too nearly nothing to both, to have any comfort in having been sought by either. They must now rehearse together. Edmund proposed, urged, entreated it—till the lady, not very unwilling at first, could refuse no longer—and Fanny was wanted only to prompt and observe them. She was invested, indeed, with the office of judge and critic, and earnestly desired to exercise it and tell them all their faults; but from doing so every feeling within her shrank, she could not, would not, dared not attempt it; had she been otherwise qualified for criticism, her conscience must have re-strained her from venturing at disapprobation. She believed herself to feel too much of it in the aggregate for honesty or safety in particulars. To prompt them must be enough for her; and it was sometimes *more* than enough; for she could not always pay attention to the book. In watching them she forgot herself; and agitated by the increasing spirit of Edmund's manner, had once closed the page and turned away ex-actly as he wanted help. It was imputed to very reasonable weariness, and she was thanked and pitied; but she deserved their pity, more than she hoped they would ever surmise. At last the scene was over, and Fanny forced herself to add her praise to the compliments each was giving the other; and when again alone and able to recall the whole, she was inclined to believe their performance would, indeed, have such nature and feeling in it, as must ensure their credit, and make it a very suffering exhibition to herself. Whatever might be its effect, however, she must stand the brunt of it again that very day.

The first regular rehearsal of the three first acts was certainly to take place in the evening; Mrs. Grant and the Crawfords were engaged to return for that purpose as soon as they could after dinner; and every one concerned was looking forward with eagerness. There seemed a general diffusion of cheerfulness on the occasion; Tom was enjoying such an advance towards the end, Edmund was in spirits from the morning's rehearsal, and little vexations seemed every where smoothed away. All were alert and impatient; the ladies moved soon, the gentle-men soon followed them, and with the exception of Lady Bertram, Mrs. Norris, and Julia, every body was in the theatre at an early hour, and having lighted it up as well as its unfinished state admitted, were waiting only the arrival of Mrs. Grant and the Crawfords to begin.

They did not wait long for the Crawfords, but there was no Mrs. Grant. She could not come. Dr. Grant, professing an indisposition, for which he had little credit with his fair sister-in-law, could not spare his wife.

"Dr. Grant is ill," said she, with mock solemnity. "He has been ill ever since; he did not eat any of the pheasant to day. He fancied it tough—sent away his plate—and has been suffering ever since."

Here was disappointment! Mrs. Grant's non-attendance was sad in-deed. Her pleasant manners and cheerful conformity made her always valuable amongst them—but *now* she was absolutely necessary. They could not act, they could not rehearse with any satisfaction without her. The comfort of the whole evening was destroyed. What was to be done? Tom, as Cottager, was in despair. After a pause of perplexity, some eyes began to be turned towards Fanny, and a voice or two, to say, "If Miss Price would be so good as to *read* the part." She was immediately surrounded by supplications, every body asked it, even Edmund said, "Do Fanny, if it is not *very* disagreeable to you."

But Fanny still hung back. She could not endure the idea of it. Why was not Miss Crawford to be applied to as well? Or why had not she rather gone to her own room, as she had felt to be safest, instead of attending the rehearsal at all? She had known it would irritate and distress her—she had known it her duty to keep away. She was properly punished.

"You have only to *read* the part," said Henry Crawford, with renewed entreaty.

"And I do believe she can say every word of it," added Maria, "for she could put Mrs. Grant right the other day in twenty places. Fanny, I am sure you know the part."

Fanny could not say she did *not*—and as they all persevered—as Edmund repeated his wish, and with a look of even fond dependence on her good nature, she must yield. She would do her best. Every body was satisfied—and she was left to the tremors of a most palpitating heart, while the others prepared to begin.

They *did* begin—and being too much engaged in their own noise, to be struck by an usual* noise in the other part of the house, had proceeded some way, when the door of the room was thrown open, and Julia appearing at it, with a face all aghast, exclaimed, "My father is come! He is in the hall at this moment."

END OF VOL. I.

Volume II

Chapter I.

How is the consternation of the party to be described? To the greater number it was a moment of absolute horror. Sir Thomas in the house! All felt the instantaneous conviction. Not a hope of imposition or mistake was harboured any where. Julia's looks were an evidence of the fact that made it indisputable; and after the first starts and exclamations, not a word was spoken for half a minute; each with an altered countenance was looking at some other, and almost each was feeling it a stroke the most unwelcome, most ill-timed, most appalling! Mr. Yates might consider it only as a vexatious interruption for the evening, and Mr. Rushworth might imagine it a blessing, but every other heart was sinking under some degree of self-condemnation or undefined alarm, every other heart was suggesting "What will become of us? what is to be done now?" It was a terrible pause; and terrible to every ear were the corroborating sounds of opening doors and passing footsteps.

Julia was the first to move and speak again. Jealousy and bitterness had been suspended: selfishness was lost in the common cause; but at the moment of her appearance, Frederick was listening with looks of devotion to Agatha's narrative, and pressing her hand to his heart, and as soon as she could notice this, and see that, in spite of the shock of her words, he still kept his station and retained her sister's hand, her wounded heart swelled again with injury, and looking as red as she had been white before, she turned out of the room, saying "I need not be afraid of appearing before him."

Her going roused the rest; and at the same moment, the two brothers stepped forward, feeling the necessity of doing something. A very few words between them were sufficient. The case admitted no difference of opinion; they must go to the drawing-room directly. Maria joined them with the same intent, just then the stoutest of the three; for the very circumstance which had driven Julia away, was to her the sweetest support. Henry Crawford's retaining her hand at such a moment, a moment of such peculiar proof and importance, was worth ages of doubt and anxiety. She hailed it as an earnest of the most serious determination, and was equal even to encounter her father. They walked off, utterly heedless of Mr. Rushworth's repeated question of, "Shall I

121

go too?—Had not I better go too?—Will not it be right for me to go too?" but they were no sooner through the door than Henry Crawford undertook to answer the anxious inquiry, and encouraging him by all means to pay his respects to Sir Thomas without delay, sent him after the others with delighted haste.

Fanny was left with only the Crawfords and Mr. Yates. She had been quite overlooked by her cousins; and as her own opinion of her claims on Sir Thomas's affection was much too humble to give her any idea of classing herself with his children, she was glad to remain behind and gain a little breathing time. Her agitation and alarm exceeded all that was endured by the rest, by the right of a disposition which not even innocence could keep from suffering. She was nearly fainting: all her former habitual dread of her uncle was returning, and with it compassion for him and for almost every one of the party on the development[1] before him*—with solicitude on Edmund's account indescribable. She had found a seat, where in excessive trembling she was enduring all these fearful thoughts, while the other three, no longer under any restraint, were giving vent to their feelings of vexation, lamenting over such an unlooked-for premature arrival as a most untoward event, and without mercy wishing poor Sir Thomas had been twice as long on his passage, or were still in Antigua.

The Crawfords were more warm on the subject than Mr. Yates, from better understanding the family and judging more clearly of the mischief that must ensue. The ruin of the play was to them a certainty, they felt the total destruction of the scheme to be inevitably at hand; while Mr. Yates considered it only as a temporary interruption, a disaster for the evening, and could even suggest the possibility of the rehearsal being renewed after tea, when the bustle of receiving Sir Thomas were over and he might be at leisure to be amused by it. The Crawfords laughed at the idea; and having soon agreed on the propriety of their walking quietly home and leaving the family to themselves, proposed Mr. Yates's accompanying them and spending the evening at the Parsonage. But Mr. Yates, having never been with those who thought much of parental claims, or family confidence, could not perceive that any thing of the kind was necessary, and therefore, thanking them, said, "he preferred remaining where he was that he might pay his respects to the old gentleman handsomely since he *was* come; and besides, he did not think it would be fair by the others to have every body run away."

Fanny was just beginning to collect herself, and to feel that if she staid longer behind it might seem disrespectful, when this point was settled, and being commissioned with the brother and sister's apology,

1. Realization, disclosure.

saw them preparing to go as she quitted the room herself to perform the dreadful duty of appearing before her uncle.

Too soon did she find herself at the drawing-room door, and after pausing a moment for what she knew would not come, for a courage which the outside of no door had ever supplied to her, she turned the lock in desperation, and the lights of the drawing-room and all the collected family were before her. As she entered, her own name caught her ear. Sir Thomas was at that moment looking round him, and saying "But where is Fanny?—Why do not I see my little Fanny?" And on perceiving her, came forward with a kindness which astonished and penetrated her, calling her his dear Fanny, kissing her affectionately, and observing with decided pleasure how much she was grown! Fanny knew not how to feel, nor where to look. She was quite oppressed. He had never been so kind, so *very* kind to her in his life. His manner seemed changed; his voice was quick from the agitation of joy, and all that had been awful in his dignity seemed lost in tenderness. He led her nearer the light and looked at her again—inquired particularly after her health, and then correcting himself, observed, that he need *not* inquire, for her appearance spoke sufficiently on that point. A fine blush having succeeded the previous paleness of her face, he was justified in his belief of her equal improvement in health and beauty. He inquired next after her family, especially William; and his kindness altogether was such as made her reproach herself for loving him so little, and thinking his return a misfortune; and when, on having courage to lift her eyes to his face, she saw that he was grown thinner and had the burnt, fagged, worn look of fatigue and a hot climate, every tender feeling was increased, and she was miserable in considering how much unsuspected vexation was probably ready to burst on him.

Sir Thomas was indeed the life of the party, who at his suggestion now seated themselves round the fire. He had the best right to be the talker; and the delight of his sensations in being again in his own house, in the centre of his family, after such a separation, made him communicative and chatty in a very unusual degree; and he was ready to give every information as to his voyage, and answer every question of his two sons almost before it was put. His business in Antigua had latterly been prosperously rapid, and he came directly from Liverpool,[2] having had an opportunity of making his passage thither in a private vessel, instead of waiting for the packet; and all the little particulars of his proceedings and events, his arrivals and departures, were most promptly delivered, as he sat by Lady Bertram and looked with heartfelt satisfaction on the faces around him—interrupting himself more than once, however, to remark on his good fortune in finding them all at

2. Port city in northwest England associated with the slave trade.

home—coming unexpectedly as he did—all collected together exactly as he could have wished, but dared not depend on. Mr. Rushworth was not forgotten; a most friendly reception and warmth of hand-shaking had already met him, and with pointed attention he was now included in the objects most intimately connected with Mansfield. There was nothing disagreeable in Mr. Rushworth's appearance, and Sir Thomas was liking him already.

By not one of the circle was he listened to with such unbroken unalloyed enjoyment as by his wife, who was really extremely happy to see him, and whose feelings were so warmed by his sudden arrival, as to place her nearer agitation than she had been for the last twenty years. She had been *almost* fluttered for a few minutes, and still remained so sensibly animated as to put away her work, move Pug from her side, and give all her attention and all the rest of her sofa to her husband. She had no anxieties for any body to cloud *her* pleasure; her own time had been irreproachably spent during his absence; she had done a great deal of carpet work and made many yards of fringe; and she would have answered as freely for the good conduct and useful pursuits of all the young people as for her own. It was so agreeable to her to see him again, and hear him talk, to have her ear amused and her whole comprehension filled by his narratives, that she began particularly to feel how dreadfully she must have missed him, and how impossible it would have been for her to bear a lengthened absence.

Mrs. Norris was by no means to be compared in happiness to her sister. Not that *she* was incommoded by many fears of Sir Thomas's disapprobation when the present state of his house should be known, for her judgment had been so blinded, that except by the instinctive caution with which she had whisked away Mr. Rushworth's pink satin cloak as her brother-in-law entered, she could hardly be said to shew any sign of alarm; but she was vexed by the *manner* of his return. It had left her nothing to do. Instead of being sent for out of the room, and seeing him first, and having to spread the happy news through the house, Sir Thomas, with a very reasonable dependence perhaps on the nerves of his wife and children, had sought no confidant but the butler, and had been following him almost instantaneously into the drawing-room. Mrs. Norris felt herself defrauded of an office on which she had always depended, whether his arrival or his death were to be the thing unfolded; and was now trying to be in a bustle without having any thing to bustle about, and labouring to be important where nothing was wanted but tranquillity and silence. Would Sir Thomas have consented to eat, she might have gone to the house-keeper with troublesome directions, and insulted the footmen with injunctions of dispatch; but Sir Thomas resolutely declined all dinner; he would take nothing, nothing till tea came—he would rather wait for tea. Still Mrs. Norris was at intervals urging something different, and in the most interesting

moment of his passage to England, when the alarm of a French privateer[3] was at the height, she burst through his recital with the proposal
of soup. "Sure, my dear Sir Thomas, a basin[4] of soup would be a much
better thing for you than tea. Do have a basin of soup."

Sir Thomas could not be provoked. "Still the same anxiety for every
body's comfort, my dear Mrs. Norris," was his answer. "But indeed I
would rather have nothing but tea."

"Well then, Lady Bertram, suppose you speak for tea directly, suppose you hurry Baddeley a little, he seems behind hand to-night." She
carried this point, and Sir Thomas's narrative proceeded.

At length there was a pause. His immediate communications were
exhausted, and it seemed enough to be looking joyfully around him,
now at one, now at another of the beloved circle; but the pause was
not long: in the elation of her spirits Lady Bertram became talkative,
and what were the sensations of her children upon hearing her say,
"How do you think the young people have been amusing themselves
lately, Sir Thomas? They have been acting. We have been all alive with
acting."

"Indeed! and what have you been acting?"

"Oh! They'll tell you all about it."

"The *all* will be soon told," cried Tom hastily, and with affected
unconcern; "but it is not worth while to bore my father with it now.
You will hear enough of it to-morrow, sir. We have just been trying,
by way of doing something, and amusing my mother, just within the
last week, to get up a few scenes, a mere trifle. We have had such
incessant rains almost since October began, that we have been nearly
confined to the house for days together. I have hardly taken out a gun
since the 3d. Tolerable sport the first three days, but there has been no
attempting any thing since. The first day I went over Mansfield Wood,
and Edmund took the copses beyond Easton, and we brought home
six brace between us, and might each have killed six times as many;
but we respect your pheasants, sir, I assure you, as much as you could
desire. I do not think you will find your woods by any means worse
stocked than they were. I never saw Mansfield Wood so full of pheasants in my life as this year. I hope you will take a day's sport there
yourself, sir, soon."

For the present the danger was over, and Fanny's sick feelings subsided; but when tea was soon afterwards brought in, and Sir Thomas,
getting up, said that he found he could not be any longer in the house
without just looking into his own dear room, every agitation was returning. He was gone before any thing had been said to prepare him
for the change he must find there; and a pause of alarm followed his
disappearance. Edmund was the first to speak:

3. An armed private ship.
4. A small circular dish.

"Something must be done," said he.

"It is time to think of our visitors," said Maria, still feeling her hand pressed to Henry Crawford's heart, and caring little for any thing else.—"Where did you leave Miss Crawford, Fanny?"

Fanny told of their departure, and delivered their message.

"Then poor Yates is all alone," cried Tom. "I will go and fetch him. He will be no bad assistant when it all comes out."

To the Theatre he went, and reached it just in time to witness the first meeting of his father and his friend. Sir Thomas had been a good deal surprized to find candles burning in his room; and on casting his eye round it, to see other symptoms of recent habitation, and a general air of confusion in the furniture. The removal of the book-case from before the billiard room door struck him especially, but he had scarcely more than time to feel astonished at all this, before there were sounds from the billiard room to astonish him still further. Some one was talking there in a very loud accent—he did not know the voice—*more* than talking—almost hallooing. He stept to the door, rejoicing at that moment in having the means of immediate communication, and opening it, found himself on the stage of a theatre, and opposed to a ranting young man, who appeared likely to knock him down backwards. At the very moment of Yates perceiving Sir Thomas, and giving perhaps the very best start he had ever given in the whole course of his rehearsals, Tom Bertram entered at the other end of the room; and never had he found greater difficulty in keeping his countenance. His father's looks of solemnity and amazement on this his first appearance on any stage, and the gradual metamorphosis of the impassioned Baron Wildenheim into the well-bred and easy Mr. Yates, making his bow and apology to Sir Thomas Bertram, was such an exhibition, such a piece of true acting as he would not have lost upon any account. It would be the last—in all probability the last scene on that stage; but he was sure there could not be a finer. The house would close with the greatest eclat.

There was little time, however, for the indulgence of any images of merriment. It was necessary for him to step forward too and assist the introduction, and with many awkward sensations he did his best. Sir Thomas received Mr. Yates with all the appearance of cordiality which was due to his own character, but was really as far from pleased with the necessity of the acquaintance as with the manner of its commencement. Mr. Yates's family and connections were sufficiently known to him, to render his introduction as the "particular friend," another of the hundred particular friends of his son, exceedingly unwelcome; and it needed all the felicity of being again at home, and all the forbearance it could supply, to save Sir Thomas from anger on finding himself thus bewildered in his own house, making part of a ridiculous exhibition in the midst of theatrical nonsense, and forced in so untoward a moment to admit the acquaintance of a young man whom he felt sure of disapproving, and whose easy indifference and volubility in the course of the first five minutes seemed to mark him the most at home of the two.

Tom understood his father's thoughts, and heartily wishing he might be always as well disposed to give them but partial expression, began to see more clearly than he had ever done before that there might be some ground of offence—that there might be some reason for the glance his father gave towards the ceiling and stucco of the room; and that when he inquired with mild gravity after the fate of the billiard table, he was not proceeding beyond a very allowable curiosity. A few minutes were enough for such unsatisfactory sensations on each side; and Sir Thomas, having exerted himself so far as to speak a few words of calm approbation in reply to an eager appeal of Mr. Yates, as to the happiness of the arrangement, the three gentlemen returned to the drawing-room together, Sir Thomas with an increase of gravity which was not lost on all.

"I come from your theatre," said he composedly, as he sat down; "I found myself in it rather unexpectedly. Its vicinity to my own room— but in every respect indeed it took me by surprize, as I had not the smallest suspicion of your acting having assumed so serious a character. It appears a neat job, however, as far as I could judge by candle-light, and does my friend Christopher Jackson credit." And then he would have changed the subject, and sipped his coffee in peace over domestic matters of a calmer hue; but Mr. Yates, without discernment to catch Sir Thomas's meaning, or diffidence, or delicacy, or discretion enough to allow him to lead the discourse while he mingled among the others with the least obtrusiveness himself, would keep him on the topic of the theatre, would torment him with questions and remarks relative to it, and finally would make him hear the whole history of his disappointment at Ecclesford. Sir Thomas listened most politely, but found much to offend his ideas of decorum and confirm his ill opinion of Mr. Yates's habits of thinking from the beginning to the end of the story; and when it was over, could give him no other assurance of sympathy than what a slight bow conveyed.

"This was in fact the origin of *our* acting," said Tom after a moment's thought. "My friend Yates brought the infection from Ecclesford, and it spread as those things always spread you know, sir—the faster probably from *your* having so often encouraged the sort of thing in us formerly. It was like treading old ground again."

Mr. Yates took the subject from his friend as soon as possible, and immediately gave Sir Thomas an account of what they had done and were doing, told him of the gradual increase of their views, the happy conclusion of their first difficulties, and present promising state of affairs; relating every thing with so blind an interest as made him not only totally unconscious of the uneasy movements of many of his friends as they sat, the change of countenance, the fidget, the hem! of unquietness, but prevented him even from seeing the expression of the face on which his own eyes were fixed—from seeing Sir Thomas's dark brow contract as he looked with inquiring earnestness at his daughters and Edmund, dwelling particularly on the latter, and speaking a language, a remonstrance, a reproof, which *he* felt at his heart. Not less acutely was it felt by Fanny, who had edged back her chair behind her aunt's end of the sofa, and, screened from notice herself, saw all that was passing before her. Such a look of reproach at Edmund from his father she could never have expected to witness; and to feel that it was in any degree deserved, was an aggravation indeed. Sir Thomas's look implied, "On your judgment, Edmund, I depended; what have you been about?"—She knelt in spirit to her uncle, and her bosom swelled to utter, "Oh! not to *him*. Look so to all the others, but not to *him*!"

Mr. Yates was still talking. "To own the truth, Sir Thomas, we were in the middle of a rehearsal when you arrived this evening. We were going through the three first acts, and not unsuccessfully upon the whole. Our company is now so dispersed from the Crawfords being gone home, that nothing more can be done to-night; but if you will give us the honour of your company to-morrow evening, I should not be afraid of the result. We bespeak your indulgence, you understand, as young performers; we bespeak your indulgence."

"My indulgence shall be given, sir," replied Sir Thomas gravely, "but without any other rehearsal."—And with a relenting smile he added, "I come home to be happy and indulgent." Then turning away towards any or all of the rest, he tranquilly said, "Mr. and Miss Crawford were mentioned in my last letters from Mansfield. Do you find them agreeable acquaintance?"

Tom was the only one at all ready with an answer, but he being entirely without particular regard for either, without jealousy either in love or acting, could speak very handsomely of both. "Mr. Crawford was a most pleasant gentleman-like man;—his sister a sweet, pretty, elegant, lively girl."

Mr. Rushworth could be silent no longer. "I do not say he is not gentleman-like, considering; but you should tell your father he is not above five feet eight, or he will be expecting a well-looking man."

Sir Thomas did not quite understand this, and looked with some surprize at the speaker.

"If I must say what I think," continued Mr. Rushworth, "in my opinion it is very disagreeable to be always rehearsing. It is having too much of a good thing. I am not so fond of acting as I was at first. I think we are a great deal better employed, sitting comfortably here among ourselves, and doing nothing."

Sir Thomas looked again, and then replied with an approving smile, "I am happy to find our sentiments on this subject so much the same. It gives me sincere satisfaction. That I should be cautious and quick-sighted, and feel many scruples which my children do *not* feel, is perfectly natural; and equally so that *my* value for domestic tranquillity, for a home which shuts out noisy pleasures, should much exceed theirs. But at your time of life to feel all this, is a most favourable circumstance for yourself and for every body connected with you; and I am sensible of the importance of having an ally of such weight."

Sir Thomas meant to be giving Mr. Rushworth's opinion in better words than he could find himself. He was aware that he must not expect a genius in Mr. Rushworth; but as a well-judging steady young man, with better notions than his elocution would do justice to, he intended to value him very highly. It was impossible for many of the others not to smile. Mr. Rushworth hardly knew what to do with so much meaning; but by looking, as he really felt, most exceedingly pleased with Sir Thomas's good opinion, and saying scarcely any thing, he did his best towards preserving that good opinion a little longer.

Chapter II.

Edmund's first object the next morning was to see his father alone, and give him a fair statement of the whole acting scheme, defending his own share in it as far only as he could then, in a soberer moment, feel his motives to deserve, and acknowledging with perfect ingenuousness that his concession had been attended with such partial good as to make his judgment in it very doubtful. He was anxious, while vindicating himself, to say nothing unkind of the others; but there was only one amongst them whose conduct he could mention without some necessity of defence or palliation. "We have all been more or less to blame," said he, "every one of us, excepting Fanny. Fanny is the only one who has judged rightly throughout, who has been consistent. *Her* feelings have been steadily against it from first to last. She never ceased to think of what was due to you. You will find Fanny every thing you could wish."

Sir Thomas saw all the impropriety of such a scheme among such a party, and at such a time, as strongly as his son had ever supposed he must; he felt it too much indeed for many words; and having shaken hands with Edmund, meant to try to lose the disagreeable impression, and forget how much he had been forgotten himself as soon as he could, after the house had been cleared of every object enforcing the remembrance, and restored to its proper state. He did not enter into any remonstrance with his other children: he was more willing to believe they felt their error, than to run the risk of investigation. The reproof of an immediate conclusion of every thing, the sweep of every preparation would be sufficient.

There was one person, however, in the house whom he could not leave to learn his sentiments merely through his conduct. He could not help giving Mrs. Norris a hint of his having hoped, that her advice might have been interposed to prevent what her judgment must certainly have disapproved. The young people had been very inconsiderate in forming the plan; they ought to have been capable of a better decision themselves; but they were young, and, excepting Edmund, he believed of unsteady characters; and with greater surprize therefore he must regard her acquiescence in their wrong measures, her countenance of their unsafe amusements, than that such measures and such amusements should have been suggested. Mrs. Norris was a little confounded, and as nearly being silenced as ever she had been in her life; for she was ashamed to confess having never seen any of the impropriety which was so glaring to Sir Thomas, and would not have admitted that her influence was insufficient, that she might have talked in vain. Her only resource was to get out of the subject as fast as possible, and turn the current of Sir Thomas's ideas into a happier channel. She had a great deal to insinuate in her own praise as to *general* attention to the interest and comfort of his family, much exertion and many sacrifices to glance at in the form of hurried walks and sudden removals from her own fire-side, and many excellent hints of distrust and economy to Lady Bertram and Edmund to detail, whereby a most considerable saving had always arisen, and more than one bad servant been detected. But her chief strength lay in Sotherton. Her greatest support and glory was in having formed the connection with the Rushworths. *There* she was impregnable. She took to herself all the credit of bringing Mr. Rushworth's admiration of Maria to any effect. "If I had not been active," said she, "and made a point of being introduced to his mother, and then prevailed on my sister to pay the first visit, I am as certain as I sit here, that nothing would have come of it—for Mr. Rushworth is the sort of amiable modest young man who wants a great deal of encouragement, and there were girls enough on the catch for him if we had been idle. But I left no stone unturned. I was ready to move heaven and earth to persuade my sister, and at last I did persuade her. You know the distance to Sotherton; it was in the middle of winter, and the roads almost impassable, but I did persuade her."

"I know how great, how justly great your influence is with Lady Bertram and her children, and am the more concerned that it should not have been"——

"My dear Sir Thomas, if you had seen the state of the roads *that* day! I thought we should never have got through them, though we had the four horses of course; and poor old coachman would attend us, out of his great love and kindness, though he was hardly able to sit the box on account of the rheumatism which I had been doctoring him for, ever since Michaelmas.[1] I cured him at last; but he was very bad all the winter—and this was such a day, I could not help going to him up in his room before we set off to advise him not to venture: he was putting on his wig—so I said, 'Coachman, you had much better not go, your Lady and I shall be very safe; you know how steady Stephen is, and Charles has been upon the leaders[2] so often now, that I am sure there is no fear.' But, however, I soon found it would not do; he was bent upon going, and as I hate to be worrying and officious, I said no more; but my heart quite ached for him at every jolt, and when we got into the rough lanes about Stoke, where what with frost and snow upon beds of stones, it was worse than any thing you can imagine, I was quite in an agony about him. And then the poor horses too!—To see them straining away! You know how I always feel for the horses. And when we got to the bottom of Sandcroft Hill, what do you think I did? You will laugh at me—but I got out and walked up. I did indeed. It might not be saving them much, but it was something, and I could not bear to sit at my ease, and be dragged up at the expense of those noble animals. I caught a dreadful cold, but *that* I did not regard. My object was accomplished in the visit."

"I hope we shall always think the acquaintance worth any trouble that might be taken to establish it. There is nothing very striking in Mr. Rushworth's manners, but I was pleased last night with what appeared to be his opinion on *one* subject—his decided preference of a quiet family-party to the bustle and confusion of acting. He seemed to feel exactly as one could wish."

"Yes, indeed,—and the more you know of him, the better you will like him. He is not a shining character, but he has a thousand good qualities! and is so disposed to look up to you, that I am quite laughed at about it, for every body considers it as my doing. 'Upon my word, Mrs. Norris,' said Mrs. Grant, the other day, 'if Mr. Rushworth were a son of your own he could not hold Sir Thomas in greater respect.' "

Sir Thomas gave up the point, foiled by her evasions, disarmed by her flattery; and was obliged to rest satisfied with the conviction that where the present pleasure of those she loved was at stake, her kindness did sometimes overpower her judgment.

It was a busy morning with him. Conversation with any of them occupied but a small part of it. He had to reinstate himself in all the wonted concerns of his Mansfield life, to see his steward and his bailiff—to examine and compute—and, in the intervals of business, to walk into his stables and his gardens, and nearest plantations; but active and methodical, he had not only done all this before he resumed his

1. September 29, the day celebrated as the feast day of St. Michael the Archangel; in a general sense, autumn.
2. Front horses.

seat as master of the house at dinner, he had also set the carpenter to work in pulling down what had been so lately put up in the billiard room, and given the scene painter his dismissal, long enough to justify the pleasing belief of his being then at least as far off as Northampton. The scene painter was gone, having spoilt only the floor of one room, ruined all the coachman's sponges, and made five of the under-servants idle and dissatisfied; and Sir Thomas was in hopes that another day or two would suffice to wipe away every outward memento of what had been, even to the destruction of every unbound copy of "Lovers' Vows" in the house, for he was burning all that met his eye.

Mr. Yates was beginning now to understand Sir Thomas's intentions, though as far as ever from understanding their source. He and his friend had been out with their guns the chief of the morning, and Tom had taken the opportunity of explaining, with proper apologies for his father's particularity, what was to be expected. Mr. Yates felt it as acutely as might be supposed. To be a second time disappointed in the same way was an instance of very severe ill-luck; and his indignation was such, that had it not been for delicacy towards his friend and his friend's youngest sister, he believed he should certainly attack the Baronet on the absurdity of his proceedings, and argue him into a little more rationality. He believed this very stoutly while he was in Mansfield Wood, and all the way home; but there was a something in Sir Thomas, when they sat round the same table, which made Mr. Yates think it wiser to let him pursue his own way, and feel the folly of it without opposition. He had known many disagreeable fathers before, and often been struck with the inconveniences they occasioned, but never in the whole course of his life, had he seen one of that class, so unintelligibly moral, so infamously tyrannical as Sir Thomas. He was not a man to be endured but for his children's sake, and he might be thankful to his fair daughter Julia that Mr. Yates did yet mean to stay a few days longer under his roof.

The evening passed with external smoothness, though almost every mind was ruffled; and the music which Sir Thomas called for from his daughters helped to conceal the want of real harmony. Maria was in a good deal of agitation. It was of the utmost consequence to her that Crawford should now lose no time in declaring himself, and she was disturbed that even a day should be gone by without seeming to advance that point. She had been expecting to see him the whole morning—and all the evening too was still expecting him. Mr. Rushworth had set off early with the great news for Sotherton; and she had fondly hoped for such an immediate eclaircissement[3] as might save him the trouble of ever coming back again. But they had seen no one from the Parsonage—not a creature, and had heard no tidings beyond a

---

3. Enlightenment; a clearing up or explanation.

friendly note of congratulation and inquiry from Mrs. Grant to Lady Bertram. It was the first day for many, many weeks, in which the families had been wholly divided. Four-and-twenty hours had never passed before, since August began, without bringing them together in some way or other. It was a sad anxious day; and the morrow, though differing in the sort of evil, did by no means bring less. A few moments of feverish enjoyment were followed by hours of acute suffering. Henry Crawford was again in the house; he walked up with Dr. Grant, who was anxious to pay his respects to Sir Thomas, and at rather an early hour they were ushered into the breakfast-room, where were most of the family. Sir Thomas soon appeared, and Maria saw with delight and agitation the introduction of the man she loved to her father. Her sensations were indefinable, and so were they a few minutes afterwards upon hearing Henry Crawford, who had a chair between herself and Tom, ask the latter in an under voice, whether there were any plan for resuming the play after the present happy interruption, (with a courteous glance at Sir Thomas,) because in that case, he should make a point of returning to Mansfield, at any time required by the party; he was going away immediately, being to meet his uncle at Bath without delay, but if there were any prospect of a renewal of "Lovers' Vows," he should hold himself positively engaged, he should break through every other claim, he should absolutely condition with his uncle for attending them whenever he might be wanted. The play should not be lost by *his* absence.

"From Bath, Norfolk, London, York—wherever I may be," said he, "I will attend you from any place in England, at an hour's notice."

It was well at that moment that Tom had to speak and not his sister. He could immediately say with easy fluency, "I am sorry you are going—but as to our play, *that* is all over—entirely at an end (looking significantly at his father). The painter was sent off yesterday, and very little will remain of the theatre to-morrow.—I knew how *that* would be from the first.—It is early for Bath.—You will find nobody there."

"It is about my uncle's usual time."

"When do you think of going?"

"I may perhaps get as far as Banbury to-day."

"Whose stables do you use at Bath?" was the next question; and while this branch of the subject was under discussion, Maria, who wanted neither pride nor resolution, was preparing to encounter her share of it with tolerable calmness.

To her he soon turned, repeating much of what he had already said, with only a softened air and stronger expressions of regret. But what availed his expressions or his air?—He was going—and if not voluntarily going, voluntarily intending to stay away; for, excepting what might be due to his uncle, his engagements were all self-imposed.—He might talk of necessity, but she knew his independence.—The hand which had so pressed her's to his heart!—The hand and the heart were alike motionless and passive now! Her spirit supported her, but the agony of her mind was severe.—She had not long to endure what arose from listening to language, which his actions contradicted, or to bury the tumult of her feelings under the restraint of society; for general civilities soon called his notice from her, and the farewell visit, as it then became openly acknowledged, was a very short one.—He was gone—he had touched her hand for the last time, he had made his parting bow, and she might seek directly all that solitude could do for her. Henry Crawford was gone—gone from the house, and within two hours afterwards from the parish; and so ended all the hopes his selfish vanity had raised in Maria and Julia Bertram.

Julia could rejoice that he was gone.—His presence was beginning to be odious to her; and if Maria gained him not, she was now cool enough to dispense with any other revenge.—She did not want exposure to be added to desertion.—Henry Crawford gone, she could even pity her sister.

With a purer spirit did Fanny rejoice in the intelligence.—She heard it at dinner and felt it a blessing. By all the others it was mentioned with regret, and his merits honoured with due gradation of feeling, from the sincerity of Edmund's too partial regard, to the unconcern of his mother speaking entirely by rote. Mrs. Norris began to look about her and wonder that his falling in love with Julia had come to nothing; and could almost fear that she had been remiss herself in forwarding it; but with so many to care for, how was it possible for even *her* activity to keep pace with her wishes?

Another day or two, and Mr. Yates was gone likewise. In *his* departure Sir Thomas felt the chief interest; wanting to be alone with his family, the presence of a stranger superior to Mr. Yates must have been irksome; but of him, trifling and confident, idle and expensive, it was every way vexatious. In himself he was wearisome, but as the friend of Tom and the admirer of Julia he became offensive. Sir Thomas had been quite indifferent to Mr. Crawford's going or staying—but his good wishes for Mr. Yates's having a pleasant journey, as he walked with him to the hall door, were given with genuine satisfaction. Mr. Yates had staid to see the destruction of every theatrical preparation at Mansfield, the removal of every thing appertaining to the play; he left the house in all the soberness of its general character; and Sir Thomas hoped, in seeing him out of it, to be rid of the worst object connected with the scheme, and the last that must be inevitably reminding him of its existence.

Mrs. Norris contrived to remove one article from his sight that might have distressed him. The curtain over which she had presided with such talent and such success, went off with her to her cottage, where she happened to be particularly in want of green baize.

Chapter III.

Sir Thomas's return made a striking change in the ways of the family, independent of Lovers' Vows. Under his government, Mansfield was an altered place. Some members of their society sent away and the spirits of many others saddened, it was all sameness and gloom, compared with the past; a sombre family-party rarely enlivened. There was little intercourse with the Parsonage. Sir Thomas drawing back from intimacies in general, was particularly disinclined, at this time, for any engagements but in one quarter. The Rushworths were the only addition to his own domestic circle which he could solicit.

Edmund did not wonder that such should be his father's feelings, nor could he regret any thing but the exclusion of the Grants. "But they," he observed to Fanny, "have a claim. They seem to belong to us—they seem to be part of ourselves. I could wish my father were more sensible of their very great attention to my mother and sisters while he was away. I am afraid they may feel themselves neglected. But the truth is that my father hardly knows them. They had not been here a twelvemonth when he left England. If he knew them better, he would value their society as it deserves, for they are in fact exactly the sort of people he would like. We are sometimes a little in want of animation among ourselves; my sisters seem out of spirits, and Tom is certainly not at his ease. Dr. and Mrs. Grant would enliven us, and make our evenings pass away with more enjoyment even to my father."

"Do you think so?" said Fanny. "In my opinion, my uncle would not like *any* addition. I think he values the very quietness you speak of, and that the repose of his own family-circle is all he wants. And it does not appear to me that we are more serious than we used to be; I mean before my uncle went abroad. As well as I can recollect, it was always much the same. There was never much laughing in his presence; or, if there is any difference, it is not more I think than such an absence has a tendency to produce at first. There must be a sort of shyness. But I cannot recollect that our evenings formerly were ever merry, except when my uncle was in town. No young people's are, I suppose, when those they look up to are at home."

"I believe you are right, Fanny," was his reply, after a short consideration. "I believe our evenings are rather returned to what they were, than assuming a new character. The novelty was in their being lively. —Yet, how strong the impression that only a few weeks will give! I have been feeling as if we had never lived so before."

"I suppose I am graver than other people," said Fanny. "The evenings do not appear long to me. I love to hear my uncle talk of the West Indies. I could listen to him for an hour together. It entertains *me* more than many other things have done—but then I am unlike other people I dare say."

"Why should you dare say *that*? (smiling)—Do you want to be told that you are only unlike other people in being more wise and discreet? But when did you or any body ever get a compliment from me, Fanny? Go to my father if you want to be complimented. He will satisfy you. Ask your uncle what he thinks, and you will hear compliments enough; and though they may be chiefly on your person, you must put up with it, and trust to his seeing as much beauty of mind in time."

Such language was so new to Fanny that it quite embarrassed her.

"Your uncle thinks you very pretty, dear Fanny—and that is the long and the short of the matter. Any body but myself would have made something more of it, and any body but you would resent that you had not been thought very pretty before; but the truth is, that your uncle never did admire you till now—and now he does. Your complexion is so improved!—and you have gained so much countenance!—and your figure—Nay, Fanny, do not turn away about it—it is but an uncle. If you cannot bear an uncle's admiration what is to become of you? You must really begin to harden yourself to the idea of being worth looking at.—You must try not to mind growing up into a pretty woman."

"Oh! don't talk so, don't talk so," cried Fanny, distressed by more feelings than he was aware of; but seeing that she was distressed, he had done with the subject, and only added more seriously, "Your uncle is disposed to be pleased with you in every respect; and I only wish you would talk to him more.—You are one of those who are too silent in the evening circle."

"But I do talk to him more than I used. I am sure I do. Did not you hear me ask him about the slave-trade[1] last night?"

"I did—and was in hopes the question would be followed up by others. It would have pleased your uncle to be inquired of farther."

"And I longed to do it—but there was such a dead silence! And while my cousins were sitting by without speaking a word, or seeming at all interested in the subject, I did not like—I thought it would appear as if I wanted to set myself off at their expense, by shewing a curiosity and pleasure in his information which he must wish his own daughters to feel."

"Miss Crawford was very right in what she said of you the other day—that you seemed almost as fearful of notice and praise as other women were of neglect. We were talking of you at the Parsonage, and those were her words. She has great discernment. I know nobody who distinguishes characters better.—For so young a woman it is remarkable! She certainly understands *you* better than you are understood by the greater part of those who have known you so long; and with regard

---

1. Though abolished by Parliament in 1807, the slave trade continued surreptitiously.

to some others, I can perceive, from occasional lively hints, the un-guarded expressions of the moment, that she could define *many* as accurately, did not delicacy forbid it. I wonder what she thinks of my father! She must admire him as a fine looking man, with most gentle-man-like, dignified, consistent manners; but perhaps having seen him so seldom, his reserve may be a little repulsive. Could they be much together I feel sure of their liking each other. He would enjoy her liveliness—and she has talents to value his powers. I wish they met more frequently!—I hope she does not suppose there is any dislike on his side."

"She must know herself too secure of the regard of all the rest of you," said Fanny with half a sigh, "to have any such apprehension. And Sir Thomas's wishing just at first to be only with his family is so very natural, that she can argue nothing from that. After a little while I dare say we shall be meeting again in the same sort of way, allowing for the difference of the time of year."

"This is the first October that she has passed in the country since her infancy. I do not call Tunbridge or Cheltenham the country; and November is a still more serious month, and I can see that Mrs. Grant is very anxious for her not finding Mansfield dull as winter comes on."

Fanny could have said a great deal, but it was safer to say nothing, and leave untouched all Miss Crawford's resources, her accomplish-ments, her spirits, her importance, her friends, lest it should betray her into any observations seemingly unhandsome. Miss Crawford's kind opinion of herself deserved at least a grateful forbearance, and she be-gan to talk of something else.

"To-morrow, I think, my uncle dines at Sotherton, and you and Mr. Bertram too. We shall be quite a small party at home. I hope my uncle may continue to like Mr. Rushworth."

"That is impossible, Fanny. He must like him less after to-morrow's visit, for we shall be five hours in his company. I should dread the stupidity of the day, if there were not a much greater evil to follow—the impression it must leave on Sir Thomas. He cannot much longer deceive himself. I am sorry for them all, and would give something that Rushworth and Maria had never met."

In this quarter, indeed, disappointment was impending over Sir Tho-mas. Not all his good-will for Mr. Rushworth, not all Mr. Rushworth's deference for him, could prevent him from soon discerning some part of the truth—that Mr. Rushworth was an inferior young man, as igno-rant in business as in books, with opinions in general unfixed, and without seeming much aware of it himself.

He had expected a very different son-in-law; and beginning to feel grave on Maria's account, tried to understand *her* feelings. Little ob-servation there was necessary to tell him that indifference was the most favourable state they could be in. Her behaviour to Mr. Rushworth was careless and cold. She could not, did not like him. Sir Thomas resolved to speak seriously to her. Advantageous as would be the alliance, and long standing and public as was the engagement, her happiness must not be sacrificed to it. Mr. Rushworth had perhaps been accepted on too short an acquaintance, and on knowing him better she was re-penting.

With solemn kindness Sir Thomas addressed her; told her his fears, inquired into her wishes, entreated her to be open and sincere, and assured her that every inconvenience should be braved, and the con-nection entirely given up, if she felt herself unhappy in the prospect of it. He would act for her and release her. Maria had a moment's struggle as she listened, and only a moment's: when her father ceased, she was able to give her answer immediately, decidedly, and with no apparent agitation. She thanked him for his great attention, his paternal kindness, but he was quite mistaken in supposing she had the smallest desire of breaking through her engagement, or was sensible of any change of opinion or inclination since her forming it. She had the highest esteem for Mr. Rushworth's character and disposition, and could not have a doubt of her happiness with him.

Sir Thomas was satisfied; too glad to be satisfied perhaps to urge the matter quite so far as his judgment might have dictated to others. It was an alliance which he could not have relinquished without pain; and thus he reasoned. Mr. Rushworth was young enough to improve; —Mr. Rushworth must and would improve in good society; and if Ma-ria could now speak so securely of her happiness with him, speaking certainly without the prejudice, the blindness of love, she ought to be believed. Her feelings probably were not acute; he had never supposed them to be so; but her comforts might not be less on that account, and if she could dispense with seeing her husband a leading, shining char-acter, there would certainly be every thing else in her favour. A well-disposed young woman, who did not marry for love, was in general but the more attached to her own family, and the nearness of Sotherton to Mansfield must naturally hold out the greatest temptation, and would, in all probability, be a continual supply of the most amiable and in-nocent enjoyments. Such and such-like were the reasonings of Sir Thomas—happy to escape the embarrassing evils of a rupture, the won-der, the reflections, the reproach that must attend it, happy to secure a marriage which would bring him such an addition of respectability and influence, and very happy to think any thing of his daughter's disposition that was most favourable for the purpose.

To her the conference closed as satisfactorily as to him. She was in a state of mind to be glad that she had secured her fate beyond recall —that she had pledged herself anew to Sotherton—that she was safe from the possibility of giving Crawford the triumph of governing her actions, and destroying her prospects; and retired in proud resolve, determined only to behave more cautiously to Mr. Rushworth in future, that her father might not be again suspecting her.

Had Sir Thomas applied to his daughter within the first three or four days after Henry Crawford's leaving Mansfield, before her feelings were at all tranquillized, before she had given up every hope of him, or absolutely resolved on enduring his rival, her answer might have been different; but after another three or four days, when there was no return, no letter, no message—no symptom of a softened heart—no hope of advantage from separation—her mind became cool enough to seek all the comfort that pride and self-revenge could give.

Henry Crawford had destroyed her happiness, but he should not know that he had done it; he should not destroy her credit, her appearance, her prosperity too. He should not have to think of her as pining in the retirement of Mansfield for *him*, rejecting Sotherton and London, independence and splendour for *his* sake. Independence was more needful than ever; the want of it at Mansfield more sensibly felt. She was less and less able to endure the restraint which her father imposed. The liberty which his absence had given was now become absolutely necessary. She must escape from him and Mansfield as soon as possible, and find consolation in fortune and consequence, bustle and the world, for a wounded spirit. Her mind was quite determined and varied not.

To such feelings, delay, even the delay of much preparation, would have been an evil, and Mr. Rushworth could hardly be more impatient for the marriage than herself. In all the important preparations of the mind she was complete; being prepared for matrimony by an hatred of home, restraint, and tranquillity; by the misery of disappointed affection, and contempt of the man she was to marry. The rest might wait. The preparations of new carriages and furniture might wait for London and spring, when her own taste could have fairer play.

The principals being all agreed in this respect, it soon appeared that a very few weeks would be sufficient for such arrangements as must precede the wedding.

Mrs. Rushworth was quite ready to retire, and make way for the fortunate young woman whom her dear son had selected;—and very early in November removed herself, her maid, her footman, and her chariot, with true dowager propriety, to Bath—there to parade over the wonders of Sotherton in her evening-parties—enjoying them as thoroughly perhaps in the animation of a card-table as she had ever done on the spot—and before the middle of the same month the ceremony had taken place, which gave Sotherton another mistress.

It was a very proper wedding. The bride was elegantly dressed—the two bridemaids were duly inferior—her father gave her away—her mother stood with salts in her hand, expecting to be agitated—her aunt tried to cry—and the service was impressively read by Dr. Grant. Nothing could be objected to when it came under the discussion of the neighbourhood, except that the carriage which conveyed the bride and bridegroom and Julia from the church door to Sotherton, was the same chaise which Mr. Rushworth had used for a twelvemonth before. In every thing else the etiquette of the day might stand the strictest investigation.

It was done, and they were gone. Sir Thomas felt as an anxious father must feel, and was indeed experiencing much of the agitation which his wife had been apprehensive of for herself, but had fortunately escaped. Mrs. Norris, most happy to assist in the duties of the day, by spending it at the Park to support her sister's spirits, and drinking the health of Mr. and Mrs. Rushworth in a supernumerary glass or two, was all joyous delight—for she had made the match—she had done every thing—and no one would have supposed, from her confident triumph, that she had ever heard of conjugal infelicity in her life, or could have the smallest insight into the disposition of the niece who had been brought up under her eye.

The plan of the young couple was to proceed after a few days to Brighton,[2] and take a house there for some weeks. Every public place was new to Maria, and Brighton is almost as gay in winter as in summer. When the novelty of amusement there were over, it* would be time for the wider range of London.

Julia was to go with them to Brighton. Since rivalry between the sisters had ceased, they had been gradually recovering much of their former good understanding; and were at least sufficiently friends to make each of them exceedingly glad to be with the other at such a time. Some other companion than Mr. Rushworth was of the first consequence to his lady, and Julia was quite as eager for novelty and pleasure as Maria, though she might not have struggled through so much to obtain them, and could better bear a subordinate situation.

Their departure made another material change at Mansfield, a chasm which required some time to fill up. The family circle became greatly contracted, and though the Miss Bertrams had latterly added little to its gaiety, they could not but be missed. Even their mother missed them—and how much more their tender-hearted cousin, who wandered about the house, and thought of them, and felt for them, with a degree of affectionate regret which they had never done much to deserve!

---

2. A fashionable seaside resort on the English Channel. Patronized by the Prince Regent, Brighton was a natural choice for the Rushworths' honeymoon.

Chapter IV.

Fanny's consequence increased on the departure of her cousins. Becoming, as she then did, the only young woman in the drawing-room, the only occupier of that interesting division of a family in which she had hitherto held so humble a third, it was impossible for her not to be more looked at, more thought of and attended to, than she had ever been before; and "where is Fanny?" became no uncommon question, even without her being wanted for any one's convenience.

Not only at home did her value increase, but at the Parsonage too. In that house which she had hardly entered twice a year since Mr. Norris's death, she became a welcome, an invited guest; and in the gloom and dirt of a November day, most acceptable to Mary Crawford. Her visits there, beginning by chance, were continued by solicitation. Mrs. Grant, really eager to get any change for her sister, could by the easiest self-deceit persuade herself that she was doing the kindest thing by Fanny, and giving her the most important opportunities of improvement in pressing her frequent calls.

Fanny, having been sent into the village on some errand by her aunt Norris, was overtaken by a heavy shower close to the Parsonage, and being descried from one of the windows endeavouring to find shelter under the branches and lingering leaves of an oak just beyond their premises, was forced, though not without some modest reluctance on her part, to come in. A civil servant she had withstood; but when Dr. Grant himself went out with an umbrella, there was nothing to be done but to be very much ashamed and to get into the house as fast as possible; and to poor Miss Crawford, who had just been contemplating the dismal rain in a very desponding state of mind, sighing over the ruin of all her plan of exercise for that morning, and of every chance of seeing a single creature beyond themselves for the next twenty-four hours; the sound of a little bustle at the front door, and the sight of Miss Price dripping with wet in the vestibule, was delightful. The value of an event on a wet day in the country, was most forcibly brought before her. She was all alive again directly, and among the most active in being useful to Fanny, in detecting her to be wetter than she would at first allow, and providing her with dry clothes; and Fanny, after being obliged to submit to all this attention, and to being assisted and waited on by mistresses and maids, being also obliged on returning down stairs, to be fixed in their drawing-room for an hour while the rain continued, the blessing of something fresh to see and think of was thus extended to Miss Crawford, and might carry on her spirits to the period of dressing and dinner.

The two sisters were so kind to her and so pleasant, that Fanny might have enjoyed her visit could she have believed herself not in the way, and could she have foreseen that the weather would certainly clear at the end of the hour, and save her from the shame of having Dr. Grant's carriage and horses out to take her home, with which she was threatened. As to anxiety for any alarm that her absence in such weather might occasion at home, she had nothing to suffer on that score; for as her being out was known only to her two aunts, she was perfectly aware that none would be felt, and that in whatever cottage aunt Norris might chuse to establish her during the rain, her being in such cottage would be indubitable to aunt Bertram.

It was beginning to look brighter, when Fanny, observing a harp in the room, asked some questions about it, which soon led to an acknowledgment of her wishing very much to hear it, and a confession, which could hardly be believed, of her having never yet heard it since its being in Mansfield. To Fanny herself it appeared a very simple and natural circumstance. She had scarcely ever been at the Parsonage since the instrument's arrival, there had been no reason that she should; but Miss Crawford, calling to mind an early-expressed wish on the subject, was concerned at her own neglect;—and "shall I play to you now?"—and "what will you have?" were questions immediately following with the readiest good humour.

She played accordingly; happy to have a new listener, and a listener who seemed so much obliged, so full of wonder at the performance, and who shewed herself not wanting in taste. She played till Fanny's eyes, straying to the window on the weather's being evidently fair, spoke what she felt must be done.

"Another quarter of an hour," said Miss Crawford, "and we shall see how it will be. Do not run away the first moment of its holding up. Those clouds look alarming."

"But they are passed over," said Fanny.—"I have been watching them.—This weather is all from the south."

"South or north, I know a black cloud when I see it; and you must not set forward while it is so threatening. And besides, I want to play something more to you—a very pretty piece—and your cousin Edmund's prime favourite. You must stay and hear your cousin's favourite."

Fanny felt that she must; and though she had not waited for that sentence to be thinking of Edmund, such a memento made her particularly awake to his idea, and she fancied him sitting in that room again and again, perhaps in the very spot where she sat now, listening with constant delight to the favourite air, played, as it appeared to her, with superior tone and expression; and though pleased with it herself, and glad to like whatever was liked by him, she was more sincerely impatient to go away at the conclusion of it than she had been before; and on this being evident, she was so kindly asked to call again, to take them in her walk whenever she could, to come and hear more of the harp, that she felt it necessary to be done, if no objection arose at home.

Such was the origin of the sort of intimacy which took place between them within the first fortnight after the Miss Bertrams' going away, an intimacy resulting principally from Miss Crawford's desire of something new, and which had little reality in Fanny's feelings. Fanny went to her every two or three days; it seemed a kind of fascination; she could not be easy without going, and yet it was without loving her, without ever thinking like her, without any sense of obligation for being sought after now when nobody else was to be had; and deriving no higher pleasure from her conversation than occasional amusement, and *that* often at the expense of her judgment, when it was raised by pleasantry on people or subjects which she wished to be respected. She went however, and they sauntered about together many an half hour in Mrs. Grant's shrubbery, the weather being unusually mild for the time of year; and venturing sometimes even to sit down on one of the benches now comparatively unsheltered, remaining there perhaps till in the midst of some tender ejaculation of Fanny's, on the sweets of so protracted an autumn, they were forced by the sudden swell of a cold gust shaking down the last few yellow leaves about them, to jump up and walk for warmth.

"This is pretty—very pretty," said Fanny, looking around her as they were thus sitting together one day: "Every time I come into this shrubbery I am more struck with its growth and beauty. Three years ago, this was nothing but a rough hedgerow along the upper side of the field, never thought of as any thing, or capable of becoming any thing; and now it is converted into a walk, and it would be difficult to say whether most valuable as a convenience or an ornament; and perhaps in another three years we may be forgetting—almost forgetting what it was before. How wonderful, how very wonderful the operations of time, and the changes of the human mind!" And following the latter train of thought, she soon afterwards added: "If any one faculty of our nature may be called *more* wonderful than the rest, I do think it is memory. There seems something more speakingly incomprehensible in the powers, the failures, the inequalities of memory, than in any other of our intelligences. The memory is sometimes so retentive, so serviceable, so obedient—at others, so bewildered and so weak—and at others again, so tyrannic, so beyond controul!—We are to be sure a miracle every way—but our powers of recollecting and of forgetting, do seem peculiarly past finding out."

Miss Crawford, untouched and inattentive, had nothing to say; and Fanny, perceiving it, brought back her own mind to what she thought must interest.

"It may seem impertinent in *me* to praise, but I must admire the taste Mrs. Grant has shewn in all this. There is such a quiet simplicity in the plan of the walk!—not too much attempted!"

"Yes," replied Miss Crawford carelessly, "it does very well for a place of this sort. One does not think of extent *here*—and between ourselves, till I came to Mansfield, I had not imagined a country parson ever aspired to a shrubbery or any thing of the kind."

"I am so glad to see the evergreens thrive!" said Fanny in reply. "My uncle's gardener always says the soil here is better than his own, and so it appears from the growth of the laurels and evergreens in general.—The evergreen!—How beautiful, how welcome, how wonderful the evergreen!—When one thinks of it, how astonishing a variety of nature!—In some countries we know the tree that sheds its leaf is the variety, but that does not make it less amazing, that the same soil and the same sun should nurture plants differing in the first rule and law of their existence. You will think me rhapsodizing; but when I am out of doors, especially when I am sitting out of doors, I am very apt to get into this sort of wondering strain. One cannot fix one's eyes on the commonest natural production without finding food for a rambling fancy."[1]

"To say the truth," replied Miss Crawford, "I am something like the famous Doge at the court of Lewis XIV;[2] and may declare that I see no wonder in this shrubbery equal to seeing myself in it. If any body had told me a year ago that this place would be my home, that I should be spending month after month here, as I have done, I certainly should not have believed them!—I have now been here nearly five months! and moreover the quietest five months I ever passed."

"*Too* quiet for you I believe."

"I should have thought so *theoretically* myself, but"—and her eyes brightened as she spoke—"take it all and all, I never spent so happy a summer.—But then"—with a more thoughtful air and lowered voice—"there is no saying what it may lead to."

Fanny's heart beat quick, and she felt quite unequal to surmizing or soliciting any thing more. Miss Crawford however, with renewed animation, soon went on:

"I am conscious of being far better reconciled to a country residence than I had ever expected to be. I can even suppose it pleasant to spend *half* the year in the country, under certain circumstances—very pleasant. An elegant, moderate-sized house in the centre of family connections—continual engagements among them—commanding the first society in the neighbourhood—looked-up to perhaps as leading it even more than those of larger fortune, and turning from the cheerful round of such amusements to nothing worse than a tête-à-tête with the person one feels most agreeable in the world. There is nothing frightful in

---

1. Fanny's rhapsodies on memory and the evergreen have a bookish sound, but no source has been traced.
2. In Voltaire's *Louis XIV*, a Venetian magistrate, when asked what he considered the most remarkable thing about Versailles, replied, "It is to see myself here."

such a picture, is there, Miss Price? One need not envy the new Mrs. Rushworth with such a home as *that*." "Envy Mrs. Rushworth!" was all that Fanny attempted to say. "Come, come, it would be very unhandsome in us to be severe on Mrs. Rushworth, for I look forward to our owing her a great many gay, brilliant, happy hours. I expect we shall be all very much at Sotherton another year. Such a match as Miss Bertram has made is a public blessing, for the first pleasures of Mr. Rushworth's wife must be to fill her house, and give the best balls in the country."

Fanny was silent—and Miss Crawford relapsed into thoughtfulness, till suddenly looking up at the end of a few minutes, she exclaimed, "Ah! here he is." It was not Mr. Rushworth, however, but Edmund, who then appeared walking towards them with Mrs. Grant. "My sister and Mr. Bertram—I am so glad your eldest cousin is gone that he *may* be Mr. Bertram again. There is something in the sound of Mr. *Edmund* Bertram so formal, so pitiful, so younger-brother-like, that I detest it."

"How differently we feel!" cried Fanny. "To me, the sound of *Mr*. Bertram is so cold and nothing-meaning—so entirely without warmth or character!—It just stands for a gentleman, and that's all. But there is nobleness in the name of Edmund. It is a name of heroism and renown—of kings, princes, and knights; and seems to breathe the spirit of chivalry and warm affections."

"I grant you the name is good in itself, and *Lord* Edmund or *Sir* Edmund sound delightfully; but sink it under the chill, the annihilation of a Mr.—and Mr. Edmund is no more than Mr. John or Mr. Thomas. Well, shall we join and disappoint them of half their lecture upon sitting down out of doors at this time of year, by being up before they can begin?"

Edmund met them with particular pleasure. It was the first time of his seeing them together since the beginning of that better acquaintance which he had been hearing of with great satisfaction. A friendship between two so very dear to him was exactly what he could have wished; and to the credit of the lover's understanding be it stated, that he did not by any means consider Fanny as the only, or even as the greater gainer by such a friendship.

"Well," said Miss Crawford, "and do not you scold us for our imprudence? What do you think we have been sitting down for but to be talked to about it, and entreated and supplicated never to do so again?"

"Perhaps I might have scolded," said Edmund, "if either of you had been sitting down alone; but while you do wrong together I can overlook a great deal."

"They cannot have been sitting long," cried Mrs. Grant, "for when I went up for my shawl I saw them from the staircase window, and then they were walking."

"And really," added Edmund, "the day is so mild, that your sitting down for a few minutes can be hardly thought imprudent. Our weather must not always be judged by the Calendar. We may sometimes take greater liberties in November than in May."

"Upon my word," cried Miss Crawford, "you are two of the most disappointing and unfeeling kind friends I ever met with! There is no giving you a moment's uneasiness. You do not know how much we have been suffering, nor what chills we have felt! But I have long thought Mr. Bertram one of the worst subjects to work on, in any little manœuvre against common sense that a woman could be plagued with. I had very little hope of *him* from the first; but you, Mrs. Grant, my sister, my own sister, I think I had a right to alarm you a little."

"Do not flatter yourself, my dearest Mary. You have not the smallest chance of moving me. I have my alarms, but they are quite in a different quarter: and if I could have altered the weather, you would have had a good sharp east wind blowing on you the whole time—for here are some of my plants which Robert *will* leave out because the nights are so mild, and I know the end of it will be that we shall have a sudden change of weather, a hard frost setting in all at once, taking every body (at least Robert) by surprise, and I shall lose every one; and what is worse, cook has just been telling me that the turkey, which I particularly wished not to be dressed till Sunday, because I know how much more Dr. Grant would enjoy it on Sunday after the fatigues of the day, will not keep beyond to-morrow. These are something like grievances, and make me think the weather most unseasonably close."

"The sweets of housekeeping in a country village!" said Miss Crawford archly. "Commend me to the nurseryman and the poulterer."

"My dear child, commend Dr. Grant to the deanery of Westminster or St. Paul's, and I should be as glad of your nurseryman and poulterer as you could be. But we have no such people in Mansfield. What would you have me do?"

"Oh! you can do nothing but what you do already; be plagued very often and never lose your temper."

"Thank you—but there is no escaping these little vexations, Mary, live where we may; and when you are settled in town and I come to see you, I dare say I shall find you with yours, in spite of the nurseryman and the poulterer—or perhaps on their very account. Their remoteness and unpunctuality, or their exorbitant charges and frauds will be drawing forth bitter lamentations."

"I mean to be too rich to lament or to feel any thing of the sort. A large income is the best recipé for happiness I ever heard of. It certainly may secure all the myrtle and turkey part of it."

"You intend to be very rich," said Edmund, with a look which, to Fanny's eye, had a great deal of serious meaning.

"To be sure. Do not you?—Do not we all?"

"I cannot intend any thing which it must be so completely beyond my power to command. Miss Crawford may chuse her degree of wealth. She has only to fix on her number of thousands a year, and there can be no doubt of their coming. My intentions are only not to be poor."

"By moderation and economy, and bringing down your wants to your income, and all that. I understand you—and a very proper plan it is for a person at your time of life, with such limited means and indifferent connections.—What can *you* want but a decent maintenance? You have not much time before you; and your relations are in no situation to do any thing for you, or to mortify you by the contrast of their own wealth and consequence. Be honest and poor, by all means—but I shall not envy you; I do not much think I shall even* respect you. I have a much greater respect for those that are honest and rich."

"Your degree of respect for honesty, rich or poor, is precisely what I have no manner of concern with. I do not mean to be poor. Poverty is exactly what I have determined against. Honesty, in the something between, in the middle state of worldly circumstances, is all that I am anxious for your not looking down on."

"But I do look down upon it, if it might have been higher. I must look down upon any thing contented with obscurity when it might rise to distinction."

"But how may it rise?—How may my honesty at least rise to any distinction?"

This was not so very easy a question to answer, and occasioned an "Oh!" of some length from the fair lady before she could add "You ought to be in parliament, or you should have gone into the army ten years ago."

"*That* is not much to the purpose now; and as to my being in parliament, I believe I must wait till there is an especial assembly for the representation of younger sons who have little to live on. No, Miss Crawford," he added, in a more serious tone, "there *are* distinctions which I should be miserable if I thought myself without any chance—absolutely without chance or possibility of obtaining—but they are of a different character."

A look of consciousness as he spoke, and what seemed a consciousness of manner on Miss Crawford's side as she made some laughing answer, was sorrowful food for Fanny's observation; and finding herself quite unable to attend as she ought to Mrs. Grant, by whose side she was now following the others, she had nearly resolved on going home immediately, and only waited for courage to say so, when the sound of the great clock at Mansfield Park, striking three, made her feel that she had really been much longer absent than usual, and brought the previous self-inquiry of whether she should take leave or not just then, and how, to a very speedy issue. With undoubting decision she directly began her adieus; and Edmund began at the same time to recollect, that his mother had been inquiring for her, and that he had walked down to the Parsonage on purpose to bring her back.

Fanny's hurry increased; and without in the least expecting Edmund's attendance, she would have hastened away alone; but the general pace was quickened, and they all accompanied her into the house through which it was necessary to pass. Dr. Grant was in the vestibule, and as they stopt to speak to him, she found from Edmund's manner that he *did* mean to go with her.—He too was taking leave.—She could not but be thankful.—In the moment of parting, Edmund was invited by Dr. Grant to eat his mutton with him the next day; and Fanny had barely time for an unpleasant feeling on the occasion, when Mrs. Grant, with sudden recollection, turned to her and asked for the pleasure of her company too. This was so new an attention, so perfectly new a circumstance in the events of Fanny's life, that she was all surprize and embarrassment; and while stammering out her great obligation, and her—"but she did not suppose it would be in her power," was looking at Edmund for his opinion and help.—But Edmund, delighted with her having such an happiness offered, and ascertaining with half a look, and half a sentence, that she had no objection but on her aunt's account, could not imagine that his mother would make any difficulty of sparing her, and therefore gave his decided open advice that the invitation should be accepted; and though Fanny would not venture, even on his encouragement, to such a flight of audacious independence, it was soon settled that if nothing were heard to the contrary, Mrs. Grant might expect her.

"And you know what your dinner will be," said Mrs. Grant, smiling—"the turkey—and I assure you a very fine one; for, my dear" —turning to her husband—"cook insists upon the turkey's being dressed to-morrow."

"Very well, very well," cried Dr. Grant, "all the better. I am glad to hear you have any thing so good in the house. But Miss Price and Mr. Edmund Bertram, I dare say, would take their chance. We none of us want to hear the bill of fare. A friendly meeting, and not a fine dinner, is all we have in view. A turkey or a goose, or a leg of mutton, or whatever you and your cook chuse to give us."

The two cousins walked home together; and except in the immediate discussion of this engagement, which Edmund spoke of with the warmest satisfaction, as so particularly desirable for her in the intimacy which he saw with so much pleasure established, it was a silent walk —for having finished that subject, he grew thoughtful and indisposed for any other.

Chapter V.

"But why should Mrs. Grant ask Fanny?" said Lady Bertram. "How came she to think of asking Fanny?—Fanny never dines there, you know, in this sort of way. I cannot spare her, and I am sure she does not want to go.—Fanny, you do not want to go, do you?"

"If you put such a question to her," cried Edmund, preventing his cousin's speaking, "Fanny will immediately say, no; but I am sure, my dear mother, she would like to go; and I can see no reason why she should not."

"I cannot imagine why Mrs. Grant should think of asking her.—She never did before.—She used to ask your sisters now and then, but she never asked Fanny."

"If you cannot do without me, ma'am," said Fanny, in a self-denying tone—

"But my mother will have my father with her all the evening."

"To be sure, so I shall."

"Suppose you take my father's opinion, ma'am."

"That's well thought of. So I will, Edmund. I will ask Sir Thomas, as soon as he comes in, whether I can do without her."

"As you please, ma'am, on that head; but I meant my father's opinion as to the *propriety* of the invitation's being accepted or not; and I think he will consider it a right thing by Mrs. Grant, as well as by Fanny, that being the *first* invitation it should be accepted."

"I do not know. We will ask him. But he will be very much surprised that Mrs. Grant should ask Fanny at all."

There was nothing more to be said, or that could be said to any purpose, till Sir Thomas were present; but the subject involving, as it did, her own evening's comfort for the morrow, was so much uppermost in Lady Bertram's mind, that half an hour afterwards, on his looking in for a minute in his way from his plantation to his dressing-room, she called him back again, when he had almost closed the door, with "Sir Thomas, stop a moment—I have something to say to you."

Her tone of calm languor, for she never took the trouble of raising her voice, was always heard and attended to; and Sir Thomas came back. Her story began; and Fanny immediately slipped out of the room; for to hear herself the subject of any discussion with her uncle, was more than her nerves could bear. She was anxious, she knew—more anxious perhaps than she ought to be—for what was it after all whether she went or staid?—but if her uncle were to be a great while considering and deciding, and with very grave looks, and those grave looks directed to her, and at last decide against her, she might not be able to appear properly submissive and indifferent. Her cause meanwhile went on well. It began, on Lady Bertram's part, with, "I have something to tell you that will surprize you. Mrs. Grant has asked Fanny to dinner!"

"Well," said Sir Thomas, as if waiting more to accomplish the surprize.

"Edmund wants her to go. But how can I spare her?"

"She will be late," said Sir Thomas, taking out his watch, "but what is your difficulty?"

Edmund found himself obliged to speak and fill up the blanks in his mother's story. He told the whole, and she had only to add, "So strange! for Mrs. Grant never used to ask her."

"But is not it very natural," observed Edmund, "that Mrs. Grant should wish to procure so agreeable a visitor for her sister?"

"Nothing can be more natural," said Sir Thomas, after a short deliberation; "nor, were there no sister in the case, could any thing in my opinion be more natural. Mrs. Grant's shewing civility to Miss Price, to Lady Bertram's niece, could never want explanation. The only surprize I can feel is that this should be the *first* time of its being paid. Fanny was perfectly right in giving only a conditional answer. She appears to feel as she ought. But as I conclude that she must wish to go, since all young people like to be together, I can see no reason why she should be denied the indulgence."

"But can I do without her, Sir Thomas?"

"Indeed I think you may."

"She always makes tea, you know, when my sister is not here."

"Your sister perhaps may be prevailed on to spend the day with us, and I shall certainly be at home."

"Very well, then, Fanny may go, Edmund."

The good news soon followed her. Edmund knocked at her door in his way to his own.

"Well, Fanny, it is all happily settled, and without the smallest hesitation on your uncle's side. He had but one opinion. You are to go."

"Thank you, I am *so* glad," was Fanny's instinctive reply; though when she had turned from him and shut the door, she could not help feeling, "And yet, why should I be glad? for am I not certain of seeing or hearing something there to pain me?"

In spite of this conviction, however, she was glad. Simple as such an engagement might appear in other eyes, it had novelty and importance in her's, for excepting the day at Sotherton, she had scarcely ever dined out before; and though now going only half a mile and only to three people, still it was dining out, and all the little interests of preparation were enjoyments in themselves. She had neither sympathy nor assistance from those who ought to have entered into her feelings and directed her taste; for Lady Bertram never thought of being useful to any body, and Mrs. Norris, when she came on the morrow, in consequence

of an early call and invitation from Sir Thomas, was in a very ill humour, and seemed intent only on lessening her niece's pleasure, both
present and future, as much as possible.

"Upon my word, Fanny, you are in high luck to meet with such
attention and indulgence! You ought to be very much obliged to Mrs.
Grant for thinking of you, and to your aunt for letting you go, and you
ought to look upon it as something extraordinary: for I hope you are
aware that there is no real occasion for your going into company in
this sort of way, or ever dining out at all; and it is what you must not
depend upon ever being repeated. Nor must you be fancying, that the
invitation is meant as any particular compliment to *you*; the compliment is intended to your uncle and aunt, and me. Mrs. Grant thinks
it a civility due to *us* to take a little notice of you, or else it would never
have come into her head, and you may be very certain, that if your
cousin Julia had been at home, you would not have been asked at all."

Mrs. Norris had now so ingeniously done away all Mrs. Grant's part
of the favour, that Fanny, who found herself expected to speak, could
only say that she was very much obliged to her aunt Bertram for sparing
her, and that she was endeavouring to put her aunt's evening work in
such a state as to prevent her being missed.

"Oh! depend upon it, your aunt can do very well without you, or
you would not be allowed to go. *I* shall be here, so you may be quite
easy about your aunt. And I hope you will have a very *agreeable* day
and find it all mighty *delightful*. But I must observe, that five is the
very awkwardest of all possible numbers to sit down to table; and I
cannot but be surprized that such an *elegant* lady as Mrs. Grant should
not contrive better! And round their enormous great wide table too,
which fills up the room so dreadfully! Had the Doctor been contented
to take my dining table when I came away, as any body in their senses
would have done, instead of having that absurd new one of his own,
which is wider, literally wider than the dinner table here—how infinitely better it would have been! and how much more he would have
been respected! for people are never respected when they step out of
their proper sphere. Remember *that*, Fanny. Five, only five to be sitting
round that table! However, you will have dinner enough on it for ten
I dare say."

Mrs. Norris fetched breath and went on again.

"The nonsense and folly of people's stepping out of their rank and
trying to appear above themselves, makes me think it right to give *you*
a hint, Fanny, now that you are going into company without any of us;
and I do beseech and intreat you not to be putting yourself forward,
and talking and giving your opinion as if you were one of your
cousins—as if you were dear Mrs. Rushworth or Julia. *That* will never
do, believe me. Remember, wherever* you are, you must be the lowest

and last; and though Miss Crawford is in a manner at home, at the Parsonage, you are not to be taking place of her.[1] And as to coming away at night, you are to stay just as long as Edmund chuses. Leave him to settle *that*."

"Yes, ma'am, I should not think of any thing else."

"And if it should rain, which I think exceedingly likely, for I never saw it more threatening for a wet evening in my life—you must manage as well as you can, and not be expecting the carriage to be sent for you. I certainly do not go home to night, and, therefore, the carriage will not be out on my account; so you must make up your mind to what may happen, and take your things accordingly."

Her niece thought it perfectly reasonable. She rated her own claims to comfort as low even as Mrs. Norris could; and when Sir Thomas, soon afterwards, just opening the door, said, "Fanny, at what time would you have the carriage come round?" she felt a degree of astonishment which made it impossible for her to speak.

"My dear Sir Thomas!" cried Mrs. Norris, red with anger, "Fanny can walk."

"Walk!" repeated Sir Thomas, in a tone of most unanswerable dignity, and coming farther into the room.—"My niece walk to a dinner engagement at this time of the year! Will twenty minutes after four suit you?"

"Yes, sir," was Fanny's humble answer, given with the feelings almost of a criminal towards Mrs. Norris; and not bearing to remain with her in what might seem a state of triumph, she followed her uncle out of the room, having staid behind him only long enough to hear these words spoken in angry agitation:

"Quite unnecessary!—a great deal too kind! But Edmund goes;—true—it is upon Edmund's account. I observed he was hoarse on Thursday night."

But this could not impose on Fanny. She felt that the carriage was for herself and herself alone; and her uncle's consideration of her, coming immediately after such representations from her aunt, cost her some tears of gratitude when she was alone.

The coachman drove round to a minute; another minute brought down the gentleman, and as the lady had, with a most scrupulous fear of being late, been many minutes seated in the drawing room, Sir Thomas saw them off in as good time as his own correctly punctual habits required.

"Now I must look at you, Fanny," said Edmund, with the kind smile of an affectionate brother, "and tell you how I like you; and as well as

---

1. To go before Mary when entering a room. Mrs. Norris is referring to the rules of decorum based on rank. Hosts entered a room with the most important female guest first, and hostesses entered last with the least important.

I can judge by this light, you look very nicely indeed. What have you got on?"

"The new dress that my uncle was so good as to give me on my cousin's marriage. I hope it is not too fine; but I thought I ought to wear it as soon as I could, and that I might not have such another opportunity all the winter. I hope you do not think me too fine."

"A woman can never be too fine while she is all in white. No, I see no finery about you; nothing but what is perfectly proper. Your gown seems very pretty. I like these glossy spots. Has not Miss Crawford a gown something the same?"

In approaching the Parsonage they passed close by the stable-yard and coach-house.—

"Hey day!" said Edmund, "here's company, here's a carriage! who have they got to meet us?" And letting down the side-glass to distinguish, " 'Tis Crawford's, Crawford's barouche, I protest! There are his own two men pushing it back into its old quarters. He is here of course. This is quite a surprise, Fanny. I shall be very glad to see him."

There was no occasion, there was no time for Fanny to say how very differently she felt; but the idea of having such another to observe her, was a great increase of the trepidation with which she performed the very aweful ceremony of walking into the drawing-room.

In the drawing-room Mr. Crawford certainly was; having been just long enough arrived to be ready for dinner; and the smiles and pleased looks of the three others standing round him, shewed how welcome was his sudden resolution of coming to them for a few days on leaving Bath. A very cordial meeting passed between him and Edmund; and with the exception of Fanny, the pleasure was general; and even to *her*, there might be some advantage in his presence, since every addition to the party must rather forward her favourite indulgence of being suffered to sit silent and unattended to. She was soon aware of this herself; for though she must submit, as her own propriety of mind directed, in spite of her aunt Norris's opinion, to being the principal lady in company, and to all the little distinctions consequent thereon, she found, while they were at table, such a happy flow of conversation prevailing in which she was not required to take any part—there was so much to be said between the brother and sister about Bath, so much between the two young men about hunting, so much of politics between Mr. Crawford and Dr. Grant, and of every thing, and all together between Mr. Crawford and Mrs. Grant, as to leave her the fairest prospect of having only to listen in quiet, and of passing a very agreeable day. She could not compliment the newly-arrived gentleman however with any appearance of interest in a scheme for extending his stay at Mansfield, and sending for his hunters from Norfolk, which, suggested by Dr. Grant, advised by Edmund, and warmly urged by the two sisters, was soon in possession of his mind, and which he seemed to want to be encouraged even by her to resolve on. Her opinion was sought as to the probable continuance of the open weather, but her answers were as short and indifferent as civility allowed. She could not wish him to stay, and would much rather not have him speak to her.

Her two absent cousins, especially Maria, were much in her thoughts on seeing him; but no embarrassing remembrance affected *his* spirits. Here he was again on the same ground where all had passed before, and apparently as willing to stay and be happy without the Miss Bertrams, as if he had never known Mansfield in any other state. She heard them spoken of by him only in a general way, till they were all re-assembled in the drawing-room, when Edmund, being engaged apart in some matter of business with Dr. Grant, which seemed entirely to engross them, and Mrs. Grant occupied at the tea-table, he began talking of them with more particularity to his other sister. With a significant smile, which made Fanny quite hate him, he said, "So! Rushworth and his fair bride are at Brighton, I understand—Happy man!"

"Yes, they have been there—about a fortnight, Miss Price, have they not?—And Julia is with them."

"And Mr. Yates, I presume, is not far off."

"Mr. Yates!—Oh! we hear nothing of Mr. Yates. I do not imagine he figures much in the letters to Mansfield Park; do you, Miss Price? —I think my friend Julia knows better than to entertain her father with Mr. Yates."

"Poor Rushworth and his two-and-forty speeches!" continued Crawford. "Nobody can ever forget them. Poor fellow!—I see him now;— his toil and his despair. Well, I am much mistaken if his lovely Maria will ever want him to make two-and-forty speeches to her"—adding, with a momentary seriousness, "She is too good for him—much too good." And then changing his tone again to one of gentle gallantry, and addressing Fanny, he said, "You were Mr. Rushworth's best friend. Your kindness and patience can never be forgotten, your indefatigable patience in trying to make it possible for him to learn his part—in trying to give him a brain which nature had denied—to mix up an understanding for him out of the superfluity of your own! *He* might not have sense enough himself to estimate your kindness, but I may venture to say that it had honour from all the rest of the party."

Fanny coloured, and said nothing.

"It is as a dream, a pleasant dream!" he exclaimed, breaking forth again after few minutes musing. "I shall always look back on our theatricals with exquisite pleasure. There was such an interest, such an animation, such a spirit diffused! Every body felt it. We were all alive. There was employment, hope, solicitude, bustle, for every hour of the day. Always some little objection, some little doubt, some little anxiety to be got over. I never was happier."

With silent indignation, Fanny repeated to herself, "Never happier! —never happier than when doing what you must know was not justifiable!—never happier than when behaving so dishonourably and unfeelingly!—Oh! what a corrupted mind!"

"We were unlucky, Miss Price," he continued in a lower tone, to avoid the possibility of being heard by Edmund, and not at all aware of her feelings, "we certainly were very unlucky. Another week, only one other week, would have been enough for us. I think if we had had the disposal of events—if Mansfield Park had had the government of the winds just for a week or two about the equinox, there would have been a difference. Not that we would have endangered his safety by any tremendous weather—but only by a steady contrary wind, or a calm. I think, Miss Price, we would have indulged ourselves with a week's calm in the Atlantic at that season."

He seemed determined to be answered; and Fanny, averting her face, said with a firmer tone than usual, "As far as *I* am concerned, sir, I would not have delayed his return for a day. My uncle disapproved it all so entirely when he did arrive, that in my opinion, every thing had gone quite far enough."

She had never spoken so much at once to him in her life before, and never so angrily to any one; and when her speech was over, she trembled and blushed at her own daring. He was surprized; but after a few moments silent consideration of her, replied in a calmer, graver tone, and as if the candid result of conviction, "I believe you are right. It was more pleasant than prudent. We were getting too noisy." And then turning the conversation, he would have engaged her on some other subject, but her answers were so shy and reluctant that he could not advance in any.

Miss Crawford, who had been repeatedly eyeing Dr. Grant and Edmund, now observed, "Those gentlemen must have some very interesting point to discuss."

"The most interesting in the world," replied her brother—"how to make money—how to turn a good income into a better. Mr. Grant is giving Bertram instructions about the living he is to step into so soon. I find he takes orders in a few weeks. They were at it in the dining-parlour. I am glad to hear Bertram will be so well off. He will have a very pretty income to make ducks and drakes with, and earned without much trouble. I apprehend he will not have less than seven hundred a year. Seven hundred a year is a fine thing for a younger brother; and as of course he will still live at home, it will be all for his *menus plaisirs*;[2] and a sermon at Christmas and Easter, I suppose, will be the sum total of sacrifice."

His sister tried to laugh off her feelings by saying, "Nothing amuses

2. Pocket money.

me more than the easy manner with which every body settles the abundance of those who have a great deal less than themselves. You would look rather blank, Henry, if your menus plaisirs were to be limited to seven hundred a year."

"Perhaps I might; but all *that* you know is entirely comparative. Birthright and habit must settle the business. Bertram is certainly well off for a cadet[3] of even a Baronet's family. By the time he is four or five-and-twenty he will have seven hundred a year, and nothing to do for it."

Miss Crawford *could* have said that there would be a something to do and to suffer for it, which she could not think lightly of; but she checked herself and let it pass; and tried to look calm and unconcerned when the two gentlemen shortly afterwards joined them.

"Bertram," said Henry Crawford, "I shall make a point of coming to Mansfield to hear you preach your first sermon. I shall come on purpose to encourage a young beginner. When is it to be? Miss Price, will not you join me in encouraging your cousin? Will not you engage to attend with your eyes steadily fixed on him the whole time—as I shall do—not to lose a word; or only looking off just to note down any sentence pre-eminently beautiful? We will provide ourselves with tablets and a pencil. When will it be? You must preach at Mansfield, you know, that Sir Thomas and Lady Bertram may hear you."

"I shall keep clear of you, Crawford, as long as I can," said Edmund, "for you would be more likely to disconcert me, and I should be more sorry to see you trying at it, than almost any other man."

"Will he not feel this?" thought Fanny. "No, he can feel nothing as he ought."

The party being now all united, and the chief talkers attracting each other, she remained in tranquillity; and as a whist table was formed after tea—formed really for the amusement of Dr. Grant, by his attentive wife, though it was not to be supposed so—and Miss Crawford took her harp, she had nothing to do but to listen, and her tranquillity remained undisturbed the rest of the evening, except when Mr. Crawford now and then addressed to her a question or observation, which she could not avoid answering. Miss Crawford was too much vexed by what had passed to be in a humour for any thing but music. With that, she soothed herself and amused her friend.

The assurance of Edmund's being so soon to take orders, coming upon her like a blow that had been suspended, and still hoped uncertain and at a distance, was felt with resentment and mortification. She was very angry with him. She had thought her influence more. She *had* begun to think of him—she felt that she had—with great regard, with almost decided intentions; but she would now meet him with his

3. A younger son.

own cool feelings. It was plain that he could have no serious views, no true attachment, by fixing himself in a situation which he must know she would never stoop to. She would learn to match him in his indifference. She would henceforth admit his attentions without any idea beyond immediate amusement. If *he* could so command his affections, *her's* should do her no harm.

Chapter VI.

Henry Crawford had quite made up his mind by the next morning to give another fortnight to Mansfield, and having sent for his hunters and written a few lines of explanation to the Admiral, he looked round at his sister as he sealed and threw the letter from him, and seeing the coast clear of the rest of the family, said, with a smile, "And how do you think I mean to amuse myself, Mary, on the days that I do not hunt? I am grown too old to go out more than three times a week; but I have a plan for the intermediate days, and what do you think it is?"

"To walk and ride with me, to be sure."

"Not exactly, though I shall be happy to do both, but *that* would be exercise only to my body, and I must take care of my mind. Besides *that* would be all recreation and indulgence, without the wholesome alloy of labour, and I do not like to eat the bread of idleness. No, my plan is to make Fanny Price in love with me."

"Fanny Price! Nonsense! No, no. You ought to be satisfied with her two cousins."

"But I cannot be satisfied without Fanny Price, without making a small hole in Fanny Price's heart. You do not seem properly aware of her claims to notice. When we talked of her last night, you none of you seemed sensible of the wonderful improvement that has taken place in her looks within the last six weeks. You see her every day, and therefore do not notice it, but I assure you, she is quite a different creature from what she was in the autumn. She was then merely a quiet, modest, not plain looking girl, but she is now absolutely pretty. I used to think she had neither complexion nor countenance; but in that soft skin of her's, so frequently tinged with a blush as it was yesterday, there is decided beauty; and from what I observed of her eyes and mouth, I do not despair of their being capable of expression enough when she has any thing to express. And then—her air, her manner, her tout ensemble[1] is so indescribably improved! She most be grown two inches, at least, since October."

"Phoo! phoo! This is only because there were no tall women to compare her with, and because she has got a new gown, and you never

1. Her everything.

saw her so well dressed before. She is just what she was in October, believe me. The truth is, that she was the only girl in company for you to notice, and you must have a somebody. I have always thought her pretty—not strikingly pretty—but 'pretty enough' as people say; a sort of beauty that grows on one. Her eyes should be darker, but she has a sweet smile; but as for this wonderful degree of improvement, I am sure it may all be resolved into a better style of dress and your having nobody else to look at; and therefore, if you do set about a flirtation with her, you never will persuade me that it is in compliment to her beauty, or that it proceeds from any thing but your own idleness and folly."

Her brother gave only a smile to this accusation, and soon afterwards said, "I do not quite know what to make of Miss Fanny. I do not understand her. I could not tell what she would be at yesterday. What is her character?—Is she solemn?—Is she queer?—Is she prudish? Why did she draw back and look so grave at me? I could hardly get her to speak. I never was so long in company with a girl in my life—trying to entertain her—and succeed so ill! Never met with a girl who looked so grave on me! I must try to get the better of this. Her looks say, 'I will not like you, I am determined not to like you,' and I say, she shall.

"Foolish fellow! And so this is her attraction after all! This it is—her not caring about you—which gives her such a soft skin and makes her so much taller, and produces all these charms and graces! I do desire that you will not be making her really unhappy; a *little* love perhaps may animate and do her good, but I will not have you plunge her deep, for she is as good a little creature as ever lived, and has a great deal of feeling."

"It can be but for a fortnight," said Henry, "and if a fortnight can kill her, she must have a constitution which nothing could save. No, I will not do her any harm, dear little soul! I only want her to look kindly on me, to give me smiles as well as blushes, to keep a chair for me by herself wherever we are, and be all animation when I take it and talk to her; to think as I think, be interested in all my possessions and pleasures, try to keep me longer at Mansfield, and feel when I go away that she shall be never happy again. I want nothing more."

"Moderation itself!" said Mary. "I can have no scruples now. Well, you will have opportunities enough of endeavouring to recommend yourself, for we are a great deal together."

And without attempting any further remonstrance, she left Fanny to her fate—a fate which, had not Fanny's heart been guarded in a way unsuspected by Miss Crawford, might have been a little harder than she deserved; for although there doubtless are such unconquerable young ladies of eighteen (or one should not read about them) as are never to be persuaded into love against their judgment by all that talent, manner, attention, and flattery can do, I have no inclination to believe

Fanny one of them, or to think that with so much tenderness of disposition, and so much taste as belonged to her, she could have escaped heart-whole from the courtship (though the courtship only of a fortnight) of such a man as Crawford, in spite of there being some previous ill-opinion of him to be overcome, had not her affection been engaged elsewhere. With all the security which love of another and disesteem of him could give to the peace of mind he was attacking, his continued attentions—continued, but not obtrusive, and adapting themselves more and more to the gentleness and delicacy of her character,—obliged her very soon to dislike him less than formerly. She had by no means forgotten the past, and she thought as ill of him as ever; but she felt his powers; he was entertaining, and his manners were so improved, so polite, so seriously and blamelessly polite, that it was impossible not to be civil to him in return.

A very few days were enough to effect this; and at the end of those few days, circumstances arose which had a tendency rather to forward his views of pleasing her, inasmuch as they gave her a degree of happiness which must dispose her to be pleased with every body. William, her brother, the so long absent and dearly loved brother, was in England again. She had a letter from him herself, a few hurried happy lines, written as the ship came up Channel, and sent into Portsmouth, with the first boat that left the Antwerp, at anchor, in Spithead;[2] and when Crawford walked up with the newspaper in his hand, which he had hoped would bring the first tidings, he found her trembling with joy over this letter, and listening with a glowing, grateful countenance to the kind invitation which her uncle was most collectedly dictating in reply.

It was but the day before, that Crawford had made himself thoroughly master of the subject, or had in fact become at all aware of her having such a brother, or his being in such a ship, but the interest then excited had been very properly lively, determining him on his return to town to apply for information as to the probable period of the Antwerp's return from the Mediterranean, &c.; and the good luck which attended his early examination of ship news, the next morning, seemed the reward of his ingenuity in finding out such a method of pleasing her, as well as of his dutiful attention to the Admiral, in having for many years taken in the paper esteemed to have the earliest naval intelligence. He proved, however, to be too late. All those fine first feelings, of which he had hoped to be the excitor, were already given. But his intention, the kindness of his intention, was thankfully acknowledged—quite thankfully and warmly, for she was elevated beyond the common timidity of her mind by the flow of her love for William.

2. A point at the outer end of the Portsmouth harbor where ships anchored.

This dear William would soon be amongst them. There could be no doubt of his obtaining leave of absence immediately, for he was still only a midshipman; and as his parents, from living on the spot, must already have seen him and be seeing him perhaps daily, his direct holidays might with justice be instantly given to the sister, who had been his best correspondent through a period of seven years, and the uncle who had done most for his support and advancement; and accordingly the reply to her reply, fixing a very early day for his arrival, came as soon as possible; and scarcely ten days had passed since Fanny had been in the agitation of her first dinner visit, when she found herself in an agitation of a higher nature—watching in the hall, in the lobby, on the stairs, for the first sound of the carriage which was to bring her a brother.

It came happily while she was thus waiting; and there being neither ceremony nor fearfulness to delay the moment of meeting, she was with him as he entered the house, and the first minutes of exquisite feeling had no interruption and no witnesses, unless the servants chiefly intent upon opening the proper doors could be called such. This was exactly what Sir Thomas and Edmund had been separately conniving at, as each proved to the other by the sympathetic alacrity with which they both advised Mrs. Norris's continuing where she was, instead of rushing out into the hall as soon as the noises of the arrival reached them.

William and Fanny soon shewed themselves; and Sir Thomas had the pleasure of receiving, in his protégé, certainly a very different person from the one he had equipped seven years ago, but a young man of an open, pleasant countenance, and frank, unstudied, but feeling and respectful manners, and such as confirmed him his friend.

It was long before Fanny could recover from the agitating happiness of such an hour as was formed by the last thirty minutes of expectation and the first of fruition; it was some time even before her happiness could be said to make her happy, before the disappointment inseparable from the alteration of person had vanished, and she could see in him the same William as before, and talk to him, as her heart had been yearning to do, through many a past year. That time, however, did gradually come, forwarded by an affection on his side as warm as her own, and much less incumbered by refinement or self-distrust. She was the first object of his love, but it was a love which his stronger spirits, and bolder temper, made it as natural for him to express as to feel. On the morrow they were walking about together with true enjoyment, and every succeeding morrow renewed a tête-à-tête, which Sir Thomas could not but observe with complacency, even before Edmund had pointed it out to him.

Excepting the moments of peculiar delight, which any marked or unlooked-for instance of Edmund's consideration of her in the last few months had excited, Fanny had never known so much felicity in her life, as in this unchecked, equal, fearless intercourse with the brother and friend, who was opening all his heart to her, telling her all his hopes and fears, plans, and solicitudes respecting that long thought of, dearly earned, and justly valued blessing of promotion—who could give her direct and minute information of the father and mother, brothers and sisters, of whom she very seldom heard—who was interested in all the comforts and all the little hardships of her home, at Mansfield— ready to think of every member of that home as she directed, or differing only by a less scrupulous opinion, and more noisy abuse of their aunt Norris—and with whom (perhaps the dearest indulgence of the whole) all the evil and good of their earliest years could be gone over again, and every former united pain and pleasure retraced with the fondest recollection. An advantage this, a strengthener of love, in which even the conjugal tie is beneath the fraternal. Children of the same family, the same blood, with the same first associations and habits, have some means of enjoyment in their power, which no subsequent connections can supply; and it must be by a long and unnatural estrangement, by a divorce which no subsequent connection can justify, if such precious remains of the earliest attachments are ever entirely outlived. Too often, alas! it is so.—Fraternal love, sometimes almost every thing, is at others worse than nothing. But with William and Fanny Price, it was still a sentiment in all its prime and freshness, wounded by no opposition of interest, cooled by no separate attachment, and feeling the influence of time and absence only in its increase.

An affection so amiable was advancing each in the opinion of all who had hearts to value any thing good. Henry Crawford was as much struck with it as any. He honoured the warm hearted, blunt fondness of the young sailor, which led him to say, with his hand stretched towards Fanny's head, "Do you know, I begin to like that queer fashion already, though when I first heard of such things being done in England I could not believe it, and when Mrs. Brown, and the other women at the Commissioner's, at Gibraltar,[3] appeared in the same trim, I thought they were mad; but Fanny can reconcile me to any thing"—and saw, with lively admiration, the glow of Fanny's cheek, the brightness of her eye, the deep interest, the absorbed attention, while her brother was describing any of the imminent hazards, or terrific scenes, which such a period, at sea, must supply.

It was a picture which Henry Crawford had moral taste enough to value. Fanny's attractions increased—increased two-fold—for the sensibility which beautified her complexion and illumined her countenance,

3. Austen initially wrote "Government House," but then told Cassandra, "I learn from Sir J. Carr that there is no Government House at Gibraltar; I must alter it to the Commissioner's" (*Letters*, January 24, 1813). Austen had just read Sir John Carr's *Descriptive Travels in the Southern and Eastern Parts of Spain* (1811).

was an attraction in itself. He was no longer in doubt of the capabilities of her heart. She had feeling, genuine feeling. It would be something to be loved by such a girl, to excite the first ardours of her young, unsophisticated mind! She interested him more than he had foreseen. A fortnight was not enough. His stay became indefinite.

William was often called on by his uncle to be the talker. His recitals were amusing in themselves to Sir Thomas, but the chief object in seeking them, was to understand the recitor, to know the young man by his histories; and he listened to his clear, simple, spirited details with full satisfaction—seeing in them, the proof of good principles, professional knowledge, energy, courage, and cheerfulness—every thing that could deserve or promise well. Young as he was, William had already seen a great deal. He had been in the Mediterranean—in the West Indies—in the Mediterranean again—had been often taken on shore by the favour of his Captain, and in the course of seven years had known every variety of danger, which sea and war together could offer. With such means in his power he had a right to be listened to; and though Mrs. Norris could fidget about the room, and disturb every body in quest of two needlefulls of thread or a second hand shirt button in the midst of her nephew's account of a shipwreck or an engagement, every body else was attentive; and even Lady Bertram could not hear of such horrors unmoved, or without sometimes lifting her eyes from her work to say, "Dear me! how disagreeable.—I wonder any body can ever go to sea."

To Henry Crawford they gave a different feeling. He longed to have been at sea, and seen and done and suffered as much. His heart was warmed, his fancy fired, and he felt the highest respect for a lad who, before he was twenty, had gone through such bodily hardships, and given such proofs of mind. The glory of heroism, of usefulness, of exertion, of endurance, made his own habits of selfish indulgence appear in shameful contrast; and he wished he had been a William Price, distinguishing himself and working his way to fortune and consequence with so much self-respect and happy ardour, instead of what he was!

The wish was rather eager than lasting. He was roused from the reverie of retrospection and regret produced by it, by some inquiry from Edmund as to his plans for the next day's hunting; and he found it was as well to be a man of fortune at once with horses and grooms at his command. In one respect it was better, as it gave him the means of conferring a kindness where he wished to oblige. With spirits, courage, and curiosity up to any thing, William expressed an inclination to hunt; and Crawford could mount him without the slightest inconvenience to himself, and with only some scruples to obviate in Sir Thomas, who knew better than his nephew the value of such a loan, and some alarms to reason away in Fanny. She feared for William; by no means convinced by all that he could relate of his own horsemanship in various countries, of the scrambling parties in which he had been engaged, the rough horses and mules he had ridden, or his many narrow escapes from dreadful falls, that he was at all equal to the management of a high-fed hunter in an English fox-chase; nor till he returned safe and well, without accident or discredit, could she be reconciled to the risk, or feel any of that obligation to Mr. Crawford for lending the horse which he had fully intended it should produce. When it was proved however to have done William no harm, she could allow it to be a kindness, and even reward the owner with a smile when the animal was one minute tendered to his use again; and the next, with the greatest cordiality, and in a manner not to be resisted, made over to his use entirely so long as he remained in Northamptonshire.

Chapter VII.

The intercourse of the two families was at this period more nearly restored to what it had been in the autumn, than any member of the old intimacy had thought ever likely to be again. The return of Henry Crawford, and the arrival of William Price, had much to do with it, but much was still owing to Sir Thomas's more than toleration of the neighbourly attempts at the Parsonage. His mind, now disengaged from the cares which had pressed on him at first, was at leisure to find the Grants and their young inmates really worth visiting; and though infinitely above scheming or contriving for any the most advantageous matrimonial establishment that could be among the apparent possibilities of any one most dear to him, and disdaining even as a littleness the being quick-sighted on such points, he could not avoid perceiving in a grand and careless way that Mr. Crawford was somewhat distinguishing his niece—nor perhaps refrain (though unconsciously) from giving a more willing assent to invitations on that account.

His readiness, however, in agreeing to dine at the Parsonage, when the general invitation was at last hazarded, after many debates and many doubts as to whether it were worth while, "because Sir Thomas seemed so ill inclined! and Lady Bertram was so indolent!"—proceeded from good breeding and good-will alone, and had nothing to do with Mr. Crawford, but as being one in an agreeable group; for it was in the course of that very visit, that he first began to think, that any one in the habit of such idle observations *would have thought* that Mr. Crawford was the admirer of Fanny Price.

The meeting was generally felt to be a pleasant one, being composed in a good proportion of those who would talk and those who would listen; and the dinner itself was elegant and plentiful, according to the usual style of the Grants, and too much according to the usual habits of all to raise any emotion except in Mrs. Norris, who could never

behold either the wide table or the number of dishes on it with patience, and who did always contrive to experience some evil from the
passing of the servants behind her chair, and to bring away some fresh
conviction of its being impossible among so many dishes but that some
must be cold.

In the evening it was found, according to the predetermination of
Mrs. Grant and her sister, that after making up the Whist table there
would remain sufficient for a round game, and every body being as
perfectly complying and without a choice as on such occasions they
always are, Speculation was decided on almost as soon as Whist;[1] and
Lady Bertram soon found herself in the critical situation of being applied to for her own choice between the games, and being required
either to draw a card for Whist or not. She hesitated. Luckily Sir Thomas was at hand.

"What shall I do, Sir Thomas?—Whist and Speculation; which will
amuse me most?"

Sir Thomas, after a moment's thought, recommended Speculation.
He was a Whist player himself, and perhaps might feel that it would
not much amuse him to have her for a partner.

"Very well," was her ladyship's contented answer—"then Speculation
if you please, Mrs. Grant. I know nothing about it, but Fanny must
teach me."

Here Fanny interposed however with anxious protestations of her
own equal ignorance; she had never played the game nor seen it played
in her life; and Lady Bertram felt a moment's indecision again—but
upon every body's assuring her that nothing could be so easy, that it
was the easiest game on the cards, and Henry Crawford's stepping forward with a most earnest request to be allowed to sit between her
ladyship and Miss Price, and teach them both, it was so settled; and
Sir Thomas, Mrs. Norris, and Dr. and Mrs. Grant, being seated at the
table of prime intellectual state and dignity, the remaining six, under
Miss Crawford's direction, were arranged round the other. It was a fine
arrangement for Henry Crawford, who was close to Fanny, and with
his hands full of business, having two persons'* cards to manage as well
as his own—for though it was impossible for Fanny not to feel herself
mistress of the rules of the game in three minutes, he had yet to inspirit
her play, sharpen her avarice, and harden her heart, which, especially
in any competition with William, was a work of some difficulty; and as

1. Whist is a card game dating from the seventeenth century; regarded as a forerunner to bridge.
The OED defines speculation as "a round game of cards, the chief feature of which is the
buying and selling of trump cards, the player who possesses the highest trump in a round
winning the pool." One of many games of banking and commerce popular in the early
nineteenth century, speculation does not appear in Hoyle's Games until the 1800 edition,
where it is described as "noisy," no doubt because of its raucous bargaining. Sir Thomas
prefers the older and more staid game of whist, but his "business" in Antigua — the sugar
trade — relies extensively on commercial speculation.

for Lady Bertram, he must continue in charge of all her fame and fortune through the whole evening; and if quick enough to keep her from looking at her cards when the deal began, must direct her in whatever was to be done with them to the end of it.

He was in high spirits, doing every thing with happy ease, and pre-eminent in all the lively turns, quick resources, and playful impudence that could do honour to the game; and the round table was altogether a very comfortable contrast to the steady sobriety and orderly silence of the other.

Twice had Sir Thomas inquired into the enjoyment and success of his lady, but in vain; no pause was long enough for the time his measured manner needed; and very little of her state could be known till Mrs. Grant was able, at the end of the first rubber, to go to her and pay her compliments.

"I hope your ladyship is pleased with the game."

"Oh! dear, yes.—Very entertaining indeed. A very odd game. I do not know what it is all about. I am never to see my cards; and Mr. Crawford does all the rest."

"Bertram," said Crawford some time afterwards, taking the opportunity of a little languor in the game, "I have never told you what happened to me yesterday in my ride home." They had been hunting together, and were in the midst of a good run, and at some distance from Mansfield, when his horse being found to have flung a shoe, Henry Crawford had been obliged to give up, and make the best of his way back. "I told you I lost my way after passing that old farm house, with the yew trees, because I can never bear to ask; but I have not told you that, with my usual luck—for I never do wrong without gaining by it—I found myself in due time in the very place which I had a curiosity to see. I was suddenly, upon turning the corner of a steepish downy field, in the midst of a retired little village between gently rising hills; a small stream before me to be forded, a church standing on a sort of knoll to my right—which church was strikingly large and handsome for the place, and not a gentleman or half a gentleman's house to be seen excepting one—to be presumed the Parsonage, within a stone's throw of the said knoll and church. I found myself in short in Thornton Lacey."

"It sounds like it," said Edmund; "but which way did you turn after passing Sewell's farm?"

"I answer no such irrelevant and insidious questions; though were I to answer all that you could put in the course of an hour, you would never be able to prove that it was *not* Thornton Lacey—for such it certainly was."

"You inquired then?"

"No, I never inquire. But I *told* a man mending a hedge that it was Thornton Lacey, and he agreed to it."

"You have a good memory. I had forgotten having ever told you half so much of the place."

Thornton Lacey was the name of his impending living, as Miss Crawford well knew; and her interest in* a negociation for William Price's knave increased.

"Well," continued Edmund, "and how did you like what you saw?"

"Very much indeed. You are a lucky fellow. There will be work for five summers at least before the place is live-able."

"No, no, not so bad as that. The farm-yard must be moved, I grant you; but I am not aware of any thing else. The house is by no means bad, and when the yard is removed, there may be a very tolerable approach to it."

"The farm-yard must be cleared away entirely, and planted up to shut out the blacksmith's shop. The house must be turned to front the east instead of the north—the entrance and principal rooms, I mean, must be on that side, where the view is really very pretty; I am sure it may be done. And *there* must be your approach—through what is at present the garden. You must make* a new garden at what is now the back of the house; which will be giving it the best aspect in the world—sloping to the south-east. The ground seems precisely formed for it. I rode fifty yards up the lane between the church and the house in order to look about me; and saw how it might all be. Nothing can be easier. The meadows beyond what *will be* the garden, as well as what now *is*, sweeping round from the lane I stood in to the north-east, that is, to the principal road through the village, must be all laid together of course; very pretty meadows they are, finely sprinkled with timber. They belong to the living, I suppose. If not, you must purchase them. Then the stream—something must be done with the stream; but I could not quite determine what. I had two or three ideas."

"And I have two or three ideas also," said Edmund, "and one of them is that very little of your plan for Thornton Lacey will ever be put in practice. I must be satisfied with rather less ornament and beauty. I think the house and premises may be made comfortable, and given the air of a gentleman's residence without any very heavy expense, and that must suffice me; and I hope may suffice all who care about me."

Miss Crawford, a little suspicious and resentful of a certain tone of voice and a certain half-look attending the last expression of his hope, made a hasty finish of her dealings with William Price, and securing his knave at an exorbitant rate, exclaimed, "There, I will stake my last like a woman of spirit. No cold prudence for me. I am not born to sit still and do nothing. If I lose the game, it shall not be from not striving for it."

The game was her's, and only did not pay her for what she had given to secure it. Another deal proceeded, and Crawford began again about Thornton Lacey.

"My plan may not be the best possible; I had not many minutes to form it in: but you must do a good deal. The place deserves it, and you will find yourself not satisfied with much less than it is capable of.—(Excuse me, your ladyship must not see your cards. There, let them lie just before you.) The place deserves it, Bertram. You talk of giving it the air of a gentleman's residence. *That* will be done, by the removal of the farm-yard, for, independent of that terrible nuisance, I never saw a house of the kind which had in itself so much the air of a gentleman's residence, so much the look of a something above a mere Parsonage House, above the expenditure of a few hundreds a year. It is not a scrambling collection of low single rooms, with as many roofs as windows—it is not cramped into the vulgar compactness of a square farm-house—it is a solid*, roomy, mansion-like looking house, such as one might suppose a respectable old country family had lived in from generation to generation, through two centuries at least, and were now spending from two to three thousand a year in." Miss Crawford listened, and Edmund agreed to this. "The air of a gentleman's residence, therefore, you cannot but give it, if you do any thing. But it is capable of much more. (Let me see, Mary; Lady Bertram bids a dozen for that queen; no, no, a dozen is more than it is worth. Lady Bertram does *not* bid a dozen. She will have nothing to say to it. Go on, go on.) By some such improvements as I have suggested, (I do not really require you to proceed upon my plan, though by the bye I doubt any body's striking out a better)—you may give it a higher character. You may raise it into a *place*. From being the mere gentleman's residence, it becomes, by judicious improvement, the residence of a man of education, taste, modern manners, good connections. All this may be stamped on it; and that house receive such an air as to make its owner be set down as the great land-holder of the parish, by every creature travelling the road; especially as there is no real squire's house to dispute the point; a circumstance between ourselves to enhance the value of such a situation in point of privilege and independence beyond all calculation. *You* think with me, I hope—(turning with a softened voice to Fanny).— Have you ever seen the place?"

Fanny gave a quick negative, and tried to hide her interest in the subject by an eager attention to her brother, who was driving as hard a bargain and imposing on her as much as he could; but Crawford pursued with "No, no, you must not part with the queen. You have bought her too dearly, and your brother does not offer half her value. No, no, sir, hands off—hands off. Your sister does not part with the queen. She is quite determined. The game will be yours, turning to her again—it will certainly be yours."

"And Fanny had much rather it were William's," said Edmund, smiling at her. "Poor Fanny! not allowed to cheat herself as she wishes!"

"Mr. Bertram," said Miss Crawford, a few minutes afterwards, "you know Henry to be such a capital improver, that you cannot possibly engage in any thing of the sort at Thornton Lacey, without accepting his help. Only think how useful he was at Sotherton! Only think what grand things were produced there by our all going with him one hot day in August to drive about the grounds, and see his genius take fire. There we went, and there we came home again; and what was done there is not to be told!"

Fanny's eyes were turned on Crawford for a moment with an expression more than grave, even reproachful; but on catching his were instantly withdrawn. With something of consciousness he shook his head at his sister, and laughingly replied, "I cannot say there was much done at Sotherton; but it was a hot day, and we were all walking after each other and bewildered." As soon as a general buz gave him shelter, he added, in a low voice directed solely at Fanny, "I should be sorry to have my powers of *planning* judged of by the day at Sotherton. I see things very differently now. Do not think of me as I appeared then."

Sotherton was a word to catch Mrs. Norris, and being just then in the happy leisure which followed securing the odd trick by Sir Thomas's capital play and her own, against Dr. and Mrs. Grant's great hands, she called out in high good-humour, "Sotherton! "Yes, that is a place indeed, and we had a charming day there. William, you are quite out of luck; but the next time you come I hope dear Mr. and Mrs. Rushworth will be at home, and I am sure I can answer for your being kindly received by both. Your cousins are not of a sort to forget their relations, and Mr. Rushworth is a most amiable man. They are at Brighton now, you know—in one of the best houses there, as Mr. Rushworth's fine fortune gives them a right to be. I do not exactly know the distance, but when you get back to Portsmouth, if it is not very far off, you ought to go over and pay your respects to them; and I could send a little parcel by you that I want to get conveyed to your cousins."

"I should be very happy, aunt—but Brighton is almost by Beachey Head;[2] and if I could get so far, I could not expect to be welcome in such a smart place as that—poor scrubby midshipman as I am."

Mrs. Norris was beginning an eager assurance of the affability he might depend on, when she was stopped by Sir Thomas's saying with authority, "I do not advise your going to Brighton, William, as I trust you may soon have more convenient opportunities of meeting, but my daughters would be happy to see their cousins any where; and you will find Mr. Rushworth most sincerely disposed to regard all the connections of our family as his own."

"I would rather find him private secretary to the first Lord than any thing else," was William's only answer, in an under voice, not meant to reach far, and the subject dropped.

2. A chalky and steep headland on the English Channel, close to Brighton.

As yet Sir Thomas had seen nothing to remark in Mr. Crawford's behaviour; but when the Whist table broke up at the end of the second rubber, and leaving Dr. Grant and Mrs. Norris to dispute over their last play, he became a looker-on at the other, he found his niece the object of attentions, or rather of professions of a somewhat pointed character.

Henry Crawford was in the first glow of another scheme about Thornton Lacey, and not being able to catch Edmund's ear, was detailing it to his fair neighbour with a look of considerable earnestness. His scheme was to rent the house himself the following winter, that he might have a home of his own in that neighbourhood; and it was not merely for the use of it in the hunting season, (as he was then telling her,) though *that* consideration had certainly some weight, feeling as he did, that in spite of all Dr. Grant's very great kindness, it was impossible for him and his horses to be accommodated where they now were without material inconvenience; but his attachment to that neighbourhood did not depend upon one amusement or one season of the year: he had set his heart upon having a something there that he could come to at any time, a little homestall[3] at his command where all the holidays of his year might be spent, and he might find himself continuing, improving, and *perfecting* that friendship and intimacy with the Mansfield Park family which was increasing in value to him every day. Sir Thomas heard and was not offended. There was no want of respect in the young man's address; and Fanny's reception of it was so proper and modest, so calm and uninviting, that he had nothing to censure in her. She said little, assented only here and there, and betrayed no inclination either of appropriating any part of the compliment to herself or of strengthening his views in favour of Northamptonshire. Finding by whom he was observed, Henry Crawford addressed himself on the same subject to Sir Thomas, in a more every day tone, but still with feeling.

"I want to be your neighbour, Sir Thomas, as you have perhaps heard me telling Miss Price. May I hope for your acquiescence and for your not influencing your son against such a tenant?"

Sir Thomas, politely bowing, replied—"It is the only way, sir, in which I could *not* wish you established as a permanent neighbour; but I hope, and believe, that Edmund will occupy his own house at Thornton Lacey. Edmund, am I saying too much?"

Edmund, on this appeal, had first to hear what was going on, but on understanding the question, was at no loss for an answer.

"Certainly, sir, I have no idea but of residence.[4] But, Crawford,

3. A homestead.
4. I.e., Edmund will live full-time in his parish. Many clergy—Austen's relations included—held several livings at once to supplement their income, and were not always resident. Nonresidence was an important social issue, debated in Parliament and decried by evangelical reformers. Sir Thomas's "harangue" suggests he is aware of this.

though I refuse you as a tenant, come to me as a friend. Consider the house as half your own every winter, and we will add to the stables on your own improved plan, and with all the improvements of your improved plan that may occur to you this spring."

"We shall be the losers," continued Sir Thomas. "His going, though only eight miles, will be an unwelcome contraction of our family circle; but I should have been deeply mortified, if any son of mine could reconcile himself to doing less. It is perfectly natural that you should not have thought much on the subject, Mr. Crawford. But a parish has wants and claims which can be known only by a clergyman constantly resident, and which no proxy can be capable of satisfying to the same extent. Edmund might, in the common phrase, do the duty of Thornton, that is, he might read prayers and preach, without giving up Mansfield Park; he might ride over, every Sunday, to a house nominally inhabited, and go through divine service; he might be the clergyman of Thornton Lacey every seventh day, for three or four hours, if that would content him. But it will not. He knows that human nature needs more lessons than a weekly sermon can convey, and that if he does not live among his parishioners and prove himself by constant attention their well-wisher and friend, he does very little either for their good or his own."

Mr. Crawford bowed his acquiescence.

"I repeat again," added Sir Thomas, "that Thornton Lacey is the only house in the neighbourhood in which I should *not* be happy to wait on Mr. Crawford as occupier."

Mr. Crawford bowed his thanks.

"Sir Thomas," said Edmund, "undoubtedly understands the duty of a parish priest.—We must hope his son may prove that *he* knows it too."

Whatever effect Sir Thomas's little harangue might really produce on Mr. Crawford, it raised some awkward sensations in two of the others, two of his most attentive listeners, Miss Crawford and Fanny.—One of whom, having never before understood that Thornton was so soon and so completely to be his home, was pondering with downcast eyes on what it would be, *not* to see Edmund every day; and the other, startled from the agreeable fancies she had been previously indulging on the strength of her brother's description, no longer able, in the picture she had been forming of a future Thornton, to shut out the church, sink the clergyman, and see only the respectable, elegant, modernized, and occasional residence of a man of independent fortune— was considering Sir Thomas, with decided ill-will, as the destroyer of all this, and suffering the more from that involuntary forbearance which his character and manner commanded, and from not daring to relieve herself by a single attempt at throwing ridicule on his cause.

All the agreeable of *her* speculation was over for that hour. It was time to have done with cards if sermons prevailed, and she was glad to find it necessary to come to a conclusion and be able to refresh her spirits by a change of place and neighbour*.

The chief of the party were now collected irregularly round the fire, and waiting the final break up. William and Fanny were the most detached. They remained together at the otherwise deserted card-table, talking very comfortably and not thinking of the rest, till some of the rest began to think of them. Henry Crawford's chair was the first to be given a direction towards them, and he sat silently observing them for a few minutes; himself in the meanwhile observed by Sir Thomas, who was standing in chat with Dr. Grant.

"This is the Assembly night," said William. "If I were at Portsmouth, I should be at it perhaps."

"But you do not wish yourself at Portsmouth, William?"

"No, Fanny, that I do not. I shall have enough of Portsmouth, and of dancing too, when I cannot have you. And I do not know that there would be any good in going to the Assembly, for I might not get a partner. The Portsmouth girls turn up their noses at any body who has not a commission. One might as well be nothing as a midshipman. One *is* nothing indeed. You remember the Gregorys; they are grown up amazing fine girls, but they will hardly speak to *me*, because Lucy is courted by a lieutenant."

"Oh! shame, shame!—But never mind it, William. (Her own cheeks in a glow of indignation as she spoke.) It is not worth minding. It is no reflection on *you*; it is no more than what the greatest admirals have all experienced, more or less, in their time. You must think of that; you must try to make up your mind to it as one of the hardships which fall to every sailor's share—like bad weather and hard living—only with this advantage that there will be an end to it, that there will come a time when you will have nothing of that sort to endure. When you are a lieutenant!—only think, William, when you are a lieutenant, how little you will care for any nonsense of this kind."

"I begin to think I shall never be a lieutenant, Fanny. Every body gets made[5] but me."

"Oh! my dear William, do not talk so, do not be so desponding. My uncle says nothing, but I am sure he will do every thing in his power to get you made. He knows, as well as you do, of what consequence it is."

She was checked by the sight of her uncle much nearer to them than she had any suspicion of, and each found it necessary to talk of something else.

"Are you fond of dancing, Fanny?"

"Yes, very;—only I am soon tired."

5. Promoted.

"I should like to go to a ball with you and see you dance. Have you never any balls at Northampton?—I should like to see you dance, and I'd dance with you if you *would*, for nobody would know who I was here, and I should like to be your partner once more. We used to jump about together many a time, did not we? when the hand-organ was in the street? I am a pretty good dancer in my way, but I dare say you are a better."—And turning to his uncle, who was now close to them—"Is not Fanny a very good dancer, sir?"

Fanny, in dismay at such an unprecedented question, did not know which way to look, or how to be prepared for the answer. Some very grave reproof, or at least the coldest expression of indifference must be coming to distress her brother, and sink her to the ground. But, on the contrary, it was no worse than, "I am sorry to say that I am unable to answer your question. I have never seen Fanny dance since she was a little girl; but I trust we shall both think she acquits herself like a gentlewoman when we do see her, which perhaps we may have an opportunity of doing ere long."

"I have had the pleasure of seeing your sister dance, Mr. Price," said Henry Crawford, leaning forward, "and will engage to answer every inquiry which you can make on the subject, to your entire satisfaction. But I believe (seeing Fanny look distressed) it must be at some other time. There is *one* person in company who does not like to have Miss Price spoken of."

True enough, he had once seen Fanny dance; and it was equally true that he would now have answered for her gliding about with quiet, light elegance, and in admirable time, but in fact he could not for the life of him recall what her dancing had been, and rather took it for granted that she had been present than remembered any thing about her.

He passed, however, for an admirer of her dancing; and Sir Thomas, by no means displeased, prolonged the conversation on dancing in general, and was so well engaged in describing the balls of Antigua, and listening to what his nephew could relate of the different modes of dancing which had fallen within his observation, that he had not heard his carriage announced, and was first called to the knowledge of it by the bustle of Mrs. Norris.

"Come, Fanny, Fanny, what are you about? We are going. Do not you see your aunt is going? Quick, quick. I cannot bear to keep good old Wilcox waiting. You should always remember the coachman and horses. My dear Sir Thomas, we have settled it that the carriage should come back for you, and Edmund, and William."

Sir Thomas could not dissent, as it had been his own arrangement, previously communicated to his wife and sister; but *that* seemed forgotten by Mrs. Norris, who must fancy that she settled it all herself.

Fanny's last feeling in the visit was disappointment—for the shawl which Edmund was quietly taking from the servant to bring and put round her shoulders, was seized by Mr. Crawford's quicker hand, and she was obliged to be indebted to his more prominent attention.

Chapter VIII.

William's desire of seeing Fanny dance, made more than a momentary impression on his uncle. The hope of an opportunity, which Sir Thomas had then given, was not given to be thought of no more. He remained steadily inclined to gratify so amiable a feeling—to gratify any body else who might wish to see Fanny dance, and to give pleasure to the young people in general; and having thought the matter over and taken his resolution in quiet independence, the result of it appeared the next morning at breakfast, when, after recalling and commending what his nephew had said, he added, "I do not like, William, that you should leave Northamptonshire without this indulgence. It would give me pleasure to see you both dance. You spoke of the balls at Northampton. Your cousins have occasionally attended them; but they would not altogether suit us now. The fatigue would be too much for your aunt. I believe, we must not think of a Northampton ball. A dance at home would be more eligible, and if"—

"Ah! my dear Sir Thomas," interrupted Mrs. Norris, "I knew what was coming. I knew what you were going to say. If dear Julia were at home, or dearest Mrs. Rushworth at Sotherton, to afford a reason, an occasion for such a thing, you would be tempted to give the young people a dance at Mansfield. I know you would. If *they* were at home to grace the ball, a ball you would have this very Christmas. Thank your uncle, William, thank your uncle."

"My daughters," replied Sir Thomas, gravely interposing, "have their pleasures at Brighton, and I hope are very happy; but the dance which I think of giving at Mansfield, will be for their cousins. Could we be all assembled, our satisfaction would undoubtedly be more complete, but the absence of some is not to debar the others of amusement."

Mrs. Norris had not another word to say. She saw decision in his looks, and her surprize and vexation required some minutes silence to be settled into composure. A ball at such a time! His daughters absent and herself not consulted! There was comfort, however, soon at hand. *She* must be the doer of every thing; Lady Bertram would of course be spared all thought and exertion, and it would all fall upon *her*. She should have to do the honours of the evening, and this reflection quickly restored so much of her good humour as enabled her to join in with the others, before their happiness and thanks were all expressed.

Edmund, William, and Fanny, did, in their different ways, look and speak as much grateful pleasure in the promised ball, as Sir Thomas could desire. Edmund's feelings were for the other two. His father had never conferred a favour or shewn a kindness more to his satisfaction.

Lady Bertram was perfectly quiescent and contented, and had no objections to make. Sir Thomas engaged for its giving her very little trouble, and she assured him, "that she was not at all afraid of the trouble, indeed she could not imagine there would be any."

Mrs. Norris was ready with her suggestions as to the rooms he would think fittest to be used, but found it all prearranged; and when she would have conjectured and hinted about the day, it appeared that the day was settled too. Sir Thomas had been amusing himself with shaping a very complete outline of the business; and as soon as she would listen quietly, could read his list of the families to be invited, from whom he calculated, with all necessary allowance for the shortness of the notice, to collect young people enough to form twelve or fourteen couple; and could detail the considerations which had induced him to fix on the 22d, as the most eligible day. William was required to be at Portsmouth on the 24th; the 22d would therefore be the last day of his visit; but where the days were so few it would be unwise to fix on any earlier. Mrs. Norris was obliged to be satisfied with thinking just the same, and with having been on the point of proposing the 22d herself, as by far the best day for the purpose.

The ball was now a settled thing, and before the evening a proclaimed thing to all whom it concerned. Invitations were sent with dispatch, and many a young lady went to bed that night with her head full of happy cares as well as Fanny.—To her, the cares were sometimes almost beyond the happiness; for young and inexperienced, with small means of choice and no confidence in her own taste—the "how she should be dressed" was a point of painful solicitude; and the almost solitary ornament in her possession, a very pretty amber cross[1] which William had brought her from Sicily, was the greatest distress of all, for she had nothing but a bit of ribbon to fasten it to; and though she had worn it in that manner once, would it be allowable at such a time, in the midst of all the rich ornaments which she supposed all the other young ladies would appear in? And yet not to wear it! William had wanted to buy her a gold chain too, but the purchase had been beyond his means, and therefore not to wear the cross might be mortifying him. These were anxious considerations; enough to sober her spirits even under the prospect of a ball given principally for her gratification.

The preparations meanwhile went on, and Lady Bertram continued to sit on her sofa without any inconvenience from them. She had some extra visits from the housekeeper, and her maid was rather hurried in making up a new dress for her; Sir Thomas gave orders and Mrs. Norris

---

1. R. W. Chapman points out that Austen's sailor brother Charles bought "gold chains & Topaze crosses" for his sisters in 1801; see *Letters*, May 26–27, 1801.

ran about, but all this gave *her* no trouble, and as she had foreseen, "there was in fact no trouble in the business."

Edmund was at this time particularly full of cares; his mind being deeply occupied in the consideration of two important events now at hand, which were to fix his fate in life—ordination and matrimony— events of such a serious character as to make the ball, which would be very quickly followed by one of them, appear of less moment in his eyes than in those of any other person in the house. On the 23d he was going to a friend near Peterborough in the same situation as himself, and they were to receive ordination in the course of the Christmas week. Half his destiny would then be determined—but the other half might not be so very smoothly wooed. His duties would be established, but the wife who was to share, and animate, and reward those duties might yet be unattainable. He knew his own mind, but he was not always perfectly assured of knowing Miss Crawford's. There were points on which they did not quite agree, there were moments in which she did not seem propitious, and though trusting altogether to her affection, so far as to be resolved (almost resolved) on bringing it to a decision within a very short time, as soon as the variety of business before him were* arranged, and he knew what he had to offer her—he had many anxious feelings, many doubting hours as to the result. His conviction of her regard for him was sometimes very strong; he could look back on a long course of encouragement, and she was as perfect in disinterested attachment as in every thing else. But at other times doubt and alarm intermingled with his hopes, and when he thought of her acknowledged disinclination for privacy and retirement, her decided preference of a London life—what could he expect but a determined rejection? unless it were an acceptance even more to be deprecated, demanding such sacrifices of situation and employment on his side as conscience must forbid.

The issue of all depended on one question. Did she love him well enough to forego what had used to be essential points—did she love him well enough to make them no longer essential? And this question, which he was continually repeating to himself, though oftenest answered with a "Yes," had sometimes its "No."

Miss Crawford was soon to leave Mansfield, and on this circumstance the "no" and the "yes" had been very recently in alternation. He had seen her eyes sparkle as she spoke of the dear friend's letter, which claimed a long visit from her in London, and of the kindness of Henry, in engaging to remain where he was till January, that he might convey her thither; he had heard her speak of the pleasure of such a journey with an animation which had "no" in every tone. But this had occurred on the first day of its being settled, within the first hour of the burst of such enjoyment, when nothing but the friends she was to visit, was before her. He had since heard her express herself differently—with other feelings—more chequered feelings; he had heard her tell Mrs. Grant that she should* leave her with regret; that she began to believe neither the friends nor the pleasures she was going to were worth those she left behind; and that though she felt she must go, and knew she should enjoy herself when once away, she was already looking forward to being at Mansfield again. Was there not a "yes" in all this?

With such matters to ponder over, and arrange, and re-arrange, Edmund could not, on his own account, think very much of the evening, which the rest of the family were looking forward to with a more equal degree of strong interest. Independent of his two cousins'* enjoyment in it, the evening was to him of no higher value than any other appointed meeting of the two families might be. In every meeting there was a hope of receiving further confirmation of Miss Crawford's attachment; but the whirl of a ball-room perhaps was not particularly favourable to the excitement or expression of serious feelings. To engage her early for the two first dances, was all the command of individual happiness which he felt in his power, and the only preparation for the ball which he could enter into, in spite of all that was passing around him on the subject, from morning till night.

Thursday was the day of the ball: and on Wednesday morning, Fanny, still unable to satisfy herself, as to what she ought to wear, determined to seek the counsel of the more enlightened, and apply to Mrs. Grant and her sister, whose acknowledged taste would certainly bear her blameless; and as Edmund and William were gone to Northampton, and she had reason to think Mr. Crawford likewise out, she walked down to the Parsonage without much fear of wanting an opportunity for private discussion; and the privacy of such a discussion was a most important part of it to Fanny, being more than half ashamed of her own solicitude.

She met Miss Crawford within a few yards of the Parsonage, just setting out to call on her, and as it seemed to her, that her friend, though obliged to insist on turning back, was unwilling to lose her walk, she explained her business at once and observed that if she would be so kind as to give her opinion, it might be all talked over as well without doors as within. Miss Crawford appeared gratified by the application, and after a moment's thought, urged Fanny's returning with her in a much more cordial manner than before, and proposed their going up into her room, where they might have a comfortable coze,² without disturbing Dr. and Mrs. Grant, who were together in the drawing-room. It was just the plan to suit Fanny; and with a great deal of gratitude on her side for such ready and kind attention, they proceeded in doors and upstairs, and were soon deep in the interesting subject. Miss Crawford,

2. Chat.

pleased with the appeal, gave her all her best judgment and taste, made every thing easy by her suggestions, and tried to make every thing agreeable by her encouragement. The dress being settled in all its grander parts,—"But what shall you have by way of necklace?" said Miss Crawford. "Shall not you wear your brother's cross?" And as she spoke she was undoing a small parcel, which Fanny had observed in her hand when they met. Fanny acknowledged her wishes and doubts on this point; she did not know how either to wear the cross, or to refrain from wearing it. She was answered by having a small trinket-box placed before her, and being requested to chuse from among several gold chains and necklaces. Such had been the parcel with which Miss Crawford was provided, and such the object of her intended visit; and in the kindest manner she now urged Fanny's taking one for the cross and to keep for her sake, saying every thing she could think of to obviate the scruples which were making Fanny start back at first with a look of horror at the proposal.

"You see what a collection I have," said she, "more by half than I ever use or think of. I do not offer them as new. I offer nothing but an old necklace. You must forgive the liberty and oblige me."

Fanny still resisted, and from her heart. The gift was too valuable. But, Miss Crawford persevered, and argued the case with so much affectionate earnestness through all the heads of William and the cross, and the ball, and herself, as to be finally successful. Fanny found herself obliged to yield, that she might not be accused of pride or indifference, or some other littleness; and having with modest reluctance given her consent, proceeded to make the selection. She looked and looked, longing to know which might be least valuable; and was determined in her choice at last, by fancying there was one necklace more frequently placed before her eyes than the rest. It was of gold prettily worked; and though Fanny would have preferred a longer and a plainer chain as more adapted for her purpose, she hoped in fixing on this, to be chusing what Miss Crawford least wished to keep. Miss Crawford smiled her perfect approbation; and hastened to complete the gift by putting the necklace round her and making her see how well it looked. Fanny had not a word to say against its becomingness, and excepting what remained of her scruples, was exceedingly pleased with an acquisition so very apropos. She would rather perhaps have been obliged to some other person. But this was an unworthy feeling. Miss Crawford had anticipated her wants with a kindness which proved her a real friend. "When I wear this necklace I shall always think of you," said she, "and feel how very kind you were."

"You must think of somebody else too when you wear that necklace," replied Miss Crawford. "You must think of Henry, for it was his choice in the first place. He gave it to me, and with the necklace I make over to you all the duty of remembering the original giver. It is to be a family remembrancer. The sister is not to be in your mind without bringing the brother too."

Fanny, in great astonishment and confusion, would have returned the present instantly.[3] To take what had been the gift of another person—of a brother too—impossible!—it must not be!—and with an eagerness and embarrassment quite diverting to her companion, she laid down the necklace again on its cotton, and seemed resolved either to take another or none at all. Miss Crawford thought she had never seen a prettier consciousness. "My dear child," said she laughing, "what are you afraid of? Do you think Henry will claim the necklace as mine, and fancy you did not come honestly by it?—or are you imagining he would be too much flattered by seeing round your lovely throat an ornament which his money purchased three years ago, before he knew there was such a throat in the world?—or perhaps—looking archly—you suspect a confederacy between us, and that what I am now doing is with his knowledge and at his desire?"

With the deepest blushes Fanny protested against such a thought.

"Well then," replied Miss Crawford more seriously but without at all believing her, "to convince me that you suspect no trick, and are as unsuspicious of compliment as I have always found you, take the necklace, and say no more about it. Its being a gift of my brother's need not make the smallest difference in your accepting it, as I assure you it makes none in my willingness to part with it. He is always giving me something or other. I have such innumerable presents from him that it is quite impossible for me to value, or for him to remember half. And as for this necklace, I do not suppose I have worn it six times; it is very pretty—but I never think of it; and though you would be most heartily welcome to any other in my trinket-box, you have happened to fix on the very one which, if I have a choice, I would rather part with and see in your possession than any other. Say no more against it, I entreat you. Such a trifle is not worth half so many words."

Fanny dared not make any further* opposition; and with renewed but less happy thanks accepted the necklace again, for there was an expression in Miss Crawford's eyes which she could not be satisfied with.

It was impossible for her to be insensible of Mr. Crawford's change of manners. She had long seen it. He evidently tried to please her—he was gallant—he was attentive—he was something like what he had been to her cousins: he wanted, she supposed, to cheat her of her tranquillity as he had cheated them; and whether he might not have some concern in this necklace!—She could not be convinced that he had not, for Miss Crawford, complaisant as a sister, was careless as a woman and a friend.

3. Fanny is uneasy because it was not proper for a woman to receive gifts or letters from a gentleman unless they were engaged.

Reflecting and doubting, and feeling that the possession of what she had so much wished for, did not bring much satisfaction, she now walked home again—with a change rather than a diminution of cares since her treading that path before.

Chapter IX.

On reaching home, Fanny went immediately up stairs to deposit this unexpected acquisition, this doubtful good of a necklace, in some favourite box in the east room which held all her smaller treasures; but on opening the door, what was her surprize to find her cousin Edmund there writing at the table! Such a sight having never occurred before, was almost as wonderful as it was welcome.

"Fanny," said he directly, leaving his seat and his pen, and meeting her with something in his hand, "I beg your pardon for being here. I came* to look for you, and after waiting a little while in hope of your coming in, was making use of your inkstand to explain my errand. You will find the beginning of a note to yourself; but I can now speak my business, which is merely to beg your acceptance of this little trifle—a chain for William's cross. You ought to have had it a week ago, but there has been a delay from my brother's not being in town by several days so soon as I expected; and I have only just now received it at Northampton. I hope you will like the chain itself, Fanny. I endeavoured to consult the simplicity of your taste, but at any rate I know you will be kind to my intentions, and consider it, as it really is, a token of the love of one of your oldest friends."

And so saying, he was hurrying away, before Fanny, overpowered by a thousand feelings of pain and pleasure, could attempt to speak; but quickened by one sovereign wish she then called out, "Oh! cousin, stop a moment, pray stop."

He turned back.

"I cannot attempt to thank you," she continued in a very agitated manner, "thanks are out of the question. I feel much more than I can possibly express. Your goodness in thinking of me in such a way is beyond"—

"If this is all you have to say, Fanny," smiling and turning away again—

"No, no, it is not. I want to consult you."

Almost unconsciously she had now undone the parcel he had just put into her hand, and seeing before her, in all the niceness of jeweller's* packing, a plain gold chain perfectly simple and neat, she could not help bursting forth again. "Oh! this is beautiful indeed! this is the very thing, precisely what I wished for! this is the only ornament I have ever had a desire to possess. It will exactly suit my cross. They must

and shall be worn together. It comes too in such an acceptable moment. Oh! cousin, you do not know how acceptable it is."

"My dear Fanny, you feel these things a great deal too much. I am
most happy that you like the chain, and that it should be here in time
for to-morrow: but your thanks are far beyond the occasion. Believe me,
I have no pleasure in the world superior to that of contributing to yours.
No, I can safely say, I have no pleasure so complete, so unalloyed. It
is without a drawback."

Upon such expressions of affection, Fanny could have lived an hour
without saying another word; but Edmund, after waiting a moment,
obliged her to bring down her mind from its heavenly flight by saying,
"But what is it that you want to consult me about?"

It was about the necklace, which she was now most earnestly longing
to return, and hoped to obtain his approbation of her doing. She gave
the history of her recent visit, and now her raptures might well be over,
for Edmund was so struck with the circumstance, so delighted with
what Miss Crawford had done, so gratified by such a coincidence of
conduct between them, that Fanny could not but admit the superior
power of *one* pleasure over his own mind, though it might have its
drawback. It was some time before she could get his attention to her
plan, or any answer to her demand of his opinion; he was in a reverie
of fond reflection, uttering only now and then a few half sentences of
praise; but when he did awake and understand, he was very decided in
opposing what she wished.

"Return the necklace! No, my dear Fanny, upon no account. It
would be mortifying her severely. There can hardly be a more unpleasant sensation than the having any thing returned on our hands, which
we have given with a reasonable hope of its contributing to the comfort
of a friend. Why should she lose a pleasure which she has shewn herself
so deserving of?"

"If it had been given to me in the first instance," said Fanny, "I
should not have thought of returning it; but being her brother's present,
is not it fair to suppose that she would rather not part with it, when it
is not wanted?"

"She must not suppose it not wanted, not acceptable at least; and its
having been originally her brother's gift makes no difference, for as she
was not prevented from offering, nor you from taking it on that account,
it ought not to affect your keeping it. No doubt it is handsomer than
mine, and fitter for a ball-room."

"No, it is not handsomer, not at all handsomer in its way, and for
my purpose not half so fit. The chain will agree with William's cross
beyond all comparison better than the necklace."

"For one night, Fanny, for only one night, if it *be* a sacrifice—I am
sure you will, upon consideration, make that sacrifice rather than give
pain to one who has been so studious of your comfort. Miss Crawford's

attentions to you have been—not more than you were justly entitled
to—I am the last person to think that *could be*—but they have been
invariable; and to be returning them with what must have something
the *air* of ingratitude, though I know it could never have the *meaning*,
is not in your nature I am sure. Wear the necklace, as you are engaged
to do to-morrow evening, and let the chain, which was not ordered
with any reference to the ball, be kept for commoner occasions. This
is my advice. I would not have the shadow of a coolness between the
two whose intimacy I have been observing with the greatest pleasure,
and in whose characters there is so much general resemblance in true
generosity and natural delicacy as to make the few slight differences,
resulting principally from situation, no reasonable hindrance to a perfect friendship. I would not have the shadow of a coolness arise," he
repeated, his voice sinking a little, "between the two dearest objects I
have on earth."

He was gone as he spoke; and Fanny remained to tranquillise herself
as she could. She was one of his two dearest—that must support her.
But the other!—the first! She had never heard him speak so openly
before, and though it told her no more than what she had long perceived, it was a stab;—for it told of his own convictions and views. They
were decided. He would marry Miss Crawford. It was a stab, in spite
of every long-standing expectation; and she was obliged to repeat again
and again that she was one of his two dearest, before the words gave
her any sensation. Could she believe Miss Crawford to deserve him, it
would be—Oh! how different would it be—how far more tolerable! But
he was deceived in her; he gave her merits which she had not; her
faults were what they had ever been, but he saw them no longer. Till
she had shed many tears over this deception, Fanny could not subdue
her agitation; and the dejection which followed could only be relieved
by the influence of fervent prayers for his happiness.

It was her intention, as she felt it to be her duty, to try to overcome
all that was excessive, all that bordered on selfishness in her affection
for Edmund. To call or to fancy it a loss, a disappointment, would be
a presumption; for which she had not words strong enough to satisfy
her own humility. To think of him as Miss Crawford might be justified
in thinking, would in her be insanity. To her, he could be nothing
under any circumstances—nothing dearer than a friend. Why did such
an idea occur to her even enough to be reprobated and forbidden? It
ought not to have touched on the confines of her imagination. She
would endeavour to be rational, and to deserve the right of judging of
Miss Crawford's character and the privilege of true solicitude for him
by a sound intellect and an honest heart.

She had all the heroism of principle, and was determined to do her
duty; but having also many of the feelings of youth and nature, let her
not be much wondered at if, after making all these good resolutions on

the side of self-government, she seized the scrap of paper on which Edmund had begun writing to her, as a treasure beyond all her hopes, and reading with the tenderest emotion these words, "My very dear Fanny, you must do me the favour to accept"—locked it up with the chain, as the dearest part of the gift. It was the only thing approaching to a letter which she had ever received from him; she might never receive another; it was impossible that she ever should receive another so perfectly gratifying in the occasion and the style. Two lines more prized had never fallen from the pen of the most distinguished author—never more completely blessed the researches of the fondest biographer. The enthusiasm of a woman's love is even beyond the biographer's. To her, the hand-writing itself, independent of any thing it may convey, is a blessedness. Never were such characters cut by any other human being, as Edmund's commonest hand-writing gave! This specimen, written in haste as it was, had not a fault; and there was a felicity in the flow of the first four words, in the arrangement of "My very dear Fanny," which she could have looked at for ever.

Having regulated her thoughts and comforted her feelings by this happy mixture of reason and weakness, she was able, in due time, to go down and resume her usual employments near her aunt Bertram, and pay her the usual observances without any apparent want of spirits.

Thursday, predestined to hope and enjoyment, came; and opened with more kindness to Fanny than such self-willed, unmanageable days often volunteer, for soon after breakfast a very friendly note was brought from Mr. Crawford to William stating, that as he found himself obliged to go to London on the morrow for a few days, he could not help trying to procure a companion; and therefore hoped that if William could make up his mind to leave Mansfield half a day earlier than had been proposed, he would accept a place in his carriage. Mr. Crawford meant to be in town by his uncle's accustomary late dinner-hour, and William was invited to dine with him at the Admiral's. The proposal was a very pleasant one to William himself, who enjoyed the idea of travelling post with four horses and such a good humoured agreeable friend; and in likening it to going up with dispatches, was saying at once every thing in favour of its happiness and dignity which his imagination could suggest; and Fanny, from a different motive, was exceedingly pleased: for the original plan was that William should go up by the mail from Northampton the following night which would not have allowed him an hour's rest before he must have got into a Portsmouth coach; and though this offer of Mr. Crawford's would rob her of many hours of his company, she was too happy in having William spared from the fatigue of such a journey, to think of any thing else. Sir Thomas approved of it for another reason. His nephew's introduction to Admiral Crawford might be of service. The Admiral he believed had interest. Upon the whole, it was a very joyous note. Fanny's spirits lived on it half the morning, deriving some accession of pleasure from its writer being himself to go away.

As for the ball so near at hand, she had too many agitations and fears to have half the enjoyment in anticipation which she ought to have had, or must have been supposed to have, by the many young ladies looking forward to the same event in situations more at ease, but under circumstances of less novelty, less interest, less peculiar gratification than would be attributed to her. Miss Price, known only by name to half the people invited, was now to make her first appearance, and must be regarded as the Queen of the evening. Who could be happier than Miss Price? But Miss Price had not been brought up to the trade of *coming out;*[1] and had she known in what light this ball was, in general, considered respecting her, it would very much have lessened her comfort by increasing the fears she already had, of doing wrong and being looked at. To dance without much observation or any extraordinary fatigue, to have strength and partners for about half the evening, to dance a little with Edmund, and not a great deal with Mr. Crawford, to see William enjoy himself, and be able to keep away from her aunt Norris, was the height of her ambition, and seemed to comprehend her greatest possibility of happiness. As these were the best of her hopes, they could not always prevail; and in the course of a long morning, spent principally with her two aunts, she was often under the influence of much less sanguine views. William, determined to make this last day a day of thorough enjoyment, was out snipe shooting; Edmund, she had too much reason to suppose, was at the Parsonage; and left alone to bear the worrying of Mrs. Norris, who was cross because the house-keeper would have her own way with the supper, and whom *she* could not avoid though the house-keeper might, Fanny was worn down at last to think every thing an evil belonging to the ball, and when sent off with a parting worry to dress, moved as languidly towards her own room, and felt as incapable of happiness as if she had been allowed no share in it.

As she walked slowly up stairs she thought of yesterday; it had been about the same hour that she had returned from the Parsonage, and found Edmund in the east room.—"Suppose I were to find him there again to-day!" said she to herself in a fond indulgence of fancy.

"Fanny," said a voice at that moment near her. Starting and looking up, she saw across the lobby she had just reached Edmund himself, standing at the head of a different staircase. He came* towards her. "You look tired and fagged, Fanny. You have been walking too far."

"No, I have not been out at all."

"Then you have had fatigues within doors, which are worse. You had better have gone out."

1. See above, p. 36, n. 2.

Fanny, not liking to complain, found it easiest to make no answer; and though he looked at her with his usual kindness, she believed he had soon ceased to think of her countenance. He did not appear in spirits; something unconnected with her was probably amiss. They proceeded up stairs together, their rooms being on the same floor above.

"I come from Dr. Grant's," said Edmund presently. "You may guess my errand there, Fanny." And he looked so conscious, that Fanny could think but of one errand, which turned her too sick for speech.—"I wished to engage Miss Crawford for the two first dances," was the explanation that followed, and brought Fanny to life again, enabling her, as she found she was expected to speak, to utter something like an inquiry as to the result.

"Yes," he answered, "she is engaged to me; but (with a smile that did not sit easy) she says it is to be the last time that she ever will dance with me. She is not serious. I think, I hope, I am sure she is not serious—but I would rather not hear it.* She never has danced with a clergyman she says, and she never *will*. For my own sake, I could wish there had been no ball just at—I mean not this very week, this very day—to-morrow I leave home."

Fanny struggled for speech, and said, "I am very sorry that any thing has occurred to distress you. This ought to be a day of pleasure. My uncle meant it so."

"Oh! yes, yes, and it will be a day of pleasure. It will all end right. I am only vexed for a moment. In fact, it is not that I consider the ball as ill-timed;—what does it signify? But, Fanny,"—stopping her by taking her hand, and speaking low and seriously, "you know what all this means. You see how it is; and could tell me, perhaps better than I could tell you, how and why I am vexed. Let me talk to you a little. You are a kind, kind listener. I have been pained by her manner this morning, and cannot get the better of it. I know her disposition to be as sweet and faultless as your own, but the influence of her former companions makes her seem, gives to her conversation, to her professed opinions, sometimes a tinge of wrong. She does not *think* evil, but she speaks it—speaks it in playfulness—and though I know it to be playfulness, it grieves me to the soul."

"The effect of education," said Fanny gently.

Edmund could not but agree to it. "Yes, that uncle and aunt! They have injured the finest mind!—for sometimes, Fanny, I own to you, it does appear more than manner; it appears as if the mind itself was tainted."

Fanny imagined this to be an appeal to her judgment, and therefore, after a moment's consideration, said, "If you only want me as a listener, cousin, I will be as useful as I can; but I am not qualified for an adviser. Do not ask advice of *me*. I am not competent."

"You are right, Fanny, to protest against such an office, but you need not be afraid. It is a subject on which I should never ask advice. It is the sort of subject on which it had better never be asked; and few I imagine do ask it, but when they want to be influenced against their conscience. I only want to talk to you."

"One thing more. Excuse the liberty—but take care *how* you talk to me. Do not tell me any thing now, which hereafter you may be sorry for. The time may come—"

The colour rushed into her cheeks as she spoke.

"Dearest Fanny!" cried Edmund, pressing her hand to his lips, with almost as much warmth as if it had been Miss Crawford's, "you are all considerate thought!—But it is unnecessary here. The time will never come. No such time as you allude to will ever come. I begin to think it most improbable; the chances grow less and less. And even if it should—there will be nothing to be remembered by either you or me, that we need be afraid of, for I can never be ashamed of my own scruples; and if they are removed, it must be by changes that will only raise her character the more by the recollection of the faults she once had. You are the only being upon earth to whom I should say what I have said; but you have always known my opinion of her; you can bear me witness, Fanny, that I have never been blinded. How many a time have we talked over her little errors! You need not fear me. I have almost given up every serious idea of her; but I must be a blockhead indeed if, whatever befell me, I could think of your kindness and sympathy without the sincerest gratitude."

He had said enough to shake the experience of eighteen. He had said enough to give Fanny some happier feelings than she had lately known, and with a brighter look, she answered, "Yes, cousin, I am convinced that *you* would be incapable of any thing else, though perhaps some might not. I cannot be afraid of hearing any thing you wish to say. Do not check yourself. Tell me whatever you like."

They were now on the second floor, and the appearance of a house-maid prevented any further conversation. For Fanny's present comfort it was concluded perhaps at the happiest moment; had he been able to talk another five minutes, there is no saying that he might not have talked away all Miss Crawford's faults and his own despondence. But as it was, they parted with looks on his side of grateful affection, and with some very precious sensations on her's. She had felt nothing like it for hours. Since the first joy from Mr. Crawford's note to William had worn away, she had been in a state absolutely their reverse; there had been no comfort around, no hope within her. Now, every thing was smiling. William's good fortune returned again upon her mind, and seemed of greater value than at first. The ball too—such an evening of pleasure before her! It was now a real animation! and she began to dress for it with much of the happy flutter which belongs to a ball. All went well—she did not dislike her own looks; and when she came to the necklaces again, her good fortune seemed complete, for upon trial the one given her by Miss Crawford would by no means go through the ring of the cross. She had, to oblige Edmund, resolved to wear it —but it was too large for the purpose. His therefore must be worn; and having, with delightful feelings, joined the chain and the cross, those memorials of the two most beloved of her heart, those dearest tokens so formed for each other by every thing real and imaginary—and put them round her neck, and seen and felt how full of William and Edmund they were, she was able, without an effort, to resolve on wearing Miss Crawford's necklace too. She acknowledged it to be right. Miss Crawford had a claim; and when it was no longer to encroach on, to interfere with the stronger claims, the truer kindness of another, she could do her justice even with pleasure to herself. The necklace really looked very well; and Fanny left her room at last, comfortably satisfied with herself and all about her.

Her aunt Bertram had recollected her on this occasion, with an unusual degree of wakefulness. It had really occurred to her, unprompted, that Fanny, preparing for a ball, might be glad of better help than the upper housemaid's, and when dressed herself, she actually sent her own maid* to assist her; too late of course to be of any use. Mrs. Chapman had just reached the attic floor, when Miss Price came out of her room completely dressed, and only civilities were necessary—but Fanny felt her aunt's attention almost as much as Lady Bertram or Mrs. Chapman could do themselves.

Chapter X.

Her uncle and both her aunts were in the drawing-room when Fanny went down. To the former she was an interesting object, and he saw with pleasure the general elegance of her appearance and her being in remarkably good looks. The neatness and propriety of her dress was all that he would allow himself to commend in her presence, but upon her leaving the room again soon afterwards, he spoke of her beauty with very decided praise.

"Yes," said Lady Bertram, "she looks very well. I sent Chapman to her."

"Look well! Oh yes," cried Mrs. Norris, "she has good reason to look well with all her advantages: brought up in this family as she has been, with all the benefit of her cousins' manners before her. Only think, my dear Sir Thomas, what extraordinary advantages you and I have been the means of giving her. The very gown you have been taking notice of, is your own generous present to her when dear Mrs. Rushworth married. What would she have been if we had not taken her by the hand?"

Sir Thomas said no more; but when they sat down to table the eyes of the two young men assured him, that the subject might be gently touched again when the ladies withdrew, with more success. Fanny saw that she was approved; and the consciousness of looking well, made her look still better. From a variety of causes she was happy, and she was soon made still happier; for in following her aunts out of the room, Edmund, who was holding open the door, said as she passed him, "You must dance with me, Fanny; you must keep two dances for me; any two that you like, except the first." She had nothing more to wish for. She had hardly ever been in a state so nearly approaching high spirits in her life. Her cousins' former gaiety on the day of a ball was no longer surprizing to her; she felt it to be indeed very charming, and was actually practising her steps about the drawing-room as long as she could be safe from the notice of her aunt Norris, who was entirely taken up at first in fresh arranging and injuring the noble fire which the butler had prepared.

Half an hour followed, that would have been at least languid under any other circumstances, but Fanny's happiness still prevailed. It was but to think of her conversation with Edmund; and what was the restlessness of Mrs. Norris? What were the yawns of Lady Bertram?

The gentlemen joined them; and soon after began the sweet expectation of a carriage, when a general spirit of ease and enjoyment seemed diffused, and they all stood about and talked and laughed, and every moment had its pleasure and its hope. Fanny felt that there must be a struggle in Edmund's cheerfulness, but it was delightful to see the effort so successfully made.

When the carriages were really heard, when the guests began really to assemble, her own gaiety of heart was much subdued; the sight of so many strangers threw her back into herself; and besides the gravity and formality of the first great circle, which the manners of neither Sir Thomas nor Lady Bertram were of a kind to do away, she found herself occasionally called on to endure something worse. She was introduced here and there by her uncle, and forced to be spoken to, and to curtsey, and speak again. This was a hard duty, and she was never summoned to it, without looking at William, as he walked about at his ease in the back ground of the scene, and longing to be with him.

The entrance of the Grants and Crawfords was a favourable epoch. The stiffness of the meeting soon gave way before their popular manners and more diffused intimacies:—little groups were formed and every body grew comfortable. Fanny felt the advantage; and, drawing back from the toils of civility, would have been again most happy, could she have kept her eyes from wandering between Edmund and Mary Crawford. *She* looked all loveliness—and what might not be the end of it? Her own musings were brought to an end on perceiving Mr. Crawford before her, and her thoughts were put into another channel by his engaging her almost instantly for the two first dances. Her happiness on this occasion was very much à-la-mortal, finely chequered. To be secure of a partner at first, was a most essential good—for the moment of beginning was now growing seriously near, and she so little understood her own claims as to think, that if Mr. Crawford had not asked her, she must have been the last to be sought after, and should have received a partner only through a series of inquiry, and bustle, and interference which would have been terrible; but at the same time there was a pointedness in his manner of asking her, which she did not like, and she saw his eye glancing for a moment at her necklace—with a smile—she thought there was a smile—which made her blush and feel wretched. And though there was no second glance to disturb her, though his object seemed then to be only quietly agreeable, she could not get the better of her embarrassment, heightened as it was by the idea of his perceiving it, and had no composure till he turned away to some one else. Then she could gradually rise up to the genuine satisfaction of having a partner, a voluntary partner secured against the dancing began.

When the company were moving into the ball-room she found herself for the first time near Miss Crawford, whose eyes and smiles were immediately and more unequivocally directed as her brother's had been, and who was beginning to speak on the subject, when Fanny, anxious to get the story over, hastened to give the explanation of the second necklace—the real chain. Miss Crawford listened; and all her intended compliments and insinuations to Fanny were forgotten; she felt only one thing; and her eyes, bright as they had been before, shewing they could yet be brighter, she exclaimed with eager pleasure, "Did he? Did Edmund? That was like himself. No other man would have thought of it. I honour him beyond expression." And she looked around as if longing to tell him so. He was not near, he was attending a party of ladies out of the room; and Mrs. Grant coming up to the two girls and taking an arm of each, they followed with the rest.

Fanny's heart sunk, but there was no leisure for thinking long even of Miss Crawford's feelings. They were in the ball-room, the violins were playing, and her mind was in a flutter that forbad its fixing on any thing serious. She must watch the general arrangements and see how every thing was done.

In a few minutes Sir Thomas came to her, and asked if she were engaged; and the "Yes, sir, to Mr. Crawford," was exactly what he had intended to hear. Mr. Crawford was not far off; Sir Thomas brought him to her, saying something which discovered to Fanny, that *she* was to lead the way and open the ball; an idea that had never occurred to her before. Whenever she had thought on the minutiæ of the evening, it had been as a matter of course that Edmund would begin with Miss Crawford, and the impression was so strong, that though *her uncle* spoke the contrary, she could not help an exclamation of surprize, a hint of her unfitness, an entreaty even to be excused. To be urging her opinion against Sir Thomas's, was a proof of the extremity of the case, but such was her horror at the first suggestion, that she could actually look him in the face and say she hoped it might be settled otherwise; in vain however;—Sir Thomas smiled, tried to encourage her, and then looked too serious and said too decidedly—"It must be so, my dear," for her to hazard another word; and she found herself the next moment conducted by Mr. Crawford to the top of the room, and standing there to be joined by the rest of the dancers, couple after couple as they were formed.

She could hardly believe it. To be placed above so many elegant young women! The distinction was too great. It was treating her like her cousins! And her thoughts flew to those absent cousins with most unfeigned and truly tender regret, that they were not at home to take their own place in the room, and have their share of a pleasure which would have been so very delightful to them. So often as she had heard them wish for a ball at home as the greatest of all felicities! And to have them away when it was given—and for *her* to be opening the ball—and with Mr. Crawford too! She hoped they would not envy her that distinction *now*; but when she looked back to the state of things in the autumn, to what they had all been to each other when once dancing in that house before, the present arrangement was almost more than she could understand herself.

The ball began. It was rather honour than* happiness to Fanny, for the first dance at least; her partner was in excellent spirits and tried to impart them to her, but she was a great deal too much frightened to have any enjoyment, till she could suppose herself no longer looked at. Young, pretty, and gentle, however, she had no awkwardnesses that were not as good as graces, and there were few persons present that were not disposed to praise her. She was attractive, she was modest, she was Sir Thomas's niece, and she was soon said to be admired by Mr. Crawford. It was enough to give her general favour. Sir Thomas himself was watching her progress down the dance with much complacency; he was proud of his niece, and without attributing all her personal beauty, as Mrs. Norris seemed to do, to her transplantation to Mansfield, he was pleased with himself for having supplied every thing else; —education and manners she owed to him.

Miss Crawford saw much of Sir Thomas's thoughts as he stood, and having, in spite of all his wrongs towards her, a general* prevailing desire of recommending herself to him, took an opportunity of stepping aside to say something agreeable of Fanny. Her praise was warm, and he received it as she could wish, joining in it as far as discretion, and politeness, and slowness of speech would allow, and certainly appearing to greater advantage on the subject, than his lady did, soon afterwards, when Mary, perceiving her on a sofa very near, turned round before she began to* dance, to compliment her on Miss Price's looks.

"Yes, she does look very well," was Lady Bertram's placid reply. "Chapman helped her dress. I sent Chapman to her." Not but that she was really pleased to have Fanny admired; but she was so much more struck with her own kindness in sending Chapman to her, that she could not get it out of her head.

Miss Crawford knew Mrs. Norris too well to think of gratifying *her* by commendation of Fanny; to her, it was as the occasion offered.— "Ah!* ma'am, how much we want dear Mrs. Rushworth and Julia to night!" and Mrs. Norris paid her with as many smiles and courteous words as she had time for, amid so much occupation as she found for herself, in making up card-tables, giving hints to Sir Thomas, and trying to move all the chaperons to a better part of the room.

Miss Crawford blundered most towards Fanny herself, in her intentions to please. She meant to be giving her little heart a happy flutter, and filling her with sensations of delightful self-consequence; and misinterpreting Fanny's blushes, still thought she must be doing so—when she went to her after the two first dances and said, with a significant look, "perhaps *you* can tell me why my brother goes to town to-morrow. He says, he has business there, but will not tell me what. The first time he ever denied me his confidence! But this is what we all come to. All are supplanted sooner or later. Now, I must apply to you for information. Pray what is Henry going for?"

Fanny protested her ignorance as steadily as her embarrassment allowed.

"Well, then," replied Miss Crawford laughing, "I must suppose it to be purely for the pleasure of conveying your brother and talking of you by the way."

Fanny was confused, but it was the confusion of discontent; while Miss Crawford wondered she did not smile, and thought her overanxious, or thought her odd, or thought her any thing rather than insensible of pleasure in Henry's attentions. Fanny had a good deal of enjoyment in the course of the evening—but Henry's attentions had very little to do with it. She would much rather *not* have been asked by him again so very soon, and she wished she had not been obliged to suspect that his previous inquiries of Mrs. Norris, about the supper-hour, were all for the sake of securing her at that part of the evening. But it was not to be avoided; he made her feel that she was the object of all; though she could not say that it was unpleasantly done, that there was indelicacy or ostentation in his manner—and sometimes, when he talked of William, he was really not un-agreeable, and shewed even a warmth of heart which did him credit. But still his attentions made no part of her satisfaction. She was happy whenever she looked at William, and saw how perfectly he was enjoying himself, in every five minutes that she could walk about with him and hear his account of his partners; she was happy in knowing herself admired, and she was happy in having the two dances with Edmund still to look forward to, during the greatest part of the evening, her hand being so eagerly sought after, that her indefinite engagement with *him* was in continual perspective. She was happy even when they did take place; but not from any flow of spirits on his side, or any such expressions of tender gallantry as had blessed the morning. His mind was fagged, and her happiness sprung from being the friend with whom it could find repose. "I am worn out with civility," said he. "I have been talking incessantly all night, and with nothing to say. But with *you*, Fanny, there may be peace. You will not want to be talked to. Let us have the luxury of silence." Fanny would hardly even speak her agreement. A weariness arising probably, in great measure, from the same feelings which he had acknowledged in the morning, was peculiarly to be respected, and they went down their two dances together with such sober tranquility as might satisfy any looker-on, that Sir Thomas had been bringing up no wife for his younger son.

The evening had afforded Edmund little pleasure. Miss Crawford had been in gay spirits when they first danced together, but it was not her gaiety that could do him good; it rather sank than raised his comfort; and afterwards—for he found himself still impelled to seek her again, she had absolutely pained him by her manner of speaking of the profession to which he was now on the point of belonging. They had talked—and they had been silent—he had reasoned—she had ridiculed—and they had parted at last with mutual vexation. Fanny, not able to refrain entirely from observing them, had seen enough to be tolerably satisfied. It was barbarous to be happy when Edmund was suffering. Yet some happiness must and would arise, from the very conviction, that he did suffer.

When her two dances with him were over, her inclination and strength for more were pretty well at an end; and Sir Thomas having seen her rather walk than dance down the shortening set, breathless and with her hand at her side, gave his orders for her sitting down entirely. From that time, Mr. Crawford sat down likewise.

"Poor Fanny!" cried William, coming for a moment to visit her and working away his partner's fan as if for life:—"how soon she is knocked up! Why, the sport is but just begun. I hope we shall keep it up these two hours. How can you be tired so soon?"

"So soon! my good friend," said Sir Thomas, producing his watch with all necessary caution—"it is three o'clock, and your sister is not used to these sort of hours."

"Well then, Fanny, you shall not get up to-morrow before I go. Sleep as long as you can and never mind me."

"Oh! William."

"What! Did she think of being up before you set off?"

"Oh! yes, sir," cried Fanny, rising eagerly from her seat to be nearer her uncle, "I must get up and breakfast with him. It will be the last time you know, the last morning."

"You had better not.—He is to have breakfasted and be gone by half past nine.—Mr. Crawford, I think you call for him at half past nine?"

Fanny was too urgent, however, and had too many tears in her eyes for denial; and it ended in a gracious, "Well, well," which was permission.

"Yes, half past nine," said Crawford to William, as the latter was leaving them, "and I shall be punctual, for there will be no kind sister to get up for *me*." And in a lower tone to Fanny, "I shall have only a desolate house to hurry from. Your brother will find my ideas of time and his own very different to-morrow."

After a short consideration, Sir Thomas asked Crawford to join the early breakfast party in that house instead of eating alone; he should himself be of it; and the readiness with which his invitation was accepted, convinced him that the suspicions whence, he must confess to himself, this very ball had in great measure sprung, were well founded. Mr. Crawford was in love with Fanny. He had a pleasing anticipation of what would be. His niece, meanwhile, did not thank him for what he had just done. She had hoped to have William all to herself, the last morning. It would have been an unspeakable indulgence. But though her wishes were overthrown there was no spirit of murmuring within her. On the contrary, she was so totally unused to have her pleasure consulted, or to have any thing take place at all in the way she could desire, that she was more disposed to wonder and rejoice in having carried her point so far, than to repine at the counteraction which followed.

Shortly afterwards, Sir Thomas was again interfering a little with her inclination, by advising her to go immediately to bed. "Advise" was his word, but it was the advice of absolute power, and she had only to rise and, with Mr. Crawford's very cordial adieus, pass quietly away; stopping at the entrance door, like the Lady of Branxholm Hall, "one moment and no more,"[1] to view the happy scene, and take a last look at the five or six determined couple, who were still hard at work—and then, creeping slowly up the principal staircase, pursued by the ceaseless country-dance, feverish with hopes and fears, soup and negus,[2] sorefooted and fatigued, restless and agitated, yet feeling, in spite of every thing, that a ball was indeed delightful.

In thus sending her away, Sir Thomas perhaps might not be thinking merely of her health. It might occur to him, that Mr. Crawford had

---

1. Fanny is again thinking of Scott's *Lay of the Last Minstrel*: "The lady forgot her purpose high, / One moment and no more; / One moment gaz'd with a mother's eye, / As she paused at the arched door; / Then from amid the armed train / She call'd to her William of Deloraine" (1.20).
2. A hot, sweet drink, made of wine, water, and spices.

been sitting by her long enough, or he might mean to recommend her as a wife by shewing her persuadableness.

Chapter XI.

The ball was over—and the breakfast was soon over too; the last kiss was given, and William was gone. Mr. Crawford had, as he foretold, been very punctual, and short and pleasant had been the meal.

After seeing William to the last moment, Fanny walked back into the breakfast-room with a very saddened heart to grieve over the melancholy change; and there her uncle kindly left her to cry in peace, conceiving perhaps that the deserted chair of each young man might exercise her tender enthusiasm, and that the remaining cold pork bones and mustard in William's plate, might but divide her feelings with the broken egg-shells in Mr. Crawford's. She sat and cried *con amore* as her uncle intended, but it was con amore fraternal and no other. William was gone, and she now felt as if she had wasted half his visit in idle cares and selfish solicitudes unconnected with him.

Fanny's disposition was such that she could never even think of her aunt Norris in the meagreness and cheerlessness of her own small house, without reproaching herself for some little want of attention to her when they had been last together; much less could her feelings acquit her of having done and said and thought every thing by William, that was due to him for a whole fortnight.

It was a heavy, melancholy day.—Soon after the second breakfast, Edmund bad them good bye for a week, and mounted his horse for Peterborough, and then all were gone. Nothing remained of last night but remembrances, which she had nobody to share in. She talked to her aunt Bertram—she must talk to somebody of the ball, but her aunt had seen so little of what passed, and had so little curiosity, that it was heavy work. Lady Bertram was not certain of any body's dress, or any body's place at supper, but her own. "She could not recollect what it was that she had heard about one of the Miss Maddoxes*, or what it was that Lady Prescott had noticed in Fanny; she was not sure whether Colonel Harrison had been talking of Mr. Crawford or of William, when he said he was the finest young man in the room; somebody had whispered something to her, she had forgot to ask Sir Thomas what it could be." And these were her longest speeches and clearest communications; the rest was only a languid "Yes—yes—very well—did you? did he?—I did not see *that*—I should not know one from the other." This was very bad. It was only better than Mrs. Norris's sharp answers would have been; but she being gone home with all the supernumerary jellies to nurse a sick maid, there was peace and good humour in their little party, though it could not boast much beside.

The evening was heavy like the day—"I cannot think what is the matter with me!" said Lady Bertram, when the tea-things were removed. "I feel quite stupid. It must be sitting up so late last night. Fanny, you must do something to keep me awake. I cannot work. Fetch the cards,—I feel so very stupid."

The cards were brought, and Fanny played at cribbage with her aunt till bed-time; and as Sir Thomas was reading to himself, no sounds were heard in the room for the next two hours beyond the reckonings of the game—"And *that* makes thirty-one;—four in hand and eight in crib.—You are to deal, ma'am; shall I deal for you?" Fanny thought and thought again of the difference which twenty-four hours had made in that room, and all that part of the house. Last night it had been hope and smiles, bustle and motion, noise and brilliancy in the drawing-room, and out of the drawing room, and every where. Now it was languor, and all but solitude.

A good night's rest improved her spirits. She could think of William the next day more cheerfully, and as the morning afforded her an opportunity of talking over Thursday night with Mrs. Grant and Miss Crawford, in a very handsome style, with all the heightenings of imagination and all the laughs of playfulness which are so essential to the shade of a departed ball, she could afterwards bring her mind without much effort into its everyday state, and easily conform to the tranquillity of the present quiet week.

They were indeed a smaller party than she had ever known there for a whole day together, and *he* was gone on whom the comfort and cheerfulness of every family-meeting and every meal chiefly depended. But this must be learned to be endured. He would soon be always gone; and she was thankful that she could now sit in the same room with her uncle, hear his voice, receive his questions, and even answer them without such wretched feelings as she had formerly known.

"We miss our two young men," was Sir Thomas's observation on both the first and second day, as they formed their very reduced circle after dinner; and in consideration of Fanny's swimming eyes, nothing more was said on the first day than to drink their good health; but on the second it led to something farther. William was kindly commended and his promotion hoped for. "And there is no reason to suppose," added Sir Thomas, "but that his visits to us may now be tolerably frequent. As to Edmund, we must learn to do without him. This will be the last winter of his belonging to us, as he has done." "Yes," said Lady Bertram, "but I wish he was not going away. They are all going away I think. I wish they would stay at home."

This wish was levelled principally at Julia, who had just applied for permission to go to town with Maria; and as Sir Thomas thought it best for each daughter that the permission should be granted, Lady Bertram, though in her own good nature she would not have prevented it, was lamenting the change it made in the prospect of Julia's return, which would otherwise have taken place about this time. A great deal of good sense followed on Sir Thomas's side, tending to reconcile his wife to the arrangement. Every thing that a considerate parent *ought* to feel was advanced for her use; and every thing that an affectionate mother *must* feel in promoting her children's enjoyment, was attributed to her nature. Lady Bertram agreed to it all with a calm "Yes"—and at the end of a quarter of an hour's silent consideration, spontaneously observed, "Sir Thomas, I have been thinking—and I am very glad we took Fanny as we did, for now the others are away, we feel the good of it."

Sir Thomas immediately improved this compliment by adding, "Very true. We shew Fanny what a good girl we think her by praising her to her face—she is now a very valuable companion. If we have been kind to *her*, she is now quite as necessary to *us*."

"Yes," said Lady Bertram presently—"and it is a comfort to think that we shall always have *her*."

Sir Thomas paused, half smiled, glanced at his niece, and then gravely replied, "She will never leave us, I hope, till invited to some other home that may reasonably promise her greater happiness than she knows here."

"And *that* is not very likely to be, Sir Thomas. Who should invite her? Maria might be very glad to see her at Sotherton now and then, but she would not think of asking her to live there—and I am sure she is better off here—and besides I cannot do without her."

The week which passed so quietly and peaceably at the great house in Mansfield, had a very different character at the Parsonage. To the young lady at least in each family, it brought very different feelings. What was tranquillity and comfort to Fanny was tediousness and vexation to Mary. Something arose from difference of disposition and habit—one so easily satisfied, the other so unused to endure; but still more might be imputed to difference of circumstances. In some points of interest they were exactly opposed to each other. To Fanny's mind, Edmund's absence was really in its cause and its tendency a relief. To Mary it was every way painful. She felt the want of his society every day, almost every hour; and was too much in want of it to derive any thing but irritation from considering the object for which he went. He could not have devised any thing more likely to raise his consequence than this week's absence, occurring as it did at the very time of her brother's going away, of William Price's going too, and completing the sort of general break-up of a party which had been so animated. She felt it keenly. They were now a miserable trio, confined within doors by a series of rain and snow, with nothing to do and no variety to hope for. Angry as she was with Edmund for adhering to his own notions and acting on them in defiance of her, (and she had been so angry that they had hardly parted friends at the ball,) she could not help thinking of him continually when absent, dwelling on his merit and affection, and longing again for the almost daily meetings they lately had. His absence was unnecessarily long. He should not have planned such an absence—he should not have left home for a week, when her own departure from Mansfield was so near. Then she began to blame herself. She wished she had not spoken so warmly in their last conversation. She was afraid she had used some strong—some contemptuous expressions in speaking of the clergy, and *that* should not have been. It was ill-bred—it was wrong. She wished such words unsaid with all her heart.

Her vexation did not end with the week. All this was bad, but she had still more to feel when Friday came round again and brought no Edmund—when Saturday came and still no Edmund—and when, through the slight communication with the other family which Sunday produced, she learnt that he had actually written home to defer his return, having promised to remain some days longer with his friend!

If she had felt impatience and regret before—if she had been sorry for what she said, and feared its too strong effect on him, she now felt and feared it all tenfold more. She had, moreover, to contend with one disagreeable emotion entirely new to her—jealousy. His friend Mr. Owen had sisters—He might find them attractive. But at any rate his staying away at a time, when, according to all preceding plans, she was to remove to London, meant something that she could not bear. Had Henry returned, as he talked of doing, at the end of three or four days, she should now have been leaving Mansfield. It became absolutely necessary for her to get to Fanny and try to learn something more. She could not live any longer in such solitary wretchedness; and she made her way to the Park, through difficulties of walking which she had deemed unconquerable a week before, for the chance of hearing a little in addition, for the sake of at least hearing his name.

The first half hour was lost, for Fanny and Lady Bertram were together, and unless she had Fanny to herself she could hope for nothing. But at last Lady Bertram left the room—and then almost immediately Miss Crawford thus began, with a voice as well regulated as she could—"And how do *you* like your cousin Edmund's staying away so long?—Being the only young person at home, I consider *you* as the greatest sufferer.—You must miss him. Does his staying longer surprize you?"

"I do not know," said Fanny hesitatingly.—"Yes—I had not particularly expected it."

"Perhaps he will always stay longer than he talks of. It is the general way all young men do*."

"He did not, the only time he went to see Mr. Owen before."

"He finds the house more agreeable *now*.—He is a very—a very pleasing young man himself, and I cannot help being rather concerned at not seeing him again before I go to London, as will now undoubtedly be the case.—I am looking for Henry every day, and as soon as he comes there will be nothing to detain me at Mansfield. I should like to have seen him once more, I confess. But you must give my compliments to him. Yes—I think it must be compliments. Is not there a something wanted, Miss Price, in our language—a something between compliments and—and love—to suit the sort of friendly acquaintance we have had together?—So many months acquaintance!—But compliments may be sufficient here.—Was his letter a long one?—Does he give you much account of what he is doing?—Is it Christmas gaieties that he is staying for?"

"I only heard a part of the letter; it was to my uncle—but I believe it was very short; indeed I am sure it was but a few lines. All that I heard was that his friend had pressed him to stay longer, and that he had agreed to do so. A *few* days longer, or *some* days longer, I am not quite sure which."

"Oh! if he wrote to his father—But I thought it might have been to Lady Bertram or you. But if he wrote to his father, no wonder he was concise. Who could write chat to Sir Thomas? If he had written to you, there would have been more particulars. You would have heard of balls and parties.—He would have sent you a description of every thing and every body. How many Miss Owens are there?"

"Three grown up."

"Are they musical?"

"I do not at all know. I never heard."

"That is the first question, you know," said Miss Crawford, trying to appear gay and unconcerned, "which every woman who plays herself is sure to ask about another. But it is very foolish to ask questions about any young ladies—about any three sisters just grown up; for one knows, without being told, exactly what they are—all very accomplished and pleasing, and *one* very pretty. There is a beauty in every family.—It is a regular thing. Two play on the piano-forte, and one on the harp—and all sing—or would sing if they were taught—or sing all the better for not being taught—or something like it."

"I know nothing of the Miss Owens," said Fanny calmly.

"You know nothing and you care less, as people say. Never did tone express indifference plainer. Indeed how can one care for those one has never seen?—Well, when your cousin comes back, he will find Mansfield very quiet;—all the noisy ones gone, your brother and mine and myself. I do not like the idea of leaving Mrs. Grant now the time draws near. She does not like my going."

Fanny felt obliged to speak. "You cannot doubt your being missed by many," said she. "You will be very much missed."

Miss Crawford turned her eye on her, as if wanting to hear or see more, and then laughingly said, "Oh! yes, missed as every noisy evil is missed when it is taken away; that is, there is a great difference felt. But I am not fishing; don't compliment me. If I *am* missed, it will appear. I may be discovered by those who want to see me. I shall not be in any doubtful, or distant, or unapproachable region."

Now Fanny could not bring herself to speak, and Miss Crawford was disappointed; for she had hoped to hear some pleasant assurance of her power, from one who she thought must know; and her spirits were clouded again.

"The Miss Owens," said she soon afterwards—"Suppose you were to have one of the Miss Owens settled at Thornton Lacey; how should you like it? Stranger things have happened. I dare say they are trying for it. And they are quite in the right, for it would be a very pretty establishment for them. I do not at all wonder or blame them.—It is every body's duty to do as well for themselves as they can. Sir Thomas Bertram's son is somebody; and now, he is in their own line. Their father is a clergyman and their brother is a clergyman, and they are all clergymen together. He is their lawful property, he fairly belongs to them. You don't speak, Fanny—Miss Price—you don't speak.—But honestly now, do not you rather expect it than otherwise?"

"No," said Fanny stoutly, "I do not expect it at all*."

"Not at all!"—cried Miss Crawford with alacrity. "I wonder at that. But I dare say you know exactly—I always imagine you are—perhaps you do not think him likely to marry at all—or not at present."

"No, I do not," said Fanny softly—hoping she did not err either in the belief or the acknowledgment of it.

Her companion looked at her keenly; and gathering greater spirit from the blush soon produced from such a look, only said, "He is best off as he is," and turned the subject.

Chapter XII.

Miss Crawford's uneasiness was much lightened by this conversation, and she walked home again in spirits which might have defied almost another week of the same small party in the same bad weather, had they been put to the proof; but as that very evening brought her brother down from London again in quite, or more than quite, his usual cheerfulness, she had nothing further to try her own. His still refusing to tell her what he had gone for, was but the promotion of gaiety; a day before it might have irritated, but now it was a pleasant joke—suspected only of concealing something planned as a pleasant surprize to herself. And the next day *did* bring a surprize to her. Henry had said he should just go and ask the Bertrams how they did, and be back in ten minutes— but he was gone above an hour; and when his sister, who had been waiting for him to walk with her in the garden, met him at last most impatiently in the sweep, and cried out, "My dear Henry, where can you possibly have been all this time?" he had only to say that he had been sitting with Lady Bertram and Fanny.

"Sitting with them an hour and half!" exclaimed Mary.

But this was only the beginning of her surprize.

"Yes, Mary," said he, drawing her arm within his, and walking along the sweep as if not knowing where he was—"I could not get away sooner—Fanny looked so lovely!—I am quite determined, Mary. My mind is entirely made up. Will it astonish you? No—You must be aware that I am quite determined to marry Fanny Price."

The surprize was now complete; for in spite of whatever his consciousness might suggest, a suspicion of his having any such views had never entered his sister's imagination; and she looked so truly the astonishment she felt, that he was obliged to repeat what he had said, and more fully and more solemnly. The conviction of his determination once admitted, it was not unwelcome. There was even pleasure with the surprize. Mary was in a state of mind to rejoice in a connection with the Bertram family, and to be not displeased with her brother's marrying a little beneath him.

"Yes, Mary," was Henry's concluding assurance. "I am fairly caught. You know with what idle designs I began—but this is the end of them. I have (I flatter myself) made no inconsiderable progress in her affections; but my own are entirely fixed."

"Lucky, lucky girl!" cried Mary as soon as she could speak—"what a match for her! My dearest Henry, this must be my *first* feeling; but my *second*, which you shall have as sincerely, is that I approve your choice from my soul, and foresee your happiness as heartily as I wish and desire it. You will have a sweet little wife; all gratitude and devotion. Exactly what you deserve. What an amazing match for her! Mrs. Norris often talks of her luck; what will she say now? The delight of all the family indeed! And she has some *true* friends in it. How *they* will rejoice! But tell me all about it. Talk to me for ever. When did you begin to think seriously about her?"

Nothing could be more impossible than to answer such a question, though nothing be more agreeable than to have it asked. "How the pleasing plague had stolen on him"[1] he could not say, and before he had expressed the same sentiment with a little variation of words three times over, his sister eagerly interrupted him with, "Ah! my dear Henry, and this is what took you to London! This was your business! You chose to consult the Admiral, before you made up your mind."

But this he stoutly denied. He knew his uncle too well to consult him on any matrimonial scheme. The Admiral hated marriage, and

---

1. From William Whitehead's "The Je ne Scai Quoi," printed in Dodsley's *Collection*, vol. 2. See above, p. 113, n. 1. The Crawfords' taste for satiric Augustan verse contrasts with Fanny's more romantic taste in poetry.

thought it never pardonable in a young man of independent fortune.

"When Fanny is known to him," continued Henry, "he will doat on her. She is exactly the woman to do away every prejudice of such a man as the Admiral, for she is exactly such a woman as he thinks does not exist in the world. She is the very impossibility he would describe —if indeed he has now delicacy of language enough to embody his own ideas. But till it is absolutely settled—settled beyond all interference, he shall know nothing of the matter. No, Mary, you are quite mistaken. You have not discovered my business yet!"

"Well, well, I am satisfied. I know now to whom it must relate, and am in no hurry for the rest. Fanny Price—Wonderful—quite wonderful!—That Mansfield should have done so much for—that *you* should have found your fate in Mansfield! But you are quite right, you could not have chosen better. There is not a better girl in the world, and you do not want for fortune; and as to her connections, they are more than good. The Bertrams are undoubtedly some of the first people in this country. She is niece to Sir Thomas Bertram; that will be enough for the world. But go on, go on. Tell me more. What are your plans? Does she know her own happiness?"

"No."

"What are you waiting for?"

"For—for very little more than opportunity. Mary, she is not like her cousins; but I think I shall not ask in vain."

"Oh! no, you cannot. Were you even less pleasing—supposing her not to love you already, (of which however I can have little doubt,) you would be safe. The gentleness and gratitude of her disposition would secure her all your own immediately. From my soul I do not think she would marry you *without* love; that is, if there is a girl in the world capable of being uninfluenced by ambition, I can suppose it her; but ask her to love you, and she will never have the heart to refuse."

As soon as her eagerness could rest in silence, he was as happy to tell as she could be to listen, and a conversation followed almost as deeply interesting to her as to himself, though he had in fact nothing to relate but his own sensations, nothing to dwell on but Fanny's charms.—Fanny's beauty of face and figure, Fanny's graces of manner and goodness of heart were the exhaustless theme. The gentleness, modesty, and sweetness of her character were warmly expatiated on, that sweetness which makes so essential a part of every woman's worth in the judgment of man, that though he sometimes loves where it is not, he can never believe it absent. Her temper he had good reason to depend on and to praise. He had often seen it tried. Was there one of the family, excepting Edmund, who had not in some way or other continually exercised her patience and forbearance? Her affections were evidently strong. To see her with her brother! What could more delightfully prove that the warmth of her heart was equal to its gentleness?—What could be more encouraging to a man who had her love in view? Then, her understanding was beyond every suspicion, quick and clear; and her manners were the mirror of her own modest and elegant mind. Nor was this all. Henry Crawford had too much sense not to feel the worth of good principles in a wife, though he was too little accustomed to serious reflection to know them by their proper name; but when he talked of her having such a steadiness and regularity of conduct, such a high notion of honour, and such an observance of decorum as might warrant any man in the fullest dependence on her faith and integrity, he expressed what was inspired by the knowledge of her being well principled and religious.

"I could so wholly and absolutely confide in her," said he; "and *that* is what I want."

Well might his sister, believing as she really did that his opinion of Fanny Price was scarcely beyond her merits, rejoice in her prospects.

"The more I think of it," she cried, "the more am I convinced that you are doing quite right, and though I should never have selected Fanny Price as the girl most likely to attach you, I am now persuaded she is the very one to make you happy. Your wicked project upon her peace turns out a clever thought indeed. You will both find your good in it."

"It was bad, very bad in me against such a creature! but I did not know her then. And she shall have no reason to lament the hour that first put it into my head. I will make her very happy, Mary, happier than she has ever yet been herself, or ever seen any body else. I will not take her from Northamptonshire. I shall let Everingham, and rent a place in this neighbourhood—perhaps Stanwix Lodge. I shall let a seven years' lease of Everingham. I am sure of an excellent tenant at half a word. I could name three people now, who would give me my own terms and thank me."

"Ha!" cried Mary, "settle in Northamptonshire! That is pleasant! Then we shall be all together."

When she had spoken it, she recollected herself, and wished it unsaid; but there was no need of confusion, for her brother saw her only as the supposed inmate of Mansfield Parsonage, and replied but to invite her in the kindest manner to his own house, and to claim the best right in her.

"You must give us more than half your time," said he; "I cannot admit Mrs. Grant to have an equal claim with Fanny and myself, for we shall both have a right in you. Fanny will be so truly your sister!"

Mary had only to be grateful and give general assurances; but she was now very fully purposed to be the guest of neither brother nor sister many months longer.

"You will divide your year between London and Northamptonshire?"

"Yes."

"That's right; and in London, of course, a house of your own; no longer with the Admiral. My dearest Henry, the advantage to you of getting away from the Admiral before your manners are hurt by the contagion of his, before you have contracted any of his foolish opinions, or learnt to sit over your dinner, as if it were the best blessing of life! —*You* are not sensible of the gain, for your regard for him has blinded you; but, in my estimation, your marrying early may be the saving of you. To have seen you grow like the Admiral in word or deed, look or gesture, would have broken* my heart."

"Well, well, we do not think quite alike here. The Admiral has his faults, but he is a very good man, and has been more than a father to me. Few fathers would have let me have my own way half so much. You must not prejudice Fanny against him. I must have them love one another."

Mary refrained from saying what she felt, that there could not be two persons in existence, whose characters and manners were less accordant; time would discover it to him; but she could not help *this* reflection on the Admiral. "Henry, I think so highly of Fanny Price, that if I could suppose the next Mrs. Crawford would have half the reason which my poor ill used aunt had to abhor the very name, I would prevent the marriage, if possible; but I know you, I know that a wife you *loved* would be the happiest of women, and that even when you ceased to love, she would yet find in you the liberality and good-breeding of a gentleman."

The impossibility of not doing every thing in the world to make Fanny Price happy, or of ceasing to love Fanny Price, was of course the ground-work of his eloquent answer.

"Had you seen her this morning, Mary," he continued, "attending with such ineffable sweetness and patience, to all the demands of her aunt's stupidity, working with her, and for her, her colour beautifully heightened as she leant over the work, then returning to her seat to finish a note which she was previously engaged in writing for that stupid woman's service, and all this with such unpretending gentleness, so much as if it were a matter of course that she was not to have a moment at her own command, her hair arranged as neatly as it always is, and one little curl falling forward as she wrote, which she now and then shook back, and in the midst of all this, still speaking at intervals to *me*, or listening, and as if she liked to listen to what I said. Had you seen her so, Mary, you would not have implied the possibility of her power over my heart ever ceasing."

"My dearest Henry," cried Mary, stopping short, and smiling in his face, "how glad I am to see you so much in love! It quite delights me. But what will Mrs. Rushworth and Julia say?"

"I care neither what they say, nor what they feel. They will now see what sort of woman it is that can attach me, that can attach a man of sense. I wish the discovery may do them any good. And they will now see their cousin treated as she ought to be, and I wish they may be heartily ashamed of their own abominable neglect and unkindness. They will be angry," he added, after a moment's silence, and in a cooler tone, "Mrs. Rushworth will be very angry. It will be a bitter pill to her; that is, like other bitter pills, it will have two moments'* ill-flavour, and then be swallowed and forgotten; for I am not such a coxcomb as to suppose her feelings more lasting than other women's, though *I* was the object of them. Yes, Mary, my Fanny will feel a difference indeed, a daily, hourly difference, in the behaviour of every being who approaches her; and it will be the completion of my happiness to know that I am the doer of it, that I am the person to give the consequence so justly her due. Now she is dependent, helpless, friendless, neglected, forgotten."

"Nay, Henry, not by all, not forgotten by all, not friendless or forgotten. Her cousin Edmund never forgets her."

"Edmund—True, I believe he is (generally speaking) kind to her; and so is Sir Thomas in his way, but it is the way of a rich, superior, longworded, arbitrary uncle. What can Sir Thomas and Edmund together do, what *do* they do for her happiness, comfort, honour, and dignity in the world to what I *shall* do?"

Chapter XIII.

Henry Crawford was at Mansfield Park again the next morning, and at an earlier hour than common visiting warrants. The two ladies were together in the breakfast-room, and fortunately for him, Lady Bertram was on the very point of quitting it as he entered. She was almost at the door, and not chusing by any means to take so much trouble in vain, she still went on, after a civil reception, a short sentence about being waited for, and a "Let Sir Thomas know," to the servant.

Henry, overjoyed to have her go, bowed and watched her off, and without losing another moment, turned instantly to Fanny, and taking out some letters said, with a most animated look, "I must acknowledge myself infinitely obliged to any creature who gives me such an opportunity of seeing you alone: I have been wishing it more than you can have any idea. Knowing as I do what your feelings as a sister are, I could hardly have borne that any one in the house should share with you in the first knowledge of the news I now bring. He is made. Your brother is a Lieutenant. I have the infinite satisfaction of congratulating you on your brother's promotion. Here are the letters which announce it, this moment come to hand. You will, perhaps, like to see them."

Fanny could not speak, but he did not want her to speak. To see the expression of her eyes, the change of her complexion, the progress of her feelings, their doubt, confusion, and felicity, was enough. She took the letters as he gave them. The first was from the Admiral to inform his nephew, in a few words, of his having succeeded in the object he had undertaken, the promotion of young Price, and inclosing two more, one from the Secretary of the First Lord to a friend, whom the Admiral had set to work in the business, the other from that friend to himself, by which it appeared that his Lordship had the very great happiness of attending to the recommendation of Sir Charles, that Sir Charles was much delighted in having such an opportunity of proving his regard for Admiral Crawford, and that the circumstance of Mr. William Price's commission as second Lieutenant of H. M. sloop Thrush, being made out, was spreading general joy through a wide circle of great people.

While her hand was trembling under these letters, her eye running from one to the other, and her heart swelling with emotion, Crawford thus continued, with unfeigned eagerness, to express his interest in the event.

"I will not talk of my own happiness," said he, "great as it is, for I think only of yours. Compared with you, who has a right to be happy? I have almost grudged myself my own prior knowledge of what you ought to have known before all the world. I have not lost a moment, however. The post was late this morning, but there has not been since, a moment's delay. How impatient, how anxious, how wild I have been on the subject, I will not attempt to describe; how severely mortified, how cruelly disappointed, in not having it finished while I was in London! I was kept there from day to day in the hope of it, for nothing less dear to me than such an object would have detained me half the time from Mansfield. But though my uncle entered into my wishes with all the warmth I could desire, and exerted himself immediately, there were difficulties from the absence of one friend, and the engagements of another, which at last I could no longer bear to stay the end of, and knowing in what good hands I left the cause, I came away on Monday, trusting that many posts would not pass before I should be followed by such very letters as these. My uncle, who is the very best man in the world, has exerted himself, as I knew he would after seeing your brother. He was delighted with him. I would not allow myself yesterday to say *how* delighted, or to repeat half that the Admiral said in his praise. I deferred it all, till his praise should be proved the praise of a friend, as this day *does* prove it. Now I may say that even *I* could not require William Price to excite a greater interest, or be followed by warmer wishes and higher commendation, than were most voluntarily bestowed by my uncle, after the evening they passed together."

"Has this been all *your* doing then?" cried Fanny. "Good Heaven! how very, very kind! Have you really—was it by *your* desire—I beg your pardon, but I am bewildered. Did Admiral Crawford apply?—how was it?—I am stupified."

Henry was most happy to make it more intelligible, by beginning at an earlier stage, and explaining very particularly what he had done. His last journey to London had been undertaken with no other view than that of introducing her brother in Hill-street, and prevailing on the Admiral to exert whatever interest he might have for getting him on. This had been his business. He had communicated it to no creature; he had not breathed a syllable of it even to Mary; while uncertain of the issue, he could not have borne any participation of his feelings, but this had been his business; and he spoke with such a glow of what his solicitude had been, and used such strong expressions, was so abounding in the *deepest interest,* in *twofold motives,* in *views and wishes more than could be told,* that Fanny could not have remained insensible of his drift, had she been able to attend; but her heart was so full and her senses still so astonished, that she could listen but imperfectly even to what he told her of William, and saying only when he paused, "How kind! how very kind! Oh! Mr. Crawford, we are infinitely obliged to you. Dearest, dearest William!" She jumped up and moved in haste towards the door, crying out, "I will go to my uncle. My uncle ought to know it as soon as possible." But this could not be suffered. The opportunity was too fair, and his feelings too impatient. He was after her immediately. "She must not go, she must allow him five minutes longer," and he took her hand and led her back to her seat, and was in the middle of his further* explanation, before she had suspected for what she was detained. When she did understand it, however, and found herself expected to believe that *she* had created sensations which his heart had never known before, and that every thing he had done for William, was to be placed to the account of his excessive and un-equalled attachment to her, she was exceedingly distressed, and for some moments unable to speak. She considered it all as nonsense, as mere trifling and gallantry, which meant only to deceive for the hour; she could not but feel that it was treating her improperly and unwor-thily, and in such a way as she had not deserved; but it was like himself, and entirely of a piece with what she had seen before; and she would not allow herself to shew half the displeasure she felt, because he had been conferring an obligation, which no want of delicacy on his part could make a trifle to her. While her heart was still bounding with joy and gratitude on William's behalf, she could not be severely resentful of any thing that injured only herself; and after having twice drawn back her hand, and twice attempted in vain to turn away from him, she got up and said only, with much agitation, "Don't, Mr. Crawford, pray don't. I beg you would not. This is a sort of talking which is very unpleasant to me. I must go away. I cannot bear it." But he was still talking on, describing his affection, soliciting a return, and, finally, in words so plain as to bear but one meaning even to *her,* offering himself, hand, fortune, every thing to her acceptance. It was so; he had said it.

Her astonishment and confusion increased; and though still not knowing how to suppose him serious, she could hardly stand. He pressed for
an answer.

"No, no, no," she cried, hiding her face. "This is all nonsense. Do
not distress me. I can hear no more of this. Your kindness to William
makes me more obliged to you than words can express; but I do not
want, I cannot bear, I must not listen to such—No, no, don't think of
me. But you are *not* thinking of me. I know it is all nothing."

She had burst away from him, and at that moment Sir Thomas was
heard speaking to a servant in his way towards the room they were in.
It was no time for further assurances or entreaty, though to part with
her at a moment when her modesty alone seemed to his sanguine and
pre-assured mind to stand in the way of the happiness he sought, was
a cruel necessity.—She rushed out at an opposite door from the one
her uncle was approaching, and was walking up and down the east
room in the utmost confusion of contrary feelings*, before Sir Thomas's
politeness and* apologies were over, or he had reached the beginning
of the joyful intelligence, which his visitor came to communicate.

She was feeling, thinking, trembling, about every thing; agitated,
happy, miserable, infinitely obliged, absolutely angry. It was all beyond
belief! He was inexcusable, incomprehensible!—But such were his
habits, that he could do nothing without a mixture of evil. He had
previously made her the happiest of human beings, and now he had
insulted—she knew not what to say—how to class or how to regard it.
She would not have him be serious, and yet what could excuse the use
of such words and offers, if they meant but to trifle?

But William was a Lieutenant.—*That* was a fact beyond a doubt and
without an alloy. She would think of it for ever and forget all the rest.
Mr. Crawford would certainly never address her so again: he must have
seen how unwelcome it was to her; and in that case, how gratefully she
could esteem him for his friendship to William!

She would not stir farther from the east-room than the head of the
great staircase, till she had satisfied herself of Mr. Crawford's having
left the house; but when convinced of his being gone, she was eager
to go down and be with her uncle, and have all the happiness of his
joy as well as her own, and all the benefit of his information or his
conjectures as to what would now be William's destination. Sir Thomas
was as joyful as she could desire, and very kind and communicative;
and she had so comfortable a talk with him about William as to make
her feel as if nothing had occurred to vex her, till she found towards
the close that Mr. Crawford was engaged to return and dine there that
very day. This was a most unwelcome hearing, for though *he* might
think nothing of what had passed, it would be quite distressing to her
to see him again so soon.

She tried to get the better of it, tried very hard as the dinner hour approached, to feel and appear as usual; but it was quite impossible for her not to look most shy and uncomfortable when their visitor entered the room. She could not have supposed it in the power of any concurrence of circumstances to give her so many painful sensations on the first day of hearing of William's promotion.

Mr. Crawford was not only in the room; he was soon close to her. He had a note to deliver from his sister. Fanny could not look at him, but there was no consciousness of past folly in his voice. She opened her note immediately, glad to have any thing to do, and happy as she read it, to feel that the fidgettings of her aunt Norris, who was also to dine there, screened her a little from view.

"My dear Fanny, for so I may now always call you, to the infinite relief of a tongue that has been stumbling at *Miss Price* for at least the last six weeks—I cannot let my brother go without sending you a few lines of general congratulation, and giving my most joyful consent and approval.—Go on, my dear Fanny, and without fear; there can be no difficulties worth naming. I chuse to suppose that the assurance of *my* consent will be something; so, you may smile upon him with your sweetest smiles this afternoon, and send him back to me even happier than he goes.

Yours affectionately,
M.C."

These were not expressions to do Fanny any good; for though she read in too much haste and confusion to form the clearest judgment of Miss Crawford's meaning, it was evident that she meant to compliment her on her brother's attachment and even to *appear* to believe it serious. She did not know what to do, or what to think. There was wretchedness in the idea of its being serious; there was perplexity and agitation every way. She was distressed whenever Mr. Crawford spoke to her, and he spoke to her much too often; and she was afraid there was a something in his voice and manner in addressing her, very different from what they were when he talked to the others. Her comfort in that day's dinner was quite destroyed; she could hardly eat any thing; and when Sir Thomas good humouredly observed, that joy had taken away her appetite, she was ready to sink with shame, from the dread of Mr. Crawford's interpretation; for though nothing could have tempted her to turn her eyes to the right hand where he sat, she felt that *his* were immediately directed towards her.

She was more silent than ever. She would hardly join even when William was the subject, for his commission came all from the right hand too, and there was pain in the connection.

She thought Lady Bertram sat longer than ever, and began to be in despair of ever getting away; but at last they were in the drawing-room she was able to think as she would, while her aunts finished the subject of William's appointment in their own style.

Mrs. Norris seemed as much delighted with the saving it would be to Sir Thomas, as with any part of it. "Now William would be able to keep himself, which would make a vast difference to his uncle, for it was unknown how much he had cost his uncle; and indeed it would make some difference in *her* presents too. She was very glad that she had given William what she did at parting, very glad indeed that it had been in her power, without material inconvenience just at that time, to give him something rather considerable;[1] that is, for *her*, with *her* limited means, for now it would all be useful in helping to fit up his cabin. She knew he must be at some expense, that he would have many things to buy, though to be sure his father and mother would be able to put him in the way of getting every thing very cheap—but she was very glad that she had contributed her mite towards it."

"I am glad you gave him something considerable," said Lady Bertram, with must unsuspicious calmness—"for *I* gave him only 10£."

"Indeed!" cried Mrs. Norris, reddening. "Upon my word, he must have gone off with his pockets well lined! and at no expense for his journey to London either!"

"Sir Thomas told me 10£ would be enough."

Mrs. Norris, being not at all inclined to question its sufficiency, began to take the matter in another point.

"It is amazing," said she, "how much young people cost their friends, what with bringing them up and putting them out in the world! They little think how much it comes to, or what their parents, or their uncles and aunts pay for them in the course of the year. Now, here are my sister Price's children;—take them all together, I dare say nobody would believe what a sum they cost Sir Thomas every year, to say nothing of what *I* do for them."

"Very true, sister, as you say. But, poor things! they cannot help it; and you know it makes very little difference to Sir Thomas. Fanny, William must not forget my shawl, if he goes to the East Indies; and I shall give him a commission for any thing else that is worth having, I wish he may go to the East Indies, that I may have my shawl. I think I will have two shawls, Fanny."

Fanny, meanwhile, speaking only when she could not help it, was very earnestly trying to understand what Mr. and Miss Crawford were at. There was every thing in the world *against* their being serious, but his words and manner. Every thing natural, probable, reasonable was against it; all their habits and ways of thinking, and all her own demerits.—How could *she* have excited serious attachment in a man, who had seen so many, and been admired by so many, and flirted with

1. After publishing *Mansfield Park*, Austen told her nieces and nephews that the "rather considerable" sum Mrs. Norris brags about was only one pound.

so many, infinitely her superiors—who seemed so little open to serious impressions, even where pains had been taken to please him—who thought so slightly, so carelessly, so unfeelingly on all such points—who was every thing to every body, and seemed to find no one essential to him?—And further, how could it be supposed that his sister, with all her high and worldly notions of matrimony, would be forwarding any thing of a serious nature in such a quarter? Nothing could be more unnatural in either. Fanny was ashamed of her own doubts. Every thing might be possible rather than serious attachment or serious approbation of it toward her. She had quite convinced herself of this before Sir Thomas and Mr. Crawford joined them. The difficulty was in maintaining the conviction quite so absolutely after Mr. Crawford was in the room; for once or twice a look seemed forced on her which she did not know how to class among the common meaning; in any other man at least, she would have said that it meant something very earnest, very pointed. But she still tried to believe it no more than what he might often have expressed towards her cousins and fifty other women.

She thought he was wishing to speak to her unheard by the rest. She fancied he was trying for it the whole evening at intervals, whenever Sir Thomas was out of the room, or at all engaged with Mrs. Norris, and she carefully refused him every opportunity.

At last—it seemed an at last to Fanny's nervousness, though not remarkably late,—he began to talk of going away; but the comfort of the sound was impaired by his turning to her the next moment, and saying, "Have you nothing to send to Mary? No answer to her note? She will be disappointed if she receives nothing from you. Pray write to her, if it be only a line."

"Oh! yes, certainly," cried Fanny, rising in haste, the haste of embarrassment and of wanting to get away—"I will write directly."

She went accordingly to the table, where she was in the habit of writing for her aunt, and prepared her materials without knowing what in the world to say! She had read Miss Crawford's note only once; and how to reply to any thing so imperfectly understood was most distressing. Quite unpractised in such sort of note-writing, had there been time for scruples and fears as to style, she would have felt them in abundance; but something must be instantly written, and with only one decided feeling, that of wishing not to appear to think any thing really intended, she wrote thus, in great trembling both of spirits and hand:

"I am very much obliged to you, my dear Miss Crawford, for your kind congratulations, as far as they relate to my dearest William. The rest of your note I know means nothing; but I am so unequal to any thing of the sort, that I hope you will excuse my begging you to take no further notice. I have seen too much of Mr. Crawford not to understand his manners; if he understood me as well, he would, I dare say, behave differently. I do not know what I write, but it would be a great favour of you never to mention the subject again. With thanks for the honour of your note,

I remain, dear Miss Crawford,
&c. &c."

The conclusion was scarcely intelligible from increasing fright, for she found that Mr. Crawford, under pretence of receiving the note, was coming towards her.

"You cannot think I mean to hurry you," said he, in an under voice, perceiving the amazing trepidation with which she made up the note; "you cannot think I have any such object. Do not hurry yourself, I entreat."

"Oh! I thank you, I have quite done, just done—it will be ready in a moment—I am very much obliged to you—if you will be so good as to give *that* to Miss Crawford."

The note was held out and must be taken; and as she instantly and with averted eyes walked towards the fireplace, where sat the others, he had nothing to do but to go in good earnest.

Fanny thought she had never known a day of greater agitation, both of pain and pleasure; but happily the pleasure was not of a sort to die with the day—for every day would restore the knowledge of William's advancement, whereas the pain she hoped would return no more. She had no doubt that her note must appear excessively ill-written, that the language would disgrace a child, for her distress had allowed no arrangement; but at least it would assure them both of her being neither imposed on, nor gratified by Mr. Crawford's attentions.

END OF THE SECOND VOLUME.

Volume III

Chapter I.

Fanny had by no means forgotten Mr. Crawford, when she awoke the next morning; but she remembered the purport of her note, and was not less sanguine, as to its effect, than she had been the night before. If Mr. Crawford would but go away!—That was what she most earnestly desired;—go and take his sister with him, as he was to do, and as he returned to Mansfield on purpose to do. And why it was not done already, she could not devise, for Miss Crawford certainly wanted no delay.—Fanny had hoped, in the course of his yesterday's visit, to hear the day named; but he had only spoken of their journey as what would take place ere long.

Having so satisfactorily settled the conviction her note would convey, she could not but be astonished to see Mr. Crawford, as she accidentally did, coming up to the house again, and at an hour as early as the day before.—His coming might have nothing to do with her, but she must avoid seeing him if possible; and being then in her way up stairs, she resolved there to remain, during the whole of his visit, unless actually sent for; and as Mrs. Norris was still in the house, there seemed little danger of her being wanted.

She sat some time in a good deal of agitation, listening, trembling, and fearing to be sent for every moment; but as no footsteps approached the east room, she grew gradually composed, could sit down, and be able to employ herself, and able to hope that Mr. Crawford had come, and would go without her being obliged to know any thing of the matter.

Nearly half an hour had passed, and she was growing very comfortable, when suddenly the sound of a step in regular approach was heard—a heavy step, an unusual step in that part of the house; it was her uncle's; she knew it as well as his voice; she had trembled at it as often, and began to tremble again, at the idea of his coming up to speak to her, whatever might be the subject.—It was indeed Sir Thomas, who opened the door, and asked if she were there, and if he might come in. The terror of his former occasional visits to that room seemed all renewed, and she felt as if he were going to examine her again in French and English.

She was all attention, however, in placing a chair for him, and trying to appear honoured; and in her agitation, had quite overlooked the deficiences of her apartment, till he, stopping short as he entered, said, with much surprise, "Why have you no fire to-day?"

There was snow on the ground, and she was sitting in a shawl. She hesitated.

"I am not cold, Sir—I never sit here long at this time of year."

"But,—you have a fire in general?"

"No, Sir."

"How comes this about; here must be some mistake. I understood that you had the use of this room by way of making you perfectly comfortable.—In your bed-chamber I know you *cannot* have a fire. Here is some great misapprehension which must be rectified. It is highly unfit for you to sit—be it only half an hour a day, without a fire. You are not strong. You are chilly. Your aunt cannot be aware of this."

Fanny would rather have been silent, but being obliged to speak, she could not forbear, in justice to the aunt she loved best, from saying something in which the words "my aunt Norris" were distinguishable.

"I understand," cried her uncle recollecting himself, and not wanting to hear more—"I understand. Your aunt Norris has always been an advocate, and very judiciously, for young people's being brought up without unnecessary indulgences; but there should be moderation in every thing.—She is also very hardy herself, which of course will influence her in her opinion of the wants of others. And on another account too, I can perfectly comprehend.—I know what her sentiments have always been. The principle was good in itself, but it may have been, and I believe *has been* carried too far in your case.—I am aware that there has been sometimes, in some points, a misplaced distinction; but I think too well of you, Fanny, to suppose you will ever harbour resentment on that account.—You have an understanding, which will prevent you from receiving things only in part, and judging partially by the event.—You will take in the whole of the past, you will consider times, persons, and probabilities, and you will feel that *they* were not least your friends who were educating and preparing you for that mediocrity of condition which *seemed* to be your lot.—Though their caution may prove eventually unnecessary, it was kindly meant; and of this you may be assured, that every advantage of affluence will be doubled by the little privations and restrictions that may have been imposed. I am sure you will not disappoint my opinion of you, by failing at any time to treat your aunt Norris with the respect and attention that are due to her.—But enough of this. Sit down, my dear. I must speak to you for a few minutes, but I will not detain you long."

Fanny obeyed, with eyes cast down and colour rising.—After a moment's pause, Sir Thomas, trying to suppress a smile, went on.

"You are not aware, perhaps, that I have had a visitor this morning.—I had not been long in my own room, after breakfast, when Mr. Crawford was shewn in.—His errand you may probably conjecture."

Fanny's colour grew deeper and deeper; and her uncle perceiving that she was embarrassed to a degree that made either speaking or looking up quite impossible, turned away his own eyes, and without any farther pause, proceeded in his account of Mr. Crawford's visit.

Mr. Crawford's business had been to declare himself the lover of Fanny, make decided proposals for her, and intreat the sanction of the uncle, who seemed to stand in the place of her parents; and he had done it all so well, so openly, so liberally, so properly, that Sir Thomas, feeling, moreover, his own replies, and his own remarks to have been very much to the purpose—was exceedingly happy to give the particulars of their conversation—and, little aware of what was passing in his niece's mind, conceived that by such details he must be gratifying her far more than himself. He talked therefore for several minutes without Fanny's daring to interrupt him.—She had hardly even attained the wish to do it. Her mind was in too much confusion. She had changed her position, and with her eyes fixed intently on one of the windows, was listening to her uncle, in the utmost perturbation and dismay.—For a moment he ceased, but she had barely become conscious of it, when, rising from his chair, he said, "And now, Fanny, having performed one part of my commission, and shewn you every thing placed on a basis the most assured and satisfactory, I may execute the remainder by prevailing on you to accompany me down stairs, where—though I cannot but presume on having been no unacceptable companion myself, I must submit to your finding one still better worth listening to.—Mr. Crawford, as you have perhaps foreseen, is yet in the house. He is in my room, and hoping to see you there."

There was a look, a start, an exclamation, on hearing this, which astonished Sir Thomas; but what was his increase of astonishment on hearing her exclaim—"Oh! no, Sir, I cannot, indeed I cannot go down to him. Mr. Crawford ought to know—he must know that—I told him enough yesterday to convince him—he spoke to me on this subject yesterday—and I told him without disguise that it was very disagreeable to me, and quite out of my power to return his good opinion."

"I do not catch your meaning," said Sir Thomas, sitting down again.—"Out of your power to return his good opinion! what is all this? I know he spoke to you yesterday, and (as far as I understand), received as much encouragement to proceed as a well-judging young woman could permit herself to give. I was very much pleased with what I collected to have been your behaviour on the occasion; it shewed a discretion highly to be commended. But now, when he has made his overtures so properly, and honourably—what are your scruples *now?*"

"You are mistaken, Sir,"—cried Fanny, forced by the anxiety of the moment even to tell her uncle that he was wrong—"You are quite mistaken. How could Mr. Crawford say such a thing? I gave him no encouragement yesterday—On the contrary, I told him—I cannot recollect my exact words—but I am sure I told him that I would not listen to him, that it was very unpleasant to me in every respect, and that I begged him never to talk to me in that manner again.—I am sure I said as much as that and more; and I should have said still more,—if I had been quite certain of his meaning any thing seriously, but I did not like to be—I could not bear to be—imputing more than might be intended. I thought it might all pass for nothing with *him*."

She could say no more; her breath was almost gone.

"Am I to understand," said Sir Thomas, after a few moments'* silence, "that you mean to *refuse* Mr. Crawford?"

"Yes, Sir."

"Refuse him?"

"Yes, Sir."

"Refuse Mr. Crawford! Upon what plea? For what reason?"

"I—I cannot like him, Sir, well enough to marry him."

"This is very strange!" said Sir Thomas, in a voice of calm displeasure. "There is something in this which my comprehension does not reach. Here is a young man wishing to pay his addresses to you, with every thing to recommend him; not merely situation in life, fortune, and character, but with more than common agreeableness, with address and conversation pleasing to every body. And he is not an acquaintance of to-day, you have now known him some time. His sister, moreover, is your intimate friend, and he has been doing *that* for your brother, which I should suppose would have been almost sufficient recommendation to you, had there been no other. It is very uncertain when my interest might have got William on. He has done it already."

"Yes," said Fanny, in a faint voice, and looking down with fresh shame; and she did feel almost ashamed of herself, after such a picture as her uncle had drawn, for not liking Mr. Crawford.

"You must have been aware," continued Sir Thomas, presently, "you must have been some time aware of a particularity in Mr. Crawford's manners to you. This cannot have taken you by surprise. You must have observed his attentions; and though you always received them very properly, (I have no accusation to make on that head,) I never perceived them to be unpleasant to you. I am half inclined to think, Fanny, that you do not quite know your own feelings."

"Oh! yes, Sir, indeed I do. His attentions were always—what I did not like."

Sir Thomas looked at her with deeper surprise. "This is beyond me," said he. "This requires explanation. Young as you are, and having seen scarcely any one, it is hardly possible that your affections——"

He paused and eyed her fixedly. He saw her lips formed into a *no*, though the sound was inarticulate, but her face was like scarlet. That, however, in so modest a girl might be very compatible with innocence; and chusing at least to appear satisfied, he quickly added, "No, no, I know *that* is quite out of the question—quite impossible. Well, there is nothing more to be said."

And for a few minutes he did say nothing. He was deep in thought. His niece was deep in thought likewise, trying to harden and prepare herself against farther questioning. She would rather die than own the truth, and she hoped by a little reflection to fortify herself beyond betraying it.

"Independently of the interest which Mr. Crawford's *choice* seemed to justify," said Sir Thomas, beginning again, and very composedly, "his wishing to marry at all so early is recommendatory to me. I am an advocate for early marriages, where there are means in proportion, and would have every young man, with a sufficient income, settle as soon after four and twenty as he can. This is so much my opinion, that I am sorry to think how little likely my own eldest son, your cousin, Mr. Bertram, is to marry early; but at present, as far as I can judge, matrimony makes no part of his plans or thoughts. I wish he were more likely to fix." Here was a glance at Fanny. "Edmund I consider from his disposition and habits as much more likely to marry early than his brother. *He*, indeed, I have lately thought has seen the woman he could love, which, I am convinced, my eldest son has not. Am I right? Do you agree with me, my dear?"

"Yes, Sir."

It was gently, but it was calmly said, and Sir Thomas was easy on the score of the cousins. But the removal of his alarm did his niece no service; as her unaccountableness was confirmed, his displeasure increased; and getting up and walking about the room, with a frown, which Fanny could picture to herself, though she dared not lift up her eyes, he shortly afterwards, and in a voice of authority, said, "Have you any reason, child, to think ill of Mr. Crawford's temper?"

"No, Sir."

She longed to add, "but of his principles I have;" but her heart sunk under the appalling prospect of discussion, explanation, and probably nonconviction. Her ill opinion of him was founded chiefly on observations, which, for her cousins'* sake, she could scarcely dare mention to their father. Maria and Julia—and especially Maria, were so closely implicated in Mr. Crawford's misconduct, that she could not give his character, such as she believed it, without betraying them. She had hoped that to a man like her uncle, so discerning, so honourable, so good, the simple acknowledgment of settled *dislike* on her side, would have been sufficient. To her infinite grief she found it was not.

Sir Thomas came towards the table where she sat in trembling wretchedness, and with a good deal of cold sternness, said, "It is of no use, I perceive, to talk to you. We had better put an end to this most mortifying conference. Mr. Crawford must not be kept longer waiting. I will, therefore, only add, as thinking it my duty to mark my opinion of your conduct—that you have disappointed every expectation I had formed, and proved yourself of a character the very reverse of what I had supposed. For I *had*, Fanny, as I think my behaviour must have shewn, formed a very favourable opinion of you from the period of my return to England. I had thought you peculiarly free from wilfulness of temper, self-conceit, and every tendency to that independence of spirit, which prevails so much in modern days, even in young women, and which in young women is offensive and disgusting beyond all common offence. But you have now shewn me that you can be wilful and per-verse, that you can and will decide for yourself, without any consider-ation or deference for those who have surely some right to guide you —without even asking their advice. You have shewn yourself very, very different from any thing that I had imagined. The advantage or disad-vantage of your family—of your parents—your brothers and sisters—never seems to have had a moment's share in your thoughts on this occasion. How *they* might be benefited, how *they* must rejoice in such an establishment for you—is nothing to *you*. You think only of yourself; and because you do not feel for Mr. Crawford exactly what a young, heated fancy imagines to be necessary for happiness, you resolve to refuse him at once, without wishing even for a little time to consider of it—a little more time for cool consideration, and for really examining your own inclinations—and are, in a wild fit of folly, throwing away from you such an opportunity of being settled in life, eligibly, honour-ably, nobly settled, as will, probably, never occur to you again. Here is a young man of sense, of character, of temper, of manners, and of fortune, exceedingly attached to you, and seeking your hand in the most handsome and disinterested way; and let me tell you, Fanny, that you may live eighteen years longer in the world, without being addressed by a man of half Mr. Crawford's estate, or a tenth part of his merits. Gladly would I have bestowed either of my own daughters on him. Maria is nobly married—but had Mr. Crawford sought Julia's hand, I should have given it to him with superior and more heartfelt satisfaction than I gave Maria's to Mr. Rushworth." After half a moment's pause—"And I should have been very much surprised had either of my daugh-ters, on receiving a proposal of marriage at any time, which might carry with it only *half* the eligibility of *this*, immediately and peremptorily, and without paying my opinion or my regard the compliment of any consultation, put a decided negative on it. I should have been much surprised, and much hurt, by such a proceeding. I should have thought it a gross violation of duty and respect. You are not to be judged by the same rule. You do not owe me the duty of a child. But, Fanny, if your heart can acquit you of *ingratitude*—"

He ceased. Fanny was by this time crying so bitterly, that angry as he was, he would not press that article farther. Her heart was almost broke by such a picture of what she appeared to him; by such accusations, so heavy, so multiplied, so rising in dreadful gradation! Self-willed, obstinate, selfish, and ungrateful. He thought her all this. She had deceived his expectations; she had lost his good opinion. What was to become of her?

"I am very sorry," said she inarticulately through her tears, "I am very sorry indeed."

"Sorry! yes, I hope you are sorry; and you will probably have reason to be long sorry for this day's transactions."

"If it were possible for me to do otherwise," said she with another strong effort, "but I am so perfectly convinced that I could never make him happy, and that I should be miserable myself."

Another burst of tears; but in spite of that burst, and in spite of that great black word *miserable*, which served to introduce it, Sir Thomas began to think a little relenting, a little change of inclination, might have something to do with it; and to augur favourably from the personal intreaty of the young man himself. He knew her to be very timid, and exceedingly nervous; and thought it not improbable that her mind might be in such a state, as a little time, a little pressing, a little patience, and a little impatience, a judicious mixture of all on the lover's side, might work their usual effect on. If the gentleman would but persevere, if he had but love enough to persevere—Sir Thomas began to have hopes; and these reflections having passed across his mind and cheered it, "Well," said he, in a tone of becoming gravity, but of less anger, "well, child, dry up your tears. There is no use in these tears; they can do no good. You must now come down stairs with me. Mr. Crawford has been kept waiting too long already. You must give him your own answer; we cannot expect him to be satisfied with less; and you only can explain to him the grounds of that misconception of your sentiments, which, unfortunately for himself, he certainly has imbibed. I am totally unequal to it."

But Fanny shewed such reluctance, such misery, at the idea of going down to him, that Sir Thomas, after a little consideration, judged it better to indulge her. His hopes from both gentleman and lady suffered a small depression in consequence; but when he looked at his niece, and saw the state of feature and complexion which her crying had brought her into, he thought there might be as much lost as gained by an immediate interview. With a few words, therefore, of no particular meaning, he walked off by himself, leaving his poor niece to sit and cry over what had passed, with very wretched feelings.

Her mind was all disorder. The past, present, future, every thing was terrible. But her uncle's anger gave her the severest pain of all. Selfish and ungrateful! to have appeared so to him! She was miserable for ever. She had no one to take her part, to counsel, or speak for her. Her only friend was absent. He might have softened his father; but all, perhaps all, would think her selfish and ungrateful. She might have to endure the reproach again and again; she might hear it, or see it, or know it to exist for ever in every connection about her. She could not but feel some resentment against Mr. Crawford; yet, if he really loved her, and were* unhappy too!—it was all wretchedness together.

In about a quarter of an hour her uncle returned; she was almost ready to faint at the sight of him. He spoke calmly, however, without austerity, without reproach, and she revived a little. There was comfort too in his words, as well as his manner, for he began with, "Mr. Crawford is gone; he has just left me. I need not repeat what has passed. I do not want to add to any thing you may now be feeling, by an account of what he has felt. Suffice it, that he has behaved in the most gentleman-like and generous manner; and has confirmed me in a most favourable opinion of his understanding, heart, and temper. Upon my representation of what you were suffering, he immediately, and with the greatest delicacy, ceased to urge to see you for the present."

Here Fanny, who had looked up, looked down again. "Of course," continued her uncle, "it cannot be supposed but that he should request to speak with you alone, be it only for five minutes; a request too natural, a claim too just to be denied. But there is no time fixed, perhaps to-morrow, or whenever your spirits are composed enough. For the present you have only to tranquillize yourself. Check these tears; they do but exhaust you. If, as I am willing to suppose, you wish to shew me any observance, you will not give way to these emotions, but endeavour to reason yourself into a stronger frame of mind. I advise you to go out, the air will do you good; go out for an hour on the gravel, you will have the shrubbery to yourself and will be the better for air and exercise. And, Fanny, (turning back again for a moment) I shall make no mention below of what has passed; I shall not even tell your aunt Bertram. There is no occasion for spreading the disappointment; say nothing about it yourself."

This was an order to be most joyfully obeyed; this was an act of kindness which Fanny felt at her heart. To be spared from her aunt Norris's interminable reproaches!—he left her in a glow of gratitude. Any thing might be bearable rather than such reproaches. Even to see Mr. Crawford would be less overpowering.

She walked out directly as her uncle recommended, and followed his advice throughout, as far as she could; did check her tears, did earnestly try to compose her spirits, and strengthen her mind. She wished to prove to him that she did desire his comfort, and sought to regain his favour; and he had given her another strong motive for exertion, in keeping the whole affair from the knowledge of her aunts. Not to excite suspicion by her look or manner was now an object worth attaining; and she felt equal to almost any thing that might save her from her aunt Norris.

She was struck, quite struck, when on returning from her walk, and going into the east room again, the first thing which caught her eye was a fire lighted and burning. A fire! it seemed too much; just at that time to be giving her such an indulgence, was exciting even painful gratitude. She wondered that Sir Thomas could have leisure to think of such a trifle again; but she soon found, from the voluntary information of the housemaid, who came in to attend it, that so it was to be every day. Sir Thomas had given orders for it.

"I must be a brute indeed, if I can be really ungrateful!" said she in soliloquy; "Heaven defend me from being ungrateful!"

She saw nothing more of her uncle, nor of her aunt Norris, till they met at dinner. Her uncle's behaviour to her was then as nearly as possible what it had been before; she was sure he did not mean there should be any change, and that it was only her own conscience that could fancy any; but her aunt was soon quarrelling with her: and when she found how much and how unpleasantly her having only walked out without her aunt's knowledge could be dwelt on, she felt all the reason she had to bless the kindness which saved her from the same spirit of reproach, exerted on a more momentous subject.

"If I had known you were going out, I should have got you just to go as far as my house with some orders for Nanny," said she, "which I have since, to my very great inconvenience, been obliged to go and carry myself. I could very ill spare the time, and you might have saved me the trouble, if you would only have been so good as to let us know you were going out. It would have made no difference to you, I suppose, whether you had walked in the shrubbery, or gone to my house."

"I recommended the shrubbery to Fanny as the dryest place," said Sir Thomas.

"Oh," said Mrs. Norris with a moment's check, "that was very kind of you, Sir Thomas; but you do not know how dry the path is to my house. Fanny would have had quite as good a walk there, I assure you; with the advantage of being of some use, and obliging her aunt: it is all her fault. If she would but have let us know she was going out—but there is a something about Fanny, I have often observed it before,— she likes to go her own way to work; she does not like to be dictated to; she takes her own independent walk whenever she can; she certainly has a little spirit of secrecy, and independence, and nonsense, about her, which I would advise her to get the better of."

As a general reflection on Fanny, Sir Thomas thought nothing could be more unjust, though he had been so lately expressing the same sentiments himself, and he tried to turn the conversation; tried repeatedly before he could succeed; for Mrs. Norris had not discernment enough to perceive, either now, or at any other time, to what degree he thought well of his niece, or how very far he was from wishing to have his own children's merits set off by the depreciation of hers. She was talking *at* Fanny, and resenting this private walk half through the dinner.

It was over, however, at last; and the evening set in with more composure to Fanny, and more cheerfulness of spirits than she could have hoped for after so stormy a morning; but she trusted, in the first place, that she had done right, that her judgment had not misled her; for the purity of her intentions she could answer; and she was willing to hope, secondly, that her uncle's displeasure was abating, and would abate farther as he considered the matter with more impartiality, and felt, as a good man must feel, how wretched, and how unpardonable, how hopeless and how wicked it was, to marry without affection.

When the meeting with which she was threatened for the morrow was past, she could not but flatter herself that the subject would be finally concluded, and Mr. Crawford once gone from Mansfield, that every thing would soon be as if no such subject had existed. She would not, could not believe, that Mr. Crawford's affection for her could distress him long; his mind was not of that sort. London would soon bring its cure. In London he would soon learn to wonder at his infatuation, and be thankful for the right reason in her, which had saved him from its evil consequences.

While Fanny's mind was engaged in these sort of hopes, her uncle was soon after tea called out of the room; an occurrence too common to strike her, and she thought nothing of it till the butler re-appeared ten minutes afterwards, and advancing decidedly towards herself, said, "Sir Thomas wishes to speak with you, Ma'am, in his own room." Then it occurred to her what might be going on; a suspicion rushed over her mind which drove the colour from her cheeks; but instantly rising, she was preparing to obey, when Mrs. Norris called out, "Stay, stay, Fanny! what are you about?—where are you going?—don't be in such a hurry. Depend upon it, it is not you that are wanted; depend upon it it is me*; (looking at the butler) but you are so very eager to put yourself forward. What should Sir Thomas want you for? It is me, Baddeley, you mean; I am coming this moment. You mean me, Baddeley, I am sure; Sir Thomas wants me, not Miss Price."

But Baddeley was stout. "No, Ma'am, it is Miss Price, I am certain of its being Miss Price." And there was a half smile with the words which meant, "I do not think *you* would answer the purpose at all."

Mrs. Norris, much discontented, was obliged to compose herself to work again; and Fanny, walking off in agitating consciousness, found herself, as she anticipated, in another minute alone with Mr. Crawford.

Chapter II.

The conference was neither so short, nor so conclusive, as the lady had designed. The gentleman was not so easily satisfied. He had all the disposition to persevere that Sir Thomas could wish him. He had vanity, which strongly inclined him, in the first place, to think she did love him, though she might not know it herself; and which, secondly, when constrained at last to admit that she did know her own present feelings, convinced him that he should be able in time to make those feelings what he wished.

He was in love, very much in love; and it was a love which, operating on an active, sanguine spirit, of more warmth than delicacy, made her affection appear of greater consequence, because it was withheld, and determined him to have the glory, as well as the felicity, of forcing her to love him.

He would not despair: he would not desist. He had every well grounded reason for solid attachment; he knew her to have all the worth that could justify the warmest hopes of lasting happiness with her; her conduct at this very time, by speaking the disinterestedness and delicacy of her character (qualities which he believed most rare indeed), was of a sort to heighten all his wishes, and confirm all his resolutions. He knew not that he had a pre-engaged heart to attack. Of *that*, he had no suspicion. He considered her rather as one who had never thought on the subject enough to be in danger; who had been guarded by youth, a youth of mind as lovely as of person; whose modesty had prevented her from understanding his attentions, and who was still overpowered by the suddenness of addresses so wholly unexpected, and the novelty of a situation which her fancy had never taken into account.

Must it not follow of course, that when he was understood, he should succeed?—he believed it fully. Love such as his, in a man like himself, must with perseverance secure a return, and at no great distance; and he had so much delight in the idea of obliging her to love him in a very short time, that her not loving him now was scarcely regretted. A little difficulty to be overcome, was no evil to Henry Crawford. He rather derived spirits from it. He had been apt to gain hearts too easily. His situation was new and animating.

To Fanny, however, who had known too much opposition all her life, to find any charm in it, all this was unintelligible. She found that he did mean to persevere; but how he could, after such language from her as she felt herself obliged to use, was not to be understood. She told him, that she did not love him, could not love him, was sure she never should love him: that such a change was quite impossible, that the subject was most painful to her, that she must intreat him never to mention it again, to allow her to leave him at once, and let it be considered as concluded for ever. And when farther pressed, had added, that in her opinion their dispositions were so totally dissimilar, as to make mutual affection incompatible; and that they were unfitted for each other by nature, education, and habit. All this she had said, and with the earnestness of sincerity; yet this was not enough, for he immediately denied there being anything uncongenial in their characters, or anything unfriendly in their situations; and positively declared, that he would still love, and still hope!

Fanny knew her own meaning, but was no judge of her own manner. Her manner was incurably gentle, and she was not aware how much it concealed the sternness of her purpose. Her diffidence, gratitude, and softness, made every expression of indifference seem almost an effort of self-denial; seem at least, to be giving nearly as much pain to herself as to him. Mr. Crawford was no longer the Mr. Crawford who, as the clandestine, insidious, treacherous admirer of Maria Bertram, had been her abhorrence, whom she had hated to see or to speak to, in whom she could believe no good quality to exist, and whose power, even of being agreeable, she had barely acknowledged. He was now the Mr. Crawford who was addressing herself with ardent, disinterested, love; whose feelings were apparently become all that was honourable and upright, whose views of happiness were all fixed on a marriage of attachment; who was pouring out his sense of her merits, describing and describing again his affection, proving, as far as words could prove it, and in the language, tone, and spirit of a man of talent too, that he sought her for her gentleness, and her goodness; and to complete the whole, he was now the Mr. Crawford who had procured William's promotion!

Here was a change! and here were claims which could not but operate. She might have disdained him in all the dignity of angry virtue, in the grounds of Sotherton, or the theatre at Mansfield Park; but he approached her now with rights that demanded different treatment. She must be courteous, and she must be compassionate. She must have a sensation of being honoured, and whether thinking of herself or her brother, she must have a strong feeling of gratitude. The effect of the whole was a manner so pitying and agitated, and words intermingled with her refusal so expressive of obligation and concern, that to a temper of vanity and hope like Crawford's, the truth, or at least the strength of her indifference, might well be questionable; and he was not so irrational as Fanny considered him, in the professions of persevering, assiduous, and not desponding attachment which closed the interview.

It was with reluctance that he suffered her to go, but there was no look of despair in parting to bely his words, or give her hopes of his being less unreasonable than he professed himself.

Now she was angry. Some resentment did arise at a perseverance so selfish and ungenerous. Here was again a want of delicacy and regard for others which had formerly so struck and disgusted her. Here was again a something of the same Mr. Crawford whom she had so reprobated before. How evidently was there a gross want of feeling and humanity where his own pleasure was concerned—And, alas! how always known no principle to supply as a duty what the heart was deficient in.* Had her own affections been as free—as perhaps they ought to have been—he never could have engaged them.

So thought Fanny in good truth and sober sadness, as she sat musing over that too great indulgence and luxury of a fire upstairs—wondering at the past and present, wondering at what was yet to come, and in a nervous agitation which made nothing clear to her but the persuasion of her being never under any circumstances able to love Mr. Crawford, and the felicity of having a fire to sit over and think of it.

Sir Thomas was obliged or obliged himself to wait till the morrow for a knowledge of what had passed between the young people. He then saw Mr. Crawford, and received his account.—The first feeling was disappointment: he had hoped better things; he had thought that an hour's intreaty from a young man like Crawford could not have worked so little change on a gentle tempered girl like Fanny; but there was speedy comfort in the determined views and sanguine perseverance of the lover; and when seeing such confidence of success in the principal, Sir Thomas was soon able to depend on it himself.

Nothing was omitted, on his side, of civility, compliment, or kindness, that might assist the plan. Mr. Crawford's steadiness was honoured, and Fanny was praised, and the connection was still the most desirable in the world. At Mansfield Park Mr. Crawford would always be welcome; he had only to consult his own judgment and feelings as to the frequency of his visits, at present or in future. In all his niece's family and friends there could be but one opinion, one wish on the subject; the influence of all who loved her must incline one way.

Every thing was said that could encourage, every encouragement received with grateful joy, and the gentlemen parted the best of friends.

Satisfied that the cause was now on a footing the most proper and hopeful, Sir Thomas resolved to abstain from all farther importunity with his niece, and to shew no open interference. Upon her disposition he believed kindness might be the best way of working. Intreaty should be from one quarter only. The forbearance of her family on a point, respecting which she could be in no doubt of their wishes, might be their surest means of forwarding it. Accordingly, on this principle Sir Thomas took the first opportunity of saying to her, with a mild gravity, intended to be overcoming, "Well, Fanny, I have seen Mr. Crawford again, and learn from him exactly how matters stand between you. He is a most extraordinary young man, and whatever be the event, you must feel that you have created an attachment of no common character;

though, young as you are, and little acquainted with the transient, vary-ing, unsteady nature of love, as it generally exists, you cannot be struck as I am with all that is wonderful in a perseverance of this sort, against discouragement. With him, it is entirely a matter of feeling; he claims no merit in it, perhaps is entitled to none. Yet, having chosen so well, his constancy has a respectable stamp. Had his choice been less un-exceptionable, I should have condemned his persevering."

"Indeed, Sir," said Fanny, "I am very sorry that Mr. Crawford should continue to —— I know that it is paying me a very great compliment, and I feel most undeservedly honoured, but I am so perfectly con-vinced, and I have told him so, that it never will be in my power—"

"My dear," interrupted Sir Thomas, "there is no occasion for this. Your feelings are as well known to me, as my wishes and regrets must be to you. There is nothing more to be said or done. From this hour, the subject is never to be revived between us. You will have nothing to fear, or to be agitated about. You cannot suppose me capable of trying to persuade you to marry against your inclinations. Your happi-ness and advantage are all that I have in view, and nothing is required of you but to bear with Mr. Crawford's endeavours to convince you, that they may not be incompatible with his. He proceeds at his own risk. You are on safe ground. I have engaged for your seeing him when-ever he calls, as you might have done, had nothing of this sort occurred. You will see him with the rest of us, in the same manner, and as much as you can, dismissing the recollection of every thing unpleasant. He leaves Northamptonshire so soon, that even this slight sacrifice cannot be often demanded. The future must be very uncertain. And now, my dear Fanny, this subject is closed between us."

The promised departure was all that Fanny could think of with much satisfaction. Her uncle's kind expressions, however, and forbearing man-ner, were sensibly felt; and when she considered how much of the truth was unknown to him, she believed she had no right to wonder at the line of conduct he pursued. He who had married a daughter to Mr. Rushworth. Romantic delicacy was certainly not to be expected from him. She must do her duty, and trust that time might make her duty easier than it now was.

She could not, though only eighteen, suppose Mr. Crawford's at-tachment would hold out for ever; she could not but imagine that steady, unceasing discouragement from herself would put an end to it in time. How much time she might, in her own fancy, allot for its dominion, is another concern. It would not be fair to enquire into a young lady's exact estimate of her own perfections.

In spite of his intended silence, Sir Thomas found himself once more obliged to mention the subject to his niece, to prepare her briefly for its being imparted to her aunts; a measure which he would still have avoided, if possible, but which became necessary from the totally opposite feelings of Mr. Crawford, as to any secrecy of proceeding. He had no idea of concealment. It was all known at the parsonage, where he loved to talk over the future with both his sisters; and it would be rather gratifying to him to have enlightened witnesses of the progress of his success. When Sir Thomas understood this, he felt the necessity of making his own wife and sister-in-law acquainted with the business without delay; though on Fanny's account, he almost dreaded the effect of the communication to Mrs. Norris as much as Fanny herself. He deprecated her mistaken, but well-meaning zeal. Sir Thomas, indeed, was, by this time, not very far from classing Mrs. Norris as one of those well-meaning people, who are always doing mistaken and very disagreeable things.

Mrs. Norris, however, relieved him. He pressed for the strictest forbearance and silence towards their niece; she not only promised, but did observe it. She only looked her increased ill-will. Angry she was, bitterly angry; but she was more angry with Fanny for having received such an offer, than for refusing it. It was an injury and affront to Julia, who ought to have been Mr. Crawford's choice; and, independently of that, she disliked Fanny, because she had neglected her; and she would have grudged such an elevation to one whom she had been always trying to depress.

Sir Thomas gave her more credit for discretion on the occasion than she deserved; and Fanny could have blessed her for allowing her only to see her displeasure, and not to hear it.

Lady Bertram took it differently. She had been a beauty, and a prosperous beauty, all her life; and beauty and wealth were all that excited her respect. To know Fanny to be sought in marriage by a man of fortune, raised her, therefore, very much in her opinion. By convincing her that Fanny *was* very pretty, which she had been doubting about before, and that she would be advantageously married, it made her feel a sort of credit in calling her niece.

"Well, Fanny," said she, as soon as they were alone together afterwards,—and she really had known something like impatience, to be alone with her, and her countenance, as she spoke, had extraordinary animation—"Well, Fanny, I have had a very agreeable surprise this morning. I must just speak of it *once*, I told Sir Thomas I must *once*, and then I shall have done. I give you joy, my dear niece."—And looking at her complacently, she added, "Humph—We certainly are a handsome family."

Fanny coloured, and doubted at first what to say; when hoping to assail her on her vulnerable side, she presently answered—

"My dear aunt, *you* cannot wish me to do differently from what I have done, I am sure. *You* cannot wish me to marry; for you would miss me, should not you?—Yes, I am sure you would miss me too much for that."

"No, my dear, I should not think of missing you, when such an offer as this comes in your way. I could do very well without you, if you were married to a man of such good estate as Mr. Crawford. And you must be aware, Fanny, that it is every young woman's duty to accept such a very unexceptionable offer as this."

This was almost the only rule of conduct, the only piece of advice, which Fanny had ever received from her aunt in the course of eight years and a half.—It silenced her. She felt how unprofitable contention would be. If her aunt's feelings were against her, nothing could be hoped from attacking her understanding. Lady Bertram was quite talkative.

"I will tell you what, Fanny," said she.—"I am sure he fell in love with you at the ball, I am sure the mischief was done that evening. You did look remarkably well. Every body said so. Sir Thomas said so. And you know you had Chapman to help you dress. I am very glad I sent Chapman to you. I shall tell Sir Thomas that I am sure it was done that evening."—And still pursuing the same cheerful thoughts, she soon afterwards added,—"And I will tell you what, Fanny—which is more than I did for Maria—the next time pug has a litter you shall have a puppy."

Chapter III.

Edmund had great things to hear on his return. Many surprises were awaiting him. The first that occurred was not least in interest,—the appearance of Henry Crawford and his sister walking together through the village, as he rode into it.—He had concluded,—he had meant them to be far distant. His absence had been extended beyond a fortnight purposely to avoid Miss Crawford. He was returning to Mansfield with spirits ready to feed on melancholy remembrances, and tender associations, when her own fair self was before him, leaning on her brother's arm; and he found himself receiving a welcome, unquestionably friendly from the woman whom, two moments before, he had been thinking of as seventy miles off, and as farther, much farther from him in inclination than any distance could express.

Her reception of him was of a sort which he could not have hoped for, had he expected to see her. Coming as he did from such a purport fulfilled as had taken him away, he would have expected any thing rather than a look of satisfaction, and words of simple, pleasant meaning. It was enough to set his heart in a glow, and to bring him home in the properest state for feeling the full value of the other joyful surprises at hand.

William's promotion, with all its particulars, he was soon master of; and with such a secret provision of comfort within his own breast to help the joy, he found in it a source of most gratifying sensation, and unvarying cheerfulness all dinner-time.

After dinner, when he and his father were alone, he had Fanny's history; and then all the great events of the last fortnight, and the present situation of matters at Mansfield were known to him.

Fanny suspected what was going on. They sat so much longer than usual in the dining parlour, that she was sure they must be talking of her; and when tea at last brought them away, and she was to be seen by Edmund again, she felt dreadfully guilty. He came to her, sat down by her, took her hand, and pressed it kindly; and at that moment she thought that, but for the occupation and the scene* which the tea-things afforded, she must have betrayed her emotion in some unpardonable excess.

He was not intending, however, by such action, to be conveying to her that unqualified approbation and encouragement which her hopes drew from it. It was designed only to express his participation in all that interested her, and to tell her that he had been hearing what quickened every feeling of affection. He was, in fact, entirely on his father's side of the question. His surprise was not so great as his father's, at her refusing Crawford, because, so far from supposing her to consider him with anything like a preference, he had always believed it to be rather the reverse, and could imagine her to be taken perfectly unprepared, but Sir Thomas could not regard the connection as more desirable than he did. It had every recommendation to him, and while honouring her for what she had done under the influence of her present indifference, honouring her in rather stronger terms than Sir Thomas could quite echo, he was most earnest in hoping, and sanguine in believing, that it would be a match at last, and that, united by mutual affection, it would appear that their dispositions were as exactly fitted to make them blessed in each other, as he was now beginning seriously to consider them. Crawford had been too precipitate. He had not given her time to attach herself. He had begun at the wrong end. With such powers as his, however, and such a disposition as hers, Edmund trusted that every thing would work out a happy conclusion. Meanwhile, he saw enough of Fanny's embarrassment to make him scrupulously guard against exciting it a second time, by any word, or look, or movement.

Crawford called the next day, and on the score of Edmund's return, Sir Thomas felt himself more than licensed to ask him to stay dinner; it was really a necessary compliment. He staid of course, and Edmund had then ample opportunity for observing how he sped with Fanny, and what degree of immediate encouragement for him might be extracted from her manners; and it was so little, so very very little, (every chance, every possibility of it, resting upon her embarrassment only, if there was not hope in her confusion, there was hope in nothing else,) that he was almost ready to wonder at his friend's perseverance.—Fanny was worth it all; he held her to be worth every effort of patience, every exertion of mind—but he did not think he could have gone on himself with any woman breathing, without something more to warm his courage than his eyes could discern in hers. He was very willing to hope that Crawford saw clearer; and this was the most comfortable conclusion for his friend that he could come to from all that he observed to pass before, and at, and after dinner.

In the evening a few circumstances occurred which he thought more promising. When he and Crawford walked into the drawing room, his mother and Fanny were sitting as intently and silently at work as if there were nothing else to care for. Edmund could not help noticing their apparently deep tranquillity.

"We have not been so silent all the time," replied his mother. "Fanny has been reading to me, and only put the book down upon hearing you coming."—And sure enough there was a book on the table which had the air of being very recently closed, a volume of Shakespeare.[1]— "She often reads to me out of those books; and she was in the middle of a very fine speech of that man's—What's his name, Fanny?—when we heard your footsteps."

Crawford took the volume. "Let me have the pleasure of finishing that speech to your ladyship," said he. "I shall find it immediately." And by carefully giving way to the inclination of the leaves, he did find it, or within a page or two, quite near enough to satisfy Lady Bertram, who assured him, as soon as he mentioned the name of Cardinal Wolsey, that he had got the very speech.—Not a look, or an offer of help had Fanny given; not a syllable for or against. All her attention was for her work. She seemed determined to be interested by nothing else. But taste was too strong in her. She could not abstract her mind five minutes; she was forced to listen; his reading was capital, and her pleasure in good reading extreme. To *good* reading, however, she had been long used; her uncle read well—her cousins all—Edmund very well; but in Mr. Crawford's reading there was a variety of excellence beyond what she had ever met with. The King, the Queen, Buckingham, Wolsey, Cromwell, all were given in turn; for with the happiest knack, the happiest power of jumping and guessing, he could always light, at will, on the best scene, or the best speeches of each; and whether it were dignity or pride, or tenderness or remorse, or whatever were to be expressed, he could do it with equal beauty.—It was truly dramatic.—His

1. *Henry VIII* is a historical drama by William Shakespeare and, it is now agreed, John Fletcher, first performed in 1613. In addition to dramatizing the formation of the English national church, this play depicts the accusation and execution of Buckingham, Henry VIII's divorce from Queen Catherine, the pride and fall of Cardinal Wolsey, the coronation of Anne Boleyn, the vindication of Cranmer and Cromwell, and the christening of Princess—later Queen— Elizabeth. Replete with elaborate pageantry and declamatory speeches about the falls of the great, *Henry VIII* was often lavishly staged in the late eighteenth century, with leading actors taking the roles of Catherine and Wolsey.

acting had first taught Fanny what pleasure a play might give, and his reading brought all his acting before her again; nay, perhaps with greater enjoyment, for it came unexpectedly, and with no such drawback as she had been used to suffer in seeing him on the stage with Miss Bertram.

Edmund watched the progress of her attention, and was amused and gratified by seeing how she gradually slackened in the needle-work, which, at the beginning, seemed to occupy her totally; how it fell from her hand while she sat motionless over it—and at last, how the eyes which had appeared so studiously to avoid him throughout the day, were turned and fixed on Crawford, fixed on him for minutes, fixed on him in short till the attraction drew Crawford's upon her, and the book was closed, and the charm was broken. Then, she was shrinking again into herself, and blushing and working as hard as ever; but it had been enough to give Edmund encouragement for his friend, and as he cordially thanked him, he hoped to be expressing Fanny's secret feelings too.

"That play must be a favourite with you," said he; "You read as if you knew it well."

"It will be a favourite I believe from this hour," replied Crawford;— "but I do not think I have had a volume of Shakespeare in my hand before, since I was fifteen.—I once saw Henry the 8th acted.—Or I have heard of it from somebody who did—I am not certain which. But Shakespeare one gets acquainted with without knowing how. It is a part of an Englishman's constitution. His thoughts and beauties are so spread abroad that one touches them every where, one is intimate with him by instinct.—No man of any brain can open at a good part of one of his plays, without falling into the flow of his meaning immediately."

"No doubt, one is familiar with Shakespeare in a degree," said Edmund, "from one's earliest years. His celebrated passages are quoted by every body; they are in half the books we open, and we all talk Shakespeare, use his similies, and describe with his descriptions; but this is totally distinct from giving his sense as you gave it. To know him in bits and scraps, is common enough; to know him pretty thoroughly, is, perhaps, not uncommon; but to read him well aloud, is no everyday talent."

"Sir, you do me honour;" was Crawford's answer, with a bow of mock gravity.

Both gentlemen had a glance at Fanny, to see if a word of accordant praise could be extorted from her; yet both feeling that it could not be. Her praise had been given in her attention; *that* must content them.

Lady Bertram's admiration was expressed, and strongly too. "It was really like being at a play," said she.—"I wish Sir Thomas had been here."

Crawford was excessively pleased.—If Lady Bertram, with all her incompetency and languor, could feel this, the inference of what her niece, alive and enlightened as she was, must feel, was elevating.

"You have a great turn for acting, I am sure, Mr. Crawford," said her Ladyship soon afterwards—"and I will tell you what, I think you will have a theatre, some time or other, at your house in Norfolk. I mean when you are settled there. I do, indeed. I think you will fit up a theatre at your house in Norfolk."

"Do you, Ma'am?" cried he with quickness. "No, no, that will never be. Your Ladyship is quite mistaken. No theatre at Everingham! Oh! no."—And he looked at Fanny with an expressive smile, which evidently meant, "that lady will never allow a theatre at Everingham."

Edmund saw it all, and saw Fanny so determined *not* to see it, as to make it clear that the voice was enough to convey the full meaning of the protestation; and such a quick consciousness of compliment, such a ready comprehension of a hint, he thought, was rather favourable than not.

The subject of reading aloud was farther discussed. The two young men were the only talkers, but they, standing by the fire, talked over the too common neglect of the qualification, the total inattention to it, in the ordinary school-system for boys, the consequently natural—yet in some instances almost unnatural degree of ignorance and uncouthness of men, of sensible and well-informed men, when suddenly called to the necessity of reading aloud, which had fallen within their notice, giving instances of blunders, and failures with their secondary causes, the want of management of the voice, of proper modulation and emphasis, of foresight and judgment, all proceeding from the first cause, want of early attention and habit; and Fanny was listening again with great entertainment.

"Even in my profession"—said Edmund with a smile—"how little the art of reading has been studied! how little a clear manner, and good delivery, have been attended to! I speak rather of the past, however, than the present.—There is now a spirit of improvement abroad; but among those who were ordained twenty, thirty, forty years ago, the larger number, to judge by their performance, must have thought reading was reading, and preaching was preaching. It is different now. The subject is more justly considered. It is felt that distinctness and energy may have weight in recommending the most solid truths; and, besides, there is more general observation and taste, a more critical knowledge diffused, than formerly; in every congregation, there is a larger proportion who know a little of the matter, and who can judge and criticize."

Edmund had already gone through the service once since his ordination; and upon this being understood, he had a variety of questions from Crawford as to his feelings and success; questions which being made—though with the vivacity of friendly interest and quick taste—without any touch of that spirit of banter or air of levity which Edmund knew to be most offensive to Fanny, he had true pleasure in satisfying; and when Crawford proceeded to ask his opinion and give his own as to the properest manner in which particular passages in the service should be delivered, shewing it to be a subject on which he had thought before, and thought with judgment, Edmund was still more and more pleased. This would be the way to Fanny's heart. She was not to be won by all that gallantry and wit, and good nature together, could do; or at least, she would not be won by them nearly so soon, without the assistance of sentiment and feeling, and seriousness on serious subjects.

"Our liturgy," observed Crawford, "has beauties, which not even a careless, slovenly style of reading can destroy; but it has also redundancies and repetitions, which require good reading not to be felt. For myself, at least, I must confess being not always so attentive as I ought to be—(here was a glance at Fanny) that nineteen times out of twenty I am thinking how such a prayer ought to be read, and longing to have it to read myself—Did you speak?" stepping eagerly to Fanny, and addressing her in a softened voice; and upon her saying, "No," he added, "Are you sure you did not speak? I saw your lips move. I fancied you might be going to tell me I *ought* to be more attentive, and not *allow* my thoughts to wander. Are not you going to tell me so?"

"No, indeed, you know your duty too well for me to—even supposing—"

She stopt, felt herself getting into a puzzle, and could not be prevailed on to add another word, not by dint of several minutes of supplication and waiting. He then returned to his former station, and went on as if there had been no such tender interruption.

"A sermon, well delivered, is more uncommon even than prayers well read. A sermon, good in itself, is no rare thing. It is more difficult to speak well than to compose well; that is, the rules and trick of composition are oftener an object of study. A thoroughly good sermon, thoroughly well delivered, is a capital gratification. I can never hear such a one without the greatest admiration and respect, and more than half a mind to take orders and preach myself. There is something in the eloquence of the pulpit, when it is really eloquence, which is entitled to the highest praise and honour. The preacher who can touch and affect* such an heterogeneous mass of hearers, on subjects limited, and longworn thread-bare in all common hands; who can say any thing new or striking, any thing that rouses the attention, without offending the taste, or wearing out the feelings of his hearers, is a man whom one could not (in his public capacity) honour enough. I should like to be such a man."

Edmund laughed.

"I should indeed. I never listened to a distinguished preacher in my life, without a sort of envy. But then, I must have a London audience. I could not preach, but to the educated; to those who were capable of estimating my composition. And I do not know that I should be fond of preaching often; now and then, perhaps, once or twice in the spring, after being anxiously expected for half a dozen Sundays together; but not for a constancy; it would not do for a constancy."

Here Fanny, who could not but listen, involuntarily shook her head, and Crawford was instantly by her side again, intreating to know her meaning; and as Edmund perceived, by his drawing in a chair, and sitting down close by her, that it was to be a very thorough attack, that looks and undertones were to be well tried, he sank as quietly as possible into a corner, turned his back, and took up a newspaper, very sincerely wishing that dear little Fanny might be persuaded into explaining away that shake of the head to the satisfaction of her ardent lover; and as earnestly trying to bury every sound of the business from himself in murmurs of his own, over the various advertisements of "a most desirable estate in South Wales"—"To Parents and Guardians"—and a "Capital season'd Hunter."

Fanny, meanwhile, vexed with herself for not having been as motionless as she was speechless, and grieved to the heart to see Edmund's arrangements, was trying, by every thing in the power of her modest gentle nature, to repulse Mr. Crawford, and avoid both his looks and enquiries; and he unrepulsable was persisting in both.

"What did that shake of the head mean?" said he. "What was it meant to express? Disapprobation, I fear. But of what?—What had I been saying to displease you?—Did you think me speaking improperly?—lightly, irreverently on the subject?—Only tell me if I was. Only tell me if I was wrong. I want to be set right. Nay, nay, I entreat you; for one moment put down your work. What did that shake of the head mean?"

In vain was her "Pray, Sir, don't—pray, Mr. Crawford," repeated twice over; and in vain did she try to move away—In the same low eager voice, and the same close neighbourhood, he went on, re-urging the same questions as before. She grew more agitated and displeased.

"How can you, Sir? You quite astonish me—I wonder how you can"—

"Do I astonish you?"—said he. "Do you wonder? Is there any thing in my present intreaty that you do not understand? I will explain to you instantly all that makes me urge you in this manner, all that gives me an interest in what you look and do, and excites my present curiosity. I will not leave you to wonder long."

In spite of herself, she could not help half a smile, but she said nothing.

"You shook your head at my acknowledging that I should not like to engage in the duties of a clergyman always for* a constancy. Yes, that was the word. Constancy, I am not afraid of the word. I would spell it, read it, write it with any body. I see nothing alarming in the word. Did you think I ought?"

"Perhaps, Sir," said Fanny, wearied at last into speaking—"perhaps, Sir, I thought it was a pity you did not always know yourself as well as you seemed to do at that moment."

Crawford, delighted to get her to speak at any rate, was determined to keep it up; and poor Fanny, who had hoped to silence him by such an extremity of reproof, found herself sadly mistaken, and that it was only a change from one object of curiosity and one set of words to another. He had always something to intreat the explanation of. The opportunity was too fair. None such had occurred since his seeing her in her uncle's room, none such might occur again before his leaving Mansfield. Lady Bertram's being just on the other side of the table was a trifle, for she might always be considered as only half awake, and Edmund's advertisements were still of the first utility.

"Well," said Crawford, after a course of rapid questions and reluctant answers—"I am happier than I was, because I now understand more clearly your opinion of me. You think me unsteady—easily swayed by the whim of the moment—easily tempted—easily put aside. With such an opinion, no wonder that——But we shall see.—It is not by protestations that I shall endeavour to convince you I am wronged, it is not by telling you that my affections are steady. My conduct shall speak for me—absence, distance, time shall speak for me.—*They* shall prove, that as far as you can be deserved by any body, I do deserve you.—You are infinitely my superior in merit; all *that* I know.—You have qualities which I had not before supposed to exist in such a degree in any human creature. You have some touches of the angel in you, beyond what—not merely beyond what one sees, because one never sees any thing like it—but beyond what one fancies might be. But still I am not frightened. It is not by equality of merit that you can be won. That is out of the question. It is he who sees and worships your merit the strongest, who loves you most devotedly, that has the best right to a return. There I build my confidence. By that right I do and will deserve you; and when once convinced that my attachment is what I declare it, I know you too well not to entertain the warmest hopes—Yes, dearest, sweetest Fanny—Nay—(seeing her draw back displeased) forgive me. Perhaps I have as yet no right—but by what other name can I call you? Do you suppose you are ever present to my imagination under any other? No, it is 'Fanny' that I think of all day, and dream of all night.—You have given the name such reality of sweetness, that nothing else can now be descriptive of you."

Fanny could hardly have kept her seat any longer, or have refrained from at least trying to get away in spite of all the too public opposition she foresaw to it, had it not been for the sound of approaching relief, the very sound which she had been long watching for, and long thinking strangely delayed.

The solemn procession, headed by Baddely, of tea-board, urn, and cake-bearers, made its appearance, and delivered her from a grievous imprisonment of body and mind. Mr. Crawford was obliged to move. She was at liberty, she was busy, she was protected.

Edmund was not sorry to be admitted again among the number of those who might speak and hear. But though the conference had seemed full long to him, and though on looking at Fanny he saw rather a flush of vexation, he inclined to hope that so much could not have been said and listened to, without some profit to the speaker.

Chapter IV.

Edmund had determined that it belonged entirely to Fanny to chuse whether her situation with regard to Crawford should be mentioned between them or not; and that if she did not lead the way, it should never be touched on by him; but after a day or two of mutual reserve, he was induced by his father to change his mind, and try what his influence might do for his friend.

A day, and a very early day, was actually fixed for the Crawfords' departure; and Sir Thomas thought it might be as well to make one more effort for the young man before he left Mansfield, that all his professions and vows of unshaken attachment might have as much hope to sustain them as possible.

Sir Thomas was most cordially anxious for the perfection of Mr. Crawford's character in that point. He wished him to be a model of constancy; and fancied the best means of effecting it would be by not trying him too long.

Edmund was not unwilling to be persuaded to engage in the business; he wanted to know Fanny's feelings. She had been used to consult him in every difficulty, and he loved her too well to bear to be denied her confidence now; he hoped to be of service to her, he thought he must be of service to her, whom else had she to open her heart to? If she did not need counsel, she must need the comfort of communication. Fanny estranged from him, silent and reserved, was an unnatural state of things; a state which he must break through, and which he could easily learn to think she was wanting him to break through.

"I will speak to her, Sir; I will take the first opportunity of speaking to her alone," was the result of such thoughts as these; and upon Sir Thomas's information of her being at that very time walking alone in the shrubbery, he instantly joined her.

"I am come to walk with you, Fanny," said he. "Shall I?"—(drawing her arm within his,) "it is a long while since we have had a comfortable walk together."

She assented to it all rather by look than word. Her spirits were low.

"But, Fanny," he presently added, "in order to have a comfortable walk, something more is necessary than merely pacing this gravel together. You must talk to me. I know you have something on your mind. I know what you are thinking of. You cannot suppose me uninformed. Am I to hear of it from every body but Fanny herself?"

Fanny, at once agitated and dejected, replied, "If you hear of it from every body, cousin, there can be nothing for me to tell."

"Not of facts, perhaps; but of feelings, Fanny. No one but you can tell me them. I do not mean to press you, however. If it is not what you wish yourself, I have done. I had thought it might be a relief."

"I am afraid we think too differently, for me to find any relief in talking of what I feel."

"Do you suppose that we think differently? I have no idea of it. I dare say, that on a comparison of our opinions, they would be found as much alike as they have been used to be: to the point—I consider Crawford's proposals as most advantageous and desirable, if you could return his affection. I consider it as most natural that all your family should wish you could return it; but that as you cannot, you have done exactly as you ought in refusing him. Can there be any disagreement between us here?"

"Oh no! But I thought you blamed me. I thought you were* against me. This is such a comfort!"

"This comfort you might have had sooner, Fanny, had you sought it. But how could you possibly suppose me against you? How could you imagine me an advocate for marriage without love? Were I even careless in general on such matters, how could you imagine me so where *your* happiness was at stake?"

"My uncle thought me wrong, and I knew he had been talking to you."

"As far as you have gone, Fanny, I think you perfectly right. I may be sorry, I may be surprised—though hardly *that*, for you had not had time to attach yourself; but I think you perfectly right. Can it admit of a question? It is disgraceful to us if it does. You did not love him—nothing could have justified your accepting him."

Fanny had not felt so comfortable for days and days.

"So far your conduct has been faultless, and they were quite mistaken who wished you to do otherwise. But the matter does not end here. Crawford's is no common attachment; he perseveres, with the hope of creating that regard which had not been created before. This, we know, must be a work of time. But (with an affectionate smile), let him succeed at last, Fanny, let him succeed at last. You have proved yourself upright and disinterested, prove yourself grateful and tender-hearted; and then you will be the perfect model of a woman, which I have always believed you born for."

"Oh! never, never, never; he never will succeed with me." And she spoke with a warmth which quite astonished Edmund, and which she blushed at the recollection of herself, when she saw his look, and heard him reply, "Never, Fanny, so very determined and positive! This is not like yourself, your rational self."

"I mean," she cried, sorrowfully, correcting herself, "that I *think*, I never shall, as far as the future can be answered for—I think I never shall return his regard."

"I must hope better things. I am aware, more aware than Crawford can be, that the man who means to make you love him (you having due notice of his intentions), must have very up-hill work, for there are all your early attachments, and habits, in battle array; and before he can get your heart for his own use, he has to unfasten it from all the holds upon things animate and inanimate, which so many years'* growth have confirmed, and which are considerably tightened for the moment by the very idea of separation. I know that the apprehension of being forced to quit Mansfield will for a time be arming you against him. I wish he had not been obliged to tell you what he was trying for. I wish he had known you as well as I do, Fanny. Between us, I think we should have won you. My theoretical and his practical knowledge together, could not have failed. He should have worked upon my plans. I must hope, however, that time proving him (as I firmly believe it will), to deserve you by his steady affection, will give him his reward. I cannot suppose that you have not the *wish* to love him—the natural wish of gratitude. You must have some feeling of that sort. You must be sorry for your own indifference."

"We are so totally unlike," said Fanny, avoiding a direct answer, "we are so very, very different in all our inclinations and ways, that I consider it as quite impossible we should ever be tolerably happy together, even if I *could* like him. There never were two people more dissimilar. We have not one taste in common. We should be miserable."

"You are mistaken, Fanny. The dissimilarity is not so strong. You are quite enough alike. You *have* tastes in common. You have moral and literary tastes in common. You have both warm hearts and benevolent feelings; and Fanny, who that heard him read, and saw you listen to Shakespeare the other night, will think you unfitted as companions? You forget yourself: there is a decided difference in your tempers, I allow. He is lively, you are serious; but so much the better; his spirits will support yours. It is your disposition to be easily dejected, and to fancy difficulties greater than they are. His cheerfulness will counteract this. He sees difficulties no where; and his pleasantness and gaiety will be a constant support to you. Your being so far unlike, Fanny, does not in the smallest degree make against the probability of your happiness together: do not imagine it. I am myself convinced that it is rather a favourable circumstance. I am perfectly persuaded that the tempers had better be unlike; I mean unlike in the flow of the spirits, in the manners, in the inclination for much or little company, in the propensity to talk or to be silent, to be grave or to be gay. Some opposition here is, I am thoroughly convinced, friendly to matrimonial happiness. I exclude extremes of course; and a very close resemblance in all those points would be the likeliest way to produce an extreme. A counteraction, gentle and continual, is the best safe-guard of manners and conduct."

Full well could Fanny guess where his thoughts were now. Miss Crawford's power was all returning. He had been speaking of her cheerfully from the hour of his coming home. His avoiding her was quite at an end. He had dined at the parsonage only the preceding day.

After leaving him to his happier thoughts for some minutes, Fanny feeling it due to herself, returned to Mr. Crawford, and said, "It is not merely in *temper* that I consider him as totally unsuited to myself; though in *that* respect, I think the difference between us too great, infinitely too great; his spirits often oppress me—but there is something in him which I object to still more. I must say, cousin, that I cannot approve his character. I have not thought well of him from the time of the play. I then saw him behaving, as it appeared to me, so very improperly and unfeelingly, I may speak of it now because it is all over—so improperly by poor Mr. Rushworth, not seeming to care how he exposed or hurt him, and paying attentions to my cousin Maria, which—in short, at the time of the play, I received an impression which will never be got over."

"My dear Fanny," replied Edmund, scarcely hearing her to the end, "let us not, any of us, be judged by what we appeared at that period of general folly. The time of the play, is a time which I hate to recollect. Maria was wrong, Crawford was wrong, we were all wrong together; but none so wrong as myself. Compared with me, all the rest were blameless. I was playing the fool with my eyes open."

"As a by-stander," said Fanny, "perhaps I saw more than you did; and I do think that Mr. Rushworth was sometimes very jealous."

"Very possibly. No wonder. Nothing could be more improper than the whole business. I am shocked whenever I think that Maria could be capable of it; but if she could undertake the part, we must not be surprised at the rest."

"Before the play, I am much mistaken, if *Julia* did not think he was paying her attentions."

"Julia!—I have heard before from some one of his being in love with Julia, but I could never see any thing of it. And Fanny, though I hope I do justice to my sisters' good qualities, I think it very possible that they might, one or both, be more desirous of being admired by Crawford, and might shew that desire rather more unguardedly than was perfectly prudent. I can remember that they were evidently fond of his society; and with such encouragement, a man like Crawford, lively, and it may be a little unthinking, might be led on to—There could be nothing very striking, because it is clear that he had no pretensions; his heart was reserved for you. And I must say, that its being for you, has raised him inconceivably in my opinion. It does him the highest honour; it shews his proper estimation of the blessing of domestic happiness, and pure attachment. It proves him unspoilt by his uncle. It proves him, in short, every thing that I had been used to wish to believe him, and feared he was not."

"I am persuaded that he does not think as he ought, on serious subjects."

"Say rather, that he has not thought at all upon serious subjects, which I believe to be a good deal the case. How could it be otherwise, with such an education and adviser? Under the disadvantages; indeed, which both have had, is it not wonderful that they should be what they are? Crawford's *feelings*, I am ready to acknowledge, have hitherto been too much his guides. Happily, those feelings have generally been good. You will supply the rest; and a most fortunate man he is to attach himself to such a creature—to a woman, who firm as a rock in her own principles, has a gentleness of character so well adapted to recommend them. He has chosen his partner, indeed, with rare felicity. He will make you happy, Fanny, I know he will make you happy; but you will make him every thing."

"I would not engage in such a charge," cried Fanny in a shrinking accent—"in such an office of high responsibility!"

"As usual, believing yourself unequal to anything!—fancying everything too much for you! Well, though I may not be able to persuade you into different feelings, you will be persuaded into them I trust. I confess myself sincerely anxious that you may. I have no common interest in Crawford's well doing. Next to your happiness, Fanny, his has the first claim on me. You are aware of my having no common interest in Crawford."

Fanny was too well aware of it, to have anything to say; and they walked on together some fifty yards in mutual silence and abstraction. Edmund first began again:—

"I was very much pleased by her manner of speaking of it yesterday, particularly pleased, because I had not depended upon her seeing every thing in so just a light. I knew she was very fond of you, but yet I was afraid of her not estimating your worth to her brother, quite as it deserved, and of her regretting that he had not rather fixed on some woman of distinction, or fortune. I was afraid of the bias of those worldly maxims, which she has been too much used to hear. But it was very different. She spoke of you, Fanny, just as she ought. She desires the connection as warmly as your uncle or myself. We had a long talk about it. I should not have mentioned the subject, though very anxious to know her sentiments—but I had not been in the room five minutes, before she began, introducing it with all that openness of heart, and sweet peculiarity of manner, that spirit and ingenuousness, which are so much a part of herself. Mrs. Grant laughed at her for her rapidity."

"Was Mrs. Grant in the room, then?"

"Yes, when I reached the house I found the two sisters together by themselves; and when once we had begun, we had not done with you, Fanny, till Crawford and Dr. Grant came in."

"It is above a week since I saw Miss Crawford."

"Yes, she laments it; yet owns it may have been best. You will see her, however, before she goes. She is very angry with you, Fanny; you must be prepared for that. She calls herself very angry, but you can imagine her anger. It is the regret and disappointment of a sister, who thinks her brother has a right to every thing he may wish for, at the first moment. She is hurt, as you would be for William; but she loves and esteems you with all her heart."

"I knew she would be very angry with me."

"My dearest Fanny," cried Edmund, pressing her arm closer to him, "do not let the idea of her anger distress you. It is anger to be talked of, rather than felt. Her heart is made for love and kindness, not for resentment. I wish you could have overheard her tribute of praise; I wish you could have seen her countenance, when she said that you *should* be Henry's wife. And I observed, that she always spoke of you as 'Fanny,' which she was never used to do; and it had a sound of most sisterly cordiality."

"And Mrs. Grant, did she say—did she speak—was she there all the time?"

"Yes, she was agreeing exactly with her sister. The surprise of your refusal, Fanny, seems to have been unbounded. That you could refuse such a man as Henry Crawford, seems more than they can understand. I said what I could for you; but in good truth, as they stated the case —you must prove yourself to be in your senses as soon as you can, by a different conduct; nothing else will satisfy them. But this is teazing you. I have done. Do not turn away from me."

"I *should* have thought," said Fanny, after a pause of recollection and exertion, "that every woman must have felt the possibility of a man's not being approved, not being loved by some one of her sex, at least, let him be ever so generally agreeable. Let him have all the perfections in the world, I think it ought not to be set down as certain, that a man must be acceptable to every woman he may happen to like himself. But even supposing it is so, allowing Mr. Crawford to have all the claims which his sisters think he has, how was I to be prepared to meet him with any feeling answerable to his own? He took me wholly by surprise. I had not an idea that his behaviour to me before had any meaning; and surely I was not to be teaching myself to like him only because he was taking, what seemed, very idle notice of me. In my situation, it would have been the extreme of vanity to be forming expectations on Mr. Crawford. I am sure his sisters, rating him as they do, must have thought it so, supposing he had meant nothing. How then was I to be—to be in love with him the moment he said he was with me? How was I to have an attachment at his service, as soon as it was asked for? His sisters should consider me as well as him. The higher his deserts, the more improper for me ever to have thought of him. And, and—we think very differently of the nature of women, if they can imagine a woman so very soon capable of returning an affection as this seems to imply."

"My dear, dear Fanny, now I have the truth. I know this to be the truth; and most worthy of you are such feelings. I had attributed them to you before. I thought I could understand you. You have now given exactly the explanation which I ventured to make for you to your friend and Mrs. Grant, and they were both better satisfied, though your warm-hearted friend was still run away with a little, by the enthusiasm of her fondness for Henry. I told them, that you were of all human creatures the one, over whom habit had most power, and novelty least: and that the very circumstance of the novelty of Crawford's addresses was against him. Their being so new and so recent was all in their disfavour; that you could tolerate nothing that you were not used to; and a great deal more to the same purpose, to give them a knowledge of your character. Miss Crawford made us laugh by her plans of encouragement for her brother. She meant to urge him to persevere in the hope of being loved in time, and of having his addresses most kindly received at the end of about ten years' happy marriage."

Fanny could with difficulty give the smile that was here asked for. Her feelings were all in revolt. She feared she had been doing wrong, saying too much, overacting the caution which she had been fancying necessary, in guarding against one evil, laying herself open to another, and to have Miss Crawford's liveliness repeated to her at such a moment, and on such a subject, was a bitter aggravation.

Edmund saw weariness and distress in her face, and immediately resolved to forbear all farther discussion; and not even to mention the name of Crawford again, except as it might be connected with what *must* be agreeable to her. On this principle, he soon afterwards observed, "They go on Monday. You are sure therefore of seeing your friend either to-morrow or Sunday. They really go on Monday! and I was within a trifle of being persuaded to stay at Lessingby till that very day! I had almost promised it. What a difference it might have made!

Those five or six days more at Lessingby might have been felt all my
life!"

"You were near staying there?"

"Very. I was most kindly pressed, and had nearly consented. Had I
received any letter from Mansfield, to tell me how you were all going
on, I believe I should certainly have stayed; but I knew nothing that
had happened here for a fortnight, and felt that I had been away long
enough."

"You spent your time pleasantly there."

"Yes; that is, it was the fault of my own mind if I did not. They were
all very pleasant. I doubt their finding me so. I took uneasiness with
me, and there was no getting rid of it till I was in Mansfield again."

"The Miss Owens—you liked them, did not you?"

"Yes, very well. Pleasant, good-humoured, unaffected girls. But I am
spoilt, Fanny, for common female society. Good-humoured, unaffected
girls, will not do for a man who has been used to sensible women.
They are two distinct orders of being. You and Miss Crawford have
made me too nice."[1]

Still, however, Fanny was oppressed and wearied; he saw it in her
looks, it could not be talked away, and attempting it no more, he led
her directly with the kind authority of a privileged guardian into the
house.

Chapter V.

Edmund now believed himself perfectly acquainted with all that Fanny
could tell, or could leave to be conjectured of her sentiments, and he
was satisfied.—It had been, as he before presumed, too hasty a measure
on Crawford's side, and time must be given to make the idea first
familiar, and then agreeable to her. She must be used to the consideration of his being in love with her, and then a return of affection
might not be very distant.

He gave this opinion as the result of the conversation, to his father;
and recommended there being nothing more said to her, no farther
attempts to influence or persuade; but that every thing should be left
to Crawford's assiduities, and the natural workings of her own mind.

Sir Thomas promised that it should be so. Edmund's account of
Fanny's disposition he could believe to be just, he supposed she had
all those feelings, but he must consider it as very unfortunate that she
had; for, less willing than his son to trust to the future, he could not
help fearing that if such very long allowances of time and habit were

1. Discriminating; fastidious.

necessary for her, she might not have persuaded herself into receiving his addresses properly, before the young man's inclination for paying them were over. There was nothing to be done, however, but to submit quietly, and hope the best.

The promised visit from her "friend," as Edmund called Miss Crawford, was a formidable threat to Fanny, and she lived in continual terror of it. As a sister, so partial and so angry, and so little scrupulous of what she said; and in another light, so triumphant and secure, she was in every way an object of painful alarm. Her displeasure, her penetration, and her happiness were all fearful to encounter; and the dependence of having others present when they met, was Fanny's only support in looking forward to it. She absented herself as little as possible from Lady Bertram, kept away from the east room, and took no solitary walk in the shrubbery, in her caution to avoid any sudden attack.

She succeeded. She was safe in the breakfast-room, with her aunt, when Miss Crawford did come; and the first misery over; and Miss Crawford looking and speaking with much less particularity of expression than she had anticipated, Fanny began to hope there would be nothing worse to be endured than an half-hour of moderate agitation. But here she hoped too much, Miss Crawford was not the slave of opportunity. She was determined to see Fanny alone, and therefore said to her tolerably soon, in a low voice, "I must speak to you for a few minutes somewhere;" words that Fanny felt all over her, in all her pulses, and all her nerves. Denial was impossible. Her habits of ready submission, on the contrary, made her almost instantly rise and lead the way out of the room. She did it with wretched feelings, but it was inevitable.

They were no sooner in the hall than all restraint of countenance was over on Miss Crawford's side. She immediately shook her head at Fanny with arch, yet affectionate reproach, and taking her hand, seemed hardly able to help beginning directly. She said nothing, however, but, "Sad, sad girl! I do not know when I shall have done scolding you," and had discretion enough to reserve the rest till they might be secure of having four walls to themselves. Fanny naturally turned up stairs, and took her guest to the apartment which was now always fit for comfortable use; opening the door, however, with a most aching heart, and feeling that she had a more distressing scene before her than ever that spot had yet witnessed. But the evil ready to burst on her, was at least delayed by the sudden change in Miss Crawford's ideas; by the strong effect on her mind which the finding herself in the east room again produced.

"Ha!" she cried, with instant animation, "am I here again? The east-room. Once only was I in this room before!"—and after stopping to look about her, and seemingly to retrace all that had then passed, she added, "Once only before. Do you remember it? I came to rehearse.

Your cousin came too; and we had a rehearsal. You were our audience and prompter. A delightful rehearsal. I shall never forget it. Here we were, just in this part of the room; here was your cousin, here was I, here were the chairs.—Oh! why will such things ever pass away?"

Happily for her companion, she wanted no answer. Her mind was entirely self-engrossed. She was in a reverie of sweet remembrances.

"The scene we were rehearsing was so very remarkable! The subject of it so very—very—what shall I say? He was to be describing and recommending matrimony to me. I think I see him now, trying to be as demure and composed as Anhalt ought, through the two long speeches. 'When two sympathetic hearts meet in the marriage state, matrimony may be called a happy life.'[1] I suppose no time can ever wear out the impression I have of his looks and voice, as he said those words. It was curious, very curious, that we should have such a scene to play! If I had the power of recalling any one week of my existence, it should be that week, that acting week. Say what you would, Fanny, it should be *that*; for I never knew such exquisite happiness in any other. His sturdy spirit to bend as it did! Oh! it was sweet beyond expression. But alas! that very evening destroyed it all. That very evening brought your most unwelcome uncle. Poor Sir Thomas, who was glad to see you? Yet, Fanny, do not imagine I would now speak disrespectfully of Sir Thomas, though I certainly did hate him for many a week. No, I do him justice now. He is just what the head of such a family should be. Nay, in sober sadness, I believe I now love you all." And having said so, with a degree of tenderness and consciousness which Fanny had never seen in her before, and now thought only too becoming, she turned away for a moment to recover herself. "I have had a little fit since I came into this room, as you may perceive," said she presently, with a playful smile, "but it is over now; so let us sit down and be comfortable; for as to scolding you, Fanny, which I came fully intending to do, I have not the heart for it when it comes to the point." And embracing her very affectionately,—"Good, gentle Fanny! when I think of this being the last time of seeing you; for I do not know how long —I feel it quite impossible to do any thing but love you."

Fanny was affected. She had not foreseen anything of this, and her feelings could seldom withstand the melancholy influence of the word "last." She cried as if she had loved Miss Crawford more than she possibly could; and Miss Crawford, yet farther softened by the sight of such emotion, hung about her with fondness, and said, "I hate to leave you. I shall see no one half so amiable where I am going. Who says we shall not be sisters? I know we shall. I feel that we are born to be connected; and those tears convince me that you feel it too, dear Fanny."

1. *Lovers' Vows* 3.2. See "Contexts," below, p. 351.

Fanny roused herself, and replying only in part, said, "But you are only going from one set of friends to another. You are going to a very particular friend."

"Yes, very true. Mrs. Fraser has been my intimate friend for years. But I have not the least inclination to go near her. I can think only of the friends I am leaving; my excellent sister, yourself, and the Bertrams in general. You have all so much more *heart* among you, than one finds in the world at large. You all give me a feeling of being able to trust and confide in you; which, in common intercourse, one knows nothing of. I wish I had settled with Mrs. Fraser not to go to her till after Easter, a much better time for the visit—but now I cannot put her off. And when I have done with her, I must go to her sister, Lady Stornaway, because *she* was rather my most particular friend of the two; but I have not cared much for *her* these three years."

After this speech, the two girls sat many minutes silent, each thoughtful; Fanny meditating on the different sorts of friendship in the world, Mary on something of less philosophic tendency. *She* first spoke again.

"How perfectly I remember my resolving to look for you up stairs; and setting off to find my way to the east room, without having an idea whereabouts it was! How well I remember what I was thinking of as I came along; and my looking in and seeing you here, sitting at this table at work; and then your cousin's astonishment when he opened the door at seeing me here! To be sure, your uncle's returning that very evening! There never was anything quite like it."

Another short fit of abstraction followed—when, shaking it off, she thus attacked her companion.

"Why, Fanny, you are absolutely in a reverie! Thinking, I hope, of one who is always thinking of you. Oh! that I could transport you for a short time into our circle in town, that you might understand how your power over Henry is thought of there! Oh! the envyings and heart-burnings of dozens and dozens! the wonder, the incredulity that will be felt at hearing what you have done! For as to secrecy, Henry is quite the hero of an old romance, and glories in his chains. You should come to London, to know how to estimate your conquest. If you were to see how he is courted, and how I am courted for his sake! Now I am well aware, that I shall not be half so welcome to Mrs. Fraser in consequence of his situation with you. When she comes to know the truth, she will very likely wish me in Northamptonshire again; for there is a daughter of Mr. Fraser by a first wife, whom she is wild to get married, and wants Henry to take. Oh! she has been trying for him to such a degree! Innocent and quiet as you sit here, you cannot have an idea of the *sensation* that you will be occasioning, of the curiosity there will be to see you, of the endless questions I shall have to answer! Poor Margaret Fraser will be at me for ever about your eyes and your teeth, and how you do your hair, and who makes your shoes. I wish Margaret

were* married, for my poor friend's sake, for I look upon the Frasers
to be about as unhappy as most other married people. And yet it was
a most desirable match for Janet at the time. We were all delighted.
She could not do otherwise than accept him, for he was rich, and she
had nothing; but he turns out ill-tempered, and *exigeant*;[2] and wants a
young woman, a beautiful young woman of five-and-twenty, to be as
steady as himself. And my friend does not manage him well; she does
not seem to know how to make the best of it. There is a spirit of
irritation, which, to say nothing worse, is certainly very ill-bred. In their
house I shall call to mind the conjugal manners of Mansfield Parsonage
with respect. Even Dr. Grant does shew a thorough confidence in my
sister, and a certain consideration for her judgment, which makes one
feel there *is* attachment; but of that, I shall see nothing with the Frasers.
I shall be at Mansfield for ever, Fanny. My own sister as a wife, Sir
Thomas Bertram as a husband, are my standards of perfection. Poor
Janet has been sadly taken in; and yet there was nothing improper on
her side; she did not run into the match inconsiderately, there was no
want of foresight. She took three days to consider of his proposals; and
during those three days asked the advice of every body connected with
.her, whose opinion was worth having; and especially applied to my late
dear aunt, whose knowledge of the world made her judgment very
generally and deservedly looked up to by all the young people of her
acquaintance; and she was decidedly in favour of Mr. Fraser. This
seems as if nothing were a security for matrimonial comfort! I have not
so much to say for my friend Flora, who jilted a very nice young man
in the Blues,[3] for the sake of that horrid Lord Stornaway, who has about
as much sense, Fanny, as Mr. Rushworth, but much worse looking,
and with a black-guard character. I *had* my doubts at the time about
her being right, for he has not even the air of a gentleman, and now,
I am sure, she was wrong. By the by, Flora Ross was dying for Henry
the first winter she came out. But were I to attempt to tell you of all
the women whom I have known to be in love with him, I should never
have done. It is you only, you, insensible Fanny, who can think of him
with any thing like indifference. But are you so insensible as you profess
yourself? No, no, I see you are not."

There was indeed so deep a blush over Fanny's face at that moment,
as might warrant strong suspicion in a pre-disposed mind.

"Excellent creature! I will not teaze you. Every thing shall take its
course. But dear Fanny, you must allow that you were not so absolutely
unprepared to have the question asked as your cousin fancies. It is not
possible, but that you must have had some thoughts on the subject,
some surmises as to what might be. You must have seen that he was

2. Demanding.
3. Belonging to one of the three divisions of the English fleet (the others being the Red and the
White).

trying to please you, by every attention in his power. Was not he devoted to you at the ball? And then before the ball, the necklace! Oh! you received it just as it was meant. You were as conscious as heart could desire. I remember it perfectly."

"Do you mean then that your brother knew of the necklace beforehand? Oh! Miss Crawford, *that* was not fair."

"Knew of it! it was his own doing entirely, his own thought. I am ashamed to say, that it had never entered my head; but I was delighted to act on his proposal, for both your sakes."

"I will not say," replied Fanny, "that I was not half afraid at the time of its being so; for there was something in your look that frightened me—but not at first—I was as unsuspicious of it at first!—indeed, indeed I was. It is as true as that I sit here. And had I had an idea of it, nothing should have induced me to accept the necklace. As to your brother's behaviour, certainly I was sensible of a particularity, I had been sensible of it some little time, perhaps two* or three weeks; but then I considered it as meaning nothing, I put it down as simply being his way, and was as far from supposing as from wishing him to have any serious thoughts of me. I had not, Miss Crawford, been an inattentive observer of what was passing between him and some part of this family in the summer and autumn. I was quiet, but I was not blind. I could not but see that Mr. Crawford allowed himself in gallantries which did mean nothing."

"Ah! I cannot deny it. He has now and then been a sad flirt, and cared very little for the havock he might be making in young ladies' affections. I have often scolded him for it, but it is his only fault; and there is this to be said, that very few young ladies have any affections worth caring for. And then, Fanny, the glory of fixing one who has been shot at by so many; of having it in one's power to pay off the debts of one's sex! Oh, I am sure it is not in woman's nature to refuse such a triumph."

Fanny shook her head. "I cannot think well of a man who sports with any woman's feelings; and there may often be a great deal more suffered than a stander-by can judge of."

"I do not defend him. I leave him entirely to your mercy; and when he has got you at Everingham, I do not care how much you lecture him. But this I will say, that his fault, the liking to make girls a little in love with him, is not half so dangerous to a wife's happiness, as a tendency to fall in love himself, which he has never been addicted to. And I do seriously and truly believe that he is attached to you in a way that he never was to any woman before; that he loves you with all his heart, and will love you as nearly for ever as possible. If any man ever loved a woman for ever, I think Henry will do as much for you."

Fanny could not avoid a faint smile, but had nothing to say.

"I cannot imagine Henry ever to have been happier," continued

Mary, presently, "than when he had succeeded in getting your brother's commission."

She had made a sure push at Fanny's feelings here.

"Oh! yes. How very, very kind of him!"

"I know he must have exerted himself very much, for I know the parties he had to move. The Admiral hates trouble, and scorns asking favours; and there are so many young men's claims to be attended to in the same way, that a friendship and energy, not very determined, is easily put by. What a happy creature William must be! I wish we could see him."

Poor Fanny's mind was thrown into the most distressing of all its varieties. The recollection of what had been done for William was always the most powerful disturber of every decision against Mr. Crawford; and she sat thinking deeply of it till Mary, who had been first watching her complacently, and then musing on something else, suddenly called her attention, by saying, "I should like to sit talking with you here all day, but we must not forget the ladies below, and so good bye, my dear, my amiable, my excellent Fanny, for though we shall nominally part in the breakfast parlour, I must take leave of you here. And I do take leave, longing for a happy re-union, and trusting, that when we meet again, it will be under circumstances which may open our hearts to each other without any remnant or shadow of reserve."

A very, very kind embrace, and some agitation of manner, accompanied these words.

"I shall see your cousin in town soon; he talks of being there tolerably soon; and Sir Thomas, I dare say, in the course of the spring; and your eldest cousin and the Rushworths and Julia I am sure of meeting again and again, and all but you. I have two favours to ask, Fanny; one is your correspondence. You must write to me. And the other, that you will often call on Mrs. Grant and make her amends for my being gone."

The first, at least, of these favours Fanny would rather not have been asked; but it was impossible for her to refuse the correspondence; it was impossible for her even not to accede to it more readily than her own judgment authorised. There was no resisting so much apparent affection. Her disposition was peculiarly calculated to value a fond treatment, and from having hitherto known so little of it, she was the more overcome by Miss Crawford's. Besides, there was gratitude towards her, for having made their tête à tête so much less painful than her fears had predicted.

It was over, and she had escaped without reproaches and without detection. Her secret was still her own; and while that was the case, she thought she could resign herself to almost every thing.

In the evening there was another parting. Henry Crawford came and sat some time with them; and her spirits not being previously in the strongest state, her heart was softened for a while towards him—because he really seemed to feel.—Quite unlike his usual self, he scarcely said any thing. He was evidently oppressed, and Fanny must grieve for him, though hoping she might never see him again till he were the husband of some other woman.

When it came to the moment of parting, he would take her hand, he would not be denied it; he said nothing, however, or nothing that she heard, and when he had left the room, she was better pleased that such a token of friendship had passed.

On the morrow the Crawfords were gone.

Chapter VI.

Mr. Crawford gone, Sir Thomas's next object was, that he should be missed, and he entertained great hope that his niece would find a blank in the loss of those attentions which at the time she had felt, or fancied an evil. She had tasted of consequence in its most flattering form; and he did hope that the loss of it, the sinking again into nothing, would awaken very wholesome regrets in her mind.—He watched her with this idea—but he could hardly tell with what success. He hardly knew whether there were any difference in her spirits or not. She was always so gentle and retiring, that her emotions were beyond his discrimination. He did not understand her; he felt that he did not; and therefore applied to Edmund to tell him how she stood affected on the present occasion, and whether she were more or less happy than she had been.

Edmund did not discern any symptom of regret, and thought his father a little unreasonable in supposing the first three or four days could produce any.

What chiefly surprised Edmund was, that Crawford's sister, the friend and companion, who had been so much to her, should not be more visibly regretted. He wondered that Fanny spoke so seldom of *her*, and had so little voluntarily to say of her concern at this separation.

Alas! it was this sister, this friend and companion, who was now the chief bane of Fanny's comfort.—If she could have believed Mary's future fate as unconnected with Mansfield, as she was determined the brother's should be, if she could have hoped her return thither, to be as distant as she was much inclined to think his, she would have been light of heart indeed; but the more she recollected and observed, the more deeply was she convinced that every thing was now in a fairer train for Miss Crawford's marrying Edmund than it had ever been before.—On his side, the inclination was stronger, on hers less equivocal. His objections, the scruples of his integrity, seemed all done away—nobody could tell how; and the doubts and hesitations of her ambition were equally got over—and equally without apparent reason. It could only be imputed to increasing attachment. His good and her bad feelings yielded to love, and such love must unite them. He was to go to town, as soon as some business relative to Thornton Lacey were completed—perhaps, within a fortnight, he talked of going, he loved to talk of it; and when once with her again, Fanny could not doubt the rest.—Her acceptance must be as certain as his offer; and yet, there were bad feelings still remaining which made the prospect of it most sorrowful to her, independently—she believed independently of self.

In their very last conversation, Miss Crawford, in spite of some amiable sensations, and much personal kindness, had still been Miss Crawford, still shewn a mind led astray and bewildered, and without any suspicion of being so; darkened, yet fancying itself light. She might love, but she did not deserve Edmund by any other sentiment. Fanny believed there was scarcely a second feeling in common between them; and she may be forgiven by older sages, for looking on the chance of Miss Crawford's future improvement as nearly desperate, for thinking that if Edmund's influence in this season of love, had already done so little in clearing her judgment, and regulating her notions, his worth would be finally wasted on her even in years of matrimony.

Experience might have hoped more for any young people, so circumstanced, and impartiality would not have denied to Miss Crawford's nature, that participation of the general nature of women, which would lead her to adopt the opinions of the man she loved and respected, as her own.—But as such were Fanny's persuasions, she suffered very much from them, and could never speak of Miss Crawford without pain.

Sir Thomas, meanwhile, went on with his own hopes, and his own observations, still feeling a right, by all his knowledge of human nature, to expect to see the effect of the loss of power and consequence, on his niece's spirits, and the past attentions of the lover producing a craving for their return; and he was soon afterwards able to account for his not yet completely and indubitably seeing all this, by the prospect of another visitor, whose approach he could allow to be quite enough to support the spirits he was watching.—William had obtained a ten days' leave of absence to be given to Northamptonshire, and was coming, the happiest of lieutenants, because the latest made, to shew his happiness and describe his uniform.

He came; and he would have been delighted to shew his uniform there too, had not cruel custom prohibited its appearance except on duty. So the uniform remained at Portsmouth, and Edmund conjectured that before Fanny had any chance of seeing it, all its own freshness, and all the freshness of its wearer's feelings, must be worn away. It would be sunk into a badge of disgrace; for what can be more unbecoming, or more worthless, than the uniform of a lieutenant, who has been a lieutenant a year or two, and sees others made commanders

before him? So reasoned Edmund, till his father made him the confident of a scheme which placed Fanny's chance of seeing the 2d lieutenant of H. M. S. Thrush, in all his glory in another light.

This scheme was that she should accompany her brother back to
Portsmouth, and spend a little time with her own family. It had occurred to Sir Thomas, in one of his dignified musings, as a right and
desirable measure; but before he absolutely made up his mind, he
consulted his son. Edmund considered it every way, and saw nothing
but what was right. The thing was good in itself, and could not be done
at a better time; and he had no doubt of it being highly agreeable to
Fanny. This was enough to determine Sir Thomas; and a decisive "then
so it shall be," closed that stage of the business; Sir Thomas retiring
from it with some feelings of satisfaction, and views of good over and
above what he had communicated to his son, for his prime motive in
sending her away, had very little to do with the propriety of her seeing
her parents again, and nothing at all with any idea of making her happy.
He certainly wished her to go willingly, but he as certainly wished her
to be heartily sick of home before her visit ended; and that a little
abstinence from the elegancies and luxuries of Mansfield Park, would
bring her mind into a sober state, and incline her to a juster estimate
of the value of that home of greater permanence, and equal comfort,
of which she had the offer.

It was a medicinal project upon his niece's understanding, which he
must consider as at present diseased. A residence of eight or nine years
in the abode of wealth and plenty had a little disordered her powers of
comparing and judging. Her Father's house would, in all probability,
teach her the value of a good income; and he trusted that she would
be the wiser and happier woman, all her life, for the experiment he
had devised.

Had Fanny been at all addicted to raptures, she must have had a
strong attack of them, when she first understood what was intended,
when her uncle first made her the offer of visiting the parents and
brothers, and sisters, from whom she had been divided, almost half her
life, of returning for a couple of months to the scenes of her infancy,
with William for the protector and companion of her journey; and the
certainty of continuing to see William to the last hour of his remaining
on land. Had she ever given way to bursts of delight, it must have been
then, for she was delighted, but her happiness was of a quiet, deep,
heart-swelling sort; and though never a great talker, she was always more
inclined to silence when feeling most strongly. At the moment she
could only thank and accept. Afterwards, when familiarized with the
visions of enjoyment so suddenly opened, she could speak more largely
to William and Edmund of what she felt; but still there were emotions
of tenderness that could not be clothed in words—The remembrance
of all her earliest pleasures, and of what she had suffered in being torn

from them, came over her with renewed strength, and it seemed as if to be at home again, would heal every pain that had since grown out of the separation. To be in the centre of such a circle, loved by so many, and more loved by all than she had ever been before, to feel affection without fear or restraint, to feel herself the equal of those who surrounded her, to be at peace from all mention of the Crawfords, safe from every look which could be fancied a reproach on their account! —This was a prospect to be dwelt on with a fondness that could be but half acknowledged.

Edmund too—to be two months from *him*, (and perhaps, she might be allowed to make her absence three) must do her good. At a distance unassailed by his looks or his kindness, and safe from the perpetual irritation of knowing his heart, and striving to avoid his confidence, she should be able to reason herself into a properer state; she should be able to think of him as in London, and arranging every thing there, without wretchedness. —— What might have been hard to bear at Mansfield, was to become a slight evil at Portsmouth.

The only drawback was the doubt of her Aunt Bertram's being comfortable without her. She was of use to no one else; but *there* she might be missed to a degree that she did not like to think of; and that part of the arrangement was, indeed, the hardest for Sir Thomas to accomplish, and what only *he* could have accomplished at all.

But he was master at Mansfield Park. When he had really resolved on any measure, he could always carry it through; and now by dint of long talking on the subject, explaining and dwelling on the duty of Fanny's sometimes seeing her family, he did induce his wife to let her go; obtaining it rather from submission, however, than conviction, for Lady Bertram was convinced of very little more than that Sir Thomas thought Fanny ought to go, and therefore that she must. In the calmness of her own dressing-room, in the impartial flow of her own meditations, unbiassed by his bewildering statements, she could not acknowledge any necessity for Fanny's ever going near a Father and Mother who had done without her so long, while she was so useful to herself.—And as to the not missing her, which under Mrs. Norris's discussion was the point attempted to be proved, she set herself very steadily against admitting any such thing.

Sir Thomas had appealed to her reason, conscience, and dignity. He called it a sacrifice, and demanded it of her goodness and self-command as such. But Mrs. Norris wanted to persuade her that Fanny could be very well spared—(*She* being ready to give up all her own time to her as requested) and in short could not really be wanted or missed.

"That may be, sister,"—was all Lady Bertram's reply—"I dare say you are very right, but I am sure I shall miss her very much."

The next step was to communicate with Portsmouth. Fanny wrote to offer herself; and her mother's answer, though short, was so kind, a

few simple lines expressed so natural and motherly a joy in the prospect
of seeing her child again, as to confirm all the daughter's views of
happiness in being with her—convincing her that she should now find
a warm and affectionate friend in the "Mamma" who had certainly
shewn no remarkable fondness for her formerly; but this she could
easily suppose to have been her own fault, or her own fancy. She had
probably alienated Love by the helplessness and fretfulness of a fearful
temper, or been unreasonable in wanting a larger share than any one
among so many could deserve. Now, when she knew better how to be
useful and how to forbear, and when her mother could be no longer
occupied by the incessant demands of a house full of little children,
there would be leisure and inclination for every comfort, and they
should soon be what mother and daughter ought to be to each other.

William was almost as happy in the plan as his sister. It would be
the greatest pleasure to him to have her there to the last moment before
he sailed, and perhaps find her there still when he came in, from his
first cruise! And besides, he wanted her so very much to see the Thrush
before she went out of harbour (the Thrush was certainly the finest
sloop in the service). And there were several improvements in the dock-
yard,[1] too, which he quite longed to shew her.

He did not scruple to add, that her being at home for a while would
be a great advantage to every body.

"I do not know how it is," said he, "but we seem to want some of
your nice ways and orderliness at my father's. The house is always in
confusion. You will set things going in a better way, I am sure. You
will tell my mother how it all ought to be, and you will be so useful
to Susan, and you will teach Betsey, and make the boys love and mind
you. How right and comfortable it will all be!"

By the time Mrs. Price's answer arrived, there remained but a very
few days more to be spent at Mansfield; and for part of one of those
days the young travellers were in a good deal of alarm on the subject
of their journey, for when the mode of it came to be talked of, and
Mrs. Norris found that all her anxiety to save her Brother-in-law's
money was vain, and that in spite of her wishes and hints for a less
expensive conveyance of Fanny, they were to travel post, when she saw
Sir Thomas actually give William notes for the purpose, she was struck
with the idea of there being room for a third in the carriage, and
suddenly seized with a strong inclination to go with them—to go and
see her poor dear sister Price. She proclaimed her thoughts. She must
say that she had more than half a mind to go with the young people;
it would be such an indulgence to her; she had not seen her poor dear
sister Price for more than twenty years; and it would be a help to the
young people in their journey to have her older head to manage for

1. The Naval Dockyard, located in Portsea.

them; and she could not help thinking her poor dear sister Price would feel it very unkind of her not to come by such an opportunity.

William and Fanny were horror-struck at the idea.

All the comfort of their comfortable journey would be destroyed at once. With woeful countenances they looked at each other. Their suspense lasted an hour or two. No one interfered to encourage or dissuade. Mrs. Norris was left to settle the matter by herself; and it ended to the infinite joy of her nephew and niece, in the recollection that she could not possibly be spared from Mansfield Park at present; that she was a great deal too necessary to Sir Thomas and Lady Bertram for her to be able to answer it to herself to leave them even for a week, and therefore must certainly sacrifice every other pleasure to that of being useful to them.

It had, in fact, occurred to her, that, though taken to Portsmouth for nothing, it would be hardly possible for her to avoid paying her own expenses back again. So, her poor dear sister Price was left to all the disappointment of her missing such an opportunity; and another twenty years' absence, perhaps, begun.

Edmund's plans were affected by this Portsmouth journey, this absence of Fanny's. He too had a sacrifice to make to Mansfield Park, as well as his aunt. He had intended, about this time, to be going to London, but he could not leave his father and mother just when every body else of most importance to their comfort, was leaving them; and with an effort, felt but not boasted of, he delayed for a week or two longer a journey which he was looking forward to, with the hope of its fixing his happiness for ever.

He told Fanny of it. She knew so much already, that she must know every thing. It made the substance of one other confidential discourse about Miss Crawford; and Fanny was the more affected from feeling it to be the last time in which Miss Crawford's name would ever be mentioned between them with any remains of liberty. Once afterwards, she was alluded to by him. Lady Bertram had been telling her niece in the evening to write to her soon and often, and promising to be a good correspondent herself; and Edmund, at a convenient moment, then added, in a whisper, "And *I* shall write to you, Fanny, when I have any thing worth writing about; any thing to say, that I think you will like to hear, and that you will not hear so soon from any other quarter." Had she doubted his meaning while she listened, the glow in his face, when she looked up at him, would have been decisive.

For this letter she must try to arm herself. That a letter from Edmund should be a subject of terror! She began to feel that she had not yet gone through all the changes of opinion and sentiment, which the progress of time and variation of circumstances occasion in this world of changes. The vicissitudes of the human mind had not yet been exhausted by her.

Poor Fanny! though going, as she did, willingly and eagerly, the last evening at Mansfield Park must still be wretchedness. Her heart was completely sad at parting. She had tears for every room in the house, much more for every beloved inhabitant. She clung to her aunt, because she would miss her; she kissed the hand of her uncle with struggling sobs, because she had displeased him; and as for Edmund, she could neither speak, nor look, nor think, when the last moment came with *him*, and it was not till it was over that she knew he was giving her the affectionate farewell of a brother.

All this passed over night, for the journey was to begin very early in the morning; and when the small, diminished party met at breakfast, William and Fanny were talked of as already advanced one stage.

Chapter VII.

The novelty of travelling, and the happiness of being with William, soon produced their natural effect on Fanny's spirits, when Mansfield Park was fairly left behind, and by the time their first stage was ended, and they were to quit Sir Thomas's carriage, she was able to take leave of the old coachman, and send back proper messages, with cheerful looks.

Of pleasant talk between the brother and sister, there was no end. Every thing supplied an amusement to the high glee of William's mind, and he was full of frolic and joke, in the intervals of their higher-toned subjects, all of which ended, if they did not begin, in praise of the Thrush, conjectures how she would be employed, schemes for an action with some superior force, which (supposing the first lieutenant out of the way—and William was not very* merciful to the first lieutenant) was to give himself the next step as soon as possible, or speculations upon prize money, which was to be generously distributed at home, with only the reservation of enough to make the little cottage comfortable, in which he and Fanny were to pass all their middle and latter life together.

Fanny's immediate concerns, as far as they involved Mr. Crawford, made no part of their conversation. William knew what had passed, and from his heart lamented that his sister's feelings should be so cold towards a man whom he must consider as the first of human characters; but he was of an age to be all for love, and therefore unable to blame; and knowing her wish on the subject, he would not distress her by the slightest allusion.

She had reason to suppose herself not yet forgotten by Mr. Crawford.—She had heard repeatedly from his sister within the three weeks which had passed since their leaving Mansfield, and in each letter there had been a few lines from himself, warm and determined like his

speeches. It was a correspondence which Fanny found quite as unpleasant as she had feared. Miss Crawford's style of writing, lively and
affectionate, was itself an evil, independent of what she was thus forced
into reading from the brother's pen, for Edmund would never rest till
she had read the chief of the letter to him, and then she had to listen
to his admiration of her language, and the warmth of her attachments.—There had, in fact, been so much of message, of allusion, of
recollection, so much of Mansfield in every letter, that Fanny could
not but suppose it meant for him to hear; and to find herself forced
into a purpose of that kind, compelled into a correspondence which
was bringing her the addresses of the man she did not love, and obliging
her to administer to the adverse passion of the man she did, was cruelly
mortifying. Here, too, her present removal promised advantage. When
no longer under the same roof with Edmund, she trusted that Miss
Crawford would have no motive for writing, strong enough to overcome
the trouble, and that at Portsmouth their correspondence would dwin-
dle into nothing.

With such thoughts as these among ten hundred others, Fanny proceeded in her journey, safely and cheerfully, and as expeditiously as
could rationally be hoped in the dirty month of February. They entered
Oxford, but she could take only a hasty glimpse of Edmund's College
as they passed along, and made no stop any where, till they reached
Newbury,[1] where a comfortable meal, uniting dinner and supper,
wound up the enjoyments and fatigues of the day.

The next morning saw them off again at an early hour; and with no
events and no delays they regularly advanced, and were in the environs
of Portsmouth while there was yet daylight for Fanny to look around
her, and wonder at the new buildings.—They passed the Drawbridge,[2]
and entered the town; and the light was only beginning to fail, as,
guided by William's powerful voice, they were rattled into a narrow
street, leading from the high street, and drawn up before the door of a
small house now inhabited by Mr. Price.

Fanny was all agitation and flutter—all hope and apprehension. The
moment they stopt, a trollopy-looking maid-servant, seemingly in waiting for them at the door, stept forward, and more intent on telling the
news, than giving them any help, immediately began with "the Thrush
is gone out of harbour, please Sir, and one of the officers has been
here to" —— She was interrupted by a fine tall boy of eleven years old,
who rushing out of the house, pushed the maid aside, and while William was opening the chaise door himself, called out, "you are just in
time. We have been looking for you this half hour. The Thrush went

1. Fanny's journey from Northamptonshire through Oxford and Newbury to Portsmouth was a
trip of 120 miles, with Newbury somewhat beyond the halfway point.
2. Portsmouth was heavily fortified, defended by two drawbridges and the Landsport Gate, the
barrier closest to town.

out of harbour this morning. I saw her. It was a beautiful sight. And they think she will have her orders in a day or two. And Mr. Campbell was here at four o'clock, to ask for you; he has got one of the Thrush's boats, and is going off to her at six, and hoped you would be here in time to go with him."

A stare or two at Fanny, as William helped her out of the carriage, was all the voluntary notice which this brother bestowed;—but he made no objection to her kissing him, though still entirely engaged in detailing farther particulars of the Thrush's going out of harbour, in which he had a strong right of interest, being to commence his career of seamanship in her at this very time.

Another moment, and Fanny was in the narrow entrance-passage of the house, and in her mother's arms, who met her there with looks of true kindness, and with features which Fanny loved the more, because they brought her aunt Bertram's before her; and there were her two sisters, Susan, a well-grown fine girl of fourteen, and Betsey, the youngest of the family, about five—both glad to see her in their way, though with no advantage of manner in receiving her. But manner Fanny did not want. Would they but love her, she should be satisfied.

She was then taken into a parlour, so small that her first conviction was of its being only a passage-room to something better, and she stood for a moment expecting to be invited on; but when she saw there was no other door, and that there were signs of habitation before her, she called back her thoughts, reproved herself, and grieved lest they should have been suspected. Her mother, however, could not stay long enough to suspect any thing. She was gone again to the street door, to welcome William. "Oh! my dear William, how glad I am to see you. But have you heard about the Thrush? She is gone out of harbour already, three days before we had any thought of it; and I do not know what I am to do about Sam's things, they will never be ready in time; for she may have her orders to-morrow, perhaps. It takes me quite unawares. And now you must be off for Spithead too. Campbell has been here, quite in a worry about you; and now, what shall we do? I thought to have had such a comfortable evening with you, and here every thing comes upon me at once."

Her son answered cheerfully, telling her that every thing was always for the best; and making light of his own inconvenience, in being obliged to hurry away so soon.

"To be sure, I had much rather she had stayed in harbour, that I might have sat a few hours with you in comfort; but as there is a boat ashore, I had better go off at once, and there is no help for it. Whereabouts does the Thrush lay at Spithead? Near the Canopus?[3] But no matter—here's Fanny in the parlour, and why should we stay in the

---

3. An actual ship on which Austen's brother Francis sailed, as was the *Elephant* on p. 258, below.

passage?—Come, mother, you have hardly looked at your own dear Fanny yet."

In they both came, and Mrs. Price having kindly kissed her daughter again, and commented a little on her growth, began with very natural solicitude to feel for their fatigues and wants as travellers.

"Poor dears! how tired you must both be!—and now what will you have? I began to think you would never come. Betsey and I have been watching for you this half hour. And when did you get anything to eat? And what would you like to have now? I could not tell whether you would be for some meat, or only a dish of tea after your journey, or else I would have got something ready. And now I am afraid Campbell will be here, before there is time to dress a steak, and we have no butcher at hand. It is very inconvenient to have no butcher in the street. We were better off in our last house. Perhaps you would like some tea, as soon as it can be got."

They both declared they should prefer it to anything. "Then, Betsey, my dear, run into the kitchen, and see if Rebecca has put the water on; and tell her to bring in the tea-things as soon as she can. I wish we could get the bell mended—but Betsey is a very handy little messenger."

Betsey went with alacrity; proud to shew her abilities before her fine new sister.

"Dear me!" continued the anxious mother, "what a sad fire we have got, and I dare say you are both starved with cold. Draw your chair nearer, my dear. I cannot think what Rebecca has been about. I am sure I told her to bring some coals half an hour ago. Susan, *you* should have taken care of the fire."

"I was up stairs, mamma, moving my things;" said Susan, in a fearless, self-defending tone, which startled Fanny. "You know you had but just settled that my sister Fanny and I should have the other room; and I could not get Rebecca to give me any help."

Farther discussion was prevented by various bustles; first, the driver came to be paid—then there was a squabble between Sam and Rebecca, about the manner of carrying up his sister's trunk, which he would manage all his own way; and lastly in walked Mr. Price himself, his own loud voice preceding him, as with something of the oath kind he kicked away his son's portmanteau, and his daughter's band-box in the passage, and called out for a candle; no candle was brought, however, and he walked into the room.

Fanny, with doubting feelings, had risen to meet him, but sank down again on finding herself undistinguished in the dusk, and unthought of. With a friendly shake of his son's hand, and an eager voice, he instantly began—"Ha! welcome back, my boy. Glad to see you. Have you heard the news? The Thrush went out of harbour this morning. Sharp* is the word, you see. By G—, you are just in time. The doctor has been here enquiring for you; he has got one of the boats, and is to be off for Spithead by six, so you had better go with him. I have been to Turner's[4] about your mess[5]*; it is all in a way to be done. I should not wonder if you had your orders to-morrow; but you cannot sail with this wind, if you are to cruize to the westward; and Captain Walsh thinks you will certainly have a cruize to the westward, with the Elephant. By G—, I wish you may. But old Scholey was saying just now, that he thought you would be sent first to the Texel.[6] Well, well, we are ready, whatever happens. But by G—, you lost a fine sight by not being here in the morning to see the Thrush go out of harbour. I would not have been out of the way for a thousand pounds. Old Scholey ran in at breakfast time, to say she had slipped her moorings and was coming out. I jumped up, and made but two steps to the platform.[7] If ever there was a perfect beauty afloat, she is one; and there she lays at Spithead, and anybody in England would take her for an eight-and-twenty.[8] I was upon the platform two hours this afternoon, looking at her. She lays close to the Endymion, between her and the Cleopatra,[9] just to the eastward of the sheer hulk."*[1]

"Ha!" cried William, "*that's* just where I should have put her myself. It's the best birth at Spithead.* But here is my sister, Sir, here is Fanny," turning and leading her forward;—"it is so dark you do not see her."

With an acknowledgment that he had quite forgot her, Mr. Price now received his daughter; and, having given her a cordial hug, and observed that she was grown into a woman, and he supposed would be wanting a husband soon, seemed very much inclined to forget her again.

Fanny shrunk back to her seat, with feelings sadly pained by his language and his smell of spirits; and he talked on only to his son, and only of the Thrush, though William, warmly interested, as he was, in that subject, more than once tried to make his father think of Fanny, and her long absence and long journey.

After sitting some time longer, a candle was obtained; but, as there was still no appearance of tea, nor, from Betsey's reports from the kitchen, much hope of any under a considerable period, William determined to go and change his dress, and make the necessary prepa-

4. A naval supplier or agent whose shop was at 85 High Street. Austen mentions Turner's twice in her letters, in both cases relative to her sailor brothers.
5. Provisions.
6. The channel between the Dutch mainland and the Dutch island of Texel, through which ships could enter from the North Sea. Because Napoleon held the Netherlands during this time, the Texel was the site of British naval blockades.
7. The Saluting Platform, overlooking the harbor, built in the 1490s.
8. A frigate with twenty-eight guns. William's ship, the *Thrush*, was a modern sloop built in 1806, which is why the proud Mr. Price says it could be mistaken for a twenty-eight-gun frigate, even though sloops are smaller, differently rigged, and generally mount fewer guns.
9. Actual ships on which Austen's brother Charles served.
1. The hull of an old ship, fitted up with devices for the maintenance and repair of other ships; i.e., a floating dockyard.

rations for his removal on board directly, that he might have his tea in comfort afterwards.

As he left the room, two rosy-faced boys, ragged and dirty, about eight and nine years old, rushed into it just released from school, and coming eagerly to see their sister, and tell that the Thrush was gone out of harbour; Tom and Charles: Charles had been born since Fanny's going away, but Tom she had often helped to nurse, and now felt a particular pleasure in seeing again. Both were kissed very tenderly, but Tom she wanted to keep by her, to try to trace the features of the baby she had loved, and talked to,* of his infant preference of herself. Tom, however, had no mind for such treatment: he came home, not to stand and be talked to, but to run about and make a noise; and both boys had soon burst away from her, and slammed the parlour door till her temples ached.

She had now seen all that were at home; there remained only two brothers between herself and Susan, one of whom was a clerk in a public office in London, and the other midshipman on board an Indiaman.[2] But though she had *seen* all the members of the family, she had not yet *heard* all the noise they could make. Another quarter of an hour brought her a great deal more. William was soon calling out from the landing-place of the second story, for his mother and for Rebecca. He was in distress for something that he had left there, and did not find again. A key was mislaid, Betsey accused of having got at his new hat, and some slight, but essential alteration of his uniform waist-coat, which he had been promised to have done for him, entirely neglected.

Mrs. Price, Rebecca, and Betsey, all went up to defend themselves, all talking together, but Rebecca loudest, and the job was to be done, as well as it could, in a great hurry; William trying in vain to send Betsey down again, or keep her from being troublesome where she was; the whole of which, as almost every door in the house was open, could be plainly distinguished in the parlour, except when drowned at intervals by the superior noise of Sam, Tom, and Charles chasing each other up and down stairs, and tumbling about and hallooing.

Fanny was almost stunned. The smallness of the house, and thinness of the walls, brought every thing so close to her, that, added to the fatigue of her journey, and all her recent agitation, she hardly knew how to bear it. *Within* the room all was tranquil enough, for Susan having disappeared with the others, there were soon only her father and herself remaining; and he taking out a newspaper—the accustomary loan[3] of a neighbour, applied himself to studying it, without seeming to recollect her existence. The solitary candle was held between himself and the paper, without any reference to her possible convenience; but

2. A ship of large tonnage belonging to the East India Company.
3. Being very expensive, newspapers were often shared among friends.

she had nothing to do, and was glad to have the light screened from her aching head, as she sat in bewildered, broken, sorrowful contemplation.

She was at home. But alas! it was not such a home, she had not such a welcome, as——she checked herself; she was unreasonable. What right had she to be of importance to her family? She could have none, so long lost sight of! William's concerns must be dearest—they always had been—and he had every right. Yet to have so little said or asked about herself—to have scarcely an enquiry made after Mansfield! It did pain her to have Mansfield forgotten; the friends who had done so much—the dear, dear friends! But here, one subject swallowed up all the rest. Perhaps it must be so. The destination of the Thrush must be now pre-eminently interesting. A day or two might shew the difference. *She* only was to blame. Yet she thought it would not have been so at Mansfield. No, in her uncle's house there would have been a consideration of times and seasons, a regulation of subject, a propriety, an attention towards every body which there was not here.

The only interruption which thoughts like these received for nearly half an hour, was from a sudden burst of her father's, not at all calculated to compose them. At a more than ordinary pitch of thumping and hallooing in the passage, he exclaimed, "Devil take those young dogs! How they are singing out! Ay, Sam's voice louder than all the rest! That boy is fit for a boat-swain.[4] Holla—you there—Sam—stop your confounded pipe, or I shall be after you."

This threat was so palpably disregarded, that though within five minutes afterwards the three boys all burst into the room together and sat down, Fanny could not consider it as a proof of any thing more than their being for the time thoroughly fagged, which their hot faces and panting breaths seemed to prove—especially as they were still kicking each other's shins, and hallooing out at sudden starts immediately under their father's eye.

The next opening of the door brought something more welcome; it was for the tea-things, which she had begun almost to despair of seeing that evening. Susan and an attendant girl, whose inferior appearance informed Fanny, to her great surprise, that she had previously seen the upper servant brought in every thing necessary for the meal; Susan looking as she put the kettle on the fire and glanced at her sister, as if divided between the agreeable triumph of shewing her activity and usefulness, and the dread of being thought to demean herself by such an office. "She had been into the kitchen," she said, "to hurry Sally and help make the toast, and spread the bread and butter—or she did not know when they should have got tea—and she was sure her sister must want something after her journey."

4. A petty officer on a ship who is in charge of the sails and riggings and who summons men to their duties with a whistle; a naval joke alluding to Sam's "pipe."

Fanny was very thankful. She could not but own that she should be very glad of a little tea, and Susan immediately set about making it, as if pleased to have the employment all to herself; and with only a little unnecessary bustle, and some few injudicious attempts at keeping her brothers in better order than she could, acquitted herself very well. Fanny's spirit was as much refreshed as her body; her head and heart were soon the better for such well-timed kindness. Susan had an open, sensible countenance; she was like William—and Fanny hoped to find her like him in disposition and good will towards herself.

In this more placid state of things William re-entered, followed not far behind by his mother and Betsey. He, complete in his Lieutenant's uniform, looking and moving all the taller, firmer, and more graceful for it, and with the happiest smile over his face, walked up directly to Fanny—who, rising from her seat, looked at him for a moment in speechless admiration, and then threw her arms round his neck to sob out her various emotions of pain and pleasure.

Anxious not to appear unhappy, she soon recovered herself: and wiping away her tears, was able to notice and admire all the striking parts of his dress—listening with reviving spirits to his cheerful hopes of being on shore some part of every day before they sailed, and even of getting her to Spithead to see the sloop.

The next bustle brought in Mr. Campbell, the Surgeon of the Thrush, a very well behaved young man, who came to call for his friend, and for whom there was with some contrivance found a chair, and with some hasty washing of the young tea-maker's, a cup and saucer; and after another quarter of an hour of earnest talk between the gentlemen, noise rising upon noise, and bustle upon bustle, men and boys at last all in motion together, the moment came for setting off; every thing was ready, William took leave, and all of them were gone —for the three boys, in spite of their mother's intreaty, determined to see their brother and Mr. Campbell to the sally-port[5] and Mr. Price walked off at the same time to carry back his neighbour's newspaper.

Something like tranquillity might now be hoped for, and accordingly, when Rebecca had been prevailed on to carry away the tea-things, and Mrs. Price had walked about the room some time looking for a shirt sleeve, which Betsey at last hunted out from a drawer in the kitchen, the small party of females were pretty well composed, and the mother having lamented again over the impossibility of getting Sam ready in time, was at leisure to think of her eldest daughter and the friends she had come from.

A few enquiries began; but one of the earliest—"How did her sister Bertram manage about her servants? Was she as much plagued as herself to get tolerable servants?"—soon led her mind away from North-

5. An opening in a wall or fortification from which attacks (sallies) are made; an embarkation point.

amptonshire, and fixed it on her own domestic grievances; and the shocking character of all the Portsmouth servants, of whom she believed her own two were the very worst, engrossed her completely. The Bertrams were all forgotten in detailing the faults of Rebecca, against whom Susan had also much to depose, and little Betsey a great deal more, and who did seem so thoroughly without a single recommendation, that Fanny could not help modestly presuming that her mother meant to part with her when her year was up.

"Her year!" cried Mrs. Price; "I am sure I hope I shall be rid of her before she has staid a year, for that will not be up till November. Servants are come to such a pass, my dear, in Portsmouth, that it is quite a miracle if one keeps them more than half-a-year. I have no hope of ever being settled; and if I was to part with Rebecca, I should only get something worse. And yet I do not think I am a very difficult mistress to please—and I am sure the place is easy enough, for there is always a girl under her, and I often do half the work myself."

Fanny was silent; but not from being convinced that there might not be a remedy found for some of these evils. As she now sat looking at Betsey, she could not but think particularly of another sister, a very pretty little girl, whom she had left there not much younger when she went into Northamptonshire, who had died a few years afterwards. There had been something remarkably amiable about her. Fanny, in those early days, had preferred her to Susan; and when the news of her death had at last reached Mansfield, had for a short time been quite afflicted.—The sight of Betsey brought the image of little Mary back again, but she would not have pained her mother by alluding to her, for the world.—While considering her with these ideas, Betsey, at a small distance, was holding out something to catch her eyes, meaning to screen it at the same time from Susan's.

"What have you got there, my love?" said Fanny, "come and shew it to me."

It was a silver knife. Up jumped Susan, claiming it as her own, and trying to get it away; but the child ran to her mother's protection, and Susan could only reproach, which she did very warmly, and evidently hoping to interest Fanny on her side. "It was very hard that she was not to have her *own* knife; it was her own knife; little sister Mary had left it to her upon her death-bed, and she ought to have had it to keep herself long ago. But mamma kept it from her, and was always letting Betsey get hold of it; and the end of it would be that Betsey would spoil it, and get it for her own, though mamma had *promised* her that Betsey should not have it in her own hands."

Fanny was quite shocked. Every feeling of duty, honour, and tenderness was wounded by her sister's speech and her mother's reply.

"Now, Susan," cried Mrs. Price in a complaining voice, "now, how can you be so cross? You are always quarrelling about that knife. I wish you would not be so quarrelsome. Poor little Betsey; how cross Susan is to you! But you should not have taken it out, my dear, when I sent you to the drawer. You know I told you not to touch it, because Susan is so cross about it. I must hide it another time, Betsey. Poor Mary little thought it would be such a bone of contention when she gave it me to keep, only two hours before she died. Poor little soul! she could but just speak to be heard, and she said so prettily, 'Let sister Susan have my knife, mamma, when I am dead and buried.'—Poor little dear! she was so fond of it, Fanny, that she would have it lay by her in bed, all through her illness. It was the gift of her good godmother, old Mrs. Admiral Maxwell, only six weeks before she was taken for death. Poor little sweet creature! Well, she was taken away from evil to come. My own Betsey, (fondling her), you have not the luck of such a good godmother. Aunt Norris lives too far off, to think of such little people as you."

Fanny had indeed nothing to convey from aunt Norris, but a message to say she hoped her god-daughter was a good girl, and learnt her book. There had been at one moment a slight murmur in the drawing-room at Mansfield Park, about sending her a Prayer-book; but no second sound had been heard of such a purpose. Mrs. Norris, however, had gone home and taken down two old Prayer-books of her husband, with that idea, but upon examination, the ardour of generosity went off. One was found to have too small a print for a child's eyes, and the other to be too cumbersome for her to carry about.

Fanny fatigued and fatigued again, was thankful to accept the first invitation of going to bed; and before Betsey had finished her cry at being allowed to sit up only one hour extraordinary in honour of sister, she was off, leaving all below in confusion and noise again, the boys begging for toasted cheese, her father calling out for his rum and water, and Rebecca never where she ought to be.

There was nothing to raise her spirits in the confined and scantily-furnished chamber that she was to share with Susan. The smallness of the rooms above and below indeed, and the narrowness of the passage and staircase, struck her beyond her imagination. She soon learnt to think with respect of her own little attic at Mansfield Park, in *that* house reckoned too small for anybody's comfort.

Chapter VIII.

Could Sir Thomas have seen all his niece's feelings, when she wrote her first letter to her aunt, he would not have despaired; for though a good night's rest, a pleasant morning, the hope of soon seeing William again, and the comparatively quiet state of the house, from Tom and Charles being gone to school, Sam on some project of his own, and her father on his usual lounges,[1] enabled her to express herself cheerfully on the subject of home, there were still to her own perfect consciousness, many drawbacks suppressed. Could he have seen only half that she felt before the end of a week, he would have thought Mr. Crawford sure of her, and been delighted with his own sagacity.

Before the week ended, it was all disappointment. In the first place, William was gone. The Thrush had had her orders, the wind had changed, and he was sailed within four days from their reaching Portsmouth; and during those days, she had seen him only twice, in a short and hurried way, when he had come ashore on duty. There had been no free conversation, no walk on the ramparts, no visit to the dockyard, no acquaintance with the Thrush—nothing of all that they had planned and depended on. Every thing in that quarter failed her, except William's affection. His last thought on leaving home was for her. He stepped back again to the door to say, "Take care of Fanny, mother. She is tender, and not used to rough it like the rest of us. I charge you, take care of Fanny."

William was gone;—and the home he had left her in was—Fanny could not conceal it from herself—in almost every respect, the very reverse of what she could have wished. It was the abode of noise, disorder, and impropriety. Nobody was in their right place, nothing was done as it ought to be. She could not respect her parents, as she had hoped. On her father, her confidence had not been sanguine, but he was more negligent of his family, his habits were worse, and his manners coarser, than she had been prepared for. He did not want abilities; but he had no curiosity, and no information beyond his profession; he read only the newspaper and the navy-list; he talked only of the dockyard, the harbour, Spithead, and the Motherbank;[2] he swore and he drank, he was dirty and gross. She had never been able to recal anything approaching to tenderness in his former treatment of herself. There had remained only a general impression of roughness and loudness; and now he scarcely ever noticed her, but to make her the object of a coarse joke.

Her disappointment in her mother was greater; *there* she had hoped much, and found almost nothing. Every flattering scheme of being of consequence to her soon fell to the ground. Mrs. Price was not unkind—but, instead of gaining on her affection and confidence, and becoming more and more dear, her daughter never met with greater kindness from her, than on the first day of her arrival. The instinct of nature was soon satisfied, and Mrs. Price's attachment had no other source. Her heart and her time were already quite full; she had neither leisure nor affection to bestow on Fanny. Her daughters never had been much to her. She was fond of her sons, especially of William, but

1. Strolls.
2. West of the Isle of Wight, the stretch of shallow water where the fleet would moor.

Betsey was the first of her girls whom she had ever much regarded. To her she was most injudiciously indulgent. William was her pride; Betsey, her darling; and John, Richard, Sam, Tom, and Charles, occupied all the rest of her maternal solicitude, alternately her worries and her comforts. These shared her heart; her time was given chiefly to her house and her servants. Her days were spent in a kind of slow bustle; always* busy without getting on, always behindhand and lamenting it, without altering her ways; wishing to be an economist, without contrivance or regularity; dissatisfied with her servants, without skill to make them better, and whether helping, or reprimanding, or indulging them, without any power of engaging their respect.

Of her two sisters, Mrs. Price very much more resembled Lady Bertram than Mrs. Norris. She was a manager by necessity, without any of Mrs. Norris's inclination for it, or any of her activity. Her disposition was naturally easy and indolent, like Lady Bertram's; and a situation of similar affluence and do-nothing-ness would have been much more suited to her capacity, than the exertions and self-denials of the one, which her imprudent marriage had placed her in. She might have made just as good a woman of consequence as Lady Bertram, but Mrs. Norris would have been a more respectable mother of nine children, on a small income.

Much of all this, Fanny could not but be sensible of. She might scruple to make use of the words, but she must and did feel that her mother was a partial, ill-judging parent, a dawdle, a slattern, who neither taught nor restrained her children, whose house was the scene of mismanagement and discomfort from beginning to end, and who had no talent, no conversation, no affection towards herself; no curiosity to know her better, no desire of her friendship, and no inclination for her company that could lessen her sense of such feelings.

Fanny was very anxious to be useful, and not to appear above her home, or in any way disqualified or disinclined, by her foreign education, from contributing her help to its comforts, and therefore set about working for Sam immediately, and by working early and late, with perseverance and great dispatch, did so much, that the boy was shipped off at last, with more than half his linen ready. She had great pleasure in feeling her usefulness, but could not conceive how they would have managed without her.

Sam, loud and overbearing as he was, she rather regretted when he went, for he was clever and intelligent, and glad to be employed in any errand in the town; and though spurning the remonstrances of Susan, given as they were—though very reasonable in themselves, with ill-timed and powerless warmth, was beginning to be influenced by Fanny's services, and gentle persuasions; and she found that the best of the three younger ones was gone in him; Tom and Charles being at* least as many years as they were his juniors distant from that age of feeling and reason, which might suggest the expediency of making friends, and of endeavouring to be less disagreeable. Their sister soon despaired of making the smallest impression on *them*; they were quite untameable by any means of address which she had spirits or time to attempt. Every afternoon brought a return of their riotous games all over the house; and she very early learnt to sigh at the approach of Saturday's constant half holiday.[3]

Betsey too, a spoilt child, trained up to think the alphabet her greatest enemy, left to be with the servants at her pleasure, and then encouraged to report any evil of them, she was almost as ready to despair of being able to love or assist; and of Susan's temper, she had many doubts. Her continual disagreements with her mother, her rash squabbles with Tom and Charles, and petulance with Betsey, were at least so distressing to Fanny, that though admitting they were by no means without provocation, she feared the disposition that could push them to such length must be far from amiable, and from affording any repose to herself.

Such was the home which was to put Mansfield out of her head, and teach her to think of her cousin Edmund with moderated feelings. On the contrary, she could think of nothing but Mansfield, its beloved inmates, its happy ways. Every thing where she now was was in full contrast to it. The elegance, propriety, regularity, harmony—and perhaps, above all, the peace and tranquillity of Mansfield, were brought to her remembrance every hour of the day, by the prevalence of every thing opposite to them *here*.

The living in incessant noise was to a frame and temper, delicate and nervous like Fanny's, an evil which no super-added elegance or harmony could have entirely atoned for. It was the greatest misery of all. At Mansfield, no sounds of contention, no raised voice, no abrupt bursts, no tread of violence was ever heard; all proceeded in a regular course of cheerful orderliness; every body had their due importance; every body's feelings were consulted. If tenderness could be ever supposed wanting, good sense and good breeding supplied its place; and as to the little irritations, sometimes introduced by aunt Norris, they were short, they were trifling, they were as a drop of water to the ocean, compared with the ceaseless tumult of her present abode. Here, every body was noisy, every voice was loud, (excepting, perhaps, her mother's, which resembled the soft monotony of Lady Bertram's, only worn into fretfulness.)—Whatever was wanted, was halloo'd for, and the servants halloo'd out their excuses from the kitchen. The doors were in constant banging, the stairs were never at rest, nothing was done without a clatter, nobody sat still, and nobody could command attention when they spoke.

In a review of the two houses, as they appeared to her before the

---

3. Schoolboys had the latter part of Saturday off from school.

end of a week, Fanny was tempted to apply to them Dr. Johnson's celebrated judgment as to matrimony and celibacy, and say, that though Mansfield Park might have some pains, Portsmouth could have no pleasures.[4]

Chapter IX.

Fanny was right enough in not expecting to hear from Miss Crawford now, at the rapid rate in which their correspondence had begun; Mary's next letter was after a decidedly longer interval than the last, but she was not right in supposing that such an interval would be felt a great relief to herself.—Here was another strange revolution of mind!—She was really glad to receive the letter when it did come. In her present exile from good society, and distance from every thing that had been wont to interest her, a letter from one belonging to the set where her heart lived, written with affection, and some degree of elegance, was thoroughly acceptable.—The usual plea of increasing engagements was made in excuse for not having written to her earlier, "and now that I have begun," she continued, "my letter will not be worth your reading, for there will be no little offering of love at the end, no three or four lines passionées from the most devoted H. C. in the world, for Henry is in Norfolk; business called him to Everingham ten days ago, or perhaps he only pretended the call, for the sake of being travelling at the same time that you were. But there he is, and, by the by, his absence may sufficiently account for any remissness of his sister's in writing, for there has been no 'well, Mary, when do you write to Fanny?—is not it time for you to write to Fanny?' to spur me on. At last, after various attempts at meeting, I have seen your cousins, 'dear Julia and dearest Mrs. Rushworth;' they found me at home yesterday, and we were glad to see each other again. We *seemed very* glad to see each other, and I do really think we were a little.—We had a vast deal to say.—Shall I tell you how Mrs. Rushworth looked when your name was mentioned? I did not use to think her wanting in self-possession, but she had not quite enough for the demands of yesterday. Upon the whole Julia was in the best looks of the two, at least after you were spoken of. There was no recovering the complexion from the moment that I spoke of 'Fanny,' and spoke of her as a sister should.—But Mrs. Rushworth's day of good looks will come; we have cards for her first party on the 28th.—Then she will be in beauty, for she will open one of the best houses in Wimpole Street. I was in it two years ago, when it was Lady

4. From Samuel Johnson's *Rasselas* (1759), where the Princess, debating the felicity of the married versus the unmarried state, declares "Marriage has many pains, but celibacy has no pleasures" (ch. 26). Fanny's disappointing homecoming may also echo Imlac's in *Rasselas*, ch. 12. Johnson was one of Austen's favorite authors.

Lascelles's, and prefer it to almost any I know in London, and certainly she will then feel—to use a vulgar phrase—that she has got her pennyworth for her penny. Henry could not have afforded her such a house. I hope she will recollect it, and be satisfied, as well she may, with moving the queen of a palace, though the king may appear best in the back ground; and as I have no desire to tease her, I shall never *force* your name upon her again. She will grow sober by degrees.— From all that I hear and guess, Baron Wildenhaim's attentions to Julia continue, but I do not know that he has any serious encouragement. She ought to do better. A poor honourable is no catch, and I cannot imagine any liking in the case, for, take away his rants, and the poor Baron has nothing. What a difference a vowel makes!—if his rents were but equal to his rants!—Your cousin Edmund moves slowly; detained, perchance, by parish duties. There may be some old woman at Thornton Lacey to be converted. I am unwilling to fancy myself neglected for a *young* one. Adieu, my dear sweet Fanny, this is a long letter from London; write me a pretty one in reply to gladden Henry's eyes, when he comes back—and send me an account of all the dashing young captains whom you disdain for his sake."

There was great food for meditation in this letter, and chiefly for unpleasant meditation; and yet, with all the uneasiness it supplied, it connected her with the absent, it told her of people and things about whom she had never felt so much curiosity as now, and she would have been glad to have been sure of such a letter every week. Her correspondence with her aunt Bertram was her only concern of higher interest.

As for any society in Portsmouth, that could at all make amends for deficiencies at home, there were none within the circle of her father's and mother's acquaintance to afford her the smallest satisfaction; she saw nobody in whose favour she could wish to overcome her own shyness and reserve. The men appeared to her all coarse, the women all pert, every body under-bred; and she gave as little contentment as she received from introductions either to old or new acquaintance. The young ladies who approached her at first with some respect, in consideration of her coming from a Baronet's family, were soon offended by what they termed "airs"—for as she neither played on the piano-forte nor wore fine pelisses,[1] they could, on farther observation, admit no right of superiority.

The first solid consolation which Fanny received for the evils of home, the first which her judgment could entirely approve, and which gave any promise of durability, was in a better knowledge of Susan, and a hope of being of service to her. Susan had always behaved pleasantly to herself, but the determined character of her general manners had

1. Ankle-length mantles worn by women.

astonished and alarmed her, and it was at least a fortnight before she began to understand a disposition so totally different from her own. Susan saw that much was wrong at home, and wanted to set it right. That a girl of fourteen, acting only on her own unassisted reason, should err in the method of reform was not wonderful; and Fanny soon became more disposed to admire the natural light of the mind which could so early distinguish justly, than to censure severely the faults of conduct to which it led. Susan was only acting on the same truths, and pursuing the same system, which her own judgment acknowledged, but which her more supine and yielding temper would have shrunk from asserting. Susan tried to be useful, where *she* could only have gone away and cried; and that Susan was useful she could perceive; that things, bad as they were, would have been worse but for such interposition, and that both her mother and Betsey were restrained from some excesses of very offensive indulgence and vulgarity.

In every argument with her mother, Susan had in point of reason the advantage, and never was there any maternal tenderness to buy her off. The blind fondness which was for ever producing evil around her, *she* had never known. There was no gratitude for affection past or present, to make her better bear with its excesses to the others.

All this became gradually evident, and gradually placed Susan before her sister as an object of mingled compassion and respect. That her manner was wrong, however, at times very wrong—her measures often ill-chosen and ill-timed, and her looks and language very often indefensible, Fanny could not cease to feel; but she began to hope they might be rectified. Susan, she found, looked up to her and wished for her good opinion; and new as any thing like an office of authority was to Fanny, new as it was to imagine herself capable of guiding or informing any one, she did resolve to give occasional hints to Susan, and endeavour to exercise for her advantage the juster notions of what was due to every body, and what would be wisest for herself, which her own more favoured education had fixed in her.

Her influence, or at least the consciousness and use of it, originated in an act of kindness by Susan, which after many hesitations of delicacy, she at last worked herself up to. It had very early occurred to her, that a small sum of money might, perhaps, restore peace for ever on the sore subject of the silver knife, canvassed as it now was continually, and the riches which she was in possession of herself, her uncle having given her 10*l*. at parting, made her as able as she was willing to be generous. But she was so wholly unused to confer favours, except on the very poor, so unpractised in removing evils, or bestowing kindnesses among her equals, and so fearful of appearing to elevate herself as a great lady at home, that it took some time to determine that it would not be unbecoming in her to make such a present. It was made, however, at last; a silver knife was bought for Betsey, and accepted with great delight, its newness giving it every advantage over the other that could be desired; Susan was established in the full possession of her own.* Betsey handsomely declaring that now she had got one so much prettier herself, she should never want *that* again—and no reproach seemed conveyed to the equally satisfied mother, which Fanny had almost feared to be impossible. The deed thoroughly answered; a source of domestic altercation was entirely done away, and it was the means of opening Susan's heart to her, and giving her something more to love and be interested in. Susan shewed that she had delicacy; pleased as she was to be mistress of property which she had been struggling for at least two years, she yet feared that her sister's judgment had been against her, and that a reproof was designed her for having so struggled as to make the purchase necessary for the tranquillity of the house.

Her temper was open. She acknowledged her fears, blamed herself for having contended so warmly, and from that hour Fanny understanding the worth of her disposition, and perceiving how fully she was inclined to seek her good opinion and refer to her judgment, began to feel again the blessing of affection, and to entertain the hope of being useful to a mind so much in need of help, and so much deserving it. She gave advice; advice too sound to be resisted by a good understanding, and given so mildly and considerately as not to irritate an imperfect temper; and she had the happiness of observing its good effects not unfrequently; more was not expected by one, who, while seeing all the obligation and expediency of submission and forbearance, saw also with sympathetic acuteness of feeling, all that must be hourly grating to a girl like Susan. Her greatest wonder on the subject soon became—not that Susan should have been provoked into disrespect and impatience against her better knowledge—but that so much better knowledge, so many good notions, should have been hers at all; and that, brought up in the midst of negligence and error, she should have formed such proper opinions of what ought to be—she, who had had no cousin Edmund to direct her thoughts or fix her principles.

The intimacy thus begun between them was a material advantage to each. By sitting together up stairs, they avoided a great deal of the disturbance of the house; Fanny had peace, and Susan learnt to think it no misfortune to be quietly employed. They sat without a fire; but *that* was a privation familiar even to Fanny, and she suffered the less because reminded by it of the east-room. It was the only point of resemblance. In space, light, furniture, and prospect, there was nothing alike in the two apartments; and she often heaved a sigh at the remembrance of all her books and boxes, and various comforts there. By degrees the girls came to spend the chief of the morning up stairs, at first only in working and talking; but after a few days, the remembrance of the said books grew so potent and stimulative, that Fanny found it impossible not to try for books again. There were none in her father's house; but wealth is luxurious and daring—and some of hers found its way to a circulating library.[2] She became a subscriber—amazed at being any thing *in* propria persona*, amazed at her own doings in every way; to be a renter, a chuser of books! And to be having any one's improvement in view in her choice! But so it was. Susan had read nothing, and Fanny longed to give her a share in her own first pleasures, and inspire a taste for the biography and poetry which she delighted in herself.

In this occupation she hoped, moreover, to bury some of the recollections of Mansfield which were too apt to seize her mind if her fingers only were busy; and especially at this time, hoped it might be useful in diverting her thoughts from pursuing Edmund to London, whither, on the authority of her aunt's last letter, she knew he was gone. She had no doubt of what would ensue. The promised notification was hanging over her head. The postman's knock within the neighbourhood was beginning to bring its daily terrors—and if reading could banish the idea for even half an hour, it was something gained.

Chapter X.

A week was gone since Edmund might be supposed in town, and Fanny had heard nothing of him. There were three different conclusions to be drawn from his silence, between which her mind was in fluctuation; each of them at times being held the most probable. Either his going had been again delayed, or he had yet procured no opportunity of seeing Miss Crawford alone—or, he was too happy for letter writing!

One morning about this time, Fanny having now been nearly four weeks from Mansfield—a point which she never failed to think over and calculate every day—as she and Susan were preparing to remove as usual up stairs, they were stopt by the knock of a visitor, whom they felt they could not avoid, from Rebecca's alertness in going to the door, a duty which always interested her beyond any other.

It was a gentleman's voice; it was a voice that Fanny was just turning pale about, when Mr. Crawford walked into the room.

Good sense, like hers, will always act when really called upon; and she found that she had been able to name him to her mother, and recal her remembrance of the name, as that of "William's friend," though she could not previously have believed herself capable of uttering a syllable at such a moment. The consciousness of his being known there only as William's friend, was some support. Having introduced him, however, and being all re-seated, the terrors that occurred of what

2. Private lending libraries. Though Austen used them, as an author she could also complain of readers more willing to borrow than to buy.

this visit might lead to were overpowering, and she fancied herself on the point of fainting away.

While trying to keep herself alive, their visitor, who had at first approached her with as animated a countenance as ever, was wisely and kindly keeping his eyes away, and giving her time to recover, while he devoted himself entirely to her mother, addressing her, and attending to her with the utmost politeness and propriety, at the same time with a degree of friendliness—of interest at least—which was making his manner perfect.

Mrs. Price's manners were also at their best. Warmed by the sight of such a friend to her son, and regulated by the wish of appearing to advantage before him, she was overflowing with gratitude, artless, maternal gratitude, which could not be unpleasing. Mr. Price was out, which she regretted very much. Fanny was just recovered enough to feel that *she* could not regret it; for to her many other sources of uneasiness was added the severe one of shame for the home in which he found her. She might scold herself for the weakness, but there was no scolding it away. She was ashamed, and she would have been yet more ashamed of her father, than of all the rest.

They talked of William, a subject on which Mrs. Price could never tire; and Mr. Crawford was as warm in his commendation, as even her heart could wish. She felt that she had never seen so agreeable a man in her life; and was only astonished to find, that so great and so agreeable as he was, he should be come down to Portsmouth neither on a visit to the port-admiral, nor the commissioner, nor yet with the intention of going over to the island, nor of seeing the Dock-yard. Nothing of all that she had been used to think of as the proof of importance, or the employment of wealth, had brought him to Portsmouth.[1] He had reached it late the night before, was come for a day or two, was staying at the Crown,[2] had accidentally met with a navy officer or two of his acquaintance, since his arrival, but had no object of that kind in coming.

By the time he had given all this information, it was not unreasonable to suppose, that Fanny might be looked at and spoken to; and she was tolerably able to bear his eye, and hear that he had spent half an hour with his sister, the evening before his leaving London; that she had sent her best and kindest love, but had had no time for writing; that he thought himself lucky in seeing Mary for even half an hour, having spent scarcely twenty-four hours in London after his return from Norfolk, before he set off again; that her cousin Edmund was in town, had been in town, he understood, a few days; that he had not seen him,

1. Though the home of the Royal Navy, Portsmouth, unlike nearby Southampton, was not a fashionable town during Austen's time—hence Mrs. Price's surprise that Crawford visits without specific business.
2. The Crown Inn was popular with naval officers; it was also the home of the assemblies William misses when visiting Mansfield Park.

himself, but that he was well, had left them all well at Mansfield, and was to dine, as yesterday, with the Frasers.

Fanny listened collectedly even to the last-mentioned circumstance; nay, it seemed a relief to her worn mind to be at any certainty; and the words, "then by this time it is all settled," passed internally, without more evidence of emotion than a faint blush.

After talking a little more about Mansfield, a subject in which her interest was most apparent, Crawford began to hint at the expediency of an early walk;—"It was a lovely morning, and at that season of the year a fine morning so often turned off, that it was wisest for everybody not to delay their exercise;" and such hints producing nothing, he soon proceeded to a positive recommendation to Mrs. Price and her daughters, to take their walk without loss of time. Now they came to an understanding. Mrs. Price, it appeared, scarcely ever stirred out of doors, except of a Sunday; she owned she could seldom, with her large family, find time for a walk.—"Would she not then persuade her daughters to take advantage of such weather, and allow him the pleasure of attending them?"—Mrs. Price was greatly obliged, and very complying. "Her daughters were very much confined—Portsmouth was a sad place—they did not often get out—and she knew they had some errands in the town, which they would be very glad to do."—And the consequence was, that Fanny, strange as it was—strange, awkward, and distressing—found herself and Susan, within ten minutes, walking towards the High Street, with Mr. Crawford.

It was soon pain upon pain, confusion upon confusion; for they were hardly in the High Street, before they met her father, whose appearance was not the better from its being Saturday. He stopt; and, ungentlemanlike as he looked, Fanny was obliged to introduce him to Mr. Crawford. She could not have a doubt of the manner in which Mr. Crawford must be struck. He must be ashamed and disgusted altogether. He must soon give her up, and cease to have the smallest inclination for the match; and yet, though she had been so much wanting his affection to be cured, this was a sort of cure that would be almost as bad as the complaint; and I believe, there is scarcely a young lady in the united kingdoms, who would not rather put up with the misfortune of being sought by a clever, agreeable man, than have him driven away by the vulgarity of her nearest relations.

Mr. Crawford probably could not regard his future father-in-law with any idea of taking him for a model in dress; but (as Fanny instantly, and to her great relief discerned), her father was a very different man, a very different Mr. Price in his behaviour to this most highly-respected stranger, from what he was in his own family at home. His manners now, though not polished, were more than passable; they were grateful, animated, manly; his expressions were those of an attached father, and a sensible man;—his loud tones did very well in the open air, and there was not a single oath to be heard. Such was his instinctive compliment to the good manners of Mr. Crawford; and be the consequence what it might, Fanny's immediate feelings were infinitely soothed.

The conclusion of the two gentlemen's civilities was an offer of Mr. Price's to take Mr. Crawford into the dock-yard, which Mr. Crawford, desirous of accepting as a favour, what was intended as such, though he had seen the dock-yard again and again; and hoping to be so much the longer with Fanny, was very gratefully disposed to avail himself of, if the Miss Prices were not afraid of the fatigue; and as it was somehow or other ascertained, or inferred, or at least acted upon, that they were not at all afraid, to the dock-yard they were all to go; and, but for Mr. Crawford, Mr. Price would have turned thither directly, without the smallest consideration for his daughters'* errands in the High Street. He took care, however, that they should be allowed to go to the shops they came out expressly to visit; and it did not delay them long, for Fanny could so little bear to excite impatience, or be waited for, that before the gentlemen, as they stood at the door, could do more than begin upon the last naval regulations, or settle the number of three deckers[3] now in commission, their companions were ready to proceed.

They were then to set forward for the dock-yard at once, and the walk would have been conducted (according to Mr. Crawford's opinion) in a singular manner, had Mr. Price been allowed the entire regulation of it, as the two girls, he found, would have been left to follow, and keep up with them, or not, as they could, while they walked on together at their own hasty pace. He was able to introduce some improvement occasionally, though by no means to the extent he wished; he absolutely would not walk away from them; and, at any crossing, or any crowd, when Mr. Price was only calling out, "Come, girls—come, Fan—come, Sue—take care of yourselves—keep a sharp look out," he would give them his particular attendance.

Once fairly in the dock-yard, he began to reckon upon some happy intercourse with Fanny, as they were very soon joined by a brother lounger of Mr. Price's, who was come to take his daily survey of how things went on, and who must prove a far more worthy companion than himself; and after a time the two officers seemed very well satisfied in going about together and discussing matters of equal and never-failing interest, while the young people sat down upon some timbers in the yard, or found a seat on board a vessel in the stocks which they all went to look at. Fanny was most conveniently in want of rest. Crawford could not have wished her more fatigued or more ready to sit down; but he could have wished her sister away. A quick looking girl of Susan's age was the very worst third in the world—totally different from Lady Bertram—all eyes and ears; and there was no introducing

3. War ships with three decks of cannons.

the main point before her. He must content himself with being only generally agreeable, and letting Susan have her share of entertainment, with the indulgence, now and then, of a look or hint for the better informed and conscious Fanny. Norfolk was what he had mostly to talk of; there he had been some time, and every thing there was rising in importance from his present schemes. Such a man could come from no place, no society, without importing something to amuse; his journeys and his acquaintance were all of use, and Susan was entertained in a way quite new to her. For Fanny, somewhat more was related than the accidental agreeableness of the parties he had been in. For her approbation, the particular reason of his going into Norfolk at all, at this unusual time of year, was given. It had been real business, relative to the renewal of a lease in which the welfare of a large and (he believed) industrious family was at stake. He had suspected his agent of some underhand dealing—of meaning to bias him against the deserving—and he had determined to go himself, and thoroughly investigate the merits of the case. He had gone, had done even more good than he had foreseen, had been useful to more than his first plan had comprehended, and was now able to congratulate himself upon it, and to feel, that in performing a duty, he had secured agreeable recollections for his own mind. He had introduced himself to some tenants, whom he had never seen before; he had begun making acquaintance with cottages whose very existence, though on his own estate, had been hitherto unknown to him. This was aimed, and well aimed, at Fanny. It was pleasing to hear him speak so properly; here, he had been acting as he ought to do. To be the friend of the poor and oppressed! Nothing could be more grateful to her, and she was on the point of giving him an approving look when it was all frightened off, by his adding a something too pointed of his hoping soon to have an assistant, a friend, a guide in every plan of utility or charity for Everingham, a somebody that would make Everingham and all about it, a dearer object than it had ever been yet.

She turned away, and wished he would not say such things. She was willing to allow he might have more good qualities than she had been wont to suppose. She began to feel the possibility of his turning out well at last; but he was and must ever be completely unsuited to her, and ought not to think of her.

He perceived that enough had been said of Everingham, and that it would be as well to talk of something else, and turned to Mansfield. He could not have chosen better; that was a topic to bring back her attention and her looks almost instantly. It was a real indulgence to her to hear or to speak of Mansfield. Now so long divided from every body who knew the place, she felt it quite the voice of a friend when he mentioned it, and led the way to her fond exclamations in praise of its beauties and comforts, and by his honourable tribute to its inhabitants allowed her to gratify her own heart in the warmest eulogium, in speaking of her uncle as all that was clever and good, and her aunt as having the sweetest of all sweet tempers.

He had a great attachment to Mansfield himself; he said so; he looked forward with the hope of spending much, very much of his time there—always there, or in the neighbourhood. He particularly built upon a very happy summer and autumn there this year; he felt that it would be so; he depended upon it; a summer and autumn infinitely superior to the last. As animated, as diversified, as social—but with circumstances of superiority undescribable.

"Mansfield, Sotherton, Thornton Lacey," he continued, "what a society will be comprised in those houses! And at Michaelmas, perhaps, a fourth may be added, some small hunting-box[4] in the vicinity of every thing so dear—for as to any partnership in Thornton Lacey, as Edmund Bertram once good-humouredly proposed, I hope I foresee two objections, two fair, excellent, irresistible objections to that plan."

Fanny was doubly silenced here; though when the moment was passed, could regret that she had not forced herself into the acknowledged comprehension of one half of his meaning, and encouraged him to say something more of his sister and Edmund. It was a subject which she must learn to speak of, and the weakness that shrunk from it would soon be quite unpardonable.

When Mr. Price and his friend had seen all that they wished, or had time for, the others were ready to return; and in the course of their walk back, Mr. Crawford contrived a minute's privacy for telling Fanny that his only business in Portsmouth was to see her, that he was come down for a couple of days on her account and hers only, and because he could not endure a longer total separation. She was sorry, really sorry; and yet, in spite of this and the two or three other things which she wished he had not said, she thought him altogether improved since she had seen him; he was much more gentle, obliging, and attentive to other people's feelings than he had ever been at Mansfield; she had never seen him so agreeable—so *near* being agreeable; his behaviour to her father could not offend, and there was something particularly kind and proper in the notice he took of Susan. He was decidedly improved. She wished the next day over, she wished he had come only for one day—but it was not so very bad as she would have expected; the pleasure of talking of Mansfield was so very great!

Before they parted, she had to thank him for another pleasure, and one of no trivial kind. Her father asked him to do them the honour of taking his mutton with them, and Fanny had time for only one thrill of horror, before he declared himself prevented by a prior engagement. He was engaged to dinner already both for that day and the next; he

---

4. A small country house, occupied during hunting season.

had met with some acquaintance at the Crown who would not be denied; he should have the honour, however, of waiting on them again on the morrow, &c. and so they parted—Fanny in a state of actual felicity from escaping so horrible an evil!

To have had him join their family dinner-party and see all their deficiencies would have been dreadful! Rebecca's cookery and Rebecca's waiting, and Betsey's eating at table without restraint, and pulling every thing about as she chose, were what Fanny herself was not yet enough inured to, for her often to make a tolerable meal. *She* was nice only from natural delicacy, but *he* had been brought up in a school of luxury and epicurism.

Chapter XI.

The Prices were just setting off for church the next day when Mr. Crawford appeared again. He came—not to stop—but to join them; he was asked to go with them to the Garrison chapel,[1] which was exactly what he had intended, and they all walked thither together.

The family were now seen to advantage. Nature had given them no inconsiderable share of beauty, and every Sunday dressed them in their cleanest skins and best attire. Sunday always brought this comfort to Fanny, and on this Sunday she felt it more than ever. Her poor mother now did not look so very unworthy of being Lady Bertram's sister as she was but too apt to look. It often grieved her to the heart—to think of the contrast between them—to think that where nature had made so little difference, circumstances should have made so much, and that her mother, as handsome as Lady Bertram, and some years her junior, should have an appearance so much more worn and faded, so comfortless, so slatternly, so shabby. But Sunday made her a very creditable and tolerably cheerful looking Mrs. Price, coming abroad with a fine family of children, feeling a little respite of her weekly cares, and only discomposed if she saw her boys run into danger, or Rebecca pass by with a flower in her hat.

In chapel they were obliged to divide, but Mr. Crawford took care not to be divided from the female branch; and after chapel he still continued with them, and made one in the family party on the ramparts.

Mrs. Price took her weekly walk on the ramparts every fine Sunday throughout the year, always going directly after morning service and staying till dinner-time. It was her public place; there she met her

---

1. Built in 1212 as a hospice. After the dissolution of monasteries in the 1530s, it was used as a garrison and later as a residence for the military governor of Portsmouth; the chapel was used by military personnel.

acquaintance, heard a little news, talked over the badness of the Portsmouth servants, and wound up her spirits for the six days ensuing.

Thither they now went; Mr. Crawford most happy to consider the Miss Prices as his peculiar charge; and before they had been there long—somehow or other—there was no saying how—Fanny could not have believed it—but he was walking between them with an arm of each under his, and she did not know how to prevent or put an end to it. It made her uncomfortable for a time—but yet there were enjoyments in the day and in the view which would be felt.

The day was uncommonly lovely. It was really March; but it was April in its mild air, brisk soft wind, and bright sun, occasionally clouded for a minute; and every thing looked so beautiful under the influence of such a sky, the effects of the shadows pursuing each other, on the ships at Spithead and the island beyond, with the ever-varying hues of the sea now at high water, dancing in its glee and dashing against the ramparts with so fine a sound, produced altogether such a combination of charms for Fanny, as made her gradually almost careless of the circumstances under which she felt them. Nay, had she been without his arm, she would soon have known that she needed it, for she wanted strength for a two hours' saunter of this kind, coming as it generally did upon a week's previous inactivity. Fanny was beginning to feel the effect of being debarred from her usual, regular exercise; she had lost ground as to health since her being in Portsmouth, and but for Mr. Crawford and the beauty of the weather, would soon have been knocked up now.

The loveliness of the day, and of the view, he felt like herself. They often stopt with the same sentiment and taste, leaning against the wall, some minutes, to look and admire; and considering he was not Edmund, Fanny could not but allow that he was sufficiently open to the charms of nature, and very well able to express his admiration. She had a few tender reveries now and then, which he could sometimes take advantage of, to look in her face without detection; and the result of these looks was, that though as bewitching as ever, her face was less blooming than it ought to be.—She *said* she was very well, and did not like to be supposed otherwise; but take it all in all, he was convinced that her present residence could not be comfortable, and, therefore, could not be salutary for her, and he was growing anxious for her being again at Mansfield, where her own happiness, and his in seeing her, must be so much greater.

"You have been here a month, I think?" said he.

"No. Not quite a month.—It is only four weeks to-morrow since I left Mansfield."

"You are a most accurate and honest reckoner. I should call that a month."

"I did not arrive here till Tuesday evening."

"And it is to be a two months' visit, is not it?"

"Yes.—My uncle talked of two months. I suppose it will not be less."

"And how are you to be conveyed back again? Who comes for you?"

"I do not know. I have heard nothing about it yet from my aunt. Perhaps I may be to stay longer. It may not be convenient for me to be fetched exactly at the two months' end."

After a moment's reflection, Mr. Crawford replied, "I know Mansfield, I know its way, I know its faults towards *you*. I know the danger of your being so far forgotten, as to have your comforts give way to the imaginary convenience of any single being in the family. I am aware that you may be left here week after week, if Sir Thomas cannot settle every thing for coming himself, or sending your aunt's maid for you, without involving the slightest alteration of the arrangements which he may have laid down for the next quarter of a year. This will not do. Two months is an ample allowance, I should think six weeks quite enough.—I am considering your sister's health," said he, addressing himself to Susan, "which I think the confinement of Portsmouth unfavourable to. She requires constant air and exercise. When you know her as well as I do, I am sure you will agree that she does, and that she ought never to be long banished from the free air, and liberty of the country.—If, therefore, (turning again to Fanny) you find yourself growing unwell, and any difficulties arise about your returning to Mansfield—without waiting for the two months to be ended—*that* must not be regarded as of any consequence, if you feel yourself at all less strong, or comfortable than usual, and will only let my sister know it, give her only the slightest hint, she and I will immediately come down, and take you back to Mansfield. You know the ease, and the pleasure with which this would be done. You know all that would be felt on the occasion."

Fanny thanked him, but tried to laugh it off.

"I am perfectly serious,"—he replied,—"as you perfectly know.—And I hope you will not be cruelly concealing any tendency to indisposition.—Indeed, you shall *not*, it shall not be in your power, for so long only as you positively say, in every letter to Mary, 'I am well.'— and I know you cannot speak or write a falsehood,—so long only shall you be considered as well."

Fanny thanked him again, but was affected and distressed to a degree that made it impossible for her to say much, or even to be certain of what she ought to say.—This was towards the close of their walk. He attended them to the last, and left them only at the door of their own house, when he knew them to be going to dinner, and therefore pretended to be waited for elsewhere.

"I wish you were not so tired,"—said he, still detaining Fanny after all the others were in the house; "I wish I left you in stronger health. —Is there any thing I can do for you in town? I have half an idea of going into Norfolk again soon. I am not satisfied about Maddison.—I am sure he still means to impose on me if possible, and get a cousin of his own into a certain mill, which I design for somebody else.—I must come to an understanding with him. I must make him know that I will not be tricked on the south side of Everingham, any more than on the north, that I will be master of my own property. I was not explicit enough with him before.—The mischief such a man does on an estate, both as to the credit of his employer, and the welfare of the poor, is inconceivable. I have a great mind to go back into Norfolk directly, and put every thing at once on such a footing as cannot be afterwards swerved from.—Maddison is a clever fellow; I do not wish to displace him—provided he does not try to displace *me*;—but it would be simple to be duped by a man who has no right of creditor to dupe me—and worse than simple to let him give me a hard-hearted, griping fellow for a tenant, instead of an honest man, to whom I have given half a promise already.—Would not it be worse than simple? Shall I go?—Do you advise it?"

"I advise!—you know very well what is right."

"Yes. When you give me your opinion, I always know what is right. Your judgment is my rule of right."

"Oh, no!—do not say so. We have all a better guide in ourselves, if we would attend to it, than any other person can be. Good bye; I wish you a pleasant journey to-morrow."

"Is there nothing I can do for you in town?"

"Nothing, I am much obliged to you."

"Have you no message for anybody?"

"My love to your sister, if you please; and when you see my cousin —my cousin Edmund, I wish you would be so good as to say that—I suppose I shall soon hear from him."

"Certainly; and if he is lazy or negligent, I will write his excuses myself—"

He could say no more, for Fanny would be no longer detained. He pressed her hand, looked at her, and was gone. *He* went to while away the next three hours as he could, with his other acquaintance, till the best dinner that a capital inn afforded, was ready for their enjoyment, and *she* turned in to her more simple one immediately.

Their general fare bore a very different character; and could he have suspected how many privations, besides that of exercise, she endured in her father's house, he would have wondered that her looks were not much more affected than he found them. She was so little equal to Rebecca's puddings, and Rebecca's hashes, brought to table as they all were, with such accompaniments of half-cleaned plates, and not half-cleaned knives and forks, that she was very often constrained to defer her heartiest meal, till she could send her brothers in the evening for biscuits and buns. After being nursed up at Mansfield, it was too late in the day to be hardened at Portsmouth; and though Sir Thomas, had he known all, might have thought his niece in the most promising way of being starved, both mind and body, into a much juster value for Mr. Crawford's good company and good fortune, he would probably have feared to push his experiment farther, lest she might die under the cure.

Fanny was out of spirits all the rest of the day. Though tolerably secure of not seeing Mr. Crawford again, she could not help being low. It was parting with somebody of the nature of a friend; and though in one light glad to have him gone, it seemed as if she was now deserted by everybody; it was a sort of renewed separation from Mansfield; and she could not think of his returning to town, and being frequently with Mary and Edmund, without feelings so near akin to envy, as made her hate herself for having them.

Her dejection had no abatement from anything passing around her; a friend or two of her father's, as always happened if he was not with them, spent the long, long evening there; and from six o'clock to half past nine, there was little intermission of noise or grog. She was very low. The wonderful improvement which she still fancied in Mr. Craw-ford, was the nearest to administering comfort of anything within the current of her thoughts. Not considering in how different a circle she had been just seeing him, nor how much might be owing to contrast, she was quite persuaded of his being astonishingly more gentle, and regardful of others, than formerly. And if in little things, must it not be so in great? So anxious for her health and comfort, so very feeling as he now expressed himself, and really seemed, might not it be fairly supposed, that he would not much longer persevere in a suit* so dis-tressing to her?

Chapter XII.

It was presumed that Mr. Crawford was travelling back to London, on the morrow, for nothing more was seen of him at Mr. Price's; and two days afterwards, it was a fact ascertained to Fanny by the following letter from his sister, opened and read by her, on another account, with the most anxious curiosity:—

"I have to inform you, my dearest Fanny, that Henry has been down to Portsmouth to see you; that he had a delightful walk with you to the Dock-yard last Saturday, and one still more to be dwelt on the next day, on the ramparts; when the balmy air, the sparkling sea, and your sweet looks and conversation were altogether in the most delicious har-mony, and afforded sensations which are to raise ecstacy even in ret-rospect. This, as well as I understand, is to be the substance of my information. He makes me write, but I do not know what else is to be communicated, except this said visit to Portsmouth, and these two said walks, and his introduction to your family, especially to a fair sister of your's, a fine girl of fifteen, who was of the party on the ramparts, taking her first lesson, I presume, in love. I have not time for writing much, but it would be out of place if I had, for this is to be a mere letter of business, penned for the purpose of conveying necessary information, which could not be delayed without risk of evil. My dear, dear Fanny, if I had you here, how I would talk to you!—You should listen to me till you were tired, and advise me till you were tired still* more; but it is impossible to put an hundredth part of my great mind on paper, so I will abstain altogether, and leave you to guess what you like. I have no news for you. You have politics of course; and it would be too bad to plague you with the names of people and parties, that fill up my time. I ought to have sent you an account of your cousin's first party, but I was lazy, and now it is too long ago; suffice it, that every thing was just as it ought to be, in a style that any of her connections must have been gratified to witness, and that her own dress and manners did her the greatest credit. My friend Mrs. Fraser is mad for such a house, and it would not make *me* miserable. I go to Lady Stornaway after Easter. She seems in high spirits, and very happy. I fancy Lord S. is very good-humoured and pleasant in his own family, and I do not think him so very ill-looking as I did, at least one sees many worse. He will not do by the side of your cousin Edmund. Of the last-mentioned hero, what shall I say? If I avoided his name entirely, it would look suspicious. I will say, then, that we have seen him two or three times, and that my friends here are very much struck with his gentleman-like appearance. Mrs. Fraser (no bad judge), declares she knows but three men in town who have so good a person, height, and air; and I must confess, when he dined here the other day, there were none to compare with him, and we were a party of sixteen. Luckily there is no distinction of dress now-a-days to tell tales, but—but—but.

Your's, affectionately."

"I had almost forgot (it was Edmund's fault, he gets into my head more than does me good), one very material thing I had to say from Henry and myself, I mean about our taking you back into Northamptonshire. My dear little creature, do not stay at Portsmouth to lose your pretty looks. Those vile sea-breezes are the ruin of beauty and health. My poor aunt always felt affected, if within ten miles of the sea, which the Admiral of course never believed, but I know it was so. I am at your service and Henry's, at an hour's notice. I should like the scheme, and we would make a little circuit, and shew you Everingham in our way, and perhaps you would not mind passing through London, and seeing the inside of St. George's, Hanover-Square. Only keep your cousin Edmund from me at such a time, I should not like to be tempted. What a long letter!—one word more. Henry I find has some idea of going into Norfolk again upon some business that *you* approve, but this cannot possibly be permitted before the middle of next week, that is, he cannot any how be spared till after the 14th, for we have a party that evening. The value of a man like Henry on such an occasion, is what you can have no conception of; so you must take it upon my word, to be inestimable. He will see the Rushworths, which I own I am not sorry for—having a little curiosity—and so I think has he, though he will not acknowledge it."

This was a letter to be run through eagerly, to be read deliberately, to supply matter for much reflection, and to leave every thing in greater suspense than ever. The only certainty to be drawn from it was, that nothing decisive had yet taken place. Edmund had not yet spoken. How Miss Crawford really felt—how she meant to act, or might act without or against her meaning—whether his importance to her were* quite what it had been before the last separation—whether if lessened it were likely to lessen more, or to recover itself, were subjects for endless conjecture, and to be thought of on that day and many days to come, without producing any conclusion. The idea that returned the oftenest, was that Miss Crawford, after proving herself cooled and staggered by a return to London habits, would yet prove herself in the end too much attached to him, to give him up. She would try to be more ambitious than her heart would allow. She would hesitate, she would teaze, she would condition, she would require a great deal, but she would finally accept. This was Fanny's most frequent expectation*. A house in town!—that she thought must be impossible. Yet there was no saying what Miss Crawford might not ask. The prospect for her cousin grew worse and worse. The woman who could speak of him, and speak only of his appearance!—What an unworthy attachment!—To be deriving support from the commendations of Mrs. Fraser! She who had known him intimately half a year! Fanny was ashamed of her. Those parts of the letter which related only to Mr. Crawford and herself, touched her in comparison, slightly. Whether Mr. Crawford went into Norfolk before or after the 14th, was certainly no concern of her's, though, every thing considered, she thought he would go without delay. That Miss Crawford should endeavour to secure a meeting between him and Mrs. Rushworth, was all in her worst line of conduct, and grossly unkind and ill-judged; but she hoped he would not be actuated by any such degrading curiosity. He acknowledged no such inducement, and his sister ought to have given him credit for better feelings than her own.

She was yet more impatient for another letter from town after receiving this, than she had been before; and for a few days, was so unsettled by it altogether, by what had come, and what might come, that her usual readings and conversation with Susan were much suspended. She could not command her attention as she wished. If Mr. Crawford remembered her message to her cousin, she thought it very likely, most likely, that he would write to her at all events; it would be most consistent with his usual kindness, and till she got rid of this idea, till it gradually wore off, by no letters appearing in the course of three or four days more, she was in a most restless, anxious state.

At length, a something like composure succeeded. Suspense must be submitted to, and must not be allowed to wear her out, and make her useless. Time did something, her own exertions something more, and she resumed her attentions to Susan, and again awakened the same interest in them.

Susan was growing very fond of her, and though without any of the early delight in books, which had been so strong in Fanny, with a disposition much less inclined to sedentary pursuits, or to information for information's sake, she had so strong a desire of not *appearing* ignorant, as with a good clear understanding, made her a most attentive, profitable, thankful pupil. Fanny was her oracle. Fanny's explanations and remarks were a most important addition to every essay, or every chapter of history. What Fanny told her of former times, dwelt more on her mind than the pages of Goldsmith;[1] and she paid her sister the compliment of preferring her style to that of any printed author. The early habit of reading was wanting.

Their conversations, however, were not always on subjects so high as history or morals. Others had their hour; and of lesser matters, none returned so often, or remained so long between them, as Mansfield Park, a description of the people, the manners, the amusements, the ways of Mansfield Park. Susan, who had an innate taste for the genteel and well-appointed, was eager to hear, and Fanny could not but indulge herself in dwelling on so beloved a theme. She hoped it was not wrong; though after a time, Susan's very great admiration of every thing said or done in her uncle's house, and earnest longing to go into Northamptonshire, seemed almost to blame her for exciting feelings which could not be gratified.

Poor Susan was very little better fitted for home than her elder sister; and as Fanny grew thoroughly to understand this, she began to feel that when her own release from Portsmouth came, her happiness would have a material drawback in leaving Susan behind. That a girl so capable of being made, every thing good, should be left in such hands, distressed her more and more. Were *she* likely to have a home to invite her to, what a blessing it would be!—And had it been possible for her to return Mr. Crawford's regard, the probability of his being very far from objecting to such a measure, would have been the greatest increase of all her own comforts. She thought he was really goodtempered, and could fancy his entering into a plan of that sort, most pleasantly.

---

1. Oliver Goldsmith (1730?–1774) was a novelist, poet, playwright, essayist, and historian. His *History of England in a series of letters from a nobleman to his son* (1764) was widely read.

Chapter XIII.

Seven weeks of the two months were very nearly gone, when the one letter, the letter from Edmund so long expected, was put into Fanny's hands. As she opened and saw its length she prepared herself for a minute detail of happiness and a profusion of love and praise towards the fortunate creature, who was now mistress of his fate. These were the contents.

"*Mansfield Park.*

"My dear Fanny,

"Excuse me that I have not written before.* Crawford told me that you were wishing to hear from me, but I found it impossible to write from London, and persuaded myself that you would understand my silence.—Could I have sent a few happy lines, they should not have been wanting, but nothing of that nature was ever in my power.—I am returned to Mansfield in a less assured state than when I left it. My hopes are much weaker.—You are probably aware of this already.—So very fond of you as Miss Crawford is, it is most natural that she should tell you enough of her own feelings, to furnish a tolerable guess at mine.—I will not be prevented, however, from making my own communication. Our confidences in you need not clash.—I ask no questions.—There is something soothing in the idea, that we have the same friend, and that whatever unhappy differences of opinion may exist between us, we are united in our love of you.—It will be a comfort to me to tell you how things now are, and what are my present plans, if plans I can be said to have.—I have been returned since Saturday. I was three weeks in London, and saw her (for London) very often. I had every attention from the Frasers that could be reasonably expected. I dare say I was *not* reasonable in carrying with me hopes of an intercourse at all like that of Mansfield. It was her manner, however, rather than any unfrequency of meeting. Had she been different* when I did see her, I should have made no complaint, but from the very first she was altered; my first reception was so unlike what I had hoped, that I had almost resolved on leaving London again directly.—I need not particularize. You know the weak side of her character, and may imagine the sentiments and expressions which were torturing me. She was in high spirits, and surrounded by those who were giving all the support of their own bad sense to her too lively mind. I do not like Mrs. Fraser. She is a cold-hearted, vain woman, who has married entirely from convenience, and though evidently unhappy in her marriage, places her disappointment, not to faults of judgement or temper, or disproportion of age, but to her being after all, less affluent than many of her acquaintance, especially than her sister, Lady Stornaway, and is the determined supporter of every thing mercenary and ambitious, provided it be only mercenary and ambitious enough. I look upon her intimacy with those two sisters, as the greatest misfortune of her life and mine. They have been leading her astray for years. Could she be detached from them!—and sometimes I do not despair of it, for the affection appears to me principally on their side. They are very fond of her; but I am sure she does not love them as she loves you. When I think of her great attachment to you, indeed, and the whole of her judicious, upright conduct as a sister, she appears a very different creature, capable of every thing noble, and I am ready to blame myself for a too harsh construction of a playful manner. I cannot give her up, Fanny. She is the only woman in the world whom I could ever think of as a wife. If I did not believe that she had some regard for me, of course I should not say this, but I do believe it. I am convinced, that she is not without a decided preference. I have no jealousy of any individual. It is the influence of the fashionable world altogether that I am jealous of. It is the habits of wealth that I fear. Her ideas are not higher than her own fortune may warrant, but they are beyond what our incomes united could authorise. There is comfort, however, even here. I could better bear to lose her, because not rich enough, than because of my profession. That would only prove her affection not equal to sacrifices, which, in fact, I am scarcely justified in asking; and if I am refused, *that*, I think, will be the honest motive. Her prejudices, I trust, are not so strong as they were. You have my thoughts exactly as they arise, my dear Fanny; perhaps they are some times contradictory, but it will not be a less faithful picture of my mind. Having once begun, it is a pleasure to me to tell you all I feel. I cannot give her up. Connected, as we already are, and, I hope, are to be, to give up Mary Crawford, would be to give up the society of some of those most dear to me, to banish myself from the very houses and friends whom, under any other distress, I should turn to for consolation. The loss of Mary I must consider as comprehending the loss of Crawford and of Fanny. Were it a decided thing, an actual refusal, I hope I should know how to bear it, and how to endeavour to weaken her hold on my heart—and in the course of a few years—but I am writing nonsense—were I refused, I must bear it; and till I am, I can never cease to try for her. This is the truth. The only question is *how*? What may be the likeliest means? I have some-times thought of going to London again after Easter, and sometimes resolved on doing nothing till she returns to Mansfield. Even now, she speaks with pleasure of being in Mansfield in June; but June is at a great distance, and I believe I shall write to her. I have nearly deter-mined on explaining myself by letter. To be at an early certainty is a material object. My present state is miserably irksome. Considering every thing, I think a letter will be decidedly the best method of expla-nation. I shall be able to write much that I could not say, and shall be giving her time for reflection before she resolves on her answer, and I am less afraid of the result of reflection than of an immediate hasty impulse; I think I am. My greatest danger would lie in her consulting Mrs. Fraser, and I at a distance, unable to help my own cause. A letter exposes to all the evil of consultation, and where the mind is any thing short of perfect decision, an adviser may, in an unlucky moment, lead it to do what it may afterwards regret. I must think this matter over a little. This long letter, full of my own concerns alone, will be enough to tire even the friendship of a Fanny. The last time I saw Crawford was at Mrs. Fraser's party. I am more and more satisfied with all that I see and hear of him. There is not a shadow of wavering. He thoroughly knows his own mind, and acts up to his resolutions—an inestimable quality. I could not see him, and my eldest sister in the same room, without recollecting what you once told me, and I acknowledge that they did not meet as friends. There was marked coolness* on her side. They scarcely spoke. I saw him draw back surprised, and I was sorry that Mrs. Rushworth should resent any former supposed slight to Miss Bertram. You will wish to hear my opinion of Maria's degree of comfort as a wife. There is no appearance of unhappiness. I hope they get on pretty well together. I dined twice in Wimpole Street, and might have been there oftener, but it is mortifying to be with Rushworth as a brother. Julia seems to enjoy London exceedingly. I had little enjoyment there—but have less here. We are not a lively party. You are very much wanted. I miss you more than I can express. My mother desires her best love, and hopes to hear from you soon. She talks of you almost every hour, and I am sorry to find how many weeks more she is likely to be without you. My Father means to fetch you himself, but it will not be till after Easter, when he has business in town. You are happy at Portsmouth, I hope, but this must not be a yearly visit. I want you at home, that I may have your opinion about Thornton Lacey. I have little heart for extensive improvements till I know that it will ever have a mistress. I think I shall certainly write. It is quite settled that the Grants go to Bath; they leave Mansfield on Monday. I am glad of it. I am not comfortable enough to be fit for any body; but your aunt seems to feel out of luck that such an article of Mansfield news should fall to my pen instead of her's. Your's ever, my dearest Fanny."

"I never will—no, I certainly never will wish for a letter again," was Fanny's secret declaration, as she finished this. "What do they bring but disappointment and sorrow?—Not till after Easter!—How shall I bear it?—And my poor aunt talking of me every hour!"

Fanny checked the tendency of these thoughts as well as she could, but she was within half a minute of starting the idea, that Sir Thomas was quite unkind, both to her aunt and to herself.—As for the main subject of the letter—there was nothing in that to soothe irritation. She was almost vexed into displeasure, and anger, against Edmund. "There is no good in this delay," said she. "Why is not it settled?"—He is blinded, and nothing will open his eyes, nothing can, after having had truths before him so long in vain.—He will marry her, and be poor and miserable. God grant that her influence do not make him cease to be respectable!"—She looked over the letter again. " 'So very fond of me!' 'tis nonsense all. She loves nobody but herself and her brother. Her friends leading her astray for years! She is quite as likely to have led *them* astray. They have all, perhaps, been corrupting one another; but if they are so much fonder of her than she is of them, she is the less likely to have been hurt, except by their flattery. 'The only woman in the world, whom he could ever think of as a wife.' I firmly believe it. It is an attachment to govern his whole life. Accepted or refused, his heart is wedded to her for ever. 'The loss of Mary, I must consider as comprehending the loss of Crawford and Fanny.'* Edmund, you do not know *me*. The families would never be connected, if you did not connect them! Oh! write, write. Finish it at once. Let there be an end of this suspense. Fix, commit, condemn yourself."

Such sensations, however, were too near a kin to resentment to be long guiding Fanny's soliloquies. She was soon more softened and sorrowful.—His warm regard, his kind expressions, his confidential treatment touched her strongly. He was only too good to every body.— It was a letter, in short, which she would not but have had for the world, and which could never be valued enough. This was the end of it.

Every body at all addicted to letter writing, without having much to say, which will include a large proportion of the female world at least, must feel with Lady Bertram, that she was out of luck in having such a capital piece of Mansfield news, as the certainty of the Grants going to Bath, occur at a time when she could make no advantage of it, and will admit that it must have been very mortifying to her to see it fall to the share of her thankless son, and treated as concisely as possible at the end of a long letter, instead of having it to spread over the largest part of a page of her own.—For though Lady Bertram rather shone in the epistolary line, having early in her marriage, from the want of other employment, and the circumstance of Sir Thomas's being in Parliament, got into the way of making and keeping correspondents, and formed for herself a very creditable, common-place, amplifying style, so that a very little matter was enough for her; she could not do entirely without any; she must have something to write about, even to her niece, and being so soon to lose all the benefit of Dr. Grant's gouty symptoms and Mrs. Grant's morning calls, it was very hard upon her to be deprived of one of the last epistolary uses she could put them to.

There was a rich amends, however, preparing for her. Lady Bertram's hour of good luck came. Within a few days from the receipt of Edmund's letter, Fanny had one from her aunt, beginning thus:—

"My dear Fanny,
"I take up my pen to communicate some very alarming intelligence, which I make no doubt will give you much concern."

This was a great deal better than to have to take up the pen to acquaint her with all the particulars of the Grants' intended journey, for the present intelligence was of a nature to promise occupation for the pen for many days to come, being no less than the dangerous illness of her eldest son, of which they had received notice by express, a few hours before.

Tom had gone from London with a party of young men to Newmarket, where a neglected fall, and a good deal of drinking, had brought on a fever; and when the party broke up, being unable to move, had been left by himself at the house of one of these young men, to the comforts of sickness and solitude, and the attendance only of servants. Instead of being soon well enough to follow his friends, as he had then hoped, his disorder increased considerably, and it was not long before he thought so ill of himself, as to be as ready as his physician to have a letter dispatched to Mansfield.

"This distressing intelligence, as you may suppose," observed her Ladyship, after giving the substance of it, "has agitated us exceedingly, and we cannot prevent ourselves from being greatly alarmed, and apprehensive for the poor invalid, whose state Sir Thomas fears may be very critical; and Edmund kindly proposes attending his brother immediately, but I am happy to add, that Sir Thomas will not leave me on this distressing occasion, as it* would be too trying for me. We shall greatly miss Edmund in our small circle, but I trust and hope he will find the poor invalid in a less alarming state than might be apprehended, and that he will be able to bring him to Mansfield shortly, which Sir Thomas proposes should be done, and thinks best on every account, and I flatter myself, the poor sufferer will soon be able to bear the removal without material inconvenience or injury. As I have little doubt of your feeling for us, my dear Fanny, under these distressing circumstances, I will write again very soon."

Fanny's feelings on the occasion were indeed considerably more warm and genuine than her aunt's style of writing. She felt truly for them all. Tom dangerously ill, Edmund gone to attend him, and the sadly small party remaining at Mansfield, were cares to shut out every other care, or almost every other. She could just find selfishness enough to wonder whether Edmund *had* written to Miss Crawford before this summons came, but no sentiment dwelt long with her, that was not purely affectionate and disinterestedly anxious. Her aunt did not neglect her; she wrote again and again; they were receiving frequent accounts from Edmund, and these accounts were as regularly transmitted to Fanny, in the same diffuse style, and the same medley of trusts, hopes, and fears, all following and producing each other at hap-hazard. It was a sort of playing at being frightened. The sufferings which Lady Bertram did not see, had little power over her fancy; and she wrote very comfortably about agitation and anxiety, and poor invalids, till Tom was actually conveyed to Mansfield, and her own eyes had beheld his altered appearance. Then, a letter which she had been previously preparing for Fanny, was finished in a different style, in the language of real feeling and alarm; then, she wrote as she might have spoken. "He is just come, my dear Fanny, and is taken up stairs; and I am so shocked to see him, that I do not know what to do. I am sure he has been very ill. Poor Tom, I am quite grieved for him, and very much frightened, and so is Sir Thomas; and how glad I should be, if you were here to comfort me. But Sir Thomas hopes he will be better to-morrow, and says we must consider his journey."

The real solicitude now awakened in the maternal bosom was not soon over. Tom's extreme impatience to be removed to Mansfield, and experience those comforts of home and family which had been little thought of in uninterrupted health, had probably induced his being conveyed thither too early, as a return of fever came on, and for a week he was in a more alarming state than ever. They were all very seriously frightened. Lady Bertram wrote her daily terrors to her niece, who might now be said to live upon letters, and pass all her time between suffering from that of to-day, and looking forward to to-morrow's. Without any particular affection for her eldest cousin, her tenderness of heart made her feel that she could not spare him; and the purity of her principles added yet a keener solicitude, when she considered how little useful, how little self-denying his life had (apparently) been.

Susan was her only companion and listener on this, as on more common occasions. Susan was always ready to hear and to sympathize. Nobody else could be interested in so remote an evil as illness, in a family above an hundred miles off—not even Mrs. Price, beyond a brief question or two if she saw her daughter with a letter in her hand, and now and then the quiet observation of "My poor sister Bertram must be in a great deal of trouble."

So long divided, and so differently situated, the ties of blood were little more than nothing. An attachment, originally as tranquil as their tempers, was now become a mere name. Mrs. Price did quite as much for Lady Bertram, as Lady Bertram would have done for Mrs. Price. Three or four Prices might have been swept away, any or all, except Fanny and William, and Lady Bertram would have thought little about it; or perhaps might have caught from Mrs. Norris's lips the cant of its being a very happy thing, and a great blessing to their poor dear sister Price to have them so well provided for.

Chapter XIV.*

At about the week's end from his return to Mansfield, Tom's immediate danger was over, and he was so far pronounced safe, as to make his mother perfectly easy; for being now used to the sight of him in his suffering, helpless state, and hearing only the best, and never thinking beyond what she heard, with no disposition for alarm, and no aptitude at a hint, Lady Bertram was the happiest subject in the world for a little medical imposition. The fever was subdued; the fever had been his complaint, of course he would soon be well again; Lady Bertram could think nothing less, and Fanny shared her aunt's security, till she received a few lines from Edmund, written purposely to give her a clearer idea of his brother's situation, and acquaint her with the apprehensions which he and his father had imbibed from the physician, with respect to some strong hectic[1] symptoms, which seemed to seize the frame on the departure of the fever. They judged it best that Lady Bertram should not be harassed by alarms which, it was to be hoped, would prove unfounded; but there was no reason why Fanny should not know the truth. They were apprehensive for his lungs.

A very few lines from Edmund shewed her the patient and the sick room in a juster and stronger light than all Lady Bertram's sheets of paper could do. There was hardly any one in the house who might not have described, from personal observation, better than herself; not one who was not more useful at times to her son. She could do nothing but glide in quietly and look at him; but, when able to talk or be talked to, or read to, Edmund was the companion he preferred. His aunt worried him by her cares, and Sir Thomas knew not how to bring down his conversation or his voice to the level of irritation and feebleness. Edmund was all in all. Fanny would certainly believe him so at least, and must find that her estimation of him was higher than ever when he appeared as the attendant, supporter, cheerer of a suffering brother. There was not only the debility of recent illness to assist; there was also, as she now learnt, nerves much affected, spirits much depressed to calm and raise; and her own imagination added that there must be a mind to be properly guided.

The family were not consumptive, and she was more inclined to hope than fear for her cousin—except when she thought of Miss Crawford—but Miss Crawford gave her the idea of being the child of

---

1. Wasting, consumptive.

good luck, and to her selfishness and vanity it would be good luck to have Edmund the only son.

Even in the sick chamber, the fortunate Mary was not forgotten. Edmund's letter had this postcript. "On the subject of my last, I had actually begun a letter when called away by Tom's illness, but I have now changed my mind, and fear to trust the influence of friends. When Tom is better, I shall go."

Such was the state of Mansfield, and so it continued, with scarcely any change till Easter. A line occasionally added by Edmund to his mother's letter was enough for Fanny's information. Tom's amendment was alarmingly slow.

Easter came—particularly late this year, as Fanny had most sorrowfully considered, on first learning that she had no chance of leaving Portsmouth till after it. It came, and she had yet heard nothing of her return—nothing even of the going to London, which was to precede her return. Her aunt often expressed a wish for her, but there was no notice, no message from the uncle on whom all depended. She supposed he could not yet leave his son, but it was a cruel, a terrible delay to her. The end of April was coming on; it would soon be almost three months instead of two that she had been absent from them all, and that her days had been passing in a state of penance, which she loved them too well to hope they would thoroughly understand;—and who could yet say when there might be leisure to think of, or fetch her?

Her eagerness, her impatience, her longings to be with them, were such as to bring a line or two of Cowper's Tirocinium for ever before her.—"With what intense desire she wants her home,"[2] was continually on her tongue, as the truest description of a yearning which she could not suppose any school-boy's bosom to feel more keenly.

When she had been coming to Portsmouth, she had loved to call it her home, had been fond of saying that she was going home; the word had been very dear to her; and so it still was, but it must be applied to Mansfield. *That* was now the home. Portsmouth was Portsmouth; Mansfield was home. They had been long so arranged in the indulgence of her secret meditations; and nothing was more consolatory to her than to find her aunt using the same language.—"I cannot but say, I much regret your being from home at this distressing time, so very trying to my spirits.—I trust and hope, and sincerely wish you may never be absent from home so long again"—were most delightful sentences to her. Still, however, it was her private regale.—Delicacy to her parents made her careful not to betray such a preference of her uncle's house: it was always, "when I go back into Northamptonshire, or when I return

---

2. William Cowper's "Tirocinium, Or a Review of Schools" (1784/85) attacked "public" education, recommending private tutors instead: "Th'indented stick that loses day by day / Notch after notch, 'till all are smooth'd away, / Bears witness, long ere his dismission come, / With what intense desire he wants his home" (lines 559–62).

to Mansfield, I shall do so and so."—For a great while it was so; but at last the longing grew stronger, it overthrew caution, and she found herself talking of what she should do when she went home, before she was aware.—She reproached herself, coloured and looked fearfully towards her Father and Mother. She need not have been uneasy. There was no sign of displeasure, or even of hearing her. They were perfectly free from any jealousy of Mansfield. She was as welcome to wish herself there, as to be there.

It was sad to Fanny to lose all the pleasures of spring. She had not known before what pleasures she *had* to lose in passing March and April in a town. She had not known before, how much the beginnings and progress of vegetation had delighted her.—What animation both of body and mind, she had derived from watching the advance of that season which cannot, in spite of its capriciousness, be unlovely, and seeing its increasing beauties, from the earliest flowers, in the warmest divisions of her aunt's garden, to the opening of leaves of her uncle's plantations, and the glory of his woods.—To be losing such pleasures was no trifle; to be losing them, because she was in the midst of closeness and noise, to have confinement, bad air, bad smells, substituted for liberty, freshness, fragrance, and verdure, was infinitely worse;—but even these incitements to regret, were feeble, compared with what arose from the conviction of being missed, by her best friends, and the longing to be useful to those who were wanting her!

Could she have been at home, she might have been of service to every creature in the house. She felt that she must have been of use to all. To all, she must have saved some trouble of head or hand; and were it only in supporting the spirits of her aunt Bertram, keeping her from the evil of solitude, or the still greater evil of a restless, officious companion, too apt to be heightening danger in order to enhance her own importance, her being there would have been a general good. She loved to fancy how she could have read to her aunt, how she could have talked to her, and tried at once to make her feel the blessing of what was, and prepare her mind for what might be; and how many walks up and down stairs she might have saved her, and how many messages she might have carried.

It astonished her that Tom's sisters could be satisfied with remaining in London at such a time—through an illness, which had now, under different degrees of danger, lasted several weeks. *They* might return to Mansfield when they chose; travelling could be no difficulty to *them*, and she could not comprehend how both could still keep away. If Mrs. Rushworth could imagine any interfering obligations, Julia was certainly able to quit London whenever she chose.—It appeared from one of her aunt's letters, that Julia had offered to return if wanted—but this was all.—It was evident that she would rather remain where she was.

Fanny was disposed to think the influence of London very much at war with all respectable attachments. She saw the proof of it in Miss Crawford, as well as in her cousins; *her* attachment to Edmund had been respectable, the most respectable part of her character, her friendship for herself*, had at least been blameless. Where was either sentiment now? It was so long since Fanny had had any letter from her, that she had some reason to think lightly of the friendship which had been so dwelt on.—It was weeks since she had heard any thing of Miss Crawford or of her other connections in town, except through Mansfield, and she was beginning to suppose that she might never know whether Mr. Crawford had gone into Norfolk again or not, till they met, and might never hear from his sister any more this spring, when the following letter was received to revive old, and create some new sensations.

"Forgive me, my dear Fanny, as soon as you can, for my long silence, and behave as if you could forgive me directly. This is my modest request and expectation, for you are so good, that I depend upon being treated better than I deserve—and I write now to beg an immediate answer. I want to know the state of things at Mansfield Park, and you, no doubt, are perfectly able to give it. One should be a brute not to feel for the distress they are in—and from what I hear, poor Mr. Bertram has a bad chance of ultimate recovery. I thought little of his illness at first. I looked upon him as the sort of person to be made a fuss with, and to make a fuss himself in any trifling disorder, and was chiefly concerned for those who had to nurse him; but now it is confidently asserted that he is really in a decline, that the symptoms are most alarming, and that part of the family, at least, are aware of it. If it be so, I am sure you must be included in that part, that discerning part, and therefore intreat you to let me know how far I have been rightly informed. I need not say how rejoiced I shall be to hear there has been any mistake, but the report is so prevalent, that I confess I cannot help trembling. To have such a fine young man cut off in the flower of his days, is most melancholy. Poor Sir Thomas will feel it dreadfully. I really am quite agitated on the subject. Fanny, Fanny, I see you smile, and look cunning, but upon my honour, I never bribed a physician in my life. Poor young man!—If he is to die, there will be *two* poor young men less in the world; and with a fearless face and bold voice would I say to any one, that wealth and consequence could fall into no hands more deserving of them. It was a foolish precipitation last Christmas, but the evil of a few days may be blotted out in part. Varnish and gilding hide many stains. It will be but the loss of the Esquire after his name. With real affection, Fanny, like mine, more might be overlooked. Write to me by return of post, judge of my anxiety, and do not trifle with it. Tell me the real truth, as you have it from the fountain head. And now, do not trouble yourself to be ashamed of either my feelings or your own. Believe me, they are not only natural, they are philanthropic and virtuous. I put it to your conscience, whether 'Sir Edmund' would not do more good with all the Bertram property, than any other possible 'Sir.' Had the Grants been at home, I would not have troubled you, but you are now the only one I can apply to for the truth, his sisters not being within my reach. Mrs. R. has been spending the Easter with the Aylmers at Twickenham[3] (as to be sure you know), and is not yet returned; and Julia is with the cousins, who live near Bedford Square; but I forgot their name and street. Could I immediately apply to either, however, I should still prefer you, because it strikes me, that they have all along been so unwilling to have their own amusements cut up, as to shut their eyes to the truth. I suppose, Mrs. R.'s Easter holidays will not last much longer; no doubt they are thorough holidays to her. The Aylmers are pleasant people; and her husband away, she can have nothing but enjoyment. I give her credit for promoting his going dutifully down to Bath, to fetch his mother; but how will she and the dowager agree in one house? Henry is not at hand, so I have nothing to say from him. Do not you think Edmund would have been in town again long ago, but for this illness?—Yours ever, Mary."

"I had actually began folding my letter, when Henry walked in; but he brings no intelligence to prevent my sending it. Mrs. R. knows a decline is apprehended; he saw her this morning, she returns to Wimpole Street today, the old lady is come. Now do not make yourself uneasy with any queer fancies, because he has been spending a few days at Richmond.[4] He does it every spring. Be assured, he cares for nobody but you. At this very moment, he is wild to see you, and occupied only in contriving the means for doing so, and for making his pleasure conduce to yours. In proof, he repeats, and more eagerly, what he said at Portsmouth, about our conveying you home, and I join him in it with all my soul. Dear Fanny, write directly, and tell us to come. It will do us all good. He and I can go to the Parsonage, you know, and be no trouble to our friends at Mansfield Park. It would really be gratifying to see them all again, and a little addition of society might be of infinite use to them; and, as to yourself, you must feel yourself to be so wanted there, that you cannot in conscience (conscientious as you are,) keep away, when you have the means of returning. I have not time or patience to give half Henry's messages; be satisfied, that the spirit of each and every one is unalterable affection."

Fanny's disgust at the greater part of this letter, with her extreme reluctance to bring the writer of it and her cousin Edmund together, would have made her (as she felt), incapable of judging impartially

---

3. A village east of London where prominent families built their villas. The rakish Admiral Crawford's cottage is also located in Twickenham (see above, p. 42), which is why Mary Crawford expects Fanny to feel suspicious.

4. Another fashionable village east of London. Richmond is directly across the Thames from Twickenham—hence Mary Crawford's efforts to assure Fanny that Henry's visit there is coincidental.

whether the concluding offer might be accepted or not. To herself, individually, it was most tempting. To be finding herself, perhaps, within three days, transported to Mansfield, was an image of the greatest felicity—but it would have been a material drawback, to be owing such felicity to persons in whose feelings and conduct, at the present moment, she saw so much to condemn; the sister's feelings—the brother's conduct—*her* cold-hearted ambition—*his* thoughtless vanity. To have him still the acquaintance, the flirt, perhaps, of Mrs. Rushworth!—She was mortified. She had thought better of him. Happily, however, she was not left to weigh and decide between opposite inclinations and doubtful notions of right; there was no occasion to determine, whether she ought to keep Edmund and Mary asunder or not. She had a rule to apply to, which settled every thing. Her awe of her uncle, and her dread of taking a liberty with him, made it instantly plain to her, what she had to do. She must absolutely decline the proposal. If he wanted, he would send for her; and even to offer an early return, was a presumption which hardly any thing would have seemed to justify. She thanked Miss Crawford, but gave a decided negative.—"Her uncle, she understood, meant to fetch her; and as her cousin's illness had continued so many weeks without her being thought at all necessary, she must suppose her return would be unwelcome at present, and that she should be felt an incumbrance."

Her representation of her cousin's state at this time, was exactly according to her own belief of it, and such as she supposed would convey to the sanguine mind of her correspondent, the hope of every thing she was wishing for. Edmund would be forgiven for being a clergyman, it seemed, under certain conditions of wealth; and this,* she suspected, was all the conquest of prejudice, which he was so ready to congratulate himself upon. She had only learnt to think nothing of consequence but money.

Chapter XV.

As Fanny could not doubt that her answer was conveying a real disappointment, she was rather in expectation, from her knowledge of Miss Crawford's temper, of being urged again; and though no second letter arrived for the space of a week, she had still the same feeling when it did come.

On receiving it, she could instantly decide on its containing little writing, and was persuaded of its having the air of a letter of haste and business. Its object was unquestionable; and two moments were enough to start the probability of its being merely to give her notice that they should be in Portsmouth that very day, and to throw her into all the agitation of doubting what she ought to do in such a case. If two moments, however, can surround with difficulties, a third can disperse them; and before she had opened the letter, the possibility of Mr. and Miss Crawford's having applied to her uncle and obtained his permission, was giving her ease. This was the letter.

"A most scandalous, ill-natured rumour has just reached me, and I write, dear Fanny, to warn you against giving the least credit to it, should it spread into the country. Depend upon it there is some mistake, and that a day or two will clear it up—at any rate, that Henry is blameless, and in spite of a moment's *etourderie*[1] thinks of nobody but you. Say not a word of it—hear nothing, surmise nothing, whisper nothing, till I write again. I am sure it will be all hushed up, and nothing proved but Rushworth's folly. If they are gone, I would lay my life they are only gone to Mansfield Park, and Julia with them. But why would not you let us come for you? I wish you may not repent it.

"Yours, &c."

Fanny stood aghast. As no scandalous, ill-natured rumour had reached her, it was impossible for her to understand much of this strange letter. She could only perceive that it must relate to Wimpole Street and Mr. Crawford, and only conjecture that something very imprudent had just occurred in that quarter to draw the notice of the world, and to excite her jealousy, in Miss Crawford's apprehension, if she heard it. Miss Crawford need not be alarmed for her. She was only sorry for the parties concerned and for Mansfield, if the report should spread so far; but she hoped it might not. If the Rushworths were gone themselves to Mansfield, as was to be inferred from what Miss Crawford said, it was not likely that any thing unpleasant should have preceded them, or at least should make any impression.

As to Mr. Crawford, she hoped it might give him a knowledge of his own disposition, convince him that he was not capable of being steadily attached to any one woman in the world, and shame him from persisting any longer in addressing herself.

It was very strange! She had begun to think he really loved her, and to fancy his affection for her something more than common—and his sister still said that he cared for nobody else. Yet there must have been some marked display of attentions to her cousin, there must have been some strong indiscretion, since her correspondent was not of a sort to regard a slight one.

Very uncomfortable she was and must continue till she heard from Miss Crawford again. It was impossible to banish the letter from her thoughts, and she could not relieve herself by speaking of it to any human being. Miss Crawford need not have urged secrecy with so much warmth, she might have trusted to her sense of what was due to her cousin.

---

1. Thoughtlessness; giddiness.

The next day came and brought no second letter. Fanny was disappointed. She could still think of little else all the morning; but when her father came back in the afternoon with the daily newspaper as usual, she was so far from expecting any elucidation through such a channel, that the subject was for a moment out of her head.

She was deep in other musing. The remembrance of her first evening in that room, of her father and his newspaper came across her. No candle was *now* wanted. The sun was yet an hour and half above the horizon. She felt that she had, indeed, been three months there; and the sun's rays falling strongly into the parlour, instead of cheering, made her still more melancholy; for sun shine appeared to her a totally different thing in a town and in the country. Here, its power was only a glare, a stifling, sickly glare, serving but to bring forward stains and dirt that might otherwise have slept. There was neither health nor gaiety in sun-shine in a town. She sat in a blaze of oppressive heat, in a cloud of moving dust; and her eyes could only wander from the walls marked by her father's head, to the table cut and knotched by her brothers, where stood the tea-board never thoroughly cleaned, the cups and saucers wiped in streaks, the milk a mixture of motes floating in thin blue, and the bread and butter growing every minute more greasy than even Rebecca's hands had first produced it. Her father read his newspaper, and her mother lamented over the ragged carpet as usual, while the tea was in preparation—and wished Rebecca would mend it; and Fanny was first roused by his calling out to her, after humphing and considering over a particular paragraph—"What's the name of your great cousins in town, Fan?"

A moment's recollection enabled her to say, "Rushworth, Sir."

"And don't they live in Wimpole Street?"

"Yes, Sir."

"Then, there's the devil to pay among them, that's all. There, (holding out the paper to her)—much good may such fine relations do you. I don't know what Sir Thomas may think of such matters; he may be too much of the courtier and fine gentleman to like his daughter the less. But by G— if she belonged to *me*, I'd give her the rope's end as long as I could stand over her. A little flogging for man and woman too, would be the best way of preventing such things."

Fanny read to herself that "it was with infinite concern the newspaper had to announce to the world, a matrimonial *fracas*[2] in the family of Mr. R. of Wimpole Street; the beautiful Mrs. R. whose name had not long been enrolled in the lists of hymen,[3] and who had promised to become so brilliant a leader in the fashionable world, having quitted her husband's roof in company with the well known and captivating Mr. C. the intimate friend and associate of Mr. R. and it was not

2. Disturbance.
3. Married.

known, even to the editor of the newspaper, whither they were gone."

"It is a mistake, Sir," said Fanny instantly; "it must be a mistake—it cannot be true—it must mean some other people."

She spoke from the instinctive wish of delaying shame, she spoke with a resolution which sprung from despair, for she spoke what she did not, could not believe herself. It had been the shock of conviction as she read. The truth rushed on her; and how she could have spoken at all, how she could even have breathed—was afterwards matter of wonder to herself.

Mr. Price cared too little about the report, to make her much answer. "It might be all a lie, he acknowledged; but so many fine ladies were going to the devil now-a-days that way, that there was no answering for anybody."

"Indeed, I hope it is not true," said Mrs. Price plaintively, "it would be so very shocking!—If I have spoken once to Rebecca about that carpet, I am sure I have spoke at least a dozen times; have not I, Betsey?—And it would not be ten minutes work."

The horror of a mind like Fanny's, as it received the conviction of such guilt, and began to take in some part of the misery that must ensue, can hardly be described. At first, it was a sort of stupefaction; but every moment was quickening her perception of the horrible evil. She could not doubt; she dared not indulge a hope of the paragraph being false. Miss Crawford's letter, which she had read so often as to make every line her own, was in frightful conformity with it. Her eager defence of her brother, her hope of its being *hushed up*, her evident agitation, were all of a piece with something very bad; and if there was a woman of character in existence, who could treat as a trifle this sin of the first magnitude, who could try to gloss it over, and desire to have it unpunished, she could believe Miss Crawford to be the woman! Now she could see her own mistake as to *who* were gone—or *said* to be gone. It was not Mr. and Mrs. Rushworth, it was Mrs. Rushworth and Mr. Crawford.

Fanny seemed to herself never to have been shocked before. There was no possibility of rest. The evening passed, without a pause of misery, the night was totally sleepless. She passed only from feelings of sickness to shudderings of horror; and from hot fits of fever to cold. The event was so shocking, that there were moments even when her heart revolted from it as impossible—when she thought it could not be. A woman married only six months ago, a man professing himself devoted, even *engaged*, to another—that other her near relation—the whole family, both families connected as they were by tie upon tie, all friends, all intimate together!—it was too horrible a confusion of guilt, too gross a complication of evil, for human nature, not in a state of utter barbarism, to be capable of!—yet her judgment told her it was so. *His* unsettled affections, wavering with his vanity, *Maria's* decided attachment, and no sufficient principle on either side, gave it possibility—Miss Crawford's letter stampt it a fact.

What would be the consequence? Whom would it not injure? Whose views might it not affect*? Whose peace would it not cut up for ever? Miss Crawford herself—Edmund; but it was dangerous, perhaps, to tread such ground. She confined herself, or tried to confine herself to the simple, indubitable family-misery which must envelope all, if it were indeed a matter of certified guilt and public exposure. The mother's sufferings, the father's—there, she paused. Julia's, Tom's, Edmund's—there, a yet longer pause. They were the two on whom it would fall most horribly. Sir Thomas's parental solicitude, and high sense of honour and decorum, Edmund's upright principles, unsuspicious temper, and genuine strength of feeling, made her think it scarcely possible for them to support life and reason under such disgrace; and it appeared to her, that as far as this world alone was concerned, the greatest blessing to every one of kindred with Mrs. Rushworth would be instant annihilation.

Nothing happened the next day, or the next, to weaken her terrors. Two posts came in, and brought no refutation, public or private. There was no second letter to explain away the first, from Miss Crawford; there was no intelligence from Mansfield, though it was now full time for her to hear again from her aunt. This was an evil omen. She had, indeed, scarcely the shadow of a hope to soothe her mind, and was reduced to so low and wan and trembling a condition as no mother—not unkind, except Mrs. Price, could have overlooked, when the third day did bring the sickening knock, and a letter was again put into her hands. It bore the London postmark, and came from Edmund.

"Dear Fanny,

You know our present wretchedness. May God support you under your share. We have been here two days, but there is nothing to be done. They cannot be traced. You may not have heard of the last blow—Julia's elopement; she is gone to Scotland with Yates. She left London a few hours before we entered it. At any other time, this would have been felt dreadfully. Now it seems nothing, yet it is an heavy aggravation. My father is not overpowered. More cannot be hoped. He is still able to think and act; and I write, by his desire, to propose your returning home. He is anxious to get you there for my mother's sake. I shall be at Portsmouth the morning after you receive this, and hope to find you ready to set off for Mansfield. My Father wishes you to invite Susan to go with you, for a few months. Settle it as you like; say what is proper; I am sure you will feel such an instance of his kindness at such a moment! Do justice to his meaning, however I may confuse it. You may imagine something of my present state. There is no end of the evil let loose upon us. You will see me early, by the mail. Your's, &c.

Never had Fanny more wanted a cordial.[4] Never had she felt such a one as this letter contained. To-morrow! to leave Portsmouth to-morrow! She was, she felt she was, in the greatest danger of being exquisitely happy, while so many were miserable. The evil which brought such good to her! She dreaded lest she should learn to be insensible of it. To be going so soon, sent for so kindly, sent for as a comfort, and with leave to take Susan, was altogether such a combination of blessings as set her heart in a glow, and for a time, seemed to distance every pain, and make her incapable of suitably sharing the distress even of those whose distress she thought of most. Julia's elopement could affect her comparatively but little; she was amazed and shocked; but it could not occupy her, could not dwell on her mind. She was obliged to call herself to think of it, and acknowledge it to be terrible and grievous, or it was escaping her, in the midst of all the agitating, pressing, joyful cares attending this summons to herself.

There is nothing like employment, active, indispensable employment, for relieving sorrow. Employment, even melancholy, may dispel melancholy, and her occupations were hopeful. She had so much to do, that not even the horrible story of Mrs. Rushworth (now fixed to the last point of certainty), could affect her as it had done before. She had not time to be miserable. Within twenty-four hours she was hoping to be gone; her father and mother must be spoken to, Susan prepared; every thing got ready. Business followed business; the day was hardly long enough. The happiness she was imparting too, happiness very little alloyed by the black communication which must briefly precede it— the joyful consent of her father and mother to Susan's going with her —the general satisfaction with which the going of both seemed regarded—and the ecstasy of Susan herself, was all serving to support her spirits.

The affliction of the Bertrams was little felt in the family. Mrs. Price talked of her poor sister for a few minutes—but how to find any thing to hold Susan's clothes, because Rebecca took away all the boxes and spoilt them, was much more in her thoughts, and as for Susan, now unexpectedly gratified in the first wish of her heart, and knowing noth-ing personally of those who had sinned, or of those who were sorrowing—if she could help rejoicing from beginning to end, it was as much as ought to be expected from human virtue at fourteen.

As nothing was really left for the decision of Mrs. Price, or the good offices of Rebecca, every thing was rationally and duly accomplished, and the girls were ready for the morrow. The advantage of much sleep to prepare them for their journey, was impossible. The cousin who was travelling towards them, could hardly have less than visited their agi-

---

4. A liqueur taken medicinally to revive one's spirits.

tated spirits, one all happiness, the other all varying and indescribable perturbation.

By eight in the morning, Edmund was in the house. The girls heard his entrance from above, and Fanny went down. The idea of immediately seeing him, with the knowledge of what he must be suffering, brought back all her own first feelings. He so near her, and in misery. She was ready to sink, as she entered the parlour. He was alone, and met her instantly; and she found herself pressed to his heart with only these words, just articulate, "My Fanny—my only sister—my only comfort now." She could say nothing; nor for some minutes could he say more.

He turned away to recover himself, and when he spoke again, though his voice still faltered, his manner showed the wish of self-command, and the resolution of avoiding any farther allusion. "Have you breakfasted?—When shall you be ready?—Does Susan go?"—were questions following each other rapidly. His great object was to be off as soon as possible. When Mansfield was considered, time was precious; and the state of his own mind made him find relief only in motion. It was settled that he should order the carriage to the door in half an hour; Fanny answered for their having breakfasted, and being quite ready in half an hour. He had already ate, and declined staying for their meal. He would walk round the ramparts, and join them with the carriage. He was gone again, glad to get away even from Fanny.

He looked very ill; evidently suffering under violent emotions, which he was determined to suppress. She knew it must be so, but it was terrible to her.

The carriage came; and he entered the house again at the same moment, just in time to spend a few minutes with the family, and be a witness—but that he saw nothing—of the tranquil manner in which the daughters were parted with, and just in time to prevent their sitting down to the breakfast table, which by dint of much unusual activity, was quite and completely ready as the carriage drove from the door. Fanny's last meal in her father's house was in character with her first; she was dismissed from it as hospitably as she had been welcomed.

How her heart swelled with joy and gratitude, as she passed the barriers[5] of Portsmouth, and how Susan's face wore its broadest smiles, may be easily conceived. Sitting forwards, however, and screened by her bonnet, those smiles were unseen.

The journey was likely to be a silent one. Edmund's deep sighs often reached Fanny. Had he been alone with her, his heart must have opened in spite of every resolution; but Susan's presence drove him quite into himself, and his attempts to talk on indifferent subjects could never be long supported.

5. See above, p. 255, n. 2.

Fanny watched him with never-failing solicitude, and sometimes catching his eye, revived* an affectionate smile, which comforted her; but the first day's journey passed without her hearing a word from him on the subjects that were weighing him down. The next morning produced a little more. Just before their setting out from Oxford, while Susan was stationed at a window, in eager observation of the departure of a large family from the inn, the other two were standing by the fire; and Edmund, particularly struck by the alteration in Fanny's looks, and from his ignorance of the daily evils of her father's house, attributing an undue share of the change, attributing *all* to the recent event, took her hand, and said in a low, but very expressive tone, "No wonder— you must feel it—you must suffer. How a man who had once loved, could desert you! But *your's*—your regard was new compared with —— Fanny, think of *me!*"

The first division of their journey occupied a long day, and brought them almost knocked up, to Oxford; but the second was over at a much earlier hour. They were in the environs of Mansfield long before the usual dinner-time, and as they approached the beloved place, the hearts of both sisters sank a little. Fanny began to dread the meeting with her aunts and Tom, under so dreadful a humiliation; and Susan to feel with some anxiety, that all her best manners, all her lately acquired knowledge of what was practised here, was on the point of being called into action. Visions of good and ill breeding, of old vulgarisms and new gentilities were before her; and she was meditating much upon silver forks, napkins, and finger glasses.[6] Fanny had been every where awake to the difference of the country since February; but, when they entered the Park, her perceptions and her pleasures were of the keenest sort. It was three months, full three months, since her quitting it; and the change was from winter to summer. Her eye fell every where on lawns and plantations of the freshest green; and the trees, though not fully clothed, were in that delightful state, when farther beauty is known to be at hand, and when, while much is actually given to the sight, more yet remains for the imagination. Her enjoyment, however, was for herself alone. Edmund could not share it. She looked at him, but he was leaning back, sunk in a deeper gloom than ever, and with eyes closed as if the view of cheerfulness oppressed him, and the lovely scenes of home must be shut out.

It made her melancholy again; and the knowledge of what must be enduring there, invested even the house, modern, airy, and well situated as it was, with a melancholy aspect.

By one of the suffering party within, they were expected with such impatience as she had never known before. Fanny had scarcely passed the solemn-looking servants, when Lady Bertram came from the draw-

---

6. Glasses holding water, for rinsing the fingers after dessert. Susan takes a lively interest in the material aspects of gentility at Mansfield Park.

ing room to meet her; came with no indolent step; and, falling on her neck, said, "Dear Fanny! now I shall be comfortable."

Chapter XVI.

It had been a miserable party, each of the three believing themselves most miserable. Mrs. Norris, however, as most attached to Maria, was really the greatest sufferer. Maria was her first favourite, the dearest of all; the match had been her own contriving, as she had been wont with such pride of heart to feel and say, and this conclusion of it almost overpowered her.

She was an altered creature, quieted, stupified, indifferent to every thing that passed. The being left with her sister and nephew, and all the house under her care, had been an advantage entirely thrown away; she had been unable to direct or dictate, or even fancy herself useful. When really touched by affliction, her active powers had been all benumbed; and neither Lady Bertram nor Tom had received from her the smallest support or attempt at support. She had done no more for them, than they had done for each other. They had been all solitary, helpless, and forlorn alike; and now the arrival of the others only established her superiority in wretchedness. Her companions were relieved, but there was no good for *her*. Edmund was almost as welcome to his brother, as Fanny to her aunt; but Mrs. Norris, instead of having comfort from either, was but the more irritated by the sight of the person whom, in the blindness of her anger, she could have charged as the dæmon of the piece. Had Fanny accepted Mr. Crawford, this could not have happened.

Susan, too, was a grievance. She had not spirits to notice her in more than a few repulsive looks, but she felt her as a spy, and an intruder, and an indigent niece, and every thing most odious. By her other aunt, Susan was received with quiet kindness. Lady Bertram could not give her much time, or many words, but she felt her, as Fanny's sister, to have a claim at Mansfield, and was ready to kiss and like her; and Susan was more than satisfied, for she came perfectly aware, that nothing but ill humour was to be expected from Aunt Norris; and was so provided with happiness, so strong in that best of blessings, an escape from many certain evils, that she could have stood against a great deal more indifference than she met with from the others.

She was now left a good deal to herself, to get acquainted with the house and grounds as she could, and spent her days very happily in so doing, while those who might otherwise have attended to her, were shut up, or wholly occupied each with the person quite dependant on them, at this time, for every thing like comfort; Edmund trying to bury his own feelings in exertions for the relief of his brother's, and Fanny devoted to her aunt Bertram, returning to every former office, with more than former zeal, and thinking she could never do enough for one who seemed so much to want her.

To talk over the dreadful business with Fanny, talk and lament, was all Lady Bertram's consolation. To be listened to and borne with, and hear the voice of kindness and sympathy in return, was every thing that could be done for her. To be otherwise comforted was out of the question. The case admitted of no comfort. Lady Bertram did not think deeply, but, guided by Sir Thomas, she thought justly on all important points; and she saw, therefore, in all its enormity, what had happened, and neither endeavoured herself, nor required Fanny to advise her, to think little of guilt and infamy.

Her affections were not acute, nor was her mind tenacious. After a time, Fanny found it not impossible to direct her thoughts to other subjects, and revive some interest in the usual occupations; but whenever Lady Bertram *was* fixed on the event, she could see it only in one light, as comprehending the loss of a daughter, and a disgrace never to be wiped off.

Fanny learnt from her, all the particulars which had yet transpired. Her aunt was no very methodical narrator; but with the help of some letters to and from Sir Thomas, and what she already knew herself, and could reasonably combine, she was soon able to understand quite as much as she wished of the circumstances attending the story.

Mrs. Rushworth had gone, for the Easter holidays, to Twickenham, with a family whom she had just grown intimate with—a family of lively, agreeable manners, and probably of morals and discretion to suit—for to *their* house Mr. Crawford had constant access at all times. His having been in the same neighbourhood, Fanny already knew. Mr. Rushworth had been gone, at this time, to Bath, to pass a few days with his mother, and bring her back to town, and Maria was with these friends without any restraint, without even Julia; for Julia had removed from Wimpole Street two or three weeks before, on a visit to some relations of Sir Thomas; a removal which her father and mother were now disposed to attribute to some view of convenience on Mr. Yates's account. Very soon after the Rushworths'* return to Wimpole Street, Sir Thomas had received a letter from an old and most particular friend in London, who hearing and witnessing a good deal to alarm him in that quarter, wrote to recommend Sir Thomas's coming to London himself, and using his influence with his daughter, to put an end to an intimacy which was already exposing her to unpleasant remarks, and evidently making Mr. Rushworth uneasy.

Sir Thomas was preparing to act upon this letter, without communicating its contents to any creature at Mansfield, when it was followed by another, sent express from the same friend, to break to him the almost desperate situation in which affairs then stood with the young people. Mrs. Rushworth had left her husband's house; Mr. Rushworth had been in great anger and distress to *him* (Mr. Harding), for his advice; Mr. Harding feared there had been *at least*, very flagrant indiscretion. The maid-servant of Mrs. Rushworth, senior, threatened alarmingly. He was doing all in his power to quiet every thing, with the hope of Mrs. Rushworth's return, but was so much counteracted in Wimpole Street by the influence of Mr. Rushworth's mother, that the worst consequences might be apprehended.

This dreadful communication could not be kept from the rest of the family. Sir Thomas set off; Edmund would go with him; and the others had been left in a state of wretchedness, inferior only to what followed the receipt of the next letters from London. Every thing was by that time public beyond a hope. The servant of Mrs. Rushworth, the mother, had exposure in her power, and, supported by her mistress, was not to be silenced. The two ladies, even in the short time they had been together, had disagreed; and the bitterness of the elder against her daughter-in-law might,* perhaps, arise almost as much from the personal disrespect with which she had herself been treated, as from sensibility for her son.

However that might be, she was unmanageable. But had she been less obstinate, or of less weight with her son, who was always guided by the last speaker, by the person who could get hold of and shut him up, the case would still have been hopeless, for Mrs. Rushworth did not appear again, and there was every reason to conclude her to be concealed somewhere with Mr. Crawford, who had quitted his uncle's house, as for a journey, on the very day of her absenting herself.

Sir Thomas, however, remained yet a little longer in town, in the hope of discovering, and snatching her from farther vice, though all was lost on the side of character.

His present state, Fanny could hardly bear to think of. There was but one of his children who was not at this time a source of misery to him. Tom's complaints had been greatly heightened by the shock of his sister's conduct, and his recovery so much thrown back by it, that even Lady Bertram had been struck by the difference, and all her alarms were regularly sent off to her husband; and Julia's elopement, the additional blow which had met him on his arrival in London, though its force had been deadened at the moment, must, she knew, be sorely felt. She saw that it was. His letters expressed how much he deplored it. Under any circumstances it would have been an unwelcome alliance, but to have it so clandestinely formed, and such a period chosen for its completion, placed Julia's feelings in a most unfavourable light, and severely aggravated the folly of her choice. He called it a bad thing, done in the worst manner, and at the worst time; and though Julia was yet as more pardonable than Maria as folly than vice, he could not but regard the step she had taken, as opening the worst probabilities of a conclusion hereafter, like her sister's. Such was his opinion of the set into which she had thrown herself.

Fanny felt for him most acutely. He could have no comfort but in Edmund. Every other child must be racking his heart. His displeasure against herself she trusted, reasoning differently from Mrs. Norris, would now be done away. *She* should be justified. Mr. Crawford would have fully acquitted her conduct in refusing him, but this, though most material to herself, would be poor consolation to Sir Thomas. Her uncle's displeasure was terrible to her; but what could her justification, or her gratitude and attachment do for him? His stay must be on Edmund alone.

She was mistaken, however, in supposing that Edmund gave his father no present pain. It was of a much less poignant nature than what the others excited; but Sir Thomas was considering his happiness as very deeply involved in the offence of his sister and friend, cut off by it as he must be from the woman, whom he had been pursuing with undoubted attachment, and strong probability of success; and who in every thing but this despicable brother, would have been so eligible a connection. He was aware of what Edmund must be suffering on his own behalf in addition to all the rest, when they were in town; he had seen or conjectured his feelings, and having reason to think that *one* interview with Miss Crawford had taken place, from which Edmund derived only increased distress, had been as anxious on that account as on others, to get him out of town, and had engaged him in taking Fanny home to her aunt, with a view to his relief and benefit, no less than theirs. Fanny was not in the secret of her uncle's feelings, Sir Thomas not in the secret of Miss Crawford's character. Had he been privy to her conversation with his son, he would not have wished her to belong to him, though her twenty thousand pounds had been forty.

That Edmund must be for ever divided from Miss Crawford, did not admit of a doubt with Fanny; and yet, till she knew that he felt the same, her own conviction was insufficient. She thought he did, but she wanted to be assured of it. If he would now speak to her with the unreserve which had sometimes been too much for her before, it would be most consoling; but *that* she found was not to be. She seldom saw him—never alone—he probably avoided being alone with her. What was to be inferred? That his judgment submitted to all his own peculiar and bitter share of this family affliction, but that it was too keenly felt to be a subject of the slightest communication. This must be his state. He yielded, but it was with agonies, which did not admit of speech. Long, long would it be ere Miss Crawford's name passed his lips again, or she could hope for a renewal of such confidential intercourse as had been.

It *was** long. They reached Mansfield on Thursday, and it was not till Sunday evening that Edmund began to talk to her on the subject.

Sitting with her on Sunday evening—a wet Sunday evening—the very time of all others when if a friend is at hand the heart must be opened, and every thing told—no one else in the room, except his mother, who, after hearing an affecting sermon, had cried herself to sleep—it was impossible not to speak; and so, with the usual beginnings, hardly to be traced as to what came first, and the usual declaration that if she would listen to him for a few minutes, he should be very brief, and certainly never tax her kindness in the same way again—she need not fear a repetition—it would be a subject prohibited entirely—he entered upon the luxury of relating circumstances and sensations of the first interest to himself, to one of whose affectionate sympathy he was quite convinced.

How Fanny listened, with what curiosity and concern, what pain and what delight, how the agitation of his voice was watched, and how carefully her own eyes were fixed on any object but himself, may be imagined. The opening was alarming. He had seen Miss Crawford. He had been invited to see her. He had received a note from Lady Storn-away to beg him to call; and regarding it as what was meant to be the last, last interview of friendship, and investing her with all the feelings of shame and wretchedness which Crawford's sister ought to have known, he had gone to her in such a state of mind, so softened, so devoted, as made it for a few moments impossible to Fanny's fears, that it should be the last. But as he proceeded in his story, these fears were over. She had met him, he said, with a serious—certainly a serious—even an agitated air; but before he had been able to speak one intelli-gible sentence, she had introduced the subject in a manner which he owned had shocked him. "I heard you were in town," said she—"I wanted to see you. Let us talk over this sad business. What can equal the folly of our two relations?"—"I could not answer, but I believe my looks spoke. She felt reproved. Sometimes how quick to feel! With a graver look and voice she then added—'I do not mean to defend Henry at your sister's expence.' So she began—but how she went on, Fanny, is not fit—is hardly fit to be repeated to you. I cannot recall all her words. I would not dwell upon them if I could. Their substance was great anger at the *folly* of each. She reprobated her brother's folly in being drawn on by a woman whom he had never cared for, to do what must lose him the woman he adored; but still more the folly of—poor Maria, in sacrificing such a situation, plunging into such difficulties, under the idea of being really loved by a man who had long ago made his indifference clear. Guess what I must have felt. To hear the woman whom—no harsher name than folly given!—So voluntarily, so freely, so coolly to canvass it!—No reluctance, no horror, no feminine—shall I say? no modest loathings!—This is what the world does. For where, Fanny, shall we find a woman whom nature had so richly endowed? —Spoilt, spoilt!—"

After a little reflection, he went on with a sort of desperate calmness—"I will tell you every thing, and then have done for ever. She saw it only as folly, and that folly stamped only by exposure. The want of common discretion, of caution—his going down to Richmond for the whole time of her being at Twickenham—her putting herself in the power of a servant;—it was the detection in short—Oh! Fanny, it was the detection, not the offence which she reprobated. It was the imprudence which had brought things to extremity, and obliged her brother to give up every dearer plan, in order to fly with her."

He stopt.—"And what," said Fanny, (believing herself required to speak), "what could you say?"

"Nothing, nothing to be understood. I was like a man stunned. She went on, began to talk of you;—yes, then she began to talk of you, regretting, as well she might, the loss of such a ——. There she spoke very rationally. But she has always done justice to you. 'He has thrown away,' said she, 'such a woman as he will never see again. She would have fixed him, she would have made him happy for ever.'—My dearest Fanny, I am giving you I hope more pleasure than pain by this retrospect of what might have been—but what never can be now. You do not wish me to be silent?—if you do, give me but a look, a word, and I have done."

No look or word was given.

"Thank God!" said he. "We were all disposed to wonder—but it seems to have been the merciful appointment[1] of Providence that the heart which knew no guile, should not suffer. She spoke of you with high praise and warm affection; yet, even here, there was alloy, a dash of evil—for in the midst of it she could exclaim 'Why,* would not she have him? It is all her fault. Simple girl!—I shall never forgive her. Had she accepted him as she ought, they might now have been on the point of marriage, and Henry would have been too happy and too busy to want any other object. He would have taken no pains to be on terms with Mrs. Rushworth again. It would have all ended in a regular standing flirtation, in yearly meetings at Sotherton and Everingham.' Could you have believed it possible?—But the charm is broken. My eyes are opened."

"Cruel!" said Fanny—"quite cruel! At such a moment to give way to gaiety and to speak with lightness, and to you!—Absolute cruelty."

"Cruelty, do you call it?—We differ there. No, her's is not a cruel nature. I do not consider her as meaning to wound my feelings. The evil lies yet deeper; in her total ignorance, unsuspiciousness of there being such feelings, in a perversion of mind which made it natural to her to treat the subject as she did. She was speaking only, as she had been used to hear others speak, as she imagined every body else would

1. Dispensation.

speak. Her's are not faults of temper. She would not voluntarily give unnecessary pain to any one, and though I may deceive myself, I cannot but think that for me, for my feelings, she would—Her's are faults of principle, Fanny, of blunted delicacy and a corrupted, vitiated mind. Perhaps it is best for me—since it leaves me so little to regret.—Not so, however. Gladly would I submit to all the increased pain of losing her, rather than have to think of her as I do. I told her so."

"Did you?"

"Yes, when I left her I told her so."

"How long were you together?"

"Five and twenty minutes. Well, she went on to say, that what remained now to be done, was to bring about a marriage between them. She spoke of it, Fanny, with a steadier voice than I can." He was obliged to pause more than once as he continued. "We must persuade Henry to marry her," said she, "and what with honour, and the certainty of having shut himself out for ever from Fanny, I do not despair of it. Fanny he must give up. I do not think that even *he* could now hope to succeed with one of her stamp, and therefore I hope we may find no insuperable difficulty. My influence, which is not small, shall all go that way; and, when once married, and properly supported by her own family, people of respectability as they are, she may recover her footing in society to a certain degree. In some circles, we know, she would never be admitted, but with good dinners, and large parties, there will always be those who will be glad of her acquaintance; and there is, undoubtedly, more liberality and candour on those points than formerly. What I advise is, that your father be quiet. Do not let him injure his own cause by interference. Persuade him to let things take their course. If by any officious exertions of his, she is induced to leave Henry's protection, there will be much less chance of his marrying her, than if she remain with him. I know how he is likely to be influenced. Let Sir Thomas trust to his honour and compassion, and it may all end well; but if he get his daughter away, it will be destroying the chief hold."

After repeating this, Edmund was so much affected, that Fanny, watching him with silent, but most tender concern, was almost sorry that the subject had been entered on at all. It was long before he could speak again. At last, "Now Fanny," said he, "I shall soon have done. I have told you the substance of all that she said. As soon as I could speak, I replied that I had not supposed it possible, coming in such a state of mind into that house, as I had done, that any thing could occur to make me suffer more, but that she had been inflicting deeper wounds in almost every sentence. That, though I had, in the course of our acquaintance, been often sensible of some difference in our opinions, on points too*, of some moment, it had not entered my imagination to conceive the difference could be such as she had now proved it.

That the manner in which she treated the dreadful crime committed by her brother and my sister—(with whom lay the greater seduction I pretended not to say)—but the manner in which she spoke of the crime itself, giving it every reproach but the right, considering its ill consequences only as they were to be braved or overborne by a defiance of decency and impudence in wrong; and, last of all, and above* all, recommending to us a compliance, a compromise, an acquiescence, in the continuance of the sin, on the chance of a marriage which, thinking as I now thought of her brother, should rather be prevented than sought—all this together most grievously convinced me that I had never understood her before, and that, as far as related to mind, it had been the creature of my own imagination, not Miss Crawford, that I had been too apt to dwell on for many months past. That, perhaps it was best for me; I had less to regret in sacrificing a friendship—feelings—hopes which must, at any rate, have been torn from me now. And yet, that I must and would confess, that, could I have restored her to what she had appeared to me before, I would infinitely prefer any increase of the pain of parting, for the sake of carrying with me the right of tenderness and esteem. This is what I said—the purport of it—but, as you may imagine, not spoken so collectedly or methodically as I have repeated it to you. She was astonished, exceedingly astonished—more than astonished. I saw her change countenance. She turned extremely red. I imagined I saw a mixture of many feelings—a great, though short struggle—half a wish of yielding to truths, half a sense of shame—but habit, habit carried it. She would have laughed if she could. It was a sort of laugh, as she answered, 'A pretty good lecture upon my word. Was it part of your last sermon? At this rate, you will soon reform every body at Mansfield and Thornton Lacey; and when I hear of you next, it may be as a celebrated preacher in some great society of Methodists,[2] or as a missionary into foreign parts.' She tried to speak carelessly; but she was not so careless as she wanted to appear. I only said in reply, that from my heart I wished her well, and earnestly hoped that she might soon learn to think more justly, and not owe the most valuable knowledge we could any of us acquire—the knowledge of ourselves and of our duty to the lessons of affliction—and immediately left the room. I had gone a few steps, Fanny, when I heard the door open behind me. 'Mr. Bertram,' said she. I looked back. 'Mr. Bertram,' said she, with a smile—but it was a smile ill-suited to the conversation that had passed, a saucy playful smile, seeming to invite, in order to subdue me; at least, it appeared so to me. I resisted; it was the impulse of the moment to resist, and still walked on. I have since

2. Founded by John Wesley in the mid-1700s as a revivalist movement within the Anglican church, the Society of Methodists was (in)famous for preaching, discipline, and missionary work, and for censuring the laxity and worldliness of the Church of England, from which it seceded in 1795.

—sometimes—for a moment—regretted that I did not go back; but I know I was right; and such has been the end of our acquaintance! And what an acquaintance has it been! How have I been deceived! Equally in brother and sister deceived! I thank you for your patience, Fanny. This has been the greatest relief, and now we will have done."

And such was Fanny's dependance on his words, that for five minutes she thought they *had* done. Then, however, it all came on again, or something very like it, and nothing less than Lady Bertram's rousing thoroughly up, could really close such a conversation. Till that happened, they continued to talk of Miss Crawford alone, and how she had attached him, and how delightful nature had made her, and how excellent she would have been, had she fallen into good hands earlier. Fanny, now at liberty to speak openly, felt more than justified in adding to his knowledge of her real character, by some hint of what share his brother's state of health might be supposed to have in her wish for a complete reconciliation. This was not an agreeable intimation. Nature resisted it for a while. It would have been a vast deal pleasanter to have had her more disinterested in her attachment; but his vanity was not of a strength to fight long against reason. He submitted to believe, that Tom's illness had influenced her; only reserving for himself this consoling thought, that considering the many counteractions of opposing habits, she had certainly been *more** attached to him than could have been expected, and for his sake been more near doing right. Fanny thought exactly the same; and they were also quite agreed in their opinion of the lasting effect, the indelible impression, which such a disappointment must make on his mind. Time would undoubtedly abate somewhat of his sufferings, but still it was a sort of thing which he never could get entirely the better of; and as to his ever meeting with any other woman who could—it was too impossible to be named but with indignation. Fanny's friendship was all that he had to cling to.

Chapter XVII.

Let other pens dwell on guilt and misery. I quit such odious subjects as soon as I can, impatient to restore every body, not greatly in fault themselves, to tolerable comfort, and to have done with all the rest.

My Fanny indeed at this very time, I have the satisfaction of knowing, must have been happy in spite of every thing. She must have been a happy creature in spite of all that she felt or thought she felt, for the distress of those around her. She had sources of delight that must force their way. She was returned to Mansfield Park, she was useful, she was beloved; she was safe from Mr. Crawford, and when Sir Thomas came back she had every proof that could be given in his then melancholy state of spirits, of his perfect approbation and increased regard; and happy as all this must make her, she would still have been happy without any of it, for Edmund was no longer the dupe of Miss Crawford.

It is true, that Edmund was very far from happy himself. He was suffering from disappointment and regret, grieving over what was, and wishing for what could never be. She knew it was so, and was sorry; but it was with a sorrow so founded on satisfaction, so tending to ease, and so much in harmony with every dearest sensation, that there are few who might not have been glad to exchange their greatest gaiety for it.

Sir Thomas, poor Sir Thomas, a parent, and conscious of errors in his own conduct as a parent, was the longest to suffer. He felt that he ought not to have allowed the marriage, that his daughter's sentiments had been sufficiently known to him to render him culpable in authorising it, that in so doing he had sacrificed the right to the expedient, and been governed by motives of selfishness and worldly wisdom. These were reflections that required some time to soften; but time will do almost every thing, and though little comfort arose on Mrs. Rushworth's side for the misery she had occasioned, comfort was to be found greater than he had supposed, in his other children. Julia's match became a less desperate business than he had considered it at first. She was humble and wishing to be forgiven, and Mr. Yates, desirous of being really received into the family, was disposed to look up to him and* be guided. He was not very solid; but there was a hope of his becoming less trifling—of his being at least tolerably domestic and quiet; and, at any rate, there was comfort in finding his estate rather more, and his debts much less, than he had feared, and in being consulted and treated as the friend best worth attending to. There was comfort also in Tom, who gradually regained his health, without regaining the thoughtlessness and selfishness of his previous habits. He was the better for ever for his illness. He had suffered, and he had learnt to think, two advantages that he had never known before; and the self-reproach arising from the deplorable event in Wimpole Street, to which he felt himself accessary by all the dangerous intimacy of his unjustifiable theatre, made an impression on his mind which, at the age of six-and-twenty, with no want of sense, or good companions, was durable in its happy effects. He became what he ought to be, useful to his father, steady and quiet, and not living merely for himself.

Here was comfort indeed! and quite as soon as Sir Thomas could place dependence on such sources of good, Edmund was contributing to his father's ease by improvement in the only point in which *he* had given him pain before—improvement in his spirits. After wandering about and sitting under trees with Fanny all the summer evenings, he had so well talked his mind into submission, as to be very tolerably cheerful again.

These were the circumstances and the hopes which gradually brought their alleviation to Sir Thomas, deadening his sense of what was lost, and in part reconciling him to himself; though the anguish arising from the conviction of his own errors in the education of his daughters, was never to be entirely done away.

Too late he became aware how unfavourable to the character of any young people, must be the totally opposite treatment which Maria and Julia had been always experiencing at home, where the excessive indulgence and flattery of their aunt had been continually contrasted with his own severity. He saw how ill he had judged, in expecting to counteract what was wrong in Mrs. Norris, by its reverse in himself, clearly saw that he had but increased the evil, by teaching them to repress their spirits in his presence, as to make their real disposition unknown to him, and sending them for all their indulgences to a person who had been able to attach them only by the blindness of her affection, and the excess of her praise.

Here had been grievous mismanagement; but, bad as it was, he gradually grew to feel that it had not been the most direful mistake in his plan of education. Something must have been wanting *within*, or time would have worn away much of its ill effect. He feared that principle, active principle, had been wanting, that they had never been properly taught to govern their inclinations and tempers, by that sense of duty which can alone suffice. They had been instructed theoretically in their religion, but never required to bring it into daily practice. To be distinguished for elegance and accomplishments—the authorised object of their youth—could have had no useful influence that way, no moral effect on the mind. He had meant them to be good, but his cares had been directed to the understanding and manners, not the disposition; and of the necessity of self-denial and humility, he feared they had never heard from any lips that could profit them.

Bitterly did he deplore a deficiency which now he could scarcely comprehend to have been possible. Wretchedly did he feel, that with all the cost and care of an anxious and expensive education, he had brought up his daughters, without their understanding their first duties, or his being acquainted with their character and temper.

The high spirit and strong passions of Mrs. Rushworth especially, were made known to him only in their sad result. She was not to be prevailed on to leave Mr. Crawford. She hoped to marry him, and they continued together till she was obliged to be convinced that such hope was vain, and till the disappointment and wretchedness arising from the conviction, rendered her temper so bad, and her feelings for him so like hatred, as to make them for a while each other's punishment, and then induce a voluntary separation.

She had lived with him to be reproached as the ruin of all his happiness in Fanny, and carried away no better consolation in leaving him, than that she *had* divided them. What can exceed the misery of such a mind in such a situation.

Mr. Rushworth had no difficulty in procuring a divorce[1] and so ended a marriage contracted under such circumstances as to make any better end, the effect of good luck, not to be reckoned on. She had despised him, and loved another—and he had been very much aware that it was so. The indignities of stupidity, and the disappointments of selfish passion, can excite little pity. His punishment followed his conduct, as did a deeper punishment, the deeper guilt of his wife. *He* was released from the engagement to be mortified and unhappy, till some other pretty girl could attract him into matrimony again, and he might set forward on a second, and it is to be hoped, more prosperous trial of the state—if duped, to be duped at least with good humour and good luck; while *she* must withdraw with infinitely stronger feelings to a retirement and reproach, which could allow no second spring of hope or character.

Where she could be placed, became a subject of most melancholy and momentous consultation. Mrs. Norris, whose attachment seemed to augment with the demerits of her niece, would have had her received at home, and countenanced by them all. Sir Thomas would not hear of it, and Mrs. Norris's anger against Fanny was so much the greater, from considering *her* residence there as the motive. She persisted in placing his scruples to *her* account, though Sir Thomas very solemnly assured her, that had there been no young woman in question, had there been no young person of either sex belonging to him, to be endangered by the society, or hurt by the character of Mrs. Rushworth, he would never have offered so great an insult to the neighbourhood, as to expect it to notice her. As a daughter—he hoped a penitent one —she should be protected by him, and secured in every comfort, and supported by every encouragement to do right, which their relative situations admitted; but farther than *that*, he would not go. Maria had destroyed her own character, and he would not by a vain attempt to restore what never could be restored, be affording his sanction to vice, or in seeking to lessen its disgrace, be anywise accessary to introducing such misery in another man's family, as he had known himself.

It ended in Mrs. Norris's resolving to quit Mansfield, and devote herself to her unfortunate Maria, and in an establishment being formed for them in another country—remote and private, where, shut up together with little society, on one side no affection, on the other, no judgment, it may be reasonably supposed that their tempers became their mutual punishment.

Mrs. Norris's removal from Mansfield was the great supplementary comfort of Sir Thomas's life. His opinion of her had been sinking from

---

1. A wife's (but not a husband's) adultery was grounds for divorce, but divorces were costly and rare, requiring a private act of Parliament.

the day of his return from Antigua; in every transaction together from that period, in their daily intercourse, in business, or in chat, she had been regularly losing ground in his esteem, and convincing him that either time had done her much disservice, or that he had considerably over-rated her sense, and wonderfully borne with her manners before. He had felt her as an hourly evil, which was so much the worse, as there seemed no chance of its ceasing but with life; she seemed a part of himself, that must be borne for ever. To be relieved from her, therefore, was so great a felicity, that had she not left bitter remembrances behind her, there might have been danger of his learning almost to approve the evil which produced such a good.

She was regretted by no one at Mansfield. She had never been able to attach even those she loved best, and since Mrs. Rushworth's elopement, her temper had been in a state of such irritation, as to make her every where tormenting. Not even Fanny had tears for aunt Norris—not even when she was gone for ever.

That Julia escaped better than Maria was owing, in some measure, to a favourable difference of disposition and circumstance, but in a greater to her having been less the darling of that very aunt, less flattered, and less spoilt. Her beauty and acquirements had held but a second place. She had been always used to think herself a little inferior to Maria. Her temper was naturally the easiest of the two; her feelings, though quick, were more controulable; and education had not given her so very hurtful a degree of self-consequence.

She had submitted the best to the disappointment in Henry Crawford. After the first bitterness of the conviction of being slighted was over, she had been tolerably soon in a fair way of not thinking of him again; and when the acquaintance was renewed in town, and Mr. Rushworth's house became Crawford's object, she had had the merit of withdrawing herself from it, and of chusing that time to pay a visit to her other friends, in order to secure herself from being again too much attracted. This had been her motive in going to her cousins. Mr. Yates's convenience had had nothing to do with it. She had been allowing his attentions some time, but with very little idea of ever accepting him; and, had not her sister's conduct burst forth as it did, and her increased dread of her father and of home, on that event—imagining its certain consequence to herself would be greater severity and restraint—made her hastily resolve on avoiding such immediate horrors at all risks, it is probable that Mr. Yates would never have succeeded. She had not eloped with any worse feelings than those of selfish alarm. It had appeared to her the only thing to be done. Maria's guilt had induced Julia's folly.

Henry Crawford, ruined by early independence and bad domestic example, indulged in the freaks of a cold-blooded vanity a little too long. Once it had, by an opening undesigned and unmerited, led him into the way of happiness. Could he have been satisfied with the conquest of one amiable woman's affections, could he have found sufficient exultation in overcoming the reluctance, in working himself into the esteem and tenderness of Fanny Price, there would have been every probability of success and felicity for him. His affection had already done something. Her influence over him had already given him some influence over her. Would he have deserved more, there can be no doubt that more would have been obtained; especially when that marriage had taken place, which would have given him the assistance of her conscience in subduing her first inclination, and brought them very often together. Would he have persevered, and uprightly, Fanny must have been his reward—and a reward very voluntarily bestowed—within a reasonable period from Edmund's marrying Mary.

Had he done as he intended, and as he knew he ought, by going down to Everingham after his return from Portsmouth, he might have been deciding his own happy destiny. But he was pressed to stay for Mrs. Fraser's party; his staying was made of flattering consequence, and he was to meet Mrs. Rushworth there. Curiosity and vanity were both engaged, and the temptation of immediate pleasure was too strong for a mind unused to make any sacrifice to right; he resolved to defer his Norfolk journey, resolved that writing should answer the purpose of it, or that its purpose was unimportant—and staid. He saw Mrs. Rushworth, was received by her with a coldness which ought to have been repulsive, and have established apparent indifference between them for ever; but he was mortified, he could not bear to be thrown off by the woman whose smiles had been so wholly at his command; he must exert himself to subdue so proud a display of resentment; it was anger on Fanny's account; he must get the better of it, and make Mrs. Rushworth Maria Bertram again in her treatment of himself.

In this spirit he began the attack; and by animated perseverance had soon re-established the sort of familiar intercourse—of gallantry—of flirtation which bounded his views, but in triumphing over the discretion, which, though beginning in anger, might have saved them both, he had put himself in the power of feelings on her side, more strong than he had supposed.—She loved him; there was no withdrawing attentions, avowedly dear to her. He was entangled by his own vanity, with as little excuse of love as possible, and without the smallest inconstancy of mind towards her cousin.—To keep Fanny and the Bertrams from a knowledge of what was passing became his first object. Secrecy could not have been more desirable for Mrs. Rushworth's credit than he felt it for his own.—When he returned from Richmond, he would have been glad to see Mrs. Rushworth no more.—All that followed was the result of her imprudence; and he went off with her at last, because he could not help it, regretting Fanny, even at the moment, but regretting her infinitely more, when all the bustle of the intrigue was over, and a very few months had taught him, by the force of contrast, to place a yet higher value on the sweetness of her temper, the purity of her mind, and* the excellence of her principles.

That punishment, the public punishment of disgrace, should in a just measure attend *his* share of the offence, is, we know, not one of the barriers, which society gives to virtue. In this world, the penalty is less equal than could be wished; but without presuming to look forward to a juster appointment hereafter, we may fairly consider a man of sense like Henry Crawford, to be providing for himself no small portion of vexation and regret—vexation that must rise sometimes to self-reproach, and regret to wretchedness—in having so requited hospitality, so injured family peace, so forfeited his best, most estimable and endeared acquaintance, and so lost the woman whom he had rationally, as well as passionately loved.

After what had passed to wound and alienate the two families, the continuance of the Bertrams and Grants in such close neighbourhood would have been most distressing; but the absence of the latter, for some months purposely lengthened, ended very fortunately in the necessity, or at least the practicability of a permanent removal. Dr. Grant, through an interest on which he had almost ceased to form hopes, succeeded to a stall² in Westminster, which, as affording an occasion for leaving Mansfield, an excuse for residence in London, and an increase of income to answer the expenses of the change, was highly acceptable to those who went, and those who staid.

Mrs. Grant, with a temper to love and be loved, must have gone with some regret, from the scenes and people she had been used to; but the same happiness of disposition must in any place and any society, secure her a great deal to enjoy, and she had again a home to offer Mary; and Mary had had enough of her own friends, enough of vanity, ambition, love, and disappointment in the course of the last half year, to be in need of the true kindness of her sister's heart, and the rational tranquillity of her ways.—They lived together; and when Dr. Grant had brought on apoplexy and death, by three great institutionary dinners in one week, they still lived together; for Mary, though perfectly resolved against ever attaching herself to a younger brother again, was long in finding among the dashing representatives, or idle heir apparents, who were at the command of her beauty, and her 20,000*l.* any one who could satisfy the better taste she had acquired at Mansfield, whose character and manners could authorise a hope of the domestic happiness she had there learnt to estimate, or put Edmund Bertram sufficiently out of her head.

Edmund had greatly the advantage of her in this respect. He had not to wait and wish with vacant affections for an object worthy to

2. A pew or enclosed seat in the choir of a church for use by the clergy; i.e., Dr. Grant has received a prestigious living at Westminster Abbey.

succeed her in them. Scarcely had he done regretting Mary Crawford, and observing to Fanny how impossible it was that he should ever meet with such another woman, before it began to strike him whether a very different kind of woman might not do just as well—or a great deal better; whether Fanny herself were not growing as dear, as important to him in all her smiles, and all her ways, as Mary Crawford had ever been; and whether it might not be a possible, an hopeful undertaking to persuade her that her warm and sisterly regard for him would be foundation enough for wedded love.

I purposely abstain from dates on this occasion, that every one may be at liberty to fix their own, aware that the cure of unconquerable passions, and the transfer of unchanging attachments, must vary much as to time in different people.—I only intreat every body to believe that exactly at the time when it was quite natural that it should be so, and not a week earlier, Edmund did cease to care about Miss Crawford, and became as anxious to marry Fanny, as Fanny herself could desire.

With such a regard for her, indeed, as his had long been, a regard founded on the most endearing claims of innocence and helplessness, and completed by every recommendation of growing worth, what could be more natural than the change? Loving, guiding, protecting her, as he had been doing ever since her being ten years old, her mind in so great a degree formed by his care, and her comfort depending on his kindness, an object to him of such close and peculiar interest, dearer by all his own importance with her than any one else at Mansfield, what was there now to add, but that he should learn to prefer soft light eyes to sparkling dark ones.—And being always with her, and always talking confidentially, and his feelings exactly in that favourable state which a recent disappointment gives, those soft light eyes could not be very long in obtaining the pre-eminence.

Having once set out, and felt that he had done so, on this road to happiness, there was nothing on the side of prudence to stop him or make his progress slow; no doubts of her deserving, no fears from opposition of taste, no need of drawing new hopes of happiness from dissimilarity of temper. Her mind, disposition, opinions, and habits wanted no half concealment, no self deception on the present, no reliance on* future improvement. Even in the midst of his late infatuation, he had acknowledged Fanny's mental superiority. What must be his sense of it now, therefore? She was of course only too good for him; but as nobody minds having what is too good for them, he was very steadily earnest in the pursuit of the blessing, and it was not possible that encouragement from her should be long wanting. Timid, anxious, doubting as she was, it was still impossible that such tenderness as hers should not, at times, hold out the strongest hope of success, though it remained for a later period to tell him the whole delightful and astonishing truth. His happiness in knowing himself to have been so long the beloved of such a heart, must have been great enough to warrant any strength of language in which he could clothe it to her or to himself; it must have been a delightful happiness! But there was happiness elsewhere which no description can reach. Let no one presume to give the feelings of a young woman on receiving the assurance of that affection of which she has scarcely allowed herself to entertain a hope.

Their own inclinations ascertained, there were no difficulties behind, no drawback of poverty or parent. It was a match which Sir Thomas's wishes had even forestalled. Sick of ambitious and mercenary connections, prizing more and more the sterling good of principle and temper, and chiefly anxious to bind by the strongest securities all that remained to him of domestic felicity, he had pondered with genuine satisfaction on the more than possibility of the two young friends finding their mutual consolation in each other for all that had occurred of disappointment to either; and the joyful consent which met Edmund's application, the high sense of having realised a great acquisition in the promise of Fanny for a daughter, formed just such a contrast with his early opinion on the subject when the poor little girl's coming had been first agitated, as time is for ever producing between the plans and decisions of mortals, for their own instruction, and their neighbours'* entertainment.

Fanny was indeed the daughter that he wanted. His charitable kindness had been rearing a prime comfort for himself. His liberality had a rich repayment, and the general goodness of his intentions by her, deserved it. He might have made her childhood happier; but it had been an error of judgment only which had given him the appearance of harshness, and deprived him of her early love; and now, on really knowing each other, their mutual attachment became very strong. After settling her at Thornton Lacey with every kind attention to her comfort, the object of almost every day was to see her there, or to get her away from it.

Selfishly dear as she had long been to Lady Bertram, she could not be parted with willingly by *her.* No happiness of son or niece could make her wish the marriage. But it was possible to part with her, because Susan remained to supply her place.—Susan became the stationary niece—delighted to be so!—and equally well adapted for it by a readiness of mind, and an inclination for usefulness, as Fanny had been by sweetness of temper, and strong feelings of gratitude. Susan could never be spared. First as a comfort to Fanny, then as an auxiliary, and last as her substitute, she was established at Mansfield, with every appearance of equal permanency. Her more fearless disposition and happier nerves made every thing easy to her there.—With quickness in understanding the tempers of those she had to deal with, and no natural timidity to restrain any consequent wishes, she was soon welcome, and useful to all; and after Fanny's removal, succeeded so naturally to her influence over the hourly comfort of her aunt, as gradually to become, perhaps, the most beloved of the two.—In *her** usefulness, in Fanny's excellence, in William's continued good conduct, and rising fame, and in the general well-doing and success of the other members of the family, all assisting to advance each other, and doing credit to his countenance and aid, Sir Thomas saw repeated, and for ever repeated reason to rejoice in what he had done for them all, and acknowledge the advantages of early hardship and discipline, and the consciousness of being born to struggle and endure.

With so much true merit and true love, and no want of fortune or friends, the happiness of the married cousins must appear as secure as earthly happiness can be.—Equally formed for domestic life, and attached to country pleasures, their home was the home of affection and comfort; and to complete the picture of good, the acquisition of Mansfield living by the death of Dr. Grant, occurred just after they had been married long enough to begin to want an increase of income, and feel their distance from the paternal abode an inconvenience.

On that event they removed to Mansfield, and the parsonage there, which under each of its two former owners, Fanny had never been able to approach but with some painful sensation of restraint or alarm, soon grew as dear to her heart, and as thoroughly perfect in her eyes, as every thing else, within the view and patronage of Mansfield Park, had long been.

FINIS.

Textual Notes

A = First Edition of *Mansfield Park*, 1814
B = Second Edition of *Mansfield Park*, 1816

The text of this edition of *Mansfield Park* was arrived at by collating copies of the first and second editions held by Cornell University and Princeton University. Austen's second edition (1816) is the basis for this text, as it is for all modern editions of the novel. This edition, however, strives to make editorial intervention explicit and to allow those inconsistencies that cannot be adjudicated on the basis of known information about the text to stand.

These textual notes, and my discussion in the Introduction (pp. xvi–xxi), record the evidence for my decisions. The notes detail the instances where A's readings are improved by those in B, but include only examples of A's significant errors in word choice, grammar, and punctuation, rather than of A's minor grammatical errors, frequent typographical mistakes, and inconsequential spelling differences against B. Such infelicities in A are usually corrected by B. Similarly, errors at this level that remain in B or, as is rarely the case, are introduced by B, I have silently corrected.

All instances where A's reading is to be preferred to B's are listed. In each case where A and B err independently or jointly and I have had, thus, to emend the text, their readings are noted.

These notes do not contain an exhaustive account of the differences between the Chapman edition (1923; revised Mary Lascelles, 1966) and AB, although the character of Chapman's edition is discussed in my Introduction (pp. xx–xxi). Nevertheless, as an aid to the reader, Chapman's editorial decisions and comments are noted whenever the passage offers interpretative difficulties.

I.i.6: however,] *omitted in* A
I.i.9: bear] bare A
I.i.9: us,] A; us?" B
I.i.10: help to dress] help dress A (*Chapman adopts* A.)
I.i.10: daughters] daughter AB (Chapman also emends.)
I.ii.11: as unhappy] as an unhappy A
I.iii.23: considering Sir Thomas] considering. Sir Thomas A (*Chapman adopts* A, *which is plausible.*)
I.iv.27: cousins'] cousin's AB (*Chapman also emends.*)
I.iv.27: perceived] perceive A (*Chapman adopts* A.)
I.vi.41: respectable] respectably A
I.vii.53: Edmund," . . . "it] Edmund . . . it AB (*Chapman also emends.*)
I.viii.54: she] he A (*Chapman adopts* A.)
I.viii.54: civility especially,] civility, especially A
I.viii.55: Mrs.] Miss AB (*Chapman also emends.*)

323

I.viii.56: would] could A

I.viii.57: his] her AB (*Chapman also emends.*)

I.viii.58: men] man A

I.ix.61: disappointed,] disappointed, cousin, A

I.xiii.87: My] my AB (*Chapman also emends.*)

I.xiii.89: do" . . . " To] do . . . To AB (*Chapman also emends.*)

I.xiii.90: not] not AB (*Chapman also emends.*)

I.xiii.90: sister's] AB (*Chapman emends to sisters'. Although I generally emend faulty plural possessives, as does B, I retain the singular of AB because, though Julia plays, there is no internal evidence that the piano belongs to both sisters.*)

I.xiv.93: characters,] AB (*Chapman moves the comma, emending the phrase to* characters too many,.)

I.xiv.94: To] A; The B (*Chapman adopts A.*)

I.xv.98: to be] to be called A

I.xv.100: can),] can). AB (*Chapman also emends.*)

I.xv.104: again — She] AB (*Chapman emends to* again — she *thus correcting the grammar. Perhaps Austen's MS read* again. — She *as Austen typically uses a period and a dash for an end stop.*)

I.xvi.107: What] AB (*Although AB agree in this reading, Chapman emends to* what *thus repairing the grammar and stressing the parallelism with the previous sentence. It is probable that Austen's MS read* for? — What.)

I.xvi.108: unpleasantness] unpleasantnesses A (*Chapman adopts A.*)

I.xvi.109: spared." . . .] spared." A

I.xvii.111: unconnected] connected A

I.xix.118: help him to prepare] help him prepare A (*Chapman adopts A.*)

I.xviii.120: an usual] AB (*Chapman emends to* unusual noise *noting that* an unusual noise *is yet another possibility. I retain AB because the reading makes sense without intervention:* too busy with their own noise, the Bertram children do not notice the usual noise their father makes entering the house.)

II.i.122: him] them A (*Chapman adopts A.*)

II.i.140: it] A; is B (*Chapman adopts A.*)

II.iv.147: even] ever A

II.v.151: wherever] where-| ever AB

II.vii.164: persons'] persons AB (*Chapman also emends.*)

II.vii.166: in] for A

II.vii.166: you must make] you must make you A (*Chapman adopts A without notice.*)

II.vii.167: solid] solid walled A (*Chapman adopts A.*)

II.vii.171: neighbour] neighbours A

II.viii.175: were] was A

II.viii.176: should] would A

II.viii.176: cousins'] cousins AB (*Chapman also emends.*)

II.viii.178: further] farther A

II.ix.179: came] come AB (*Chapman also emends.*)

II.ix.179: jeweller's] A; jewellers' B (*Chapman adopts A.*)

II.ix.183: came] come A

II.ix.184: hear it.] hear. A

II.ix.186: maid] woman A

II.x.189: than] then A

II.x.189: general] generally A

II.x.190: to] the A

II.x.190: offered.—"Ah!] AB (*Chapman emends to* offered,—"Ah! *noting that this changes the sense.*)

II.xi.193: Maddoxes] Maddox' A

II.xi.196: way all] AB (*Chapman emends to* way, all *though he notes that AB may be "just possible."*)

II.xi.198: it at all] it all A

II.xii.202: broken] broke A (*Chapman adopts B, noting A's plausibility.*)

II.xii.203: moments'] moments AB (*Although Chapman generally corrects for grammar, here he adopts AB without correction.*)

II.xiii.205: further] farther A

II.xiii.206: feelings] A; feeling B (*Chapman adopts A.*)

II.xiii.206: and] A; or B (*Chapman adopts A, noting that B's* or *may have been introduced by the typesetter because of* or *three words later.*)

III.i.214: moments'] moments AB (*Chapman adopts AB.*)

III.i.215: cousins'] cousin's AB

III.i.218: were] was A

III.i.220: Depend upon it it is me] A; Depend upon it is me B (*Chapman adopts* A.)

III.ii.223: *This sentence is controversial. Though Chapman let it stand, he regarded it as so vexed as to require emendation. AB agree, however; and in context the sentence, while difficult, is not unintelligible.*

III.iii.227: scene] AB (*Although AB agree on this reading, Chapman notes that* screen *may have been intended.*)

III.iii.231: affect] effect A

III.iii.232: always for] AB (*Chapman emends to* always, for *which changes the sense.*)

III.iv.235: were] was A

III.iv.236: years'] A; years B

III.v.245: were] was A

III.v.246: two] too A

III.vii.254: very] always A (*Chapman adopts* A.)

III.vii.257: Sharp] Alert A

III.vii.258: mess] things A

III.vii.258: Old Scholey . . . sheer hulk"] Old Scholey ran in at breakfast time, to say that she was under weigh. I jumped up, and made but two steps to the point. If ever there was a perfect beauty afloat, she is one; and there she lays at Spithead, and anybody in England would take her for an eight-and-twenty. I was upon the platform two hours this afternoon, looking at her. She lays just astern of the Endymion, with the Cleopatra to larboard." A

III.vii.258: It's the best birth at Spithead.] *omitted in* A

III.vii.259: talk to, of his infant] AB (*Chapman considers this a crux, emending it to* talk to him. *AB make adequate sense if we suppose that Fanny is saying that she used to soothe and talk to Tom when he was an infant, a possibility Chapman finds illogical. Given that this is a section Austen seemed to have revised with some care, it is hard to imagine that she would let stand an obscurity of the magnitude Chapman supposes.*)

III.viii.265: always] A; all was B (*Chapman adopts* A.)

III.ix.265: at] as A

III.ix.270: own.] AB (*Although AB agree and make sense, Chapman emends to* own,.)

III.ix.271: in] in AB (*Chapman also emends, noting that Austen might not have regarded* in *as part of the Latin.*)

III.x.274: daughters'] daughter's AB (*Chapman also emends.*)

III.xi.281: suit] pursuit A

III.xii.282 tired still] A; still tired B (*Chapman adopts* A.)

III.xii.283: were] was A

III.xii.283: expectation] A; expectations B (*Chapman adopts* A.)

III.xiii.285: before.] A; before, B (*Chapman adopts* A.)

III.xiii.285: had she been different] AB (*Mary Lascelles observes that the sense clearly calls for* had she not been different.)

III.xiii.287: coolness] coldness A

III.xiii.288: 'The loss . . . and Fanny.'] The loss . . . and Fanny. A

III.xiii.289: it] is A

III.xiv.291: XIV.] XVI. AB (*Chapman also emends.*)

III.xiv.294: for herself] for her herself A

III.xiv.296 this,] A; this B (*Chapman adopts* A.)

III.xv.300: affect] effect AB (*Chapman also emends.*)

III.xv.303: revived] received A (*Chapman adopts* A. *This is a genuine crux, for both A and B make sense. Revive a smile is a somewhat unusual usage, one Austen never employed in any other novel, though she often talks of reviving spirits or subjects. Austen used the phrase* received a smile *in Emma (III.6). It is, moreover, true that the typesetter of the third volume is not as careful as other typesetters, and this lends A more weight. On the other hand, the substitution of* revived *for* received *is not the common sort of error the typesetter of this volume often commits, and we would have to imagine the error eluding not only his notice but that of correctors as well, supposing that Austen herself did not catch it. Finally, Austen made many changes in this volume, and it is not implausible that she made this one as well. I retain B because I cannot prove it in error.*)

III.xvi.305: Rushworths'] Rushworths AB

III.xvi.306: might,] A; might B (*Chapman adopts* A. *The dropped comma occurs at the end of a line, a common site for typesetting errors.*)

III.xvi.307: was] was A

III.xvi.309: 'Why,] 'Why A

III.xvi.310: too] to A

III.xvi.311: above all,] A; above, B (*Chapman adopts* A.)

III.xvi.312: more] more A

III.xvii.313: him and] him to A
III.xvii.318: mind, and] and *omitted in* A
III.xvii.319: reliance on] A; on *omitted in* B (*Chapman adopts* A.)
III.xvii.320: neighbours'] neighbour's AB (*Chapman also emends.*)
III.xvi.321: *her*] her A

CONTEXTS

ELIZABETH INCHBALD

Lovers' Vows; A Play, in Five Acts; Altered from the German of Kotzebue†

Preface on the First Publication of Lovers' Vows

It would appear like affectation to offer an apology for any scenes or passages omitted or added, in this play, different from the original: its reception has given me confidence to suppose what I have done is right; for Kotzebue's "Child of Love," in Germany, was never more attractive, than "Lovers' Vows" has been in England.

I could trouble my reader with many pages to disclose the motives, which induced me to alter, with the exception of a few common-place sentences only, the characters of Count Cassel, Amelia, and Verdun the Butler—I could explain why the part of the Count, as in the original, would have inevitably condemned the whole play—I could inform my reader why I have pourtrayed the Baron, in many particulars, different from the German author, and carefully prepared the audience for the grand effect of the last scene in the fourth act, by totally changing his conduct towards his son, as a robber—why I gave sentences of a humourous kind to the parts of the two Cottagers—why I was compelled, on many occasions, to compress the substance of a speech of three or four pages, into one of three or four lines—and why, in no once instance, I would suffer my respect for Kotzebue to interfere with my profound respect for the judgment of a British audience. But I flatter myself such a vindication is not requisite to the enlightened reader, who, I trust, on comparing this drama with the original, will, at once, see all my motives—and the dull admirer of mere verbal translation, it would be vain to endeavour to inspire with taste by instruction.

Wholly unacquainted with the German language, a literal translation of the "Child of Love" was given to me by the manager of Covent Garden Theatre, to be adapted, as my opinion should direct, for his stage. This translation, tedious and vapid, as most literal translations are, had the peculiar disadvantage of having been put into our language by a German—of course, it came to me in broken English. It was no

---

† Elizabeth Inchbald (1753–1821) was an actress, playwright, novelist, critic, and anthologist allied with progressive causes. *Lovers' Vows* (1798) is loosely based on a German sentimental melodrama, *Das Kind der Liebe* (1791) by August Friedrich Ferdinand von Kotzebue. Inchbald's play enjoyed considerable success on stage in the late eighteenth and early nineteenth centuries. The text reprinted here was published in 1798. Typographical errors have been silently corrected, and the bracketing of stage directions has been regularized.

slight misfortune, to have an example of bad grammar, false metaphors and similes, with all the usual errors of imperfect diction, placed before a female writer. But if, disdaining the construction of sentences,—the precise decorum of the cold grammarian,—she has caught the spirit of her author,—if, in every altered scene,—still adhering to the nice propriety of his meaning, and still keeping in view his great catastrophe, —she has agitated her audience with all the various passions he depicted, the rigid criticism of the closet will be but a slender abatement of the pleasure resulting from the sanction of an applauding theatre.

It has not been one of the least gratifications I have received from the success of this play, that the original German, from which it is taken, was printed in the year 1791; and yet, that, during all the period which has intervened, no person of talents or literary knowledge (though there are in this country many of that description, who profess to search for German dramas,) has thought it worth employment to make a translation of the work. I can only account for such an apparent neglect of Kotzebue's "Child of Love," by the consideration of its being in the original discordant with an English stage, and the difficulty of making it otherwise—a difficulty, which once appeared so formidable, that I thought I must have declined it, even after I had proceeded some length in the undertaking.

Independently of objections to the character of the Count, the dangerous insignificance of the Butler, in the original, embarrassed me much. I found, if he was retained in the *Dramatis Personæ*, something more must be supplied than the author had assigned him: I suggested the verses I have introduced; but not being blessed with the Butler's happy art of rhyming, I am indebted for them, except the seventh and eleventh stanzas in the first of his poetic stories, to the author of the prologue.

The part of Amelia has been a very particular object of my solicitude and alteration: the same situations which the author gave her, remain, but almost all the dialogue of the character I have changed: the forward and unequivocal manner, in which she announces her affection to her lover, in the original, would have been revolting to an English audience: the passion of love, represented on the stage, is certain to be either insipid or hateful, unless it creates smiles or tears: Amelia's love, by Kotzebue, is indelicately blunt, and yet, void of mirth or sadness: I have endeavoured to attach the attention and sympathy of the audience, by whimsical insinuations, rather than coarse abruptness: she is still the same woman, I conceive, whom the author drew, with the self-same sentiments, but with manners conforming to the English, rather than the German taste; and if the favour in which this character is held by the audience, together with every sentence and incident, which I have presumed to introduce in the play, may be offered as the criterion of my skill, I am sufficiently rewarded for the task I have performed.

In stating the foregoing circumstances relating to this production, I hope not to be suspected of arrogating to my own exertions only, the popularity which has attended "The Child of Love," under the title of "Lovers' Vows:"—the exertions of every performer engaged in the play deservedly claim a share in its success; and I most sincerely thank them for the high importance of their aid.

Remarks

Plays, founded on German dramas, have long been a subject both of ridicule and of serious animadversion. Ridicule is a jocund slanderer; and who does not love to be merry? but the detraction, that is dull, is inexcusable calumny.

The grand moral of this play is—to set forth the miserable consequences which arise from the neglect, and to enforce the watchful care, of illegitimate offspring; and surely, as the pulpit has not had eloquence to eradicate the crime of seduction, the stage may be allowed an humble endeavour to prevent its most fatal effects.

But there are some pious declaimers against theatrical exhibitions, so zealous to do good,—they grudge the poor dramatist his share in the virtuous concern.

Not furnished with one plea throughout four acts of "Lovers' Vows" for accusation, those critics arraign its catastrophe, and say,—"the wicked should be punished."—They forget there is a punishment called *conscience*, which, though it seldom troubles the defamer's peace, may weigh heavy on the fallen female and her libertine seducer.

But as a probationary prelude to the supposed happiness of the frail personages of this drama, the author has plunged the offender, Agatha, in bitterest poverty and woe; which she receives as a contrite penitent, atoning for her sins. The Baron Wildenhaim, living in power and splendour, is still more rigorously visited by remorse: and, in the reproaches uttered by his outcast son, (become, by the father's criminal disregard of his necessities, a culprit subject to death by the law,) the Baron's guilt has sure exemplary chastisement. But yet, after all the varied anguish of his mind, should tranquillity promise, at length, to crown his future days, where is the immorality? If holy books teach, that the wicked too often prosper, why are plays to be withheld from inculcating the self-same doctrine? Not that a worldly man would class it amongst the prosperous events of life, to be (like the Baron) compelled to marry his cast-off mistress, after twenty years absence.

It may not here be wholly useless to observe—that, in the scene in the fourth act, just mentioned, between the Baron and his son—the actor, who plays Frederick, too frequently forms his notion of the passion he is to pourtray, through the interview, from the following lines, at the end of one of his speeches:

"And, when he dies, a funeral sermon will praise his great benevolence, his christian charities"

The sarcasm here to be expressed, should be evinced in no one sentence else. Where, in a preceding speech, he says, the Baron is—"a man, kind, generous, beloved by his tenants:"—he certainly means *this* to be his character. Frederick is not ironical, except by accident. Irony and sarcasm do not appertain to youth: open, plain, downright habits, are the endearing qualities of the young. Moreover, a son, urged by cruel injuries, may upbraid his father even to rage, and the audience will yet feel interest for them both; but if he contemn or deride him, all respect is lost, both for the one and the other.

The passions which take possession of this young soldier's heart, when admitted to the presence of the Baron, knowing him to be his father, are various; but scorn is not amongst the number. Awe gives the first sensation, and is subdued by pride: filial tenderness would next force its way, and is overwhelmed by anger. These passions strive in his breast, till grief for his mother's wrongs, and his own ignominious state, burst all restraint—and as fury drives him to the point of distraction, he changes his accents to a tone of irony, in the lines just quoted.

"Oh! there be actors I have seen, and heard others praise, who, (not to speak it profanely,) have"—scornfully sneered at their father through this whole scene, and yet, been highly applauded.

While it is the fashion to see German plays, both the German and the English author will patiently bear the displeasure of a small party of critics, as the absolute conditions on which they enjoy popularity. Nor, till the historian is forbid to tell, how tyrants have success in vanquishing nations; or the artist be compelled to paint the beauteous courtezan with hideous features, as the emblem of her mind, shall the free dramatist be untrue to his science; which, like theirs, is to follow nature through all her rightful course. Deception, beyond the result of genuine imitative art, he will disclaim, and say with Shakespeare to the self-approving zealot:

> "Virtue itself turns vice, being misapplied,
> And vice sometime's by action dignified."

Lovers' Vows

Persons Represented†

BARON WILDENHAIM

COUNT CASSEL

ANHALT

FREDERICK

VERDUN, the Butler

LANDLORD

COTTAGER

FARMER

COUNTRYMAN

AGATHA FRIBURG

AMELIA WILDENHAIM

COTTAGER'S WIFE

COUNTRY GIRL

Huntsmen, Servants, &c.

SCENE—Germany.

Act the First

SCENE I

*A high road, a town at a distance.—A small inn on one
side the road.—A cottage on the other.*

[*The* LANDLORD *of the inn leads* AGATHA *by the hand out of his house.*]

LAND. No, no! no room for you any longer—It is the fair to-day in the
next village; as great a fair as any in the German dominions. The
country people with their wives and children take up every corner
we have.

AGATHA. You will turn a poor sick woman out of doors, who has spent
her last farthing in your house?

LAND. For that very reason; because she *has* spent her last farthing.

AGATHA. I can work.

LAND. You can hardly move your hands.

AGATHA. My strength will come again.

LAND. Then *you* may come again

AGATHA. What am I to do? where shall I go?

LAND. It is fine weather—you may go any where.

AGATHA. Who will give me a morsel of bread to satisfy my hunger?

LAND. Sick people eat but little.

† As the play was staged at Mansfield Park, Baron Wildenhaim was played by Mr. Yates; Count
Cassel by Mr. Rushworth; Anhalt by Edmund Bertram; Frederick by Henry Crawford; Verdun
the Butler by Tom Bertram, who also takes the Cottager's part; Agatha by Maria Bertram;
Amelia by Mary Crawford. Fanny Price reluctantly agrees to read the part of the Cottager's
Wife—an irreverent role curiously at odds with Fanny's meek character—but Sir Thomas's
return home stops the performance.

AGATHA. Hard, unfeeling man, have pity.

LAND. When times are hard, pity is too expensive for a poor man. Ask alms of the different people that go by.

AGATHA. Beg! I would rather starve.

LAND. You may beg, and starve too. What a fine lady you are! Many an honest woman has been obliged to beg. Why should not you? [AGATHA *sits down upon a large stone under a tree.*] For instance, here comes somebody; and I will teach you how to begin. [A COUNTRY- MAN, *with working tools, crosses the road.*] Good day, neighbour Nicholas.

COUNTR. Good day.   [*Stops.*]

LAND. Won't you give a trifle to this poor woman? [COUNTRYMAN *takes no notice, but walks off.*] That would not do—the poor man has nothing himself but what he gets by hard labour. Here comes a rich farmer; perhaps he will give you something.

[*Enter* FARMER.]

LAND. Good morning to you, sir. Under yon tree sits a poor woman in distress, who is in need of your charity.

FAR. Is she not ashamed of herself? Why don't she work?

LAND. She has had a fever. If you would but pay for one dinner—

FAR. The harvest has been but indifferent, and my cattle and sheep have suffered by a distemper.   [*Exit.*]

LAND. My fat smiling face was not made for begging: you'll have more luck with your thin, sour one—so, I'll leave you to yourself.   [*Exit.*]

[AGATHA *rises, and comes forward.*]

AGATHA. Oh Providence! thou hast till this hour protected me, and hast given me fortitude not to despair. Receive my humble thanks, and restore me to health, for the sake of my poor son, the innocent cause of my sufferings, and yet my only comfort. [*Kneeling.*] Oh, grant, that I may see him once more! See him improved in strength of mind and body; and that by thy gracious mercy he may never be visited with afflictions great as mine. [*After a pause.*] Protect his father too, merciful Providence, and pardon his crime of perjury to me! Here, in the face of Heaven (supposing my end approaching, and that I can but a few days longer struggle with want and sorrow,) here, I solemnly forgive my seducer for all the ills, the accumulated evils, which his allurements, his deceit and cruelty, have for twenty years past drawn upon me.

[*Enter a* COUNTRY GIRL, *with a basket.*]

AGATHA. [*Near fainting.*] My dear child, if you could spare me a trifle—
GIRL. I have not a farthing in the world—But I am going to market to
sell my eggs, and as I come back I'll give you three-pence—And I'll
be back as soon as ever I can.   [*Exit.*]
AGATHA. There was a time, when I was as happy as this country girl,
and as willing to assist the poor in distress.
[*Retires to the tree, and sits down.*]

[*Enter* FREDERICK—*He is dressed in a German soldier's uniform, has a
knapsack on his shoulders, appears in high spirits, and stops at the door
of the inn.*]

FRED. Halt! Stand at ease! It is a very hot day—A draught of good wine
will not be amiss. But first let me consult my purse. [*Takes out a
couple of pieces of money, which he turns about in his hand.*] This
will do for a breakfast—the other remains for my dinner; and in the
evening I shall be at home. [*Calls out.*] Ha! Halloo! Landlord! [*Takes
notice of* AGATHA, *who is leaning against the tree.*] Who is that? A
poor sick woman! She don't beg; but her appearance makes me think
she is in want. Must one always wait to give till one is asked? Shall
I go without my breakfast now, or lose my dinner? The first I think
is best. Ay, I don't want a breakfast, for dinner-time will soon be here.
To do good satisfies both hunger and thirst. [*Going towards her with
the money in his hand.*] Take this, good woman.

[*She stretches her hand for the gift, looks stedfastly at him, and cries out
with astonishment and joy.*]

AGATHA. Frederick!
FRED. Mother! [*With amazement and grief.*] Mother! For God's sake
what is this! How is this! And why do I find my mother thus? Speak!
AGATHA. I cannot speak, dear son! [*Rising, and embracing him.*] My
dear Frederick! The joy is too great—I was not prepared—
FRED. Dear mother, compose yourself: [*Leans her head against his
breast.*] now then, be comforted. How she trembles! She is fainting.
AGATHA. I am so weak, and my head so giddy—I had nothing to eat all
yesterday.
FRED. Good heavens! Here is my little money, take it all! Oh mother!
mother! [*Runs to the inn.*] Landlord! Landlord! [*Knocking violently
at the door.*]
LAND. What is the matter?
FRED. A bottle of wine—quick, quick!
LAND. [*Surprised.*] A bottle of wine! For who?
FRED. For me. Why do you ask? Why don't you make haste?
LAND. Well, well, Mr. Soldier: but can you pay for it?

FRED. Here is money—make haste, or I'll break every window in your house.

LAND. Patience! Patience!   [*Goes off.*]

FRED. [*To* AGATHA.] You were hungry yesterday, when I sat down to a comfortable dinner. You were hungry, when I partook of a good supper. Oh! Why is so much bitter mixed with the joy of my return?

AGATHA. Be patient, my dear Frederick. Since I see you, I am well. But I *have been* very ill: so ill, that I despaired of ever beholding you again.

FRED. Ill, and I was not with you? I will, now, never leave you more. Look, mother, how tall and strong I am grown. These arms can now afford you support. They can, and shall, procure you subsistence.

[LANDLORD, *coming out of the house with a small pitcher.*]

LAND. Here is wine—a most delicious nectar. [*Aside.*] It is only Rhenish; but it will pass for the best old Hock.

FRED. [*Impatiently snatching the pitcher.*] Give it me.

LAND. No, no—the money first. One shilling and two-pence, if you please.   [FRED. *gives him money.*]

FRED. This is all I have.—Here, here, mother.

[*While she drinks,* LANDLORD *counts the money.*]

LAND. Three halfpence too short! However, one must be charitable.
                                          [*Exit* LANDLORD.]

AGATHA. I thank you, my dear Frederick—Wine revives me—Wine from the hand of my son gives me almost a new life.

FRED. Don't speak too much, mother—Take your time.

AGATHA. Tell me, dear child, how you have passed the five years, since you left me.

FRED. Both good and bad, mother. To-day plenty—to-morrow not so much—And sometimes nothing at all.

AGATHA. You have not written to me this long while.

FRED. Dear mother, consider the great distance I was from you!—And then, in the time of war, how often letters miscarry.—Besides ——

AGATHA. No matter, now I see you. But have you obtained your discharge?

FRED. Oh, no, mother—I have leave of absence only for two months; and that for a particular reason. But I will not quit you so soon, now I find you are in want of my assistance.

AGATHA. No, no, Frederick; your visit will make me so well, that I shall in a very short time recover strength to work again; and you must return to your regiment, when your furlough is expired. But you told me leave of absence was granted you for a particular reason.—What reason?

FRED. When I left you, five years ago, you gave me every thing you could afford, and all you thought would be necessary for me. But one trifle you forgot, which was, the certificate of my birth from the church-book. You know in this country there is nothing to be done without it. At the time of parting from you, I little thought it could be of that consequence to me, which I have since found it would have been. Once I became tired of a soldier's life, and in the hope I should obtain my discharge, offered myself to a master to learn a profession; but his question was, "Where is your certificate from the church-book of the parish, in which you were born?" It vexed me that I had not it to produce, for my comrades laughed at my disappointment. My captain behaved kinder, for he gave me leave to come home to fetch it—and you see, mother, here I am.

[*During this speech,* AGATHA *is confused and agitated.*]

AGATHA. So you are come for the purpose of fetching your certificate from the church-book.
FRED. Yes, mother.
AGATHA. Oh! oh!
FRED. What is the matter? [*She bursts into tears.*] For Heaven's sake, mother, tell me what's the matter?
AGATHA. You have no certificate.
FRED. No!
AGATHA. No.—The laws of Germany excluded you from being registered at your birth—for—you are a natural son.
FRED. [*Starts*]—[*After a pause.*] So!—And who is my father?
AGATHA. Oh, Frederick, your wild looks are daggers to my heart. Another time.
FRED. [*Endeavouring to conceal his emotion.*] No, no—I am still your son—and you are still my mother. Only tell me, who is my father?
AGATHA. When we parted, five years ago, you were too young to be intrusted with a secret of so much importance.—But the time is come, when I can, in confidence, open my heart, and unload that burthen, with which it has been long oppressed. And yet, to reveal my errors to my child, and sue for his mild judgment on my conduct—
FRED. You have nothing to sue for; only explain this mystery.
AGATHA. I will. I will. But—my tongue is locked with remorse and shame. You must not look at me.
FRED. Not look at you! Cursed be that son, who could find his mother guilty, although the world should call her so.
AGATHA. Then listen to me, and take notice of that village, [*Pointing.*] of that castle, and of that church. In that village I was born—In that church I was baptized. My parents were poor, but reputable farmers.—The lady of that castle and estate requested them to let me live with her, and she would provide for me through life. They re-

signed me; and, at the age of fourteen, I went to my patroness. She took pleasure to instruct me in all kind of female literature and accomplishments, and three happy years had passed, under her protection, when her only son, who was an officer in the Saxon service, obtained permission to come home. I had never seen him before—he was a handsome young man—in my eyes a prodigy; for he talked of love, and promised me marriage. He was the first man, who had ever spoke to me on such a subject.—His flattery made me vain, and his repeated vows —— Don't look at me, dear Frederick!—I can say no more. [FREDERICK, *with his eyes cast down, takes her hand, and puts it to his heart.*] Oh! oh! my son! I was intoxicated by the fervent caresses of a young, inexperienced, capricious man, and did not recover from the delirium till it was too late.

FRED. [*After a pause.*] Go on.—Let me know more of my father.

AGATHA. When the time drew near that I could no longer conceal my guilt and shame, my seducer prevailed on me not to expose him to the resentment of his mother. He renewed his former promises of marriage at her death;—on which relying, I gave him my word to be secret—and I have to this hour buried his name deep in my heart.

FRED. Proceed, proceed! give me full information —— I will have courage to hear it all.   [*Greatly agitated.*]

AGATHA. His leave of absence expired, he returned to his regiment, depending on my promise, and well assured of my esteem. As soon as my situation became known, I was questioned, and received many severe reproaches; but I refused to confess who was my undoer; and for that obstinacy was turned from the castle.—I went to my parents; but their door was shut against me. My mother, indeed, wept as she bade me quit her sight for ever; but my father wished,—that increased affliction might befal me.

FRED. [*Weeping.*] Be quick with your narrative, or you'll break my heart.

AGATHA. I now sought protection from the old clergyman of the parish He received me with compassion. On my knees I begged forgiveness for the scandal I had caused to his parishioners; promised amendment; and he said he did not doubt me. Through his recommendation I went to town; and, hid in humble lodgings, procured the means of subsistence by teaching to the neighbouring children what I had learnt under the tuition of my benefactress.—To instruct you, my Frederick, was my care and my delight; and, in return for your filial love, I would not thwart your wishes, when they led to a soldier's life: but I saw you go from me with an aching heart. Soon after, my health declined, I was compelled to give up my employment, and, by degrees, became the object you now see me. But, let me add, before I close my calamitous story, that—when I left the good old clergyman, taking along with me his kind advice and his blessing, I left him with a firm determination to fulfil the vow I had made of repentance and amendment. I *have* fulfilled it—and now, Frederick, you may look at me again.

[*He embraces her.*]

FRED. But my father all this time? [*Mournfully.*] I apprehend he died.

AGATHA. No—he married.

FRED. Married!

AGATHA. A woman of virtue —— of noble birth and immense fortune. Yet, [*Weeps.*] I had written to him many times; had described your infant innocence and wants; had glanced obliquely at former promises ——

FRED. [*Rapidly.*] No answer to these letters?

AGATHA. Not a word.—But in the time of war, you know, letters miscarry.

FRED. Nor did he ever return to this estate?

AGATHA. No—since the death of his mother this castle has only been inhabited by servants—for he settled as far off as Alsace, upon the estate of his wife.

FRED. I will carry you in my arms to Alsace. No—why should I ever know my father, if he is a villain! My heart is satisfied with a mother.—No—I will not go to him. I will not disturb his peace—I leave that task to his conscience. What say you, mother, can't we do without him? [*Struggling between his tears and his pride.*] We don't want him. I will write directly to my captain. Let the consequence be what it will, leave you again I cannot. Should I be able to get my discharge, I will work all day at the plough, and all the night with my pen. It will do, mother, it will do! Heaven's goodness will assist me—it will prosper the endeavours of a dutiful son for the sake of a helpless mother.

AGATHA. [*Presses him to her breast.*] Where could be found such another son?

FRED. But tell me my father's name, that I may know how to shun him.

AGATHA. Baron Wildenhaim.

FRED. Baron Wildenhaim! I shall never forget it.—Oh! you are near fainting. Your eyes are cast down. What's the matter? Speak, mother!

AGATHA. Nothing particular.—Only fatigued with talking, I wish to take a little rest.

FRED. I did not consider, that we have been all this time in the open road. [*Goes to the inn, and knocks at the door.*] Here, Landlord!

[LANDLORD *re-enters.*]

LAND. Well, what is the matter now?

FRED. Make haste, and get a bed ready for this good woman.

LAND. [*With a sneer.*] A bed for this good woman! Ha! ha! ha! She slept last night in that pent-house; so she may to-night.

[*Exit, shutting the door.*]

FRED. You are an infamous—[*Goes back to his mother.*] Oh! my poor
mother—[*Runs to the cottage at a little distance, and knocks.*] Ha!
halloo! Who is there?

[*Enters* COTTAGER.]

COT. Good day, young soldier.—What is it you want?
FRED. Good friend, look at that poor woman. She is perishing in the
public road! It is my mother.—Will you give her a small corner in
your hut? I beg for mercy's sake—Heaven will reward you.
COT. Can't you speak quietly? I understand you very well. [*Calls at the
door of the hut.*] Wife, shake up our bed—here's a poor sick woman
wants it.

[*Enter* WIFE.]

Why could not you say all this in fewer words? Why such a long
preamble? Why for mercy's sake, and Heaven's reward; Why talk
about reward for such trifles as these Come, let us lead her in; and
welcome she shall be to a bed, as good as I can give her; and to our
homely fare.
FRED. Ten thousand thanks, and blessings on you!
WIFE. Thanks and blessings! here's a piece of work indeed about nothing! Good sick lady, lean on my shoulder. [*To* FREDERICK.] Thanks
and reward, indeed! Do you think husband and I have lived to these
years, and don't know our duty? Lean on my shoulder.

[*Exeunt into the cottage.*]

Act the Second

SCENE I

A room in the Cottage.

[AGATHA, COTTAGER, *his* WIFE, *and* FREDERICK *discovered*—AGATHA *re-
clining upon a wooden bench.* FREDERICK *leaning over her.*]

FRED. Good people, have you nothing to give her? Nothing that's
nourishing?
WIFE. Run, husband, run, and fetch a bottle of wine from the landlord
of the inn.
FRED. No, no his wine is as bad as his heart: she has drank some of it,
which I am afraid has turned to poison.
COT. Suppose, wife, you look for a new laid egg?
WIFE. Or a drop of brandy, husband—that mostly cures me.
FRED. Do you hear, mother—will you, mother? [AGATHA *makes a sign*

with her hand as if she could not take any thing.] She will not. Is there no doctor in this neighbourhood?

WIFE. At the end of the village there lives a horse doctor. I have never heard of any other.

FRED. What shall I do? She is dying. My mother is dying—Pray for her, good people!

AGATHA. Make yourself easy, dear Frederick, I am well, only weak—Some wholesome nourishment—

FRED. Yes, mother, directly—directly. [*Aside.*] Oh! where shall I—no money—not a farthing left.

WIFE. Oh, dear me! Had you not paid the rent yesterday, husband—

COT. I then should know what to do. But as I hope for mercy, I have not a penny in my house.

FRED. Then I must—[*Apart, coming forward.*]—Yes, I will go, and beg.—But should I be refused—I will then—I leave my mother in your care, good people—Do all you can for her, I beseech you! I shall soon be with you again. [*Goes off in haste and confusion.*]

COT. If he should go to our parson, I am sure he would give him something.

[AGATHA *having revived by degrees during the scenes, rises.*]

AGATHA. Is that good old man still living, who was minister here some time ago?

WIFE. No—It pleased Providence to take that worthy man to Heaven two years ago. We have lost in him both a friend and a father. We shall never get such another.

COT. Wife, wife, our present rector is likewise a very good man.

WIFE. Yes! But he is so very young.

COT. Our late parson was young once.

WIFE. [*To* AGATHA.] This young man being tutor in our Baron's family, he is very much beloved by them all; and so the Baron gave him this living in consequence.

COT. And well he deserved it, for his pious instructions to our young lady; who is, in consequence, good, and friendly to every body.

AGATHA. What young lady do you mean?

COT. Our Baron's daughter.

AGATHA. Is she here?

WIFE. Dear me! Don't you know that? I thought every body had known that. It is almost five weeks since the Baron and all his family arrived at the castle.

AGATHA. Baron Wildenhaim?

WIFE. Yes, Baron Wildenhaim.

AGATHA. And his lady?

COT. His lady died in France, many miles from hence, and her death, I suppose, was the cause of his coming to this estate—For the Baron has not been here till within these five weeks ever since he was married. We regretted his absence much, and his arrival has caused great joy.

WIFE. [*Addressing her discourse to* AGATHA.] By all accounts the Baroness was very haughty, and very whimsical.

COT. Wife, wife, never speak ill of the dead. Say what you please against the living, but not a word against the dead.

WIFE. And yet, husband, I believe the dead care the least what is said against them.—And so, if you please, I'll tell my story. The late Baroness was, they say, haughty and proud; and they do say, the Baron was not so happy as he might have been;—but he, bless him, our good Baron is still the same as when a boy. Soon after madam had closed her eyes, he left France, and came to Wildenhaim, his native country.

COT. Many times has he joined in our village dances. Afterwards, when he became an officer, he was rather wild, as most young men are.

WIFE. Yes, I remember when he fell in love with poor Agatha, Friburg's daughter: what a piece of work that was—It did not do him much credit. That was a wicked thing.

COT. Have done—no more of this—It is not well to stir up old grievances.

WIFE. Why you said I might speak ill of the living. 'Tis very hard indeed, if one must not speak ill of one's neighbours, dead, or alive.

COT. Who knows whether he was the father of Agatha's child? She never said he was.

WIFE. Nobody but him—that I am sure—I would lay a wager—no, no, husband, you must not take his part—it is very wicked! Who knows what is now become of that poor creature? She has not been heard of this many a year. May be she is starving for hunger. Her father might have lived longer too, if that misfortune had not happened.

[AGATHA *faints.*]

COT. See here! Help! She is fainting—take hold.

WIFE. Oh, poor woman!

COT. Let us take her into the next room.

WIFE. Oh, poor woman!—I am afraid she will not live. Come cheer up, cheer up You are with those who feel for you. [*They lead her off.*]

SCENE II

An apartment in the Castle.

[*A table spread for breakfast—Several Servants in livery disposing the equipage—*BARON WILDENHAIM *enters, attended by a* GENTLEMEN *in waiting.*]

BARON. Has not Count Cassel left his chamber yet?

GENT. No, my lord, he has but now rung for his valet.

BARON. The whole castle smells of his perfumery. Go, call my daughter hither. [*Exit* GENTLEMAN.] And am I after all to have an ape for a son-in-law? No, I shall not be in a hurry—I love my daughter too well. We must be better acquainted before I give her to him. I shall not sacrifice my Amelia to the will of others, as I myself was sacrificed. The poor girl might, in thoughtlessness, say yes, and afterwards be miserable. What a pity she is not a boy! The name of Wildenhaim will die with me. My fine estates, my good peasants, all will fall into the hands of strangers. Oh! why was not Amelia a boy?

[*Enter* AMELIA—*She kisses the* BARON'S *hand.*]

AMELIA. Good morning, dear my lord.

BARON. Good morning, Amelia. Have you slept well?

AMELIA. Oh! yes, papa. I always sleep well.

BARON. Not a little restless last night?

AMELIA. No.

BARON. Amelia, you know you have a father, who loves you, and I believe you know you have a suitor who is come to ask permission to love you. Tell me candidly how you like Count Cassel.

AMELIA. Very well.

BARON. Do not you blush, when I talk of him?

AMELIA. No.

BARON. No:—I am sorry for that. [*Aside.*]—Have you dreamt of him?

AMELIA. No.

BARON. Have you not dreamt at all to-night?

AMELIA. Oh yes—I have dreamt of our Chaplain, Mr. Anhalt.

BARON. Ah ha! As if he stood before you and the Count to ask for the ring.

AMELIA. No: not that—I dreamt we were all still in France, and he, my tutor, just going to take his leave of us for ever.—I 'woke with the fright, and found my eyes full of tears.

BARON. Pshaw! I want to know if you can love the Count. You saw him at the last ball we were at in France: when he capered round you; when he danced minuets; when he——. But I cannot say what his conversation was.

AMELIA. Nor I either—I do not remember a syllable of it.

BARON. No? Then I do not think you like him.

AMELIA. I believe not.

BARON. But I think proper to acquaint you, he is rich, and of great consequence; rich, and of great consequence; do you hear?

AMELIA. Yes, dear papa. But my tutor has always told me, that birth and fortune are inconsiderable things, and cannot give happiness.

BARON. There he is right—But if it happens, that birth and fortune are joined with sense and virtue——

AMELIA. But is it so with Count Cassel?

BARON. Hem! Hem! [*Aside.*] I will ask you a few questions on this subject; but be sure to answer me honestly—Speak the truth.

AMELIA. I never told an untruth in my life.

BARON. Nor ever *conceal* the truth from me, I command you.

AMELIA. [*Earnestly.*] Indeed, my lord, I never will.

BARON. I take you at your word—And now reply to me truly—Do you like to hear the Count spoken of?

AMELIA. Good, or bad?

BARON. Good. Good.

AMELIA. Oh yes; I like to hear good of every body.

BARON. But do not you feel a little fluttered, when he is talked of?

AMELIA. No.   [*Shaking her head.*]

BARON. Are not you a little embarrassed?

AMELIA. No.

BARON. Don't you wish sometimes to speak to him, and have not the courage to begin?

AMELIA. No.

BARON. Do not you wish to take his part, when his companions laugh at him?

AMELIA. No—I love to laugh at him myself.

BARON. Provoking! [*Aside.*] Are not you afraid of him, when he comes near you?

AMELIA. No, not at all.—Oh, yes—once.   [*Recollecting herself.*]

BARON. Ah! Now it comes!

AMELIA. Once at a ball he trod on my foot; and I was so afraid he should tread on me again.

BARON. You put me out of patience. Hear me, Amelia! [*Stops short, and speaks softer.*] To see you happy is my wish. But matrimony, without concord, is like a duetto badly performed; for that reason, nature, the great composer of all harmony, has ordained, that, when bodies are allied, hearts should be in perfect unison. However, I will send Mr. Anhalt to you ——

AMELIA. [*Much pleased.*] Do, papa.

BARON. He shall explain to you my sentiments. [*Rings.*] A clergyman can do this better than ——

[*Enter* SERVANT.]

Go directly to Mr. Anhalt, tell him I shall be glad to see him for a quarter of an hour, if he is not engaged.   [*Exit* SERVANT.]

AMELIA. [*Calls after him.*] Wish him a good morning from me.

BARON. [*Looking at his watch.*] The Count is a tedious time dressing.—Have you breakfasted, Amelia?

AMELIA. No, papa.   [*They sit down to breakfast.*]

BARON. How is the weather? Have you walked this morning?

AMELIA. Oh, yes—I was in the garden at five o'clock; it is very fine.

BARON. Then I'll go out shooting. I do not know in what other way to amuse my guest.

[*Enter* COUNT CASSEL.]

COUNT. Ah, my dear Colonel! Miss Wildenhaim, I kiss your hand.
BARON. Good morning! good morning! though it is late in the day, Count. In the country we should rise earlier.

[AMELIA *offers the* COUNT *a cup of tea.*]

COUNT. It is Hebe herself, or Venus, or ——
AMELIA. Ha! ha! ha! Who can help laughing at his nonsense?
BARON. [*Rather angry.*] Neither Venus, nor Hebe; but Amelia Wildenhaim, if you please.
COUNT. [*Sitting down to breakfast.*] You are beautiful, Miss Wildenhaim.—Upon my honour, I think so. I have travelled, and seen much of the world, and yet I can positively admire you.
AMELIA. I am sorry I have not seen the world.
COUNT. Wherefore?
AMELIA. Because I might then, perhaps, admire you.
COUNT. True;—for I am an epitome of the world. In my travels I learnt delicacy in Italy—hauteur, in Spain—in France, enterprize—in Russia, prudence—in England, sincerity—in Scotland, frugality—and in the wilds of America, I learnt love.
AMELIA. Is there any country where love is taught?
COUNT. In all barbarous countries. But the whole system is exploded in places that are civilized
AMELIA. And what is substituted in its stead?
COUNT. Intrigue.
AMELIA. What a poor, uncomfortable substitute!
COUNT. There are other things—Song, dance, the opera, and war.

[*Since the entrance of the* COUNT, *the* BARON *has removed to a table at a little distance.*]

BARON. What are you talking of there?
COUNT. Of war, Colonel.
BARON. [*Rising.*] Ay, we like to talk on what we don't understand.
COUNT. [*Rising.*] Therefore, to a lady, I always speak of politics; and to her father, on love.
BARON. I believe, Count, notwithstanding your sneer, I am still as much of a proficient in that art as yourself.
COUNT. I do not doubt it, my dear Colonel, for you are a soldier: and, since the days of Alexander, whoever conquers men, is certain to overcome women.

BARON. An achievement to animate a poltron.

COUNT. And, I verily believe, gains more recruits than the king's pay.

BARON. Now we are on the subject of arms, should you like to go out a shooting with me for an hour before dinner?

COUNT. Bravo, Colonel! A charming thought! This will give me an opportunity to use my elegant gun: the butt is inlaid with mother-of-pearl. You cannot find better work, or better taste.—Even my coat of arms is engraved.

BARON. But can you shoot?

COUNT. That I have never tried—except, with my eyes, at a fine woman.

BARON. I am not particular what game I pursue.—I have an old gun; it does not look fine; but I can always bring down my bird.

[*Enter* SERVANT.]

SERV. Mr. Anhalt begs leave ——

BARON. Tell him to come in.—I shall be ready in a moment.

[*Exit* SERVANT.]

COUNT. Who is Mr. Anhalt?

AMELIA. Oh, a very good man. [*With warmth.*]

COUNT. A good man! In Italy, that means a religious man; in France, it means a cheerful man; in Spain, it means a wise man; and in England, it means a rich man.—Which good man of all these is Mr. Anhalt?

AMELIA. A good man in every country, except England.

COUNT. And give me the English good man, before that of any other nation.

BARON. And of what nation would you prefer your good woman to be, Count?

COUNT. Of Germany [*Bowing to* AMELIA.]

AMELIA. In compliment to me?

COUNT. In justice to my own judgment.

BARON. Certainly. For have we not an instance of one German woman, who possesses every virtue that ornaments the whole sex; whether as a woman of illustrious rank, or in the more exalted character of a wife, and a mother?

[*Enter* MR. ANHALT.]

ANHALT. I come by your command, Baron ——

BARON. Quick, Count.—Get your elegant gun.—I pass your apartments, and will soon call for you.

COUNT. I fly.—Beautiful Amelia, it is a sacrifice I make to your father, that I leave for a few hours his amiable daughter. [*Exit.*]

BARON. My dear Amelia, I think it scarcely necessary to speak to Mr.

Anhalt, or that he should speak to you, on the subject of the Count; but as he is here, leave us alone.

AMELIA. [*As she retires.*] Good morning, Mr. Anhalt.—I hope you are very well. [*Exit.*]

BARON. I'll tell you in a few words, why I sent for you. Count Cassel is here, and wishes to marry my daughter.

ANHALT. [*Much concerned.*] Really!

BARON. He is—he—in a word, I don't like him.

ANHALT. [*With emotion.*] And Miss Wildenhaim——

BARON. I shall not command, neither persuade her to the marriage—I know too well the fatal influence of parents on such a subject. Objections to be sure, if they could be removed—But when you find a man's head without brains, and his bosom without a heart, these are important articles to supply. Young as you are, Anhalt, I know no one so able to restore, or to bestow, those blessings on his fellow creatures, as you. [ANHALT *bows.*] The Count wants a little of my daughter's simplicity and sensibility.—Take him under your care while he is here, and make him something like yourself.—You have succeeded to my wish in the education of my daughter.—Form the Count after your own manner.—I shall then have what I have sighed for all my life—a son.

ANHALT. With your permission, Baron, I will ask one question. What remains to interest you in favour of a man, whose head and heart are good for nothing?

BARON. Birth and fortune. Yet, if I thought my daughter absolutely disliked him, or that she loved another, I would not thwart a first affection;—no, for the world, I would not. [*Sighing.*] But that her affections are already bestowed, is not probable.

ANHALT. Are you of opinion, that she will never fall in love?

BARON. Oh! no. I am of opinion, no woman ever arrived at the age of twenty without that misfortune.—But this is another subject.—Go to Amelia—explain to her the duties of a wife, and of a mother.—If she comprehends them, as she ought, then ask her, if she thinks she could fulfil those duties, as the wife of Count Cassel.

ANHALT. I will.—But—I—Miss Wildenhaim—[*Confused.*] I—I shall—I —I shall obey your commands.

BARON. Do so. [*Gives a deep sigh.*] Ah! so far this weight is removed; but there lies still a heavier next my heart.—You understand me.— How is it, Mr. Anhalt? Have you not yet been able to make any discoveries on that unfortunate subject?

ANHALT. I have taken infinite pains; but in vain. No such person is to be found.

BARON. Believe me, this burthen presses on my thoughts so much, that many nights I go without sleep. A man is sometimes tempted to commit such depravity when young.—Oh, Anhalt! had I, in my youth, had you for a tutor;—but I had no instructor but my passions; no governor but my own will. [*Exit.*]

ANHALT. This commission of the Baron's, in respect to his daughter, I am—[*Looks about.*]—If I should meet her now, I cannot—I must recover myself first, and then prepare.—A walk in the fields, and a fervent prayer—After these, I trust, I shall return, as a man, whose views are solely placed on a future world; all hopes in this, with fortitude resigned. [*Exit.*]

Act the Third

SCENE I

An open Field.

[FREDERICK *alone, with a few pieces of money, which he turns about in his hands.*]

FRED. To return with this trifle, for which I have stooped to beg! return to see my mother dying! I would rather fly to the world's end. [*Looking at the money.*] What can I buy with this? It is hardly enough to pay for the nails, that will be wanted for her coffin. My great anxiety will drive me to distraction. However, let the consequence of our affliction be what it may, all will fall upon my father's head; and may he pant for Heaven's forgiveness, as my poor mother —— [*At a distance is heard the firing of a gun, then the cry of halloo, halloo—* GAMEKEEPER *and* SPORTSMEN *run across the stage—he looks about.*] Here they come—a nobleman, I suppose, or a man of fortune. Yes, yes—and I will once more beg for my mother.—May Heaven send relief!

[*Enter the* BARON, *followed slowly by the* COUNT. *The* BARON *stops.*]

BARON. Quick, quick, Count! Aye, aye, that was a blunder, indeed. Don't you see the dogs? There they run—they have lost the scent.

[*Exit* BARON, *looking after the dogs.*]

COUNT. So much the better, Colonel, for I must take a little breath.

[*He leans on his gun—*FREDERICK *goes up to him with great modesty.*]

FRED. Gentleman, I beg you will bestow from your superfluous wants something to relieve the pain, and nourish the weak frame, of an expiring woman.

[*The* BARON *re-enters.*]

COUNT. What police is here! that a nobleman's amusements should be interrupted by the attack of vagrants.

FRED. [*To the* BARON.] Have pity, noble sir, and relieve the distress of an unfortunate son, who supplicates for his dying mother.

BARON. [*Taking out his purse.*] I think, young soldier, it would be better if you were with your regiment on duty, instead of begging.

FRED. I would with all my heart: but at this present moment my sorrows are too great.—[BARON *gives something.*] I entreat your pardon. What you have been so good as to give me, is not enough.

BARON. [*Surprised.*] Not enough!

FRED. No, it is not enough.

COUNT. The most singular beggar I ever met in all my travels.

FRED. If you have a charitable heart, give me one dollar.

BARON. This is the first time I was ever dictated by a beggar what to give him.

FRED. With one dollar you will save a distracted man.

BARON. I don't choose to give any more. Count, go on.

[*Exit* COUNT—*as the* BARON *follows,* FREDERICK *seizes him by the breast, and draws his sword.*]

FRED. Your purse, or your life.

BARON. [*Calling.*] Here! here! seize and secure him.

[*Some of the* GAMEKEEPERS *run on, lay hold of* FREDERICK, *and disarm him.*]

FRED. What have I done!

BARON. Take him to the castle, and confine him in one of the towers. I shall follow you immediately.

FRED. One favour I have to beg, one favour only.—I know that I am guilty, and am ready to receive the punishment, my crime deserves. But I have a mother, who is expiring for want—pity her, if you cannot pity me—bestow on her relief. If you will send to yonder hut, you will find that I do not impose on you a falsehood. For her it was I drew my sword—for her I am ready to die.

BARON. Take him away, and imprison him where I told you.

FRED. [*As he is forced off.*] Woe to that man, to whom I owe my birth. [*Exit.*]

BARON. [*Calls another* KEEPER.] Here, Frank, run directly to yonder hamlet, inquire in the first, second, and third, cottage for a poor sick woman—and if you really find such a person, give her this purse.

[*Exit* GAMEKEEPER.]

BARON. A most extraordinary event!—and what a well-looking youth! something in his countenance and address, which struck me inconceivably!—If it is true, that he begged for his mother—But if he did——for the attempt upon my life, he must die. Vice is never half so dangerous, as when it assumes the garb of morality.   [*Exit.*]

SCENE II

A room in the Castle.

[AMELIA *alone.*]

AMELIA. Why am I so uneasy; so peevish; who has offended me? I did not mean to come into this room. In the garden I intended to go. [*Going, turns back.*] No, I will not—yes, I will—just go, and look if my auriculas are still in blossom; and if the apple-tree is grown, which Mr. Anhalt planted.—I feel very low-spirited—something must be the matter.—Why do I cry?—Am I not well?

[*Enter* MR. ANHALT.]

Ah! good morning, my dear sir—Mr. Anhalt, I meant to say—I beg pardon.

ANHALT. Never mind, Miss Wildenhaim—I don't dislike to hear you call me as you did.

AMELIA. In earnest!

ANHALT. Really. You have been crying. May I know the reason? The loss of your mother, still?—

AMELIA. No—I have left off crying for her.

ANHALT. I beg pardon if I have come at an improper hour; but I wait upon you by the commands of your father.

AMELIA. You are welcome at all hours. My father has more than once told me, that he, who forms my mind, I should always consider as my greatest benefactor. [*Looking down.*] And my heart tells me the same.

ANHALT. I think myself amply rewarded by the good opinion you have of me.

AMELIA. When I remember what trouble I have sometimes given you, I cannot be too grateful.

ANHALT. [*To himself*] Oh! Heavens! [*To* AMELIA.] I—I come from your father with a commission.—If you please, we will sit down [*He places chairs, and they sit*] Count Cassel is arrived.

AMELIA. Yes I know.

ANHALT. And do you know for what reason?

AMELIA. He wishes to marry me.

ANHALT. Does he? [*Hastily.*] But, believe me, the Baron will not persuade you—No, I am sure he will not.

AMELIA. I know that.

ANHALT. He wishes, that I should ascertain whether you have an inclination —

AMELIA. For the Count, or for matrimony, do you mean?

ANHALT. For matrimony.

AMELIA. All things, that I don't know, and don't understand, are quite indifferent to me.

ANHALT. For that very reason I am sent to you to explain the good and the bad, of which matrimony is composed.

AMELIA. Then I beg first to be acquainted with the good.

ANHALT. When two sympathetic hearts meet in the marriage state, matrimony may be called a happy life. When such a wedded pair find thorns in their path, each will be eager, for the sake of the other, to tear them from the root. Where they have to mount hills, or wind a labyrinth, the most experienced will lead the way, and be a guide to his companion. Patience and love will accompany them in their journey, while melancholy and discord they leave far behind.—Hand in hand they pass on from morning till evening, through their summer's day, till the night of age draws on, and the sleep of death overtakes the one. The other, weeping and mourning, yet looks forward to the bright region, where he shall meet his still surviving partner, among trees and flowers, which themselves have planted, in the fields of eternal verdure.

AMELIA. You may tell my father—I'll marry. [*Rises.*]

ANHALT. [*Rising.*] This picture is pleasing; but I must beg you not to forget, that there is another on the same subject.—When convenience, and fair appearance joined to folly and ill humour, forge the fetters of matrimony, they gall with their weight the married pair. Discontented with each other—at variance in opinions—their mutual aversion increases with the years they live together. They contend most, where they should most unite; torment, where they should most soothe. In this rugged way, choked with the weeds of suspicion, jealousy, anger, and hatred, they take their daily journey, till one of these also sleep in death. The other then lifts up his dejected head, and calls out in acclamations of joy—Oh, liberty! dear liberty!

AMELIA. I will not marry.

ANHALT. You mean to say, you will not fall in love.

AMELIA. Oh no! [*Ashamed.*] I am in love.

ANHALT. Are in love! [*Starting.*] And with the Count?

AMELIA. I wish I was.

ANHALT. Why so?

AMELIA. Because *he* would, perhaps, love me again.

ANHALT. [*Warmly.*] Who is there that would not?

AMELIA. Would you?

ANHALT. I—I—me—I—I am out of the question.

AMELIA. No; you are the very person to whom I have put the question.

ANHALT. What do you mean?

AMELIA. I am glad you don't understand me. I was afraid I had spoken too plain. [*In confusion.*]

ANHALT. Understand you!—As to that—I am not dull.

AMELIA. I know you are not—And as you have for a long time instructed me, why should not I now begin to teach you?

ANHALT. Teach me what?

AMELIA. Whatever I know, and you don't.

ANHALT. There are some things, I had rather never know.

AMELIA. So you may remember I said, when you began to teach me mathematics. I said, I had rather not know it—But now I have learnt it, it gives me a great deal of pleasure—and [*Hesitating.*] perhaps, who can tell, but that I might teach something as pleasant to you, as resolving a problem is to me.

ANHALT. Woman herself is a problem.

AMELIA. And I'll teach you to make her out.

ANHALT. You teach?

AMELIA. Why not? None but a woman can teach the science of herself: and though I own I am very young, a young woman may be as agreeable for a tutoress as an old one.—I am sure I always learnt faster from you than from the old clergyman, who taught me before you came.

ANHALT. This is nothing to the subject!

AMELIA. What is the subject?

ANHALT. ——— Love.

AMELIA. [*Going up to him.*] Come, then, teach it me—teach it me as you taught me geography, languages, and other important things.

ANHALT. [*Turning from her.*] Pshaw!

AMELIA. Ah! you won't—You know you have already taught me that, and you won't begin again.

ANHALT. You misconstrue—you misconceive every thing, I say or do. The subject I came to you upon was marriage.

AMELIA. A very proper subject for the man, who has taught me love, and I accept the proposal.

[*Courtesying.*]

ANHALT. Again you misconceive and confound me.

AMELIA. Ay, I see how it is—You have no inclination to experience with me "the good part of matrimony:" I am not the female, with whom you would like to go "hand in hand up hills, and through labyrinths"—with whom you would like to "root up thorns; and with whom you would delight to plant lilies and roses." No, you had rather call out, "Oh, liberty! dear liberty!"

ANHALT. Why do you force from me, what it is villanous to own?—I love you more than life—Oh, Amelia! had we lived in those golden times, which the poets picture, no one but you —— But, as the world is changed, your birth and fortune make our union impossible—To preserve the character, and, more, the feelings of an honest man, I would not marry you without the consent of your father—And could I, dare I, propose it to him?

AMELIA. He has commanded me never to conceal or disguise the truth. I will propose it to him. The subject of the Count will force me to speak plainly, and this will be the most proper time, while he can compare the merit of you both.

ANHALT. I conjure you not to think of exposing yourself and me to his resentment.

AMELIA. It is my father's will that I should marry—It is my father's wish to see me happy—If, then, you love me as you say, I will marry; and will be happy—but only with you.—I will tell him this.—At first he will start; then grow angry; then be in a passion—In his passion he will call me "undutiful:" but he will soon recollect himself, and resume his usual smiles, saying, "Well, well, if he love you, and you love him, in the name of Heaven, let it be."—Then I shall hug him round the neck, kiss his hands, run away from him, and fly to you; it will soon be known, that I am your bride, the whole village will come to wish me joy, and Heaven's blessing will follow.

[*Enter* VERDUN, *the Butler.*]

AMELIA. [*Discontented.*] Ah! is it you?

BUTLER. Without vanity, I have taken the liberty to enter this apartment, the moment the good news reached my ears.

AMELIA. What news?

BUTLER. Pardon an old servant, your father's old butler, gracious lady, who has had the honour to carry the Baron in his arms—and afterwards with humble submission to receive many a box o' the ear from you—if he thinks it his duty to make his congratulations with due reverence on this happy day, and to join with the muses in harmonious tunes on the lyre.

AMELIA. Oh! my good butler, I am not in a humour to listen to the muses, and your lyre.

BUTLER. There has never been a birth-day, nor wedding-day, nor christening-day, celebrated in your family, in which I have not joined with the muses in full chorus.—In forty-six years, three hundred and ninety-seven congratulations on different occasions have dropped from my pen. To-day, the three hundred and ninety-eighth is coming forth;—for Heaven has protected our noble master, who has been in great danger.

AMELIA. Danger! My father in danger! What do you mean?

BUTLER. One of the gamekeepers has returned to inform the whole castle of a base and knavish trick, of which the world will talk, and my poetry hand down to posterity.

AMELIA. What, what is all this?

BUTLER. The Baron, my lord and master, in company with the strange

Count, had not been gone a mile beyond the lawn, when one of them ——

AMELIA. What happened? Speak, for Heaven's sake!

BUTLER. My verse shall tell you.

AMELIA. No, no; tell us in prose.

ANHALT. Yes, in prose.

BUTLER. Ah, you have neither of you ever been in love, or you would prefer poetry to prose. But excuse [*Pulls out a paper.*] the haste in which it was written. I heard the news in the fields—always have paper and a pencil about me, and composed the whole forty lines crossing the meadows and the park in my way home. [*Reads.*]

> *Oh Muse, ascend the forked mount,*
> *And lofty strains prepare,*
> *About a Baron and a Count,*
> *Who went to hunt the hare.*
>
> *The hare she ran with utmost speed,*
> *And sad and anxious looks,*
> *Because the furious hounds indeed*
> *Were near to her, gadzooks.*
>
> *At length the Count and Baron bold*
> *Their footsteps homeward bended;*
> *For why, because, as you were told,*
> *The hunting it was ended.*
>
> *Before them strait a youth appears,*
> *Who made a piteous pother,*
> *And told a tale with many tears,*
> *About his dying mother.*
>
> *The youth was in severe distress,*
> *And seem'd as he had spent all,*
> *He look'd a soldier by his dress,*
> *For that was regimental.*
>
> *The Baron's heart was full of ruth,*
> *And from his eye fell brine o!*
> *And soon he gave the mournful youth*
> *A little ready rino.*
>
> *He gave a shilling, as I live,*
> *Which sure, was mighty well;*
> *But to some people if you give*
> *An inch—they'll take an ell.*
>
> *The youth then drew his martial knife,*
> *And seiz'd the Baron's collar,*
> *He swore he'd have the Baron's life,*
> *Or else another dollar.*

Then did the Baron, in a fume,
  Soon raise a mighty din,
Whereon came butler, huntsman, groom,
  And eke the whipper-in.

Maugre this young man's warlike coat,
  They bore him off to prison;
And held so strongly by his throat,
  And almost stopp'd his whizzen.

Soon may a neckcloth, call'd a rope,
  Of robbing cure this elf;
If so, I'll write, without a trope,
  His dying speech myself.

And had the Baron chanc'd to die,
  Oh! grief to all the nation,
I must have made an elegy,
  And not this fine narration.

MORAL.

Henceforth let those who all have spent,
  And would by begging live,
Take warning here, and be content
  With what folks chuse to give.

AMELIA. Your muse, Mr. Butler, is in a very inventive humour this morning.

ANHALT. And your tale too improbable even for fiction.

BUTLER. Improbable! It's a real fact.

AMELIA. What, a robber in our grounds at noonday? Very likely indeed!

BUTLER. I don't say it was likely—I only say it is true.

ANHALT. No, no, Mr. Verdun, we find no fault with your poetry; but don't attempt to impose it upon us for truth.

AMELIA. Poets are allowed to speak falsehood, and we forgive yours.

BUTLER. I won't be forgiven, for I speak truth—and here the robber comes, in custody, to prove my words. [*Goes off, repeating*] "I'll write his dying speech myself."

AMELIA. Look! as I live, so he does—They come nearer; he's a young man, and has something interesting in his figure. An honest countenance, with grief and sorrow in his face. No, he is no robber—I pity him! Oh! look how the keepers drag him unmercifully into the tower—Now they lock it—Oh! how that poor, unfortunate man must feel!

ANHALT. [*Aside.*] Hardly worse than I do.

[*Enter the* BARON.]

AMELIA. [*Runs up to him.*] A thousand congratulations, my dear papa.

BARON. For Heaven's sake, spare your congratulations. The old butler, in coming up stairs, has already overwhelmed me with them.

ANHALT. Then, it is true, my lord? I could hardly believe the old man.

AMELIA. And the young prisoner, with all his honest looks, is a robber?

BARON. He is; but I verily believe for the first and last time. A most extraordinary event, Mr. Anhalt. This young man begged; then drew his sword upon me; but he trembled so, when he seized me by the breast, a child might have overpowered him. I almost wish he had made his escape—this adventure may cost him his life, and I might have preserved it with one dollar: but now, to save him would set a bad example.

AMELIA. Oh no! my lord, have pity on him! Plead for him, Mr. Anhalt.

BARON. Amelia, have you had any conversation with Mr. Anhalt?

AMELIA. Yes, my lord.

BARON. Respecting matrimony?

AMELIA. Yes; and I have told him ——

ANHALT. [*Very hastily.*] According to your commands, Baron ——

AMELIA. But he has conjured me ——

ANHALT. I have endeavoured, my lord, to find out ——

AMELIA. Yet, I am sure, dear papa, your affection for me ——

ANHALT. You wish to say something to me in your closet, my lord?

BARON. What the devil is all this conversation? You will not let one another speak—I don't understand either of you.

AMELIA. Dear father, have you not promised you will not thwart my affections when I marry, but suffer me to follow their dictates?

BARON. Certainly.

AMELIA. Do you hear, Mr. Anhalt?

ANHALT. I beg pardon—I have a person who is waiting for me—I am obliged to retire.

[*Exit in confusion.*]

BARON. [*Calls after him.*] I shall expect you in my closet. I am going there immediately.

[*Retiring towards the opposite door.*]

AMELIA. Pray, my lord, stop a few minutes longer: I have something of great importance to say to you.

BARON. Something of importance! to plead for the young man, I suppose! But that's a subject I must not listen to.   [*Exit.*]

AMELIA. I wish to plead for two young men—For one, that he may be let out of prison: for the other, that he may be made a prisoner for life. [*Looks out.*] The tower is still locked. How dismal it must be to be shut up in such a place! and perhaps—[*Calls.*] Butler! Butler!

come this way. I wish to speak to you. This young soldier has risked his life for his mother, and that accounts for the interest I take in his misfortunes.

[*Enter the* BUTLER.]

Pray, have you carried any thing to the prisoner to eat?

BUTLER. Yes.

AMELIA. What was it?

BUTLER. Some fine black bread; and water as clear as crystal.

AMELIA. Are you not ashamed! Even my father pities him. Go directly down to the kitchen, and desire the cook to give you something good and comfortable; and then go into the cellar for a bottle of wine.

BUTLER. Good and comfortable indeed!

AMELIA. And carry both to the tower.

BUTLER. I am willing at any time dear lady, to obey your orders; but, on this occasion, the prisoner's food must remain bread and water— It is the Baron's particular command.

AMELIA. Ah! My father was in the height of passion, when he gave it.

BUTLER. Whatsoever his passion might be, it is the duty of a true and honest dependent to obey his lord's mandates. I will not suffer a servant in this house, nor will I, myself, give the young man any thing except bread and water—But I'll tell you what I'll do—I'll read my verses to him.

AMELIA. Give me the key of the cellar—I'll go myself.

BUTLER. [*Gives the key.*] And there's my verses—[*Taking them from his pocket.*] carry them with you, they may comfort him as much as the wine. [*She throws them down.*]   [*Exit* AMELIA.]

BUTLER. [*In amazement.*] Not take them! Refuse to take them!—[*He lifts them from the floor with the utmost respect*]—

> "I must have made an elegy,
> And not this fine narration."   [*Exit.*]

Act the Fourth

SCENE I

A Prison in one of the Towers of the Castle.

[FREDERICK *alone.*]

FRED. How a few moments destroy the happiness of a man! When I, this morning, set out from my inn, and saw the sun rise, I sung with joy.—Flattered with the hope of seeing my mother, I formed a scheme how I would lovingly surprise her. But, farewell all pleasant prospects—I return to my native country, and the first object I behold, is my dying parent; my first lodging, a prison; and my next walk will perhaps be—oh, merciful Providence! have I deserved all this?

[*Enter* AMELIA, *with a small basket covered with a napkin.—She speaks to some one without.*]

AMELIA. Wait there, Francis, I shall soon be back.

FRED. [*Hearing the door open, and turning round.*] Who's there?

AMELIA. You must be both hungry and thirsty, I fear.

FRED. Oh, no! neither.

AMELIA. Here is a bottle of wine, and something to eat. [*Places the basket on the table.*] I have often heard my father say, that wine is quite a cordial to the heart.

FRED. A thousand thanks, dear stranger. Ah! could I prevail on you to have it sent to my mother, who is upon her death-bed, under the roof of an honest peasant, called Hubert! Take it hence, my kind benefactress, and save my mother.

AMELIA. But first assure me, that you did not intend to murder my father.

FRED. Your father! Heaven forbid.—I meant but to preserve her life, who gave me mine.—Murder your father! No, no—I hope not.

AMELIA. And I thought not—or, if you had murdered any one, you had better have killed the Count; nobody would have missed him.

FRED. Who, may I inquire, were those gentlemen, whom I hoped to frighten into charity?

AMELIA. Ay, if you only intended to frighten them, the Count was the very person for your purpose. But you caught hold of the other gentleman.—And could you hope to intimidate Baron Wildenhaim?

FRED. Baron Wildenhaim?—Almighty powers!

AMELIA. What's the matter?

FRED. The man to whose breast I held my sword— [*Trembling.*]

AMELIA. Was Baron Wildenhaim—the owner of this estate—my father!

FRED. [*With the greatest emotion.*] My father!

AMELIA. Good Heaven, how he looks! I am afraid he's mad. Here! Francis, Francis. [*Exit, calling.*]

FRED. [*All agitation.*] My father! Eternal Judge! thou dost not slumber! The man, against whom I drew my sword this day, was my father! One moment longer, and provoked, I might have been the murderer of my father! [*Sinks down on a chair.*]

[*Enter* MR. ANHALT.]

Welcome, sir! By your dress you are of the church, and consequently a messenger of comfort. You are most welcome, sir.

ANHALT. I wish to bring comfort, and avoid upbraidings; for your own conscience will reproach you more than the voice of a preacher. From the sensibility of your countenance, together with a language and address superior to the vulgar, it appears, young man, you have had an education, which should have preserved you from a state like this.

FRED. My education I owe to my mother. Filial love, in return, has plunged me into the state you see. A civil magistrate will condemn according to the law—A priest, in judgment, is not to consider the act itself, but the impulse, which led to the act.

ANHALT. I shall judge with all the lenity my religion dictates: and you are the prisoner of a nobleman, who compassionates you for the affection which you bear towards your mother; for he has sent to the village where you directed him, and has found the account you have relating to her true.—With this impression in your favour, it is my advice, that you endeavour to see and supplicate the Baron for your release from prison, and all the peril of his justice.

FRED. [Starting.] I—I see the Baron! I!—I supplicate for my deliverance.—Will you favour me with his name?—Is it not Baron ——

ANHALT. Baron Wildenhaim.

FRED. Baron Wildenhaim! He lived formerly in Alsace?

ANHALT. The same.—About a year after the death of his wife, he left Alsace; and arrived here a few weeks ago to take possession of this his paternal estate.

FRED. So! his wife is dead;—and that generous young lady, who came to my prison just now, is his daughter?

ANHALT. Miss Wildenhaim, his daughter.

FRED. And that young gentleman, I saw with him this morning, is his son?

ANHALT. He has no son.

FRED. [Hastily.] Oh, yes, he has—[Recollecting himself.]—I mean him that was out shooting to-day.

ANHALT. He is not his son.

FRED. [To himself.] Thank Heaven!

ANHALT. He is only a visitor.

FRED. I thank you for this information; and if you will undertake to procure me a private interview with Baron Wildenhaim ——

ANHALT. Why private? However, I will venture to take you for a short time from this place, and introduce you; depending on your innocence, or your repentance—on his conviction in your favour, or his mercy towards your guilt. Follow me.   [Exit.]

FRED. [Following.] I have beheld an affectionate parent in deep adversity.—Why should I tremble thus?—Why doubt my fortitude, in the presence of an unnatural parent in prosperity?   [Exit.]

A Room in the Castle.

[*Enter* BARON WILDENHAIM *and* AMELIA.]

BARON. I hope you judge more favourably of Count Cassel's understanding, since the private interview you have had with him. Confess
to me the exact effect of the long conference between you.

AMELIA. To make me hate him.

BARON. What has he done?

AMELIA. Oh! told me of such barbarous deeds he has committed.

BARON. What deeds?

AMELIA. Made vows of love to so many women, that, on his marriage
with me, a hundred female hearts will at least be broken.

BARON. Pshaw! do you believe him?

AMELIA. Suppose I do not; is it to his honour that I believe he tells a
falsehood?

BARON. He is mistaken merely.

AMELIA. Indeed, my lord, in one respect I am sure he speaks truth. For
our old butler told my waiting-maid of a poor young creature who
has been deceived, undone; and she, and her whole family, involved
in shame and sorrow by his perfidy.

BARON. Are you sure the butler said this?

AMELIA. See him, and ask him. He knows the whole story, indeed he
does; the names of the persons, and every circumstance.

BARON. Desire he may be sent to me.

AMELIA. [*Goes to the door and calls.*] Order old Verdun to come to the
Baron directly.

BARON. I know tale-bearers are apt to be erroneous. I'll hear from himself the account you speak of.

AMELIA. I believe it is in verse.

BARON. [*Angry.*] In verse!

AMELIA. But, then, indeed it's true.

[*Enter* BUTLER.]

AMELIA. Verdun, pray have you not some true poetry?

BUTLER. All my poetry is true—and so far, better than some people's
prose.

BARON. But I want prose on this occasion, and command you to give
me nothing else. [BUTLER *bows.*] Have you heard of an engagement
which Count Cassel is under to any other woman than my daughter?

BUTLER. I am to tell your honour in prose?

BARON. Certainly. [BUTLER *appears uneasy and loath to speak.*] Amelia,
he does not like to divulge what he knows in presence of a third
person—leave the room. [*Exit* AMELIA.]

BUTLER. No, no—that did not cause my reluctance to speak.

BARON. What then?

BUTLER. Your not allowing me to speak in verse—for here is the poetic poem. [*Holding up a paper.*]

BARON. How dare you pretend to contend with my will? Tell me in plain language all you know on the subject I have named.

BUTLER. Well then, my lord, if you must have the account in quiet prose, thus it was—Phœbus, one morning, rose in the east, and having handed in the long-expected day, he called up his brother Hymen——

BARON. Have done with your rhapsody.

BUTLER. Ay; I knew you'd like it best in verse—

> There liv'd a lady in this land,
>   Whose charms the heart made tingle;
> At church she had not given her hand,
>   And therefore still was single.

BARON. Keep to prose.

BUTLER. I will, my lord; but I have repeated it so often in verse, I scarce know how.—Count Cassel, influenced by the designs of Cupid in his very worst humour.

> "Count Cassel woo'd this maid so rare,
>   And in her eye found grace;
> And if his purpose was not fair,"

BARON. No verse.

BUTLER. "*It probably was base.*"
I beg your pardon, my lord; but the verse will intrude, in spite of my efforts to forget it. 'Tis as difficult for me at times to forget, as 'tis for other men at times to remember. But in plain truth, my lord, the Count was treacherous, cruel, forsworn.

BARON. I am astonished!

BUTLER. And would be more so if you would listen to the whole poem. [*Most earnestly.*] Pray, my lord, listen to it.

BARON. You know the family? All the parties?

BUTLER. I will bring the father of the damsel to prove the veracity of my muse. His name is Baden—poor old man!

> "The sire consents to bless the pair,
>   And names the nuptial day,
> When, lo! the bridegroom was not there,
>   Because he was away."

BARON. But tell me—Had the father his daughter's innocence to deplore?

BUTLER. Ah! my lord, ah! and you *must* hear that part in rhyme. Loss of innocence never sounds well except in verse.

> *"For, ah! the very night before,*
>   *No prudent guard upon her,*
> *The Count he gave her oaths a score,*
>   *And took in change her honour.*

MORAL.
> *Then you, who now lead single lives,*
>   *From this sad tale beware;*
> *And do not act as you were wives,*
>   *Before you really are."*

[*Enter* COUNT CASSEL.]

BARON. [*To the* BUTLER.] Leave the room instantly.

COUNT. Yes, good Mr. family poet, leave the room, and take your dog-gerels with you.

BUTLER. Don't affront my poem, your honour; for I am indebted to you for the plot.

> *"The Count he gave her oaths a score,*
>   *And took in change her honour."*
> [*Exit* BUTLER.]

BARON. Count, you see me agitated.

COUNT. What can be the cause?

BARON. I'll not keep you in doubt a moment. You are accused, sir, of being engaged to another woman, while you offer marriage to my child.

COUNT. To only *one* other woman?

BARON. What do you mean?

COUNT. My meaning is, that when a man is young and rich, has trav-elled, and is no personal object of disapprobation,—to have made vows but to one woman is an absolute slight upon the rest of the sex.

BARON. Without evasion, sir, do you know the name of Baden? Was there ever a promise of marriage made by you to his daughter? An-swer me plainly: or must I take a journey to inquire of the father?

COUNT. No—he can tell you no more than, I dare say, you already know; and which I shall not contradict.

BARON. Amazing insensibility! And can you hold your head erect, while you acknowledge perfidy?

COUNT. My dear Baron,—if every man, who deserves to have a charge such as this brought against him, was not permitted to look up—it is a doubt whom we might not meet crawling on all fours.

[*He accidentally taps the* BARON'S *shoulder.*]

BARON. [*Starts—recollects himself—then in a faultering voice.*] Yet—nevertheless—the act is so atrocious—

COUNT. But nothing new.

BARON. [*Faintly.*] Yes—I hope—I hope it is new.

COUNT. What, did you never meet with such a thing before?

BARON. [*Agitated.*] If I have—I pronounced the man, who so offended
—a villain.

COUNT. You are singularly scrupulous. I question if the man thought
himself so.

BARON. Yes he did.

COUNT. How do you know?

BARON. [*Hesitating.*] I have heard him say so.

COUNT. But he ate, drank, and slept, I suppose?

BARON. [*Confused.*] Perhaps he did.

COUNT. And was merry with his friends; and his friends as fond of him
as ever?

BARON. Perhaps [*Confused.*]—perhaps they were.

COUNT. And perhaps he now and then took upon him to lecture young
men for their gallantries?

BARON. Perhaps he did.

COUNT. Why, then, after all, Baron, your villain is a mighty good, prudent, honest fellow; and I have no objection to your giving me that
name.

BARON. But do you not think of some atonement to the unfortunate
girl?

COUNT. Did *your* villain atone?

BARON. No: when his reason was matured, he wished to make some
recompense, but his endeavours were too late.

COUNT. I will follow his example, and wait till my reason is matured,
before I think myself competent to determine what to do.

BARON. And till that time I defer your marriage with my daughter.

COUNT. Would you delay her happiness so long? Why, my dear Baron,
considering the fashionable life I lead, it may be these ten years
before my judgment arrives to its necessary standard.

BARON. I have the head-ache, Count—These tidings have discomposed,
disordered me—I beg your absence for a few minutes.

COUNT. I obey—And let me assure you, my lord, that, although, from
the extreme delicacy of your honour, you have ever through life
shuddered at seduction; yet, there are constitutions, and there are
circumstances, in which it can be palliated.

BARON. Never.   [*Violently.*]

COUNT. Not in a grave, serious, reflecting man such as *you*, I grant. But
in a gay, lively, inconsiderate, flimsy, frivolous coxcomb, such as
myself, it is excusable: for me to keep my word to a woman, would
be deceit: 'tis not expected of me. It is in my character to break oaths
in love; as it is in your nature, my lord, never to have spoken any
thing but wisdom and truth.   [*Exit.*]

BARON. Could I have thought a creature so insignificant as that, had
power to excite sensations such as I feel at present! I am, indeed,

worse than he is, as much as the crimes of a man exceed those of an idiot.

[*Enter* AMELIA.]

AMELIA. I heard the Count leave you, my lord, and so I am come to inquire——

BARON. [*Sitting down, and trying to compose himself.*] You are not to marry Count Cassel—And now, mention his name to me no more.

AMELIA. I won't—indeed I won't—for I hate his name.—But thank you, my dear father, for this good news. [*Draws a chair, and sits on the opposite side of the table, on which he leans.—After a pause.*] And who am I to marry?

BARON. [*His head on his hand.*] I can't tell.

[AMELIA *appears to have something on her mind which she wishes to disclose.*]

AMELIA. I never liked the Count.

BARON. No more did I.

AMELIA. [*After a pause.*] I think love comes just as it pleases, without being asked.

BARON. [*In deep thought.*] It does so.

AMELIA. [*After another pause.*] And there are instances, where, perhaps, the object of love makes the passion meritorious.

BARON. To be sure there are.

AMELIA. For example; my affection for Mr. Anhalt as my tutor.

BARON. Right.

AMELIA. [*After another pause.*] I should like to marry.   [*Sighing.*]

BARON. So you shall. [*A pause.*] It is proper for every body to marry.

AMELIA. Why, then, does not Mr. Anhalt marry?

BARON. You must ask him that question yourself.

AMELIA. I have.

BARON. And what did he say?

AMELIA. Will you give me leave to tell you what he said?

BARON. Certainly.

AMELIA. And what I said to him?

BARON. Certainly.

AMELIA. And won't you be angry?

BARON. Undoubtedly not.

AMELIA. Why, then—you know you commanded me never to disguise or conceal the truth.

BARON. I did so.

AMELIA. Why, then he said——

BARON. What did he say?

AMELIA. He said—he would not marry me without your consent for the world.

BARON. [*Starting from his chair.*] And pray, how came this the subject of your conversation?

AMELIA. [*Rising.*] I brought it up.

BARON. And what did you say?

AMELIA. I said, that birth and fortune were such old-fashioned things to me, I cared nothing about either: and that I had once heard my father declare he should consult my happiness in marrying me, beyond any other consideration.

BARON. I will once more repeat to you my sentiments. It is the custom in this country for the children of nobility to marry only with their equals; but as my daughter's content is more dear to me than an ancient custom, I would bestow you on the first man I thought calculated to make you happy; by this I do not mean to say, that I should not be severely nice in the character of the man to whom I gave you; and Mr. Anhalt, from his obligations to me, and his high sense of honour, thinks too nobly——

AMELIA. Would it not be noble to make the daughter of his benefactor happy?

BARON. But when that daughter is a child, and thinks like a child——

AMELIA. No, indeed, papa, I begin to think very like a woman. Ask *him* if I don't.

BARON. Ask him! You feel gratitude for the instructions you have received from him, and you fancy it love.

AMELIA. Are there two gratitudes?

BARON. What do you mean?

AMELIA. Because I feel gratitude to you; but that is very unlike the gratitude I feel towards him.

BARON. Indeed!

AMELIA. Yes; and then he feels another gratitude towards me. What's that?

BARON. Has he told you so?

AMELIA. Yes.

BARON. That was not right of him.

AMELIA. Oh! if you did but know how I surprised him!

BARON. Surprised him!

AMELIA. He came to me by your command, to examine my heart respecting Count Cassel. I told him, that I would never marry the Count.

BARON. But him?

AMELIA. Yes, him.

BARON. Very fine indeed! And what was his answer?

AMELIA. He talked of my rank in life; of my aunts and cousins; of my grandfather, and great grandmother; of his duty to you; and endeavoured to persuade me to think no more of him.

BARON. He acted honestly.

AMELIA. But not politely.

BARON. No matter.

AMELIA. Dear father! I shall never be able to love another—Never be happy with any one else. [*Throwing herself on her knees.*]

BARON. Rise, I insist.

[*As she rises, enter* ANHALT.]

ANHALT. My lord, forgive me! I have ventured, on the privilege of my office, as a minister of holy charity, to bring the poor soldier, whom your justice has arrested, into the adjoining room; and I presume to entreat you will admit him to your presence, and hear his apology, or his supplication.

BARON. Anhalt, you have done wrong. I pity the unhappy boy; but you know I cannot, must not, forgive him.

ANHALT. I beseech you then, my lord, to tell him so yourself. From your lips he may receive his doom with resignation.

AMELIA. Oh father! See him and take pity on him; his sorrows have made him frantic.

BARON. Leave the room, Amelia, I command you. [*On her attempting to speak, he raises his voice.*] Instantly.— [*Exit* AMELIA.]

ANHALT. He asked a private audience: perhaps he has some confession to make that may relieve his mind, and may be requisite for you to hear.

BARON. Well, bring him in,—and do you wait in the adjoining room, till our conference is over. I must then, sir, have a conference with you.

ANHALT. I shall obey your commands. [*He goes to the door, and re-enters with* FREDERICK. ANHALT *then retires at the same door.*]

BARON. [*Haughtily to* FREDERICK.] I know, young man, you plead your mother's wants in excuse for an act of desperation: but powerful as this plea might be in palliation of a fault, it cannot extenuate a crime like yours.

FRED. I have a plea for my conduct even more powerful than a mother's wants.

BARON. What's that?

FRED. My father's cruelty.

BARON. You have a father then?

FRED. I have, and a rich one—Nay, one that's reputed virtuous, and honourable. A great man, possessing estates and patronage in abundance; much esteemed at court, and beloved by his tenants; kind, benevolent, honest, generous—

BARON. And with all those great qualities, abandons you?

FRED. He does, with all the qualities I mention.

BARON. Your father may do right; a dissipated, desperate youth, whom kindness cannot draw from vicious habits, severity may.

FRED. You are mistaken—My father does not discard me for my vices

—He does not know me—has never seen me—He abandoned me, even before I was born.

BARON. What do you say?

FRED. The tears of my mother are all that I inherit from my father. Never has he protected or supported me—never protected her.

BARON. Why don't you apply to his relations?

FRED. They disown me, too—I am, they say, related to no one—All the world disclaim me, except my mother—and there again, I have to thank my father.

BARON. How so?

FRED. Because I am an illegitimate son.—My seduced mother has brought me up in patient misery. Industry enabled her to give me an education; but the days of my youth commenced with hardships, sorrow, and danger.—My companions lived happy around me, and had a pleasing prospect in their view, while bread and water only were my food, and no hopes joined to sweeten it. But my father felt not that!

BARON. [*To himself.*] He touches my heart.

FRED. After five years' absence from my mother, I returned this very day, and found her dying in the streets for want—Not even a hut to shelter her, or a pallet of straw—But my father feels not that! He lives in a palace, sleeps on the softest down, enjoys all the luxuries of the great; and, when he dies, a funeral sermon will praise his great benevolence, his christian charities.

BARON. [*Greatly agitated.*] What is your father's name?

FRED. —He took advantage of an innocent young woman, gained her affection by flattery and false promises; gave life to an unfortunate being,—who was on the point of murdering his father.

BARON. [*Shuddering.*] Who is he?

FRED. Baron Wildenhaim.

[*The* BARON'S *emotion expresses the sense of amazement, guilt, shame, and horror.*]

FRED. In this house did you rob my mother of her honour; and in this house I am a sacrifice for the crime. I am your prisoner—I will not be free—I am a robber—I give myself up.—You shall deliver me into the hands of justice—You shall accompany me to the spot of public execution. You shall hear in vain the chaplain's consolation and in-junctions. You shall find how I, in despair, will, to the last moment, call for retribution on my father.

BARON. Stop! Be pacified—

FRED. —And when you turn your head from my extended corse, you will behold my weeping mother.—Need I paint how her eyes will greet you?

BARON. Desist—barbarian, savage, stop!

[*Enter* ANHALT, *alarmed.*]

ANHALT. What do I hear? What is this?—Young man, I hope you have
not made a second attempt?
FRED. Yes; I have done what it was your place to do. I have made a
sinner tremble. [*Points to the* BARON, *and exit.*]
ANHALT. What can this mean?—I do not comprehend—
BARON. He is my son!—He is my son!—Go, Anhalt,—advise me—help
me—Go to the poor woman, his mother—He can show you the
way—make haste—speed to protect her—
ANHALT. But what am I to——
BARON. Go.—Your heart will tell you how to act. [*Exit* ANHALT.]
[BARON *distractedly.*] Who am I? What am I? Mad—raving—no—I
have a son—A son! The bravest—I will—I must—oh! [*With tenderness.*] Why have I not embraced him yet? [*Increasing his voice.*] why
not pressed him to my heart? Ah! see—[*Looking after him.*]—He flies
from the castle—Who's there? Where are my attendants?

[*Enter two* SERVANTS.]

Follow him—bring the prisoner back.—But observe my command—
treat him with respect—treat him as my son—and your master.
[*Exeunt.*]

Act the Fifth

SCENE I

Inside of the Cottage.

[AGATHA, COTTAGER, *and his* WIFE, *discovered.*]

AGATHA. Pray look and see if he is coming.
COT. It is of no use. I have been in the road; have looked up and down;
but neither see nor hear any thing of him.
WIFE. Have a little patience.
AGATHA. I wish you would step out once more—I think he cannot be
far off.
COT. I will; I will go. [*Exit.*]
WIFE. If your son knew what Heaven had sent you, he would be here
very soon.
AGATHA. I feel so anxious——
WIFE. But why? I should think a purse of gold, such as you have re-
ceived, would make any body easy.
AGATHA. Where can he be so long? He has been gone four hours. Some
ill must have befallen him.
WIFE. It is still broad day-light—don't think of any danger.—This eve-

ning we must all be merry. I'll prepare the supper. What a good gentleman our Baron must be! I am sorry I ever spoke a word against him.

AGATHA. How did he know I was here?

WIFE. Heaven only can tell. The servant that brought the money was
very secret.

AGATHA. [To herself.] I am astonished! I wonder! Oh! surely he has been
informed—Why else should he have sent so much money?

[Re-enter COTTAGER.]

AGATHA. Well!—not yet!

COT. I might look till I am blind for him—but I saw our new Rector
coming along the road; he calls in sometimes. May be, he will this
evening.

WIFE. He is a very good gentleman; pays great attention to his parishioners; and where he can assist the poor, he is always ready.

[Enter MR. ANHALT.]

ANHALT. Good evening, friends.

BOTH. Thank you, reverend sir.

[They both run to fetch a chair.]

ANHALT. I thank you, good people—I see you have a stranger here.

COT. Yes, your reverence; it is a poor sick woman, whom I took in
doors.

ANHALT. You will be rewarded for it. [To AGATHA.] May I beg leave to
ask your name?

AGATHA. Ah! If we were alone——

ANHALT. Good neighbours, will you leave us alone for a few minutes?
I have something to say to this poor woman.

COT. Wife, do you hear? Come along with me.

[Exeunt COTTAGER and his WIFE.]

ANHALT. Now——

AGATHA. Before I tell who I am, what I am, and what I was——I must
beg to ask——Are you of this country?

ANHALT. No—I was born in Alsace.

AGATHA. Did you know the late rector personally, whom you have
succeeded?

ANHALT. No.

AGATHA. Then you are not acquainted with my narrative?

ANHALT. Should I find you to be the person whom I have long been
in search of, your history is not altogether unknown to me.

AGATHA. "That you have been in search of!" Who gave you such a
commission?

ANHALT. A man, who, if it so prove, is much concerned for your misfortunes.

AGATHA. How? Oh, sir! tell me quickly—Whom do you think to find in me?

ANHALT. Agatha Friburg.

AGATHA. Yes, I am that unfortunate woman; and the man, who pretends to take concern in my misfortunes, is —— Baron Wildenhaim — he who betrayed me, abandoned me and my child, and killed my parents. He would now repair our sufferings with this purse of gold. [*Takes out the purse.*] Whatever may be your errand, sir, whether to humble, or to protect me, it is alike indifferent. I therefore request you to take this money to him, who sent it. Tell him, my honour has never been saleable. Tell him, destitute as I am, even indigence will not tempt me to accept charity from my seducer. He despised my heart—I despise his gold.—He has trampled on me.—I trample on his representative.

[*Throws the purse on the ground.*]

ANHALT. Be patient—I give you my word, that when the Baron sent this present to an unfortunate woman, for whom her son had supplicated, he did not know that woman was Agatha.

AGATHA. My son? what of my son!

ANHALT. Do not be alarmed—The Baron met with an affectionate son, who begged for his sick mother, and it affected him.

AGATHA. Begged of the Baron! of his father!

ANHALT. Yes; but they did not know each other; and the mother received the present on the son's account.

AGATHA. Did not know each other? Where is my son?

ANHALT. At the castle.

AGATHA. And still unknown?

ANHALT. Now he is known—an explanation has taken place; and I am sent here by the Baron, not to a stranger, but to Agatha Friburg—not with gold! his commission was —— "do what your heart directs you."

AGATHA. How is my Frederick? How did the Baron receive him?

ANHALT. I left him just in the moment the discovery was made. By this time your son is, perhaps, in the arms of his father.

AGATHA. Oh! is it possible, that a man, who has been near eighteen years deaf to the voice of nature, should change so suddenly?

ANHALT. I do not mean to justify the Baron. But—he has loved you—and fear of his noble kindred alone caused his breach of faith to you.

AGATHA. But to desert me wholly, and wed another—

ANHALT. War called him away—Wounded in the field, he was taken to the adjacent seat of a noble-man, whose only daughter by anxious attention to his recovery, won his gratitude; and, influenced by the advice of his worldly friends, he married. But no sooner was I re-

ceived into the family, and admitted to his confidence, than he related to me your story; and at times would exclaim in anguish—"The
proud imperious Baroness avenges the wrongs of my deserted Agatha." Again, when he presented me this living, and I left France to
take possession of it, his last words, before we parted, were—"The
moment you arrive at Wildenhaim, make all inquiries to find out
my poor Agatha." Every letter I afterwards received from him contained "Still, still, no tidings of my Agatha." And fate ordained it
should be so till this fortunate day.

AGATHA. What you have said has made my heart overflow—where will
this end?

ANHALT. I know not yet the Baron's intentions: but your sufferings demand immediate remedy; and one way only is left—Come with me
to the castle. Do not start—you shall be concealed in my apartments,
till you are called for.

AGATHA. I go to the Baron's;—No.

ANHALT. Go for the sake of your son—reflect, that his fortunes may
depend upon your presence.

AGATHA. And he is the only branch on which my hope still blossoms:
the rest are withered.—I will forget my wrongs as a woman, if the
Baron will atone to the mother—he shall have the woman's pardon,
if he will merit the mother's thanks—[*After a struggle.*]—I *will* go to
the castle—for the sake of my Frederick, go even to his father. But
where are my good host and hostess, that I may take leave, and thank
them for their kindness?

ANHALT. [*Taking up the purse which* AGATHA *had thrown down.*] Here,
good friend! Good woman!

[*Enter the* COTTAGER *and his* WIFE.]

WIFE. Yes, yes, here am I.

ANHALT. Good people, I will take your guest with me. You have acted
an honest part, and therefore receive this reward for your trouble.
[*He offers the purse to the* COTTAGER, *who puts it by, and turns away.*]

ANHALT. [*To the* WIFE.] Do *you* take it.

WIFE. I always obey my pastor. [*Taking it.*]

AGATHA. Good bye. [*Shaking hands with the* COTTAGERS.] For your
hospitality to me, may ye enjoy continued happiness!

COT. Fare you well—fare you well.

WIFE. If you find friends and get health, we won't trouble you to call
on us again: but if you should fall sick or be in poverty, we shall take
it very unkind if we don't see you.

[*Exeunt* AGATHA *and* ANHALT *on one side,* COTTAGER *and his* WIFE *on
the other.*]

SCENE II

A Room in the Castle.

[BARON *sitting upon a sofa.*—FREDERICK *standing near him, with one hand pressed between his—the* BARON *rises.*]

BARON. Been in battle too!—I am glad to hear it. You have known hard services, but now they are over, and joy and happiness will succeed.—The reproach of your birth shall be removed, for I will acknowledge you my son, and heir to my estate.

FRED. And my mother——

BARON. She shall live in peace and affluence. Do you think I would leave your mother unprovided, unprotected? No! About a mile from this castle I have an estate called Weldendorf—there she shall live, and call her own whatever it produces. There she shall reign, and be sole mistress of the little paradise. There her past sufferings shall be changed to peace and tranquillity. On a summer's morning, we, my son, will ride to visit her; pass a day, a week with her; and in this social intercourse time will glide pleasantly.

FRED. And, pray, my lord, under what name is my mother to live then?

BARON. [*Confused.*] How?

FRED. In what capacity?—As your domestic—or as——

BARON. That we will settle afterwards.

FRED. Will you allow me sir, to leave the room a little while, that you may have leisure to consider *now*?

BARON. I do not know how to explain myself in respect to your mother, more than I have done already.

FRED. My fate, whatever it may be, shall never part me from her's. My lord, it must be Frederick of Wildenhaim, and Agatha of Wildenhaim—or Agatha Friburg, and Frederick Friburg. This is my firm resolution, upon which I call Heaven to witness. [*Exit.*]

BARON. Young man!—Frederick!—[*Calling after him.*] Hasty indeed! would make conditions with his father. No, no, that must not be. I just now thought how well I had arranged my plans—had relieved my heart of every burden, when, a second time, he throws a mountain upon it. Stop, friend conscience, why do you take his part?—For near twenty years thus you have used me, and been my torture.

[*Enter* MR. ANHALT.]

Ah! Anhalt, I am glad you are come. My conscience and myself are at variance.

ANHALT. Your conscience is in the right.

BARON. You don't know yet what the quarrel is.

ANHALT. Conscience is always right—because it never speaks unless it *is* so

BARON. Ay, a man of your order can more easily attend to its whispers, than an old warrior. The sound of cannon has made him hard of hearing.—I have found my son again, Mr. Anhalt, a fine, brave young man—I mean to make him my heir—Am I in the right?

ANHALT. Perfectly.

BARON. And his mother shall live in happiness—My estate, Weldendorf, shall be her's—I'll give it to her, and she shall make it her residence. Don't I do right?

ANHALT. No.

BARON. [Surprised.] No? And what else should I do?

ANHALT. [Forcibly.] Marry her.

BARON. [Starting.] I marry her!

ANHALT. Baron Wildenhaim is a man, who will not act inconsistently —As this is my opinion, I expect your reasons, if you do not.

BARON. Would you have me marry a beggar?

ANHALT. [After a pause.] Is that your only objection?

BARON. [Confused.] I have more—many more.

ANHALT. May I entreat to know them likewise?

BARON. My birth!

ANHALT. Go on.

BARON. My relations would despise me.

ANHALT. Go on.

BARON. [In anger.] Sdeath! are not these reasons enough?—I know no other.

ANHALT. Now, then, it is my turn to state mine for the advice I have given you. But first I presume to ask a few questions.—Did Agatha, through artful insinuation, gain your affection? or did she give you cause to suppose her inconstant?

BARON. Neither—but for me, she had been always virtuous and good.

ANHALT. Did it cost you trouble and earnest entreaty to make her otherwise?

BARON. [Angrily.] Yes.

ANHALT. You pledged your honour?

BARON. [Confused.] Yes.

ANHALT. Called God to witness?

BARON. [More confused.] Yes.

ANHALT. The witness you called at that time was the Being, who sees you now. What you gave in pledge was your honour, which you must redeem. Therefore, thank Heaven that it is in your power to redeem it. By marrying Agatha the ransom's paid: and she brings a dower greater than any princess can bestow—peace to your conscience. If you then esteem the value of this portion, you will not hesitate a moment to exclaim,—Friends, wish me joy, I will marry Agatha.

[BARON, *in great agitation, walks backwards and forwards, then takes* ANHALT *by the hand.*]

BARON. "Friend, wish me joy—I will marry Agatha."

ANHALT. I do wish you joy.

BARON. Where is she?

ANHALT. In the castle—In my apartments here—I conducted her through the garden, to avoid curiosity.

BARON. Well, then, this is the wedding-day. This very evening you shall give us your blessing.

ANHALT. Not so soon, not so private. The whole village was witness of Agatha's shame—the whole village must be witness of Agatha's re-established honour. Do you consent to this?

BARON. I do.

ANHALT. Now the quarrel is decided. Now is your conscience quiet?

BARON. As quiet as an infant's. I only wish the first interview was over.

ANHALT. Compose yourself. Agatha's heart is to be your judge.

[*Enter* AMELIA.]

BARON. Amelia, you have a brother.

AMELIA. I have just heard so, my lord; and rejoice to find the news confirmed by you.

BARON. I know, my dear Amelia, I can repay you for the loss of Count Cassel; but what return can I make to you for the loss of half your fortune?

AMELIA. My brother's love will be ample recompense.

BARON. I will reward you better. Mr. Anhalt, the battle I have just fought, I owe to myself: the victory, I gained, I owe to you. A man of your principles, at once a teacher and an example of virtue, exalts his rank in life to a level with the noblest family—and I shall be proud to receive you as my son.

ANHALT. [*Falling on his knees, and taking the* BARON'S *hand.*] My lord, you overwhelm me with confusion, as well as with joy.

BARON. My obligations to you are infinite—Amelia shall pay the debt.

[*Gives her to him.*]

AMELIA. Oh, my dear father! [*Embracing the* BARON.] what blessings you have bestowed on me in one day. [*To* ANHALT.] I will be your scholar still, and use more diligence than ever to please my master.

ANHALT. His present happiness admits of no addition.

BARON. Nor does mine—And there is yet another task to perform that will require more fortitude, more courage, than this has done! A trial that—[*Bursts into tears.*]—I cannot prevent them—Let me—let me—A few minutes will bring me to myself—Where is Agatha?

ANHALT. I will go, and fetch her.

[*Exit* ANHALT *at an upper entrance.*]

BARON. Stop! Let me first recover a little. [*Walks up and down, sighing bitterly—looks at the door through which* ANHALT *left the room.*] That door she will come from—That was once the dressing-room of my mother—From that door I have seen her come many times—have been delighted with her lovely smiles—How shall I now behold her altered looks! Frederick must be my mediator.—Where is he?— Where is my son?—Now I am ready—my heart is prepared to receive her—Haste! haste! Bring her in.

[*He looks stedfastly at the door*—ANHALT *leads in* AGATHA—*The* BARON *runs and clasps her in his arms—Supported by him, she sinks on a chair which* AMELIA *places in the middle of the stage—The* BARON *kneels by her side, holding her hand.*]

BARON. Agatha, Agatha, do you know this voice?
AGATHA. Wildenhaim.
BARON. Can you forgive me?
AGATHA. Forgive you! [*Embracing him.*]

[*Enter* FREDERICK.]

FRED. [*As he enters.*] I hear the voice of my mother!—Ha! Mother! Father!

[FREDERICK *throws himself on his knees by the other side of his mother —She clasps him in her arms.*—AMELIA *is placed by the side of her father attentively viewing* AGATHA.—ANHALT *stands on the side of* FREDER- ICK *with his hands gratefully raised to Heaven.* —— *The curtain slowly drops.*]

THE END

JANE AUSTEN

Opinions of *Mansfield Park* (1814, 1815)†

"We certainly do not think it as a *whole*, equal to P. & P.—but it has many & great beauties. Fanny is a delightful Character! and Aunt Norris is a great favourite of mine. The Characters are natural & well supported, & many of the Dialogues excellent.—You need not fear the publication being considered as discreditable to the talents of it's Au- thor." F. W. A.[1]

---

† Reprinted from *The Works of Jane Austen*, vol. VI, *Minor Works*, ed. R. W. Chapman (Oxford: Oxford UP, 1954); rev. B. C. Southam (1969). By permission of Oxford University Press. Austen collected and recorded these comments, reported to her by friends, family, and ac- quaintances, soon after *Mansfield Park* first appeared, probably in 1814 and 1815.
1. Francis William Austen.

Not so clever as P. & P.—but pleased with it altogether. Liked the character of Fanny. Admired the Portsmouth Scene.—Mr K.[2]—

Edward & George.[3]—Not liked it near so well as P. & P.—Edward admired Fanny—George disliked her.—George interested by nobody but Mary Crawford.—Edward pleased with Henry C.—Edmund objected to, as cold & formal.—Henry C.s going off with Mrs R.—at such a time, when so much in love with Fanny, thought unnatural by Edward.—

Fanny Knight.—Liked it, in many parts, very much indeed, delighted with Fanny;—but not satisfied with the end—wanting more Love between her & Edmund—& could not think it natural that Edmd. shd. be so much attached to a woman without Principle like Mary C.—or promote Fanny's marrying Henry.—

Anna[4] liked it better than P. & P.—but not so well as S. & S.—could not bear Fanny.—Delighted with Mrs Norris, the scene at Portsmouth, & all the humourous parts.—

Mrs James Austen, very much pleased. Enjoyed Mrs Norris particularly, & the scene at Portsmouth. Thought Henry Crawford's going off with Mrs Rushworth, very natural.—

Miss Clewes's objections much the same as Fanny's.—

Miss Lloyd preferred it altogether to either of the others.—Delighted with Fanny.—Hated Mrs Norris.—

My Mother—not liked it so well as P. & P.—Thought Fanny insipid.—Enjoyed Mrs Norris.—

Cassandra—thought it quite as clever, tho' not so brilliant as P. & P.—Fond of Fanny.—Delighted much in Mr Rushworth's stupidity.—

My Eldest Brother[5]—a warm admirer of it in general.—Delighted with the Portsmouth Scene.

Edward[6]—Much like his Father.—Objected to Mrs Rushworth's Elopement as unnatural.

Mr B. L.[7]—Highly pleased with Fanny Price—& a warm admirer of the Portsmouth Scene.—Angry with Edmund for not being in love with her, & hating Mrs Norris for teazing her.—

Miss Burdett—Did not like it so well as P. & P.

Mrs James Tilson—Liked it better than P. & P.

Fanny Cage—did not much like it—not to be compared to P. & P.—nothing interesting in the Characters—Language poor.—Characters natural & well supported—Improved as it went on.—

Mr & Mrs Cooke—very much pleased with it—particularly with the

2. Austen's brother Edward Austen (Knight 1812).
3. Edward Knight's sons.
4. Anna Lefroy, Austen's niece.
5. James.
6. James Edward Austen (-Leigh 1837), Austen's biographer.
7. Benjamin Lefroy.

Manner in which the Clergy are treated.—Mr Cooke called it "the most sensible Novel he had ever read."—Mrs Cooke wished for a good Matronly Character.—

Mary Cooke—quite as much pleased with it, as her Father & Mother; seemed to enter into Lady B.'s character, & enjoyed Mr Rushworth's folly. Admired Fanny in general; but thought she ought to have been more determined on overcoming her own feelings, when she saw Edmund's attachment to Miss Crawford.—

Miss Burrel—admired it very much—particularly Mrs Norris & Dr Grant.—

Mrs Bramstone—much pleased with it; particularly with the character of Fanny, as being so very natural. Thought Lady Bertram like herself.—Preferred it to either of the others—but imagined *that* might be her want of Taste—as she does not understand Wit.—

Mrs Augusta Bramstone—owned that she thought S & S.—and P. & P. downright nonsense, but expected to like M P. better, & having finished the 1st vol.—flattered herself she had got through the worst.

The families at Deane—all pleased with it.—Mrs Anna Harwood delighted with Mrs Norris & the green Curtain.

The Kintbury Family[8]—very much pleased with it;—preferred it to either of the others.—

Mr Egerton the Publisher—praised it for it's Morality, & for being so equal a Composition.—No weak parts.

Lady Rob: Kerr wrote—"You may be assured I read every line with the greatest interest & am more delighted with it than my humble pen can express. The excellent delineation of Character, sound sense, Elegant Language & the pure morality with which it abounds, makes it a most desirable as well as useful work, & reflects the highest honour &c. &c.—Universally admired in Edinburgh, by all the *wise ones*.—Indeed, I have not heard a single fault given to it."—

Miss Sharpe—"I think it excellent—& of it's good sense & moral Tendency there can be no doubt.—Your Characters are drawn to the Life—so *very, very* natural & just—but as you beg me to be perfectly honest, I must confess I prefer P & P."—

Mrs Carrick.—"All who think deeply & feel much will give the Preference to Mansfield Park."

Mr J. Plumptre.—"I never read a novel which interested me so very much throughout, the characters are all so remarkably well kept up & so well drawn, & the plot is so well contrived that I had not an idea till the end which of the two w^d marry Fanny, H. C. or Edm^d. Mrs Norris amused me particularly, & Sir Thos is very clever, & his conduct proves admirably the defects of the modern system of Education."—Mr J. P. made *two* objections, but only one of them was remembered, the

8. Fowle.

want of some character more striking & interesting to the generality of Readers, than Fanny was likely to be.—

Sir James Langham & Mr H. Sanford, having been told that it was much inferior to P. & P.—began it expecting to dislike it, but were very soon extremely pleased with it—& I *beleive*, did not think it at all inferior.—

Alethea Bigg.—"I have read M P. & heard it very much talked of, very much praised, I like it myself & think it very good indeed, but as I never say what I do not think, I will add that although it is superior in a great many points in my opinion to the other two Works, I think it has not the Spirit of P & P., except perhaps the *Price* family at Portsmouth, & they are delightful in their way."—

Charles[9]—did not like it near so well as P. & P.—thought it wanted Incident.—

Mrs Dickson.—"I have bought M P.—but it is not equal to P. & P.—

Mrs Lefroy—liked it, but thought it a mere Novel.—

Mrs Portal—admired it very much—objected cheifly to Edmund's not being brought more forward.—

Lady Gordon wrote "In most novels you are amused for the time with a set of Ideal People whom you never think of afterwards or whom you the least expect to meet in common life, whereas in Miss A-s works, & especially in M P. you actually *live* with them, you fancy yourself one of the family; & the scenes are so exactly descriptive, so perfectly natural, that there is scarcely an Incident or conversation, or a person that you are not inclined to imagine you have at one time or other in your Life been a witness to, born a part in, & been acquainted with."

Mrs Pole wrote, "There is a particular satisfaction in reading all Miss A—s works—they are so evidently written by a Gentlewoman—most Novellists fail & betray themselves in attempting to describe familiar scenes in high Life, some little vulgarism escapes & shews that they are not experimentally acquainted with what they describe, but here it is quite different. Everything is natural, & the situations & incidents are told in a manner which clearly evinces the Writer to *belong* to the Society whose Manners she so ably delineates." Mrs Pole also said that no Books had ever occasioned so much canvassing & doubt, & that everybody was desirous to attribute them to some of their own friends, or to some person of whom they thought highly.—

Adm^l. Foote—surprised that I had the power of drawing the Portsmouth-Scenes so well.—

Mrs Creed—preferred S & S. and P & P.—to Mansfield Park.

---

9. Austen's brother Charles John.

JANE AUSTEN

Evening Prayer No. I†

Give us grace almighty father, so to pray, as to deserve to be heard, to address thee with our hearts, as with our lips. Thou art every where present, from thee no secret can be hid. May the knowledge of this, teach us to fix our thoughts on thee, with reverence and devotion that we pray not in vain.

Look with mercy on the sins we have this day committed and in mercy make us feel them deeply, that our repentance may be sincere, & our resolution steadfast of endeavouring against the commission of such in future. Teach us to understand the sinfulness of our own hearts, and bring to our knowledge every fault of temper and every evil habit in which we have indulged to the discomfort of our fellow-creatures, and the danger of our own souls. May we now, and on each return of night, consider how the past day has been spent by us, what have been our prevailing thoughts, words and actions during it, and how far we can acquit ourselves of evil. Have we thought irreverently of thee, have we disobeyed thy commandments, have we neglected any known duty, or willingly given pain to any human being? Incline us to ask our hearts these questions oh! God, and save us from deceiving ourselves by pride or vanity.

Give us a thankful sense of the blessings in which we live, of the many comforts of our lot; that we may not deserve to lose them by discontent or indifference.

Be gracious to our necessities, and guard us, and all we love, from evil this night. May the sick and afflicted, be now, and ever thy care; and heartily do we pray for the safety of all that travel by land or by sea, for the comfort & protection of the orphan and widow and that thy pity may be shewn upon all captives and prisoners.

Above all other blessings oh! God, for ourselves and our fellow-creatures, we implore thee to quicken our sense of thy mercy in the redemption of the world, of the value of that holy religion in which we have been brought up, that we may not, by our own neglect, throw away the salvation thou hast given us, nor be Christians only in name.

---

† Reprinted from *The Works of Jane Austen*, vol. VI, *Minor Works*, ed. R. W. Chapman (Oxford: Oxford UP, 1954); rev. B. C. Southam (1969). By permission of Oxford University Press. Because her father and brothers were Anglican priests, Austen was as a matter of course thoroughly familiar with *The Book of Common Prayer*, from which the divine service is drawn. It is not surprising that she also wrote some prayers herself, presumably for private use at home. Prayer in particular and mental discipline in general are subjects discussed in *Mansfield Park*. This prayer is the first of three written all or in part by Austen, and transcribed after her death in 1817. Across the back of the folded sheet on which this is written, the copyist—probably Austen's sister—wrote "Prayers composed by my ever dearest sister Jane." The watermark in the paper is 1818.

Hear us almighty God, for his sake who has redeemed us, and taught us thus to pray. Our Father which art in heaven &c.

From A Companion to the Altar: Showing the Nature and Necessity of a Sacramental Preparation†

On Family Prayer

* * *

And when the Communicant has thus far advanced towards the Altar, in his *Examination, Repentance,* &c. he must not forget another excellent Preparative belonging to this Duty of communicating worthily, which although it be not mentioned in our Church Catechism, yet it is always implied as a necessary Part of our Sacramental Preparation, that is, *Prayer,* private and public; a Duty upon which all our present and future Blessings depend, *Matt.* vii. 7, 8. and 21, 22. And so near a Relation hath this Duty of Prayer with this Sacrament, that all those Blessings therein contained and promised, are only in return to our Prayers; and no doubt but that Man, who makes a conscientious Practice of this Duty in his Closet, and at Church, can never be unprepared for this Sacrament, nor want a Title to God's peculiar Favour and Blessing: *For the Eyes of the Lord are over the Righteous, and his Ears are open unto their Prayers,* I Pet. iii. 12. The constant Exercise of *Prayer* is the best Method to get the Mastery over our evil Inclinations and corrupt Affections, and to overcome our vicious Habits: It preserves a lively Sense of God and Religion in our Minds, and fortifies us against those Temptations that assault us; it spiritualizes our Nature, raiseth our Souls above this World, and supports us under the Troubles and Calamities of this Life, by sanctifying such Afflictions; it leads us gradually to the Perfection of a Christian Life, and preserves that Union between God and our Souls, which feeds our spiritual Life with Grace and Goodness; without it, we in vain pretend to discharge those Christian Duties incumbent on us, or to prosper in our temporal Affairs, which must have God's Blessing to crown them with Success.—And as Prayer in general has these great Blessings and Advantages attending it, so give me leave to suggest to you under this Head, that those Public Prayers and Devotions, which we offer unto God in our Churches, are not only more acceptable to him, but also much more edifying and

† From [William Vickers,] A *Companion to the Alter, Shewing the Nature and Necessity of a Sacramental Preparation in Order to Our Worthy Receiving of the Holy Communion* (London, 1793?). This devotional book is intended to be read by young men and women in preparation for their confirmation. The selection printed here is taken from Austen's personal copy of this book, which is in the Rare Book Room of Firestone Library at Princeton University. Austen signed and dated this book on April 24, 1794, at the age of nineteen. The author's notes have been omitted.

advantageous to ourselves: They cannot but be more acceptable to God, because thereby his Honour and Glory is much more considerably advanced and maintained in the World, than by our private Devotions: By these outward *Signs* and *Tokens*, we publicly declare to all the World that inward Regard and Esteem which we have for his divine Perfections and Goodness; hereby we *let our Light so shine before Men, that they may see our good Works, and glorify our Father which is in Heaven,* Matt. v. 16.—There is no Duty in Scripture more frequently commanded, none more earnestly pressed upon us, than this of public Prayer. We have the Example of all good Men in all Ages for it, and of Christ himself, who was daily in the Temple and in the Synagogues, and, no question, frequented those Places at the usual Hours of Prayer, because then he had the fairest Opportunity, from those public Assemblies, to instruct, and to exhort to *Faith* and *Repentance*. 2dly, We may expect greater Blessings and Success to our Requests and Desires, when we join in the public Prayers of our Church, than from private, because our Saviour has in a special Manner promised to such Assemblies his immediate Presence, that *where two or three are gathered together in his Name, there will he be in the Midst of them;* which he hath no where said of private Prayer, though both are very good, nay, both are absolutely necessary for the beginning and ending of a Christian Life; and it is a very bad Sign of some evil Principle or other, for any Man to be much a Stranger to the House of Prayer, which is one of the greatest Blessings and Privileges (if we know how to value the same) that we can have in this World, and has always been accounted such among all wise and good Men. It is certain that the *Turks*, whom we call Infidels, go to their public Devotions five Times every Day; and shall not they rise in Judgment against us Christians, who cannot afford to go once or twice a Day to God's House, when we have both Leisure and Opportunity? If Men shall be judged for every idle Word, to be sure they shall not pass unpunished for all the Neglects and Omissions of their Duty of this Nature.

✳ ✳ ✳

HUMPHRY REPTON

From Sketches and Hints on Landscape Gardening (1795)†

From *Chapter III*

PROPER SITUATIONS FOR A HOUSE

* * *

It seems to have been as much the fashion of the present century to condemn avenues as it was in the last to plant them; and yet the subject is so little understood that most people think they sufficiently justify their opinion, in either case, by merely saying, "I like an avenue," or, "I hate an avenue": it is my business to analyse this approbation or disgust.

The several degrees of pleasure which the mind derives from the love of order, of unity, antiquity, greatness of parts, and continuity are all in some measure gratified by the long perspective view of a stately avenue: for the truth of this assertion I appeal to the sensations that every one must have felt who has visited the lofty avenues of Windsor, Hatfield, Burleigh, etc., before experience had pointed out that tedious sameness and the many inconveniences which have deservedly brought avenues into disrepute. This sameness is so obvious that, by the effect of avenues, all novelty or diversity of situation is done away; and the views from every house in the kingdom may be reduced to the same landscape, if looking up or down a straight line, betwixt two green walls, deserves the name of landscape.

Among the inconveniences of long straight avenues may very properly be reckoned that of their acting as wind-spouts to direct cold blasts with more violence upon the dwelling, as driven through a long tube. But I propose rather to consider the objections in point of beauty. If at the end of a long avenue be placed an obelisk, or temple, or any other eye-trap, ignorance or childhood alone will be caught or pleased by it: the eye of taste or experience hates compulsion, and turns away with disgust from every artificial means of attracting its notice. For this rea-

† Humphry Repton (1752–1818) was the most acclaimed landscape designer in England, and his services were eagerly sought by the gentry of Austen's time. Associated with the "picturesque" school, Repton contrived landscapes to look wild and unstudied and often separated the house from the surrounding grounds through the use of balustrades and terraces. His most famous works are *Sketches and Hints on Landscape Gardening* (1795), *Observations on the Theory and Practice of Landscape Gardening* (1803), and *Fragments on the Theory and Practice of Landscape Gardening* (1816). Austen had direct knowledge of Repton's work at Adlestrop in Gloucestershire, where her mother's cousin was rector. Though Austen apparently approved of some improvements — Pemberley in *Pride and Prejudice* exemplifies judicious improvement — she mocks the fashion in *Mansfield Park*.

son an avenue is most pleasing, which, like that at Langley Park, climbs up a hill, and, passing over its summit, leaves the fancy to conceive its termination.

One great mischief of an avenue is that it divides a park and cuts it into separate parts, destroying that unity of lawn or wood which is necessary to please in every composition: this is so obvious that, where a long avenue runs through a park from east to west, it would be hardly possible to avoid distinguishing it into the north and south lawn, or north and south division of the park.

But the greatest objection to an avenue is that (especially in uneven ground) it will often act as a curtain drawn across to exclude what is infinitely more interesting than any row of trees, however venerable or beautiful in themselves; and it is in undrawing this curtain at proper places that the utility of what is called breaking an avenue consists: for it is in vain we shall endeavour, by removing nine tenths of the trees in rows, to prevent its having the effect of an avenue when seen from either end. The illustration (see pp. 384–85) may serve to shew the effect of cutting down some chestnut-trees in the avenue at Langley, to let in the hill, richly covered with oaks, and that majestic tree which steps out before its brethren like the leader of a host. Such openings may be made in several parts of this avenue with wonderful effect; and yet its venerable appearance from the windows of the saloon will not be injured, because the trees removed from the rows will hardly be missed in the general perspective view from the house. And though I should not advise the planting such an avenue, yet there will always be so much of ancient grandeur in the front trees, and in looking up this long vista at Langley, that I do not wish it should be further disturbed, especially as the views on each side are sufficiently capable of yielding beauty; and, when seen from the end rooms of the house, the avenue will act as a foreground to either landscape.

*   *   *

The effect of removing trees in the oblique view of an avenue at Langley Park. [In Repton's text, the first plate was designed to overlay the second, and by unfolding the flap the reader could see the second plate beneath and thereby

HUMPHRY REPTON

From Observations on the Theory and Practice of Landscape Gardening (1803)

From *Chapter VII*

FARM AND PARK DISTINCT OBJECTS—BEAUTY AND PROFIT SELDOM COMPATIBLE

* * *

The chief beauty of a park consists in uniform verdure; undulating lines contrasting with each other in variety of forms; trees so grouped as to produce light and shade to display the varied surface of the ground; and an undivided range of pasture. The animals fed in such a park appear free from confinement, at liberty to collect their food from the rich herbage of the valley, and to range uncontrolled to the drier soil of the hills.

The farm, on the contrary, is forever changing the colour of its surface in motley and discordant hues; it is subdivided by straight lines of fences. The trees can only be ranged in formal rows along the hedges; and these the farmer claims a right to cut, prune, and disfigure. Instead of cattle enlivening the scene by their peaceful attitudes or sportive gambols, animals are bending beneath the yoke or closely confined to fatten within narrow enclosures, objects of profit, not of beauty.

* * *

I am aware that, in the prevailing rage for agriculture, it is unpopular to assert that a farm and a park may not be united; but after various efforts to blend the two, without violation of good taste, I am convinced that they are and must be distinct objects, and ought never to be brought together in the same point of view.

To guard against misrepresentation, let me be allowed to say each may fill its appropriate station in a gentleman's estate; we do not wish to banish the nectarine from our desserts, although we plant out the wall which protects it; nor would I expunge the common farm from the pleasures of the country, though I cannot encourage its motley hues and domestic occupations to disturb the repose of park scenery. It is the union not the existence of beauty and profit, of laborious exertion and pleasurable recreation, against which I would interpose the influence of my art; nor let the fastidious objector condemn the effort till he can convince the judgement that, without violation of good taste, he could introduce the dairy and the pig-sty (those useful appendages of rural economy) into the recesses of the drawing-room or the area of the saloon. The difficulty of uniting a park and a farm arises from this material circumstance, that the one is an object of beauty, the other of profit. The scenery of both consists of ground, trees, water, and cattle; but these are very differently arranged. And since a park is less profitable than arable land, the more we can diminish the quantity of the former, provided it still be in character with the style of the mansion, the less we shall regret the sacrifice of profit to beauty.

The shape and colour of corn-fields and the straight lines of fences are so totally at variance with all ideas of picturesque beauty that I shall not venture to suggest any hints on the subject of a farm as an ornament; yet I think there might be a distinction made between the farm of a tenant, who must derive benefit from every part of his land, and that occupied by a gentleman for the purposes of amusement or experiment.

* * *

Since the beauty of pleasure-ground and the profit of a farm are incompatible, it is the business of taste and prudence so to disguise the latter and to limit the former that park scenery may be obtained without much waste or extravagance; but I disclaim all idea of making that which is most beautiful also most profitable: a ploughed field and a field of grass are as distinct objects as a flower-garden and a potato-ground.

* * *

WILLIAM COWPER

From The Task (1785)†

From *Book I. The Sofa*

[ON THE SHARED ENJOYMENT OF FAMILIAR RURAL SCENES]

* * *

[S]cenes that sooth'd
Or charm'd me young, no longer young, I find
Still soothing and of power to charm me still.
And witness, dear companion of my walks,
Whose arm this twentieth winter I perceive   145
Fast lock'd in mine, with pleasure such as love
Confirm'd by long experience of thy worth

† William Cowper (1731–1800) was among the most widely read poets of the late eighteenth century and was one of Austen's most beloved authors. *The Task* (1785), which celebrates the everyday incidents of country life, was his best-known long poem, containing many passages presaging the romantic poems of Wordsworth and Coleridge. The selections here are taken from the first edition, and the subject descriptions within brackets are by the editor of this Norton Critical Edition.

And well-tried virtues could alone inspire—
Witness a joy that thou hast doubled long.
Thou know'st my praise of nature most sincere,   150
And that my raptures are not conjured up
To serve occasions of poetic pomp,
But genuine, and art partner of them all.
How oft upon yon eminence, our pace
Has slacken'd to a pause, and we have borne   155
The ruffling wind scarce conscious that it blew,
While admiration feeding at the eye,
And still unsated, dwelt upon the scene.
Thence with what pleasure have we just discern'd
The distant plough slow-moving, and beside   160
His lab'ring team that swerv'd not from the track,
The sturdy swain diminish'd to a boy!
Here Ouse, slow winding through a level plain
Of spacious meads with cattle sprinkled o'er,
Conducts the eye along his sinuous course   165
Delighted. There, fast rooted in his bank
Stand, never overlook'd, our fav'rite elms
That screen the herdsman's solitary hut;
While far beyond and overthwart the stream
That as with molten glass inlays the vale,   170
The sloping land recedes into the clouds;
Displaying on its varied side, the grace
Of hedge-row beauties numberless, square tow'r,
Tall spire, from which the sound of chearful bells
Just undulates upon the list'ning ear;   175
Groves, heaths, and smoking villages remote.
Scenes must be beautiful which daily view'd
Please daily, and whose novelty survives
Long knowledge and the scrutiny of years.
Praise justly due to those that I describe.   180

*   *   *

From *Book III. The Garden*

[ON GARDENING; ON THE VIRTUES OF A RETIRED LIFE;
AGAINST THE NATIONAL DISGRACE OF "IMPROVEMENTS"]

*   *   *

So manifold, all pleasing in their kind,
All healthful, are th' employs of rural life,   625
Reiterated as the wheel of time
Runs round, still ending, and beginning still.
Nor are these all. To deck the shapely knoll
That softly swell'd and gayly dress'd, appears

A flow'ry island from the dark green lawn   630
Emerging, must be deemed a labor due
To no mean hand, and asks the touch of taste.
Here also gratefull mixture of well match'd
And sorted hues, (each giving each relief,
And by contrasted beauty shining more)   635
Is needful. Strength may wield the pond'rous spade,
May turn the clod, and wheel the compost home,
But elegance, chief grace the garden shows
And most attractive, is the fair result
Of thought, the creature of a polish'd mind.   640
Without it, all is Gothic as the scene
To which th' insipid citizen resorts
Near yonder heath; where industry mispent,
But proud of his uncouth ill-chosen task,
Has made a heav'n on earth. With suns and moons   645
Of close-ramm'd stones has charged th' incumber'd soil,
And fairly laid the Zodiac in the dust.
He therefore who would see his flow'rs disposed
Sightly and in just order, 'ere he gives
The beds the trusted treasure of their seeds   650
Forecasts the future whole. That when the scene
Shall break into its preconceived display,
Each for itself, and all as with one voice
Conspiring, may attest his bright design.
Nor even then, dismissing as perform'd   655
His pleasant work, may he suppose it done.
Few self-supported flow'rs endure the wind
Uninjured, but expect th' upholding aid
Of the smooth-shaven prop, and neatly tied
Are wedded thus like beauty to old age,   660
For int'rest sake, the living to the dead.
Some cloath the soil that feeds them, far diffused
And lowly creeping, modest and yet fair,
Like virtue, thriving most where little seen.
Some more aspiring catch the neighbour shrub   665
With clasping tendrils, and invest his branch
Else unadorn'd, with many a gay festoon
And fragrant chaplet, recompensing well
The strength they borrow with the grace they lend.
All hate the rank society of weeds   670
Noisome, and ever greedy to exhaust
Th' impov'rish'd earth; an overbearing race,
That like the multitude made faction-mad
Disturb good order, and degrade true worth.

Oh blest seclusion from a jarring world   675
Which he thus occupied, enjoys! Retreat
Cannot indeed to guilty man restore
Lost innocence, or cancel follies past,
But it has peace, and much secures the mind
From all assaults of evil, proving still   680
A faithful barrier, not o'erleap'd with ease
By vicious custom, raging uncontroul'd
Abroad, and desolating public life.

            ❈   ❈   ❈

          [W]ere England now
What England was, plain, hospitable, kind,
And undebauch'd. But we have bid farewell
To all the virtues of those better days,   745
And all their honest pleasures. Mansions once
Knew their own masters, and laborious hinds
That had surviv'd the father, serv'd the son.
Now the legitimate and rightful Lord
Is but a transient guest, newly arrived   750
And soon to be supplanted. He that saw
His patrimonial timber cast its leaf,
Sells the last scantling, and transfers the price
To some shrew'd sharper, 'ere it buds again.
Estates are landscapes, gazed upon awhile,   755
Then advertised, and auctioneer'd away.
The country starves, and they that feed th' o'ercharged
And surfeited lew'd town with her fair dues,
By a just judgment strip and starve themselves.
The wings that waft our riches out of sight   760
Grow on the gamester's elbows, and th' alert
And nimble motion of those restless joints
That never tire, soon fans them all away.
Improvement too, the idol of the age,
Is fed with many a victim. Lo! he comes—   765
The omnipotent magician, Brown[1] appears.
Down falls the venerable pile, th' abode
Of our forefathers, a grave whisker'd race,
But tasteless. Springs a palace in its stead,
But in a distant spot; where more exposed   770
It may enjoy th' advantage of the north
And agueish East, till time shall have transform'd
Those naked acres to a shelt'ring grove.
He speaks. The lake in front becomes a lawn,

---

1. Lancelot ("Capability") Brown (1715–1783) was the most famous English landscape designer
   before Humphry Repton. He favored "natural" designs that contrasted sharply with the formal,
   geometrical style of French gardening at the time. Cowper caustically laments the craze for
   "improvement" as disruptive and exorbitant.

Woods vanish, hills subside, and vallies rise,   775
And streams as if created for his use,
Pursue the track of his directing wand
Sinuous or strait, now rapid and now slow,
Now murm'ring soft, now roaring in cascades,
Ev'n as he bids. Th' enraptur'd owner smiles.   780
'Tis finish'd. And yet finish'd as it seems,
Still wants a grace, th' loveliest it could show,
A mine to satisfy the enormous cost.
Drain'd to the last poor item of his wealth
He sighs, departs, and leaves the accomplished plan   785
That he has touch'd, retouch'd, many a long day
Labor'd, and many a night pursued in dreams,
Just when it meets his hopes, and proves the heav'n
He wanted, for a wealthier to enjoy.

❊   ❊   ❊

JOHN GREGORY

From A Father's Legacy to His Daughter (1774)[†]

From *Conduct and Behaviour*

One of the chief beauties in a female character, is that modest reserve, that retiring delicacy, which avoids the public eye, and is discon-
certed even at the gaze of admiration.—I do not wish you to be
insensible to applause. If you were, you must become, if not worse, at
least less amiable women. But you may be dazzled by that admiration,
which yet rejoices your hearts.

When a girl ceases to blush, she has lost the most powerful charm
of beauty. That extreme sensibility which it indicates, may be a weakness and incumbrance in our sex, as I have too often felt; but in yours
it is peculiarly engaging. Pedants, who think themselves philosophers,
ask why a woman should blush when she is conscious of no crime. It
is a sufficient answer, that Nature has made you to blush when you are
guilty of no fault, and has forced us to love you because you do so.—
Blushing is so far from being necessarily an attendant on guilt, that it
is the usual companion of innocence.

This modesty, which I think so essential in your sex, will naturally
dispose you to be rather silent in company, especially in a large one.

† John Gregory (1724–1773) was a Scottish author, professor of medicine, and Fellow at the
    Royal Society. Among the best sellers of Austen's time, conduct books for women were didactic
    tracts — taking the form of sermons, letters, or even fiction — which admonished young ladies
    to be modest and dutiful daughters and wives. Gregory's *A Father's Legacy to His Daughter*
    (1774) was a widely respected and often reprinted text on female propriety. The excerpts here
    are from the 1774 and 1793 editions.

—People of sense and discernment will never mistake such silence for
dulness. One may take a share in conversation without uttering a syllable. The expression in the countenance shews it, and this never escapes an observing eye.

I should be glad that you had an easy dignity in your behaviour at
public places, but not that confident ease, that unabashed countenance,
which seems to set the company at defiance. If, while a gentleman is
speaking to you, one of superior rank addresses you, do not let your
eager attention and visible preference betray the flutter of your heart.
Let your pride on this occasion preserve you from that meanness into
which your vanity would sink you. Consider that you expose yourselves
to the ridicule of the company, and affront one gentleman, only to
swell the triumph of another, who perhaps thinks he does you honour
in speaking to you.

Converse with men even of the first rank with that dignified modesty
which may prevent the approach of the most distant familiarity, and
consequently prevent them from feeling themselves your superiors.

Wit is the most dangerous talent you can possess. It must be guarded
with great discretion and good nature, otherwise it will create you many
enemies. Wit is perfectly consistent with softness and delicacy; yet they
are seldom found united. Wit is so flattering to vanity, that they who
possess it become intoxicated, and lose all self-command.

Humour is a different quality. It will make your company much
solicited; but be cautious how you indulge it.—It is often a great enemy
to delicacy, and a still greater one to dignity of character. It may sometimes gain you applause, but will never procure you respect.

Be even cautious in displaying your good sense. It will be thought
you assume a superiority over the rest of the company.—But if you
happen to have any learning, keep it a profound secret, especially from
the men, who generally look with a jealous and malignant eye on a
woman of great parts, and a cultivated understanding.

*　*　*

Consider every species of indelicacy in conversation, as shameful in
itself, and as highly disgusting to us. All double entendre is of this
sort.—The dissoluteness of men's education allows them to be diverted
with a kind of wit, which yet they have delicacy enough to be shocked
at, when it comes from your mouths, or even when you hear it without
pain and contempt.—Virgin purity is of that delicate nature, that it
cannot hear certain things without contamination. It is always in your
power to avoid these. No man, but a brute or a fool, will insult a woman
with conversation which he sees gives her pain; nor will he dare to do
it, if she resent the injury with a becoming spirit.—There is a dignity
in conscious virtue which is able to awe the most shameless and abandoned of men.

You will be reproached perhaps with prudery. By prudery is usually meant an affectation of delicacy. Now I do not wish you to affect delicacy; I wish you to possess it. At any rate, it is better to run the risk of being thought ridiculous than disgusting.

The men will complain of your reserve. They will assure you that a franker behaviour would make you more amiable. But trust me, they are not sincere when they tell you so. * * *

From *Amusements*

I would particularly recommend to you those exercises that oblige you to be much abroad in the open air, such as walking, and riding on horse-back. This will give vigour to your constitutions, and a bloom to your complexions. If you accustom yourselves to go abroad always in chairs and carriages, you will soon become so enervated, as to be unable to go out of doors without them. They are like most articles of luxury, useful and agreeable when judiciously used: but when made habitual, they become both insipid and pernicious.

An attention to your health is a duty you owe to yourselves and to your friends. Bad health seldom fails to have an influence on the spirits and temper. The finest geniusses, the soft delicate minds, have very frequently a correspondent delicacy of bodily constitution which they are too apt to neglect. Their luxury lies in reading and late hours, equal enemies to health and beauty.

But though good health be one of the greatest blessings of life, never make a boast of it, but enjoy it in grateful silence. We so naturally associate the idea of female softness and delicacy, with a correspondent delicacy of constitution, that when a woman speaks of her great strength, her extraordinary appetite, her ability to bear excessive fatigue, we recoil at the description in a way she is little aware of.

MARY WOLLSTONECRAFT

From A Vindication of the Rights of Woman (1792)†

From *Chapter II. The Prevailing Opinion of a Sexual Character Discussed*

To account for, and excuse the tyranny of man, many ingenious arguments have been brought forward to prove, that the two sexes, in

† Mary Wollstonecraft (1759–1797) was a novelist and polemicist on behalf of women's legal and educational rights and other progressive causes. Her most famous work, *Vindication of the Rights of Woman* (1792), was among other things a tract on female education. It was well received until the British reaction against the Revolution in France (which she supported), along with disclosures about her unconventional personal life, turned opinion against her. She is one of the few prominent contemporary women writers Austen never mentions, though she was almost certainly familiar with her work. The selections here are from the Norton Critical Edition of *The Vindication*, 2nd ed., ed. Carol Poston.

the acquirement of virtue, ought to aim at attaining a very different character: or, to speak explicitly, women are not allowed to have sufficient strength of mind to acquire what really deserves the name of virtue. Yet it should seem, allowing them to have souls, that there is but one way appointed by Providence to lead *mankind* to either virtue or happiness.

If then women are not a swarm of ephemeron triflers, why should they be kept in ignorance under the specious name of innocence? Men complain, and with reason, of the follies and caprices of our sex, when they do not keenly satirize our headstrong passions and groveling vices.—Behold, I should answer, the natural effect of ignorance! The mind will ever be unstable that has only prejudices to rest on, and the current will run with destructive fury when there are no barriers to break its force. Women are told from their infancy, and taught by the example of their mothers, that a little knowledge of human weakness, justly termed cunning, softness of temper, *outward* obedience, and a scrupulous attention to a puerile kind of propriety, will obtain for them the protection of man; and should they be beautiful, every thing else is needless, for, at least, twenty years of their lives.

Thus Milton describes our first frail mother; though when he tells us that women are formed for softness and sweet attractive grace, I cannot comprehend his meaning, unless, in the true Mahometan strain, he meant to deprive us of souls, and insinuate that we were beings only designed by sweet attractive grace, and docile blind obedience, to gratify the senses of man when he can no longer soar on the wing of contemplation.

How grossly do they insult us who thus advise us only to render ourselves gentle, domestic brutes! For instance, the winning softness so warmly, and frequently, recommended, that governs by obeying. What childish expressions, and how insignificant is the being—can it be an immortal one? who will condescend to govern by such sinister methods!

* * *

[T]he most perfect education, in my opinion, is such an exercise of the understanding as is best calculated to strengthen the body and form the heart. Or, in other words, to enable the individual to attain such habits of virtue as will render it independent. In fact, it is a farce to call any being virtuous whose virtues do not result from the exercise of its own reason. This was Rousseau's opinion respecting men: I extend it to women, and confidently assert that they have been drawn out of their sphere by false refinement, and not by an endeavour to acquire masculine qualities.

* * *

I may be accused of arrogance; still I must declare what I firmly believe, that all the writers who have written on the subject of female education and manners from Rousseau to Dr. Gregory, have contributed to render women more artificial, weak characters, than they would otherwise have been; and, consequently, more useless members of society.

*   *   *

To do every thing in an orderly manner, is a most important precept, which women, who, generally speaking, receive only a disorderly kind of education, seldom attend to with that degree of exactness that men, who from their infancy are broken into method, observe. This negligent kind of guess-work, for what other epithet can be used to point out the random exertions of a sort of instinctive common sense, never brought to the test of reason? prevents their generalizing matters of fact—so they do to-day, what they did yesterday, merely because they did it yesterday.

This contempt of the understanding in early life has more baneful consequences than is commonly supposed; for the little knowledge which women of strong minds attain, is, from various circumstances, of a more desultory kind than the knowledge of men, and it is acquired more by sheer observations on real life, than from comparing what has been individually observed with the results of experience generalized by speculation. Led by their dependent situation and domestic employments more into society, what they learn is rather by snatches; and as learning is with them, in general, only a secondary thing, they do not pursue any one branch with that persevering ardour necessary to give vigour to the faculties, and clearness to the judgment. In the present state of society, a little learning is required to support the character of a gentleman; and boys are obliged to submit to a few years of discipline. But in the education of women, the cultivation of the understanding is always subordinate to the acquirement of some corporeal accomplishment; even while enervated by confinement and false notions of modesty, the body is prevented from attaining that grace and beauty which relaxed half-formed limbs never exhibit.

*   *   *

Rousseau declares that a woman should never, for a moment, feel herself independent, that she should be governed by fear to exercise her natural cunning, and made a coquetish slave in order to render her a more alluring object of desire, a *sweeter* companion to man, whenever he chooses to relax himself. He carries the arguments, which he pretends to draw from the indications of nature, still further, and insinuates that truth and fortitude, the corner stones of all human virtue, should be cultivated with certain restrictions, because, with respect to the female character, obedience is the grand lesson which ought to be impressed with unrelenting rigour.

What nonsense! when will a great man arise with sufficient strength of mind to puff away the fumes which pride and sensuality have thus spread over the subject! If women are by nature inferior to men, their virtues must be the same in quality, if not in degree, or virtue is a relative idea; consequently, their conduct should be founded on the same principles, and have the same aim.

Connected with man as daughters, wives, and mothers, their moral character may be estimated by their manner of fulfilling those simple duties; but the end, the grand end of their exertions should be to unfold their own faculties and acquire the dignity of conscious virtue. They may try to render their road pleasant; but ought never to forget, in common with man, that life yields not the felicity which can satisfy an immortal soul. I do not mean to insinuate, that either sex should be so lost in abstract reflections or distant views, as to forget the affections and duties that lie before them, and are, in truth, the means appointed to produce the fruit of life; on the contrary, I would warmly recommend them, even while I assert, that they afford most satisfaction when they are considered in their true, sober light.

*   *   *

The worthy Dr. Gregory fell into a similar error. I respect his heart; but entirely disapprove of his celebrated Legacy to his Daughters.

He advises them to cultivate a fondness for dress, because a fondness for dress, he asserts, is natural to them. I am unable to comprehend what either he or Rousseau mean, when they frequently use this indefinite term. If they told us that in a pre-existent state the soul was fond of dress, and brought this inclination with it into a new body, I should listen to them with a half smile, as I often do when I hear a rant about innate elegance.—But if he only meant to say that the exercise of the faculties will produce this fondness—I deny it.—It is not natural; but arises, like false ambition in men, from a love of power.

Dr. Gregory goes much further; he actually recommends dissimulation, and advises an innocent girl to give the lie to her feelings, and not dance with spirit, when gaiety of heart would make her feel eloquent without making her gestures immodest. In the name of truth and common sense, why should not one woman acknowledge that she can take more exercise than another? or, in other words, that she has a sound constitution; and why, to damp innocent vivacity, is she darkly to be told that men will draw conclusions which she little thinks of?

*   *   *

[T]he woman who strengthens her body and exercises her mind will, by managing her family and practising various virtues, become the friend, and not the humble dependent of her husband; and if she, by possessing such substantial qualities, merit his regard, she will not find it necessary to conceal her affection, nor to pretend to an unnatural coldness of constitution to excite her husband's passions. In fact, if we revert to history, we shall find that the women who have distinguished themselves have neither been the most beautiful nor the most gentle of their sex.

*   *   *

Do passive indolent women make the best wives? Confining our discussion to the present moment of existence, let us see how such weak creatures perform their part? Do the women who, by the attainment of a few superficial accomplishments, have strengthened the prevailing prejudice, merely contribute to the happiness of their husbands? Do they display their charms merely to amuse them? And have women, who have early imbibed notions of passive obedience, sufficient character to manage a family or educate children? So far from it, that, after surveying the history of woman, I cannot help, agreeing with the severest satirist, considering the sex as the weakest as well as the most oppressed half of the species. What does history disclose but marks of inferiority, and how few women have emancipated themselves from the galling yoke of sovereign man?

* * *

From *Chapter III. The Same Subject Continued*

Bodily strength from being the distinction of heroes is now sunk into such unmerited contempt that men, as well as women, seem to think it unnecessary: the latter, as it takes from their feminine graces, and from that lovely weakness the source of their undue power; and the former, because it appears inimical to the character of a gentleman.

* * *

I once knew a weak woman of fashion, who was more than commonly proud of her delicacy and sensibility. She thought a distinguishing taste and puny appetite the height of all human perfection, and acted accordingly.—I have seen this weak sophisticated being neglect all the duties of life, yet recline with self-complacency on a sofa, and boast of her want of appetite as a proof of delicacy that extended to, or, perhaps, arose from, her exquisite sensibility: for it is difficult to render intelligible such ridiculous jargon.

* * *

THOMAS GISBORNE

From An Enquiry into the Duties of Men in the Higher and Middle Classes of Society in Great Britain (1794)†

From *Chapter XI. On the Duties of the Clerical Profession*

* * *

The first points concerning which a young man designed for the clerical profession is bound to satisfy himself (and whether he looks forward to that profession from his own unbiassed determination, or is destined to it by the judgement of his parents and friends, the enquiry is equally indispensable), are the purposes and intentions with which he becomes a candidate for the office of a Clergyman. I mean not to require of him a degree of disinterestedness in selecting his occupation unattainable in the common course of human nature, and the existing circumstances of the world. Extravagant statements unfounded in reason and scripture defeat their own object; and, were they likely to promote it, ought not to be adopted. That Clergyman undoubtedly may be expected to labour in his vocation with the greatest earnestness and success, with the greatest comfort and advantage to himself and to others, who embraces it from a sober and deliberate preference founded on the nature of the office itself; and from a conviction that it will afford him opportunities more ample than he should be likely to possess in any other employment, of promoting the glory of God, and the good of mankind. Yet to him who is conscientiously resolved to discharge with zeal and fidelity the functions of the clerical order, if admitted to the exercise of them; and to cherish the temper and dispositions, and diligently to aim at acquiring the endowments, necessary to that end; and in whole heart piety has already such a predominant influence, as to give him a reasonable ground of confidence that these resolutions will be rendered by the divine blessing permanent and effectual; the prospect of obtaining, by the aid of his friends and relations, a competent provision in the church may lawfully be the motive which determines him to that line of life in preference to another. But he who, from the probability of succeeding to a family living, or the hopes of being pushed forward to preferment by powerful connections, stifles an

---

† Thomas Gisborne (1758–1846) was an Anglican clergyman, a supporter of Evangelicalism, and the author of numerous sermons, poems, and tracts undertaking to "improve" the manners and morals of his readers. *An Enquiry into the Duties of Men in the Higher and Middle Classes of Society in Great Britain* (1794) is a conduct book designed for men of the upper ranks of society; it was well received, going through six editions by 1811. The clergyman's profession is frequently discussed in *Mansfield Park*. The selection excerpted here, regarding the duties of clergymen, is drawn from the 1806 edition. The author's notes have been omitted.

inward repugnance to the office of a Minister of the Gospel, falls under
the severe censure implied in the Scripture against those who "take
"the oversight of the flock of God for filthy lucre." And he who enters
into the clerical profession, though not from motives of avarice, yet
without duly estimating its solemn nature and momentous functions,
the obligations which it imposes, and the responsibility annexed to it;
without possessing the qualifications essential to the upright performance of its duties; and without a serious purpose of habitually striving
to improve in them, and to exhibit to those whom he shall be appointed
to guide in the way of salvation and edifying example of piety and
virtue; engages in a most important concern with a degree of presump-
tuous rashness little adapted to ensure the future peace of his own
mind; to draw down the blessing of God upon his labours; or to leave
any substantial hopes that he will labour at all with zeal and assiduity.

*   *   *

Among the peculiar functions of the Minister of a parish, the cele-
bration of divine worship naturally offers itself in the first place to our
attention.

The usual times of public worship ought never to be changed by the
Minister for the purpose of suiting his own convenience, when his
hearers will be incommoded or displeased by the alteration, and of
course be apt to relax in their attendance.

*   *   *

In reading the liturgy, a natural, distinct, and moderately slow pro-
nunciation, audible throughout the church, but not overstrained; appropriate to the several parts of the service, but free from affected
emphasis; and that earnest and impressive solemnity of manner which
proves the heart of the Minister to be engaged in his employment, are
qualifications of the highest importance. This remark must be extended
to the recital of the baptismal office, and of other similar parts of the
book of common prayer; which are sometimes read with so much haste
and irreverence, as to lose all appearance of being offices of religion.

With respect to the composition of sermons, the only observations
proper to be suggested in this place are, that they should be plain, and
that they should be Christian discourses.

A sermon which is above the capacity of the congregation to which
it is addressed is useless or disgusting. In almost every congregation the
poor and unlearned form by much the larger part; and, universally, the
meaning of the preacher must be caught at once, or it is totally lost.
Hence the peculiar necessity of plainness in propounding the subject
to be discussed, and in the manner of treating it. Our rule therefore,
while it requires, in discourses addressed to ordinary congregations, a
simple and perfectly obvious arrangement, and, in most cases, the professed division of the subject into a few general heads; proscribes the
bewildering multiplicity of subdivisions, frequently destitute of actual

distinction, which was common among eminent divines early in the present century; together with all long and complicated sentences, obscure metaphors, refined ornaments of language and composition, learned references to Pagan philosophers and Christian fathers, and prolix digressions from the main topics suggested by the text.

* * *

The foregoing statement of the various duties of a parochial Minister clearly implies the general obligation of residence. Habitual residence on the spot is essential to his being able effectually to perform them. How far a temporary or permanent exemption from the general rule, in addition to those which the laws of the land expressly allow, may be reasonably granted in a particular case, is a point to be decided by the Bishop of the diocese. But such exemptions will never be sought by a conscientious Clergyman, except under extraordinary circumstances. A Curate has neither the authority in instructing and reproving which the actual possessor of the living has, nor the same ability to be charitable. He is not improbably a much younger man, and commonly therefore has less knowledge and experience; and is less likely to be impressed with a strict and serious sense of his momentous duties. And the uncertainty of his continuance in the cure lessens the force of several subordinate incitements to industry and exemplary conduct. It is far better however, in general, that a Clergyman should never visit his parish at all, but have his place supplied by a resident Curate; than that he should live at the distance of six or eight miles from it, and from thence take the whole care of it himself. For the consequence of the latter method will almost invariably be, that he will soon cease to visit his parishioners except on Sundays, and in very pressing cases at other times. They who have resided at the distance of two or three miles only from their parish, know how many real impediments even that small distance creates to the discharge of the duties of private instruction, and of friendly and improving intercourse; and how many pleas it supplies for indolence and neglect.

* * *

THOMAS GISBORNE

From An Enquiry into the Duties of the Female Sex (1797)†

From *Chapter IX*

ON AMUSEMENTS IN GENERAL.

For some years past the custom of acting plays in private theatres, fitted up by individuals of fortune, has occasionally prevailed. It is a custom liable to this objection among others; that it is almost certain to prove, in its effects, particularly injurious to the female performers. Let it be admitted, that theatres of this description no longer present the flagrant impropriety of ladies bearing a part in the drama in conjunction with professed players. Let it be admitted, that the drama selected will be in its language and conduct always irreprehensible. Let it even be admitted, that eminent theatrical talents will not hereafter gain admission upon such a Stage for men of ambiguous, or worse than ambiguous, character. Take the benefit of all these favourable circumstances; yet, what is even then the tendency of such amusements? to encourage vanity; to excite a thirst of applause and admiration on account of attainments which, if they are to be thus exhibited, it would commonly have been far better for the individual not to possess; to destroy diffidence by the unrestrained familiarity with persons of the other sex, which inevitably results from being joined with them in the drama; to create a general fondness for the perusal of plays, of which so many are improper to be read; and for attending dramatic representations, of which so many are unfit to be witnessed. Most of these remarks fully apply to the practice of causing children to act plays, or parts of plays; a practice of which parents, while labouring to vindicate it, sometimes pronounce an emphatical condemnation, by avowing a future purpose of abandoning it so soon as their children shall be far advanced in youth.

*   *   *

† See above, p. 398, n. Thomas Gisborne's *Enquiry into the Duties of the Female Sex* (1797) was very popular, going through eight editions by 1810. The excerpt here is taken from the first edition. The author's notes have been omitted.

From *Chapter X*

ON THE EMPLOYMENT OF TIME.

* * *

To every woman, whether single or married, the habit of regularly allotting to improving books a portion of each day, and, as far as may be practicable, at stated hours, cannot be too strongly recommended. I use the term *improving* in a large sense; as comprehending all writings which may contribute to her virtue, her usefulness, and her innocent satisfaction, to her happiness in this world and in the next. She who believes that she is to survive in another state of being through eternity, and is duly impressed by the awful conviction, will fix day by day her most serious thoughts on the inheritance to which she aspires. Where her treasure is, there will her heart be also. She will not be seduced from an habitual study of the Holy Scriptures, and of other works calculated to imprint on her bosom the comparatively small importance of the pains and pleasures of this period of existence. * * * At other parts of the day let history, let biography, let poetry, or some of the various branches of elegant and profitable knowledge, pay their tribute of instruction and amusement. But let her studies be confined within the strictest limits of purity. Whatever she peruses in her most private hours be such as she needs not to be ashamed of reading aloud to those whose good opinion she is most anxious to deserve. Let her remember that there is an all-seeing eye, which is ever fixed upon her, even in her closest retirement. Let her not indulge herself in the frequent perusal of writings, however interesting in their nature, however eminent in a literary point of view, which are likely to inflame pride, and to inspire false notions of generosity, of feeling, of spirit, or of any other quality deemed to contribute to excellence of character. Such unhappily are the effects to be apprehended from the works even of several of our distinguished writers, in prose or in verse. And let her accustom herself regularly to bring the sentiments which she reads, and the conduct which is described in terms, more or less strong, of applause and recommendation, to the test of Christian principles. In proportion as this practice is pursued or neglected, reading will be profitable, or pernicious.

* * *

Even in the class of novels least objectionable in point of delicacy, false sentiment unfitting the mind for sober life, applause and censure distributed amiss, morality estimated by an erroneous standard, and the capricious laws and empty sanctions of honour set up in the place of religion, are the lessons usually presented. There is yet another consequence too important to be overlooked. The catastrophe and the incidents of these fictitious narratives commonly turn on the vicissitudes and effects of a passion the most powerful of all those which agitate the human heart. Hence the study of them frequently creates a susceptibility of impression, and a premature warmth of tender emotions, which, not to speak of other possible effects, have been known to betray young women into a sudden attachment to persons unworthy of their affection, and thus to hurry them into marriages terminating in unhappiness.

In addition to the regular habit of useful reading, the custom of committing to the memory select and ample portions of poetic compositions, not for the purpose of ostentatiously quoting them in mixed company, but for the sake of private improvement, deserves, in consequence of its beneficial tendency, to be mentioned with a very high degree of praise. The mind is thus stored with a lasting treasure of sentiments and ideas, combined by writers of transcendent genius and vigorous imagination; clothed in appropriate, nervous, and glowing language; and impressed by the powers of cadence and harmony. Let the poetry, however, be well chosen. Let it be such as elevates the heart with the ardour of devotion; adds energy and grace to precepts of morality; kindles benevolence by pathetic narrative and reflection; enters with accurate and lively description into the varieties of character; or presents vivid pictures of the grand and beautiful features which characterise the scenery of nature. Such are, in general, the works of Milton, of Thomson, of Gray, of Mason, of Beattie, and of Cowper. It is thus that the beauty and grandeur of nature will be contemplated with new pleasure. It is thus that taste will be called forth, exercised, and corrected. It is thus that judgement will be strengthened, virtuous emotions cherished, piety animated and exalted. At all times, and under every circumstance, the heart, penetrated with religion, will delight itself in the recollection of passages, which display the perfections of that Being on whom it trusts, and the glorious hopes to the accomplishment of which it humbly looks forward. When affliction weighs down the spirits, or sickness the strength, it is then that the cheering influence of that recollection will be doubly felt.

*   *   *

HANNAH MORE

From Strictures on the Modern System of Female Education (1799)†

From *Chapter VI. Filial Obedience Not the Character of the Age*

Among the real improvements of modern times, and they are not a few, it is to be feared that the growth of filial obedience cannot be included. Who can forbear observing and regretting in a variety of instances, that not only sons but daughters have adopted something of that spirit of independence, and disdain of control, which characterise the times? And is it not obvious that domestic manners are not slightly tinctured with the hue of public principles? The *rights of man* have been discussed, till we are somewhat wearied with the discussion. To these have been opposed with more presumption than prudence *the rights of woman*. It follows according to the natural progression of human things, that the next stage of that irradiation which our enlighteners are pouring in upon us as will produce grave descants on the *rights of children*.

*   *   *

An early habitual restraint is peculiarly important to the future character and happiness of women. They should when very young be inured to contradiction. Instead of hearing their bon-mots treasured up and repeated to the guests till they begin to think it dull, when they themselves are not the little heroine of the theme, they should be accustomed to receive but little praise for their vivacity or their wit, though they should receive just commendation for their patience, their industry, their humility, and other qualities which have more worth than splendour. They should be led to distrust their own judgment; they should learn not to murmur at expostulation; but should be accustomed to expect and to endure opposition. It is a lesson with which the world will not fail to furnish them; and they will not practise it the worse for having learnt it the sooner. It is of the last importance to their happiness in life that they should early acquire a submissive temper and a forbearing spirit. They must even endure to be thought wrong sometimes,

† Hannah More (1745–1833) was a poet, playwright, novelist, and author of religious and didactic tracts associated with the Evangelical movement and such causes as the abolition of the slave trade and the education of the poor in the virtues of sobriety, industry, and subordination. A formidable polemicist on behalf of the English reaction against the French Revolution (some of her tracts sold millions of copies), More denounced the female "rights" of independence and social equality vindicated by Mary Wollstonecraft, but she also scorned the attractiveness recommended by writers like Gregory and Gisborne as frivolous, advocating a severity and discipline Wollstonecraft herself might approve. More's *Strictures on the Modern System of Female Education* (1799) sold more than 19,000 copies. The selection here comes from the first edition.

when they cannot but feel they are right. And while they should be anxiously aspiring to do well, they must not expect always to obtain the praise of having done so. But while a gentle demeanor is inculcated, let them not be instructed to practise gentleness merely on the low ground of its being decorous and feminine, and pleasing, and calculated to attract human favour; but let them be carefully taught to cultivate it on the high principle of obedience to Christ; on the practical ground of labouring after conformity to HIM, who, when he proposed himself as a perfect pattern of imitation, did not say, learn of me for I am great, or wise, or mighty, but "learn of me for I "am meek and lowly," and graciously promised that the reward should accompany the practice, by encouragingly adding, "and ye shall find rest to your souls." Do not teach them humility on the ordinary ground that vanity is *unamiable*, and that no one will *love* them if they are proud; for that will only go to correct the exterior and make them soft and smiling hypocrites. But inform them that "God "resisteth the proud," while "them that are meek he shall guide in judgment, and such as are gentle them shall he teach his way." In these, as in all other cases, an habitual attention to the *motives* should be carefully substituted in their young hearts, in the place of too much anxiety about the *event* of actions, and too much solicitude for that human praise which attaches to appearances as much as to realities; to success more than to desert.

*   *   *

It is one grand object to give the young probationer just and sober views of the world on which she is about to enter. Instead of making her bosom bound at the near prospect of emancipation from her instructors; instead of teaching her young heart to dance with premature flutterings as the critical winter draws near in which *she is to come out*; instead of raising a tumult in her busy imagination at the approach of her first *grown up ball*; endeavour to convince her that the world will not turn out to be that scene of unvarying and never-ending delights which she has perhaps been led to expect, not only from the sanguine temper and warm spirits natural to youth, but from the value she has seen put on those showy accomplishments which have too probably been fitting her for her exhibition in life. Teach her that this world is not a stage for the display of superficial talents, but for the strict and sober exercise of fortitude, temperance, meekness, faith, diligence, and self-denial.

*   *   *

From Parliamentary Debates (1806)†

Abolition of the Slave Trade

Mr. Secretary *Fox* rose, in pursuance of the notice he had given, to submit to the house a Resolution on this subject, and spoke as follows:

* * *

"That this house, conceiving the African Slave Trade to be contrary to the principles of justice, humanity, and sound policy, will, with all practicable expedition, proceed to take effectual measures for abolishing the said trade, in such manner, and at such period, as may be deemed advisable."

Sir *Ralph Milbanke* rose to second the motion. He should always, he said, endeavour to suppress a trade so unjust and so degrading to humanity; and he wished it to be remembered, that he had on every occasion given his vote for the abolition of it. He had been uniformly of opinion that the slave trade was a ruinous and destructive traffic, that it was contrary to every principle of sound policy, justice, and humanity, as had been stated by the right hon. secretary in a much more able manner than he could do. He was happy to say that the majority of his constituents concurred with him in these sentiments. He was persuaded that the cultivation of the colonies could be very well carried on without any fresh importation of slaves, and concluded by seconding the motion.

General *Tarleton* * * * felt it his duty to call their attention to the situation of Liverpool—a town which, from a miserable fishing hamlet of about 150 huts, had within a century risen to be the second town, in point of commercial wealth and consequence, in the British dominions, entirely by the African trade. * * * It was eminent for the prosperity of its commerce, its wealth, its loyalty; for the important aid it furnished to the British marine, by affording at all times a numerous supply of seamen, through its African and West Indian trade.

* * *

The *Solicitor General* said, he should have much more cordially supported a motion for leave to bring in a bill for the immediate abolition of this abominable traffic: yet still, he thought the motion ought to be supported, as pledging the house to take the most speedy and practicable means to abolish it. * * * An hon. general had said, that if this trade were to be abolished, his constituents of Liverpool must come to that house for compensation, and that a great source of revenue must

---

† From *The Parliamentary Debates from the Year 1803 to the Present Time* (London, 1812), vol. vii. As a member of the House of Commons as well as an owner of a plantation in Antigua, Sir Thomas Bertram would have participated in the many debates about the abolition of the slave trade. The selections excerpted here, which represent typical arguments on both sides at a relatively late stage, date from June 10, 1806. The trade was officially abolished in 1807.

be destroyed: be it so, at any expence, rather than hold the detestable principle, that the debts of England were to be paid with the blood of Africa. The noble lord had said, that the progress of abolition must be gradual, and that it could only be effected in concert with our West-India planters. In such a case, indeed, the prospect must not only be far distant, but utterly hopeless, as the Planters were a set of men whose assent could never be obtained * * *

General *Gascoyne* said, that with respect to the Abolition of the Slave Trade, unless the house did something effectual, they would do a great deal of mischief. * * * He was well assured it would prove highly injurious to our commercial interests in the colonies; and he wished to be informed, if there ever was a period in our history, in which our colonial trade had been in greater danger than it was at the present moment? but the house had been told, it must give some opinion on the subject; and the resolution said, the Slave Trade was contrary to every principle of justice, humanity, and sound policy. As to the question of justice, he could by no means acquiesce in it; but while we were so strenuous in favour of justice to the Africans, we should not lose sight of it towards one another; and it was not at all clear, in his mind, that it was just in the mother country to treat the colonies in the way she had done, by first giving legislative encouragement to the traffic in question, and afterwards, when large properties had been embarked in it, endeavouring thus to put a stop to it, and thereby involving in beggary and ruin, those who had risked their property, and thereby added greatly to the wealth, prosperity, and aggrandisement of the whole empire. * * * The hon. general then quoted the 25th chapter of Leviticus, out of which he read the 44th, 45th, and 46th verses. * * * The above clearly proved, that slavery had from the earliest times, been countenanced and authorized by religion itself. * * * Would the house say, that the justice they would extend to the Africans, they would refuse to their own countrymen. He would repeat what he had said on a former occasion, with the same qualification. If we had new colonies to cultivate, and he was asked his opinion, in respect to encouraging the Slave Trade, he would certainly advise it; and why? because our commerce had derived such immense sources of wealth and prosperity from it, as had proved a great mean of raising the country to its present state of aggrandisement and magnificence, and enabled us to contend with our enemies. * * *

Mr. *Wilberforce* said, that with regard to one part of the hon. general's speech, he was doubtful whether he should not have interrupted him by calling him to order. But if the hon. gent. could believe that slavery was sanctioned by our holy religion, he should only feel disposed to pity his weakness and error, and should endeavour to rectify his mistake in the spirit of mildness and conciliation. It was the glory of our religion, that it not only forbade all those odious means by which slaves were procured, but expressly prohibited the practice of man-stealing, and called us to act on a principle of universal philanthropy, and kind good-will to all men. * * *

Mr. *Rose* said as far as regarded the question of the Abolition of the Slave Trade, his opinion was still consistent with that which he had on all occasions expressed; * * * it was, that a progressive duty should be imposed upon the importation of slaves into the West Indies, until at last it should amount to such an impost as would prove an absolute prohibition of the traffic, and that the bounty should not be a source of emolument to the state, but be paid to the mothers of slaves born in the islands, until they had borne a certain number, when they should be considered free. * * * To the charge of a right hon. gent. that the trade was a system of rapine, bloodshed, and murder, he would only say, that he had read every tittle of the evidence collected on the subject, and was at a loss to form from it an opinion of the measure; that evidence was clogged with some unfounded relations, particularly the story of a ship under the command of admiral Nugent having lost 80 out of a cargo of slaves, from their being made to "walk "the board," in which there was not a syllable of truth. * * * He had argued against the abolition of the trade, because it would be depriving the country of a great source of revenue, amounting to two or three millions, at an inconvenient time, and because the American trade in slaves would increase exactly in the proportion that ours decreased. * * *

Mr. *W. Smith* said, he hoped after that night, the house would hear no more of the silly confusion of abolition of the trade, and emancipation of the negroes, as the latter had been as constantly denied by, as attributed to, the supporters of the former. He thought the character of the West-India planters, who had refused the suggestion of government to make the killing of negroes murder, hardly entitled them to the consideration gentlemen seemed to think they ought to have. He thought it was only by attention to the morals of the negroes that their decrease in the colonies could be prevented. * * * The only towns in England now interested in this trade, were London, Bristol, and Liverpool. Bristol had relinquished it, London was nearly approaching to the same, and he trusted ere long, Liverpool would follow so good an example, and that persons engaged in this trade of blood and rapine will soon be ashamed to shew their faces in society. * * *

Mr. *Fox* made a most able and animated reply, which, we regret it is not in our power to detail at length. * * * The house, he considered, was pledged upon this subject, and it was now their business to redeem that pledge. * * * The Abolition of the Slave Trade would lead to the abolition of slavery altogether in the West Indies; but he totally differed with some gentlemen, who thought the former could not be done without the consent of those islands, for if this was to be the case, no consent whatever would be granted. With respect to compensation; when the claim was well made out, let the abolition be enacted, and if then shewn that any injury had been sustained, let that be remunerated. * * * The question being loudly called for, the house divided, when there appeared for the motion 114, against it 15; majority 99.

* * *

THOMAS CLARKSON

From History of the . . . Abolition of the African Slave Trade . . . (1808)†

* * *

Thus ended one of the most glorious contests, after a continuance for twenty years, of any ever carried on in any age or country. A contest, not of brutal violence, but of reason. A contest between those, who felt deeply for the happiness and the honour of their fellow-creatures, and those, who, through vicious custom and the impulse of avarice, had trampled under-foot the sacred rights of their nature, and had even attempted to efface all title to the divine image from their minds.

Of the immense advantages of this contest I know not how to speak. Indeed, the very agitation of the question, which it involved, has been highly important. Never was the heart of man so expanded. Never were its generous sympathies so generally and so perseveringly excited. These sympathies, thus called into existence, have been useful in the preservation of a national virtue. For any thing we know, they may have contributed greatly to form a counteracting balance against the malignant spirit, generated by our almost incessant wars during this period, so as to have preserved us from barbarism.

It has been useful also in the discrimination of moral character. In private life it has enabled us to distinguish the virtuous from the more vicious part of the community. It has shown the general philanthropist. It has unmasked the vicious in spite of his pretension to virtue. It has afforded us the same knowledge in public life. It has separated the moral statesman from the wicked politician. It has shown us who, in the legislative and executive offices of our country are fit to save, and who to destroy, a nation.

It has furnished us also with important lessons. It has proved what a creature man is! how devoted he is to his own interest! to what a length of atrocity he can go, unless fortified by religious principle! But as if this part of the prospect would be too afflicting, it has proved to us, on

† Thomas Clarkson (1760–1846) was a tireless advocate of the abolition of the slave trade. Austen described herself as "in love with" him, and probably read his *History of the Rise, Progress, and Accomplishment of the Abolition of the African Slave Trade, by the British Parliament* (2 vols., 1808), the conclusion of which is excerpted here.

the other hand, what a glorious instrument he may become in the hands of his Maker; and that a little virtue, when properly leavened, is made capable of counteracting the effects of a mass of vice!

With respect to the end obtained by this contest, or the great measure of the abolition of the Slave-trade as it has now passed, I know not how to appreciate its importance. To our own country, indeed, it is invaluable. We have lived, in consequence of it, to see the day, when it has been recorded as a principle in our legislation, that commerce itself shall have its moral boundaries. We have lived to see the day, when we are likely to be delivered from the contagion of the most barbarous opinions. They, who supported this wicked traffic, virtually denied, that man was a moral being. They substituted the law of force for the law of reason. But the great Act now under our consideration, has banished the impious doctrine, and restored the rational creature to his moral rights. Nor is it a matter of less pleasing consideration, that, at this awful crisis, when the constitutions of kingdoms are on the point of dissolution, the stain of the blood of Africa is no longer upon us, or that we have been freed (alas, if it be not too late!) from a load of guilt, which has long hung like a mill-stone about our necks, ready to sink us to perdition.

* * *

Reader! Thou art now acquainted with the history of this contest! Rejoice in the manner of its termination! And, if thou feelest grateful for the event, retire within thy closet, and pour out thy thanksgivings to the Almighty for this his unspeakable act of mercy to thy oppressed fellow-creatures.

ELIZABETH INCHBALD

Remarks on Shakespeare's *King Henry VIII* (1806–09)†

As, to do good, for the honour and glory of a Supreme Being, and in conformity to his commandments, is the highest perfection of mortal man—so, to commit evil, under the pretence of religious duty, and in his sacred name, constitutes the most flagrant impiety of which a human creature can, in the full premeditation of guilt, be chargeable.

The crimes, which, unhappily, form all the incidents of this drama, are, by the hardened perpetrators of them, all ascribed to the holy will

† In 1806–09, Elizabeth Inchbald, who had already written many successful plays in addition to *Lovers' Vows*, compiled a twenty-five-volume anthology of *The British Theatre* and wrote prefaces to each play. Inchbald's remarks on Shakespeare's *Henry VIII* are included here as a contemporary response to this then popular play, whose treatment of deeply flawed figures of English temporal and spiritual authority parallels that of *Mansfield Park*. Fanny Price reads *Henry VIII* aloud to Lady Bertram, but Henry Crawford takes over when he enters the room and impresses Fanny with his elocution; see above, pp. 228–29.

and pleasure of Heaven. King Henry casts from his bed and throne his loving and obedient wife, because his conscience dreads the anger of his Maker:—and Cardinal Wolsey devotes himself to pomp, amasses unbounded wealth, and exacts from his neighbours every honour short of adoration, whilst his profession announces—his imitation of an humble Redeemer.

The qualities and characters of both the king and the cardinal underwent almost a total change, from their youth to their manhood, or to that period in which they are here delineated. Henry, when young, possessed personal beauty and grace—his mind was susceptible of all the softer delights, and a peculiar passion for music seemed to have tuned his soul to harmony. Wolsey, even at the age of forty, would laugh, sing, and dance—when he was younger, he would drink also—and once, for some tumult which he raised at a country fair, he suffered the disgrace of being placed in the stocks, though he was, at that very time, rector of a living in the neighbouring village.

Who that had beheld the gay, the graceful, the accomplished Henry, at a ball or concert, enraptured with sweet sounds, could have predicted, that he would divorce four virtuous wives, and behead two of them!—And who that had seen the riotous Wolsey, with his legs imprisoned in a market-place, could possibly have descried, in that object of condign punishment, a future archbishop, England's prime minister, an illustrious cardinal, and an aspirer at the popedom?

From the many artful praises of Anne Bullen, which Shakspeare has introduced in this play, but, above all, from his many prophetic insinuations, and, at length, his bold prophecy, that the infant daughter of Henry and beauteous Anne, shall prove a blessing to this realm, it is conjectured that the play of Henry the Eighth was written and performed during the reign of that very child, Queen Elizabeth.

With all his desire to please his royal mistress, Shakspeare has yet never once depreciated the virtues of the good Queen Katharine, or drawn a veil over her injuries. He has made her the most prominent, as well as the most amiable sufferer in his drama; and, in thus closely adhering to the truth of history, he pays a silent tribute to the liberality of Elizabeth, more worth than all his warmest eulogiums.

Katharine's first speech, in that excellent part of the play, her trial, is taken from history, with but trivial variation; and likewise the king's reply to it. Her dying scene, particularly her letter and message to the king, have also the sanction of history for their most pathetic passages. Commentators have, in general, preferred the latter scene to the foregoing one, in its quality of exciting compassion; but, perhaps, a mild and submissive woman, such as Katharine is described, can never be considered so much an object of pity as when bitter provocation has impelled her to assume the deportment of haughtiness and the language of anger.

The self-same words which Wolsey spoke upon his fall, are here inserted, and are the lines beginning, "Had I served my God," &c.— This statesman and churchman is by far more respectable in his adversity than in his prosperity; and yet, it may be observed, that he merely took the road to heaven when the path to all terrestrial joys had closed upon his footsteps.

High as the merit of this play is, its attraction on the stage is aided by a magnificent coronation of the elevated Anne Bullen. It is melancholy, however, to reflect, upon viewing this fictitious ceremony, that a few years only elapsed, after the spectacle had been in *reality* exhibited, when the same unthinking crowd who resorted to gaze, ran, with equal curiosity, to behold the identical object of all this splendour, and their admiration—perish upon a scaffold.

Anne Bullen, or rather Queen Anne, was the first crowned head who suffered death by the law of England; and yet her daughter, Elizabeth,—less penetrated by her mother's woes, than governed by her father's cruelty,—caused the second legal execution of a sovereign, in the person of her own cousin, Mary, Queen of Scots.

Many parts of this drama, where the principal characters are not introduced, are, nevertheless, highly interesting; such, in particular, is the final adieu of the Duke of Buckingham. The prayers and good wishes of him, and of all the injured persons in this play, for their common tyrant Henry, are not more remarkable for their charity than for their inefficacy. Henry's remaining life was divided between fits of anger, remorse, despondency; and he died, after a reign of thirty-seven years, hated by every Englishman,—with the rancour of a slave.

CRITICISM

JAN FERGUS

Power and *Mansfield Park*†

In her dealings with [Thomas] Egerton, Austen seems to have learned quickly that his interests were very different from hers. Her wry remark on the price that he charged for *Pride and Prejudice* shows her awareness that he was likely to profit from the novel more than she had—and more than she had profited from publishing *Sense and Sensibility* for herself. After the success of *Pride and Prejudice*, Egerton certainly offered to purchase the copyright of Austen's next novel, but she did not accept his offer. It was no doubt rather low—perhaps £150. She evidently had learned to prefer her own judgement of the value of her work to Egerton's, and she was prepared to risk an unfavourable response from the reading public. In other words, Austen had 'written myself into £250', as she wrote to her brother Frank, and she chose to invest that money in her own work—wisely, as it happened (*L* 317; 3 July 1813). Publishing *Mansfield Park* for herself would once again give her brother Henry the task of supervising the printers, but Henry probably urged her not to sacrifice her profit to his convenience.

Austen's letters include several details about the writing of *Mansfield Park*, most notoriously the still frequently misunderstood remark that she would write of 'ordination'. As long ago as 1973, F. B. Pinion pointed out that, taken in context, the remark does not refer to writing the novel at all but to writing her letter. Having written to Cassandra at great length about *Pride and Prejudice*, concluding with her supposition that it must be 'rather shorter than S. & S. altogether', Austen continues:

> Now I will try to write of something else, & it shall be a complete change of subject—ordination—I am glad to find your enquiries have ended so well. If you could discover whether Northamptonshire is a country of Hedgerows I should be glad again.
>
> (*L* 298; 29 Jan. 1813)[1]

In context, Austen is telling Cassandra that she will finally change the subject and write no more of *Pride and Prejudice*. Again, her use of 'I will' and 'it shall' always promises, threatens or commands, and here the promise and threat jokingly underline the effort required to get

† From *Jane Austen: A Literary Life* (New York: St. Martin's Press, 1991) 141–59. Reprinted with permission of St. Martin's Press, Incorporated, and Macmillan Press Ltd. The author's notes have been abridged. Page references to *Mansfield Park* refer to this Norton Critical Edition.

1. *Jane Austen's Letters to Her Sister Cassandra and Others*, ed. R. W. Chapman, 2nd ed. (1952; rpt. Oxford UP, 1979). Subsequent references appear in parentheses.

herself off the topic of her novel. Of course, the real joke is that Austen shifts the topic to one involving yet another novel—to the enquiries that she had asked Cassandra to make about ordination, perhaps concerning where and when Edmund Bertram's ordination should take place. In *Mansfield Park* Edmund is ordained at Peterborough 'in the course of the Christmas week' (175). Cassandra was at Steventon and could have asked her brother James whether those details were accurate.

If Austen had brought *Mansfield Park* to Edmund's departure for Peterborough by January 1813, she had reached the 11th chapter of Volume 2 and had thus completed about three-fifths of the whole. Even if her enquiries about ordination predated her writing the chapter, she was still quite far advanced. In an earlier letter to Cassandra she had referred to having to change the Government House at Gibraltar to the Commissioner's, and to the round table at Mrs Grant's, details that occur in the sixth and seventh chapters of the second volume (*L* 292, 294; 24 Jan. 1813). Cassandra must have read at least so far before she left for Steventon early in January. By the time Austen wrote to Frank on 3 July, she had certainly written the Portsmouth section: she tells him that she has mentioned 'the Elephant in it, & two or three other of your old Ships' but will remove these references if Frank objects (*L* 317). Again, Cassandra remembered that *Mansfield Park* had been completed 'soon after June 1813'. In other words, Austen may have written almost half the novel between January and July 1813, despite short visits to London in April and May, the first to attend Henry's wife Eliza in her last illness, and the second perhaps to provide company for Henry in his bereavement.

Austen probably took the finished manuscript with her when she paid her last visit to Godmersham—her first in four years—from September to November 1813. According to Anna Austen Lefroy, Austen was not a favourite with her nieces and nephews at Godmersham:

> They liked her indeed as a playfellow, & as a teller of stories, but they were not really fond of her. I believe that their Mother was not; at least that she very much preferred the elder Sister.

Nonetheless, two of Edward's daughters remembered very similar stories of their aunt's habits of writing, which they may have noticed at this time. Marianne recalled observing, at 12 years of age:

> how Aunt Jane would sit quietly working beside the fire in the library, saying nothing for a good while, and then would suddenly burst out laughing, jump up and run across the room to a table where pens and paper were lying, write something down, and then come back to the fire and go on quietly working as before.

Louisa remembered a similar detail, observed when she was eight: 'She was very absent indeed. She would sit silent awhile, then rub her hands, laugh to herself and run up to her room'. Austen was evidently able to become absorbed in the world of her novels despite an outward show of conventional womanly behaviour: she would have been 'quietly working' at her needle. These anecdotes indicate too that Austen composed in her head, not on the page, a practice evident also in her surviving drafts. These include sentences in which all but a few separated words have been crossed out, showing that Austen had composed her revision completely before she began to make changes.

Louisa Knight is also the source for the notion that Cassandra tried to persuade Austen:

> to alter the end of Mansfield Park and let Mr. Crawford marry Fanny Price. She [Louisa] remembers their arguing the matter but Miss Austen stood firmly and would not allow the change.

It is inconceivable, however, that the 'very prim' Cassandra, who preferred *Mansfield Park* among the novels published in her sister's lifetime, would seriously have argued for such an ending (MW 436). She and her sister were almost certainly enjoying a mock argument about the conclusion of the novel, and their eight-year-old niece was understandably baffled by their humour.

Having revised and made a fair copy of *Mansfield Park*, Austen offered it to Egerton perhaps in January 1814. Two to three months seem to have been a reasonable time in which to expect a book to go through the press. If Egerton sent *Mansfield Park* to the printer in January, Austen might expect to see proofs by March. At that time, Henry first began reading the novel as he travelled with his sister to London. If he read it in proof, as Deirdre Le Faye supposes, then the delay of nearly two months before the novel was published on 9 May is difficult to understand. Once proofs were corrected, the copies could be worked off the presses quite soon. Austen herself, however, wrote on 21 March, expecting a delay of at least a month:

> Perhaps before the end of April, *Mansfield Park* by the author of S & S.—P. & P. may be in the world.—Keep the *name* to yourself. I sh^d not like to have it known beforehand.

Although Egerton apparently did not produce *Mansfield Park* as speedily as he had *Pride and Prejudice*, he seems to have done so quite cheaply, perhaps at Austen's request. The paper is thinner (thus less expensive) than the thin paper used for *Pride and Prejudice*, and because each page contains 25 lines, not 23 as in the earlier novels, further savings on paper were achieved. R. W. Chapman has conjectured that Egerton printed only 1250 copies; later, Henry Austen reminded John Murray that he himself had 'expressed astonishment that so small an Edit: of such a work should have been sent into the world'. This edition sold out in only six months, more quickly than that of

Pride and Prejudice, which had been exhausted in eight or nine months despite being almost certainly smaller. Using Chapman's estimate of 1250 copies, we must assume that Egerton produced *Mansfield Park* extremely cheaply indeed, otherwise the figures do not gibe with what we know of Austen's earnings. It exceeded £310, the largest profit that she received during her lifetime for any novel.[2]

2. JA must have made over £310 from *MP,* according to the letter from Henry to John Murray that has been cited, for Henry asserts that she received from her small edition of *SS* (£140) and a moderate one of *MP* more than the £450 Murray had offered for the copyrights of *SS, MP* and *E* (Bodleian MS Autog d 11/224⁴; *Life* (1), pp. 310–11). She also invested the bulk of her profits from her first three novels in £600-worth of 'Navy Fives', according to her own 'Note on Profits'. Scholars have assumed that this £600 represents clear profit, but in fact 'Navy Fives' always sold at a discount during the period when JA could have purchased them. JA's investment cost her less than £600, and her profits were accordingly smaller than has been assumed. Although we cannot calculate her earnings precisely without knowing the date on which she made her purchase, we can nonetheless infer the size of the first edition of *MP* and arrive at an approximation of JA's profits on it.

   Egerton seems to have paid his authors yearly in March. If JA received the money due on *MP* (which had sold out by 18 Nov. 1814) in March 1815 and invested it on 31 March, she would have had to pay only £531 for £600 in the 'Navy Fives', plus perhaps a £1.0.0 commission fee and 2s6d transfer tax (see *Northampton Mercury,* 1 Apr. 1815 for previous day's stock prices of 88.5; see 15 May 1812 receipt to John Plomer Clarke for the sale of £818.19.9 in the 'Navy Fives', Northamptonshire Record Office, Clarke of Welton, Box X5437). Prices fluctuated wildly during 1815, particularly after Napoleon's escape from Elba at the end of Feb. 1815. Between 25 Nov. 1814 and 15 Mar. 1816, 'Navy Fives' were sold at a low of 83.75 (on 18 Aug. 1815) and a high of 97.13 (on 2 Dec. 1814) according to the *Northampton Mercury,* which for most of that time lists only the week's closing prices. JA lost the £13.7.0 of profits on *MP* that remained in Henry's bank when it failed on 15 Mar. 1816; she must have bought the 'Navy Fives' earlier. Accordingly, I calculate that JA earned from £310 on *MP* to a little over £347 (that is, six times the highest price per £100 for 'Navy Fives' plus £1.2.6. commission and tax and the further £13.7.0 that was not invested, less £250 received on *SS* and *PP*).

   R. W. Chapman has argued that JA also received about £30 on the second edition of *SS* in 1815 and included this sum in her investment ('JA and her Publishers', *London Mercury* 22 [1930], p. 339). That edition, however, is unlikely to have become profitable before the year 1815; profit would thus have been distributed in 1816. JA's 'Note on Profits' shows that she received a payment of £12.15.0 from Egerton in March 1816. That figure and the one of £19.13.0 for March 1817 suggests a very slow sale—about 39 copies in 1816, despite the appearance of *E.*

   JA could have made between £310 and £347 from *MP* only in an edition of 1250 copies. A larger edition of 1500 copies would have generated much more profit when sold out than we can account for—at least £440 even allowing £40 for advertisements, and perhaps more; a sold-out edition of 1000 would have produced a profit of less than £200. These calculations are based upon extant publishing records. John Murray's edition of *MP* (750 copies) required 42.75 printed sheets; Egerton's edition, having the same number of gatherings and similar type, would have required the same number of printed sheets. Murray's edition took 65.5 reams, slightly more than the 64.125 reams that, theoretically, 750 copies of a work of 42.75 sheets would need; 1250 copies would have required at most, then, about 109 reams of paper and perhaps less. Calculations for an edition of 1250 can draw upon the Longman records for a novel that the firm printed fairly cheaply: a translation of Louis Bonaparte's three-volume *Maria, or the Hollanders,* published in Feb. 1815. At 30s per ream, charged for the somewhat better paper in Longman's *Maria,* paper for Egerton's *MP* would come to £163.10.0. Printing for *Maria* was charged at 40s per sheet; the type is a bit smaller than that of *MP,* so although *Maria* prints only 24 lines to the page, not 25 as in *MP,* its charges for composing are likely to be a bit higher if anything. Using 40s as the base charge, however, printing *MP* would come to £85.10.0 plus an additional 2s6d per ream or £8.3.9 for all reams 'worked off beyond the 43.5 required by *Maria* (see Longman, reel 2, I/3/76; also Longman Letter Books, I/97/ 290, for reference to charges of '2/6 P Rm for the pressing' of a duodecimo work, dated 11 Feb. 1812). At these rates, total expenses for printing *MP* would be £257.3.9. If all 1250 copies sold at the full trade price for an 18s novel of 11s6d, receipts would come to at most £646.17.6 after deducting Egerton's ten per cent. This leaves £389.13.9, a figure that plausibly

If Austen began to write *Mansfield Park* as soon as she had arranged to publish her first novel for herself, that achievement easily accounts for the sense of power evident throughout her most controversial work. Power is central to *Mansfield Park*—domestic power, including what Mary Crawford calls the manoeuvring business' of marrying (34). Samuel Johnson recorded of Pope that he 'hardly drank tea without a stratagem', and in *Mansfield Park* too the serving of tea can form part of a courtship strategy, signalling 'approaching relief' for Fanny Price when she is constrained to listen to Henry Crawford's addresses:

> The solemn procession, headed by Baddely, of tea-board, urn, and cake-bearers, made its appearance, and delivered her from a grievous imprisonment of body and mind. Mr. Crawford was obliged to move. She was at liberty, she was busy, she was protected. (234)

Imprisonment, deliverance, liberty, protection: terms like these and many others that imply the exercise of power—authority, consequence, government, dominion, submission, independence—are continually applied in *Mansfield Park* to the details of domestic life, particularly courtship and marriage.

These concerns reflect an important change from those of the early novels, particularly in the treatment of women. I have argued that in the juvenilia Austen inverts traditional notions of women. She allows them a frequently outrageous assertiveness and power that they are conventionally denied, but she also points to their marginality within society. In *Mansfield Park*, *Emma* and to a lesser extent *Persuasion*, however, Austen is interested in exploring more profoundly the complex power relationships between women and a social world that reduces their options and makes them marginal. She is less interested, in other words, in portraying women like Elizabeth Bennet and Catherine Morland [in *Northanger Abbey*] who figuratively get away with murder—who rather easily triumph over their circumstances—than in rendering the way that women are enmeshed in circumstance. Enmeshed, not trapped, for Austen's women can to some extent shape their circumstances to accommodate their desires. Growth, assertion and achievement remain possible. But these possibilities have to be seized within a more fully realised social world, one that is less ready to permit individuals to evade its laws. *Mansfield Park* and *Emma* show women not escaping and evading but working within or re-forming their worlds.

*   *   *

covers the costs of advertising, further discounts to the trade (for example, the 'quarter book', a free copy sent to trade customers for every 24 books taken), author's copies and a profit for JA of between £310 and £347. I conclude that Chapman is right to infer an edition of 1250 copies.

A few months after *Mansfield Park* was published in May 1814, Austen's niece Anna at Steventon began a novel and, as she completed each sizeable chunk, sent it to Chawton to be read and criticised. Austen's letters of advice are well known, for they contain almost all her written comments on the art of the novel. She enjoyed her niece's work, encouraged her and clearly expected her to publish it, even advising against including a detail because 'to those who are acquainted with P. & P. it will seem an Imitation' (*L* 394; 10 Aug. 1814). The most familiar advice insists on realism of detail and on probability: the scene should not shift to Ireland where Anna is unfamiliar with manners, for 'You will be in danger of giving false representations' (*L* 395; 10 Aug. 1814); a character should not walk out just after having a broken arm set, even though Anna's father did so, for 'I think it can be so little usual as to *appear* unnatural in a book' (*L* 394; 10 Aug. 1814). Austen is also particularly responsive to language: she enjoys names like Newton Priors and Progillian; she objects to clichés like 'vortex of Dissipation' (*L* 404; 28 Sep. 1814); and she requires conciseness—'here & there, we have thought the sense might be expressed in fewer words' (*L* 394; 10 Aug. 1814).

But the principal concerns are, always, characterisation and (through it) comedy. Austen frequently wants Anna to develop her characters more: 'I should like to have had more of Devereux. I do not feel enough acquainted with him' (*L* 396; 10 Aug. 1814). She is particularly interested in Anna's use of conversation, for in writing *Emma* Austen was herself perfecting her own skill in using comic dialogue to develop not only characters but themes. Accordingly, she writes to Anna:

> Your last chapter is very entertaining—the conversation on Genius &c. Mr. St. J[ulian]—& Susan both talk in character & very well.—In some former parts, Cecilia is perhaps a little too solemn & good, but upon the whole, her disposition is very well opposed to Susan's—her want of Imagination is very natural.—I wish you could make Mrs. F[orester] talk more, but she must be difficult to manage & make entertaining, because there is so much good common sence & propriety about her that nothing can be very *broad*. Her Economy and her Ambition must not be staring.
>
> (*L* 401–2; 9 Sep. 1814)

This short passage refers to many of Austen's favourite techniques of characterisation: entertaining conversations; characters who talk 'in character'; contrasts between characters; broadly comic characters as well as mixed ones who combine sense and nonsense. And these remarks make clear that for Austen, the object of characterisation is entertainment—comedy, in short.

❋   ❋   ❋

Emma was finished in only 14 months, from 21 January 1814 to 29 March 1815. Austen was clearly at the height of her genius. During this time, she also saw *Mansfield Park* through the press, made three visits to Henry in London, and three more to other friends. She was away from home for at least three and a half months altogether. She wrote on 18 November 1814 that the first edition of *Mansfield Park* was sold out, and that her brother wanted her to come to London:

> to settle about a 2^d Edit:—but as I could not very conveniently leave home now, I have written him my Will and pleasure, & unless he still urges it, shall not go.—I am very greedy & want to make the most of it.   (L 411)

She did go, for on 30 November 1814 she wrote:

> it is not settled yet whether I *do* hazard a 2^d Edition. We are to see Egerton today, when it will probably be determined.—People are more ready to borrow & praise, than to buy.   (L 419)

Egerton must already have advised against a second edition. He may have pointed to a falling-off in demand for the first edition before it sold out. Austen had hoped that *Mansfield Park* 'on the credit of P. & P. will sell well, tho' not half so entertaining' (L 317; 3 July 1813). Probably just that happened; the 'Opinions' include a Mrs Dickson's rueful remark, 'I have bought MP.—but it is not equal to P. & P.' (MW 434). The second edition was finally issued more than a year later on 19 February 1816, by John Murray, who brought out *Emma* at the end of 1815.

Unfortunately, Egerton's advice turned out to be good. Murray's second edition of *Mansfield Park* lost money. In addition, Murray produced Austen's books more expensively during her lifetime than Egerton had, which reduced her possible profit. Nonetheless, her decision to approach Murray was not, on the face of it, a bad one. Murray's imprint carried much more prestige than Egerton's. By the time Austen submitted *Emma* to him in August or September 1815, he was Lord Byron's publisher and had co-published many of Walter Scott's works, including *Waverley*, an extremely popular novel. As Austen wrote in mock complaint to her niece Anna:

> Walter Scott has no business to write novels, especially good ones.—It is not fair.—He has Fame and Profit enough as a Poet, and should not be taking the bread out of other people's mouths.—I do not like him, & do not mean to like Waverley if I can help it—but fear I must.   (L 404; 28 Sep. 1814)

Furthermore, Murray was reputedly very open-handed to authors, offering large copyright fees. He wrote in 1820 that 'I declare to God it is my first consideration and the chief object of my gratification to recompense those persons for whom I have the honour of being the publisher'. Accordingly, once Murray received a favourable opinion of *Emma* from his editor William Gifford, who wrote that, 'Of "Emma", I have nothing but good to say', Austen might well have expected a generous fee for the copyright. Instead, on 15 October Murray offered the sum of £450 altogether for the copyrights of *Emma*, *Mansfield Park* and *Sense and Sensibility*. Austen commented, accurately enough, 'It will end in my publishing for myself I daresay' (*L* 425; 17 Oct. 1815). Despite illness, Henry dictated early in November an exasperated reply to Murray: 'The terms you offer are so very inferior to what we had expected, that I am apprehensive of having made some great Error in my Arithmetical Calculation'. He went on to point out that his sister had made more than £450 by one small edition of *Sense and Sensibility* and a moderate one of *Mansfield Park*. Henry's illness worsened, and Austen conducted most of the remaining negotiations for herself. In a letter of 3 November, she requested a meeting with Murray, at which time he must have agreed to publish *Emma* on commission, and on 23 November she was already 'vexed' by printers' delays (*L* 431, 432). Murray responded civilly, promising 'no farther cause for dissatisfaction. . . . In short, I am soothed & complimented into tolerable comfort' (*L* 433; 24 Nov. 1815).

Murray's arrangement to publish *Emma* on commission was, in fact, exceptional. His business records show that he published few works by women and very few novels. In his catalogue for May 1817, he lists among more than two hundred publications only five 'novels' apart from Austen's: one by Scott, two by Isaac Disraeli, and two anonymous works. His great admiration for *Pride and Prejudice* probably influenced him. And when he obtained Scott's review of *Emma*, the longest and best that Austen received in her lifetime, Murray did her a favour, since his own profit was not heavily involved. He could make no more than £137.10.0 from *Emma* if every copy were sold.

Hindsight indicates that Murray's offer of £450 for the three copyrights was fair if not generous. Austen would have done well to accept it. First, she would have received that sum within a year. Instead, because losses on the second edition of *Mansfield Park* were set against the profits of *Emma*, Austen received during her lifetime only £38.18.0 profit on her greatest work. Ultimately, her heirs received a total of about £385 more from the sole edition of *Emma*, from the second of *Mansfield Park* (both of which were remaindered in 1821), and from the sale in 1832 of the copyrights of the three novels for £42 each. In short, Murray's estimate in 1815 of the market value of her copyrights was if anything exaggerated.

*　　*　　*

LIONEL TRILLING

Mansfield Park†

* * *

There is one novel of Jane Austen's, *Mansfield Park*, in which [her] characteristic irony seems not to be at work. Indeed, one might say of this novel that it undertakes to discredit irony and to affirm literalness, that it demonstrates that there are no two ways about anything. And *Mansfield Park* is for this reason held by many to be the novel that is least representative of Jane Austen's peculiar attractiveness. For those who admire her it is likely to make an occasion for embarrassment. By the same token, it is the novel which the depreciators of Jane Austen may cite most tellingly in justification of their antagonism.

About this antagonism a word must be said. Few writers have been the object of an admiration so fervent as that which is given to Jane Austen. At the same time, she has been the object of great dislike. Lord David Cecil has said that the people who do not like Jane Austen are the kind of people "who do not like sunshine and unselfishness," and Dr. Chapman, the distinguished editor of Jane Austen's novels and letters, although dissenting from Lord David's opinion, has speculated that perhaps "a certain lack of charity" plays a part in the dislike. But Mark Twain, to take but one example, manifestly did not lack charity or dislike sunshine and unselfishness, and Mark Twain said of Jane Austen that she inspired in him an "animal repugnance." The personal intensity of both parties to the dispute will serve to suggest how momentous, how elemental, is the issue that Jane Austen presents.

The *animality* of Mark Twain's repugnance is probably to be taken as the male's revulsion from a society in which women seem to be at the center of interest and power, as a man's panic fear at a fictional world in which the masculine principle, although represented as admirable and necessary, is prescribed and controlled by a female mind. Professor Garrod, whose essay, "Jane Austen, A Depreciation," is a *summa* of all the reasons for disliking Jane Austen, expresses a repugnance which is very nearly as feral as Mark Twain's; he implies that a direct sexual insult is being offered to men by a woman author who "describes everything in the youth of women which does not matter" in such a way as to appeal to "that age in men when they have begun to ask themselves whether anything matters." The sexual protest is not only masculine—Charlotte Brontë despised Jane Austen for representing men and women as nothing but ladies and gentlemen.

† From *The Opposing Self: Nine Essays in Criticism* (New York: Viking, 1955) 208–30. Copyright © 1955 by Lionel Trilling, reprinted by permission of The Wylie Agency, Inc.

The sexual objection to Jane Austen is a very common one, even when it is not made explicit. It is not valid, yet it ought to be taken seriously into account. But then there is Emerson with his characteristic sexual indifference, his striking lack of animality, and Emerson's objection to Jane Austen is quick and entire, is instinctual. He says that she is "sterile" and goes on to call her "vulgar." Emerson held this opinion out of his passion of concern for the liberty of the self and the autonomy of spirit, and his holding it must make us see that the sexual reason for disliking Jane Austen must be subsumed under another reason which is larger, and, actually, even more elemental: the fear of imposed constraint. Dr. Chapman says something of this sort when he speaks of "political prejudice" and "impatient idealism" as perhaps having something to do with the dislike of Jane Austen. But these phrases, apart from the fact that they prejudge the case, do not suggest the biological force of the resistance which certain temperaments offer to the idea of society as a limiting condition of the individual spirit.

Such temperaments are not likely to take Jane Austen's irony as a melioration of her particular idea of society. On the contrary, they are likely to suppose that irony is but the engaging manner by which she masks society's crude coercive power. And they can point to *Mansfield Park* to show what the social coercion is in all its literal truth, before irony has beglamoured us about it and induced us to be comfortable with it—here it is in all its negation, in all the force of its repressiveness. Perhaps no other work of genius has ever spoken, or seemed to speak, so insistently for cautiousness and constraint, even for dullness. No other great novel has so anxiously asserted the need to find security, to establish, in fixity and enclosure, a refuge from the dangers of openness and chance.

There is scarcely one of our modern pieties that it does not offend. Despite our natural tendency to permit costume and manners to separate her world from ours, most readers have no great difficulty in realizing that all the other novels of Jane Austen are, in essential ways, of our modern time. This is the opinion of the many students with whom I have read the novels; not only do the young men controvert by their enthusiasm the judgment of Professor Garrod that Jane Austen appeals only to men of middle age, but they easily and naturally assume her to have a great deal to say to them about the modern personality. But *Mansfield Park* is the exception, and it is bitterly resented. It scandalizes the modern assumptions about social relations, about virtue, about religion, sex, and art. Most troubling of all is its preference for rest over motion. To deal with the world by condemning it, by withdrawing from it and shutting it out, by making oneself and one's mode and principles of life the very center of existence and to live the round of one's days in the stasis and peace thus contrived—this, in an earlier age, was one of the recognized strategies of life, but to us it seems not merely impracticable but almost wicked.

Yet *Mansfield Park* is a great novel, its greatness being commensurate with its power to offend.

Mansfield Park was published in 1814, only one year after the publication of *Pride and Prejudice*, and no small part of its interest derives from the fact that it seems to controvert everything that its predecessor tells us about life. One of the striking things about *Pride and Prejudice* is that it achieves a quality of transcendence through comedy. The comic mode typically insists upon the fact of human limitation, even of human littleness, but *Pride and Prejudice* makes comedy reverse itself and yield the implication of a divine enlargement. The novel celebrates the traits of spiritedness, vivacity, celerity, and lightness, and associates them with happiness and virtue. Its social doctrine is a generous one, asserting the right of at least the *good* individual to define himself according to his own essence. It is animated by an impulse to forgiveness. One understands very easily why many readers are moved to explain their pleasure in the book by reference to Mozart, especially *The Marriage of Figaro*.

Almost the opposite can be said of *Mansfield Park*. Its impulse is not to forgive but to condemn. Its praise is not for social freedom but for social stasis. It takes full notice of spiritedness, vivacity, celerity, and lightness, but only to reject them as having nothing to do with virtue and happiness, as being, indeed, deterrents to the good life.

Nobody, I believe, has ever found it possible to like the heroine of *Mansfield Park*. Fanny Price is overtly virtuous and consciously virtuous. Our modern literary feeling is very strong against people who, when they mean to be virtuous, believe they know how to reach their goal and do reach it. We think that virtue is not interesting, even that it is not really virtue, unless it manifests itself as a product of "grace" operating through a strong inclination to sin. Our favorite saint is likely to be Augustine; he is sweetened for us by his early transgressions. We cannot understand how any age could have been interested in Patient Griselda. We admire Milton only if we believe with Blake that he was of the Devil's party, of which we are fellow travelers; the paradox of the *felix culpa* and the "fortunate fall" appeals to us for other than theological reasons and serves to validate all sins and all falls, which we take to be the signs of life.

It does not reconcile us to the virtue of Fanny Price that it is rewarded by more than itself. The shade of Pamela hovers over her career. We take failure to be the mark of true virtue and we do not like it that, by reason of her virtue, the terrified little stranger in Mansfield Park grows up to be virtually its mistress.

Even more alienating is the state of the heroine's health. Fanny is in a debilitated condition through the greater part of the novel. At a certain point the author retrieves this situation and sees to it that Fanny becomes taller, prettier, and more energetic. But the first impression remains of a heroine who cannot cut a basket of roses without fatigue and headache.

Fanny's debility becomes the more striking when we consider that no quality of the heroine of *Pride and Prejudice* is more appealing than her physical energy. We think of Elizabeth Bennet as in physical movement; her love of dancing confirms our belief that she moves gracefully. It is characteristic of her to smile; she likes to tease; she loves to talk. She is remarkably responsive to all attractive men. And to outward seeming, Mary Crawford of *Mansfield Park* is another version of Elizabeth Bennet, and Mary Crawford is the antithesis of Fanny Price. The boldness with which the antithesis is contrived is typical of the uncompromising honesty of *Mansfield Park*. Mary Crawford is conceived—is calculated—to win the charmed admiration of almost any reader. She is all pungency and wit. Her mind is as lively and competent as her body; she can bring not only a horse but a conversation to the gallop. She is downright, open, intelligent, impatient. Irony is her natural mode, and we are drawn to think of her voice as being as nearly the author's own as Elizabeth Bennet's is. Yet in the end we are asked to believe that she is not to be admired, that her lively mind compounds, by very reason of its liveliness, with the world, the flesh, and the devil.

This strange, this almost perverse, rejection of Mary Crawford's vitality in favor of Fanny's debility lies at the very heart of the novel's intention. "The divine," said T. E. Hulme in *Speculations*, "is not life at its intensest. It contains in a way an almost anti-vital element." Perhaps it cannot quite be said that "the divine" is the object of Fanny's soul, yet she is a Christian heroine. Hulme expresses with an air of discovery what was once taken for granted in Christian feeling. Fanny is one of the poor in spirit. It is not a condition of the soul to which we are nowadays sympathetic. We are likely to suppose that it masks hostility—many modern readers respond to Fanny by suspecting her. This is perhaps not unjustified, but as we try to understand what Jane Austen meant by the creation of such a heroine, we must have in mind the tradition which affirmed the peculiar sanctity of the sick, the weak, and the dying. The tradition perhaps came to an end for literature with the death of Milly Theale, the heroine of Henry James's *The Wings of the Dove*, but Dickens exemplifies its continuing appeal in the nineteenth century, and it was especially strong in the eighteenth century. Clarissa's sickness and death confirm her Christian virtue, and in Fielding's *Amelia*, the novel which may be said to bear the same relation to *Tom Jones* that *Mansfield Park* bears to *Pride and Prejudice*, the sign of the heroine's Christian authority is her loss of health and beauty.

Fanny is a Christian heroine: it is therefore not inappropriate that the issue between her and Mary Crawford should be concentrated in the debate over whether or not Edmund Bertram shall become a clergyman. We are not, however, from our reading of the novel, inclined to say more than that the debate is "not inappropriate"—it startles us to discover that ordination was what Jane Austen said her novel was to be "about." In the letter in which she tells of having received the first copies of *Pride and Prejudice*, and while she is still in high spirits over her achievement, she says, "Now I will try and write something else, and it shall be a complete change of subject—ordination." A novelist, of course, presents a new subject to himself, or to his friends, in all sorts of ways that are inadequate to his real intention as it eventually will disclose itself—the most unsympathetic reader of *Mansfield Park* would scarcely describe it as being about ordination. Yet the question of ordination is of essential importance to the novel.

It is not really a religious question, but, rather, a cultural question, having to do with the meaning and effect of a *profession*. Two senses of that word are in point here, the open avowal of principles and beliefs as well as a man's commitment to a particular kind of life work. It is the latter sense that engages us first. The argument between Fanny and Mary is over what will happen to Edmund as a person, as a *man*, if he chooses to become a clergyman. To Mary, every clergyman is the Mr. Collins of *Pride and Prejudice*; she thinks of ordination as a surrender of manhood. But Fanny sees the Church as a career that claims a man's best manly energies; her expressed view of the churchman's function is that which was to develop through the century, exemplified in, say, Thomas Arnold, who found the Church to be an adequate field for what he called his talents for command.

*   *   *

The great fuss that is made over the amateur theatricals can seem to us a mere travesty on virtue. And the more so because it is never made clear why it is so very wrong for young people in a dull country house to put on a play. The mystery deepens, as does our sense that *Mansfield Park* represents an unusual state of the author's mind, when we know that amateur theatricals were a favorite amusement in Jane Austen's home. The play is Kotzebue's *Lovers' Vows* and it deals with illicit love and a bastard, but Jane Austen, as her letters and novels clearly show, was not a prude. Some of the scenes of the play permit Maria Bertram and Henry Crawford to make love in public, but this is not said to be decisively objectionable. What is decisive is a traditional, almost primitive, feeling about dramatic impersonation. We know of this, of course, from Plato, and it is one of the points on which almost everyone feels superior to Plato, but it may have more basis in actuality than we commonly allow. It is the fear that the impersonation of a bad or inferior

character will have a harmful effect upon the impersonator, that, indeed, the impersonation of any other self will diminish the integrity of
the real self.

A right understanding of the seemingly absurd episode of the play
must dispel any doubt of the largeness of the cultural significance of
Mansfield Park. The American philosopher George Mead has observed
that the "assumption of roles" was one of the most important elements
of Romanticism. Mead conceived of impersonation as a new mode of
thought appropriate to that new sense of the self which was Romanticism's characteristic achievement. It was, he said further, the self's
method of defining itself. Involved as we all are in this mode of thought
and in this method of self-definition, we are not likely to respond sym-
pathetically to Jane Austen when she puts it under attack as being
dangerous to the integrity of the self as a moral agent. Yet the testimony
of John Keats stands in her support—in one of his most notable letters
Keats says of the poet that, as poet, he cannot be a moral agent; he has
no "character," no "self," no "identity"; he is concerned not with moral
judgment but with "gusto," subordinating his own being to that of the
objects of his creative regard. Wordsworth implies something of a related sort when he contrasts the poet's volatility of mood with the bulk-
ing permanence of identity of the Old Leech Gatherer. And of course
not only the poet but the reader may be said to be involved in the
problems of identity and of (in the literal sense) integrity. Literature
offers the experience of the diversification of the self, and Jane Austen
puts the question of literature at the moral center of her novel.

The massive ado that is organized about the amateur theatricals and
the dangers of impersonation thus has a direct bearing upon the matter
of Edmund Bertram's profession. The election of a profession is of
course in a way the assumption of a role, but it is a permanent impersonation which makes virtually impossible the choice of another. It is
a commitment which fixes the nature of the self.

The ado about the play extends its significance still further. It points,
as it were, to a great and curious triumph of Jane Austen's art. The
triumph consists in this—that although on a first reading of *Mansfield
Park* Mary Crawford's speeches are all delightful, they diminish in
charm as we read the novel a second time. We begin to hear something
disagreeable in their intonation: it is the peculiarly modern bad quality
which Jane Austen was the first to represent—insincerity. This is a trait
very different from the *hypocrisy* of the earlier novelists. Mary Crawford's intention is not to deceive the world but to comfort herself; she
impersonates the woman she thinks she ought to be. And as we become
inured to the charm of her performance we see through the moral
impersonation and are troubled that it should have been thought necessary. In Mary Crawford we have the first brilliant example of a dis-

tinctively modern type, the person who cultivates the *style* of sensitivity, virtue, and intelligence.

Henry Crawford has more sincerity than his sister, and the adverse judgment which the novel makes on him is therefore arrived at with greater difficulty. He is conscious of his charm, of the winningness of his personal style, which has in it—as he knows—a large element of *natural* goodness and generosity. He is no less conscious of his lack of weight and solidity; his intense courtship of Fanny is, we may say, his effort to add the gravity of principle to his merely natural goodness. He becomes, however, the prey to his own charm, and in his cold flirtation with Maria Bertram he is trapped by his impersonation of passion—his role requires that he carry Maria off from a dull marriage to a life of boring concupiscence. It is his sister's refusal to attach any moral importance to this event that is the final proof of her deficiency in seriousness. Our modern impulse to resist the condemnation of sexuality and of sexual liberty cannot properly come into play here, as at first we think it should. For it is not sexuality that is being condemned, but precisely that form of asexuality that incurred D. H. Lawrence's greatest scorn—that is, sexuality as a game, or as a drama, sexuality as an expression of mere will or mere personality, as a sign of power, or prestige, or autonomy: as, in short, an impersonation and an insincerity.

A passage in one of her letters of 1814, written while *Mansfield Park* was in composition, enforces upon us how personally Jane Austen was involved in the question of principle as against personality, of character as against style. A young man has been paying court to her niece Fanny Knight, and the girl is troubled by, exactly, the effect of his principledness on his style. Her aunt's comment is especially interesting because it contains an avowal of sympathy with Evangelicism, an opinion which is the reverse of that which she had expressed in a letter of 1809 and had represented in *Pride and Prejudice*, yet the religious opinion is but incidental to the affirmation that is being made of the moral advantage of the profession of principle, whatever may be its effect on the personal style.

> Mr. J. P.——has advantages which do not often meet in one person. His only fault indeed seems Modesty. If he were less modest, he would be more agreeable, speak louder & look Impudenter;—and is it not a fine Character of which Modesty is the only defect?—I have no doubt that he will get more lively & more like yourselves as he is more with you;—he will catch your ways if he belongs to you. And as to there being any objection from his *Goodness,* from the danger of his becoming even Evangelical, I cannot admit *that.* I am by no means convinced that we ought not all to be Evangelicals, & am at least persuaded that they who are so from Reason and Feeling, must be happiest & safest. Do not be

frightened from the connection by your Brothers having most wit. Wisdom is better than Wit, & in the long run will certainly have the laugh on her side; & don't be frightened by the idea of his acting more strictly up to the precepts of the New Testament than others.

The great charm, the charming greatness, of *Pride and Prejudice* is that it permits us to conceive of morality as style. The relation of Elizabeth Bennet to Darcy is real, is intense, but it expresses itself as a conflict and reconciliation of styles: a formal rhetoric, traditional and rigorous, must find a way to accommodate a female vivacity, which in turn must recognize the principled demands of the strict male syntax. The high moral import of the novel lies in the fact that the union of styles is accomplished without injury to either lover.

Jane Austen knew that *Pride and Prejudice* was a unique success and she triumphed in it. Yet as she listens to her mother reading aloud from the printed book, she becomes conscious of her dissatisfaction with one element of the work. It is the element that is likely to delight us most, the purity and absoluteness of its particular syle.

> The work [she writes in a letter to her sister Cassandra] is rather too light, and bright, and sparkling; it wants to be stretched out here and there with a long chapter of sense, if it could be had; if not, of solemn specious nonsense, about something unconnected with the story; an essay on writing, a critique on Walter Scott, or the history of Buonaparté, or anything that would form a contrast, and bring the reader with increased delight to the playfulness and epigrammatism of the general style.

Her overt concern, of course, is for the increase of the effect of the "general style" itself, which she believes would have been heightened by contrast. But she has in mind something beyond this technical improvement—her sense that the novel is a genre that must not try for the shining outward perfection of style; that it must maintain a degree of roughness of texture, a certain hard literalness; that, for the sake of its moral life, it must violate its own beauty by incorporating some of the irreducible prosy actuality of the world. It is as if she were saying of *Pride and Prejudice* what Henry James says of one of the characters of his story "Crapy Cornelia": "Her grace of ease was perfect, but it was all grace of ease, not a single shred of it grace of uncertainty or of difficulty."

Mansfield Park, we may conceive, was the effort to encompass the grace of uncertainty and difficulty. The idea of morality as achieved style, as grace of ease, is not likely ever to be relinquished, not merely because some writers will always assert it anew, but also because morality itself will always insist on it—at a certain point in its development, morality seeks to express its independence of the grinding necessity by which it is engendered, and to claim for itself the autonomy and gratuitousness of art. Yet the idea is one that may easily deteriorate or be perverted. Style, which expresses the innermost truth of any creation or action, can also hide the truth; it is in this sense of the word that we speak of "mere style." *Mansfield Park* proposes to us the possibility of this deception. If we perceive this, we cannot say that the novel is without irony—we must say, indeed, that its irony is more profound than that of any of Jane Austen's other novels. It is an irony directed against irony itself.

In the investigation of the question of character as against personality, of principle as against style and grace of ease as against grace of difficulty, it is an important consideration that the Crawfords are of London. Their manner is the London manner, their style is the *chic* of the metropolis. The city bears the brunt of our modern uneasiness about our life. We think of it as being the scene and the cause of the loss of the simple integrity of the spirit—in our dreams of our right true selves we live in the country. This common mode of criticism of our culture is likely to express not merely our dissatisfaction with our particular cultural situation but our dislike of culture itself, or of any culture that is not a folk culture, that is marked by the conflict of interests and the proliferation and conflict of ideas. Yet the revulsion from the metropolis cannot be regarded merely with skepticism; it plays too large and serious a part in our literature to be thought of as nothing but a sentimentality.

To the style of London Sir Thomas Bertram is the principled antagonist. The real reason for not giving the play, as everyone knows, is that Sir Thomas would not permit it were he at home; everyone knows that a sin is being committed against the absent father. And Sir Thomas, when he returns before his expected time, confirms their consciousness of sin. It is he who identifies the objection to the theatricals as being specifically that of impersonation. His own self is an integer and he instinctively resists the diversification of the self that is implied by the assumption of roles. It is he, in his entire identification with his status and tradition, who makes of Mansfield Park the citadel it is—it exists to front life and to repel life's mutabilities, like the Peele Castle of Wordsworth's "Elegiac Verses," of which it is said that it is "cased in the unfeeling armor of old time." In this phrase Wordsworth figures in a very precise way the Stoic doctrine of *apatheia*, the principled refusal to experience more emotion than is forced upon one, the rejection of sensibility as a danger to the integrity of the self.

Mansfield stands not only against London but also against what is implied by Portsmouth on Fanny's visit to her family there. Fanny's mother, Lady Bertram's sister, had made an unprosperous marriage, and the Bertrams' minimal effort to assist her with the burdens of a large family had been the occasion of Fanny's coming to live at Mansfield nine years before. Her return to take her place in a home not of

actual poverty but of respectable sordidness makes one of the most
engaging episodes of the novel, despite our impulse to feel that it ought
to seem the most objectionable. We think we ought not be sympathetic
with Fanny as, to her slow dismay, she understands that she cannot be
happy with her own, her natural, family. She is made miserable by the
lack of cleanliness and quiet, of civility and order. We jib at this, we
remind ourselves that for the seemliness that does indeed sustain the
soul, men too often sell their souls, that warmth and simplicity of feeling may go with indifference to disorder. But if we have the most
elementary honesty, we feel with Fanny the genuine pain not merely
of the half-clean and the scarcely tidy, of confusion and intrusion, but
also of the vulgarity that thrives in these surroundings. It is beyond
human ingenuity to define what we mean by vulgarity, but in Jane
Austen's novels vulgarity has these elements: smallness of mind, insufficiency of awareness, assertive self-esteem, the wish to devalue, especially to devalue the human worth of other people. That Fanny's family
should have forgotten her during her long absence was perhaps inevitable; it is a vulgarity that they have no curiosity about her and no
desire to revive the connection, and this indifference is represented as
being of a piece with the general indecorum of their lives. We do not
blame Fanny when she remembers that in her foster father's house
there are many rooms, that hers, although it was small and for years it
had been cold, had always been clean and private, that now, although
she had once been snubbed and slighted at Mansfield, she is the daughter of Sir Thomas's stern heart.

Of all the fathers of Jane Austen's novels, Sir Thomas is the only one
to whom admiration is given. Fanny's real father, Lieutenant Price of
the Marines, is shallow and vulgar. The fathers of the heroines of *Pride
and Prejudice*, *Emma*, and *Persuasion*, all lack principle and fortitude;
they are corrupted by their belief in their delicate vulnerability—they
lack *apatheia*. Yet Sir Thomas is a father, and a father is as little safe
from Jane Austen's judgment as he is from Shelley's. Jane Austen's
masculine ideal is exemplified by husbands, by Darcy, Knightley, and
Wentworth, in whom principle and duty consort with a ready and
tender understanding. Sir Thomas's faults are dealt with explicitly—if
he learns to cherish Fanny as the daughter of his heart, he betrays the
daughters of his blood. Maria's sin and her sister Julia's bad disposition
are blamed directly upon his lack of intelligence and sensibility. His
principled submission to convention had issued in mere worldliness—
he had not seen to it that "principle, active principle" should have its
place in the rearing of his daughters, had not given then that "sense of
duty which alone can suffice" to govern inclination and temper. He
knew of no other way to counteract the low worldly flattery of their
Aunt Norris than by the show of that sternness which had alienated
them from him. He has allowed Mrs. Norris, the corrupter of his daugh-

ters and the persecutor of Fanny, to establish herself in the governance
of his home; "she seemed part of himself."

So that Mansfield is governed by an authority all too fallible. Yet
Fanny thinks of all that comes "within the view and patronage of Mans-
field Park" as "dear to her heart and thoroughly perfect in her eyes."
The judgment is not ironical. For the author as well as for the heroine,
Mansfield Park is the good place—it is The Great Good Place. It is the
house "where all's accustomed, ceremonious," of Yeats's "Prayer for
His Daughter"—

> How but in custom and ceremony
> Are innocence and beauty born?

Yet Fanny's loving praise of Mansfield, which makes the novel's last
word, does glance at ironies and encompasses ironies. Of these ironies
the chief is that Lady Bertram is part of the perfection. All of Mansfield's life makes reference and obeisance to Sir Thomas's wife, who is
gentle and without spite, but mindless and moveless, concerned with
nothing but the indulgence of her mild, inexorable wants. Middle-aged,
stupid, maternal persons are favorite butts for Jane Austen, but although
Lady Bertram is teased, she is loved. Sir Thomas's authority must be
qualified and tutored by the principled intelligence, the religious
intelligence—Fanny's, in effect—but Lady Bertram is permitted to live
unregenerate her life of cushioned ease.

I am never quite able to resist the notion that in her attitude to Lady
Bertram Jane Austen is teasing herself, that she is turning her irony
upon her own fantasy of ideal existence as it presented itself to her at
this time. It is scarcely possible to observe how *Mansfield Park* differs
from her work that had gone before and from her work that was to
come after without supposing that the difference points to a crisis in
the author's spiritual life. In that crisis fatigue plays a great part—we
are drawn to believe that for the moment she wants to withdraw from
the exigent energies of her actual self, that she claims in fancy the right
to be rich and fat and smooth and dull like Lady Bertram, to sit on a
cushion, to be a creature of habit and an object of ritual deference, not
to be conscious, especially not to be conscious of herself. Lady Bertram
is, we may imagine, her mocking representation of her wish to escape
from the requirements of personality.

* * *

In the person of Lady Bertram it [*Mansfield Park*] affirms, with all
due irony, the bliss of being able to remain unconscious of the demands
of personality (it is a bliss which is a kind of virtue, for one way of
being solid, simple, and sincere is to be a vegetable). It shuts out the
world and the judgment of the world. The sanctions upon which it
relies are not those of culture, of quality of being, of personality, but
precisely those which the new conception of the moral life minimizes,

the sanctions of principle, and it discovers in principle the path to the wholeness of the self which is peace. When we have exhausted our anger at the offense which *Mansfield Park* offers to our conscious pieties, we find it possible to perceive how intimately it speaks to our secret inexpressible hopes.

ALISTAIR DUCKWORTH

Mansfield Park: Jane Austen's Grounds of Being†

Throughout Jane Austen's fiction, estates function not only as the settings of action but as indexes to the character and social responsibility of their owners. Thus in *Pride and Prejudice* the aesthetic good sense that is evident in the landscape of Pemberley ("neither formal, nor falsely adorned" [245]) permits the reader (and Elizabeth) to infer the fundamental worth of Darcy's social and ethical character, while in *Emma* Donwell Abbey, with its "suitable, becoming, characteristic situation" (358), is the appropriate expression of Knightley's firm sense of stewardship. *Persuasion* provides a negative example, the renting of Kellynch Hall pointing to Sir Walter Elliot's abandonment of his social trust. Landscape improvements, too, figure incidentally in all the novels, but it is in *Mansfield Park* that Jane Austen chooses to make them a recurring motif and, in so doing, to suggest an attitude to the process of social change that is central to all her fiction.

The motif is raised early in the novel during a conversation in the Mansfield dining parlor (I, vi). Rushworth, the rich but stupid owner of Sotherton Court, has just returned from a visit to Smith's place, Compton, which has recently been improved by Humphry Repton, the controversial heir of Capability Brown in landscape gardening: "I never saw a place so altered in my life. I told Smith I did not know where I was" (39). His own place Rushworth now considers "a prison —quite a dismal old prison," which "wants improvement . . . beyond any thing" (39). Maria Bertram, his fiancée, suggests that he too employ Repton, and the officious Mrs. Norris, learning that Repton charges five guineas a day, is quick to support her favorite niece and to seize the opportunity of spending someone else's money: "Well, and if they were *ten* [guineas], . . . I am sure *you* need not regard it. The expense need not be any impediment. If I were you, I should not think of the expense. . . . Sotherton Court deserves every thing that taste and money can do" (39).

Interestingly, in view of her well-established viciousness in other re-

† Alistair Duckworth, *The Improvement of the Estate* (Baltimore: The Johns Hopkins University Press, 1971) 38–54. Reprinted by permission of The Johns Hopkins University Press. The author's notes have been abridged. Page references refer to this Norton Critical Edition.

spects, Mrs. Norris is (or was) something of an improver herself, having done a "vast deal in that way at the parsonage" (39):

> "[W]e made it quite a different place from what it was when we first had it. You young ones do not remember much about it, perhaps. But if dear Sir Thomas were here, he could tell you what improvements we made; . . . If it had not been for [Mr. Norris's sad state of health], we should have carried on the garden wall, and made the plantation to shut out the churchyard, just as Dr. Grant has done." (39–40)

I shall later argue that Jane Austen is using the technical vocabulary of improvements in a symbolic way; here it is sufficient to note that while Mrs. Norris says she has done a "vast deal," Henry Crawford is the true expert in this matter. Though the original condition of his own estate, Everingham, seemed "perfect" to his sister, Mrs. Grant, with "such a happy fall of ground, and such timber" (44), Crawford has nevertheless "improved" it: "My plan was laid at Westminster—a little altered perhaps at Cambridge, and at one and twenty executed" (45). Henceforward he becomes the acknowledged expert on improvements and is urged by Mrs. Grant and by Julia Bertram to lend his practical aid at Sotherton Court. Mary Crawford, it is true, finds "improvements *in hand* . . . the greatest of nuisances" (42), but she has no objections to them once "complete": "had I a place of my own in the country, I should be most thankful to any Mr. Repton who would undertake it, and give me as much beauty as he could for my money" (42).

Against this group of enthusiasts only Fanny Price and Edmund Bertram offer any opposition to improvements. Fanny, quoting Cowper, expresses her concern for the fate of the avenue at Sotherton which Rushworth plans to "improve" (he has already cut down "two or three fine old trees" which blocked the prospect (41). Her sentiments, while sufficiently romantic, are not to be read ironically. Unlike the subverted enthusiasm of the heroine in *Northanger Abbey*—Catherine "cared for no furniture of a more modern date than the fifteenth century" (182) —Fanny's respectful attitude to the traditional aspects of the estate, like her later regret over the disuse of the chapel, is largely underwritten by her author. Edmund, for his part, though willing to admit the need of "modern dress" (41) at Sotherton, argues against the employment of an improver: "had I a place to new fashion, I should not put myself into the hands of an improver. I would rather have an inferior degree of beauty, of my own choice, and acquired progressively" (41–42).

Why Repton, and the figure of the improver generally, should so divide the characters in *Mansfield Park* is a question that seems, initially, easy to answer. Throughout Jane Austen's writing life Humphry Repton (1752–1818) was a figure of controversy, the butt of satire, and a man whose name must frequently have been on the lips of anyone connected with the land. As R. W. Chapman notes, she would have come across Repton's celebrated Red Books in some of the houses she visited, and she must have been aware of the "paper war" in which he upheld his principles of landscaping against the attacks of Sir Uvedale Price and Richard Payne Knight, the chief proponents in their different ways of the new picturesque. The context of the paper war, however, is only a partial explanation of Jane Austen's intentions in *Mansfield Park,* and to the degree that it suggests that her distaste for Repton was merely aesthetic, implying a preference for the more naturalistic styles of Price and Knight, it can be misleading. However "enamoured of Gilpin on the Picturesque" she may have been, Jane Austen commonly treats an enthusiasm for this style with some irony in her fiction—not everyone has Marianne Dashwood's passion for dead leaves. As the tone of Fanny's and Edmund's dissenting remarks in the Mansfield dining parlor suggests, moreover, she is less occupied with the aesthetic merits of different styles of landscape than with the negative social implications of a particular mode of "improvement." The important question, then, is why she chose to cast Repton as a negative social example.

A glance at Repton's *Sketches and Hints on Landscape Gardening* (1795) and *Observations on the Theory and Practice of Landscape Gardening* (1803) introduces something of a problem here, for these works reveal him to be not only an engaging, if occasionally sycophantic, writer but a theorist whose principles of landscaping often seem close to Jane Austen's own views. His emphasis on "utility," his insistence, in the first chapter of *Sketches,* upon a "due attention to the character and situation of the place to be improved" align him with, for example, Edward Ferrars in *Sense and Sensibility,* whose "idea of a fine country . . . unites beauty with utility" (97)[1] and who finds "more pleasure in a snug farm-house than a watchtower" (98). In his celebrated debate with Marianne (I, xviii), Ferrars' rational view of the countryside does not, of course, wholly invalidate Marianne's enthusiasm for the picturesque; like Marianne, Jane Austen was as sensitive to the "beauties of nature" as she was aware that "admiration of landscape scenery [had] become a mere jargon" (97). But as in ethical matters Jane Austen gives priority to Elinor's sense over Marianne's sensibility, so in landscape she favors Edward's humanized, social settings to Marianne's romantic scenes. After a temporary enthusiasm for "rocks and mountains," Elizabeth Bennet in *Pride and Prejudice* settles for Darcy's tastefully improved estate.

Not all of Repton's principles of landscaping are close to Jane Austen's implied views, of course, nor was his practice always consistent with his theoretical principles. His theory, moreover, written in the

---

1. *Sense and Sensibility,* in *The Novels of Jane Austen,* ed. R. W. Chapman (Oxford: Oxford UP, 1932) 97. Subsequent quotations from novels other than *Mansfield Park* will come from this edition and will be noted parenthetically.

midst of debate, often has an apologetic air, giving rise to the suspicion of rationalizations after the fact. Undoubtedly some of Repton's improvements fully merited the criticisms they received. While it may be true, therefore, as Donald Pilcher argues, that Repton was made "the scapegoat for the sins of [a] flock of fashionable 'improvers'," and that Jane Austen, in singling him out, both capitalized upon his notoriety and, somewhat unfairly, made him a representative of a much wider movement, it is also possible that she had a reasoned dislike of Repton's methods. Why this should be is perhaps suggested by the radical improvements Repton made at his own cottage in Essex (pictured in the frontispiece). What he has "shut out" and "screened off" may have improved his view, but it has also removed him from any participation in the community. One wonders, in particular, what happened to the beggar (veteran, evidently, of many wars) after Repton's "improvement."

Repton's association with Capability Brown's methods accounted for much of his disrepute, for inevitably he became heir not only to Brown's practice but to the criticism that had long been directed at the "omnipotent magician" and at the figure of the improver generally. As early as Garrick's play *Lethe or Esop in the Shades* (1740), Brownian improvements had been subject to satire (Brown is here satirized when Lord Chalkstone takes exception to the layout of the Elysian fields as viewed from the shores of the Styx). Even earlier, in the country house poem of the seventeenth century, expensive innovations in estates had been castigated for their extravagance, selfishness, and disregard of "use." Thus, when Jane Austen used Repton as a negative figure, and Thomas Love Peacock cruelly satirized him as Marmaduke Milestone in *Headlong Hall* (1816), they took their places in a long tradition of anti-improvement literature.

Jane Austen's own treatment of improvements, I suspect, owes much to Cowper's *The Task*. In Book III ("The Garden"), her favorite author castigates "improvement" as the "idol of the age" in a passage that continues the traditional complaints of the country house poem against the ostentation and hostility to tradition of the vain trustee. Here too is an awareness of the enormous transformation that improvements could bring about in a landscape:

> The lake in front becomes a lawn;
> Woods vanish, hills subside, and vallies rise:
> And streams, as if created for his use,
> Pursue the track of his directing wand. . . . (ll. 774–77)[2]

With her knowledge of Cowper alone Jane Austen would have been well prepared to point up the insidious implications of extreme landscaping, but she was also undoubtedly aware of Richard Payne Knight's

2. See "Contexts," above, p. 388.

vituperative poem "The Landscape" (London, 1794), in which Repton is bidden to "follow to the tomb" his "fav'rite Brown":

Thy fav'rite Brown, whose innovating hand
First dealt thy curses o'er this fertile land. (Book I, ll. 287–88)

Even without Cowper and Knight, it is likely that Jane Austen's own experience would have led her to a dislike of the drastic alterations to landscape which frequently attended Brownian or Reptonian improvements. The radical nature of such improvements, even more pronounced in the work of less talented imitators, was everywhere evident at the time. Often involving not only the indiscriminate cutting down of trees and the magical creation of rivers and lakes but, on occasions, the relocation of whole villages which blocked the prospect and the redirection of roads by special acts of Parliament, such projects could hardly fail to strike her as emblems of inordinate change. If Edmund Burke in his political prose following the French Revolution could use the imagery of excessive estate improvements to illustrate the horrors of the revolution, we need not be surprised that Jane Austen should suggest in the adoption of Reptonian methods dangerous consequences for the continuity of a culture.

The example of Burke may be usefully extended here, not because he necessarily had a direct influence on Jane Austen's thought, but because his dislike of radical change, again and again expressed in terms of injuries done to an estate or house, suggests an appropriately serious context for her own treatment of improvements. Examples could be multiplied of Burke's employment of house and estate metaphors in the *Reflections*. Often, indeed, in speaking of the state, Burke is clearly using the image of the estate to control the construction of his thought:

> . . . one of the first and most leading principles on which the commonwealth and the laws are consecrated, is lest the temporary possessors and life-renters in it, unmindful of what they have received from their ancestors, or of what is due to their posterity, should act as if they were the entire masters; that they should not think it amongst their rights to . . . commit waste on the inheritance, by destroying at their pleasure the whole original fabric of their society; hazarding to leave to those who come after them, a ruin instead of an habitation—and teaching these successors as little to respect their contrivances, as they had themselves respected the institutions of their forefathers. By this unprincipled facility of changing the state as often, and as much, and in as many ways as there are floating fancies or fashions, the whole chain and continuity of the commonwealth would be broken.[3]

3. Edmund Burke, *Reflections on the Revolution in France*, ed. William B. Todd (New York: Rinehart, 1959) 115. Subsequent references to this edition will be made parenthetically.

Constantly the need of a stable "ground" structure is stressed, as in his expressed "prejudice" in favor of church establishment:

> For, taking ground on that religious system, of which we are now in possession, we continue to act on the early received, and uniformly continued sense of mankind. That sense not only, like a wise architect, hath built up the august fabric of states, but like a provident proprietor, to preserve the structure from prophanation and ruin . . . hath solemnly and for ever consecrated the commonwealth, and all that officiate in it. (R, 111)

But it is not only in his veneration of traditional structures and dislike of excessive alteration that Burke serves as a useful gloss for *Mansfield Park*. His concept of "improvement," where this is necessary, is also relevant to Jane Austen's motif.

As he was fond of stating, Burke was no enemy to change and improvement, and the unimproved existence of institutions is a condition against which he constantly warns in the *Reflections*. "A state without the means of some change is without the means of its conservation" (R, 23). An even greater danger for Burke, however, lies in the overthrow or destruction of establishments sanctioned by time and custom. Thus Burke is led, as Father Canavan has shown, to distinguish carefully between what is necessary improvement and what is more properly to be considered destruction. Burke would agree with Charles James Fox in this matter that "improvements were not to be confounded with innovations; the meaning of which was always odious, and conveyed an idea of alterations for the worse." To "improve" was to treat the deficient or corrupt parts of an established order with the character of the whole in mind; to "innovate" or "alter," on the other hand, was to destroy all that had been built up by the "collected reason of the ages." The difference is, of course, the difference between the two revolutions: the English had introduced "improvement" with their revolution, the French "innovation" and "alteration" with theirs.

It is perhaps worthwhile emphasizing the consistent antonymy of "improvement" and "innovation," or "alteration," at this period. A further passage from Burke will make the point, while a passage implicitly critical of Burke's viewpoint by William Godwin will provide the kind of exception that proves the rule. Burke writes: "A spirit of innovation is generally the result of a selfish temper and confined views. People will not look forward to posterity, who never look backward to their ancestors. Besides, the people of England well know, that the idea of inheritance furnishes a sure principle of conservation; . . . without at all excluding a principle of improvement" (R, 38). Godwin, on the other hand (surely with this precise passage in mind), writes of "government" that it is the "perpetual enemy of change." Among other abuses, governments "prompt us to seek the public welfare, *not in al-*

teration and improvement, but in a timid reverence for the decisions of our ancestors . . ." (my italics). Interestingly, this passage from the third edition of *Enquiry Concerning Political Justice* (1798) is a revision of a passage in the first edition (1793), in which "innovation" is phrasally associated with "improvement." The point is clear: Godwin's association of both "innovation" and "alteration" with "improvement" is an intentional dig at Burke, as well as an indication of his diametrically opposite political ideology.

In the context of the anti-improvement literature of the time and of the political prose that frequently makes use of metaphors drawn from the practice of estate improvements, Jane Austen's motif takes on a serious meaning. In her view, radical improvements of the kind Repton made were not improvements at all but "innovations" or "alterations" of a destructive nature. No less than a political constitution, an estate, with the immaterial systems of religion, morality, and manners that it contains and upholds, will need improvement from time to time. Cultural atrophy, resulting from neglect, is to be avoided. Even more serious, however, is a too active and thoughtless response on the part of an heir. Thinking to introduce improvement, he may well destroy the "whole original fabric" of his inheritance. What has been "acquired progressively" should not be radically changed. Not to know where one is in an estate that has been "altered" is hardly the cause for pleasure that Rushworth considers it, and Mrs. Norris's "vast" improvement at the Mansfield parsonage, which made it "quite a different place from what it was when [the Norrises] first had it" (39), strikes an insidious note in the context of Burke's prose.

Following the conversation at Mansfield there are two main episodes in the novel in which the improvements theme is taken up. The first is the visit to Sotherton, expressly made by the party from Mansfield for the purpose of assessing its "capabilities." The second occurs when Crawford proposes improvements to Thornton Lacey, the parsonage that Edmund is to occupy on ordination. The two extreme responses that are evident in these episodes help negatively to define Jane Austen's own view of what constitutes the proper improvement of a cultural inheritance.

Sotherton Court, an "ancient manorial residence of the family, with all its rights of Court-Leet and Court-Baron" (59), is "one of the largest estates and finest places in the country" (29). Its status as a representative estate is stressed. Edmund notes that the "house was built in Elizabeth's time, and is a large, regular, brick building—heavy, but respectable looking . . ." (41). Mary Crawford, while dismissing its owner, sees that "a man might represent the county with such an estate" (112). Heavy with the air of tradition and history, Sotherton is, however, aesthetically out of date. When the party from Mansfield arrive, they find the house as Edmund described it—"ill placed . . . in one of the lowest spots of the park" (41). With its brick construction, avenues, walls, palisades, and iron gates, it is self-evidently an estate that has largely missed the "improvements" of the great eighteenth century gardeners. Altogether it is a "good spot for fault-finding" (65). The interior of the house echoes the old-fashioned condition of the park, for it is "furnished in the taste of fifty years back" (60), and though "of pictures there were abundance . . . the larger part were family portraits, no longer any thing to any body but Mrs. Rushworth" (60). As for the chapel, built in James II's reign and "formerly in constant use both morning and evening" (62), its function has ceased, prayers having been discontinued by the late Mr. Rushworth. Fanny, who had wished to see Sotherton in its "old state" (41), is disappointed: "There is nothing awful here, nothing melancholy, nothing grand. Here are no aisles, no arches, no inscriptions, no banners" (61). Like her response to the avenue earlier, Fanny's remarks are somewhat romantic (on this occasion she quotes from Scott), and Edmund gently rebukes her by describing the original modest function of the chapel. Again, however, Fanny's instinctive response is in some measure valid, for Sotherton as a functioning estate has clearly fallen into a state of desuetude. In Burkean terms "the idea of inheritance" which "furnishes a sure principle of conservation" has been lost. Here it is less important that Rushworth has come to his inheritance out of the direct line than that he has utterly no awareness of his duty as trustee. Well aware of the aesthetic deficiencies of his estate, he is ignorant of far worse ills. We gather what these are from the complacent description given by Maria Bertram, as the party from Mansfield approaches Sotherton in the barouche [see pp. 59–60, above].

Rushworth's improvements will clearly have nothing to do with his run-down cottages. His attention to the road leading to his house, like his admiration of Smith's "approach" at Compton and his later delight in wearing a "blue dress, and a pink satin cloak" (98) for the play, reveal his character to be grounded in vanity. Nor will his marriage to Maria be the "improvement" (39) which Mrs. Grant predicts. Maria's pride in the handsome spire shows a love of display equal to her husband's, while the pleasure she takes in discovering that the church and great house are not close is nicely ambiguous. The propinquity of house and church, common in English estates and often emphasized in Jane Austen's fiction, signifies the necessary interdependence of the clerical and landed orders. Here the physical distance between the two need have no significance, but with Maria as mistress the bells are unlikely to summon the family to regular worship, and the threat is implied that the physical gap will become a spiritual gap—a spatial correlative of a gap between, in Lord Lindsay's terms, a morality of grace and a morality

of station.[4] Rushworth and Maria will become the antitypes of the
landed ideal proposed by generations of English poets:

> The Lord and Lady of this place delight
> Rather to be in act, than seeme in sight.[5]

Their disregard of religion, as evident in Maria's remarks as in the
present disuse of the chapel, will deny the religious dimension of
landed ownership, and the displacement of their concern from the
function to the appearance of Sotherton will neglect the traditional
emphasis on "use" as the basis of landed existence:

> 'T is Use alone that sanctifies Expence
> And Splendour borrows all its rays from Sense.[6]

If the condition of Sotherton serves as a negative emblem of cultural
atrophy, stemming from the neglect of its trustees, a second estate,
Thornton Lacey, faces the even greater danger of excessive "alteration."
The threat exists in Crawford's plans for its "improvement." Aware that
the parsonage is to be Edmund's home on ordination, Crawford predicts that "there will be work for five summers at least before the place
is live-able" (166).

What is remarkable here is how closely Crawford's proposals resemble Repton's plans for Harlestone Hall, the house most frequently considered the model of Mansfield Park. In Fragment VII of his *Fragments
on the Theory and Practice of Landscape Gardening* (1816), Repton
describes his method at Harlestone:

> The House was formerly approached and entered in the south
> front, which was encumbered by stables and farm yards; the road
> came through the village, and there was a large pool in front; this
> pool has been changed to an apparent river, and the stables have
> been removed. An ample Garden has been placed behind the
> house, the centre of the south front has been taken down, and a
> bow added with pilasters in the style of the house: the entrance is
> changed from south to the north side, and some new rooms to the
> west have been added.[7]

---

4. *The Two Moralities: Our Duty to God and Society* (London: Eyre and Spottiswoode, 1948).
5. Thomas Carew, "To My Friend G. N. from Wrest," ll. 31–32.
6. Alexander Pope, "Epistle to Burlington," ll. 179–80.
7. Quoted by R. W. Chapman in the Oxford edition of *Mansfield Park*, p. 552. Harlestone Park
has been considered the model for Mansfield Park by, among others, F. Alan Walbank in
The English Scene, ed. F. Alan Walbank, 2nd ed. (London: B. T. Batsford, 1946), p. 8.
Chapman, however, seems persuaded by Sir Frank MacKinnon's argument in favor of
Cottesbrook as a possible model (see R. W. Chapman, *Facts and Problems* [Oxford, At the
Clarendon Press, 1948], p. 84, and R. W. Chapman, *Jane Austen: A Critical Bibliography*,
2nd ed. [Oxford, At the Clarendon Press, 1955], item 148). Whether Harlestone or Cottesbrook is Jane Austen's model for Mansfield seems to me of little importance; what is important
is her clear association of Crawford's methods with those of Repton. Cf. Malins, *Landscaping
and Literature*, pp. 138–39.

Disarmed by Repton's tasteful improvements at Harlestone (pictured on the dust jacket of this book and in the frontispiece to Chapman's Oxford edition of *Mansfield Park*), we may be unwilling to grant negative significance to Crawford's "Reptonian" proposals. Given Jane Austen's symbolic mode, however, Crawford's suggestions are insidious enough. His plans to "clear away," "plant up," and "shut out" features of the landscape are to be read as a rejection of a traditional shape of reality, while his wish to re-orient the front of the house suggests a desire for complete cultural reorientation. Furthermore, if Repton is indeed echoed in Crawford's prose, it can be argued that Jane Austen has the latter go beyond Repton's stated practice in the *Fragments*. Whereas Repton—in the paragraph preceding the passage above—was careful to insist upon "unity of character" at Harlestone, arguing that "where great part of the original structure is to remain, the additions should doubtless partake of the existing character," Crawford is intent on completely changing the condition of Thornton Lacey; he wishes to give it a "higher character," "raise it into a *place*" (167). (There is, of course, an additional irony in his grandiose plans for what is, after all, a parsonage.) In other respects, however, Crawford is reminiscent of Repton. His "before and after" description of the garden is the verbal equivalent of the splendid selling device Repton invented in his Red Books. There Repton masked his illustration of the scene as it would be *after* improvement with a flap depicting the *present* (and of course unfashionable) appearance of the landscape. By merely lifting up the flap a prospective customer discovered a transformation.

Edmund Bertram, however, is not tempted by Crawford's picture of a transformed Thornton. He too has "two or three ideas," and "one of them is that very little of [Crawford's] plan for Thornton Lacey will ever be put in practice" (166). He admits that the yard should be removed in the interests of a "tolerable approach" (166)—once again he is not averse to "modern dress"—but he will not permit the wholesale redisposition of the structure that Crawford has in mind. He would agree, one might suggest, with Burke's "prejudice" in favor of an established commonwealth—that it is "with infinite caution that any man ought to venture upon pulling down an edifice which has answered in any tolerable degree for ages the common purposes of society, or on building it up again, without having models and patterns of approved utility before his eyes" (R, 73).

At Sotherton, where Crawford's help was invited, his schemes may at least have helped to bring an old-fashioned landscape up to date (though, even here, there would have been misplaced priorities and emphases); but at Thornton Lacey, uninvited, his plans are not only extravagant and ostentatious, they are also supererogatory. In terms of a value system that is to be found throughout Jane Austen's fiction, Thornton is a substantial and healthy estate. The house is surrounded by yew trees and the glebe meadows are "finely sprinkled with timber" (166). The church (unlike that at Sotherton) is "within a stone's throw" (165) of the house; and the house itself, with its air of having been "lived in from generation to generation, through two centuries at least" (167), is an instructive contrast to Rushworth's moribund home. One is reminded of the healthy conditions of other estates in Jane Austen's fiction and of the signs of essential soundness which she consistently provides. An abundance of timber is one such sign; the nearness of church and house another.

Trees, of course, have provided an emblem of organic growth throughout English literature. One thinks, for example, of the wych elm in *Howards End*, which, in surviving the excavations of the Wilcox men, gives some hope for social continuity. On the other hand, the cutting down of trees has suggested a radical break with the past, at least from the time of Donne's Satire II ("Where are those spred woods which cloth'd heretofore/Those bought lands?") to Ford Madox Ford's *Parade's End*, where the loss of the great tree at Groby signals the end of an order. In the light of this tradition, Fanny's objections to the cutting down of the avenue at Sotherton have deeper meaning.

In Jane Austen's fiction it is remarkable how often the presence of trees betokens value. Pemberley has its "beautiful oaks and Spanish chestnuts" (*PP*, 267), Donwell Abbey (noticeably "with all [its] old neglect of prospect") has an "abundance of timber in rows and avenues, which neither fashion nor extravagance had rooted up" (*E*, 358), and there is no "such timber any where in Dorsetshire, as there is now standing in Delaford Hanger" (*SS*, 375). It is a sign, in *Sense and Sensibility*, that the Norland estate is secure at the beginning of the novel that safeguards have been taken against "any charge on the estate, or . . . any sale of its valuable woods" (4). Equally it is a sign of the present owner's corrupted values that, when the old owner dies, he should cut down "the old walnut trees" in order to build a greenhouse (226).

If trees suggest organic growth and continuity, the nearness of church and house stresses the religious content of landed life, and precisely this would be lost at Thornton if Edmund were to accede to Crawford's plans and give in to the temptation that is posed by Mary Crawford. While her brother paints his picture of an improved Thornton, Mary, hoping to transform Edmund into a man of fashion, is able imaginatively to "shut out the church" and "sink the clergyman" (170). Like Mrs. Norris's improvements at Mansfield which, we are told, were intended to "shut out the churchyard" (40), like Maria's pleasure in the "distance" between church and house at Sotherton, and like Mary's own response to the leaving off of prayers in the Sotherton chapel— "every generation has its improvements" (62)—Mary's view of a future Thornton entirely excludes any sense of religious responsibility.

This, then, is why improvements of the kind the Crawfords favor are distrusted in *Mansfield Park*: they signal a radical attitude to a cultural heritage; they take no account of society as an organic structure; they effect, and indeed seem to favor, a widening of the gap between church and house, religion and the landed order.

* * *

NINA AUERBACH

Jane Austen's Dangerous Charm: Feeling as One Ought about Fanny Price†

Alone among masters of fiction, Jane Austen commands the woman's art of making herself loved. She knows how to enchant us with con- versational sparkle, to charm our assent with a glow of description, to entice our smiles with the coquette's practiced glee. No major novelist is such an adept at charming. Samuel Richardson, her greatest prede- cessor, disdained gentlemanly amenities in his revelations of the mind's interminable, intractable mixture of motives when it engages itself in duels of love; George Eliot, her mightiest successor, rejected charm as an opiate distracting us from the harsh realities her knobby, convoluted books explore. These majestic truthtellers could not write winningly if they tried, for they are too dismally aware of the dark side of enchant- ment; while even in her harshest revelations, Jane Austen is a maestro at pleasing.

Yet, from the cacophony of marriages with which it begins, to the depressed union which ends it, *Mansfield Park* is unlikable. When so knowing a charmer abrades her reader, her withdrawal from our plea- sure must be deliberate. She herself studied the gradations of liking *Mansfield Park* inspired, something she had not troubled to do with her earlier books, as we know from her meticulously compiled "Opin- ions of *Mansfield Park*": "My Mother—not liked it so well as P. & P. —Thought Fanny insipid.—Enjoyed Mrs. Norris.— . . . Miss Burdett —Did not like it so well as P. & P. Mrs. James Tilson—Liked it better than P. & P.,"[1] and so on. We do not know whether these carefully measured dollops of liking amused Jane Austen or annoyed her, but we do know that she was intrigued by the degree to which her unlikable novel was liked. Her apparent withdrawal from the reader's fellowship suggests a departure from the community and the conventions of re- alistic fiction toward a Romantic and a dissonant perspective. If we

---

† From *Jane Austen: New Perspectives*, ed. Janet Todd (New York: Holmes and Meier, 1983) 208–23. Reprinted by permission of the publisher. The author's notes have been abridged. Page references to *Mansfield Park* refer to this Norton Critical Edition.

1. See above, p. 374.

examine this difficult novel, with its particularly unaccommodating heroine, in relation to contemporaneous genres beyond the boundaries of realism, we may better understand Jane Austen's withdrawal from a commonality of delight.

The silent, stubborn Fanny Price appeals less than any of Austen's heroines. Perhaps because of this, she captivates more critics than they. "Nobody, I believe, has ever found it possible to like the heroine of *Mansfield Park*,"[2] Lionel Trilling intoned in 1955, and few would contradict this epitaph today. Yet Trilling goes on to apotheosize this literary wallflower, transfiguring her into a culturally fraught emblem who bears on her scant shoulders all the aches of modern secularism. Such later interpreters as Avrom Fleischman similarly embrace Fanny as emblem if not woman, wan transmitter of intricate cultural ideals.[3] It seems that once a heroine is divested of the power to please, she is granted an import beyond her apparently modest sphere, for, unlike Jane Austen's other, more immediately appealing heroines, Fanny has been said to possess our entire spiritual history as it shapes itself through her in historical time. Elizabeth and Emma live for readers as personal presences, but never as the Romantic, the Victorian, or the Modern *Zeitgeist*. Failing to charm, Fanny is allowed in compensation to embody worlds.

But readers who have been trained to respect the culturally fraught Fanny still shy away from her as a character. Living in uncomfortable intimacy with her as we do when we read the novel, we recall Kingsley Amis's taunt that an evening with Fanny and her clergyman husband "would not be lightly undertaken." We may understand our heritage through Fanny Price, but ought we to want to dine with her? The question is important because, for theorists like George Levine, the more bravely realism departs from the commonality of fellowship, the more radically it tilts toward a monstrosity that undermines the realistic community itself. In the very staunchness of her virtue Fanny Price seems to me to invoke the monsters that deny the charmed circle of realistic fiction.[4] Though she uses the word "ought" with unyielding authority, she evokes uncertainty and unease. Though we learn more about her life, and participate more intimately in her consciousness, than we do with Jane Austen's other heroines, the bothering question remains: How ought we to feel about Fanny Price?

Mansfield Park tilts away from commonality in part because it breaks the code established by Jane Austen's other novels. Few of us could read *Pride and Prejudice, Persuasion*, or even *Emma*, without liking the heroines enough to "travel with them," in Wayne Booth's charming

2. See above, p. 423.
3. Avrom Fleischman, *A Reading of Mansfield Park* (1967; rpt. Baltimore: The Johns Hopkins UP, 1970) 57–59.
4. George Levine, *The Realistic Imagination: English Fiction from Frankenstein to Lady Chatterley* (Chicago: U of Chicago P, 1981) 80.

phrase.[5] *Mansfield Park* embodies a wryer literary perception, one especially congenial to Jane Austen's poetic contemporaries: the creator of Fanny Price assumes that one may live with a character one doesn't like. One motive power of Romantic poetry is the fascination of the uncongenial. In "Resolution and Independence," Wordsworth can be possessed by a deformed and virtually nonhuman leech-gatherer, although the poet is too remote from the old man to absorb a word of his exhortation; an unkempt sinner, Coleridge's Ancient Mariner, can snatch our imagination from a wedding, that great congenial sacrament of human community. These gnarled figures lure us out of fellowship to adopt the perspective of the monstrous and the marginal.

Fanny captures our imaginations in this same Romantic way, by welcoming the reader into her solitary animosity against the intricacies of the normal: "Fanny was again left to her solitude, and with no increase of pleasant feelings, for she was sorry for almost all that she had seen and heard, astonished at Miss Bertram, and angry with Mr. Crawford." (71). The compelling, blighting power of Fanny's spectatorship at Sotherton is characteristic: morality dissolves into angry and unpleasant feelings whose intensity is an alternative to community. For while Fanny's Romanticism suggests itself in her isolating sensibility, her stylized effusions to nature, she is most Romantic in that, like Wordsworth's leech-gatherer or Coleridge's Mariner, there is something horrible about her, something that deprives the imagination of its appetite for ordinary life and compels it toward the deformed, the dispossessed.

This elevation of one's private bad feelings into a power alternate to social life associates Fanny not merely with early Romantic outcasts, but with such dashingly misanthropic hero-villains as Byron's Childe Harold, Mary Shelley's Frankenstein, and Maturin's Melmoth. Their flamboyant willfulness may seem utterly alien to this frail, clinging, and seemingly passive girl who annoys above all by her shyness, but like them, she is magnetically unconvivial, a spoiler of ceremonies. During the excursion to Sotherton, the rehearsals of *Lovers' Vows*, the game of Speculation, her baleful solitude overwhelms the company, perhaps because it expresses and exudes their own buried rancor. In families ranging from Sir Thomas Bertram's stately authoritarianism to the casual disorder of her father's house, Fanny exists like Frankenstein as a silent, censorious pall. Her denying spirit defines itself best in assertive negatives: "No, indeed, I cannot act" (102).

Fanny's credo resonates beyond her particular disapproval of staging *Lovers' Vows*, for, even when the play is not in question, Fanny refuses to act. Instead, and consistently, she counteracts; a creed which seems a high-minded elevation of her own honesty against the dangerous deceit of role-playing is also resistance to the comic, collective rhythms

5. Wayne Booth, A *Rhetoric of Fiction* (Chicago: U of Chicago P, 1961) 245.

of realistic fiction itself. The joyless exercises of her delicate body tacitly condemn not only acting, but activity in general; Mary Crawford's elation at horseback riding is as antagonistic to Fanny as is her flair for acting. At Sotherton, Fanny stations herself beside the dangerous ha-ha as a still bulwark against the mutual serpentine pursuit of the other characters; playing Speculation, she alone will not take the initiative that will advance the game. Fanny's refusal to act is a criticism not just of art, but of life as well. Her timidly resolute denial of acting includes activity and play, those impulses of comedy which bring us together in ceremonial motions where fellowship seems all. Her refusals are her countercharm against the corporate and genial charm with which Jane Austen's comedies win love.

Fanny's role as counteractive genius and spirit of anti-play is anomalous in a romantic heroine, but not in a hero-villain. Like Frankenstein and his monster, those spirits of solitude, Fanny is a killjoy, a blighter of ceremonies and divider of families. It is precisely this opposition to the traditional patterns of romantic comedy that lends her her disturbing strength. Her misery amid the bustle of the play is the stigma of her power (111).

But though she is stricken in the midst of play, unable and unwilling to act, Fanny never retreats from activity. Finally, her "jealousy and agitation" seem to take concrete shape in the angry intruder, Sir Thomas Bertram, who lends authority to Fanny's bad feelings and ends the play. Sir Thomas's interruption seems only the culmination of Fanny's silent, withering power over performance, for before he appears she has already drawn control to her watching self. Backstage, she alone is in possession of each actor's secret grievance; watching and prompting from her isolation, she alone knows everybody's lines. A center of fierce inactivity, Fanny broods jealously over the play until she masters both its script and the secret designs of its actors, at which point Sir Thomas's return vindicates her silent obstructive power. Fanny abdicates from stardom to assume a more potent control over the action: she appropriates to her solitude the controlling omniscience of the rapt audience.

As her novel's sole and constant watcher, the controlling spirit of antiplay, Fanny relinquishes performing heroism to become the jealous reader, whose solitary imagination resurrects the action and keeps it alive. In her own delicately assertive phrase, "I was quiet, but I was not blind" (246). As quietly seeing spectator of others' activities, Fanny plays a role as ambiguous as the reader's own: like Fanny, we vivify the action by our imaginative participation in it, while we hold as well the power to obstruct it by our censure. The anomalous position of the watcher more than justifies Mary Crawford's perplexed question: "Pray, is she out, or is she not?" (36). Withholding herself from play, Fanny ingests the play of everyone she silently sees. As omniscient spectator of all private and public performances, Fanny remains "out" of the action, while her knowledge seeps into its subtlest permutations. Our discomfort at her, then, may incorporate our discomfort at our own silent voyeurism; as a portrait of the reader as a young woman, she is our unflattering if indelible reflection. Her fierce spectatorship forces our reluctant identification.

As omniscient watcher and anti-comic spirit linked in uncomfortable community to the solitary reader, Fanny possesses a subtler power than we find in brighter and livelier heroines of fiction. That dynamic mis-reader Emma Woodhouse is forced by her own misconstructions into the limited position of actor in the comedy she is trying to control from without, while Fanny's role as omniscient outsider thrives on her continued abstention. In her role as controlling, anti-comic watcher, Fanny moves beyond the sphere of traditional heroinism to associate herself with a host of dashing British villains. Like them, this denying girl will not, perhaps cannot, eat; her abstinence makes her a spectral presence at the communal feast. Reunited with her family at Portsmouth, instead of feasting with them, as any of Dickens' or Charlotte Brontë's waifs would gladly do, she is repelled by the very suggestion of food, by "the teaboard never thoroughly cleaned, the cups and saucers wiped in streaks, the milk a mixture of motes floating in thin blue, and the bread and butter growing every minute more greasy than even Rebecca's hands had first produced it" (298). Family food induces only a strangely modern nausea. Fanny's revulsion against food, along with her psychic feasting on the activities of others, crystallizes her somewhat sinister position as outsider who strangely and silently moves into the interior. Her starved incapacity to eat familial food is suggestive of that winsome predator the vampire, an equally solitary and melancholy figure who haunts British literature in his dual role as dark abstainer from a comic dailiness of which he is secretly in possession. Like Fanny, the vampire cannot eat the common nourishment of daily life, but he feasts secretly upon human vitality in the dark.

In adopting the role of traditional literary villains, Fanny infects our imaginations in a way that no merely virtuous heroine could do. Her hungry exclusion seems unappeasable and triumphant. Insofar as she draws sustenance from her role as omniscient outsider at family, excursion, wedding, play, or feast, she stands with some venerable monsters in the English canon. Not only does she share the role of Mary Shelley's creature, that gloomy exile from family whose vocation is to control families and destroy them, but there is a shadow on her even of the melancholy Grendel in the Anglo-Saxon epic *Beowulf*. An exile from common feasting, Grendel peers jealously through the window of a lighted banquet hall. He defines his identity as outsider by appropriating the interior; he invades the lighted hall and begins to eat the eaters. At the end of *Mansfield Park*, Fanny too has won a somewhat predatory victory, moving from outsider in to guiding spirit of the humbled Bertram family. Fanny's cannibalistic invasion of the lighted, spacious estate of Mansfield is genteel and purely symbolic, but, like the primitive Grendel, she replaces common and convivial feasting with a solitary and subtler hunger that possesses its object. In this evocation of an earlier literary tradition, Fanny is Jane Austen's most Romantic heroine, for she is part of a literature newly awakened to ancient forms and fascinated by the monstrous and marginal. In the subtle streak of perversity that still disturbs readers today, she shows us the monsters within Jane Austen's realism, ineffable presences who allow the novels to participate in the darker moods of their age.

Fanny's jealous hunger, which can be assuaged only by private, psychic feasting, isolates her in comedy while it associates her with such venerable predators as the Ancient Mariner, the vampire, the Byronic hero-villain, and, in a far-off echo, *Beowulf*'s Grendel. Her initiation is not that of the usual heroine, whose marriage reconciles us to the choreography of comedy; instead, like the hero-villain, she proclaims her uniqueness through possessive spectatorship. The implications of Fanny's refusal to act are more richly glossed in Romantic poetry and fiction than in early nineteenth-century realism, but Romantic criticism also illuminates the complex genesis of a Fanny Price: her stubborn creed, "I cannot act," recalls some problematic characters of Shakespeare, in whom such critics as Coleridge and Hazlitt discovered new significance.

Like *Mansfield Park*, Shakespearean drama characteristically pivots upon the performance of a play within a play; like Jane Austen, Shakespeare increasingly pushes to center stage the character who refuses to act. Thus, in his early *A Midsummer Night's Dream*, all the rustics lumber through their parts in the thoroughly comic "Pyramus and Thisbe," but by the time we reach *Twelfth Night*, the play is marred: the austere Malvolio is made to perform in a cruel drama not of his making, posturing for the delectation of the raucous plotters just as he thinks he is being most sincere. This humiliation of an upright, if unlikable, character by the cruelty of play anticipates the complex tone of *Mansfield Park*, though Fanny's sharper eye for traps forbids her seduction by the players.

Malvolio abandons his part in outrage, bellowing as he exits, "I'll be revenged on the whole pack of you!" Perhaps in his revenge he returns as Hamlet, our most famous star who refuses to act. Like Fanny, Hamlet casts himself as a jealous and melancholy death's head in a gay, if false, company. His stern creed—"Madam, I know not seems"—epitomizes, like hers, refusal to act. Nonactive in the complex political drama of his family life, Hamlet likewise takes no part in the microcosmic play within the play, though, like Fanny, he hovers hungrily around its periphery, knowing all the parts. His avid spectatorship ultimately upstages the actors and spoils the performance, replacing communal play with rage and slaughter; at the end of her novel, Fanny too reigns at Mansfield in consequence of a family havoc begun at the ruin of the play.

Of course, Fanny is not Hamlet, nor was she meant to be. She is not a doomed prince, but a pauper, a woman, and a survivor; she neither rages nor soliloquizes, revealing her power and her plans only haltingly and indirectly. Still, in her complex relation to the play which epitomizes her novel's action, Fanny has more in common with Hamlet than she does with the helpless women he excoriates when they cross his path. For Hamlet is Shakespeare's supreme anti-actor and counter-actor, the avid and omniscient spectator of the game, who fascinates us as Fanny does because he expresses his virtue by the characteristics of conventional villainy. Jane Austen's contemporaries were obsessed by this troubling sort of hero: Samuel Taylor Coleridge reconceived Hamlet as a paragon of nonactivity, deifying for the modern age a character too pure to act, whose doom and calling are the destruction of play. Fanny Price may be one feminized expression of this new, Romantic fascination with Hamlet as a modern type. As Jane Austen's Hamlet, scourge and minister of a corrupted world, the perfection of the character who won't play, Fanny Price in her unyielding opposition, her longing for a purified and contracted world, gains majesty if not charm. She is as sternly denying as Hamlet, banishing in turn her cousins Maria and Julia, her parents, and the rakish, witty Crawfords from her own finer sphere. These multiple banishments align her with one type of Romantic hero, while denying her the warmth readers want in a heroine. Confronted with so richly disturbing a figure, we would insult her to sentimentalize her when *Mansfield Park* itself does not. For, as we shall see, Fanny's anti-human qualities are stressed in the text of the novel as well as in its contexts. In her progress toward power, her charmlessness only increases her efficacy as Mansfield's scourge and minister.

"Nobody falls in love with Fanny Price," Tony Tanner warns us.[6] We have seen that few readers have done so; Jane Austen further confounds our emotions by making clear that none of the characters within the novel falls in love with her either, though most heroines exist to win love. She wins neither the affection nor the interest of her parents, though they are not always unresponsive; the charm of a Henry Crawford evokes an answering charm in them, but when Fanny's penitential visit to Portsmouth is over at last, her parents seem as relieved to see her leave as she is to go. Kinship is equally unappetizing to all.

Within Mansfield, the gracious adoptive family to which Fanny returns with such ardor, she wins love in proportion to her cousins' shame, receiving emotional interest they failed to earn. Fanny, despised

6. Tony Tanner, "Introduction" to *Mansfield Park* (Harmondsworth: Penguin, 1966) 8.

by all, is embraced as a last resource when Sir Thomas's natural children disgrace themselves in turn. Jane Austen is coolly explicit about
the cannibalistic undercurrents of this, and perhaps of all, requited
love (313).

In this redemption from her usual depression, Fanny's only available
happy ending is the predator's comedy; surely there is deliberate irony
in Jane Austen's pitiless repetition of "happy" amid this household of
collapsed hopes. Never in the canon is the happy ending so reliant
upon the wounds and disappointments of others; though we leave
Fanny ministering avidly to these wounds, they will never heal. The
love she wins from her adoptive family is not a free tribute to her
beauty, her character, or her judgment, but the last tender impulse of
a stricken household.

The love of her two suitors, Henry and Edmund, is similarly under-
mined. Everything about Henry Crawford, that mobile and consum-
mate actor, calls his sincerity into question. He stages his love scenes
before select audiences, all carefully chosen to put the greatest possible
pressure on Fanny, only to humiliate her flamboyantly by his elopement with Maria once she has begun to respond. As Fanny and we
know, his passion for her repeats more grandly his pattern of behavior
with her silly cousins, so that only the most sentimentally credulous
reader could find this new performance credible. The watcher Fanny
knows his love is play, and thus by definition the medium of her humiliation; but in exposing the ardor of the romantic hero as a sadistic
game, Jane Austen undermines the reader's own impulse to fall in love
with Fanny by undermining love itself.

Readers of *Sense and Sensibility*, *Pride and Prejudice*, and *Emma*
expect Edmund Bertram, Fanny's proper husband and sober soulmate,
to redress the balance; the probity of this good suitor's love should
define the sham of Henry's. But if for Henry love is another variant of
private theatricals, a series of ritual attitudes staged for an audience,
Edmund's love is so restrained as to be imperceptible. Like Mr. Knightley, he is exemplary as Fanny's tender mentor, proud of his pupil's right
feelings and right attitudes, but he has none of Mr. Knightley's life as
an incipient lover. Sexual jealousy fuels the latter's sternly protective
manner and his indignant disapproval of Frank Churchill, while Edmund hints of no passions beyond what we see, showing not a glimmer
of jealousy when Henry Crawford makes demonstrative love to Fanny.
Edmund's impeccably clerical conscience interprets his future wife's
prospective marriage as a convenience to facilitate his own engagement
to Henry's seductive sister. Jane Austen is a sharp observer of men
struggling with powerful feelings; like Knightley, Darcy and Wentworth
fight to repress, through prudence or anger, a love that proves too strong
for them; but she withholds from Edmund Bertram any feelings worth
denying. The unlocated and undramatized conversion that leads to his

marriage carries as little emotional weight as it could do: "I only intreat every body to believe that exactly at the time when it was quite natural that it should be so, and not a week earlier, Edmund did cease to care about Mary Crawford, and became as anxious to marry Fanny, as Fanny herself could desire" (319).

This clipped, perfunctory summary, together with the fact that no earlier hints have prepared us for an outbreak of passion on Edmund's part, seems deliberately designed to banish love from our thoughts. The final marriage is as stately and inevitable as Edmund's ordination will be; the ritual is performed, though neither love nor guardianship quite joins the marrying couple. The narrator's reiterated appeal to nature— "what could be more natural than the change?"—is a further symptom of the hopelessness of love, for, as we shall see below, nature is a feeble contender in the manipulated world of *Mansfield Park*. Though Edmund marries the woman he ought, the stern hope he husbands is a loveless strength.

A romance from a writer of marriage comedies that so unremittingly denies love to its heroine is a brave novel indeed, particularly when this heroine is ready to love both her emotionally desiccated suitors. If two wooing men cannot manage to love Fanny, with the true suitor proving as hollow as the false, then surely the reader never will. Austerely alone in a community of fictional heroines for whom love is their chief talent and reward, Fanny is further isolated from affection by her radical homelessness. This waiflike attribute may lead us to associate *Mansfield Park* with such Victorian orphan-myths as *Jane Eyre*: Jane, like Fanny, is an unprepossessing orphan, "a discord" in her corrupted foster family, who grows into an iron-willed little savior. But like most of her orphaned analogues in Victorian fiction, Jane is baptized into strength by the recovery of family: it is not her love for Rochester, but her healing interlude with her recovered cousins, the Rivers family, that allows her identity and her destiny to cohere. The more radical Fanny similarly recovers her family during a romantic crisis, only to discover her total absence of kin. Her ideal home is her utter homelessness. She belongs everywhere she is not: "When she had been coming to Portsmouth, she had loved to call it her home, had been fond of saying that she was going home; the word had been very dear to her; and so it still was, but it must be applied to Mansfield. *That* was now the home. Portsmouth was Portsmouth; Mansfield was home" (292).

The word may be very dear, but the thing eludes her as she eludes it. Victorian orphan-fiction typically begins with the loss of home and ends with its recovery, but here, home is palpable to Fanny only by its absence. Mansfield itself is no true home. The vacuum at its heart is evident not only in the flights of all its members except the supine Lady Bertram, but in the chilling ease with which it can be transformed into a theater. Upon her return, Fanny compels the gutted Mansfield to be her home by an act of will, but in its shrunken regenerate state it bears little resemblance to the place in which she grew up. Fanny's dual returns, to her natural and then to her adoptive origins, prove only the impossibility of self-discovery through return. Thus, though she may resemble later orphan-heroes, Fanny is a more indigestible figure than these wistful waifs, for whom embracing their kin is secular salvation. In the tenacity with which she adheres to an identity validated by no family, home, or love, she denies the vulnerability of the waif for the unlovable toughness of the authentic transplant. Her fragility cloaks the will to live without the traditional sanctions for life. Underlying her pious rigidity is a dispossession so fundamental that, among nineteenth-century English novelists, only the tact of a Jane Austen could dare reveal it in a lady.

Readers are right, then, to find Fanny a relentlessly uncomfortable figure in a domestic romance and to wonder nervously where Jane Austen's comedy went. This uncompromising novel never dissolves its heroine's isolation; she merely passes from the isolation of the outcast to that of the conqueror. Her solitude is rarely alleviated by pathos; instead, she hones it into a spectator's perspective from which she can observe her world and invade it. In this above all, she is closer to the Romantic hero than to the heroine of romance: her solitude is her condition, not a state from which the marriage comedy will save her. In her relentless spectatorship, Fanny may be Jane Austen's domestic answer to Byron's more flamboyant and venturesome Childe Harold, exile from his kind, passing eternally through foreign civilizations in order to create elegies to their ruins. Though Fanny travels only to Sotherton and Portsmouth, her role too is alien and elegiac, as it is at Mansfield itself; like Byron's persona, she is a hero because she is sufficiently detached to see the death of worlds. Fabricating an identity from uprootedness, she conquers the normal world that acts, plays, and marries, through her alienation from it. In the text of her novel, she is a being without kin, but in its context, she exudes a quiet kinship with the strangers and the monsters of her age.

Like other literary monsters, Fanny is a creature without kin who longs for a mate of her own kind. The pain of her difference explains a longing in *Mansfield Park* that is common to much Romantic literature and that, in its obsessed exclusiveness, may look to modern readers unnervingly like incest: the hunger of sibling for sibling, of kin for kind. Seen in its time, the ecstatic, possessive passion Fanny divides between her brother William and her foster brother Edmund, her horror at the Crawfords' attempt to invade her emotions, seem less relevant to the Freudian family romance than to the monster's agonized attempts to alleviate his monstrosity. Mary Shelley's monster asks only that Frankenstein create for him a sister-wife; Bram Stoker's Dracula experiences his triumphant climax when turning his victims into fellow members of the Undead, thus making of them sisters as well as spouses. Fanny yearns similarly in isolation for a brother-mate, repelling the Crawfords above all because they are so different as to constitute virtually another species: "We are so totally unlike . . . we are so very, very different in all our inclinations and ways, that I consider it as quite impossible we should ever be tolerably happy together, even if I *could* like him. There never were two people more dissimilar. We have not one taste in common. We should be miserable" (236).

This rage of self-removal extends itself to Mary Crawford as well, above all perhaps in the emotional spaciousness with which Mary reaches out to Fanny as her "sister." Mary's quest for sisters of gender rather than family, her uncomfortably outspoken championship of abused wives, her sexual initiative, and her unsettling habit of calling things by their names, all suggest the pioneering sensibility of her contemporary, Mary Wollstonecraft; but Fanny cannot endure so universal an embrace, clutching only the shreds of kinship. The novel ends as it ought, with Mary's expulsion into a wider and sadder world, while Fanny, still isolated, clings jealously to her conquered family.

Fanny as Romantic monster does not dispel our discomfort in reading *Mansfield Park*, but may explain some of it. Until recently, critics have limited their recognition of the monsters that underlie Jane Austen's realism to the peripheral figures whose unreason threatens the heroine, while the heroine herself remains solidly human. Yet Fanny excites the same mixture of sympathy and aversion as does Frankenstein's loveless, homeless creature, and the pattern of her adventures is similar to his. Frankenstein's monster begins as a jealous outcast, peering in at family and civic joys. His rage for inclusion makes him the hunted prey of those he envies, and he ends as the conqueror of families. Fanny too is a jealous outcast in the first volume. In the second, she is besieged by the family that excluded her in the form of Henry Crawford's lethal marriage proposal; finally her lair, the chilly East room, is hunted down like Grendel's and invaded by Sir Thomas himself. In the third volume, Fanny, like Mary Shelley's monster, becomes the solitary conqueror of a gutted family. This movement from outcast within a charmed circle to one who is hunted by it and then conqueror of it aligns Jane Austen's most Romantic, least loved heroine with the kin she so wretchedly seeks.

Modern readers may shun Fanny as a static, solitary predator, but in the world of *Mansfield Park* her very consistency and tenacity are bulwarks against a newly opening space that is dangerous in its very fluidity: even Sir Thomas Bertram's solid home is made vulnerable by economic fluctuations in far-off Antigua. Though the large and loveless house that gives it its name has made many readers feel that *Mansfield Park* is Jane Austen's most oppressive novel, its dominant emotional atmosphere induces a certain vertigo, evident in the apparent rocklike solidity, but the true and hopeless elusiveness, of the word "ought." "Ought" tolls constantly, its very sound bringing a knell of absolutism, and nobody uses it with more assurance than the hero and heroine. Fanny can dismiss Henry Crawford simply because "he can feel nothing as he ought," while Edmund freights the word with religious and national authority: "as the clergy are, or are not what they ought to be, so are the rest of the nation" (67). As a barometer of feelings, morals, and institutions, the word seems an immutable touchstone, but in fact it has no objective validation. Its authority in the novel is entirely, and alarmingly, self-generated. The great houses Mansfield and Sotherton scarcely institutionalize the "ought" that resounds in the novel's language; the Portsmouth of the Prices and the London of the Crawfords are equally ignorant of its weight. It has no echo in the world of households and institutions.

Yet this lack of official authority does not prevent the novel's misguided characters from using the word with the same assurance as Fanny and Edmund do. Sir Thomas says of a Fanny who is brewing rebellion, "She appears to feel as she ought" (150); for Mary, the party with which Maria Rushworth inaugurates her miserable marriage finds everything "just as it ought to be" (282); Maria herself avoids only the word in seeing her mercenary marriage as "a duty" (29). Even Edmund, who has transmitted its value to Fanny, abuses the word throughout the novel, beginning with his myopic pressure on Fanny to live with her hated Aunt Norris: "She is choosing a friend and companion exactly where she ought" (20). The incoherence underlying Edmund's authoritative vocabulary tells us that the word recurs anarchically, for there is no objective code to endow it with consistency. Fanny, for example, longs for a loving reunion with her indifferent mother, hoping that "they should soon be what mother and daughter ought to be to each other" (252), but as usual the novel provides no objective image of this "ought": in *Mansfield Park* and throughout Jane Austen's canon, mothers and daughters are at best indifferent and at worst antagonistic, depriving the commanding word of validation. Fanny is repeatedly hymned as the only character who feels consistently as she ought, but in a world where the word changes its meaning so incessantly, her role as a walking "ought" merely isolates her further. Whatever authority Fanny has comes magically from herself alone. Though she can control the inchoate outside world, it is too lacking in definition to claim kinship with her.

For though Fanny possesses a quasi-magical power over the action, she represents less a moral than a shaping principle, assuming the author's prerogatives along with the reader's: the novel's action happens as she wills, and so her emotions become our only standard of right. In its essence, the world of *Mansfield Park* is terrifyingly malleable. Jane Austen detaches herself from her Romantic contemporaries to reveal both inner and outer nature as pitifully ineffectual compared to what can be made. Mrs. Price grows listless toward Fanny because the "instinct of nature was soon satisfied, and Mrs. Price's attachment had no other source" (264). The gap between Mrs. Price and Mrs. Bertram can never heal because "where nature had made so little difference, circumstances [had] made so much" (277). Mary Crawford's nature, like Maria's and Julia's, is similarly helpless against the constructive, or the deconstructive, power of her medium: "For where, Fanny, shall we find a woman whom nature had so richly endowed?—Spoilt, spoilt!—" (308). By contrast, we know that Susan Price will survive, not because of her natural qualities, but because she is "a girl so capable of being made, every thing good" (284). Nature's insufficiency may explain the deadness of Fanny's effusions to stars, trees, and "verdure," for though she laments improvements, Fanny is the most potent of the novel's improving characters. In so malleable and so defective a world, Fanny is polite to the stars, but she turns her most potent attention on the vulnerable, that which is "capable of being made."

In Mary Shelley's *Frankenstein* as well, family, nature, and even the Alps pall before the monster who is capable of being made. The monstrosity of *Mansfield Park* as a whole is one manifestation of its repelled fascination with acting, with education, and with landscape and estate improvements: the novel imagines a fluid world, one with no fixed principles, capable of awesome, endless, and dangerous manipulation. The unconvivial stiffness of its hero and heroine is their triumph: by the end, they are so successfully "made" by each other that he is her creature as completely as she has always been his. The mobility and malleability of *Mansfield Park* is a dark realization of an essentially Romantic vision, of which Fanny Price represents both the horror and the best hope. Only in *Mansfield Park* does Jane Austen force us to experience the discomfort of a Romantic universe presided over by the potent charm of a charmless heroine who was not made to be loved.

CLAUDIA L. JOHNSON

Mansfield Park: Confusions of Guilt and Revolutions of Mind†

* * *

Although not begun until early in 1811, *Mansfield Park* is animated by the preoccupations of the 1790s. On the face of it, *Mansfield Park* looks even more than *Pride and Prejudice* like the flower of conservative mythology. Sir Thomas seems to perform the duties proper to a father of his station with scrupulous decorum. He is ponderous, it is true, but not unbecomingly so. Whether adopting poor relations, repairing the family's flagging fortunes, or pontificating about the moral necessity of single incumbencies, Sir Thomas always minds his dignity. In his musings about his daughters, he thinks exactly as he ought, to use the phrase so important to him: "His daughters he felt, while they retained the name of Bertram, must be giving it new grace, and in quitting it he trusted would extend its respectable alliances" (17). Such, of course, are the classic aspirations of the father of a good family: he strives to adorn his name by cultivating everyone attached to it, and to extend his benevolence outwards through marriage until the neighborhood and eventually the nation itself become a web of amiable relations, stable and loyal because wrought from the fabric of familial affections. But just as notable as Austen's effort to establish the stereotypical outlines of Sir Thomas's character is her tendency simultaneously to sully his probity with deadpan insouciance. The instances of paternal rectitude cited above, for example, are each tainted: Fanny is charitably admitted to Mansfield, but only on Sir Thomas's specific condition that she be made always to remember she is not "a *Miss Bertram*" (10); the family fortunes he rescues depend on slave labor in the West Indies; he approves Edmund's ordination during an uncanonical season and later procures for him a multiple incumbency of the very sort he had earlier disparaged.

Austen's enterprise in *Mansfield Park* is to turn conservative myth sour, as she surely need not have done were her allegiances to the world of the country house as assured as is generally argued. This effort is evidenced, not simply in the inobtrusive profusion of ironic details, but also in the central and most conspicuous donnée of the novel, the characterization of the family at Mansfield Park. From the first pages

† From *Jane Austen: Women, Politics, and the Novel* (Chicago: U of Chicago P, 1988) 96–120. Reprinted by permission of the publisher. The author's notes have been abridged. Page references to *Mansfield Park* refer to this Norton Critical Edition.

on, Austen is at pains to employ the Burkean vocabulary of the political sublime in order to describe the sexually differentiated dynamics of the Bertram household. Everything from Sir Thomas's arched brow to his inflated diction marks him as a figurehead for the sublime. The sway this redoubtable patriarch is supposed to hold over his children is commensurate with his ability to awe them, to strike them with terror lest they offend. If we were to judge his children solely by their sensations upon his return from Antigua, this model might appear accurate. The exceptionally timorous Fanny almost faints with terror as her "former habitual dread of her uncle was returning," but the brassier Bertram children, not less affrighted, share her "excessive trembling" and "fearful thoughts" (122). They too are seized with "absolute horror" (121), and a "terrible pause" (121) ensues as they listen for his footsteps.

But the conservative description of paternal authority invoked here and throughout the novel remarkably fails. Sir Thomas's gravity operates only as an external check, not as an internal inhibition, upon the behavior of his children. He quiets but he does not quell lawlessness; his children tremble at the detection, rather than the commission, of wrongs. Their sneakiness is quite successful. One of the first things we learn about Sir Thomas, after all, is that he is in the dark about his daughters' dispositions, and that his own forbidding airs have made this so: "Sir Thomas did not know what was wanting, because, though a truly anxious father, he was not outwardly affectionate, and the reserve of his manner repressed all the flow of their spirits before him" (16). The dutifulness Sir Thomas assumes he has secured by his paternal sublimity is thus his own delusion. His dignity is undercut by the ignorance it gives rise to and further diminished by the pity it inspires in the perceptive but powerless Fanny.

Austen's scepticism also extends to the beautiful, that is to say, the feminine. As soon as she comes to Mansfield, Fanny observes that Lady Bertram "by the mere aid of a good-humoured smile, became immediately the less awful character of the two" parental figures (11). Fanny's perception rehearses debates about the aesthetic properties of sexual difference that had already been recognized to serve political agendas, for while the sublime arouses passions of dread and respect, the beautiful softens and endears. Although many political allies and opponents alike objected to Burke's gallant taste for helplessly distressed females, Wollstonecraft was the first to attack the link between Burke's aesthetic and political preferences for women. Before her *Vindication of the Rights of Woman*, Wollstonecraft assailed Burke's *Reflections* along with his *Enquiry* for holding that "*littleness* and *weakness* are the very essence of beauty" in women, and thus encouraging in them a helpless enervation that unfits them for the exertions of moral agency. The homage Burke would have men feel towards women of delicacy, Wollstonecraft sneers, "makes those beings vain inconsiderate dolls, who ought to be prudent mothers and useful members of society."[1] Austen's treatment of the vitiating tendencies of female manners follows along the same lines, for in Lady Bertram's case female delicacy becomes pampered somnambulance. Being beautiful—a "vain inconsiderate doll," as the severer Wollstonecraft would put it—engrosses her wholly: "To the education of her daughters, Lady Bertram paid not the smallest attention. She had not time for such cares. She was a woman who spent her days in sitting nicely dressed on a sofa" (16).

* * *

Conservative apologists pitched their flag on the claim that the patriarchal family nurtured moral sentiments, and that the same affections that make us dutiful children and feeling siblings make us obedient subjects and responsible members of our neighborhoods. But in *Mansfield Park*, confidence in the moral tendencies, not simply of parental figures in particular, but of the family in general, is woefully misplaced. *Mansfield Park* is set in motion when the thoughtless extravagance of an eldest son drives his entire family into debt. Sir Thomas, a sometime man of feeling, scolds his heir with every expectation that he will be susceptible to sentimental arguments: " 'I blush for you, Tom,' said he, in his most dignified manner; 'I blush for the expedient which I am driven on, and I trust I may pity your feelings as a brother on the occasion. You have robbed Edmund for ten, twenty, thirty years, perhaps for life, of more than half the income which ought to be his' " (19). But good Sir Thomas blushes in vain. A tender regard for familial dependents evidently does not come with the heir's territory. In fact, "with all the liberal dispositions of an eldest son, who feels born only for expense and enjoyment," Tom never musters much in the way of magnanimity towards any one beyond giving Fanny "some very pretty presents" and laughing at her, acts of "kindness" which are "consistent with his situation and rights" (15).

Such discrepancies between the pretenses and the substance of conservative myth remind us that *Mansfield Park* is no less a parody, though much less a comedy, than *Northanger Abbey*, and that fissures in social and political discourse can be examined as methodically as those in the discourse of gothic fiction. By questioning the moral efficacy Burkeans attach to familial figures, *Mansfield Park* engages in progressive, though muted, social criticism. In some of the most famous purple patches of the *Reflections*, Burke hailed chivalric respect for the sacredness of paternal authority and patriarchal family relations as the "decent drapery of life," tailored through the ages to cover our "naked shivering natures"—not as fixed and immutable truths, but rather as "pleasing illusions" and "superadded ideas" which serve our wishes for dignity

---

1. Mary Wollstonecraft, *Vindication of the Rights of Men* (London, 1790) 112, 54.

and raise us in our own esteem.[2] Burke's attack on the demystification of authority structures in France, like his defense of prejudice, was often adopted in women's fiction of the period, and sometimes in novels Austen certainly knew, such as Edgeworth's *Belinda* and Brunton's *Self-Control*. Where the process of demystification appears in Austen's fiction, by contrast, it is generally infused with a positive charge. Even though *Pride and Prejudice* spares Darcy's position from demystifying satire, Darcy and Elizabeth themselves angrily tear off "pleasing illusions" about each other, and this measured but satiric stripping is essentially educative. Mr. Knightley's success as a character depends on the fact that, despite the chivalric provenance of his name, he is continually presented as a plainspoken man (another mystification in itself, certainly), who gets vexed, who flushes as he buttons his gaiters, and who never does learn the worst about the woman he marries.

More than any other novel by Austen, *Mansfield Park* is a work of demystification, and here that process is conceived, not in Burkean fashion as a brutal assault upon a naked queen, and with that a challenge to the power of the king, but rather as an inquiry into the moral wardrobe of the venerable father himself. Invariably careful to say the right thing, the authority figures at Mansfield Park all don the drapery of decency. But authorially underscored differences between profession and deed invite us to consider whether their drapery is not more indecent than that which it purports to obviate by concealing. The to-do over the staging of *Lovers' Vows* should call our attention to more than the disorderly passions of the young people at Mansfield. Their enactments of illicit or improper desire are actually among the least deceptive instances of acting in the novel, for every major character is acting all the time. Lady Bertram's acts are perhaps the least offensive, deriving as they do from innocent vacuity rather than deceit. If she has nothing to conceal, she does not exactly have anything to show either, even when she feels she should. Her letters on the "dangerous illness of her eldest son" (289), for example, are a "medley of trusts, hopes, and fears . . . a sort of playing at being frightened" (290). The "playing" of the others, however, is marked by a greater degree of subterfuge, consisting not of a ludic engagement of impulses or energies, but rather of a more strategic production of obfuscating displays, designed as much for themselves as for others. Mrs. Norris plays the self-sacrificing sister and aunt, Maria and Julia the parts of proper young ladies, and Edmund the highminded priest, ever vigilant if not ever successful in maintaining what Fanny calls his "moral elevation" (110). However spontaneously thoughtless he may appear, even Tom himself does not hesitate to play up the role assigned to him. Displeased with Edmund's insubordinate objection that acting will ruin their sisters' reputations, Tom maintains

2. Edmund Burke, *Reflections on the Revolution in France* (1790), in *Works of the Right Honourable Edmund Burke*, 16 vols. (London, 1826) 5:151.

that the womenfolk are not a younger brother's business: "I'll take care
that his [Sir Thomas's] daughters do nothing to distress him. Manage
your own concerns, Edmund, and I'll take care of the rest of the family"
(90). To the extent that Tom's remark is consistent with his "situation
and rights," it is a legitimate assertion of his prerogative. But insofar as
it is belied by Tom's manifest obliviousness to his family's concerns and
his sisters' good names, it is yet another instance of the double-talk
characters in *Mansfield Park* employ when they wish to invest their self-
will in the sanctity of social form.

Sir Thomas is the most assiduous of actors at Mansfield Park, and
his shows are designed to satisfy himself as well as others of his paternal
judiciousness. Like Tom, of course, Sir Thomas is committed to "taking
care of the family," and this primarily entails looking after the womenfolk. Sir Thomas plainly perceives that Maria despises Rushworth.
But his offer to call off a marriage "so unquestionably advantageous,"
one which moreover would form a "connection exactly of the right
sort; in the same county, and the same interest" (30), is halfhearted at
best and disingenuous at worst. Sir Thomas stops well short of the
candor that could have brought Maria to think twice. As we learn in
formulations that slowly unfold his bad faith, he is too "satisfied" with
her perfunctory avowal of esteem for Rushworth, "too glad to be satisfied perhaps to urge the matter quite so far as his judgment might have
dictated to others. It was an alliance which he could not have relinquished without pain" (138). When we read just a little later that Sir
Thomas is "very happy to think any thing of his daughter's disposition
that was most favourable for the purpose" (138), the scrupulous gestures
of concern we just witnessed are unmasked as parade.

Sir Thomas's shows of kindness to Fanny are more deceptive. When
he "advises" her to retire to bed after the ball, he employs a discourse
of benevolence the narrator proceeds to strip: " 'Advise' was his word,
but it was the advice of absolute power" (192). Lest we assume that
"absolute power" exercised on behalf of a ward's frail health is permis-
sible, if not indeed desirable, we are obliged to think again, as the
narrator leads us through a sequence of suppositions which exposes Sir
Thomas's motives: "In thus sending her away, Sir Thomas perhaps
might be thinking merely of her health. It might occur to him, that
Mr. Crawford had been sitting by her long enough, or he might mean
to recommend her as a wife by shewing her persuadableness" (193).
Eager to dispose of his niece with unexpected advantage in the marriage
market, Sir Thomas stages this drama for Henry Crawford's benefit,
and it will later become even more painfully clear how little Fanny
herself has to do with Sir Thomas's "act" of solicitude. Though Sir
Thomas's acts on behalf of the moral welfare of his family are more
polished than Tom's, though he is always careful to don the drapery of

decency, his probity is just as specious as Tom's, and his exertions just as coercive.

Mansfield Park never permits paternalistic discourse completely to conceal or to mystify ugly facts about power. Instead it turns back onto itself into incoherence, one of the novel's principal stylistic devices. Maria is not the only one to be confounded "from listening to language" which "actions contradicted" (134). The "persuadableness" Sir Thomas wishes to appear to recommend, for example, is in fact a logical impossibility: since "absolute power" is, as we are told, what is really at play, the option of dissent which persuasion implies is not available to Fanny, here or elsewhere. Like Mrs. Norris, who with his authorization instructs Maria and Julia, "if you are ever so forward and clever yourselves, you should always be modest" (16), Sir Thomas too is caught between the promptings of decency and acquisitiveness, and so lapses unreflectively into the same sort of self-contradiction. He "fancies," for example, that the best way of showing Henry Crawford to be a "model of constancy" is "by not trying him too long" (234). This kind of double-talk is also typical of Tom. Having just been railroaded into playing whist, Tom fumes against polite formulations that give with one hand what they take away with the other: "A pretty modest request upon my word! . . . And to ask me in such a way too! without ceremony, before them all, so as to leave me no possibility of refusing! *That* is what I dislike most particularly . . . to have the pretence of being asked, of being given a choice, and at the same time addressed in such a way as to oblige one to do the very thing—whatever it be!" (85). Tom is not aware that when he states "in an languid way, 'If you want to dance, Fanny, I will stand up with you' " (84), he commits the same offense. But the "pretense" of choice Tom resents is essential to the paternalistic discourse represented in *Mansfield Park* because it enables people to compel others without having to regard themselves as bullies. When Mrs. Norris announces that she is not "going to urge" Fanny to act, "but I shall think her a very obstinate, ungrateful girl, if she does not do what her aunt and cousins wish her" (103); when Edmund pressures Fanny to read *Lovers' Vows* by manipulatively pleading "Do Fanny, if it is not *very* disagreeable to you" (119); or when Sir Thomas himself damns Fanny's refusal of Crawford as "self-willed, obstinate, selfish, and ungrateful" (217), while at the same time insisting "You cannot suppose me capable of trying to persuade you to marry against your inclinations" (224), they each hang onto the drapery of decency just barely held together by impressive-sounding but incoherent formulations such as these.

The system of female manners is supposed to eliminate the need for the nakedness of coercion, and the embarrassment this entails, by rendering women so quiescent and tractable that they sweetly serve in the designs of fathers or guardians without wishing to resist and without noting that they have no choice. In most of Austen's novels, of course, fathers are not inclined to tyranny, nor are daughters trained to such ductility. But the women of Mansfield Park *are* held to a code of female propriety. The subject of femininity is a matter of great concern to virtually all the male characters. Still a bit queasy about authorizing Maria's marriage, Sir Thomas consoles himself with the (inaccurate) observation that Maria's disposition is, like his wife's, so placid that she will never be unhappy with the lot to which he is anxious creditably to assign her: "Her feelings probably were not acute; he had never supposed them to have been so" (138). Of course Sir Thomas's confidence that Maria will cooperate in an alliance advantageous to himself without any ill effects is preposterous: she never really attended to lessons in female modesty in the first place, nor is her disposition so placid as he wishfully fancies. Studious to conceal rather than sublimate the rebelliousness of her temper, Maria suffers petulantly but desperately from restraint: "I cannot get out, as the starling said" (71). For her, marriage to Rushworth is not voluntary service to a new man, but "independence" from Mansfield and "escape" from Sir Thomas (139). But lessons in modesty did take on Fanny. She consistently strives to feel and do as she ought, to entrust herself to guardian males without presuming to act "*in propria persona*" (271). But modesty so extreme has intolerable costs. Refusing the unseemliness of self-assertion, Fanny trusts that guardians will think for and of her, only to discover instead that they are too full of their own, invariably wrongheaded, plans to think much about her at all. When she finds herself neglected or abused, then, she has no other recourse than to consider herself somehow at fault for having nursed an implausible sense of consequence. When Sir Thomas, Edmund, and Lady Bertram collude in Crawford's unwelcome suit, Fanny may be surprised to learn just how little is set store by her wishes, but we cannot be, because she has always denied or concealed having any wishes of her own in the first place. Fanny's efforts to be modest, then, are every bit as frustrating and corrosive as Maria's efforts simply to appear so. Between the two of them the confounding bind in which the code of propriety places women is laid bare.

Maria's status as Sir Thomas's daughter entitles her to at least the decent appearance of matrimonial choice. As an indigent niece, however, Fanny is not granted the same consideration. When Sir Thomas discovers to his amazement that Fanny has no intention of accepting Crawford's proposal, he rails at what he understands to be pernicious doctrines of the day which have infected even Fanny:

"I had thought you peculiarly free from wilfulness of temper, self-conceit, and every tendency to that independence of spirit, which prevails so much in modern days, even in young women, and which in young women is offensive and disgusting beyond all common offence. But you have now shown me that you can be wilful and perverse, that you can and will decide for yourself, without any consideration or deference for those who have surely some right to guide you—without even asking their advice." (216)

By this time, of course, Sir Thomas's term, "advice," can no longer deceive us, since we have already learned that his is "the advice of absolute power" (192). What he expects from Fanny is a cheerful readiness to be guided, so that the nakedness of force will never be necessary. Her resistance implies an assumption of self-responsibility that challenges his authority, and he is alarmed. Unlike Austen's other country gentlemen, who typify the mores of their station without much self-reflexivity, Sir Thomas is alert to revolutionary ideology. His violent antipathy to the "independence of spirit" and the determination to "decide" for oneself prevalent in modern females is anchored in much of the postrevolutionary discourse we have already reviewed, where the merits of thinking for oneself were widely debated. Sympathetic young men in Opie's *Adeline Mowbray* and Smith's *Young Philosopher*, for example, get into trouble precisely because they are committed to the principle of thinking, judging, and deciding for themselves, rather than conforming slavishly to the dictates of authority or convention. By contrast, in her *Letters Addressed to a Young Man*, Jane West denounces self-conceited independence in favor of a Burkean "concurrence" to "established forms" that have emerged over time. Counterrevolutionary writers looked upon "independence of spirit" in a woman with even more alarm. In "The Unsex'd Females," the ne plus ultra of the period's antifeminist rhetoric, Richard Polwhele denounced literary ladies in England for their sexual immodesty and republican sentiments, equally unclean violations of natural law. Less grossly, but no less fervently, Letitia Hawkins elaborated the commonplace equation between the government of the passions and the government of England, when she opposed radical sophisms about "equal rights, the abjectness of submission, the duty of every one to think for themselves," because they diminished "the respect formerly paid to authority" and encouraged a tendency to regard a "husband as an unauthorized tyrant," a tendency which could only culminate in promiscuity and adultery.

All the worst crimes pursuant upon female immodesty—illicit sex and adultery—come to pass in *Mansfield Park*. But here such effects proceed from causes contrary to what conservative writers conceived. The only character in *Mansfield Park* whose hands remain clean has to think for herself and to defy the figureheads of social and religious authority in order to remain guiltless. It is symptomatic of Sir Thomas's breathtaking impercipience that he attributes radical agendas and ungovernable passions to the dutiful and mild Fanny. Sir Thomas's interviews with Fanny and Maria on the subject of feminine choice mirror each other, for just as he attributes Maria's wish to marry a man she does not love to a commendable, because easily governable, serenity of temper, so he attributes Fanny's refusal to marry a man she does not love to a "young, heated fancy" (216) and a "wild fit of folly" (216), to headstrong passions unbecoming in themselves and inconvenient to parents or guardians, whose "advantage or disadvantage" depends on her. Fanny's hope that "to a man like her uncle, so discerning, so honourable, so good, the simple acknowledgement of settled *dislike* on her side would have been sufficient" (215) to end Crawford's suit is disastrously disappointed. Indeed, it is the very assumption that her "settled *dislike*" matters that so affronts Sir Thomas. Sir Thomas can be a man of feeling when it comes to pitying the disappointment of a younger brother deprived of his patrimony. But as Fanny herself later recollects, he cannot entertain the sentiments of girls given in marriage to undeserving husbands: "He who had married a daughter to Mr. Rushworth. Romantic delicacy was certainly not to be expected from him" (224).

Taking the opposite approach, rather like that of the good cop, Edmund tries to persuade Fanny to let Henry "succeed at last" precisely because she is so modest. He too, then, appeals to her wish for sexual approval: "You have proved yourself upright and disinterested, prove yourself grateful and tender-hearted; and then you will be the perfect model of a woman, which I have always believed you born for" (235–36). Being a model woman, by this account, entails several responsibilities. Fanny has already *seemed* to fulfill some of them by not forming romantic attachments independent of parental supervision—Edmund has no idea she is carrying a torch for him—and by not being a fortune hunter. But to be a model woman, Fanny must do yet more. Now that her guardian sanctions the match, she must feel so thankful to have been asked at all and so anxious not to disappoint the feelings of a man who has favored her with his attention that she must, in short, say "yes." Here even Fanny rankles, contending in the manner of Elizabeth Bennet that "it ought not to be set down as certain, that a man must be acceptable to every woman he may happen to like himself" (239). But Fanny goes yet further in questioning the antithetical duties exacted from modest women. First they are required not to desire at all, and next they are enjoined to feel desire on proper command: "How then was I to be—to be in love with him the moment he said he was with me? How was I to have an attachment at his service, as soon as it was asked for?" (240).

There is no adequate way to answer Fanny's questions, for the paradox of female modesty is not simply that the same purity which is supposed to place them above the suspicion of sexual desire actually inflames male desire. It is also that female purity itself is simultaneously demanded as natural and disbelieved as affected. From the outside, Fanny's refusal of Henry looks like the coquettish "no" Mr. Collins has learned to expect from "elegant" females before hearing their inevitable, grateful "yes"—in short, like another of the many acts people in *Mansfield Park* stage for propriety's sake. Fanny is dismayed to find that Henry persists in his unwelcome suit despite all her entreaties. But her pleas appear even more disingenuous to him than Mrs. Norris's "acts" of liberality or Sir Thomas's show of kindness in sending Fanny to Portsmouth do to us:

> Fanny knew her own meaning, but was no judge of her own manner. Her manner was incurably gentle, and she was not aware how much it concealed the sternness of her purpose. Her diffidence, gratitude, and softness, made every expression of indifference seem almost an effort of self-denial; seem at least, to be giving nearly as much pain to herself as to him. (222)

Fanny's own language is made to inform against her: A modest "no" is heard as a coy "yes." Diffidence, gentleness, self-effacement—the same attributes of modesty which should relieve her from the attention and consequence she shuns—turn on her even more insidiously than her "protectors" Sir Thomas and Edmund do, depriving her of the credibility Elizabeth Bennet describes when, eschewing sexual distinction, she asks to be treated like a "rational creature" worthy of the "compliment of being believed sincere." Modesty, then, dispossesses Fanny of her meaning by reversing her own assertions. As such, it legitimizes and guarantees domination by providing it with a "decent" rationale.

Another way to describe a modest young woman whose function it is to oblige the wishes of fathers, uncles, and brothers without exhibiting any "independence of spirit" or any "perverse" and "disgusting" desires to decide for herself is to say that she is a slave. Surprisingly, until very recently the subject of slavery as it bears upon Austen's novels has received little critical attention, an omission that must derive at least in part from the time-honored premise of Austen's indifference to matters of "public" interest. Fanny herself is curious about slavery. But even though she appears to favor writers famous for abolitionist sympathies, such as Johnson and Cowper, there is no reason to assume that when she asks Sir Thomas "about the slave trade" (136) she is critical of the institution or uncomfortable with his role in it. Austen does not provide us with details about Sir Thomas's treatment of slaves in the West Indies, but the fact of ownership itself serves not simply to reveal the source of the income which supports the Bertrams' stateliness, but also more importantly to illuminate the nature of Sir Thomas's kindness to Fanny. If his treatment of Fanny can be a guide, Sir Thomas is like the model paternalist Mr. Edwards, in Edgeworth's "The Grateful Negro" (1802), a man who believes that the emancipation of his slaves would not make them happy, who sees his guardianship as an act of kindness on behalf of dependents who cannot act for themselves, and who renders his slaves orderly and obedient by developing their capacity to feel grateful for his own kindness. Sir Thomas exacts compliance from Fanny in the same way, by virtue of his position not as a parent but rather as a benefactor: "You do not owe me the duty of a child. But, Fanny, if your heart can acquit you of *ingratitude—*" (216).

* * *

As could be expected from a character who takes the code of modesty so much to heart, Fanny is not in the least inclined to question Sir Thomas's authority to dictate to her. Informed ever since her arrival that "an extraordinary degree of gratitude and good behaviour" is expected from her in return for her "wonderful good fortune" (12) in being invited at all, Fanny finds nothing improper about Mrs. Norris's admonition that she be "the lowest and last" wherever she goes. Fanny rates "her own claims to comfort as low even as Mrs. Norris could" (152). Believing the grey mare more entitled to consideration than she is herself, Fanny regards even rather minimal attentions—Sir Thomas's greeting upon his return, or his wish for her to use the carriage on a cold evening—as extravagant kindnesses. Rather than wonder why Sir Thomas had never ordered a fire to burn in the east room before, when she finally finds one there, for the first time in eight years, she is so impressed that he "could have leisure to think of such a trifle" that she regards his attention as "too much," as "an indulgence" beyond her intrinsic deserts. To her, ingratitude is a particularly heinous offense— " 'I must be a brute indeed, if I can be really ungrateful!' said she in soliloquy; 'Heaven defend me from being ungrateful!' " (219)—and like a grateful slave she lets particular and small acts of kindness overshadow a larger act of cruelty.

The grateful submission of women is of such consequence to begin with because their sexual modesty alone guarantees the continuing authority of their guardians. With the exception of Tom Bertram, whose passion for horses prevents him from noticing any of Mary Crawford's attempts to ensnare him, the men in *Mansfield Park* are nervous about female sexuality. Edmund, for example, is alternately spellbound and horror striken by Mary Crawford, and poor Mr. Rushworth is at ease only with his mother. Though Henry Crawford is, of course, the major offender on the score of illicit sex, he is also, by his own admission, "of a cautious temper" (32) about women. This only makes sense, since he learned his "lessons" (32) from his uncle the admiral. Still assuming that the sisterly Austen, like Fanny, idealized the navy and extolled the manly integrity of all its officers, commentary has attended very little to Admiral Crawford, "a man of vicious conduct" (30) whose particularly sordid domestic behavior intrudes upon the central narrative here. It is, after all, the rank indecency of this paternal figure that brings the Crawfords to Mansfield. Upon the death of his much-abused wife, the admiral shows his hostility to his niece and his contempt for social rules by bringing a mistress under his roof. With such experience behind him, as he jocularly confesses, Henry is understandably "unwilling to risk [his] happiness in a hurry" (32). His commendation of the virtues he expects Fanny to practice as a wife discloses the nature of his risk:

> Henry Crawford had too much sense not to feel the worth of good principles in a wife, though he was too little accustomed to serious reflection to know them by their proper name; but when he talked of her having such a steadiness and regularity of conduct, such a high notion of honour, and such an observance of decorum as might warrant any man in the fullest dependence on her faith and integrity, he expressed what was inspired by the knowledge of her being well principled and religious. (201)

Henry's dependence on Fanny's steadiness, honor, decorum, faith, and integrity adds up to the singularly important confidence that she will be above the temptation of adultery. However careless he is about violating the domestic sovereignty of another man, Henry has "too much sense" to omit forfending against this disgrace in his own home, even though he has been taught to consider this disgrace virtually inevitable. Evidently as the admiral would have it, every woman is a rake at heart, and as a result marriage is "never pardonable in a young man of independent fortune" (200). With her surpassing modesty and rectitude, Fanny is "exactly the woman to do away every prejudice of such a man as the admiral, for she is exactly such a woman as he thinks does not exist in the world. She is the very impossibility he would describe" (200).

If the other male characters do not share the admiral's penchant for illicit sex, they do share his suspicions about the "impossibility" of female modesty and his unwillingness to let a wife's infidelity compromise his social identity. Austen makes this clear by the staging, of all possible progressive plays, *Lovers' Vows*. The radical agenda of Kotzebue's play announces itself, not simply in its characterization of the worldly baron who wishes to sell his daughter off in marriage to a rich lout, but also in its sympathetic presentation of female desire. Fanny disapproves of both female roles—"the situation of one, and the language of the other, so unfit to be expressed by any woman of modesty" (97): a deserted unwed mother and a lively young woman frankly en-

amored with the shy clergyman who has "formed" her mind both pre-
suppose the independence of female sexuality. Defenders of the
patriarchal family were particularly horrified by the "indecent" woman
who, like Emma in *Emma Courtney*, might consider herself as entitled
as men are to declare her love and to propose marriage, or who, like
Julia in *Memoirs of Modern Philosophers*, feels free to enact her desires
without male authorization. In *Lovers' Vows*, however, such indecency
is presented amiably and without reproach, and in the original, Amelia's
declaration of love verges on an outright proposal. Herself sympathetic
to, but prudently detached from, the Wollstonecraft-Godwin circle,
Inchbald was sensitive to the uneasiness of her increasingly reactionary
audience on the subject of female sexuality. Recognizing that "the forward and unequivocal manner in which she [Amelia] announces her
affection to her lover, in the original would have been revolting to an
English audience," Inchbald softens the blow in her translation, rendering Amelia's declaration of love "by whimsical insinuations, rather
than coarse abruptness" (330). Enough indelicacy remains, however, to
scandalize Fanny even as it discloses her own unenacted desires for the
clergyman who has formed *her* mind. Austen calls further attention to
the anxiety prompted by the acknowledgement of female desire within
the play when Mary Crawford's uncommonly bold question about
casting—"What gentleman among you am I to have the pleasure of
making love to" (101)—meets with stunned silence.

Mary's question poses the temptation of sexuality as well as the threat
of social disorder, and Edmund responds to both from the start. Austen
uses sexualized details more extensively here than in any other novel,
and they attest to Edmund's susceptibility to erotic enchantments. He
not only approves but encourages Mary's horseback riding. Her "pure
genuine pleasure of the exercise" (48) is engaging to him, and his own
pleasure in being "close to her . . . directing her management of the
bridle" (49), Fanny rather resentfully observes, is glaringly apparent. As
Fanny is made once again to witness, Edmund would sooner forego
contemplating the harmony of the stars than miss a few bars of the
decidedly *un*celestial music of Mary at her harp. But if Edmund can
accept Mary's unblushing vigor, he cannot tolerate what Darcy, so
much the larger figure, finds so attractive in Elizabeth Bennet: her
freedom of speech. Mary Crawford does not stand in "awe" of her own
uncle the admiral, or live, as Fanny does, in "dread of taking a liberty
with him" (296). Nor does she venerate Edmund "as an example of
every thing good and great" (28). His approbation is as little essential
to her self-definition as the support his arm is to her brisk walk (67).
She speaks without the respect for decorum on which Edmund insists.
When Mary complains about a matter as innocuous as the admiral's
messy improvements at Twickenham, Edmund is "silenced" by a freedom with her uncle that "did not suit his sense of propriety" (42).

When she indulges in irreverent and salacious puns at the expense of the navy—the *"Rears,* and *Vices"* (44) one encounters at her uncle's house—she arouses the same degree of disapproval: "Edmund again felt grave" (44).

Disturbed by these infractions, Edmund quizzes his pupil Fanny on what was "not quite right" (46) in Mary's conversation. Fanny could wish that her own loyalty and modesty could make her desirable, and as a result she is a sterner judge of female propriety than he is. Of course both agree that Mary "ought not have spoken of her uncle as she did" (46). But to Edmund, the fault is superficial: "I do not censure her *opinions*; but there certainly *is* impropriety in making them public" (46), emphasis Edmund's). Tacitly courting Mary himself, Edmund is uneasy about a prospective wife's propensity to talk without inhibition about so formidable a figure. A man's bad character should stay behind closed doors, and a woman's character as a woman is subject to review whenever she fails to respect his character in public: "She," he assures the dubious Fanny, "is perfectly feminine, except in the instances we have been speaking of" (47).

Whereas the dimsighted Edmund wishes Mary to engage in the same kind of decorous concealment that makes Maria dangerous, Fanny insists rigorously on a totality of felt respect for male authority figures. But if Edmund's position is disturbing because it recommends double-talk, Fanny's is disturbing because it has ceased to take note of the indecencies that the drapery of position can conceal. The scurrility of the admiral is not significant to Fanny, except as an inconvenience a sister should gladly endure for a brother's sake. To her, it is not merely Mary's expression of criticism about the admiral that is wrong but the sentiment itself: "whatever his faults may be," she insists, he "is so very fond of her brother" (46) that he ought to be respected. So complete is Fanny's credence in the moral puissance of patricians that she does not stop merely with reproaching Mary's "ungrateful" (46) sentiments. Indeed, she does everything she can to exculpate the admiral himself and blames his wife instead: Mary's "impropriety is a reflection itself upon Mrs. Crawford. . . . She cannot have given her [Mary] right notions of what was due to the admiral" (46).

＊　＊　＊

Mansfield Park adumbrates a phenomenon which has preoccupied modern feminists: the dependence of certain kinds of masculine discourse on feminine silence. Mansfield Park runs smoothly only so long as female dissent can be presumed not to exist. Lady Bertram, of course, has nothing to say for herself; her daughters never voice their noncompliance, and while their rebellion is obvious enough to Fanny, she herself can never say what she knows, and when she tries she is not listened to; even Mary Crawford's blatant liberties with paternal figures are unheard for as long as possible. But when women's defiance of patriarchal codes can no longer be ignored, men here are utterly sty-mied, and their confusion gives another, quite dizzying turn to the political sublime. Sir Thomas is "astonished" (213) even by mild Fan-ny's unexpected and "very strange" act of resistance, interrupting as it does, not only his command of her, but also his command of his own understanding: "There is something in this which my comprehension does not reach" (214). But when Maria commits her even more con-founding crime, Sir Thomas reportedly falls just short of paralysis— "My father is not overpowered. More cannot be hoped. He is still able to think and act" (300)—while Mrs. Norris, his mistress-at-arms, is thor-oughly deprived of her faculties of speech and reasoning, "quieted, stupified, indifferent . . . benumbed" (304). As the case of Mary Craw-ford attests, however, chastity alone is not enough to assure and ensure the interests of patriarchy. Silence too, at least on some subjects, is also required to place that chastity beyond suspicion, even though, para-doxically, that silence, like modesty itself, will also and always be liable to doubt. Finally it is Mary's ability to speak about illicit sex that seems so audacious and perverse that Edmund's very power of speech is taken away: "To hear the woman whom—no harsher name than folly given!—So voluntarily, so freely, so coolly to canvass it!—No reluctance, no horror, no feminine—shall I say? no modest loathings! . . . I was like a man stunned" (308–09).

Edmund is silenced by the same "——" that silenced that other younger son and clergyman, Henry Tilney: obliging young ladies blithely framing and uttering thoughts which they cannot so much as consider, let alone speak. Mary is dismissed from Mansfield Park, but not because she, like Marianne or the female philosophers of turn-of-the-century political novels, consciously holds an opposing ideological position—though this too, of course, would be intolerable. Rather, she is dismissed because she never has considered what the issues are in the first place, and as a result does not even realize that a modest silence on the subject of sex and grateful veneration of the moral prestige of patriarchal benefactors are required of her. At times, this obliviousness to the exigencies of gentry mythology reflects back unfavorably onto the Bertrams themselves. After all, on some subjects, such as the pursuit of wealth through the formation of advantageous marriages, Mary and the Bertrams see eye to eye. She and Sir Thomas alike reinforce Lady Bertram's admonition to Fanny that "it is every woman's duty to accept such a very unexceptionable offer" as Henry's (226), and so they form an alliance which denudes Sir Thomas of the dignifying moral preten-sions he is at such pains to maintain. But Mary makes no such preten-sions, and that is what damns her. She covets the trappings of social prestige and respects the dictates of worldly wisdom—including that portion of it which requires female chastity—but she does not recognize the mystique of social institutions and the people who embody them, and thus does not appreciate the enormity of Maria's crime. Fanny, needless to say, knows better. To her, Maria's is "a sin of the first magnitude" (299). Whereas Edmund had earlier insisted that Mary's faults consisted in manner alone, he eventually agrees with Fanny that they result instead from "a perversion of mind which made it natural to her to treat the subject" (309) lightly as a folly which is dangerous only where it is known, rather than as sin in itself, which loyalty to a patriarchal social structure should prevent her even from naming. About this there must be no mistake: the Bertrams view Maria's offense as a crime against fathers of good families. In Sir Thomas's opinion, any palliation of Maria's action would entail "an insult to the neighbourhood" and a danger of "introducing such misery in another man's family, as he had known himself" (315).

It is small wonder that, having been charged with "blunted delicacy and a corrupted, vitiated mind" (310), Mary Crawford should next appear to Edmund as a siren, flashing "a saucy playful smile, seeming to invite, in order to subdue" (311) him and emasculate his moral indignation: after all, the ability to think and speak of the violation of domestic trust lightly is tantamount to confessing a failure to be awed by it. From the Bertrams' point of view, the novel closes with a vengeance of reactionary formulas derived from conservative fiction: the demon aunt is cast out as a betrayer of the good man's trust, and the offending daughter banished to the hell of her perpetual company; the impious seductress is righteously spurned by the man of God, and her reprobate brother forever barred from happiness; the giddy heir apparent is sobered by instructive affliction, and the modest girl, in a triumph of passive aggression, is vindicated and rewarded with everything she wanted but never presumed to ask for. But the wicked are not merely segregated from the virtuous. Sir Thomas, "anxious to bind by the strongest securities all that remained to him of domestic felicity" (320), repents his ambitions, blesses the marriage of Edmund and Fanny, and stations them both next door, so that the good themselves can huddle even closer within the hallowed ties of marriage.

But *Mansfield Park* erodes rather than upholds conclusions which comprise a conservative reading of the novel. Austen calls attention to the parodic elements of her denouements here much as she does in *Northanger Abbey*, where a dubious surplus of conventionalized material and a "tell-tale compression" of pages hurrying characters to tidy destinies lurches the novel into fantasies we are not permitted to credit. When Edmund finally gets around to asking Fanny to marry him, the narrator intrudes with an unwontedly Sternean garrulity that obliges us to consider their alliance as a perfunctorily opted anticlimax the narrator washes her hands of, rather than a properly wished-for and well-deserved union towards which the parties have been moving all along: "I purposely abstain from dates on this occasion. . . . I only intreat every body to believe that exactly at the time when it was quite natural that it should be so, and not a week earlier, Edmund did cease to care about Miss Crawford" (319).

* * *

The doubts we are obliged to form about the moral stature of Mansfield further compromise the satisfaction typically proffered by a happy ending. Throughout the novel, the moral welfare of the great house has been subject to the self-will, the bad judgment, or the mercenary projects of those appointed to govern it, and every time Fanny has had to struggle with uncertainty "as to what she *ought to do*" (107), it has been because such figures urge her on to what she knows she ought *not* do. And although Fanny has been independent enough to resist them, she has never been lucid enough to recognize what is problematic about their authority even as she sees them err, even as she is obliged inwardly and outwardly to resist them. After Sir Thomas tries to force her into the arms of the man who disgraces his family, Fanny still sees him as her "rule to apply to," and stands in "dread of taking a liberty with him" (296). Edmund is yet worse. If it is true, as he proudly declares, that "as the clergy are, or are not what they ought to be, so are the rest of the nation" (67), then woe to England, for Edmund shares his father's tendency to invest personal desires with the dignity of moral imperatives. Yet to Fanny, Edmund remains "an example of every thing good and great" (28), even after he urges her to settle in with Mrs. Norris, to take part in *Lovers' Vows*, and to marry Henry Crawford.

The most unsettling irony of *Mansfield Park*, then, is that the failures of conservative ideology fall, not exclusively, but still most heavily, on the only member of the household to believe in and act by it fully to the very end. From the squalor of Portsmouth it seems to Fanny that "all proceeded in a regular course of cheerful orderliness" at Mansfield, that "every body had their due importance; every body's feelings were consulted" (266). But Fanny's trip "home," as Sir Thomas designed, taught her how to value the advantages of wealth and comfort Mansfield provides, not how to see past its dignity. The stately household she pines for from afar is about to explode; as we well know, it has never been "cheerful" or orderly, and "every one's" feelings there are *not* consulted, Fanny's least of all. To be "mistress of Pemberley," as Elizabeth Bennet puts it, might indeed "be something," but Mansfield Park has no such luster. A conventionally happy ending which ensconces Fanny there, indispensable at last, and still adulating now enervated figures whose discernment has been radically impeached, sustains rather than settles the problems the foregoing material has uncovered.

Finally, *Mansfield Park* parodies the structures of conservative fiction most subversively, though in some ways most obliquely of all, in its presentation of family itself, the ostensibly sacred bonds the weary Bertrams form at last. Conservative novelists typically set up uncomplicated moral oppositions—good girls and bad girls, good marriages and bad marriages, good parents and bad parents—to reinforce their political ideals. To the extent that the illicit liaison between Henry and Maria contrasts with the lawful marriage of Edmund and Fanny, *Mansfield Park*, of course, appears to do the same. But this polarity collapses under close examination. Although Austen writes nothing that can be construed as a palliation of adultery, the narrator shows no ladylike impulse to recoil in shame from the greatest insult that can be made to a man of Rushworth's prestige, and no inclination to moralize in the manner of Sir Thomas, Edmund, or Fanny. On the contrary, the narrator's comments discourage us from regarding Maria's offense as a "sin of the first magnitude," as Fanny would say, or even as a heinous crime against an estimable personage. Not only does the narrator imply that Rushworth had it coming—"The indignities of stupidity, and the disappointments of selfish passion, can excite little pity. His punishment followed his conduct"—but she also suggests that the good-natured dolt may be betrayed again—"if duped, to be duped at least with good humour and good luck" (315).

*   *   *

To readers·who have been readier than Austen is to privilege the viewpoint of the dutiful father and the unassuming girl who idolizes him, *Mansfield Park* has generally seemed doctrinaire. But the novel is not so placid. The highly conventionalized moral oppositions touted in the conclusion—the narrator's pronounced determination to quit "guilt and misery," to restore the good to "tolerable comfort," and "to have done with all the rest" (312)—will not bear the scrutiny Austen's own style is always inviting. When desolated at Portsmouth, Fanny feels her gladness to receive Mary Crawford's letters as "another strange revolution of mind" (267). Throughout the course of her story, when she has found that the wicked Mary can be kind, that the rakish Henry can be desirable, that the awesome Sir Thomas must be opposed, and the sterling Edmund is weak, Fanny has had to undergo revolutions of mind which lead to the kind of "confusion of guilt" and "complication of evil" (299) she and the Bertrams would like to assign and confine to the Crawfords or to Mrs. Norris. But we need not read their story the same way they do, any more than we need to think about Henry Tilney or his father the same way the deferent Catherine does [in *Northanger Abbey*]. Revolutions of ideas invite the kind of reflection which the most stereotypically sage characters, including Fanny, cannot follow through with, and which disturb the coziness of the conclusion by subverting the moral polarities on which it seems to rest. In contrast to *Pride and Prejudice*, if *Mansfield Park* appears to let conservative ideologues have it their way, it is only to give them the chance to show

how little, rather than how much, they can do, and so to oblige them to discredit themselves with their own voices.

JOSEPH LITVAK

The Infection of Acting: Theatricals and Theatricality in *Mansfield Park*†

Though *Mansfield Park* seems the least inclusive or dialectical of Jane Austen's novels, it has failed to produce the critical unanimity that so unambiguous a work ought to permit. Despite repeated attempts to lay the groundwork for scholarly consensus, this ostensibly nonironic novel continues to elicit incompatible commentaries. Paradoxically, its very dogmatism is what makes for disagreement: the question of why Austen, in championing the priggish Fanny Price, should appear to dishonor her own artistic verve, may be answered, it seems, in more than one way. Recent critics are divided between those for whom *Mansfield Park* is an emphatically anti-Jacobin, staunchly Christian work, and those who find in it a disguised yet all the more potent version of the feminist or anti-authoritarian message that other Austen novels develop less obliquely. From this discord, one is tempted to conclude that the novel's dogma is somehow shakier than it ought to be. This chapter seeks not to determine once and for all whether the presiding genius of *Mansfield Park* is Edmund Burke or Mary Wollstonecraft, but to examine the central instability within the novel itself, the instability that renders such determination impossible. I will argue that the novel is neither unequivocally conservative nor unequivocally progressive, but rather that it is governed by a conservatism so riddled with internal contradictions as to trouble the authoritarian temperament more radically than would the dialectical leniency of, say, *Pride and Prejudice* or *Emma*. To argue as much, however, will also mean showing the tenacity of that conservatism, qualifying any interpretation too eager to claim *Mansfield Park* as a document of humanistic amplitude.[1]

One recent call for a synthesis in Austen criticism asks us to imagine a "structure large enough to accommodate an affirmative text with a

---

† From *Caught in the Act: Theatricality in the Nineteenth-Century English Novel* (Berkeley and Los Angeles: U of California P, 1992) 1–26. Reprinted by permission of the publisher. The author's notes have been abridged. Page references to *Mansfield Park* refer to this Norton Critical Edition.

1. In other words, this chapter attempts a kind of balancing act between two influential styles of novel-reading, the first associated with certain versions of feminism and deconstruction, the second emerging from the writings of Michel Foucault. If I have tried to maintain a sense of the subversive implications of theatricality without underestimating the capacity of authority to domesticate forces that might overturn it, I have also sought to suggest power's genius for self-preservation without promoting the monolithic view of power that often characterizes discussions of the nineteenth-century novel as a disciplinary practice.

subversive subtext." *Mansfield Park* reveals how precarious such a structure must, by definition, be. In a novel that abounds in talk of structures—of their erection, their improvement, and their dismantlement—the most problematic structure is the makeshift "theater" set up in the billiard-room of Mansfield Park. This structure literalizes a somewhat more abstract "structure"—the episode of the theatricals, the textual locus on which so much critical attention has centered. As Jonas Barish has pointed out, "the theatricals come charged with a mysterious iniquity that challenges explanation."[2] The "crux of the book," the theatrical episode disturbs us because we cannot see why *Austen* should have been so disturbed by an art form whose energies seem so similar to her own. Yet one might also say that it disturbs us even more insistently precisely because it *is* the crux of the book—because, that is, it has the power to become more than just a local structure, to spread perplexingly throughout the novel, just as the "theater" at Mansfield Park soon extends from the billiard-room, encompassing, of all places, Sir Thomas's study. The episode, which occupies the last third of the first volume, is abruptly terminated by his return from Antigua: he wastes no time in eradicating all traces of the theatricals, not only ordering the sets to be torn down but going so far as to burn every copy of *Lovers' Vows*, the play chosen for private performance. Despite this aggressive attempt at effacement, however, and despite the destruction of the theater as place, theatricality as topic turns out to pervade the novel. In this movement from a literal structure to a more metaphorical one, we witness a process of refinement, of increasingly subtle infiltration. After describing Sir Thomas's swift campaign of destruction, Austen informs us, slyly, that at least *one* remnant of the episode has escaped his ravages: Mrs. Norris has appropriated the curtain, surreptitiously removing it to her cottage, "where she happened to be particularly in want of green baize (134)." This appropriation and transformation might stand for that adaptability which allows the theater to survive and flourish in a less conspicuous form, reaching into the most unlikely recesses of the text.

Yet if this shift from theater to theatricality suggests the triumphant expansion of a "subversive subtext," we need to specify just what theatricality entails. As we will see, the political implications of theatricality in *Mansfield Park* are ineluctably ambiguous. Critics have tended to associate it with the most attractively self-dramatizing characters in the novel, Mary and Henry Crawford, thereby construing it in terms of metropolitan glamor and decadence. Theatricality has a less glittering side, however, and this variant turns out to be surprisingly consistent with the authoritarianism represented, in different ways, by Sir Thomas, Mrs. Norris, Fanny, and Edmund. Wavering between affirmative and

---

2. Jonas Barish, *The Anti-Theatrical Prejudice* (Berkeley and Los Angeles: University of California Press, 1981) 381.

subversive poles, the generalized, ubiquitous structure of theatricality begins to expose their relationship as one not of opposition but of almost systematic interdependence. An all-embracing theatricality would seem to threaten the very foundations of a novel whose heroine epitomizes what Tony Tanner calls "immobility," yet theatricality is in fact capable of such wide diffusion only because it has certain features that not merely conform to but even enable the novel's overriding conservatism. The question, in other words, is not so much "What motivated Austen's anti-theatricalism?" as "What motivated her to create the *impression* of anti-theatricalism?" Alien enough to give her pause yet not so alien as to resist the uses to which Austen puts it, theatricality in *Mansfield Park* affords the spectacle of a distinct overdetermination.

But what in the nature of theatricality allows supposedly rival ideologies to converge upon it? When Fanny Price and Henry Crawford offer their respective descriptions of the theatricals, we note the similarity of their language as much as the difference between their tones. Here is Fanny's view of the rehearsals:

> So far from being all satisfied and all enjoying, she found every body requiring something they had not, and giving occasion of discontent to the others.—Every body had a part either too long or too short;—nobody would attend as they ought, nobody would remember on which side they were to come in—nobody but the complainer would observe any directions.   (115)

Henry recalls the same experience with nostalgic relish:

> "It is as a dream, a pleasant dream!" he exclaimed, breaking forth again after a few minutes musing. "I shall always look back on our theatricals with exquisite pleasure. There was such an interest, such an animation, such a spirit diffused! Every body felt it. We were all alive. There was enjoyment, hope, solicitude, bustle, for every hour of the day. Always some little objection, some little doubt, some little anxiety to be got over. I never was happier."
> (154)

Though one response suggests the bemused omniscience of detachment while the other evokes the giddiness of absolute involvement, both Fanny and Henry characterize the theatricals in terms of "discontent" or "anxiety." As Ruth Bernard Yeazell has written, theatricality provokes an "anxiety of boundary-confusion" that "is everywhere felt" in *Mansfield Park*.[3] Yet for Fanny and Henry the theater is not just an *object* of anxiety but the very *site* of anxiety, a site that crosses its own boundaries to figure the anxiety of the novel as a whole. For *Mansfield*

3. Ruth Bernard Yeazell, "The Boundaries of *Mansfield Park*," *Representations* 7 (Summer 1984): 137.

Park, however much it may favor repose, is, as Yeazell notes, certainly one of the most anxious novels ever written.[4] Anxiety may be the condition of all narratives, but here, in its generality as "a spirit diffused," it seems especially acute. Indeed, Fanny's composure is merely superficial, a defensive fiction: Austen tells us that, during the rehearsals, "her mind had never been farther from peace" (111), that she is agitated by "many uncomfortable, anxious, apprehensive feelings" (116), that she observes the preparations in a baffled state of "longing and dreading" (117). Fanny is anxious about the theater precisely because she knows that it is less a structure toward which one can locate a safely external position than the fluctuating space in which all positions find their tenuous footing. A Henry Crawford may thrive within this milieu while a Fanny Price may inhabit it more unhappily, but neither the libertine nor the evangelical moralist can choose to function outside of it. In *Mansfield Park*, the theater, or the theatricality by virtue of which it disperses itself and colonizes the rest of the novel, becomes virtually synonymous with the inescapable context of all social existence and all political postures. Resembling Henry Crawford in abhorring "any thing like a permanence of abode" (31), theatricality turns up where one least expects it—even in the innermost meditations of the self-effacing Fanny. Discussions of the theatricals have not stressed sufficiently their *privateness: Mansfield Park* is about the incursion of public values upon private experience, about the theatricality of everyday life, in which to say, with Fanny, "No, indeed, I cannot act" (102), is already to perform, whether one wants to or not.

Like Fanny's anti-theatricalism, then, Austen's begins to emerge as a futile protest against the theatrical imperative—futile in large part because it is disingenuous, given the extent to which the political order of *Mansfield Park* depends upon a certain theatricality. Actual theaters may be circumscribed places that one can have demolished, but in its most generalized form theatricality, like Flaubert's divine artist, is present everywhere though visible nowhere. If this invisibility induces paranoia in the Tory mind, it also makes possible a more efficient policing of the social practices by which authority sustains itself.

* * *

As a novel about theatricality, *Mansfield Park* dramatizes both the conservative appropriation of theatrical forms and the way these forms endanger the very interests that appropriate them, threatening to turn the captors into captives.

Just how does conservatism appropriate theatricality? Following Hazlitt,[5] we might see a certain homeopathic logic at work in the novel.

---

4. It is remarkable how frequently the word "anxious" and its various derivatives appear in the text. I suspect that a concordance of Austen's works would show that *Mansfield Park* draws more heavily than any of the other novels on the vocabulary of anxiety.

5. See William Hazlitt, "On Actors and Acting," in *Essays*, ed. Vallance and John Hampden (London: Folio Society, 1964).

The patriarchal authority who "keeps every body in their places" (113), Sir Thomas embodies a cunningly manipulative authority, one that will not hesitate, for example, to exile Fanny to Portsmouth in the name of a "medicinal project upon [her] understanding, which he must consider as at present diseased" (250). Though the theatrical scheme suggests a flouting of his authority, since it is conceived and begun during his absence and in spite of the likelihood of his disapproval, the theatricals may function quite differently, as a kind of medicinal project upon Mansfield Park itself, which a conscientious authority must also consider as diseased. For even before the Crawfords arrive, Mansfield Park suffers from an overdose of theatricality. Indeed, the regime in question seems more like a parody of authority than like authority in the strict sense. Sir Thomas has delegated too much power to the officious Mrs. Norris, who, with her "love of directing" (8), views the household as a showcase for her own talents of management and domestic economy. Small wonder that she becomes such an energetic sponsor and supervisor of the theatricals. She has already assisted in the education, or miseducation, of Sir Thomas's daughters, Maria and Julia, who typify the sort of "accomplished" young women about whom Hannah More complains:

> The Miss Bertrams were now fully established among the belles of the neighbourhood; and as they joined to beauty and brilliant acquirements, a manner naturally easy, and carefully formed to general civility and obligingness, they possessed its favour as well as its admiration. Their vanity was in such good order, that they seemed to be quite free from it, and gave themselves no airs; while the praises attending such behaviour, secured, and brought round by their aunt, served to strengthen them in believing they had no faults. (26)

Actresses in everything but the title, Maria and Julia manifest their illness by concealing it. Just as, for Mrs. More, the poison of subversive ideas works most effectively when introduced under a familiar disguise, so the height of vanity is to "seem quite free from it," and the perfection of theatrical artifice is an apparent artlessness.

Given this state of affairs, why not attempt to cure like with like, "treating" theatricality itself with doses of more theatricality? Obviously, Sir Thomas has nothing to do with the theatrical scheme. I am not intimating that he masterminds and controls it in some implausibly subterranean way. Yet, as the major authority *within* the book, he may well represent the authority *behind* the book—namely, Jane Austen herself. As he states at the outset, it is his duty to "authorize" (10) various practices and relationships at Mansfield Park, and this responsibility echoes a more fundamental author-izing. Perhaps Austen not only authors but also authorizes the theatrical episode, working out in terms of narrative structure a medicinal project or experiment upon the diseased body politic of Mansfield Park and, by extension, of the English gentry as a whole. The injection of the Crawfords—and, to a lesser extent, of Mr. Yates—would serve to shock the system of Mansfield Park into protecting itself against such intruders. The infection that they bring would have the theatricals as its most alarming symptom, but this attack would culminate in a return to health. Indeed, the episode does seem to have some of the desired effect, for it ends with the banishment of Yates, the retreat of the Crawfords, and the departure of Maria and Julia, and initiates both the rise of Fanny and the fall of Mrs. Norris.

The only trouble with this scheme is that it scants the considerable distance between the end of the theatrical episode and the end of the novel itself: two whole volumes stand between the ostensible purgation and the complete recovery of Mansfield Park from the evils that have plagued it. However daring the homeopathic experiment, the disease lingers. For the Crawfords are only temporarily repelled by Sir Thomas's displeasure; their exclusion, in fact, lasts for a mere two chapters. Moreover, it is immediately after this drastic attempt at cleansing that Edmund makes his remark about how the Grants, half-sister and half-brother-in-law of the Crawfords, "seem to be part of ourselves." And instead of taking steps to resolve this familial identity crisis, Sir Thomas actually exacerbates it, trying to maneuver Fanny into marrying Henry Crawford. Sir Thomas does not seem to recognize the Crawfords as the real "daemon[s] of the piece" (304), as the chief perpetrators of the "bustle and confusion of acting" (131)]. Like Maria and Julia, whose vanity is so advanced that it conceals itself, Mary and Henry are such adroit actors that they know how to dissemble their theatrical busy-ness. As a result, they are soon readmitted, while the less skillful Mr. Yates, who "bustles" more discernibly, is cast out. Of course, Yates is not merely a scapegoat, since it was he, after all, who carried the infection of acting from Ecclesford to Mansfield in the first place. But this very sanctioning of a covert theatricality at the expense of an overt one inheres in the deeper logic of the narrative: the theatricals serve not as a homeopathic cure—although Austen might want us to view them as one—but as a "diversion," as Hazlitt would say, from the subtler and more comprehensive theatricality that persists long after Sir Thomas has reclaimed his study.

Jane Austen diverts our attention from this theatricality so that we may not notice how indispensable a role it plays in the rehabilitation of Mansfield Park. The reason that the Crawfords, who, through metonymic slippage, "seem to belong to us," and the bustling Mrs. Norris, who "seemed a part of" Sir Thomas (316), are not expelled until the end of the novel is not that it takes so long to eliminate theatricality, but that theatricality requires this much time to, as it were, take effect. By the end of the novel, these characters have done their work so well—have "implanted" theatricality so firmly—that they themselves no longer need to remain at Mansfield: they have not so much overstayed their welcome as outlived their usefulness. A sort of sideshow, the homeopathic experiment fails because it was never intended to succeed.

Theatricality inhabits Mansfield Park before, during, and after the theatrical episode. Are there differences, though, between the theatricality of the Miss Bertrams and the theatricality of the Crawfords, or between the theatricality of the Crawfords and the theatricality of Fanny? We may begin to answer this question by suggesting that, where Fanny's cousins embody a dangerously centrifugal sociability, Fanny installs a steadfast and almost inaccessible inwardness at the other end of the narrative continuum. Mary and Henry Crawford do not so much stand between these two extremes as upset the very dichotomy on which this model is predicated. Mary, for example, is the subject of numerous tortured conversations between Fanny and Edmund, in which they struggle to decide whether her apparent irreverence indicates some profound flaw in her nature or merely the unfortunate effect of the company she keeps. We can understand Fanny and Edmund's perplexity: on the one hand, Mary displays what looks like genuine warmth and affection for others; on the other hand, Austen often emphasizes the enormous amount of technique that underlies this display, as when, at Fanny's coming-out party, Mary takes great pains to tell everyone what (she thinks) he or she wants to hear. In her artful artlessness, she puts even Maria and Julia to shame, seducing not only Edmund but many a suspicious, if not cantankerous, critic as well.

Yet her brother is an even better actor, in whom play and seriousness are inseparably intertwined. Thus Fanny, whose mind tolerates only either/or distinctions, is at a loss to interpret his amorous behavior toward her:

> How could *she* have excited serious attachment in a man, who had seen so many, and been admired by so many, and flirted with so many, infinitely her superiors—who seemed so little open to serious impressions, even where pains had been taken to please him—who thought so slightly, so carelessly, so unfeelingly on all such points—who was every thing to every body, and seemed to find no one essential to him? . . . Every thing might be possible rather than serious attachment or serious approbation of it toward her. She had quite convinced herself of this before Sir Thomas and Mr. Crawford joined them. The difficulty was in maintaining the conviction quite so absolutely after Mr. Crawford was in the room; for once or twice a look seemed forced on her which she did not know how to class among the common meaning; in any other man at least, she would have said that it meant something

very earnest, very pointed. But she still tried to believe it no more than what he might often have expressed towards her cousins or fifty other women.   (208–09)

An inveterate player of roles—a man who is "every thing to every body"—Henry seems incapable of meaning what he says. How could such semiotic promiscuity coexist with the "seriousness" that Fanny keeps invoking? And yet Crawford presents the anomaly of one who not only combines role-playing with sincerity but reveals sincerity as an *effect* of role-playing. Fanny is bewildered by Crawford because she assumes that, if one is not serious, then one must be acting, manipulating conventions rather than speaking from the heart. Austen's *style indirect libre*, however, discloses more than Fanny's consciousness can contain: words and deeds that one can "class among the common meaning" or insert into a conventional slot are not those that *lack* sincerity but those that convey it. Though he seems to personify an illicit deviation from the norm of seriousness into the no-man's-land of artifice and conventionality, Henry in fact exposes seriousness as a product of artifice and conventionality. He is the exception that infects the rule.

What is infectious in Henry, moreover, is not the unmanageable indeterminacy that Fanny sees in him, but something surprisingly close to the ideals of hierarchy and propriety that we associate with a character like Sir Thomas. For although Henry enters the novel trailing clouds of undecidability—as befits one whom Leo Bersani calls an "ontological floater"[6]—the aim of the authoritarian appropriation of theatricality is to demystify it, to shift its focus from glamorous excess to a more pedestrian trading in certain codified procedures. Where before there was the prospect of reckless, infinite self-invention, now we find an almost mechanical shuffling and reshuffling of a limited repertory of tricks of the trade. Once the more or less spectacular attack of the theatricals has subsided, the novel can address itself to the task of domesticating the theatrical Crawfords—not, as More would have it, in order more certainly, though more slowly, to subvert Mansfield Park, but in order to rob them of their subversive power. By the end of the novel, potentially subversive impulses—which Austen groups under the heading of the "itch for acting" (86)—will have been converted into props of authority.

The conquest of the Crawfords is a crucial intermediate phase in the ideological conflict enacted in the novel. For if Mary and Henry emblematize at first the anarchy of the unbounded self, they magnify the objectionable theatricality of Maria and Julia, who, as Sir Thomas finally admits, "had never been properly taught to govern their inclina-

6. Leo Bersani, *A Future for Astyanax: Character and Desire in Literature* (Boston: Little, Brown, 1976) 76.

tions and tempers" (314). The triumph of Fanny at the end of the novel symbolizes the triumph of governance over a selfhood run wild, but the demystification of Mary and Henry marks the turning point in that war. And though Fanny is appalled by the way the Crawfords reduce sincerity to a convention, she herself represents the consummation of that process. Of course, we have identified artful artlessness as the most distinctive trait of the Bertram sisters, yet their theatricality is too dispersive, too outer-directed, to comply with the novel's centripetal ethos. The burden of the middle section of the novel is to stage the theatricalization of the self in such a way that theatricality virtually disappears into that inner space, submerged in the form of rigorously inculcated habits of mind and modes of response. *Mansfield Park*, that is, attempts to move backward from Gisborne's theatrical young women, "ensnared into errors and excesses," to the latent actresses whose "propensity to imitation," carefully shaped and supervised, becomes the very guarantee of their virtuous "conformity." Lending themselves to a demonstration of how the theatrical self may be redefined, the Crawfords enable this corrective movement from the theatrically extroverted Maria and Julia to the theatrically introverted Fanny.

When Henry reads aloud from Shakespeare, for example, Fanny's involuntary absorption in the performance signifies more than just the transitory power of actor over spectator. An important lesson is being impressed upon her mind:

> In Mr. Crawford's reading there was a variety of excellence beyond what she had ever met with. The King, the Queen; Buckingham, Wolsey, Cromwell, all were given in turn; for with the happiest knack, the happiest power of jumping and guessing, he could always light, at will, on the best scene, or the best speeches of each; and whether it were dignity or pride, or tenderness or remorse, or whatever were to be expressed, he could do it with equal beauty.—It was truly dramatic.—His acting had first taught Fanny what pleasure a play might give, and his reading brought all his acting before her again; nay, perhaps with greater enjoyment, for it came unexpectedly, and with no such drawback as she had been used to suffer in seeing him on stage with Miss Bertram.   (228–29)

Up until now, reading, for Fanny, has represented an escape from the public exposure implicit in acting. Whenever the eroticism of the rehearsals impinges too painfully upon her claustral sensibility, Fanny withdraws into the chill of her fireless room, where her books offer the solace of silent and purely spiritual intercourse.[7] It is not surprising that

---

7. One of the most common criticisms of private theatricals was that they permitted an "unrestrained familiarity with persons of the opposite sex" (Gisborne, *Enquiry*, p. 184). [See above, p. 401 — *Editor*.]

at her greatest crisis during the theatrical episode—the point at which she nearly capitulates to the company's request that she read the part of the Cottager's wife—Fanny can think only of returning to her room. She has, of course, been helping the others learn their lines by reading opposite them, but what is disturbing about this request is that it makes reading look all too much like a form of acting. It is one thing to rehearse with individual actors, quite another to read aloud as a member, however temporary, of the entire cast. Reading aloud points to an infection of reading proper by the very values it ought to exclude. Fanny's desire to maintain a polarity between reading and acting manifests itself throughout the novel, since any kind of heightened attention in the rooms below—any compulsion to look at and to be looked at—merely reinstates the theatrical threat on a less obvious level. Yet Henry's reading aloud once again undermines her cherished opposition: as Lady Bertram says, "It was really like being at a play" (229). "His reading [brings] all his acting before [Fanny] again," revealing the didactic purposiveness of both pursuits. For where, before, her retreats to the converted schoolroom that is her own apartment were a way of "shrinking again into herself" (229), as if in flight from the free play of wandering libido, now she realizes that Henry's "acting taught . . . what pleasure a play might give."

His acting teaches her a more essential lesson as well—that the act of shrinking into oneself, of cultivating inwardness, has certain inevitable histrionic implications. All along, in eschewing acting, Fanny has in fact been playing a role, albeit "sincerely." As Sandra M. Gilbert and Susan Gubar point out, "Fanny silently plays the role of the angel by refusing to play."[8] From Henry's performance, she learns not the necessity of acting but the impossibility of *not* acting. Many critics have cited Henry's remarks about the inability of most preachers to deliver an impressive sermon as a sure sign of his moral turpitude: he is actually a "bad reader" (and thus a bad person), the argument runs, because he is "not concerned with belief, only with applause or admiration." This sort of reasoning, however, may tell us more about the conduciveness of Austen's novels to moral position-taking than about the ideological ironies that generate their moralism. For Henry's preoccupation with the "rules and trick" (231) of preaching merely foregrounds the obsessive and omnipresent conventionality upon which the moral system of the entire novel depends. Whatever taint we may detect in Henry's tendency to see theatricality in everything—even in the religious vocation that is the novel's purported theme—turns out to color the authoritarian vision of *Mansfield Park* as a whole, especially as that vision is entrusted to Sir Thomas.

Indeed, if Henry's cynicism—or, what is even worse, his conflation

8. Sandra Gilbert and Susan Gubar, *The Madwoman in the Attic: The Woman Writer and the Nineteenth-Century Literary Imagination* (New Haven: Yale UP, 1979) 166.

of cynicism and conviction—offends our moral good taste, Sir Thomas's medicinal projects should strike us as equally exploitive. If they do not, it is only because the novel has succeeded in concealing its indebtedness to what it pretends to disown. One almost senses a collusion between Henry and Sir Thomas, for while the former would seduce Fanny into marriage, the latter expends considerable energy in encouraging this seduction. Any difference between the two male characters lies in Austen's presentation of their strategies. In the case of Henry, she chooses to italicize, literally, his conscious use of rhetorical convention. When, for example, he tells Fanny that he has had William promoted to second lieutenant, he "used such strong expressions, was so abounding in the *deepest interest*, in *two-fold motives*, in *views and wishes more than could be told*, that Fanny could not have remained insensible of his drift" (205); Austen's emphasis). In the case of Sir Thomas, Austen adopts a coy tone in order to cast a somewhat more benign light on the same manipulativeness. At the end of Fanny's party, when Sir Thomas orders her, in the presence of Crawford, to go to bed—" 'Advise' was his word, but it was the advice of absolute power" (192)—Austen comments tellingly on the devices whereby patriarchal authority perpetuates itself: "In thus sending her away, Sir Thomas perhaps might not be thinking merely of her health. It might occur to him, that Mr. Crawford had been sitting by her long enough, or he might mean to recommend her as a wife by shewing her persuadableness" (193).

Readers of Austen's last complete novel know what an ominous ring the word "persuasion" can acquire. In "shewing her persuadableness," Sir Thomas puts Fanny on stage, exhibiting her just as Henry exhibits himself, deploying theatrical technique as craftily as his younger collaborator. In fact, he may be even shrewder, since he is manipulating both actress (Fanny) and audience (Henry). Displaying Fanny in the role of the obedient young woman, Sir Thomas in effect concocts, for Henry's benefit, a preview of and invitation to the marriage he seeks to bring about. With his keen sense of timing—he judges that "Mr. Crawford had been sitting by [Fanny] long enough"—and his eye for the symbolically resonant detail, Sir Thomas is the novel's preeminent juggler of theatrical conventions. Fanny's dramatic exit is merely the finale to an entire evening of skillfully directed moves, one that began with her "practising her steps about the drawing-room" (187), looking perhaps more like one of Hannah More's amateur actresses than like one of Gisborne's demure mimics. The ball in her honor, conceived and staged by her uncle, constitutes her official entrance into society, the moment at which the ugly duckling steps into the spotlight to discover herself a swan. It is thus a thoroughly theatrical event, but instead of receiving the stigma that one might think it merits, it functions both as a pivotal point in the heroine's development and as a validation of the "absolute power" by which that development has been supervised: Sir Thomas "was pleased with himself for having supplied every thing else [but Fanny's beauty];—education and manners she owed to him" (189).

Fanny, however, does not seem fully to appreciate the extent of her debt to Sir Thomas, for she of course rebels against his plan for her to marry Crawford, leading many commentators to propose that she is perhaps not so docile after all. Admittedly, her secret yet unwavering devotion to her cousin Edmund, in spite of her suitor's relentless blandishments and her uncle's merciless charge of "*ingratitude*" (216; Austen's emphasis), seems to adumbrate a rejection of theatrical management and a brave defense of the inviolate self. But we would do well to consider the long-range effects, as well as the immediate consequences, of this recalcitrance. Fanny's insubordination precipitates the medicinal project according to which Sir Thomas dispatches her to the petit bourgeois chaos of Portsmouth, where she learns to esteem rather than disdain the theatricality of the Mansfield Park regime. After only a week amid the filth and anarchy of the parental abode, where "Nobody was in their right place, nothing was done as it ought to be" (264), she longs for the scrupulous decorum of her uncle's home, where his insistently watchful authority "keeps every body in their place." If Fanny showed a regrettable tendency to disobey theatrically organized power, her exile serves as a valuable reminder of the virtues of such theatricality. Sir Thomas's project upon her diseased understanding is a success, not because Fanny relinquishes her claim to an unassailable self, but because she realizes that that very integrity is possible only on the intensely supervised stage of Mansfield Park. Ultimately, that is, she acknowledges her debt to Sir Thomas, and to the elegant conventionality for which, and by which, he stands:

> Her eagerness, her impatience, her longings to be with them, were such as to bring a line or two of Cowper's Tirocinium for ever before her. "With what intense desire she wants her home," was continually on her tongue, as the truest description of a yearning which she could not suppose any school-boy's bosom to feel more keenly. (292)

The citational mode of Fanny's yearning is itself a token of the experiment's success. It demonstrates that Austen's most inward heroine is also, as many readers have observed, her most bookishly formulaic. Whenever she feels the urge to dive deep into her innermost self, Fanny comes up with a handy touchstone, usually borrowed from Cowper. She is most herself when she is quoting someone else.

It might be objected that theatricality is not the same thing as conventionality, that, although Fanny may think in clichés, she does not therefore acquiesce to the theatrical imperative. Yet the contention of this chapter is that, in the case of *Mansfield Park*, theatricality is in fact identified with conventionality to such a degree that the two terms eventually become synonymous. That theatricality-as-conventionality replaces theatricality-as-subversion reveals itself most vividly in the shift from metaphors of infection and of seduction to metaphors of debt and repayment. By the end of the novel, an omniscient authority has placed this world sufficiently under its control so that it may be said to own its subjects just as a conventional utterance or gesture owns a fixed and stable meaning. In marrying Edmund instead of Henry Crawford, Fanny indeed helps Sir Thomas to consolidate his empire and to protect his property from dispersion at the hands of outsiders. In keeping the family circle closed, she affirms repetition over difference, and legitimates Sir Thomas's patriarchal program: "Sir Thomas saw repeated, and for ever repeated reason to rejoice in what he had done for them all" (321). At last, after the disappointments arising from the "grievous mismanagement" (314) of his own daughters, he sees in Fanny a handsome return on his investment: "Fanny was indeed the daughter that he wanted. His charitable kindness had been rearing a prime comfort for himself. His liberality had a rich repayment" (320). "Prizing" in Fanny "more and more the sterling good of principle" (320), Sir Thomas prizes as well the sterling good of principal.

Indeed, in the final chapter of the novel one has the impression that its protagonist is less Fanny than Sir Thomas himself, or the "governing body" that he represents. Fanny and Edmund live happily ever after, but they do so in order to repay the authority that created them. As we have said, Sir Thomas may be viewed as an agent of Jane Austen, insofar as both appear to endorse the fortification of a conservative social order. Just here, however, where this order seems to have prevailed over the forces of subversion, authority starts to look oddly vulnerable. We would not be the first to notice a rather mechanical quality to this last chapter, which Austen begins with a perfunctory remark about her "impatien[ce] to restore every body . . . to tolerable comfort" (312), and which she punctuates with other disquieting glimpses of the novelist ostentatiously in a hurry to tie up loose ends. When did Edmund transfer his love from Mary Crawford to Fanny?: "exactly at the time when it was quite natural that it should be so, and not a week earlier" (319). What became of the prodigal older son, Tom?: "He became what he ought to be" (313). Austen takes greater trouble to describe the fates of Maria and Julia, the Crawfords, and Mrs. Norris, but her own somewhat noisy interventions are all too reminiscent of this last character's theatrical bustle. No sooner has Sir Thomas expelled his demonic counterpart—whose "anxiety for every body's comfort" (125) mocks his own need to keep everybody in "their place"—than Mrs. Norris returns in the form of the anxious, "impatient," comfort-oriented author herself. Not only does Mrs. Norris parody the authority of Sir Thomas; as Gilbert and Gubar have written, she is a "parodic surrogate for the author, a suitable double whose manipulations match those of Aunt Jane."[9] In the embarrassing moment when the ordinarily discreet Jane Austen advances to the proscenium to ring down the curtain on the final scene of her drama, we witness something like a return of the repressed.

The lesson of *Mansfield Park*, it seems, is that subversive theatricality can *only* be repressed, temporarily neutralized by a concerted effort of demystification. This process can occur, however, precisely because theatricality is not a single, unitary phenomenon but an already self-divided set of practices capable of serving both reactionary and subversive causes. If it can serve both, it can betray both, offering at best a precarious purchase on whatever interpretation of reality it has been recruited to promote. *Mansfield Park* has been praised as a psychological study that uncovers the impurity of even the most admirable motives, yet it also performs a political analysis, yielding insight into the necessary inconsistency of any ideological position that appropriates theatricality for its own purposes. A final reference should illustrate this point. When Edmund decides that duty compels him to give up his censorious stance and join in the theatricals, he tries to persuade Fanny, and himself, that this about-face produces only the *"appearance* of . . . inconsistency"* ([108]; Austen's emphasis). He explains that, if he does not play the romantic lead opposite Mary Crawford, someone from outside the immediate circle will. Thus he must act so that he "can be the means of restraining the publicity of the business, of limiting the exhibition, of concentrating our folly" (108). And, of course, his folly *is* concentrated, not only in the sense of being circumscribed but also in the sense of being intensified. For in becoming an accomplice to the theatrical scheme, Edmund loses some of his status as moral paragon, incurring the disapproval of both Fanny and his father. He may genuinely wish to "limit the exhibition," but he may also wish to exhibit his desire for and to Mary Crawford. Acting (the word itself is suggestive) in what he imagines is his father's interest, he manages at the same time to accommodate certain designs of his own, designs that may be at odds with the preservation of law and order. In Edmund's inconsistent behavior, authority nearly subverts itself. Faced with this emergency, Jane Austen summons Sir Thomas back to Mansfield Park—so that authority may attempt, yet again, to include what could disrupt it.

9. Gilbert and Gubar, p. 171.

EDWARD SAID

Jane Austen and Empire†

* * *

Interpreting Jane Austen depends on *who* does the interpreting, *when* it is done, and no less important, from *where* it is done. If with feminists, with great cultural critics sensitive to history and class like [Raymond] Williams, with cultural and stylistic interpreters, we have been sensitized to the issues their interests raise, we should now proceed to regard the geographical division of the world—after all significant to *Mansfield Park*—as not neutral (any more than class and gender are neutral) but as politically charged, beseeching the attention and elucidation its considerable proportions require. The question is thus not only how to understand and with what to connect Austen's morality and its social basis, but also *what* to read of it.

Take once again the casual references to Antigua, the ease with which Sir Thomas's needs in England are met by a Caribbean sojourn, the uninflected, unreflective citations of Antigua (or the Mediterranean, or India, which is where Lady Bertram, in a fit of distracted impatience, requires that William should go " 'that I may have a shawl. I think I will have two shawls.' ") They stand for a significance "out there" that frames the genuinely important action *here*, but not for a great significance. Yet these signs of "abroad" include, even as they repress, a rich and complex history, which has since achieved a status that the Bertrams, the Prices, and Austen herself would not, could not recognize. To call this "the Third World" begins to deal with the realities but by no means exhausts the political or cultural history.

We must first take stock of *Mansfield Park*'s prefigurations of a later English history as registered in fiction. The Bertrams' usable colony in *Mansfield Park* can be read as pointing forward to Charles Gould's San Tomé mine in *Nostromo*, or to the Wilcoxes' Imperial and West African Rubber Company in Forster's *Howards End*, or to any of these distant but convenient treasure spots in *Great Expectations*, Jean Rhys's *Wide Sargasso Sea*, [Conrad's] *Heart of Darkness*—resources to be visited, talked about, described, or appreciated for domestic reasons, for local metropolitan benefit. If we think ahead to these other novels, Sir Thomas's Antigua readily acquires a slightly greater density than the discrete, reticent appearances it makes in the pages of *Mansfield Park*. And already our reading of the novel begins to open up at those points where ironically Austen was most economical and her critics most (dare

† From *Culture and Imperialism* by Edward W. Said (New York: Knopf, 1993) 93–97. Copyright © 1993 by Edward W. Said. Reprinted by permission of Alfred A. Knopf, Inc. and Chatto & Windus. The author's notes have been omitted.

one say it?) negligent. Her "Antigua" is therefore not just a slight but a definite way of marking the outer limits of what Williams calls domestic improvements, or a quick allusion to the mercantile venturesomeness of acquiring overseas dominions as a source for local fortunes, or one reference among many attesting to a historical sensibility suffused not just with manners and courtesies but with contests of ideas, struggles with Napoleonic France, awareness of seismic economic and social change during a revolutionary period in world history.

Second, we must see "Antigua" held in a precise place in Austen's moral geography, and in her prose, by historical changes that her novel rides like a vessel on a mighty sea. The Bertrams could not have been possible without the slave trade, sugar, and the colonial planter class; as a social type Sir Thomas would have been familiar to eighteenth- and early-nineteenth-century readers who knew the powerful influence of the class through politics, plays (like Cumberland's *The West Indian*), and many other public activities (large houses, famous parties and social rituals, well-known commercial enterprises, celebrated marriages). As the old system of protected monopoly gradually disappeared and as a new class of settler-planters displaced the old absentee system, the West Indian interest lost dominance: cotton manufacture, an even more open system of trade, and abolition of the slave trade reduced the power and prestige of people like the Bertrams, whose frequency of sojourn in the Caribbean then decreased.

Thus Sir Thomas's infrequent trips to Antigua as an absentee plantation owner reflect the diminishment in his class's power, a reduction directly expressed in the title of Lowell Ragatz's classic *The Fall of the Planter Class in the British Caribbean, 1763–1833* (1928). But is what is hidden or allusive in Austen made sufficiently explicit more than one hundred years later in Ragatz? Does the aesthetic silence or discretion of a great novel in 1814 receive adequate explication in a major work of historical research a full century later? Can we assume that the process of interpretation is fulfilled, or will it continue as new material comes to light?

For all his learning Ragatz still finds it in himself to speak of "the Negro race" as having the following characteristics: "he stole, he lied, he was simple, suspicious, inefficient, irresponsible, lazy, superstitious, and loose in his sexual relations." Such "history" as this therefore happily gave way to the revisionary work of Caribbean historians like Eric Williams and C.L.R. James, and more recently Robin Blackburn, in *The Overthrow of Colonial Slavery, 1776–1848*; in these works slavery and empire are shown to have fostered the rise and consolidation of capitalism well beyond the old plantation monopolies, as well as to have been a powerful ideological system whose original connection to specific economic interests may have gone, but whose effects continued for decades.

The political and moral ideas of the age are to be examined in
the very closest relation to the economic development. . . . An
outworn interest, whose bankruptcy smells to heaven in historical
perspective, can exercise an obstructionist and disruptive effect
which can only be explained by the powerful services it had previously rendered and the entrenchment previously gained. . . . The
ideas built on these interests continue long after the interests have
been destroyed and work their old mischief, which is all the more
mischievous because the interests to which they corresponded no
longer exist.

Thus Eric Williams in *Capitalism and Slavery* (1961). The question of
interpretation, indeed of writing itself, is tied to the question of interests,
which we have seen are at work in aesthetic as well as historical writing,
then and now. We must not say that since *Mansfield Park* is a novel,
its affiliations with a sordid history are irrelevant or transcended, not
only because it is irresponsible to do so, but because we know too much
to say so in good faith. Having read *Mansfield Park* as part of the
structure of an expanding imperialist venture, one cannot simply restore
it to the canon of "great literary masterpieces"—to which it most certainly belongs—and leave it at that. Rather, I think, the novel steadily,
if unobtrusively, opens up a broad expanse of domestic imperialist culture without which Britain's subsequent acquisition of territory would
not have been possible.

I have spent time on *Mansfield Park* to illustrate a type of analysis
infrequently encountered in mainstream interpretations, or for that matter in readings rigorously based in one or another of the advanced
theoretical schools. Yet only in the global perspective implied by Jane
Austen and her characters can the novel's quite astonishing general
position be made clear. I think of such a reading as completing or
complementing others, not discounting or displacing them. And it bears
stressing that because *Mansfield Park* connects the actualities of British
power overseas to the domestic imbroglio within the Bertram estate,
there is no way of doing such readings as mine, no way of understanding the "structure of attitude and reference" except by working through
the novel. Without reading it in full, we would fail to understand the
strength of that structure and the way it was activated and maintained
in literature. But in reading it carefully, we can sense how ideas about
dependent races and territories were held both by foreign-office exec-
utives, colonial bureaucrats, and military strategists and by intelligent
novel-readers educating themselves in the fine points of moral evalua-
tion, literary balance, and stylistic finish.

There is a paradox here in reading Jane Austen which I have been
impressed by but can in no way resolve. All the evidence says that even
the most routine aspects of holding slaves on a West Indian sugar plan-

tation were cruel stuff. And everything we know about Austen and her values is at odds with the cruelty of slavery. Fanny Price reminds her cousin that after asking Sir Thomas about the slave trade, "There was such a dead silence" (136) as to suggest that one world could not be connected with the other since there simply is no common language for both. That is true. But what stimulates the extraordinary discrepancy into life is the rise, decline, and fall of the British empire itself and, in its aftermath, the emergence of a post-colonial consciousness. In order more accurately to read works like *Mansfield Park*, we have to see them in the main as resisting or avoiding that other setting, which their formal inclusiveness, historical honesty, and prophetic suggestiveness cannot completely hide. In time there would no longer be a dead silence when slavery was spoken of, and the subject became central to a new understanding of what Europe was.

It would be silly to expect Jane Austen to treat slavery with anything like the passion of an abolitionist or a newly liberated slave. Yet what I have called the rhetoric of blame, so often now employed by subaltern, minority, or disadvantaged voices, attacks her, and others like her, retrospectively, for being white, privileged, insensitive, complicit. Yes, Austen belonged to a slave-owning society, but do we therefore jettison her novels as so many trivial exercises in aesthetic frumpery? Not at all, I would argue, if we take seriously our intellectual and interpretative vocation to make connections, to deal with as much of the evidence as possible, fully and actually, to read what is there or not there, above all, to see complementarity and interdependence instead of isolated, venerated, or formalized experience that excludes and forbids the hybridizing intrusions of human history.

* * *

BRIAN SOUTHAM

The Silence of the Bertrams†

> "Did not you hear me ask him about the slave trade last night?"
> "I did—and was in hopes the question would be followed up by others. It would have pleased your uncle to be inquired of farther."
> "And I longed to do it—but there was such a dead silence!"

* * *

There is general misunderstanding about the circumstances of the slave trade and its abolition, an issue central to the slavery/colonial

† From *Times Literary Supplement*, Feb. 17, 1995. Reprinted by permission.

approach; and without a firm historical base, any attempt at historical interpretation is liable to run aground.

But when we return to the text, we find that this confusion is entirely needless. We are able to pinpoint the course of events, not from the vague "About thirty years ago" of the opening, which is no more than a glance backwards at the antecedents of the story proper, but from a single reference in Chapter Sixteen, the chapter in which Edmund visits Fanny in the East room seeking her approval for taking the part of Anhalt in *Lovers' Vows*. On the table are some books, "her books of which she had been a collector from the first hour of her commanding a shilling". Edmund looks at three of them: Macartney's *Journal of the Embassy to China* (1807), Johnson's *Idler*, and Crabbe's *Tales* (in full, *Tales in Verse*), published in September 1812. In the next chapter, Sir Thomas surprises the household with his sudden and unannounced return from Antigua. In the strained atmosphere of the family gathering that follows, Tom tries to delay his father's discovery of their rehearsing *Lovers' Vows* and rattles on about the pheasant-shooting and the wretched weather they have been having that October.

So Jane Austen fixes the month and year of Sir Thomas's return as October 1812. October 1813 is theoretically possible, until we calculate that this would put the end of the story at mid-1814, about nine months after Austen had completed the novel; and it is highly improbable that she would use a time-scheme setting the final section of the story in the future. With October 1812 as the known point, the reader can work backwards and forwards in the story to construct a time-scheme for the main action of just under three years, within which fall six key events: Sir Thomas and Tom leave for Antigua about October 1810; Tom returns about September 1811; Sir Thomas writes home, April 1812; Fanny in possession of Crabbe's *Tales*, published September 1812; Sir Thomas returns, late October 1812; Edmund turns to Fanny, summer 1813.

* * *

To confirm the novel's chronology is not simply a pedantic exercise. With the advent of slave and colonialist perspectives, the dating of the story becomes important to our understanding of *Mansfield Park*, since the Bertrams are financed by the income from their Antigua estate and Sir Thomas takes his journey there in an attempt to halt its decline— successfully, as it turns out. Although these circumstances play a significant part in the first half of the story and resonate throughout the novel, traditional accounts of *Mansfield Park* have ignored the purpose of Sir Thomas's voyage (some describe it, using Austen's own word, as merely a visit on "business") and have treated the journey as no more than a device to get the head of the family out of the way and allow the young people to run wild. But to accept the historical force of Austen's portrait is to view Sir Thomas not just as a patriarchal English country gentleman but also in his "colonial" role as an absentee plantation owner, in Parliament an active member of the West Indian lobby, now compelled by "some recent losses on his West Indian Estate" to return to Antigua and (as we may suppose) take over the running of the plantation from the resident manager and restore it to prosperity. "Fat managers and lean employees" was the uncomfortable adage current on the island.

A variety of datings has been proposed for the action of the novel, some of which open up wholly misleading lines of interpretation: 1803–6 or 1805–7 sets Sir Thomas's visit just ahead of the abolition of the slave trade in 1807; whereas 1808–9 or 1808–10 give us post-abolitionist readings. Equally, in Chapter Twenty-One, Fanny's "slave trade" question to Sir Thomas carried a very different significance in 1812 than it would if asked in earlier years. It was a question which Fanny wanted to follow up with others. But she was deterred from doing so by the "dead silence" that followed, her cousins "sitting by without speaking a word, or seeming at all interested in the subject". We are left to wonder about Sir Thomas's reply. Charitably, we can suppose that he answers Fanny fully and to her satisfaction. But Jane Austen glides over the point, leaving it wholly unresolved, perhaps even weighing the balance against him. A moment earlier, Fanny has been telling Edmund how she loves to hear Sir Thomas talking of the West Indies, how she "could listen to him for an hour together. It entertains *me* more than many other things have done." Earlier, Sir Thomas was "communicative and chatty . . . as to his voyage". Now, the "dead silence" hints that his loquacity may have dried up at the mention of slaves. As if to underline the point, Austen later restores Sir Thomas's animation when he comes to talk to William Price about "the balls of Antigua", a recreation that the young midshipman may also have enjoyed on his West Indies tour of duty.

The precise interpretation of this scene—of Fanny's questions, asked and unasked, of the "dead silence", of the cousins' "seeming" absence of interest—turns crucially on the issue of dating. Some critics fasten immediately on Fanny's reference to the slave trade and conclude, over-hastily, that her question to Sir Thomas must have been put before the Abolition Act became law in March 1807. But this is to misunderstand the historical situation. The Act came into force in two stages: from May 1, 1807, no ship with slaves on board was permitted to sail from any port in the British Empire unless legally cleared before that date: and from March 1, 1808, no slaves were to be landed. By the letter of the Act, for Britain and its overseas possessions, the slave trade was ended: "hereby utterly abolished, prohibited, and declared to be unlawful". Declaration, of course, is one thing, enforcement another. This branch of commerce, recognized, sanctioned and encouraged for 250 years, now went underground. It was a trade that the African patrol was unable to stop. The naval presence was laughable: two elderly vessels, a frigate and a sloop, facing the slave outlets along 3,000 miles of coastline, and behind them the vast extent of the Atlantic sea lanes. Four more ships were added to the patrol in 1810, to some immediate effect. But deterrent policing was only possible years later, when the Navy was clear of its involvement in the American and Napoleonic wars and when the Admiralty, for centuries protector of the Islands, was sufficiently persuaded of the abolitionist cause to enforce the blockade wholeheartedly. A further immediate weakness lay with the Act itself, since trading was treated there as a contraband activity and carried penalties no heavier than confiscation and fines. Punitive as these costs could be, profits were so high that traders were prepared to risk capture. Even when losing two out of three of their ships and human cargoes, they could still come out with a profit. Four years later, in 1811, in an attempt to clamp down on the continuing traffic, the Slave Trade Felony Act was introduced. This made trading a crime, carrying a penalty of up to fourteen years' transportation. Its net was cast wide, applying to British subjects trading anywhere in the world and to traders of any nationality operating within the British Empire. In part, this was directed at British slave-dealers trading under neutral flags of convenience. This was a device employed well before 1807 and used by traders to avoid the Acts of 1789 and 1799 regulating the number of slaves according to the ship's weight and dimensions, humanitarian measures which cut into their profits. The Felony Act closed further loopholes and increased existing penalties. The severity of these measures had some effect. But since the demand remained—"buying is cheaper than breeding" was a mainstay of planter wisdom—the trade persisted.

* * *

For the characters and circumstances of her story, Jane Austen did not have to look far. The slave connection was to be found in the immediate history of her own family. In 1760, Jane's father, the Revd George Austen, was appointed principal trustee of a plantation in Antigua, a fact unmentioned in the family biographies and memoirs. During Jane Austen's lifetime, the full abomination of slavery struck the nation's conscience and the "harshness and despotism" of the plantation owners and their managers were reported back to the family by Francis Austen from his experience of naval duty in the West Indies. A silence not unlike the "dead silence" at Mansfield Park may have begun to gather over Mr Austen's West Indian connections—connections which extended deeper into the household. The owner of the Antigua plantation, James Langford Nibbs, a former pupil of Mr Austen at Oxford, stood in 1765 as godfather for James, the eldest Austen son. Like Sir Thomas Bertram, Mr Nibbs had a spendthrift elder son, James junior; and like Tom Bertram, James junior was taken off to Antigua by his father to detach him from his "unwholesome connections". In this circuitous way, the Austens too had a dependence, however slight, upon the prosperity of a plantation in Antigua; and events similar to the *Mansfield Park* story would have become known to Jane Austen in her childhood. Like many planters' sons, James Langford Nibbs was sent home from the West Indies for education and gentrification. He aimed to set himself up as a propertied English gentleman, and began the process with a grant of arms in 1759, crowning the elevation of the Nibbs family with a country seat in Devon, where he died in 1795. Could this be the story, typical of West Indian advancement in the mother country, that Jane Austen drew on in portraying the Bertrams in their "modern-built house"? There is something distinctly "modern-built", *nouveau* and West Indian about Sir Thomas and his social standing, a point worth making since some commentators wholly misplace Sir Thomas, writing about him as a member of the old and established landed gentry who bears an ancient title. It is not only Mr Rushworth's £12,000 a year and his large estate that make him such a catch for Maria: "It was a connection exactly of the right sort", an "alliance" with the old-established gentry, the Rushworths having lived for centuries in "their ancient manorial residence", "a marriage which could bring" Sir Thomas "such an addition of respectability and influence".

Alerted at the very opening of the story to Sir Thomas's overseas interests, his "West Indian property", Jane Austen's readers would recognize his type immediately: not at all the character "West-Injine" fresh from the Caribbean—vulgar, flamboyant, free-spending and high-living—sneered at by the King, the court and the Tory gentry, the detestation of Cobbett and the delight of satirists from Hogarth and Smollett onwards—but a Mr Nibbs, a second-generation absentee, set on rising above and obscuring the origins of his wealth; on giving his sons, via Eton and Oxford, connections and a gentleman's education; and on securing further connections and alliances through the marriage of his daughters, and through the marriage of Fanny Price to Henry Crawford. Students of patronage will also understand Sir Thomas's doubts whether his influence will run as far as obtaining a commission for Fanny's midshipman brother. In 1812, with the economic importance of the West Indies in decline, the extent of Sir Thomas's "interest" was in decline too. The portrait is subtle, deeply grounded in observation, and to see Sir Thomas in this character helps us to follow what part the Antiguan associations have to play in the comedy and in the darker side of *Mansfield Park*.

* * *

Edward Said gives us an Austen world of altogether different dimensions. In *Culture and Imperialism*, he views *Mansfield Park* in a global perspective, embracing the Mediterranean and India as well as the Caribbean, locating the house itself "at the centre of an arc of interests and concerns spanning the hemisphere, two major seas and four continents". It is a wide and exciting prospect, as stimulating as Nabokov's loving attention to fine detail, inviting us to consider *Mansfield Park* in the colonial aspect of its world setting. Physical and commercial geography here go hand-in-hand with moral geography. Between the household of Mansfield Park and the plantation on Antigua, Said finds a relaxed and balanced articulation: "What assures the domestic tranquillity and attractive harmony of one is the productivity and regulated discipline of the other."

*   *   *

Where does Jane Austen stand in this? With Sir Thomas, as Said believes? Or with her heroine? Readers of the novel will decide for themselves. But the logic of history, biography and the text itself places Austen beside Fanny Price. *Mansfield Park*'s "power to offend" is not, as Said would have us believe, to render Fanny Price (and her creator) friends of the plantocracy. At this notable moment, in the lion's den, Fanny is unmistakably a "friend of the abolition", and Austen's readers in 1814 would have applauded the heroine and her author for exactly that.

JOSEPH LEW

"That Abominable Traffic": *Mansfield Park* and the Dynamics of Slavery†

The evil in question began in avarice. It was nursed also by worldly interest.
—Thomas Clarkson

I saw in these . . . [slave-owning] provinces so many vices and corruptions, increased by this trade and this way of life, that it appeared to me as a gloom over the land.

—John Woolman

In the summer of 1814, popular opinion in England about the international slave trade rose to a fevered pitch. In June, the Houses of Parliament were deluged by more than eight hundred petitions, with more than a quarter of a million signatures, demanding international abolition. On August 1, 1814, Castlereagh, foreign minister and British plenipotentiary at the Congress of Vienna, wrote to the duke of Wellington: "The nation is bent upon this object . . . and the ministers

† From *History, Gender, & Eighteenth-Century Literature*, ed. Beth Fowkes Tobin (Athens: The U of Georgia P, 1994) 271–300. Reprinted by permission of the publisher. The author's notes have been omitted. Page references to *Mansfield Park* refer to this Norton Critical Edition.

must make it the basis of their policy." Holland agreed to abolition in June 1814. The restored Bourbon king of France, Louis XVIII, refused immediate abolition, promising only eventual abolition—presumably only after replenishing supplies and clearing uncultivated lands. Napoleon, on his return from Elba, abolished the slave trade in an attempt to curry support from Britain.

That deluge of petitions descended upon Parliament during the month following the advertisement for Jane Austen's third published novel in the *Morning Chronicle* (May 23 and 27, 1814). That novel, *Mansfield Park*, dramatizes what Thomas Clarkson, an author Austen "loved," called "the Slavery and Commerce of the Human Species." The novel's opening sentences describe "all Huntingdon's" reaction to the attainment, by Miss Maria Ward, of a husband, title, and estate to which "her uncle, the lawyer, himself allowed her to be at least three thousand pounds short of any equitable claim" (5). Two pages later, after being sent "advice and professions," but more important, "money and baby-linen," Lady Bertram's now-impoverished younger sister hands over Fanny, her second child. As Avrom Fleischman, Margaret Kirkham, and Claudia Johnson (among others) have noted, the question of slavery and the slave trade appears obliquely in the novel through references to Sir Thomas's Antigua estate and Fanny's questions about the slave trade. More than merely topical, these allusions underscore the larger political context—a context that goes beyond the explicitly gendered issues portrayed. In short, *Mansfield Park* continues debates over slavery and over women's political rights.

* * *

In concentrating on the network of connections among *Mansfield Park*, acrimonious parliamentary debates over the slave trade and the continuance of the institution of slavery itself, I am arguing, essentially, a much broader interpretation than the one usually given to the famous letter to Austen's niece, Anna. In critiquing Anna's novel-in-progress, Austen suggested: "we think you had better not leave England. Let the Portmans go to Ireland, but as you know nothing of the Manners there, you had better not go with them. You will be in danger of giving false representations. Stick to Bath & the Foresters. There you will be quite at home." As I have shown, Austen knew a great deal about both the "manners" of the West Indies, and the various "representations" of them current, not merely from her reading but from George Austen's trusteeship of an Antigua estate, her brothers' naval stations in the West Indies, and through Cassandra's fiancé and other friends of the family. *Persuasion's* Mrs. Croft echoes Austen's own knowledge and love of precision, saying: "We do not call Bermuda or Bahama, you know, the West Indies." By sticking to places where she can feel "quite at home," however, Austen devastatingly exposes the contradictions inherent both in absentee landlordism and in the ideologies and realities of family life. This section discusses first, how Austen's contemporaries conceptualized the relationship between family and state, and second, the parallels between Austen's and Montesquieu's depictions of the politics of representations of reality.

That Austen should choose to do so by depicting "3 or 4 Families in a Country Village" should not surprise us, familiar as we are with the feminist equation of the personal and the political. Gary Kelly notes that "throughout Anti-Jacobin fiction there is a tendency not only to reduce large political and public issues to their domestic, everyday, commonplace consequences in individual domestic experience (a tendency found in Burke's *Reflections* and fully developed in the Romantic historical novels), but also actually to translate the political and public issues into private and domestic equivalents." Johnson notes that Burke's *Reflections* "is striking for the degree to which it presents a vast and multifaceted series of events in France as a unitary family drama." Burke was not an anomaly; as J. C. D. Clark argues, the theoretical identification of family and state by no means died after the Glorious Revolution, as the common use of the term "patriarchy" in the period makes clear. Two decades before the publication of *Esprit des lois*, Montesquieu illustrated, in a hybridized novel form, the structure of the despotic state as family in *Lettres persanes*. Family quarrels could still lead to revolution or to civil war, as was feared when King George IV attempted to divorce his wife only three years after Austen's death suggested. Anti-abolitionists used this identification of family and state to support their positions as slaveholders, often finding biblical justifications for owning slaves. Franklyn argued: "But it appears clearly, from the context, that the *elder* brethren of Canaan were involved in the sentence; a sentence pronounced by Noah, the supreme lord of the whole earth, and the only person, since our first parent, who had a right to claim the title of universal monarch."

As Johnson notes of *Pride and Prejudice*, the presence of Lydia Bennet deflects criticism from Elizabeth's behavior; Lydia acts as "a decoy who attracts the disapproval to which Elizabeth herself could otherwise be subject." In *Mansfield Park*, Edmund similarly acts as a decoy for his father. Monaghan indicates the problems inherent in Edmund's acceptance of multiple livings, yet fails to note that this *reflects* his father's possession of multiple estates. Supervision of multiple estates within England itself, or even within the British Isles as a whole, could be maintained through annual peregrinations. Despite Sir Thomas's voyage to Antigua, he remains an absentee landowner, although now of Mansfield Park itself.[1] Sir Thomas Bertram's attempts to regulate

1. Moreover, until the introduction of steamships, a planter could, for surprisingly long periods of time, be an "absentee" of both West Indian and British estates. Having left London November 5, 1817, Lewis's arrival in Jamaica was delayed by adverse weather until January 20, 1818—a period just short of eleven weeks.

affairs at Mansfield fail as miserably as his earlier epistolary supervision
of Antigua, and for precisely the same reasons.

Sir Thomas's vision of the familial government he has established at
Mansfield Park does not coincide with the life his children experience.
In this noncoincidence between what we could call "theory" and "practice" resides a key to the novel's political system; Montesquieu's classic
definitions of forms of government help here. Sir Thomas likes to believe his Northampton estate (and we should hear that embedded syllable, "state") is monarchical: a rule by one, true—but a rule by law
both founded upon and endeavoring to instill a love of "honor" in its
subjects. While he succeeds to a limited degree with Edmund, the Miss
Bertrams experience not monarchical law but despotic caprice, a domination based upon fear. Deprived as we are of representations of Sir
Thomas's pre-voyage interactions with his daughters, we must recon-
struct his relationships with them from Maria's and Julia's reactions to
the news of his departure, their responses to his letters and return, and
from his subsequent treatment of them.

Sir Thomas, who "had never seemed the friend of [his daughters']
pleasures" (25), has adopted a distant, slightly preoccupied authoritarian stance. Never having been inspired with any "love" for their father,
Maria and Julia experience his absence, not as an emotional void but
as "welcome," as a "relief," as the negative creation of freedom by the
removal of "restraint" (25). Although still subject to the father's word,
especially now that that word is written, they paradoxically feel more
autonomous, "at their own disposal" (25). Subjected all the same, their
condition *feels* different because they are no longer objects of the despot's informing gaze. As if he had been blinded (a metaphor all the
more compelling in that it was common knowledge that many Oriental
despots, from Gibbon's Byzantine emperors to the Persian shahs of
Chardin or Montesquieu, disqualified other claimants to power by
blinding them), Sir Thomas must now order and give orders to a reality
he can no longer directly observe. And because Mrs. Norris, the Miss
Bertrams' great ally, assists in creating the representations of reality sent
across the Atlantic to Antigua, Maria's and Julia's euphoria stems in
part from the power over reality as text newly "at their disposal."

I have drawn upon Montesquieu's *Esprit des lois* (1748) in order to
highlight eighteenth-century distinctions between monarchic and despotic rule. The situation I now describe, however, bears greater resemblance to *Lettres persanes* (1721). In the "seraglio" subplot of that text
(the letters exchanged between Usbek and various eunuchs and women
in his harem), the reader gradually discovers the horrifying abyss between the representation of idyllic life in the despot's absence and the
grim yet equally represented accounts of disorder, deceit, and sexual
misconduct in the final letters. As the eunuchs jockey for power, the
Persian women take advantage of the fissure formed between rival fac-

tions, rewarding those who turn a blind eye to misconduct and who participate in misrepresenting the fictional world. Within the moral system of *Lettres persanes*, Usbek's "honor" resides in the fear-enforced chastity of his women; as time passes and his return to Ispahan is repeatedly postponed, that fear lessens and the harem becomes irremediably corrupt.

Mansfield Park depicts a similar chain of events. Sir Thomas's absence is motivated by epistolary accounts of the Antigua estate's "poor returns" (23). Father and son depart in the fall, intending to return the following September (28). Sir Thomas leaves a strange "regency" behind him, dividing his "confidence" between "Mrs. Norris's watchful attention" and Edmund's "judgement" (25). A full year passes almost without incident—indeed, in only two pages. But only Tom returns on time; Sir Thomas is delayed and delayed again, until more than two years have passed. Austen reminds us of the difficulties of long-distance governance: it is "some months" before the inhabitants of the Park receive his consent to Maria's engagement (29).

Although the first year of Sir Thomas's absence passes relatively quietly, it lays the groundwork for the swift moral decay of the second. Most obviously, it introduces Rushworth and the Crawfords (30).[2] The conspiracy between Maria and Mrs. Norris, their manipulations of the texts by which Sir Thomas must order Mansfield, begin with the request for his consent to Maria's engagement. Mrs. Norris seems to have used Edmund as a test case for Sir Thomas's response; Austen notes that "no *representation* of [Mrs. Norris's] could induce [Edmund] to find Mr. Rushworth a desirable companion" (30, my emphasis). The text suggests that Aunt Norris, accepting discretion as the better part of valor, decides that "no representation" of Rushworth's obvious personal shortcomings might be the best representation of all. Sir Thomas's response supports this reading, noting Rushworth's economic qualifications and political connections while making no comment upon his character: "Sir Thomas . . . was truly happy in the prospect of an alliance so unquestionably advantageous. . . . It was a connection exactly of the right sort; in the same county, and the same interest" (30).[3] The despot, always subjected to human limitations, cannot obtain omniscience, but must rely upon the often self-interested representations of others. Distorting these representations becomes just one technique by which the relatively powerless subvert power.

Chapters 5 to 20 are punctuated by Sir Thomas's letters home, well-intentioned attempts to run Mansfield. His efforts at long-distance di-

---

2. Rushworth's name recalls the name of a character in [Elizabeth Inchbald's] *A Simple Story*: Rushbrook.

3. It is even possible that Rushworth is himself an absentee planter or an investor in the slave trade, as the West Indian planters and slave traders were powerful enough in Parliament to be called an "interest."

rection parallel those of Usbek. As with his Oriental counterpart, Sir Thomas's letters arrive too late; they address situations already superseded. As communication, they fail utterly, producing effects in their readers entirely different from their author's intentions; even "the day at Sotherton, with all its imperfections, afforded the Miss Bertrams much more agreeable feelings than were derived from the letters from Antigua" (76). Sir Thomas's letters respond to a fictive past, to other letters that rhetorically represent reality (the novel as *we* read it). Mrs. Norris's letters in particular seem to have recreated Rushworth in a flattering light; upon returning, Sir Thomas is surprised by his prospective son-in-law's purely negative personal virtues: his possessing "not more than common sense," his having "nothing disagreeable in . . . figure or address" (29). Because these letters correspond to an alternate reality, they create unresolvable paradoxes for the tenants of Mansfield: because they are the words of the father, and because they are signed with the Name of the Father, they ought to be obeyed, yet cannot be. They add to the instability of the regency government; by their unmeaning, yet imperative significations, they change the mere absence of authority into a vacuum that threatens to suck all the narrative's characters into a moral, social, and economic abyss. Because Sir Thomas corresponds with a partially fictionalized past, his letters legitimize transgression. He leaves behind him subjects already chafing at his restraints; despite the Miss Bertrams' good intentions, never "*aiming* at one gratification that would *probably* have been forbidden by Sir Thomas" (25, my emphases), they move imperceptibly (and at Sotherton, quite literally) down the garden path, recreating at Mansfield the conditions of economic and ethical insolvency that Sir Thomas has attempted to rectify in Antigua. Maria resolves upon a loveless marriage in order to escape restraint; ultimately, she criminally elopes with Henry Crawford from London. This transgression can only be revealed in letters.

The famous theatricals, the abortive preparations for the performance of Inchbald's *Lovers' Vows* (an adaptation and translation for the English stage of Kotzebue's *Das Kind der Liebe*), do not merely strike at the moral system upholding Mansfield Park or blur boundaries between illusion and reality. We can read, in the rehearsals of an Inchbald play in a novel itself modeled in some ways upon Inchbald's fiction, an odd continuation of the tradition of eighteenth-century masquerade that Castle sees culminating in *A Simple Story*. The ecstatic liberation characteristic of earlier masquerades was predicated upon the marked visual disjunction between the carnival and everyday life: the visor covering the face, the costume disguising the body. In *Mansfield Park*, however, even these marks are "internalized." Without the formality of costume, and in the absence of "good hardened real acting" (88), the boundaries

between performer and role disappear, as Mary Crawford's playful confusion of pronouns demonstrates: "Who is to be Anhalt? What gentleman among you am I to have the pleasure of making love to?"

Mary Crawford's speech suggests another theme of the carnivalesque:
the World Upside Down. Inchbald's play not only brings together social
ranks that should be kept separate (in a way reminiscent of Richardson's
Pamela), but reverses quotidian courtship practices; the play continues
the sexual allegory of the Sotherton episode. Now, however, the possibilities of transgression are not limited to the tame "wilderness," but
spread like an infection from one Mansfield room to another, even to
Fanny's attic. Fanny must first "make love" to Edward herself, helping
him to prepare his part—then cede that role to Mary, while paradoxically remaining (as prompter) guardian of the text.

The most severe upheaval, however, occurs in the twin male sanc-
tums of Mansfield, the billiard room and Sir Thomas's bedroom. In
these rooms, striking out against a restrictive moral system becomes a
striking out of the signs of the father, of patriarchal texts. Yates trans-
forms the billiard room from a locus of ritualized combat between men
into an arena for narcissistic self-display: a stage replaces the billiard
table. The entire room is feminized, cordoned off with what later become Mrs. Norris's green curtains. Sir Thomas's room is equally transformed, uncharacteristically lit up by candles; its most distinguishing
piece of furniture, the bookcase, is removed. As if in revenge for those
disagreeable letters from Antigua, the father has been written out, not
merely of the play but of his own room. His physical return restores
apparent order to the disordered estate, scattering its inhabitants, acting
"comme la foudre qui tombe au milieu des éclats et des tempêtes,"
which Usbek had wished his letters to be. Despite letters announcing
that return, it is unexpected and strikes terror into his children's hearts.
He appears like a revenant, leaving Julia "aghast." While the written
words from Antigua reinforced the false security of absence and enabled
the endless speechifying of the theatricals, the spoken word of return
leaves all speechless, closing the first volume without authorial comment. Julia's words—"My father is come! He is in the hall at this
moment!"—echo in the space between volumes, accenting the caesura-
like pause and ringing with the deadly certainty of Judgment.

Sir Thomas's return (as his later mistreatment of Fanny makes abundantly clear) forces all of the women to realize, at least subconsciously,
that the apparent "freedom," the absence of "restraint," was illusory.
For this freedom can never, in the despotic world, be a freedom to
"act" in any way; even by escaping the father's gaze, the objects of that
gaze can never become subjects, except in being "subjected." The Antigua trip creates a freedom to desire, a sense that "every indulgence is
. . . within reach" (25). But as in *Lettres persanes*, female desire must
not be satisfied: to move beyond restraints is to transgress fatally, be-

cause sexually. The twin allegories of *Mansfield Park*, volume 1 (the wilderness of Sotherton and the theatricals), play upon this sexual transgression. *Mansfield Park* and female-authored anti-Jacobin novels make clear that both restraints and apparent liberations are constructed by and in the self-interests of men. Literally, walls and gate of the "wilderness" of Sotherton are constructed by men, just as the script of Maria's transgression is written by Henry: "prohibited," "authority," and "protection" are all Crawford's words, as is the suggestion of evading the locked gate. Maria's entrance into The Wilderness and her later elopement, like the sexual fall of Elizabeth Hamilton's Julia Delmond, are engineered by hopeful seducers. The theatricals, and eventually *Lovers' Vows* itself, are suggested by Yates, just as the casting of the major roles is at least nominally determined by men.

The narrator of Sarah Scott's *Millenium Hall* describes his "impaired constitution," explaining why the corrupting climate of Jamaica forced him to return to England. In the eighteenth century, the "corruption" inherent in certain climates increasingly came to be seen as merely the outward manifestation of moral and political corruption. This section discusses a few significant stages in the development of the multifaceted theories concerning corruption, arguing that Sir Thomas needs to be "read" as a modification of the stereotype of the returned planter. By looking at Macartney's debunking of eighteenth-century depictions of China, I claim that Fanny's reading of Macartney prepares her to resist Sir Thomas's demands.

Montesquieu's theories of the impact of climate not merely upon the physical constitution of the individual human body but also upon the political constitution of the state explained why geographical areas prone to diseases such as yellow fever were also prone to despotic forms of government. Cooler climates, such as those of Europe and of the North American colonies, produced healthier individuals and healthier governments. Because the body politic, like the human body, was exposed to agents of "corruption" both within and without, Montesquieu could explain why apparently healthy governments, such as those of late Republican Rome or of seventeenth-century France, could degenerate into despotisms. Material goods, especially luxuries, mysteriously affected both the human body and the body politic.[4]

Scientific advances, such as Harvey's discovery of the circulation of blood, seemed to reinforce and even to suggest improvements upon these theories. An empire, conceived of as a body, relied upon the circulation of goods but also of persons for its continued existence.

4. In *Journal of the Plague Year*, for example, Defoe reported beliefs that the plague had been brought first to Europe, then to England, in cloths. Montesquieu and Gibbon suggested that "corrupt" Oriental manners were imported into Greece and Rome along with luxury goods; individual and political morals depended upon the material conditions of life.

Novels, the drama, and political treatises document the circulation of individuals (their departure from and return to the mother country) as part of the normal workings of empire.[5] These men, theories and fictions agree, are adversely affected by prolonged residence in a corrupting climate and society.

In *An Inquiry into the Colonial Policy of the European Powers*, first published in 1802, Henry Brougham described how the West Indies affected the physical health and the personal morals of English residents as well as the constitution of the mother country, explicitly counterpointing the various meanings and methods of "corruption." He begins by discussing the degeneration of the Englishman's moral character in the absence of Englishwomen and the development of patterns of promiscuity that encourage the spread of specifically sexual diseases: "The want of modest female society—the necessity of gratifying the desires engendered by a burning climate—the abundance of unhappy women, whose blood boils with still stronger passions, and renders them, in the European's eyes, only an inferior race, formed for the corporeal convenience of their masters—these are other causes of dissolute morals. The want of female society, while it brutalizes the minds and manners of men, necessarily deprives them of all the virtuous pleasures of domestic life, and frees them from those restraints, which the presence of a family always imposes on the conduct of the most profligate men" (i, 70). Worse even than the sexual "brutalization" of the planters are the political "contaminations" they undergo: "Hence arises the most disgusting contamination with which the residence of the new world stains the character of the European—a love of uncontrouled power over individuals—a selfish reference of their situation to his own wants—a disgraceful carelessness about the happiness of a race, with whose enjoyments he cannot sympathize—a detestable indifference to the sufferings of his fellow-creatures—and a habit, no less odious, of indulging, at their expence, every caprice of temper or desire." Could this contamination be subject to quarantine—could the lands "beyond the pale" be cordoned off from the "mother country," the damage to England's "sons" contained? Unfortunately, however, because of the "circulation" of populations, the "character" of the mother country is also damaged: "Upon their return to their native country, their habits are too deeply rooted, to be shaken off; and their influence is not inconsiderable upon the society in which they mingle. Others find in the West Indies, a station congenial to their former lives; but they return

5. Moll Flanders goes to Virginia, Dorriforth and Sir Thomas Bertram go to the West Indies and St.-Preux circumnavigates the globe during the War of Jenkins' Ear (1740–48); Antony Harlowe suggests for James Jr. a bride whose name, d'Oyley, associates her with the Jamaican plutocracy; Antony Harlowe and Samuel Foote's Nabob (in the play named after him) exert power gained through commerce with and residence in India; William Beckford, Jr. (the novelist), was the son of a returned Jamaican who retained his colonial accent throughout life, and Matthew Lewis died returning home from his second voyage to his Jamaican estates.

still more depraved in principles and taste, armed with an influence which they did not before possess." By sending a character to the West Indies, novelists implicitly encoded what appears to be a violation of the law of conservation of character. West Indians were particularly known for heartlessness and irascibility: "A correspondent in the *Public Advertiser* (September 29, 1780) records an incident of which Goldsmith had told him, in which 'several cottages were destroyed' near the house of 'a great West Indian.' " While an underling such as St.-Preux returns tamed, perhaps even emasculated, from Anson's punitive expedition against the Spanish Main, Inchbald's Dorriforth returns from his West Indian estate a confirmed tyrant, authoring capricious laws, insisting upon observance of their letter, and pronouncing unjustifiably harsh and woefully inappropriate sentences to witting and unwitting offenders, as the twin banishments of Lady Elmwood and her daughter Matilda illustrate.[6]

In this light, Fleischman's emphasis upon Sir Thomas's new "firmness" is entirely appropriate. That Fanny possesses even a negative will becomes abhorrent to Mrs. Norris and Sir Thomas alike. Her refusal to enter into a loveless marriage with Henry Crawford (and thus promote the system of familial alliances to which he sacrifices his own daughter) produces a crisis qualitatively similar to that caused of the princess of Wales's refusal to marry in 1815. Having accustomed himself to exerting *de facto* absolute power over his Negro chattel (*de facto* in light of the inadmissibility of evidence by coloreds against whites), Sir Thomas expects an identical submission from the inhabitants of Mansfield, females especially. By saying "no," Fanny commits a treasonous act, a crime of *lèse majesté* punishable by exile and even death. For, as Austen makes clear, the very air of Portsmouth undermines Fanny's health and could lead to her demise.[7] Exiling a young woman in already dubious health to a city becomes a judicial murder or a domestic equivalent to the colonial practice of starving slaves into submission. It duplicates the contemporary practice of transportation, which deported those convicted of crimes against property to unhealthy climates—to Botany Bay, where Austen's aunt Perrot would have been sent if she had been convicted after having been accused of stealing twenty shillings worth of lace. Maria Bertram is similarly exiled for adultery, for exerting female will and asserting female sexuality. Mrs.

6. The despotism and irascibility of both the returning planter or returning Nabob became commonplace in late eighteenth-century fiction and theater. Examples include characters in Frances Sheridan's *Sidney Bidulph* (which Doody believes to be another model for *Mansfield Park*); in Foote's *The Nabob*; and throughout Inchbald's dramatic works, especially *The Wise Man of the East*.

7. Recent critics, used to the improved sanitary conditions of modern cities, tend to pooh-pooh Austen's direct assertions; epidemiology and modern statistical studies, however, assert that, well into the nineteenth century, even Paris and London were remarkably unhealthy places. Their unprecedented eighteenth- and nineteenth-century growth were due not to natural increase but to migration from the healthier countryside.

Norris travels with her to an "establishment" in "another country"; both are condemned to an islanded existence, "remote and private," and with "little society" (315). These exiles repeat the sentences imposed upon slaves convicted of participating in the 1736 Antigua uprising.

Fanny's "no" is an act of rebellion, endangering a system based upon the exchange of women between men as surely as a slave's refusal to work. It poses both an economic and an epistemological threat to the patriarchal system: saying no, "by repudiating the principle of submission it struck at the heart of the master's moral self-justification and therefore at his self-esteem." Lady Tremor, a character in Inchbald's *Such Things Are*, expresses this concisely, asking: "Is it true that the Sultan cut off the head of one of his wives the other day because she said 'I won't?' " Throughout *Mansfield Park*, Sir Thomas and Mrs. Norris discuss Fanny's economic value, usually in negative terms. At nine years old, she is as costly and as unwanted as a child slave; the "trouble and expense" she will be to the Bertrams can only be justified in terms of an alternative economy. As a resident of Mansfield Park, the child Fanny will become a visible and above all daily reminder to the neighborhood of a member of Parliament's "benevolence" (7). At the same time, the Bertrams' expense must be minimized; the governess and other instructors employed for the Miss Bertrams become more cost-efficient by being assigned a third pupil. From the very beginning, Mrs. Norris touts the possibility that she may extend the Bertram connections by marrying into a "creditable establishment," in implicit contrast to her mother. Moreover, by seeing Fanny raised as their sister, it will become "morally impossible" that either Tom or Edmund should duplicate Miss Frances's *mésalliance* by marrying not only beneath them but also endogamously.

Fanny improves her position at Mansfield by demonstrating her economic value. David Stalker, an employee on the Stapleton plantations in Nevis, had advised buying slaves young: "they are fully seasoned by 18 and in full as handy as them that is born in the country [Creoles] but them full grown fellers think it hard to work never being brought up to it they take it to heart and dy or is never good for any things." In the early chapters of the novel, we have witnessed Fanny's "seasoning"; from having been merely a debit for almost a decade, a body for which so much clothing and food (but not firewood!) must be set aside every year, Fanny becomes a "credit." After Maria's marriage, Fanny becomes an unpaid companion to Lady Bertram, providing a service *gratis* for which many impoverished young women, including Sydney Owenson, received wages. When she attracts the attentions of the wealthy Henry Crawford, her value rises still further. Doweryless as she is, Crawford's proposal converts her into an extremely marketable commodity. At very little cost to himself, Sir Thomas can gain all the advantages of a connection that, in Maria's case, cost him many thousands of pounds. Fanny's insistent refusal, as absurd and as infuriating as a cargo of sugar (or of slaves) refusing to be sold to the highest bidder, also potentially alienates Henry and the naval interests to which he is so closely connected (through Admiral Crawford)—interests crucial to the continued well-being of the British West Indies.

The text implies Fanny may on some level be aware of the revolutionary potential of her "no." She has been reading, we are told, Macartney's *Travels in China*. In the mid-1790s, Lord Macartney had been sent to the Celestial Empire in an abortive attempt to extend British commercial privileges. Barlow published a biography and extended excerpts from Macartney's journal after the lord's death in 1806; Fanny seems to have read these. Macartney's journal is noteworthy in that it opposes popular eighteenth-century notions of China as a near-utopian benevolent despotism, governed by a bureaucratic meritocracy. Instead of Voltaire's and Goldsmith's visions of a nation of philosophers, Macartney posits a nation whose inhabitants are prone to the same moral failings as those of Europe: "the boasted moral institutes of China are not much better observed than those of some other countries, and that the disciples of Confucious are composed of the same fragile materials as the children of Mammon in the western world." Macartney's China is an absolute patriarchy: "all power and authority . . . derive solely from the sovereign," who, we learn, has sired many sons. The emperor/father's word is immortal; the laws he and his predecessors have made so inviolable that "no consideration could ever induce him to infringe them."

In Great Britain, as my discussion of both pro- and anti-abolition tracts illustrated, the patriarchal family was regarded as both a microcosm of the monarchical state and necessary to the continuance of that state. Macartney indicates that the same is true in China: "A Chinese family is regulated with the same regard to subordination and economy that is observed in the government of a state[;] the paternal authority, though unlimited, is usually exercised with kindness and indulgence." Although "usually" kind and indulgent, the prose suggests, the "paternal authority" can be abusive; a father may even sell his girl-children into slavery. Where this authority is absolute, there are no legitimate means of redress—all demurrals are rebellions. All individual wills are and must be subordinated to that of the father. The child must feel grateful; any child who attempted to claim an "interest" contrary to that of the father "would be unnatural and wicked." Chinese society, Macartney asserts, has so successfully inculcated the virtues of obedience that "an undutiful child is a monster that China does not produce."

Fanny's reading, then, prepares her for her rebellion but also makes that rebellion more difficult. Through his demystification of the eighteenth-century concept of "China," Macartney teaches Fanny to recognize that a "usually" kind and indulgent despot is still a despot, that the "inviolable" word may be inapplicable to changed circumstances. Yet Macartney cannot suggest how one might resist the "unusual" injustices without becoming "unnatural," "wicked," or a "monster." Like his contemporary, Burke, Macartney believes that amelioration of the conditions of the subjected may be achieved gradually: "A sudden transition from slavery to freedom, from dependence to authority, can seldom be borne with moderation or discretion. Every change in the state of man ought to be gentle and gradual, otherwise it is commonly dangerous to himself and intolerable to others." Macartney draws connections among the dangers of reform in China and the atrocities that resulted from revolution in France and, interestingly enough, the West Indian island of Saint Domingue: "the Chinese, if not led to emancipation by degrees, but let loose on a burst of enthusiasm would probably fall into all the excesses of folly, suffer all the paroxysms of madness, and be found as unfit for the enjoyment of freedom as the French and the negroes." We can begin to imagine, then, how Fanny's reading, which suggests analogies not merely between conditions in China and those in the West Indies but also with her own odd status at Mansfield, may have prompted and shaped those unrecorded questions about the slave trade.

Critics as diverse as Halperin and Claudia Johnson share a dissatisfaction with the ending of *Mansfield Park*, especially in comparison to the uplifting endings of *Pride and Prejudice* or *Emma*. Fanny rejects Henry Crawford in order to marry a younger son, a clergyman, almost incestuously. Yet the Crawfords inhabit a realm vicious enough to corrupt young women, as Mary's shamelessly open reference to homosexual sodomy, to *"Rears* and *Vices,"* makes abundantly clear. After Fanny's marriage to her first cousin Edmund, Austen relegates them first to Thornton Lacey, then to the parsonage at Mansfield. Yet this less-than-euphoric ending is necessary to the novel's, and particularly Fanny's, integrity. *This* Pemberley is tainted. We have seen enough of Edmund's casuistry (especially where Mary Crawford or acting are concerned) to postulate that, should his elder brother Tom die childless, he could have reconciled himself to absentee landlordism or slaveholding as easily as he reconciles himself to holding plural livings.

At the conclusion of *Mansfield Park*, Austen leaves us not in the fairytale-like atmosphere of *Emma* or *Pride and Prejudice* but in one resembling the world and family she knew. The errors of Elizabeth Bennett or Emma Woodhouse have no lasting effects on the societies around them; the moral effects of slaveowning and absenteeism come close to destroying the circle at Mansfield, which is a microcosm of Great Britain itself. Literature by women in the early nineteenth century often, as I have argued elsewhere, explored the ethical dimensions of empire building. Like Sydney Owenson before her and Mary Shelley after, Jane Austen depicts the inescapable problems and the moral compromises made inevitable by the power dynamics of Britain's "second" empire: one based not upon settlement but upon subjugation.

Jane Austen: A Chronology†

1775	Jane Austen born, December 16, at Steventon, Hampshire, the seventh of eight children of the Rev. George Austen. George III is on the throne of England.
1784	Formal· education ends at age 9, at school in Reading.
1789–91	Between the ages of 14 and 16, she writes a novel called "Love and Freindship," a "History of England," and stories called "Lesley Castle" and "A Collection of Letters."
1793–96	Writes "Lady Susan" and "Elinor and Marianne," the earliest version of *Sense and Sensibility*.
1797	Writes "First Impressions," the earliest version of *Pride and Prejudice*.
1797–98	Rewrites "Elinor and Marianne" as *Sense and Sensibility* (which remains unpublished until 1811).
1798–99	Writes *Susan* (an early version of *Northanger Abbey*).
1801	Austen family moves to Bath.
1803	Sells *Susan* to Crosby of London for publication.
1804	Writes *The Watsons*.
1805	Her father dies. The following year, Jane, Cassandra, and their mother move to Southhampton.
1809	They move to Chawton Cottage in Hampshire. Austen resumes interest in publication.
1810–11	Begins revising "Elinor and Marianne" into *Sense and Sensibility*, and "First Impressions" into *Pride and Prejudice*.
1811–20	The Regency: George, Prince of Wales — who would become an admirer of Austen's novels — takes over the powers of George III, who lives on until 1820.
1813	*Pride and Prejudice* published.
1814	Writes *Emma* and publishes *Mansfield Park*.
1815	Writes *Persuasion*.
1816	*Emma* published, dedicated to Prince Regent. Buys back *Susan* and revises as *Northanger Abbey*.
1817	Jane Austen dies at the age of 42 in Winchester, of Addison's disease, leaving "Sanditon," an unfinished novel.
1818	*Northanger Abbey* and *Persuasion* published, again anonymously.

† From Jane Austen, *Persuasion*: A Norton Critical Edition, edited by Patricia Meyer Spacks (New York: Norton, 1995). Reprinted by permission of Patricia Meyer Spacks and W. W. Norton & Company, Inc.

Selected Bibliography

JANE AUSTEN'S WRITINGS

Austen, Jane. *The Novels of Jane Austen.* 5 vols. 3rd ed. Ed. R. W. Chapman. London: Oxford UP, 1932–34.
——. *Minor Works.* Ed. R. W. Chapman. Vol. 6 of *The Novels of Jane Austen.* London: Oxford UP, 1954.
——. *Jane Austen's Letters.* 3rd ed. Ed. Deirdre Le Faye. Oxford: Oxford UP, 1995.

BIOGRAPHICAL AND CRITICAL STUDIES

● indicates works included or excerpted in this volume.

● Auerbach, Nina. "Jane Austen's Dangerous Charm: Feeling as One Ought about Fanny Price." *Jane Austen: New Perspectives.* Ed. Janet Todd. New York: Holmes and Meier, 1983. 208–23.
Austen-Leigh, J. E. *A Memoir of Jane Austen.* London, 1870.
Austen-Leigh, W., and R. A. *Jane Austen: A Family Record.* Rev. and enl. by Deirdre Le Faye. London: The British Library, 1989.
Amis, Kingsley. "What Became of Jane Austen?" *Spectator* 199 (1957): 439–40.
Armstrong, Isobel. *Jane Austen: Mansfield Park.* Harmondsworth: Penguin, 1988.
Banfield, Ann. "The Moral Landscape of *Mansfield Park.*" *Nineteenth-Century Fiction* 26 (1971): 1–24.
Bloom, Harold, ed. *Modern Critical Interpretations: Jane Austen's Mansfield Park.* New York: Chelsea House, 1987.
Brown, Julia Prewitt. *Jane Austen's Novels: Social Change and Literary Form.* Cambridge: Harvard UP, 1979.
Butler, Marilyn. *Jane Austen and the War of Ideas.* Oxford: Oxford UP, 1975. Rpt. with new introduction, 1987.
——. *Romantics, Rebels, and Reactionaries: English Literature and Its Backgrounds, 1760–1830.* Oxford: Oxford UP, 1981.
Copeland, Edward, and McMaster, Juliet, eds. *A Cambridge Companion to Jane Austen.* Cambridge: Cambridge UP, 1997.
Devlin, David. *Jane Austen and Education.* New York: Barnes & Noble Books, 1975.
● Duckworth, Alistair. *The Improvement of the Estate.* Baltimore: Johns Hopkins UP, 1971.
Farrer, Reginald. "Jane Austen." *Quarterly Review* 228 (1917): 1–30.
● Fergus, Jan. *Jane Austen: A Literary Life.* New York: St. Martin's Press, 1991.
Ferguson, Moira. *Colonialism and Gender Relations from Mary Wollstonecraft to Jamaica Kincaid.* New York: Columbia UP, 1994.
Fleischman, Avrom. *A Reading of Mansfield Park: An Essay of Critical Synthesis.* Minneapolis: U of Minnesota P, 1967.
Forster, E. M. "Jane Austen." *Abinger Harvest.* London: Harcourt, 1936. 145–59.
Garrod, H. W. "Jane Austen, A Depreciation." *Essays by Divers Hands* n.s. 8 (1928): 39–40. [See also R. W. Chapman, "A Reply to Mr. Garrod." *Essays by Divers Hands* n.s. 10 (1931): 17–34.]
Gilson, David. *A Bibliography of Jane Austen.* Oxford: Clarendon, 1982.
Greenfield, Susan C. "Fanny's Misreading and the Misreading of Fanny: Women, Literature, and Interiority in *Mansfield Park.*" *Texas Studies in Literature and Language* 36 (1994): 306–27.
Grey, J. David, ed. *The Jane Austen Companion.* New York: Macmillan, 1986.

Halperin, John. *The Life of Jane Austen*. Baltimore & London: Johns Hopkins UP, 1984.

——, ed. *Jane Austen: Bicentenary Essays*. Cambridge: Cambridge UP, 1975.

Harding, D. W. "Regulated Hatred: An Aspect of the Work of Jane Austen." *Scrutiny* 8 (1940): 346–62.

Harris, Jocelyn. *Jane Austen's Art of Memory*. Cambridge: Cambridge UP, 1989.

Heath, William, ed. *Discussions of Jane Austen*. Boston: D. C. Heath & Co., 1961.

Honan, Park. *Jane Austen: Her Life*. London: Weidenfeld and Nicholson, 1987.

Jarvis, W. A. M. "The Ships in *Mansfield Park*." *Persuasions* 10 (1988): 31–33.

● Johnson, Claudia L. *Jane Austen: Women, Politics, and the Novel*. Chicago: U of Chicago P, 1988.

Jordan, Elaine. "Pulpit, Stage, and Novel: *Mansfield Park* and Mrs. Inchbald's *Lovers' Vows*." *NOVEL* 20 (1987): 138–48.

Kelly, Gary. *The English Jacobin Novel, 1780–1805*. Oxford: Oxford UP, 1976.

——. "Reading Aloud in *Mansfield Park*." *Nineteenth-Century Fiction* 37 (1982): 29–50.

Kirkham, Margaret. *Jane Austen, Feminism and Fiction*. Totowa: Barnes & Noble, 1983.

Lascelles, Mary. *Jane Austen and Her Art*. Oxford: Oxford UP, 1939.

● Lew, Joseph. "'That Abominable Traffic': *Mansfield Park* and the Dynamics of Slavery." *History, Gender, & Eighteenth-Century Literature*. Ed. Beth Fowkes Tobin. Athens: U of Georgia P, 1994. 271–300.

Lewes, George Henry. "The Novels of Jane Austen." *Blackwood's* 86 (1859): 1609–11.

● Litvak, Joseph. "The Infection of Acting: Theatricals and Theatricality in *Mansfield Park*." *Caught in the Act: Theatricality in the Nineteenth-Century Novel*. Berkeley and Los Angeles: U of California P, 1992.

Litz, A. Walton. *Jane Austen: A Study of Her Artistic Development*. New York: Oxford UP, 1965.

Looser, Devoney, ed. *Jane Austen and Discourses of Feminism*. New York: St. Martin's Press, 1995.

McMaster, Juliet. *Jane Austen on Love*. Victoria: U of Victoria P, 1978.

——. *Jane Austen the Novelist*. New York: St. Martin's Press, 1996.

——, ed. *Jane Austen's Achievement*. London: Macmillan, 1973.

Mooneyham, Laura. *Romance, Language and Education in Jane Austen's Novels*. London: Macmillan, 1988.

Mudrick, Marvin. *Jane Austen: Irony as Defense and Discovery*. Princeton: Princeton UP, 1952.

Phillips, K. C. *Jane Austen's English*. London: Andre Deutsch Ltd., 1970.

Poovey, Mary. *The Proper Lady and the Woman Writer: Ideology as Style in the Works of Mary Wollstonecraft, Mary Shelley, and Jane Austen*. Chicago: U of Chicago P, 1984.

Reitzel, William. "*Mansfield Park* and Kotzebue's *Lovers' Vows*." *Review of English Studies* 9 (1933): 451–56.

● Said, Edward. "Jane Austen and Empire." *Culture and Imperialism*. New York: Knopf, 1993. 80–97.

Southam, B. C. *Jane Austen's Literary Manuscripts*. London: Oxford UP, 1964.

——, ed. *Critical Essays on Jane Austen*. London: Routledge, 1968.

——, ed. *Jane Austen: The Critical Heritage*, vol. 1. London: Routledge, 1968.

——, ed. *Jane Austen: The Critical Heritage, 1870–1940*, vol. 2. London: Routledge, 1987.

● Southam, Brian. "The Silence of the Bertrams." *Times Literary Supplement* 17 Feb. 1995.

Stewart, Maaja. *Domestic Realities and Imperial Fictions: Jane Austen's Novels in Eighteenth-Century Contexts*. Athens: U of Georgia P, 1993.

Sulloway, Alison. *Jane Austen and the Province of Womanhood*. Philadelphia: U of Pennsylvania P, 1989.

Tanner, Tony. *Jane Austen*. Cambridge: Harvard UP, 1986.

Tave, Stuart. *Some Words of Jane Austen*. Chicago: U of Chicago P, 1973.

Thomas, B. C. "Portsmouth in Jane Austen's Time." *Persuasions* 12 (1990): 61–66.

Todd, Janet, ed. *Jane Austen: New Perspectives. Women & Literature*, n.s. 3. New York: Holmes & Meier, 1983.

● Trilling, Lionel. "*Mansfield Park*." *The Opposing Self: Nine Essays in Criticism*. New York: Viking, 1955. 206–30.

Vanita, Ruth. "*Mansfield Park* in Miranda House." *The Lie of the Land: English*

Literary Studies in India. Ed. Rajeswari Sunder Rajan. Delhi: Oxford UP, 1992. 90–98.

Watt, Ian, ed. *Jane Austen: A Collection of Critical Essays*. Englewood Cliffs, N.J.: Prentice-Hall, 1963.

Wiesenfarth, John. *The Errand of Form*. New York: Fordham UP, 1967.

Wilson, Edmund. "A Long Talk about Jane Austen." *Classics and Commercials*. New York: Farrar, 1950. 196–203.

Woolf, Virginia." "Jane Austen." *The Common Reader*. London and New York: Harcourt, 1925. 191–206.

Yeazell, Ruth. *Fictions of Modesty*. Chicago: U of Chicago P, 1991.

Norton Critical Editions